BESTSELLING
BOOK SERIES

Visual Basic .NET All-in One
Desk Reference For Du...

KU-607-396

Visual Basic .NET Data Types

Visual Basic Type	Common Language Runtime Type Structure	Storage Size	Value Range
Boolean	System.Boolean	2 bytes	True or False
Byte	System.Byte	1 byte	0 to 255 (unsigned)
Char	System.Char	2 bytes	0 to 65535 (unsigned)
Date	System.DateTime	8 bytes	January 1, 0001 to December 31, 9999
Decimal	System.Decimal	16 bytes	+/-79,228,162,514,264,337,593,543,950,335 with no decimal point; +/-7.9228162514264337593543950335 with 28 places to the right of the decimal; smallest non-zero number is +/-0.0000000000000000000000000001
Double (double-precision floating-point)	System.Double	8 bytes	-1.79769313486231E+308 to -4.94065645841247E-324 for negative values; 4.94065645841247E-324 to 1.79769313486231E+308 for positive values
Integer	System.Int32	4 bytes	-2,147,483,648 to 2,147,483,647
Long (long integer)	System.Int64	8 bytes	-9,223,372,036,854,775,808 to 9,223,372,036,854,775,807
Object	System.Object (class)	4 bytes	Any type can be stored in a variable of type Object
Short	System.Int16	2 bytes	-32,768 to 32,767
Single (single-precision floating-point)	System.Single	4 bytes	-3.402823E+38 to -1.401298E-45 for negative values; 1.401298E-45 to 3.402823E+38 for positive values
String (variable-length)	System.String (class)	Depends on implementing platform	0 to approximately 2 billion Unicode characters
User-Defined Type (structure)	(inherits from System. ValueType)	Sum of the sizes of its members	Each member of the structure has a range determined by its data type and independent of the ranges of the other members

Standardized Naming Conventions

Prefix	Corresponding Object	Example	Prefix	Corresponding Object	Example
Acd	ActiveDoc	AcdMainPage	Hpl	HyperLink	HplURL
Chk	CheckBox	ChkBoldface	Lbl	Label	LblContents
Cbo	ComboBox	CboDropper	Lst	ListBox	LstNames
Cm	ADO command (database)	CmMyCommand	Pag	Page	PagTurn
Cmd	CommandButton	CmdExit	Pgf	PageFrame	PgfRule
Cmg	CommandGroup	CmgSelectOne	Prj	ProjectHook	PrjSuzerine
Cn	Connection (database)	CnMyConnex	Rb	RadioButton	RbBlueBackground
Con	Container	CntFramed	Rs	Recordset (database)	RsTotalSales
Ctr	Control	CtlSeeThis	Sep	Separator	SepZone
Fld	Field (database)	FldTitles	Spn	Spinner	SpnWatch
Frm	Form	FrmColors	Txt	TextBox	TxtAddress
Frs	FormSet	FrsTypeIn	Tmr	Timer	TmrAnimation
Grd	Grid	GrdGoods	Tbr	ToolBar	TbrDropThis
Grc	Column (in grid)	GrcQuantity	Tbl	Table (database)	TblTitles
Grh	Header (in grid)	GrhYearsResults			

For Dummies: Bestselling Book Series for Beginners

Visual Basic .NET All-in-One Desk Reference For Dummies®

Cheat Sheet

Shortcut Keys Used in the VB.NET Editor

Command Name	Shortcut Keys	Behavior
Edit.Copy	CTRL + C CTRL + INSERT	Copies the currently selected item to the Clipboard.
Edit.Cut	CTRL + X SHIFT + DELETE	Removes the currently selected item, but saves a copy in the Clipboard in case you want to paste it somewhere.
Edit.GoToNextLocation	F8	Moves the cursor to the next item.
Edit.GoToPreviousLocation	SHIFT + F8	Moves the cursor to the previous item.
Edit.GoToReference	SHIFT + F12	Displays the reference of the selection in the code window.
Edit.OpenFile	CTRL + SHIFT + G	Displays the Open File dialog box.
Edit.Paste	CTRL + V SHIFT + INSERT	Pastes the contents of the Clipboard at the insertion point.
Edit.Redo	CTRL + SHIFT + Z CTRL + Y SHIFT + ALT + BACKSPACE	Restores a previously undone action.
Edit.SelectionCancel	ESC	Cancels the current operation or closes a dialog box.
Edit.Undo	ALT + BACKSPACE CTRL + Z	Reverses the last editing action.
File.Print	CTRL + P	Displays the Print dialog box so you can specify printer settings.
File.SaveAll	CTRL + SHIFT + S	Saves all documents in the current solution.
File.SaveSelectedItems	CTRL + S	Saves the currently active (or selected) items in the current project.
Tools.GoToCommandLine	CTRL + /	Places the caret in the Find/Command box on the Standard toolbar.
View.NextTask	CTRL + SHIFT + F12	Moves to the next task in the Task List window.
View.ViewCode	F7	Displays the selected file (in Solution Explorer) in Code editor window.
View.ViewDesigner	SHIFT + F7	Displays the selected file in the Design. (Simply double-clicking the filename in Solution Explorer is easier.)
View.WebNavigateBack	ALT + LEFT ARROW	Displays the previous page in the viewing history.
View.WebNavigateForward	ALT + RIGHT ARROW	Displays the next page in the viewing history.

For Dummies: Bestselling Book Series for Beginners

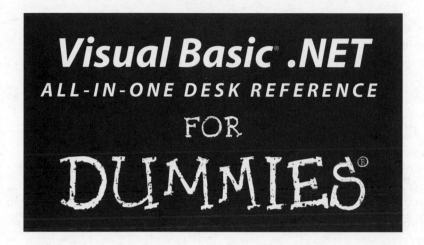

Visual Basic® .NET
ALL-IN-ONE DESK REFERENCE
FOR
DUMMIES®

by Richard Mansfield

WILEY

Wiley Publishing, Inc.

Visual Basic® .NET All-in-One Desk Reference For Dummies®

Published by
Wiley Publishing, Inc.
909 Third Avenue
New York, NY 10022
www.wiley.com

About the Author

Richard Mansfield's recent titles include *Visual Basic .NET Weekend Crash Course, Visual Basic .NET Database Programming For Dummies, Visual Basic 6 Database Programming For Dummies* (all from Wiley), *Hacker Attack* (Sybex), and *The Wi-Fi Experience: Everyone's Guide to 802.11b Wireless Networking* (Que).

From 1981 through 1987, Richard was editor of *COMPUTE! Magazine,* during which time he wrote hundreds of magazine articles and two columns. From 1987 to 1991, he was editorial director and partner in Signal Research and began writing books full-time in 1991. He has written 33 computer books since 1982. Of those, four became best-sellers: *Machine Language For Beginners* (COMPUTE! Books), *The Second Book of Machine Language* (COMPUTE! Books), *The Visual Guide to Visual Basic* (Ventana), and *The Visual Basic Power Toolkit* (Ventana, with Evangelos Petroutsos). Overall, his books have sold more than 500,000 copies worldwide and have been translated into 11 languages.

Dedication

This book is dedicated to my friend Cliff Way.

Author's Acknowledgments

I was very lucky to have two first-rate editors work with me on this book. Project Editor Andrea Boucher deserves much credit for her discernment and the exceptionally high quality of her editing. I've written 36 books now and in my experience truly outstanding editors are relatively rare. Andrea has just the right touch: She knows when you've been naughty and she knows when you've been nice. And her suggested changes are nearly always an improvement.

Technical Editor Mike Lerch is also well above the average. He thoroughly reviewed the manuscript and carefully tested all the code. He made many important suggestions and considerably enhanced the book's overall quality.

I'd also like to thank Acquisitions Editor Melody Layne for initiating this project and for her thoughtful advice throughout. To these, and all the other good people at Wiley who contributed to the book, my thanks for the time and care they took to ensure quality every step along the way to publication.

Finally, I want to give special thanks to my agent, Matt Wagner of Waterside Productions, who has been offering me good advice for over a decade.

Publisher's Acknowledgments

We're proud of this book; please send us your comments through our online registration form located at www.dummies.com/register/.

Some of the people who helped bring this book to market include the following:

Acquisitions, Editorial, and Media Development

Project Editor: Andrea C. Boucher

Acquisitions Editor: Melody Layne

Technical Editor: Mike Lerch

Editorial Manager: Carol Sheehan

Media Development Manager: Laura VanWinkle

Media Development Supervisor: Richard Graves

Editorial Assistant: Amanda Foxworth

Cartoons: Rich Tennant (www.the5thwave.com)

Production

Project Coordinator: Nancee Reeves

Layout and Graphics: Carrie Foster, Stephanie D. Jumper, LeAndra Johnson, Kristin McMullan, Jacque Schneider, Rashell Smith, Ron Terry

Proofreaders: Vickie Broyles, John Tyler Connoley, Andy Hollandbeck, Carl William Pierce, Dwight Ramsey

Indexer: Sharon Hilgenberg

Publishing and Editorial for Technology Dummies

> **Richard Swadley,** Vice President and Executive Group Publisher
>
> **Andy Cummings,** Vice President and Publisher
>
> **Mary C. Corder,** Editorial Director

Publishing for Consumer Dummies

> **Diane Graves Steele,** Vice President and Publisher
>
> **Joyce Pepple,** Acquisitions Director

Composition Services

> **Gerry Fahey,** Vice President of Production Services
>
> **Debbie Stailey,** Director of Composition Services

Contents at a Glance

Table of Contents

Introduction: Welcome to .NET

Welcome to the world of VB.NET programming. Microsoft has put many of its best cutting-edge tools into this powerhouse package, and this book shows you how to use this great new language.

It *is* a new language. If you're familiar with previous versions of Visual Basic, you will quickly discover that VB.NET is not traditional Basic. However, after you become comfortable with it, I think you'll agree that VB.NET is better. Quite a bit better.

For the past 11 years, far more programmers have chosen Visual Basic than all other programming languages combined. Estimates range from 3 million to 6 million active VB developers.

In spite of its popularity — or perhaps partly *because* of it — some programmers lifted their noses into the air, sniffed, and claimed that VB wasn't a "serious" language. In other words, the languages they used were more difficult and sometimes required much more time than VB to finish a project. But those languages could also build programs that accomplished some jobs faster and better than VB. Using the Windows Crypto API to encrypt files, for example, required an expert C++ guru. Now, though, you can use VB.NET to quite easily tap into more security power than the Crypto API ever offered. No gurus required, as you will see in Book III, Chapter 7.

Visual Basic was the first, and I believe is still the best, *rapid application development* language. Nevertheless, some programmers complained that VB would not qualify as a "real" programming language until it had true inheritance, multi-threading, and other features. With VB.NET, the VB feature set is now equivalent to all other professional programming languages. In fact, all the .NET languages compile into the *same* executable code result. So, lower your noses.

VB.NET is both powerful and diverse. If you want to do almost anything with Windows or Internet programming, you can do it with VB.NET. But, best of all, many of Visual Basic's features are still designed to be easy to use. The tools include hundreds of efficiencies, step-through wizards, and shortcuts. For example, even if you have no experience at all in adding a database to an Internet Web page, you can understand how to do just that in about two minutes.

Of course, other tasks are not as rapidly accomplished. Otherwise, this book would be five pages long, and people wouldn't be paid so much money for writing programs.

Nonetheless, if you want to create a Web service, design a brand-new database, or leverage your skills with objects, this is the book for you, and VB.NET is the language of choice. Those jobs do take longer than slapping a database connection onto a Web page (but in VB.NET, they don't take much longer). Precisely *how* much longer depends on what you want your Web service to do, how complex your database is, or how deeply into object-oriented programming you want to go. But if you can click a mouse, write ordinary Visual Basic programming, and follow straightforward directions, you can do the job. This book shows you how to create effective Windows applications and Web pages.

About This Book

My main job in this book is to show you the best way to accomplish the various techniques that, collectively, put you on the path to VB.NET programming expertise. If a task requires hands-on programming, I show you, step-by-step, how to write that programming. In other cases, I tell you when there's a simpler, better way to accomplish a job. Otherwise, you could spend days hand-programming something that's already been built — something you can create by clicking a simple menu option, adding a prebuilt component, firing up a Wizard, or using a template.

Because VB.NET is so huge, you can easily overlook the many shortcuts it contains. I've been on the betas for VB for about 10 years now, and I was on the VB.NET technical beta from its start. I've also written several books on Visual Basic. All modesty aside, I do know Visual Basic well. But VB.NET is a whole new ballgame. Many people, including yours truly, call it an entirely new language. VB.NET is big, and much of it is new. Some important techniques and tools (such as the WinCV utility described in the final chapter) I only discovered while writing this book, and this is the third VB.NET book I've written. I've been using VB.NET several hours a day since July, 2000. Two-and-a-half years. You'd think I would have pretty much mapped out the .NET world by now. But no. As you will discover yourself, .NET is a gigantic collection of interrelated technologies, and even at this late date you can still find yourself boldly going where no man has gone before.

I hope that all my work these past years will benefit you — showing you the many useful shortcuts and guiding you over the rough spots. I won't pull any punches: I confess it took me several days of wrestling with VB.NET to figure out how to get data successfully displayed in a grid. Now I can show you how to do it in a few minutes.

Also, unlike some other books about Visual Basic programming (which must remain nameless), this book is written in plain, clear English. You will find sophisticated tasks made easy: The book is filled with step-by-step examples that you can follow, even if you've never written a line of programming or designed a single computer application.

Visual Basic .NET does require some brains and practice to master, but you can handle it. To make this book as valuable for you as possible without writing a six-volume life's work on all of Visual Basic's features and functions, I geared this book toward familiarizing you with the most useful tools. You can use most of them to create either Windows or Web applications. (The approach to both platforms is quite wonderfully similar, thanks to WebForms and "code-behind" features.) VB gives you dozens of ways to get a job done, but one way always proves to be best — most sturdy, most effective, and, often, most efficiently programmed. I show you those best ways throughout the book.

How to Use This Book

This book obviously can't cover every feature in VB.NET. Instead, as you try the many step-by-step examples in this book, you become familiar with the most useful features of Visual Basic programming and many shortcuts and time-saving tricks — some that can take years to discover on your own. (Believe me, some of them have taken me years to stumble upon.)

Whether you want to create stunning Web sites or impressive Windows applications, this book tells you how to create what you want to build. Here are just a few of the goals that you can achieve with this book:

✦ Build professional-looking, effective programs.

✦ See how to move existing Windows applications to an intranet or the new Internet WebForms (and be smart enough to know when to use wizards to help).

✦ Make the transition from the traditional Microsoft ADO (ActiveX Data Objects) to the new ADO.NET technologies for database programming.

✦ Make the transition from the traditional Microsoft ASP (Active Server Pages) to the new ASP.NET technologies for Web programming.

✦ Understand how to best use the many features built into VB.NET.

✦ Kill bugs in Windows applications or Web pages.

✦ Get the most out of the new VB.NET Server Explorer, WebForm Designer, DataSet controls, .NET Framework, and other great tools.

✦ See how to use SQL, the database query language.

Many people think that programming is impossibly difficult — and that Internet programming is even more difficult. It doesn't have to be. In fact, many common programming jobs have already been written for you in VB.NET, so you don't have to do the programming at all. If you're smart, you don't reinvent the wheel. Sometimes, all you need to know is where in VB to find a particular component, Wizard, template, or other prebuilt solution. Then, drop it into your application. And when you do need to program, the Visual Basic .NET Help source code examples can often help you to get the job done more quickly than you could do it all by yourself. However, because .NET is so large and, to many programmers, so daunting (at least at first), you must learn your way around. This book can be your key to unlocking .NET's secrets.

This book tells you if a particular wheel has already been invented. It also shows you how to save time by using or modifying existing components or Help code to fit your needs instead of building new solutions from scratch. But if you're doing something totally original (congratulations!), this book also gives you step-by-step recipes for tackling many common tasks from the ground up.

Foolish Assumptions

In writing this book, I had to make a few assumptions about you, dear reader. I assume that you know how to use Windows and understand the elements of computing in general (the various ways to use a mouse, how to navigate menus, and so on).

I also assume that you don't know much, if anything, about VB.NET programming. Perhaps most importantly, I assume that you don't want lots of theory or extraneous details. You just want to get the programming jobs done.

How This Book Is Organized

The overall goal of *Visual Basic .NET All-In-One Desktop Reference For Dummies* is to provide an enjoyable and understandable guide for the Visual Basic .NET programmer. This book will be accessible to developers and programmers with little or no .NET programming experience.

The book is divided into seven books, with several chapters in each book. But the fact that the book is organized doesn't mean you have to be. You don't have to read the book in sequence from Chapter 1 to the end, just as you don't have to read a cookbook in sequence.

In fact, if you already have some experience with OOP (object-oriented programming), I suggest you read the last chapter first. Book VII, Chapter 5 helps you understand the VB.NET Help system, best employ Help's source code examples, and untangle the vast .NET Framework (collection of built-in classes). This chapter gives you guidance on how to begin navigating .NET on your own. However, because .NET is in some ways based on OOP, the last chapter will be more understandable if you are grounded in OOP as well. (OOP is the topic covered in all of Book VII.)

If you want to know how to save and load disk files, go right to Book I, Chapter 3. You're not expected to know what's in Chapter 2 before you can get results in Chapter 3. Similarly, within each chapter, you can often scan the headings and jump right to the section covering the task that you want to accomplish. There's no need to read each chapter from start to finish. I've been careful to make all the examples as self-contained as possible. And each of them works, too. They've been thoroughly tested.

All of the source code for all the examples in this book is downloadable from this book's Web site at: dummies.com/extras. The appendix at the end of this book also lists the code.

The following sections give you a brief description of the book's seven main parts.

Book I: The Fundamentals of Visual Basic .NET Programming

This book introduces .NET — explaining its purposes and its fundamental nature. You see how common tasks are accomplished, and you learn the elements of .NET programming. You are introduced to the main features of the Visual Basic .NET generous suite of programming tools. You see how to use some of the Visual Basic specialized tools to make most any programming job easier. You get a taste of .NET coding by working with file and directory management. Finally, you see how to make the transition from previous languages (particularly previous versions of Visual Basic) to the .NET programming model.

Book II: Tapping the Power of the .NET Editor

Book II covers the tools and techniques necessary to get the most out of the VB.NET IDE (integrated design editor). The IDE is your home base in VB.NET, and it's bristling with features that can make your programming jobs easier. You see how to organize your projects and how to view them in various ways (design mode, code window, solution explorer, output window, and so on). You discover how to use and customize the Toolbox, and you see how to change the way the IDE itself works by adjusting preferences and options.

Book III: Advanced Visual Basic .NET Programming

Book III explores various aspects of VB.NET that you use to tap into the power of this language. You see how to manage variables and arrays, how to *serialize* and *stream* data, and how to create controls while a program runs. In addition, you explore the new idea of *overloading*. Chapter 6 zeros in on bugs — how to trap them and what to do to fix the critters after you do trap them. Finally, you work with the intriguing .NET built-in security apparatus to encrypt and decrypt files.

Book IV: Programming for the Web

This book covers the various ways to program a Web site, including how to migrate existing traditional Windows (WinForm) applications, transforming them into WebForm-based applications. You find out how to work with the new ASP.NET technology to build intelligence into your Web site programs: persisting variables, using ASP.NET controls, connecting a database, writing Web Services, and debugging.

Book V: Visual Basic .NET Database Programming

Experts estimate that 80 percent of all programming involves databases in one way or another. That's not surprising; programming is, after all, *data* processing. This book demonstrates how to design, build, and manage databases, and it describes ways to employ DataSets (VB.NET's versatile, scalable new mini-databases). You also experiment with various approaches to indexing, data validation, querying, and the other features of the new Microsoft ADO.NET database technology. You see how to use tried-and-true database programming strategies, and you discover how to make the important transition from the older ADO to the newer ADO.NET tools.

Book VI: Fun and Games with Graphics

Book VI is all about visuals — the primary way that humans interact with computers. You focus on the various alternative drawing and imaging techniques that .NET offers to see what might be best for each particular programming job. You also see how to manage printing; few books get it right. Finally, you see how to generate graphics on the fly, by creating intriguing fractal-like Wolfram diagrams.

Book VII: Visual Basic .NET Object-Oriented Programming

Book VII introduces you to the essentials of OOP, showing you how to write classes, create objects, and handle inheritance. You write your first fully OOP project, gaining insights into the ways that OOP differs from traditional programming. The book concludes with a set of tools and resources you can use to go on by yourself, exploring the fascinating world of .NET, and continuing to expand your understanding of how to write programs within this powerful, new programming platform.

Conventions Used in This Book

This book is filled with step-by-step lists that serve as recipes to help you cook up a finished product. Each step starts off with a boldface sentence or two telling you what you should do. Directly after the bold step, you may see a sentence or two, not in boldface, telling you what happens as a result of the bold action — a menu opens, a dialog box pops up, a wizard appears, you win the lottery, whatever.

A primary convention used in this book is that I've tried to make the step-by-step examples as general as possible, but at the same time make them specific, too. Sounds impossible, and it wasn't easy. The idea is to give you a specific example that you can follow while also giving you a series of steps that you can apply directly to your own projects.

In some of the examples, I use the Pubs sample database that comes with VB.NET. For instance, a listbox is filled with particular records from Pubs, or you type some data and it's stored as a new record in Pubs and then you read the record back and see it on-screen. However, if you wish, you can follow the same steps — substituting your own particular database connection for the Pubs connection used in the examples.

Also, note that a special symbol shows you how to navigate menus. For example, when you see "Choose File⇨New⇨Project," you should click the File menu, click the New submenu, and finally click the Project option.

When I display programming code, you see it in a typeface that looks like this:

```
Dim pfont As Font
pfont = New Font("Times New Roman", 12)
```

And if I mention some programming code within a regular paragraph of text, I use a special typeface, like this: `Dim pfont As Font`.

Find All the Code Online

Every line of code that you see in this book is also available for downloading from the Dummies Web site at `dummies.com/extras`. (You can also review the code in the appendix at the end of this book.) Take advantage of this handy electronic version of the code by downloading it from the Web site so that you can then just copy and paste source code instead of typing it by hand. Saves time and avoids pesky typos.

The Searchable Dictionary

Also at this book's Web site, as well as at the end of this book, is a huge, book-length appendix that is a dictionary of traditional VB programming commands and their VB.NET equivalents. Experienced VB programmers can look in the appendix for a command that they already know (such as `InStr`), and see how that job is done the VB.NET way. But those readers who are not familiar with traditional VB will also find this searchable appendix of use. If you want to quickly find out, for example, how to change a property of `Form1` from within `Form2`, search the dictionary and you get your answer. Find the appendix at the back of the book or at this book's Web site: `dummies.com/extras`.

What You Need to Get Started

To use this book to the fullest, you need only one thing: a copy of VB.NET. (This book does not require the high-end Enterprise Version of VB.NET.)

Although Book VII covers OOP in depth, you do need to understand a few basic terms up front:

✦ A *class* is a container for source code that you write in the editor. For example, `Form1` is a class that always appears by default in any new VB.NET project.

✦ An *object* is an entity that comes into existence when you run your project by pressing F5. The object's characteristics and behaviors are based on the description of that object you provided in the *class*. For example, `Form1` becomes an object when you press F5, and thereby execute your program.

✦ Classes (and the objects that result from them) are primarily composed of two types of code: *properties* (the object's characteristics, like its `BackColor`) and *methods* (the object's behaviors, like its `Show` method). Properties are similar to traditional variables, and methods are similar to traditional functions. Collectively, an object's methods and properties are called its *members*.

Icons Used in This Book

Notice the eye-catching little icons in the margins of this book. They're next to certain paragraphs to emphasize that special information appears. Here are the icons and their meanings:

The Tip icon points you to shortcuts and insights that save you time and trouble.

A Warning icon aims to steer you away from dangerous situations.

A Technical Stuff icon highlights nerdy technical discussions that you can skip if you want to. I'm not too fond of unnecessary technical stuff, so you don't see this icon very often.

The Remember icon marks things you should keep in mind.

Where to Go from Here

Where you turn next depends on what you need. If you want the lowdown on the fundamental Visual Basic .NET tools, as well as some important terms and concepts, turn to Book I. If you're looking for the answer to a specific problem, check the index or the table of contents and then turn directly to the appropriate section.

Book I

The Fundamentals of Visual Basic .NET Programming

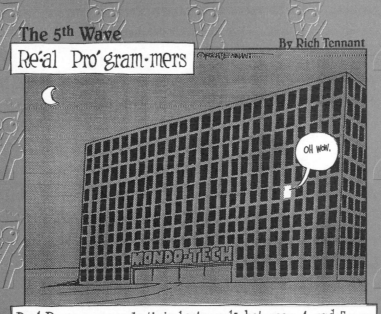

The 5th Wave   By Rich Tennant

Re´al Pro´gram·mers

OH WOW.

MONDO-TECH

Real Programmers do their best work between 1 and 5 a.m.

Contents at a Glance

Chapter 1: Getting With the Program

In This Chapter

- ✔ Understanding .NET goals
- ✔ Selling services
- ✔ Platform independence
- ✔ Software services
- ✔ Internet programming
- ✔ Database solutions
- ✔ Language independence
- ✔ Programming issues

Remember a few years ago when various Microsoft products began sporting the name *active?* Active desktop, Active directory, ActiveX, and so on. Well, now a new term has arrived, the suffix *.NET*. Visual Studio .NET, Visual Basic .NET, ASP.NET, ADO.NET, and so on.

Understanding .NET

The central concept around which all these next-generation products revolve is a technology called *.NET*. .NET, like the older COM technology, is not a single entity. Rather, it's a collection of tools and "rich" components: a programming and development environment; a runtime; a library of classes; a set of languages; a group of robust built-in security features; a highly effective way of programming for the Internet; and a commitment to support XML-based, object-oriented, easily deployed, scalable, and reliable multi-platform computing. That's quite an ambitious little solar system of new objects and technologies — all in orbit around the central idea of .NET.

.NET is a major shift. It's being called the next wave in computing — driven by an effort to make programming more coherent, and by the nature and requirements of Internet computing. Some argue that this shift from Windows-based to Internet-based computing is as profound as the shift from the text-based, colorless DOS world to the rich graphics of Windows. Perhaps. What isn't arguable is that .NET requires us programmers and developers to learn many new techniques, habits, and attitudes. Well, maybe we can at least keep some of the old attitudes.

Prepare Yourself for Some Major Changes

Think back to the late '70s when computing was mostly confined to IBM mainframes. These large centralized computers fed information to dumb terminals. The terminal stations had very little computational power of their own. They were simply display devices with a dumb keyboard. Their entire reason for existence was to act as an interface between humans and the mainframe. Both memory and processing were contained on the central mainframe.

Then at the start of the '80s, processing and memory split off into millions of personal computers. And for the past 20 years, discrete, self-contained machines have dominated computing. Perhaps we're now coming full circle in a sense. It's quite possible that in the next few years input/output units may become as small and as dumb as a cell phone. Your data may reside somewhere on the Internet, in a massive, centralized server farm — or perhaps distributed among many servers.

And that data may also be processed by services on the Internet that you "subscribe to," rather than applications that you purchase in a shrink-wrapped package. This computing model avoids the need for a dedicated personal computer, with its hard drive for storage, and lots of RAM and processing power located right there at your desk. Instead, you can access your virtual "personal computer" anywhere, anytime, using anything from a PDA to a huge wallscreen TV.

Once again, I/O terminals may become dumb, connecting to remote data storage and processing.

If these predicted changes do, in fact, occur (and some of them are already underway), programmers will be required to make quite a few adjustments to their ways of working. .NET attempts to ease this transition, while simulta-neously anticipating the platform demanded by Internet-centric computing. For one thing, traditional method-driven (or procedure-driven) programming styles may have to shift to a more message-driven (or event-driven) model.

Of course, you aren't forced to abandon your familiar programming techniques. You can use the Visual Studio .NET editor and VB.NET tools and techniques to produce traditional Windows programs just as you always have. In fact, you can produce better programs faster after you learn .NET techniques and discover how to tap into the huge .NET set of built-in classes (the Framework).

Nevertheless, .NET offers quite a variety of new skills to your programming bag of tricks. This book focuses on the .NET tools and techniques that Visual Basic programmers will want to learn.

.NET includes many familiar VB elements but sometimes gives them new names. Errors, for example, are now called *exceptions*, which sounds so much nicer. "Yes, boss, I'm going to work on some of my exceptions today."

However VB.NET brings with it many new ideas and capabilities — such as overloading and inheritance — which were never part of traditional (VB 6 and earlier) Visual Basic, although they were available in C++.

Rather than focus this book on all the differences between VB 6 and VB.NET, I've included an appendix, a dictionary of these differences, on this book's Web site. (This dictionary is as big as a book itself.) You can easily download and then search the dictionary if you want to see how something that you know how to do in traditional VB is done in VB.NET. Find this dictionary, and other helpful information, at `dummies.com/extras`. (This appendix is also included at the back of this book.)

Now back to our regular program.

Platform Independence: The Great Goal

For decades, people have been trying to design languages and operating systems that are *platform independent*. In other words, in theory it should be possible for a language or system to run on all kinds of different machines, of all sizes, made by different manufacturers, with different operating systems. Internet programming is similar: A program should adapt itself to both a large-screen TV as well as a PDA. So far, this has been an elusive goal.

But with all the new and varying sizes of computer display devices — television/internet boxes, hand-held devices, car computers, cell phones, videogame/internet devices — and all the new platforms (the Internet itself is a platform, in a sense), platform-independence is becoming more than merely an aspiration. It's becoming a necessity.

.NET must be able to run in a variety of environments. One primary thrust of .NET is that it has to be compatible with many possible devices, various programming languages, various data stores, and even different processes running at different speeds from different hard drives located in different places around the world.

The Internet is, of course, driving these changes — and the changes run deep. There must be new programming styles, new user interfaces, and new ways of communicating between applications and objects. The Internet by definition is a wildly large collection of loosely connected objects. Another way of saying this is that the Web is *highly distributed.* The Internet stores bits and pieces here and there, and each new page you visit can contain a different collection of information coming from different servers, working in different computer languages.

And, of course, large-scale applications must be able to ramp up from zero to perhaps thousands of simultaneous users — they must be *scalable.*

Software Services

Another feature of this new trend is that software will probably be increasingly sold as a *service.* You won't buy a CD/manual package in the store; instead, you'll sign up for a subscription to an application — and the application will be automatically upgraded as bugs are fixed and new features are added.

Imagine that your data, applications ("services"), and any other computing items are stored in a secure location (or spread among several locations) on the Internet, rather than on your local hard drive as they are now. This Internet-storage approach has several advantages. You can access your data from any Internet device, no matter where you are or what kind of localized storage the device has. You also lessen the *version problem* — no longer having to use a "briefcase" utility to attempt to synchronize your files between your home, office, and portable machines. Wireless Internet access is an important element in this next phase of personal computing.

Another facet of services is that small, self-contained libraries or components can reside on the Internet (or intranets) and easily be accessed thanks to the light, flexible communications protocol called SOAP (built upon XML and usable throughout the .NET technology).

.NET on the Internet

How about a .NET initiative for Internet programming? Are you kidding? All of Book IV focuses on this important technology — ASP.NET. And most of the programming in all the Books in this book can be ported quite easily to the ASP.NET WebForm container. In fact, when you use WebForms, you get the entire VB.NET language at your disposal, not just some limited scripting language as in the past. .NET is Internet-centric, to be sure, but you can also write dedicated Windows-style programs quite effectively with .NET.

.NET and Databases

Is there a new .NET initiative for database management? You bet: ADO.NET, covered extensively throughout Book V. It works well with XML and takes detached recordsets to a new level of detachment (they're now called *DataSets*). This feature is particularly useful when you're using ASP.NET Web Services to transmit and receive data. ADO.NET has been designed to accept data in many formats and from a variety of sources. It's object-oriented, of course, and also works well with relational data.

What is the main reason to move to ADO.NET? It makes database management highly scalable.

Briefly, ADO.NET neatly solves problems related to large local area networks and the Internet. Instead of maintaining a constant open connection to a database (which eats up bandwidth and resources), users "check out" a set of data as if they were borrowing a book from the library. In other words, they are only briefly connected to the database. This was not necessary when only three dental assistants in an office were connected to a central patient database. However, on the Internet, thousands of people may simultaneously attempt to interact with a database. *Scalability* means being able to ramp up from a few to many users — without bogging down or crashing from overload.

Language Independence

In keeping with the thrust toward platform and output-device independence, .NET is also language independent. It uses the CLR, the .NET Common Language Runtime. All source code from any of the supported languages is compiled into the same IL (Intermediate Language). From there, it is converted into executable code (binary object code, as it's called). This code is identical, no matter which language the source code was written in.

Several benefits result when all your programming languages compile into identical object code. You can freely inherit objects between languages (for example, borrow a VB object for use in C#).

 C# is a new language invented by Microsoft for .NET programmers who prefer the more Java-like (and, therefore, C-like) punctuation and program writing style. Some code examples in the VB.NET Help system (as well as many online examples) are written only in C#. But, don't worry, because the differences between VB.NET and C#.NET are not extreme. In fact, after you're comfortable with VB.NET and you have had a little exposure to C#, you may be able to quickly translate C# source code into VB.NET. But why even bother? If you prefer not to translate C#, the following online utility enables you to paste C# code into it, and then it translates the code for you: http://www.kamalpatel.net/ConvertCSharp2VB.aspx.

You can access one .NET language's functions from another language. For many of us, comfortable with a single language, being able to import libraries and classes from some other language may certainly expand our options and enrich our native language.

Also, studies have shown that 60 percent of developers use two languages when building their applications. Clearly, for most people, Visual Basic has been the most efficient language to work with; most people find it easier to use, read, and maintain than other languages. However, in the past, other languages have offered some performance efficiencies unavailable to the VB programmer. No longer: VB.NET has all the power of any other .NET language. So, switch and swap, or stick with VB.NET. Either way, .NET gives you all the power and efficiency you need to face the future of computing. (I doubt that 60 percent of developers will be employing dual languages when writing programs in .NET, though. VB.NET remains the easiest language to program, but now it has all the power of the other .NET languages.)

What about the Programming?

Well, you say, that's all good, but what about the actual programming? Isn't .NET programming unforgiving? Yes, but so are earlier versions of Visual Basic, or indeed any other computer language.

Of course, human languages are sometimes unforgiving, too — as any American who hitchhikes in Europe quickly discovers. If you move your thumb up and down, a passing driver may slam on his brakes, but only so he can pound you to a pulp. That thumb gesture means something very nasty in other parts of the world.

Yet, in many ways, a computer is the least flexible thing you'll ever try to communicate with. Put a comma — a little comma — in the wrong place and the computer language completely misunderstands what you're asking it to do. Misspell a word, even only slightly, and the compiler doesn't understand it at all. There's no getting around it — at this stage of their development, computer languages are extremely literal critters. Communicating with them means doing it their way or not at all.

VB.NET to the rescue

However, in spite of this literal-mindedness, VB helps you out in many ways when you're programming. First, some of the VB commands — the words in the VB language — are familiar English words like `stop`, `end`, `text`, and `timer`. Second, you can sometimes combine VB commands into statements that are quite similar to English sentences, for example: `If Dollars = 12 Then PayBill()`.

Sure, punctuation, word order, and other elements must be exact. But Visual Basic hates to let you fail. While you're learning to program, you can turn on

various kinds of training wheels that are built into VB.NET. If you make
a punctuation error or misspell a command, VB makes suggestions.
Intellisense features such as Auto Syntax Check and Auto Quick Info are
always available and are turned on by default.

If you don't remember the various capabilities (members) of a given object,
Intellisense tells you — and also shows you the parameters and the syntax.

Even experienced programmers are unlikely to turn the Intellisense features
off. And while you're still getting used to the idea of telling a machine what you
want it to do (also known as programming), these various kinds of helpers are
invaluable. As you read this book, you'll find dozens of useful VB.NET tools
that are always right there as you write your lines of source code.

Computers may be highly literal, but they make up for it by offering you
tireless and watchful assistance. If you mistype a VB command, VB itself
immediately shows you the error and suggests how to fix it. And if you're
still not exactly sure what a particular command does — or how to use it —
descriptions of each command (and often source code examples) are only
a keypress away — key F1, to be specific. Just click a command in your
programming code to select it, and then press F1. With VB, you're rarely
left twisting in the wind.

VB.NET 2003

A 2003 version of .NET offers a variety of improvements under the hood
(bug fixes, improved performance), but VB.NET programmers will find very
few changes to the language itself. Here and there throughout the book I
mention these changes. To summarize: You can now initialize a variable in
a `For Each` or `If` statement (`For I As Integer = 0 To 10`); `Try` and
`Inherits` now automatically fill in the skeletal code required to complete
their jobs (such as `Catch...End Try`); Intellisense now displays quite a few
overloaded members (rather than a drop-down list); and, my favorite, the
IDE now separates each procedure with a gray line, which makes it easier
to locate a particular procedure as you scroll through your code.

VB.NET Differs from Previous Versions

VB.NET of course represents a major shift in the commands, syntax, diction,
and other elements of Visual Basic. Most of the *punctuation* and perhaps
40 percent of the other language elements remain the same. But much is
different. The various .NET languages (specifically VB, C++, C#, and, in the
2003 version of .NET, Java) use a syntax that's more similar than ever before.
If you're familiar with traditional VB, you'll feel that VB.NET contains quite a
few C-like qualities. Here's a very brief table just to give you a little sample
of some fundamental changes:

Traditional VB	VB.NET
File `Open`.	Streaming File I/O. Much greater flexibility; more programmer control; more source code to write and test.
A largely self-describing library (few qualifiers required from the programmer).	Namespace references often required. Frequent object qualification (the VB.NET `PrintDocument1.DefaultPageSettings = PageSetupDialog1.PageSettings` as opposed to the VB 6 `Printer.Print`).
Simple procedure structures.	More complex procedure syntax.

Here's an example of a typical VB 6 procedure:

```
Sub CommandButton1_Click()
```

In VB.NET, it expands to:

```
Private Sub Button1_Click(ByVal sender As System.Object,
    ByVal e As System.EventArgs) Handles Button1.Click
```

There are many, many such changes. If you've programmed in VB before, you'll note the changes throughout this book. But don't be discouraged. After you learn the various techniques and adjust to the changes, the greater verbosity of VB.NET becomes a blessing: You get more information about all the elements of the language. Among other benefits, this helps you choose the best approach to solving programming problems, and it also provides more descriptive error messages.

In order to smooth the transition from VB to VB.NET — some people have as much as 10 years of experience with traditional VB — you can still use many traditional keywords when working within VB.NET. If you find yourself in a snit (or a bind) and want to use an old-style VB traditional command rather than the new VB.NET version, try putting this line of code at the very top of your code window:

```
Imports Microsoft.VisualBasic
```

In many cases, referencing this "compatibility library" of legacy VB functions permits you to use the older syntax, diction, and punctuation from VB 6.

Overall, I believe you'll find your journey into VB.NET as exciting and rewarding as I have. It's quite an improvement over previous programming technologies. Throughout this book, you find lots of tips and techniques to assist you in preparing for twenty-first century programming, and .NET is a big step in that direction.

Chapter 2: Common Tasks

In This Chapter

✔ Using the StringBuilder and the String functions

✔ Declaring and scoping

✔ Using RND (it's accidental on purpose)

✔ Adding menus

In this chapter, you discover how to manage several important VB.NET programming tasks. You see how to work with strings (text), how to deal with scope, the tricks of randomizing, and the new, easy way to add menus to your applications. First, you take a look at the VB.NET versatile and very swift StringBuilder.

Tackling the StringBuilder might seem a bit of a leap into the deep end of VB.NET — right here at the start of the book. But you're up to it. I want you to get a feel for the power and depth of the VB.NET language right off the bat. Don't worry, though. I felt the same way when I first saw how big and sturdy the .NET engine is. I suspect everyone is a bit awed at first.

Working with Strings: Using the StringBuilder

Manipulating strings is fundamental to any computer programming, and VB.NET includes a StringBuilder class that has been optimized to improve performance when concatenating (adding strings together or, put another way, *building* strings). The StringBuilder also performs a variety of other useful string manipulations, as this chapter shows.

A string, like most everything else in VB.NET, is an *object* and it has many *methods*. VB.NET also offers you the more efficient, faster-executing way of manipulating strings, called the StringBuilder. Use it when you are going to do some heavy-duty manipulations of a string or because you like its various convenient methods.

Instead of creating a new string each time you modify a string, the StringBuilder does not spawn multiple string objects (as do ordinary VB.NET string methods, such as ToUpper). Why? In VB.NET, when you create a string, it is *immutable* — meaning that it cannot be changed. If you ask for a change (such as "make this string all uppercase" with the ToUpper method),

VB.NET creates a brand new string with all uppercase letters, but the old string still hangs around in memory until garbage collection cleans things up. Asking VB.NET to create new strings each time you manipulate a string wastes time and space. For this reason, when you change the text held by a `StringBuilder`, it does *not* create a new string; it merely changes its existing string. (The `StringBuilder` is not any more efficient than ordinary strings when you are only reading or querying the contents of a string — such as using the `IndexOf` method. However, the `StringBuilder` is much faster when you are *changing* a string, not merely reading it.)

Traditionally, strings have been managed relatively inefficiently by VB. Fortunately, the techniques available to the new VB.NET `StringBuilder` allow your programs to run faster. The next section demonstrates how it works.

Speeding execution

If you are writing some source code that involves repeatedly changing a string, you can speed up your program's execution by creating a `StringBuilder` object rather than using normal strings. After you are through with the manipulations, you can turn the `StringBuilder`'s products back into normal strings with the `.ToString` method if you like (but usually this isn't necessary).

The `StringBuilder` sets aside some memory for itself when you instantiate it (first declare it, or *initialize* it, in your program). Then it does its work directly on the string data within that memory block. No nasty little abandoned strings hanging around waiting for the garbage truck to make its rounds.

Creating a new project

As is so often the case in VB.NET, you must initialize the `StringBuilder` before you can use it. You must create an *instance* of the `StringBuilder` class, which is a fancy way of saying that you bring a `StringBuilder` into existence. After you have the instance, you can then do all kinds of things with the text.

The following steps illustrate how to start a new VB.NET Windows-style project and how to write code for it and execute it. To try the VB.NET `StringBuilder` and see how to create a new VB.NET project, follow these steps:

1. **Start VB.NET.**

2. **Choose File⇨New⇨Project.**

The New Project dialog box appears. This is where you can select the type of project you want to work with. Most of the time, you choose either Windows Application or ASP.NET Web Application.

   3. **If it isn't already selected by default, click Visual Basic Projects in the left pane of the New Project dialog box.**

   4. **Double-click the Windows Application icon in the right pane of the New Project dialog box.**

   The dialog box closes and a brand new VB.NET project is born. It is named WindowsApplication1, unless you've created some previous projects with the name WindowsApplication.

   You see an empty form named Form1. This view, called *design view,* is where you can specify how your project looks to a user. You can add controls from the Toolbox to your forms when in design view. However, you want to just write some VB.NET code at this point. You want to switch to code view — the other primary view in VB.NET.

   5. **Double-click Form1.**

   You now see the code window. You can switch back and forth between code view and design view quite easily by simply clicking the tabs named Form1.vb(Design) or Form1.vb, which is the code view.

   6. **Your insert cursor (the flashing vertical line) is currently located in the** Form1_Load **event, but you need to type something at the very top of the code window — above all this default code. So use the up arrow key or the PageUp key to move the cursor to the first line where it says** Public Class Form1. **You want to be above this line, so press the Enter key a couple of times. Then use the up arrow key to move up into the blank white space you've just created.** *Now you're ready to rumble.*

To instantiate a StringBuilder, you must first have imported the System.Text class in your form or module. You import namespaces by using the Imports command. (A *namespace* is a collection of related functions. Don't worry about this; a namespace is merely a tag that you can optionally enter into your code using the Imports statement to simplify things.)

At the very top of your form's code module, type the following code, as shown in Figure 2-1.

```
Imports System.Text
```

If you don't import a necessary code library (namespace), you have to *qualify* (add the library name) each use of a procedure that resides in that library, like this:

```
txt = New System.Text.StringBuilder()
```

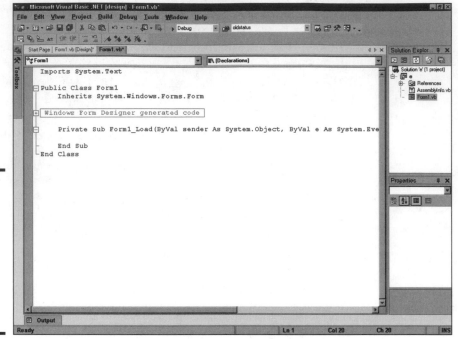

Figure 2-1:
Type any
necessary
Imports
statements
at the very
top of a
form's
source
code.

Having to qualify each time you use a procedure can get rather tedious because you have to repeat `System.Text` each time you instantiate a `StringBuilder` (or any other object that resides in the `System.Text` library). So, it's just simpler to use the `Imports` command to bring in the whole library (namespace) and after that forget about it.

After the library has been imported, you can instantiate a `StringBuilder` object and assign some text to it, and then you can concatenate (add more text using the `Append` method). Type the following into the `Form_Load` event:

```
Private Sub Form1_Load(ByVal sender As System.Object, ByVal e
    As System.EventArgs) Handles MyBase.Load

    Dim txt As New StringBuilder("This message")
    txt.Append(" and more message")

    MsgBox(txt.ToString)

End Sub
```

All the source code for this book is online, ready for you to download it and copy and paste it. Go to this book's Web site at dummies.com/extras.

Press F5 to run this program, and you see a message box displaying This message and more message.

The important point to remember here is that concatenating is a common job in computer programming, and that VB.NET does it far more quickly than previous versions of VB. It's also easier to program than the old way, which involved using the & operator:

```
Dim txt As String
txt = "This message"
txt = txt & " and more message"

MsgBox(txt)
```

The StringBuilder works with *dynamic* strings (strings that can change size while a program runs). When first instantiated, a StringBuilder object defaults to a size 16 characters large, but if you instantiate it with an initial string, it resizes to hold that string. Recall the previous example where you used Dim txt As New StringBuilder("This message"). The default string This message causes the new StringBuilder object to adjust its size dynamically. (You can also instantiate a StringBuilder with no default text, like this:

```
Dim txt As New StringBuilder().
```

In the early days of computer programming, when memory space was very expensive and therefore carefully conserved, string variables were also quite limited in the amount of text that they were permitted to hold. However, nowadays, each StringBuilder object can hold 2,147,483,647 characters. Surely two billion is big enough for most purposes. It's enough to hold two million book pages. And if you need more space for some reason, you can just instantiate a new StringBuilder.

Also, if for some reason you want to get maximum performance out of a StringBuilder's text manipulations, you can specify during instantiation the largest text size that you expect it to hold. That way, the StringBuilder doesn't have to dynamically resize itself while the program runs (and thereby exact a speed penalty). To specify maximum size, instantiate like this:

```
Dim txt As New StringBuilder(144)
```

What if your program accidentally exceeds your estimated maximum? No problem. If necessary, the StringBuilder will boost the size. But VB.NET is marvelously flexible. What if you want to *insist* that the StringBuilder not exceed a given size? Again, no problem. Just provide two numbers (initial capacity and absolute maximum capacity) as the instantiation argument, like this:

```
Dim txt As New StringBuilder(144, 2000)
```

Learning the Properties and Methods

As you may expect, there are more properties and methods available to a StringBuilder than you'll likely ever need. But this embarrassment of riches is just fine. Memory is now so cheap, why shouldn't our tools offer all kinds of "attachments"? If you ever *do* need some attachment, it's nice to have it available.

Properties

A StringBuilder can tell you the current size of the string it holds with the Length property. You can read or change a character — or group of characters — within a string using the Chars property. To change an M to a T, use this code:

```
Dim txt As New StringBuilder("Mama Mia")
Dim c As Char

c = "T"

txt.Chars(5) = c

MsgBox(txt.ToString)
```

This results in the message Mama Tia. Note that you specified position 5, even though the M is really the sixth character in your string. This is because the StringBuilder starts counting from 0, so it considers the first character the "zeroth." You just have to remember that in most collections, indexes, and other lists in VB.NET, the count starts with 0, so each item is specified as *one less* than its true position in the list.

To read the sixth character in the string, use this code:

```
MsgBox(txt.Chars(5))
```

Notice that in traditional VB strings, you can read but not change (write) characters inside a string.

Just to make life interesting, some collections and other lists violate the zero-based indexing scheme and, instead, start counting with 1 (as we humans do). So, unfortunately, you just have to always test when you're working with a set of items (such as an array, a collection, and so on) in VB.NET. You must test to see if it is a zero-based (as most are) or a one-based set.

The GetChar function returns a character from within a string at the specified index. But notice that the following example uses an index of 3 and returns the letter N, so it's one-based rather than zero-based (a zero-based index would return E as the third index position):

```
Dim s As String = "ZONE"
Dim c As Char
c = GetChar(s, 3)
msgbox(c)
```

Methods

The `Append` method, which I use in the first `StringBuilder` method earlier in this chapter, is also flexible. You can append a number, and it will be automatically turned into characters (digits):

```
Dim txt As New StringBuilder("Score: ")

    Dim n As Integer = 12

    txt.Append(n)

    MsgBox(txt.ToString)
```

You can also append a part of a string by specifying which character to start with (less one because of the "zeroth" counting, described earlier in this chapter) and how many characters to use. In this next example, I append *defgh* by specifying "start with *d* and append a total of five characters from string *c*":

```
Dim txt As New StringBuilder("Letters: ")

    Dim c As String = "abcdefghi"

    txt.Append(c, 3, 5)

    MsgBox(txt.ToString)
```

If you prefer, you can use the same syntax to append from within an array of characters instead of a simple string:

```
Dim c() As Char = "abcdefghi"
```

Don't worry at this point about arrays; Book III, Chapter 2 is devoted exclusively to the science and practice of VB.NET arrays.

Inserting

To insert text (or dates or numbers) into a `StringBuilder` object, use the `Insert` method. You specify the location where the new text should be inserted; then you provide the actual text or a variable holding that text. This example inserts 23 into a `StringBuilder`:

Learning the Properties and Methods

```
Dim txt As New StringBuilder("We invited  people.")

    Dim n As Integer = 23

    txt.Insert(11, n)

    MsgBox(txt.ToString)
```

Replacing

The `StringBuilder` easily replaces the classic VB `InStr`, `Mid` and other string manipulation functions.

Here's an example that puts the `StringBuilder` through some of its paces. I start off with `My original string` and then transform it into `Attention! Attention! This original string has now been extended and modified`. Notice the `Replace` method I use in the following example. `Replace` replaces all instances of a string with a different string.

Type this into your `Form_Load` event and press F5 to run it:

```
Private Sub Form1_Load(ByVal sender As System.Object, ByVal e
    As System.EventArgs) Handles MyBase.Load

  Dim txt As System.Text.StringBuilder
  txt = New System.Text.StringBuilder("My original string.")

  txt.Replace("My", "This") ' Edit the string by replacing
a word.
  txt.Replace(".", "") ' Edit the string by removing
punctuation
  txt.Append(" has now been extended and modified.") '
append some words
  txt.Insert(0, "Attention! ", 2) ' insert two copies at
the start (character position zero)
  MsgBox(txt.ToString)

End Sub
```

You can also limit the `Replace` activity to a specific zone within the StringBuilder's contents, if you wish:

```
txt.Replace(oldstring, newstring, startcharacter, length)
```

Removing

To cut some characters from a `StringBuilder`, specify the start position within the string and the length of the string you want removed, like this:

```
txt.Remove(startcharacter, length)
```

Appending with formatting

The `StringBuilder` includes a variation on the `Append` method called `AppendFormat`. With this method, you can apply formatting to a string prior to appending it. For example, to change an ordinary integer into dollars and cents format, use the `C` formatting command, like this:

```
Dim txt As New StringBuilder("Please pay ")

    Dim n As Integer = 1234567

    txt.AppendFormat("{0:C} ", n)
    MsgBox(txt.ToString)
```

If you run this example, you get this result: `Please pay $1,234,567.00`.

To use the formatting commands, enclose within brackets the item number you want appended. (In this example, there was only one item, n, so I used `0:` to specify that item.) Next within the brackets, specify the formatting command, which is `C` for *currency*. (For a complete list of formatting commands, look in the VB.NET Help Index for Formatting Types or enter this address in Help's address box: `ms-help://MS.VSCC/MS.MSDNVS/cpguide/html/cpconformattingtypes.htm`).

Using the String Functions

Although the `StringBuilder` class is often preferable (because it's faster), you can use the `String` class if speed isn't an issue. And while there is considerable overlap between the `StringBuilder` and `String` classes, there are some things you can do only with the `String` class. For example, both `StringBuilder` and `String` classes have a `Chars` property, but only the `String` class has the `ToUpper` method, which capitalizes an entire string in one swift pass. Turn your attention now to the `String` class and see some of the jobs it does well.

IndexOf (formerly InStr)

In the following sections, the headlines begin with the .NET command name, followed by the older, Visual Basic 6 traditional name in parentheses. In this section, for example, you look at the VB.NET `IndexOf` command, which replaces the traditional `InStr` command. Note, too, that most traditional commands are still available if you prefer to use them, but the VB.NET commands are often preferable because they are more efficient or versatile.

If you want to find out the location of one piece of text within larger text, you can use either the traditional VB `InStr` function or the new VB.NET `IndexOf` method.

Using IndexOf

The VB.NET IndexOf method can tell you where (in which character position) one piece of text is located within a larger text string.

This capability is remarkably handy when you need to *parse* some text (locate or extract a piece of text within a larger body of text). IndexOf enables you to see if a particular word, for example, exists within a file or within some text that the user has typed into a TextBox. Perhaps you need to search a TextBox to see if the user typed in the words New Jersey, and if so, to tell them that your product is not available in that state.

IndexOf is the VB.NET method that replaces the traditional VB InStr function. Here's an example that finds the first occurrence of the letter *n* in a string:

```
Dim s As String = "Hello Sonny"
Dim x As Integer
x = s.IndexOf("n")
MsgBox(x)
```

IndexOf is case-sensitive. Also, if you wish to specify the starting character position (rather than starting from the first character), add an integer to the argument list, like this:

```
Dim y as integer = 4
    x = s.IndexOf("n", y)
```

What if you want to know whether more than one instance of the search string is within the larger text? You can easily find additional instances by using the result of a previous IndexOf search. IndexOf, when it finds a match, reports the location — the character position within the larger text — where the match was found. Here's an example that reports how many times it finds the word *pieces* in some text:

```
Private Sub Form1_Load(ByVal sender As System.Object, ByVal e
    As System.EventArgs) Handles MyBase.Load

        Dim quot, MainText, SearchWord As String
        Dim X, Y, Z As Integer


        quot = Chr(34)

        MainText = "Masterpieces are built of pieces."
        SearchWord = "pieces"

        Do
            X = Y + 1
            Z = Z + 1
```

```
 Y = MainText.IndexOf(SearchWord, X)
  Loop Until Y = -1

        MsgBox("We found " & SearchWord & " " & Z - 1 & _
          " times inside " & quot & MainText & quot)


     End Sub
```

In this example, the loop continues to look through the MainText until the IndexOf method returns a -1 (which indicates that the SearchWord was not found any more). The variable Z is used to count the number of times there's a successful hit. The variable X moves the pointer one character further into the MainText (X = Y + 1). You can use this example as a template any time you need to count the number of occurrences of a string within another, larger string.

Using InStr

The traditional VB InStr format is as follows:

```
InStr([start, ]string1, string2[, compare])
```

InStr is case-sensitive by default — it makes a distinction between Upper and upper, for example. InStr tells you where (in which character position) string2 is located within string1.

To use InStr in the previous "Masterpiece" example, you need only to change these two lines:

```
Y = InStr(X, MainText, SearchWord)
  Loop Until Y = 0
```

To merely see if, in the previous example, a string appears at all within another one, you can use this technique:

```
If InStr("Masterpiece", "piece") Then MsgBox ("Yep!")
```

This code translates to: If "piece" is found within "Masterpiece," then display "Yep!"

ToLower (formerly LCase)

Sometimes you want to capitalize text in some new way. For example, you can use the ToLower method to change all uppercase letters in a string, reducing them to all lowercase characters. AfterWord becomes afterword. Likewise, there's also a ToUpper method that raises all the characters in a string to uppercase.

The VB.NET `ToLower` method replaces the traditional VB `LCase` function, and the VB.NET `ToUpper` replaces the traditional `UCase` function.

These methods or functions are used when you want to ignore the case — when you want to be *case-insensitive*. Usually, `ToLower` or `ToUpper` are valuable when the user is providing input and you can't know (and don't care) how he or she might capitalize the input. For example, string comparisons are case-sensitive:

```
If "Larry" = "larry" Then MsgBox "They are the same."
```

This message box will never be displayed. The `L` is not the same because one is uppercase and the other is lowercase. You can see the problem. You often just don't know whether your users will capitalize any letters when they type something in while the program is running. If you don't care, just use `ToLower` or `ToUpper` to force all the characters to be lowercase or uppercase, like this:

```
Private Sub Form1_Load(ByVal sender As System.Object, ByVal e
    As System.EventArgs) Handles MyBase.Load

        Dim reply As String
        Dim n As Integer

        reply = InputBox("Shall we proceed?")

reply = reply.ToUpper

        Dim x As Integer


        If reply = "YES" Then
            MsgBox("Ok. We'll proceed.")
        End If


    End Sub
```

In this example, notice that it now does not matter how the user capitalized `yes`. Any capitalization will be forced into uppercase letters, and you compare it to a literal `YES` that is also all uppercase.

Substring (formerly Left)

If you want to retrieve only a portion of a string — the first three letters, for example — you can use the new VB.NET equivalent of the traditional `Left` or `Right` string functions, which is the `SubString` method:

```
Dim n As String = "More to the point."
```

```
n = n.Substring(0, 4)
MsgBox(n)
```

The first number inside the parentheses specifies the position to start at, with 0 meaning the first character. The second number (4 here) specifies how many characters you want to extract. The result of this code puts the characters More into the string variable n.

Or to get a string from the right side, the following code retrieves all characters from the twelfth character to the end of the string:

```
n = n.Substring(12)
```

The traditional Left function works similarly; it returns a portion of a string, the number of characters defined by the Number argument. Here's an example:

```
Dim n As String = Microsoft.VisualBasic.Left("More to the
    point.", 4)
MsgBox(n)
```

There's also a Right function. Notice that both Left and Right functions require the Microsoft.VisualBasic qualifier, which was not necessary in previous versions of VB.

Length (formerly Len)

The VB.NET Length method tells you how many characters are in a string. You may want to let the users know that their response is too wordy for your database's allotted space for a particular entry. Or perhaps you want to see if they entered the full telephone number, including their area code. If they have, their numbers will have to be at least 10 characters long. You can use the less-than symbol (<) to test their entry, like this:

```
If TextBox1.Text.Length < 10 Then
```

Or use the traditional Len function, as follows:

```
If Len(TextBox1.Text) < 10 Then MsgBox("Shorter")
```

Trim (formerly LTrim)

The VB.NET Trim method removes any leading and trailing space characters from a string. The uses for this method are similar to those for ToUpper or ToLower: Sometimes people accidentally add extra spaces at the beginning or end of their typing. Those space characters will cause a string comparison to fail because computers can be quite literal. " This" is not the same thing as `"This"`. If you write code `If " This" = "This"`, and the user types `" This "`, the computer's answer will be `no`. Also, some data formats require a particular string length.

Here's an example that removes four leading spaces:

```
Dim s As String = "    Here"
s = s.Trim
MsgBox(s & s.Length)
```

You can also employ VB.NET `TrimEnd` and `TrimStart` methods, if you are interested in getting rid of spaces from only one side of a string.

`Trim, LTrim` (and its brother `RTrim`) are the traditional VB space-removal functions.

Substring (formerly Mid)

You may find yourself using the `Substring` method surprisingly often. It can extract a substring (a string within a string) from anywhere within a string.

```
Dim s As String = "1234567"
MsgBox(s.Substring(2, 4))
```

Running this code results in `3456`. You asked to start at the third character (by specifying the `2`) and to extract the 4 characters following it. VB.NET brings us many improvements over traditional VB, and some degradations. In my view, this example illustrates one of the degradations: Notice that to start with the *third* character in this string, you must specify `2` as your `Substring` argument. Recall the discussion earlier in this chapter of the "zeroth" problem when using collections, lists, and other sets. This nonsense occurs because the `Substring` method, like other methods in computer languages, begins counting characters with zero (the *first* character — as we humans think of it — must be described in VB.NET here as the "zeroth" character). Of course, in human language (and, consequently, in human thinking processes), the zero means absence or nonexistence. So we never think of the first item in a list as being the *zero* item. Nor should we have to think this way when using computer languages. In previous versions of VB, we didn't have to, at least when extracting strings. The VB 6 `Mid` function does the same thing as the VB.NET `Substring` method in this example. However, `Mid` begins counting characters with 1, as we humans do. Somebody who worked on designing VB.NET thinks we should start counting with zero, as in: "This is my zeroth time visiting Greece; I'm so glad I got to vacation here. Next year I'm coming back for my *first* visit!"

The traditional VB `Mid` format is as follows:

```
Mid(String, StartCharacter [, NumberOfCharacters])
```

The Mid function works like this:

```
MsgBox(Mid("1234567", 3, 4))
```

 There isn't space to cover *all* the string methods in VB.NET; they are too numerous. Here are some additional methods you may want to familiarize yourself with by reading about them after looking them up in the VB.NET Help index — just so you know they exist if you ever need them:

✦ Compare

✦ Concat

✦ Format

✦ Chars

✦ EndsWith

✦ Insert

✦ LastIndexOf

✦ PadLeft

✦ PadRight

✦ Remove

✦ Replace

✦ Split

✦ StartsWith

Chr and ASC

The Chr and ASC functions can come in handy in some specialized situations. In case you ever need one of them, you should be aware that they exist.

Chr

The traditional Chr VB function has no VB.NET equivalent, but it is sometimes useful. Chr returns the character represented by the ASCII code. In computer languages, all characters (all the uppercase and lowercase letters of the alphabet, punctuation marks, digits, and special symbols) have a numeric code from 0 to 255 (although this is changing to a larger set of numbers to accommodate most of the world's languages).

The computer works exclusively with numbers. The only purpose of text, from the computer's point of view, is to facilitate communication with humans. When you type in the letter **a**, the computer "remembers" it as the number 97. When that character is printed on the screen or on paper, the computer translates 97 back into the visual symbol we recognize as *a*.

Chr can be useful when encrypting messages or to solve specialized character-displaying problems, as the following example illustrates.

To display quotation marks to the user, you can define a variable containing the code for the quotation mark, which is 34:

```
Dim quot As String

    quot = Chr(34)
    MsgBox("We're selling " & quot & "wood." & quot)
```

There are built-in .NET constants you can use instead of specifying the code number. For example, use the ControlChars class like this instead of Chr(34) for a quotation mark:

```
Dim quot As String = ControlChars.Quote
```

Another common use of Chr is to force a carriage return (linefeed): in other words, to simulate pressing the Enter key to move down to the next line in a TextBox. There is no way to type the Enter key into a string, so you must define the two character codes that simulate it, like this:

```
Dim cr As String = Chr(13) & Chr(10)
TextBox1.Text = "Hi" & cr & "How are you all!"
```

Instead of Chr(13) & Chr(10), you can use the built-in VB.NET constant for these two characters, like this:

```
Dim clrf As String = ControlChars.CrLf
```

By now you're probably muttering to yourself, "Well, if they defined a constant called ControlChars.CrLf to solve this problem, why didn't they just go the whole way and really simplify things and eliminate that ControlChars? Just use CrLf so that I, the programmer, don't have to go to the trouble of remembering a more complicated name?" Well, I have no good answer except that old adage that life isn't always fair, so stop muttering.

You may have noticed that a couple of examples in this chapter have used a condensed format when declaring a variable. In VB.NET, you can both declare the variable and assign a value to it, right on the same line:

```
Dim clrf As String = ControlChars.CrLf
```

This is a handy shortcut for the following, more traditional way of declaring and then assigning a value to a variable:

```
Dim clrf As String
Clrf  = ControlChars.CrLf
```

ASC

The ASC function is related to Chr but does the opposite job: ASC looks at a text character and provides you with its code:

```
Dim n As Integer = Asc("Q")
MsgBox(n)
```

This code displays the number 81, which is the ASCII code value for the uppercase q. A set of VB.NET constants is defined in the Keys class (technically this list of constants is called an *enumeration*), which you can use instead of ASC:

```
Dim n As Integer = Keys.Q
MsgBox(n)
```

The Keys set of constants is useful when you are testing user input with the KeyDown or KeyPress events.

Using constants

VB.NET includes many *constants* — predefined values for such things as colors, keypresses, and other elements used in programming. In the preceding section, you saw that there are various constants for character codes.

It's usually best in VB.NET to use the *names* of the built-in constants. Although the constants do have numeric values you could use, your programs will be far easier to read and deal with if you stick with the built-in constant names.

How do you find these built-in constant names? You can rely on the Intellisense lists that VB.NET displays to you while you're writing a line of programming. For example, a slew of constants are associated with the Color object in VB.NET. So, for example, to choose one of these colors for the BackColor property of a form, type part of the line until you get to the dot (.), as shown in the following figure. As soon as you type that dot, VB.NET drops down a list of all the color constants from which you can choose (same for Keys. or ControlChars. as illustrated in earlier examples in this chapter).

(continued)

(continued)

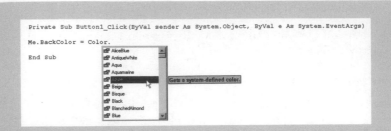

```
Private Sub Button1_Click(ByVal sender As System.Object, ByVal e As System.EventArgs)

Me.BackColor = Color.

End Sub
```

Some people like to use the VB.NET Object Browser utility instead of (or in addition to) Intellisense. Press F2 and then open the various namespaces in the left pane to see if you can find the object that interests you. For this example, look for System.Drawing.Color. Of course, you *do* run into the old paradox from time to time: How do you look up a word in the dictionary if you don't know how to spell it? With VB.NET enumerations and other such classes, if you don't remember that the enumeration is named Keys or Color or ControlChars, you may have a tough time finding the list in Help, in the Object Browser, or in the Intellisense feature. I don't know of any solution to this problem, other than memorizing the necessary names for certain classes such as Color.

Understanding Scope

VB.NET programs are subdivided into zones, just as America is divided into states, counties, and cities. And, just as law enforcement agents have different sizes of jurisdictions (city cops, state troopers, and FBI, which can go anywhere), so do VB.NET lines of programming have ranges of influence. This range of influence, called *scope,* mostly applies to variables (but can also apply to procedures — subs and functions — as well as entire classes).

Often you want to query or change the value in a variable, but whether or not that variable is accessible to you depends on its scope. For example, you can always access a variable from within the same procedure (functions, subroutines, and events are all procedures). To see how this works, type the following into your code module:

```
Private Sub Form1_Load(ByVal sender As System.Object, ByVal e
    As System.EventArgs) Handles MyBase.Load

        Dim N As String = "This"
        MsgBox(N)

End Sub
```

Press F5 and notice that the MsgBox has no problem displaying the value of the variable N.

It displays This. Now type another sub just below the Form1_Load sub in the code window:

```
Public Sub TryIt()

        MsgBox(N)

End Sub
```

Notice that there is a sawtooth line under the variable N in the TryIt sub. Hold your mouse pointer on top of the sawtooth line and VB.NET displays an error message telling you that Name 'N' is not declared.

This error message means that any lines of code within the TryIt sub (between Public Sub and End Sub) cannot read (access) or write (change) the variable N. N was declared (with the Dim command) in a separate procedure, and so the scope of N (its range of accessibility) is limited to lines of code within its same procedure.

Although Dim is the most commonly used, you can use seven additional declaration commands: Static, Public, Protected, Friend, Shared, Protected Friend, and Private. These additional commands specify *scope* (from which locations in your program a variable can be accessed).

So far in all the examples in the first two chapters, I've been declaring variables only inside procedures. Recall that when you declare a variable inside a procedure, the variable works only within that procedure. When the program executes the procedure (or event), the variable comes to life, does its thing, and then dies (disappears) as soon as the End Sub line is executed.

When variables are local

Variables that live only within a single procedure are called *local variables*. Local variables have two qualities that you need to memorize:

+ No programming outside their own procedure can interact with them, either to read their value or to change their value. Their scope is limited to their own procedure.

+ When VB finishes executing the procedure in which they reside, their value evaporates. If that procedure is executed a second time, whatever value the local variable once contained is no longer there. One execution of the procedure is their lifetime. There are some situations in which you do want a local variable's value to be preserved. Recall that in those cases, you use the Static command rather than the Dim command:

```
Private Sub Form1_Load(ByVal sender As System.Object,
    ByVal e As System.EventArgs) Handles MyBase.Load

        Dim n As Integer
        Static x As Integer

End Sub
```

In this example, the variable n loses its value when the End Sub is executed. However, the variable x retains its value until the program is shut down. Another way of putting it is this: When you use the Static command with a local variable, the value of that variable is preserved for the lifetime of your application. (*Lifetime* means how long something is in existence in a program.)

What do you think would happen if you put two Command Buttons on your Form, and then you ran the program and clicked Command1 first, and then clicked Command2, in this next program?

```
Private Sub Button1_Click(ByVal sender As System.Object,
    ByVal e As System.EventArgs) Handles Button1.Click
        Dim X As Integer
        X = 12
        X = X + 5
    End Sub

Private Sub Button2_Click(ByVal sender As System.Object,
    ByVal e As System.EventArgs) Handles Button2.Click
        Dim X As Integer
        MsgBox(X)
    End Sub
```

The message box displays nothing. The variable X in Command1's Click event is a completely different variable from the X in Command2's Click event. They are *local* in scope and simply have no relationship to each other, no more than two strangers named Mike who happen to live in the Bronx and never meet.

But what if you want both of these procedures to be able to access and manipulate the same variable? To do this, you define the variable outside your procedures. Try it. Click just above your first procedure (just above the line Private Sub Form1_Load) in the code window to move the insertion cursor there. Now type the following:

```
Dim x As Integer
```

That's where you want to put any variables that you want to give *form-wide* scope — in other words, to permit all the procedures in that form (Form1, in this case) to be able to read and modify the variable. (The area where you put form-wide variables used to be called the `General Declarations` area, prior to VB.NET.)

Now, with that `X` variable `Dim`med up there above (outside) all the Subs and other procedures, when you run the same program, click Command1, and then click Command2, you see the result you want to see: the number `17`. When you declare `X` to be form-wide in scope, the two buttons can access that variable `X`. Delete the two `Dim` statements that previously declared `X` within those two Button events. Now `X = X + 5` and `MsgBox(X)` both refer to the same variable named `X`.

When a variable has form-wide scope, it's then available to all of the procedures in that form. It's not available, however, to the procedures in any other forms in the project.

Public: The greatest scope of all

What if you want to make a variable available to all the procedures in all your forms in a given project? In such a case, you have to use the `Public` command rather than `Dim`. What's more, you have to put this `Public` declaration into a standard module, not a form.

Variables declared `Public` in a standard module are visible from anywhere in your project.

A module is similar to a form, but it doesn't have a user interface (no text boxes, buttons, or anything else visible to a user when the program runs). A module also contains no events. It's just a code window — a location where you can put public declarations (program-wide in scope) or a place to put program-wide scoped procedures. (Yes, procedures, like variables, have scope. Notice how each procedure begins with a scope declaration such as `Private`.)

To add a module to your program, follow these steps:

1. **Choose Project➪Add Module.**

The Add Module dialog box opens.

2. **Double-click the Module icon.**

A new module (named Module1) appears in your Solution Explorer window. You also see the module's code window.

Both form-wide and program-wide variables are preserved for the lifetime of your application. They never lose their values like local variables declared with `Dim` do.

3. **Now type a Public variable into the module:**

```
Module Module1
```

```
        'this variable can now be seen in both Form1 and
     Form2

     Public Password As String

  End Module
```

It's considered good programming practice to try to avoid using Public variables whenever possible. Variables with that much scope can make your programming harder to debug. Looking at the status of variables is one of the primary ways to find out where a problem is located in a program. If you use a local variable, any problem involving that variable can be found in its procedure, which really narrows your search for a bug. By contrast, you have more code — probably much more code — to search and analyze if the bug involves a form-wide (or worse, project-wide) variable. However, sometimes you have to use form-wide or even project-wide variables.

Recall that procedures also have scope. By default, VB makes some events `Private` (`Private Sub Button1_Click`) and others `Public`. If you don't want to permit code outside your current form to access a procedure, declare it (or leave it defaulting) as `Private`. If you do want to permit outside code access, declare the procedure as `Public`.

Traditional VB had only six commands that specified scope: `Public`, `Private`, `Dim`, `ReDim`, `Friend`, and `Static`. This chapter has covered all but the `ReDim` and `Friend` commands. `ReDim` is not often used, and it works only with arrays. So I postpone discussing it until Book III. `Friend` access is similar to `Public`, but only code within its project (or application) can access a variable or procedure declared with `Friend`. This means that another, separate application cannot access a `Friend`. (Separate applications *can* make use of `Public` variables or procedures.)

VB.NET adds these nine additional procedure declaration commands related to scope: `Overloads`, `Overrides`, `Overridable`, `NotOverridable`, `MustOverride`, `Shadows`, `Shared`, `Protected`, and `Protected Friend`. The majority of these commands involve inheritance (see Book VII, Chapter 1).

Randomizing

Generating a series of random numbers has uses in games, encryption, and other programming tasks. In VB.NET, use the `System.Random` function to get random numbers. To try it, type this code into your code window:

```
Private Sub Form1_Load(ByVal sender As System.Object, ByVal e
     As System.EventArgs) Handles MyBase.Load

  Dim i As Integer
```

```
      For i = 1 To 50
          Console.Write(rand(i) & " ")
      Next

  End Sub

Function rand(ByVal MySeed As Integer) As Integer
      Dim obj As New System.Random(MySeed)
      Return obj.Next(1, 12)
End Function
```

The `rand` function returns random numbers between 1 and 11. When you press F5 to run this example, you see the results in the VB.NET Output window. If the Output window isn't visible, press Ctrl+Alt+O. You should see a list of random numbers such as 3 9 4 9 4 10 5 10 5 11 6 11 ...

Although the arguments in this example say 1, 12 in the `Return obj.next(1, 12)` line, you won't get a single 12 in your results. The numbers provided by the `System.Random` function in this case range only from 1 to 11 (it provides numbers up to 12, not through 12). Just another one of those little annoying exceptions to the rule that you must memorize.

Notice that every time you press F5 to run the previous example, you always get the *same* list of random numbers. This can be useful when writing encryption schemes, but with games you want a different list each time you run your application.

Here's an example that illustrates how you can use the `Now` command to seed your random generator. `Now` returns the current date and time, and it will always be different (time doesn't run backward). Type this code in the `Form_Load` event:

```
Private Sub Form1_Load(ByVal sender As System.Object, ByVal e
    As System.EventArgs) Handles MyBase.Load

      Dim sro As New coin()
      Dim x As Integer
      Dim i As Integer

      For i = 1 To 100
          sro.toss()

          Dim n As String

          x = sro.coinvalue
          If x = 1 Then
              n = "tails"
          Else
              n = "heads"
          End If
```

```
        n = n & " "

     Console.Write(n)
  Next i

End Sub
```

Then, at the very bottom of your code window, *below* the `End Class` line, type this new class, which tosses a coin:

```
End Class

Class coin

    Private m_coinValue As Integer = 0

    Private Shared s_rndGenerator As New
System.Random(Now.Millisecond)

    Public ReadOnly Property coinValue() As Integer
        Get
            Return m_coinValue
        End Get
    End Property

    Public Sub toss()
        m_coinValue = s_rndGenerator.next(1, 3)
    End Sub

End Class
```

Now press F5 several times to run this repeatedly, and each time check the Output window. Notice that the list of coin toss results now differs each time you run this application.

Using the Menu Maker

Visual Basic .NET makes the job of adding menus to your projects quite straightforward, which is an improvement over the somewhat clumsy techniques used in previous versions of VB.

You add a control from the Toolbox and then just type in the various menus and submenus you want to add to a form. Then, to make the menus actually *do* something when the program runs, double-click any of the menu items on the Form and, as usual, you're taken down into the code window where you can then add whatever programming is needed.

You fill in the code

The MainMenu control, as it's called, merely leaves behind shell structures (a `Click` event `Sub` for each menu item). It's up to you, of course, to fill in the programming code that, for example, actually saves a file if the user clicks your Save As option in your File menu. Fortunately, several of the most common menu options — File Open, Save, Print, Print Preview, Page Setup, Color, and Change Fonts — can be handled rather easily with the `CommonDialog` controls.

Go ahead and give the `MainMenu` control a try:

1. **Click the Form1.vb(Design) tab at the top of the code window.**

You see the design view where you can add controls to your form.

2. **Press Ctrl+Alt+X.**

The Toolbox opens.

3. **Double-click the MainMenu control.**

A MainMenu control is added to your form. The tray opens below your form, displaying a MainMenu icon. Also, you see a box at the top left of the form that says "Type Here."

4. **Select the Type Here box with your mouse.**

The Type Here box is selected, ready for you to type something in.

5. **Type the word** File, **as shown in Figure 2-2.**

Figure 2-2:
As soon as you label a file item, surrounding empty squares open up inviting you to label them, too, if you wish.

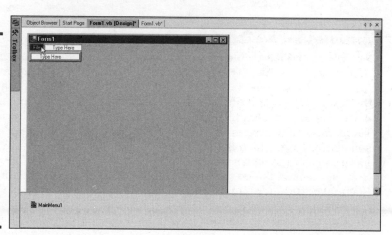

The menus across the top are *root menus*. They are usually visible to the user at all times. Most of the time, their only job is to drop down a menu to reveal their set of submenu items. Each submenu item has a `Click` event where you put the programming for the response if the user chooses that menu item.

6. **Type the word** Save **in the box just below the one you labeled File.**

   Notice once again that various adjacent empty boxes open up.

7. **Type** Text 1 **in the box to the right of Save.**

   Notice in Figure 2-3 that VB.NET automatically adds a right-arrow symbol when you create secondary menu items. This kind of menu item pops out to the right, providing the user with various options. In this case, you're offering the user the chance to save the contents of a TextBox.

Figure 2-3:
Continue
typing in
menu items
until you've
created the
menu
structure
you want.

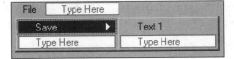

Making menu items work

You've created a little menu, but you now must provide the programming that responds if the user selects items in your menu. To create a Save feature, use the SaveFileDialog control. Double-click the SaveFileDialog icon in the Toolbox. (You'll probably have to use the down-arrow icon near the bottom of the Toolbox to scroll down to find the SaveFileDialog icon. The Toolbox holds more controls than can be displayed at one time, so you sometimes have to scroll it.)

Now you're ready to go into the code window and provide the programming that makes the Save happen.

1. **Double-click the TextBox icon in the Toolbox.**

   A TextBox is added to your form.

2. **Double-click the Text 1 menu item in your menu structure on the form.**

The code window opens, displaying that menu item's Click event. (You don't put any code into the Save menu item because its only job is to display the Text 1 submenu.)

3. **Type the following into the** MenuItem3_Click **event:**

```
Private Sub MenuItem3_Click(ByVal sender As
    System.Object, ByVal e As System.EventArgs) Handles
MenuItem3.Click

        Dim s As New SaveFileDialog()
        s = SaveFileDialog1

        s.ShowDialog()
        MsgBox(s.FileName)

    End Sub
```

4. **Press F5.**

Your program runs.

5. **Use the FileSave dialog to browse.**

Locate a folder where you want to store the file.

6. **Type in a filename.**

7. **Click Save.**

You see a message box like the one shown in Figure 2-4 (although your results will display the path and filename you used when running this test).

Figure 2-4:
Here's the result you wanted: A file can now be saved.

Of course, you need to add a bit more code to this procedure to actually *save* the file to the hard drive. All you've programmed so far is the ability to get the path and filename (s.filename) from the user. How to save and load files is covered in Book III, Chapter 3.

Chapter 3: Managing Files and Directories

In This Chapter

✔ Creating and deleting

✔ The larger picture: managing directories

*T*his chapter shows you how to handle several common file and directory tasks. You see how to create, copy, cut, move, and delete files — all from within your program. Then you create and delete entire directories.

Creating a New File

When you want to create a new file and save something into that new file, you use the new VB.NET `filestream` object.

The following example illustrates how to set the various properties of the `SaveFileDialog` control and then write the programming to actually save the contents of a `TextBox` to a file:

1. **Choose File⇨New⇨Project.**

You see the New Project dialog box.

2. **Type** FileSave **in the Name box of the dialog box.**

3. **Double-click the Windows Application icon.**

The New Project dialog box closes and your new application opens, ready for you to program it.

4. **Add a TextBox and a Button to your form by double-clicking their icons in the Toolbox. Also double-click the SaveFileDialog icon in the Toolbox to add this control to your form. (Recall that you'll have to click the black down-arrow at the bottom of the Toolbox to scroll it in order to access the SaveFileDialog icon.)**

5. **Double-click the Button control that you put on the form.**

You are taken to the `Button1_Click` event in the code window. When you double-click on a control, you cause VB.NET to create an event for that control and switch you to the code window.

6. **It is essential that you go to the very top of the code window and type in this line:**

```
Imports System.IO
```

Without this `Imports` line, VB.NET will not understand the meaning of the `FileStream` class and other elements you'll be using to save a file.

7. **Now type the following into the** `Button1_Click` **event:**

```
Private Sub Button1_Click(ByVal sender As
    System.Object, ByVal e As System.EventArgs) Handles
    Button1.Click

        SaveFileDialog1.Title = "Save the contents of
    the TextBox"
        SaveFileDialog1.FileName = "TextBox1.txt"
        SaveFileDialog1.InitialDirectory = "C:\"
        SaveFileDialog1.DefaultExt = ".txt"
        SaveFileDialog1.Filter = "Text files
    (*.txt)|*.txt|All files (*.*)|*.*"

        SaveFileDialog1.RestoreDirectory = True

        If SaveFileDialog1.ShowDialog() =
    DialogResult.OK Then
            'actually save the file:

            Dim strText As String = TextBox1.Text

            If (strText.Length < 1) Then
                MsgBox("Please type something into the
    TextBox so we can save it.")
                Exit Sub
            Else
                Dim strFileName As String =
    SaveFileDialog1.FileName
                Dim objOpenFile As FileStream = New
    FileStream(strFileName, FileMode.Append,
    FileAccess.Write, FileShare.Read)
                Dim objStreamWriter As StreamWriter =
    New StreamWriter(objOpenFile)

                objStreamWriter.WriteLine(strText)

                objStreamWriter.Close()
                objOpenFile.Close()
            End If

        End If

    End Sub
```

Notice the .Close method that concludes this example. Always use it when you are finished with a stream object such as a StreamWriter or FileStream. The .Close method causes any data held in a temporary storage area (a cache) to be saved to the hard drive. You could also use the .Flush method, but that's not generally necessary because the .Close method automatically causes a flush.

You often need to test whether the user has pressed the Cancel button in a dialog box. Here's a good way to do that:

```
If SaveFileDialog1.ShowDialog() = DialogResult.OK Then
```

If the user clicks the Cancel button, this If test will fail, and the program will skip and ignore any programming code between the If and the End If. Notice that this line of code displays the dialog box, and then when the user is finished and closes this dialog box, the code tests DialogResult.OK to see whether your program should do anything, or whether it should respond to a Cancel by doing nothing.

Let's consider what the programming in this example does. Before you displayed this dialog box (with the ShowDialog command), you set a series of properties. You created a title for the dialog box, and then you suggested a default filename. The user always has the option of changing that suggestion by overtyping in the dialog box.

After ShowDialog finishes executing, the Dialog's FileName property automatically contains the full path of where the file was actually saved, such as C:\MyFolder\Trips.Txt. You then use that information to write the code that actually accomplishes the file-saving, as this example illustrates.

Next, you set the DefaultExt property so that if users don't supply a filename extension, .TXT will be appended to their filenames automatically. The directory that is first displayed is set to C:\.

The Filter property adds a typical filter. By default, this dialog box displays only files ending in the .TXT extension when it displays the contents of a disk folder. However, if users click the Save as type field, they can choose to display all the files (*.*).

Finally, as a courtesy, you set the RestoreDirectory property to True. Windows always maintains a *current directory,* which is the one displayed by default unless a program specifies otherwise (as you did when you specified the InitialDirectory). If users browse the hard drive while using the SaveFile dialog box, they are changing the current directory each time they move to a new directory. However, by setting the RestoreDirectory property to True, you cause Windows to ignore the user's browsing — and the current directory remains what it was before your dialog box was used.

Saving a File

The actual saving is accomplished by using a C-language style of file-access, visualized as a *stream* of data (flowing, presumably, between a hard drive and the computer's RAM memory). VB programmers will wonder where their familiar Open, Write, Print, and Close commands have gone. You can still use that old style if you want by adding the following at the top of the code window:

```
Imports Microsoft.VisualBasic
```

This Imports statement adds the *compatibility* feature (allowing you to use various VB 6 programming code commands to VB.NET programs), like this:

```
Open FileName For Output As #1
Write #1, Text1.Text
Close #1
```

However, if you want to know how to save a file using VB.NET-style code, follow the example earlier in this chapter that uses the FileStream and StreamWriter objects. You can simply copy that code into your own projects, modifying it as necessary. As you can see, you create a FileStream object and a StreamWriter object. Streams are covered in depth in Book III, Chapter 3.

Reading a File

You use a similar syntax to open a disk file and read ("get") its contents into your program. Add a second button control to your form, and then type this into its Click event:

```
Private Sub Button2_Click(ByVal sender As System.Object,
    ByVal e As System.EventArgs) Handles Button2.Click

     Dim strText As String
     Dim strFileName As String = "C:\myfile2.txt"

     Dim objOpenFile As FileStream = New
FileStream(strFileName, FileMode.Open, FileAccess.Read,
FileShare.Read)
     Dim objStreamReader As StreamReader = New
StreamReader(objOpenFile)

     strText = objStreamReader.ReadLine()

     objStreamReader.Close()
     objOpenFile.Close()
```

```
MsgBox(strText)

End Sub
```

When you press F5 to test this example, be sure that you have a file on your
C: drive named myfile2.txt, or you will get an error message.

I've illustrated the primary differences between the file writing and file
reading commands in this example by putting them in boldface. Pay special
attention to this line:

```
strText = objStreamReader.ReadLine()
```

Memorize the fact that you must *assign* the value of the file (meaning, the
text in the file) you are reading to your strText variable. However, when
you are writing, you *pass* the text as a parameter to the WriteLine method
(using parentheses, rather than the = assignment operator):

```
objStreamWriter.WriteLine(strText)
```

This distinction is typical of the difference in syntax between sending data
to a procedure (writing) and getting data from a procedure (reading).

Copying, Moving, and Deleting Files

As long as you have Imports System.IO as the first line in your code
window, you can write various kinds of programming to manage files. If you
want to copy a file, type this into your Form_Load event and then press F5
to test it:

```
Private Sub Form1_Load(ByVal sender As System.Object, ByVal e
    As System.EventArgs) Handles MyBase.Load

    Dim fa As New FileInfo("c:\testqz.txt") 'create a
file object
    fa.Create()              'create a new file on the hard
    drive
End Sub
```

Press F5 to run this code, and then change the Form1_Load event to create
a copy, as follows:

```
 Private Sub Form1_Load(ByVal sender As System.Object,
ByVal e As System.EventArgs) Handles MyBase.Load

    Dim fa As New FileInfo("c:\testqz.txt") 'create a
file object
```

```
      fa.CopyTo("c:\testqz.bak") 'make a copy of it

   End Sub
```

Moving a file

Assuming that you created the file *c:\testqz.bak* in the previous example, now you can move it, using the following code:

```
Dim fa As New FileInfo("c:\testqz.bak") 'identify the file
fa.MoveTo("d:\testqz.bak") 'make a copy of it on drive D:
```

Deleting a file

Use the following code to delete the file you just moved to drive D:

```
Dim fa As New FileInfo("c:\testqz.bak") 'identify the file
fa.MoveTo("d:\testqz.bak") 'make a copy of it on drive D:
```

You can use the `FileInfo` object to perform a variety of other operations on a file, including appending text and finding out when it was created, when it was last viewed, how big it is, what directory it is in (`Dim n As String = fa.Directory.ToString`), what its extension is, when it was last modified, and so on.

Managing Directories

If you want to create a new directory, use `Imports` with the `System.IO` namespace (as you did earlier in this chapter); then use the `DirectoryInfo` object. This example creates a new directory:

```
Private Sub Form1_Load(ByVal sender As System.Object, ByVal e
   As System.EventArgs) Handles MyBase.Load

      Dim objDir As New DirectoryInfo("c:\TestDir")

      Try
         objDir.Create()

      Catch
         Throw New Exception("Failed to create new
directory")
      End Try

   End Sub
```

You see how to deal with error trapping (also known as *exception handling*) — that `Try...Catch...Throw` business in this example — in Book I, Chapter 4.

Deleting a directory

Here's how to delete a directory:

```
Dim objDir As New DirectoryInfo("C:\TestDir")
Try
    objDir.Delete(True)
Catch
    Throw New Exception("Failed to delete")
End Try
```

Creating a new subdirectory

To create a new subdirectory, use this code:

```
Dim objDir As New DirectoryInfo("c:\TestDir") 'parent
directory
    Try
        objDir.CreateSubdirectory("TestSubDir") 'name for
new subdiretory

    Catch
        Throw New Exception("Failed to create new
subdirectory")
    End Try
```

What's the current directory?

Recall that there is always a default directory — the current directory that Windows accesses unless told to switch directories. You can find out the current directory with this code:

```
MsgBox(System.Environment.CurrentDirectory)
```

The `System.Environment` object allows you to find out many other aspects of the current computer environment as well:

```
Private Sub Form1_Load(ByVal sender As System.Object,
ByVal e As System.EventArgs) Handles MyBase.Load
    Console.WriteLine(Environment.CurrentDirectory)
    Console.WriteLine(Environment.CommandLine) 'running
program
    Console.WriteLine(Environment.MachineName)
    Console.WriteLine(Environment.OSVersion)
    Console.WriteLine(Environment.SystemDirectory)
    Console.WriteLine(Environment.UserDomainName)
    Console.WriteLine(Environment.UserName)
    Console.WriteLine(Environment.Version)
End Sub
```

Chapter 4: Old Concepts in New Clothes

In This Chapter

✔ **Understanding the major shifts**

✔ **Using classic functions from the compatibility namespace**

✔ **Making the most of auto-list members and auto completion**

✔ `CheckBox.Value` **becomes** `CheckBox.Checked`, **and other changes in diction**

✔ **A more formal approach: Exploring the new structured error handling**

*T*o many people who are experienced with earlier versions of VB, coming to VB.NET causes something of a shock. Some of it looks suspiciously like C and related languages such as Java and Pascal. What's N += 4? What's an *io stream?* And why do you have to use `Imports` for code libraries when, for the past 10 years, everything you needed was right there in Visual Basic?

Understanding the Major Shifts

Most observers agree that VB.NET represents a major shift, an attempt to do two things at once: to bring Visual Basic — at least to a degree — into conformity with most other computer languages and also to make Web programming with VB as easy as possible.

Although VB has always been the easiest language to use and the quickest route from idea to finished application, some professional programmers and academics have shunned it. Why? Because VB could not easily accomplish some advanced techniques (or, in some cases, it couldn't accomplish them at all). Also, although VB has, since Version 4, increasingly added object-oriented programming (OOP) features, until VB.NET it wasn't *fully* OOP capable (because it didn't have true inheritance).

In some ways, VB has always been unique. Other languages — Pascal, Delphi, Java, C, and others — were part of a family of sister languages, similar in their design, syntax, diction, and punctuation. The odd man out was VB, with its philosophical commitment to clarity, simplicity, and English-like grammar and diction. VB also introduced the now widely copied RAD (Rapid Application Development) tools such as prewritten controls, wizards, and other add-ins that often make programming more efficient.

Consider some examples of the differences. In traditional VB, you opened a disk file like this:

```
Open "C:\TEST.TXT" As 1
```

Now, in VB.NET, you accomplish the same task using programming similar to C and the other languages:

```
Dim objFilename As FileStream = New FileStream("C:\TEST.TXT",
    FileMode.Open, FileAccess.Read, FileShare.Read)

Dim objFileRead As StreamReader = New
    StreamReader(objFilename)
```

However, VB.NET often includes several alternative ways to program a given task, and some of them are included simply to make the transition from traditional VB to VB.NET easier for programmers who are used to classic VB. For example, here's an alternative way to open a disk file in VB.NET that's similar to the traditional VB code:

```
FileOpen(FileNum, "C:\TEST", OpenMode.Random, , , RecLength)
```

Also, VB.NET includes a *compatibility namespace,* a library of traditional VB programming features, that you can use within VB.NET if you wish. When you type the following at the top of your code window, you add the compatibility namespace to any form or module:

```
Imports Microsoft.VisualBasic
```

The compatibility namespace includes many traditional VB commands. However, some traditional VB commands are automatically included in VB.NET (you don't need to import the compatibility namespace). Such included traditional features are described as *wrapped* functions. Len is an example of a legacy command that VB.NET includes.

The main point is this: If you try to use a classic VB programming command and you get an error message from VB.NET, try adding the Imports Microsoft.VisualBasic line to see if that cures the problem. But, eventually, you should make the transition to the .NET way of doing things. In the long run, .NET is generally better for future computing (as well as being more powerful and flexible), as you'll see in the next section.

Conformity

VB.NET now has all the capabilities of competing languages, including full OOP inheritance, multithreading, strict type checking, and direct access to all the object libraries underlying Windows, Internet, database, and other systems. Why, you might ask, is all this necessary? VB programmers got along just fine for over a decade without these advanced features.

True, but the requirements of group programming are fundamentally different from the requirements of individual programming. If you are sitting alone in your home, quickly putting together a simple state-capitols quiz program for little Ashley, you simply do not need multithreading, inheritance, and all the rest of it. Traditional VB is just fine for personal computing.

However, when you move beyond amateur programming into the world of professional group programming, things change. OOP practices — while somewhat controversial and, perhaps, not the ultimate solution to group programming problems — do help alleviate some of the traffic, security, and other issues that arise when more than one cook is working on the stew.

Another compelling reason to migrate to VB.NET is that it truly does live up to its name *.NET.* The Web browser appears to be well on its way to becoming the new user interface, the Web site is becoming the new application paradigm, and Internet-driven programming (distributed programming) is becoming the new de facto "operating system," so to speak. We all have to get with the program. Like it or not, the old days — when your data sat on the hard drive right there with your application — are all but over. Distributed programming is the inevitable future of computing. Parts of the data on which your program operates might be stored in various locations around the world (and the Internet makes this possible).

What's more, even the programs you write might be distributed. You might write a program that uses a Web service located in Toledo and another Web service located in Japan. Even though the main shell of your program may indeed be on your local hard drive, it could employ objects (services) that are widely scattered around the world. (And remember that when you use controls like a TextBox or the new Web services, you're effectively working with other programmers because you are incorporating their programming into your applications.)

Distributed programming, like group programming, raises security issues and related communication issues that are simply beyond the ability of traditional VB. But more to the point, when you enter the world of distributed programming, you must learn new programming techniques. The change is similar to the difference between telling your children what to do and working on legislation in the state senate: In both cases, you are passing laws, but being a senator requires that you follow many new rules that ensure cooperation with other people. OOP, stricter variable typing rules, more structured debugging, and many other new features of VB.NET are designed — like Robert's Rules of Order — to promote harmony in the new world of distributed programming.

The Migration Wizard

An attempt was made to automate (as much as possible) the process of translating a VB 6 program into VB.NET. The utility that attempts this is called the Migration Wizard, and it does its best — but you cannot expect it to actually port a VB 6 program of any complexity to VB.NET without lots of hand-programming, testing, and general personal effort on your part. The process is *not* automatic, nor, given the profound differences between VB 6 and VB.NET, could it be automatic.

If you choose File⇨Open⇨Project in VB.NET and then attempt to load in a VB 6 project file (.VBP extension), you see the Migration Wizard pop up, offering assistance, as shown in Figure 4-1.

Figure 4-1:
This wizard does its best, but you have to do a lot of the work yourself when translating a VB 6 program to .NET.

The Wizard attempts to make changes to your VB 6 source code. If you look at the source code in the Solution Explorer after the Wizard finishes, you see comments like this:

```
'UPGRADE_WARNING: Event Text1.TextChanged may fire when form
    is initialized. Click for more: 'ms-help://MS.VSCC/
    commoner/redir/redirect.htm?keyword="vbup2075"'
```

This kind of comment alerts you of possible problems that the wizard cannot resolve. Also, the wizard generates an Upgrade Report log (also found in the Solution Explorer) that will tell you of additional anomalies it found. For example, in traditional VB, it was common to set a Timer control's Interval value to zero as a way of disabling the Timer. In VB.NET, though, this is forbidden, as this Upgrade Report message indicates:

```
Timer property Timer1.Interval cannot have a value of 0
```

Like voice-to-text technology, you will find many errors to fix by hand when you set the Migration Wizard to work on a VB 6 project. Therefore, first learn VB.NET so that you can actually be of assistance to the wizard when it fails to completely translate the VB 6 code. Also, because of the magnitude of the differences between VB.NET and VB 6, don't attempt to translate applications that are fully debugged and running effectively on the VB 6 platform. Why should you? The following are probably the only two reasons to translate a VB 6 application:

+ It's a good way to learn some of the differences between the two languages.

+ You intend to significantly enhance that application by using the special new capabilities that VB.NET offers.

Intellisense to the Rescue

VB.NET gives you access to many thousands of programming commands, and many of them have multiple variations — meaning that you can use each command in various ways. It would be impossible for most of us to remember all the commands and their variations.

What was hidden, now is seen

Over the years, VB source code has grown more complex. VB 1 in 1991 had a vocabulary of approximately 350 words.

When VB made its first, tentative moves toward OOP in Version 4, the vocabulary began to balloon. Now, in VB.NET, you can program with thousands of classes, and each of them can have dozens of members (methods, properties, and events). Each of these members can include yet more diction (various *arguments* — the data passed to the members). The total vocabulary now available to the VB programmer is many thousands of words.

For example, the `Switch` class includes the following members: `Description`, `DisplayName`, `Equals`, `GetHashCode`, `GetType`, `ToString`, `SwitchSetting`, `Finalize`, `MemberwiseClone`, `OnSwitchSettingChanged`.

How are you going to remember all these words and their grammar?

Fortunately, you don't have to remember all this. You can always use the Help feature, which continues to improve with each new version of Visual Basic. Also, a technology called Intellisense, which is built into VB.NET, includes auto-completion and auto-list-members features that pop up while you're writing your source code, listing all the members; then when you've chosen a member, these features list all that member's arguments.

To see these automated helpers in action, find a sub in one of your forms and on a blank line within that sub, type the following:

```
messagebox.
```

As soon as you type the period following the word messagebox, the auto-list-members list pops up and you can double-click any member displayed to have it automatically inserted into your code, as shown in Figure 4-2.

Argument list options

Then, after the member is added to your source code, type in a left-parenthesis to bring up the *auto-completion* feature. It shows you all the arguments available for use with whatever member you used, as shown in Figure 4-3.

To review: Typing a period after a class name shows you its various members (properties and methods). Similarly, typing a left parenthesis shows you a scrollable list of all the *arguments* (data passed to a member) that can be used with a particular member. Note the "1 of 12" and the down arrow next to the argument list shown in Figure 4-3. This tells you that you have 12 different argument options to choose among (the visible one is the most commonly used). To scroll down and see the rest of the alternative argument lists, press the down-arrow key (or up-arrow key). In the 2003 version of VB.NET, scrolling is no longer necessary; the entire list is displayed at once.

Figure 4-2:
Auto-list-members helps you keep track of the properties and methods available for the thousands of classes in VB.NET.

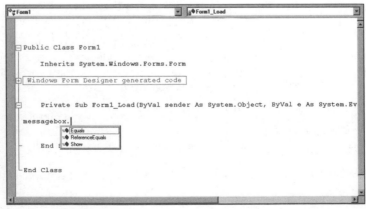

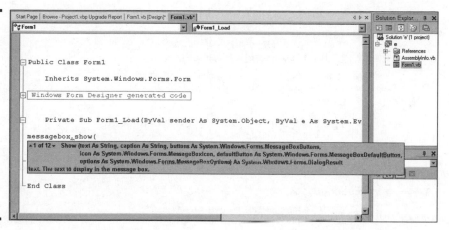

Figure 4-3:
The auto-completion feature provides you with a list of arguments you can use with a particular class member.

Ch-Ch-Ch-Ch-Changes

Alas, if you're an old hand at VB programming, you'll find that VB.NET demands that you learn many new things and remain flexible. You'll find yourself puzzled over and over as you discover the many changes in the language.

For example, since VB 1 in 1990, the CheckBox control had a Value property. Now, in VB.NET, the Value property has been renamed Checked. Also, several controls' default names have been changed. For example, instead of Check1, which all previous versions of VB named a CheckBox, VB.NET instead uses the fuller, more formal CheckBox1. Same with Text1 changing to TextBox1 and Picture1 changing to PictureBox1. You get the idea. There are always exceptions to every rule, though: The traditional CommandButton is now called, simply, the Button.

Also, VB has traditionally offered default properties. You could save some time by writing Text1 = "Barley" rather than Text1.Text = "Barley" because the Text property was the default property. It was understood. No more. VB.NET has no default properties, so you must spell everything out completely: TextBox1.Text = "Barley"

Among the many other changes, the following are gone from VB:

✦ The Autoredraw property

✦ Control arrays

✦ The venerable Directory-, Drive-, and FileListBox controls

✦ Empty

✦ Null

◆ Missing

◆ IsNull

◆ IsObject

◆ IsMissing

◆ Global

◆ The Line **control (and the** Line **command)**

◆ LSet **and** RSet

◆ Left, Top, Height, Width, Move

◆ As Any

◆ Property Let, Get, **and** Set

◆ ScaleHeight, ScaleWidth

◆ The Shape **control**

◆ Tag

◆ Type...End Type

◆ The Variant

In fact, there are so many changes in VB.NET that they cannot be covered in this chapter. This entire book describes the various elements of the VB.NET language. Now and then, you'll find references to "the way things were done in traditional VB." However, I've put together a compendium called Appendix C that contains an alphabetical list of traditional VB programming commands and their VB.NET equivalents. You can download this appendix (which is the size of a small book) from this book's Web site at dummies.com/extras.

The New Structured Error Handling

Some errors occur only during runtime. Your programming is valid, but something unexpected happens while the program is running. This is often a problem related to a peripheral, such as a hard drive. For example, suppose that the user has no file named *myfile.doc* on drive C:\ and your program executes this code trying to open that file:

```
Private Sub Form1_Load(ByVal sender As System.Object, ByVal e
    As System.EventArgs) Handles MyBase.Load

    Try

        Dim sr As New
System.IO.StreamReader("c:\myfile.doc")
```

```
Catch er As System.IO.FileNotFoundException

    MsgBox(er.ToString)

End Sub
```

The error message shown in Figure 4-4 is displayed. You need to prevent, or at least gracefully handle, runtime errors. It's no good having a smoothly running program that suddenly halts if the user, say, forgets to put a disk in drive A or fails to close the drive door. And, for heaven's sake, don't let your user see the hair-raising message shown in Figure 4-4.

Figure 4-4:
This
message is
likely to
terrify, or
at least
depress,
a user.

```
System.IO.FileNotFoundException: Could not find file "c:\myfile.doc".
File name: "c:\myfile.doc"
    at System.IO.__Error.WinIOError(Int32 errorCode, String str)
    at System.IO.FileStream..ctor(String path, FileMode mode, FileAccess access, FileShare
share, Int32 bufferSize, Boolean useAsync, String msgPath, Boolean bFromProxy)
    at System.IO.FileStream..ctor(String path, FileMode mode, FileAccess access, FileShare
share, Int32 bufferSize)
    at System.IO.StreamReader..ctor(String path, Encoding encoding, Boolean
detectEncodingFromByteOrderMarks, Int32 bufferSize)
    at System.IO.StreamReader..ctor(String path)
    at e.Form1.Form1_Load(Object sender, EventArgs e) in E:\Cryptography dotNET\Public
Key\e\Form1.vb:line 55
```
```
            OK
```

How runtime errors occur

Runtime errors include unexpected situations that can come up when the program is running. While you're writing a program, you can't know a number of things about the user's system. For example, how large is the disk drive? Is it already so full that when your program tries to save a file, enough room won't be available? Are you creating an array so large that it exceeds the computer's available memory? Is the printer turned off, but the user tries to print anyway? And what wacky mistake might some users type in when you ask them to provide a telephone number?

Whenever your program is attempting to interact with an entity outside the program — such as the user's input, disk drives, Clipboard, RAM — you need to take precautions by using the `Try-End Try` structure. This structure enables your program to deal effectively with the unexpected while it runs.

Unfortunately, your program can't correct many runtime errors. For instance, you can only let the user know that his or her disk is nearly full. The user will have to remedy this kind of problem; you can't correct it with your code.

Runtime errors can also occur because of such unexpected problems as numeric overflow (a variable grows too large for its variable type) or array boundary violations (an attempt is made to access an item from an array index outside the range of the array). Other runtime errors result from attempts to use remote objects' methods or properties incorrectly (such as when accessing a database, an API, or a Web service). Remote objects return error messages, error codes (numbers that you must then look up in an error code list), or a combination of the two.

Sometimes the error message is returned within an object or directly by a function. When you use a function that is supposed to provide you with the length of some text, but it returns -1, that's an error flag. In all these cases, you must read the documentation that describes both how error messages are returned to your project and what those messages mean. Often, however, VB.NET intercepts incoming error messages from remote classes and signals them to your project as a VB.NET-style runtime error.

Understanding Try

If you suspect that a particular location in your source code may be responsible for a runtime error, use the Try command to trap the error. Attempting to set things right by first handling the error if possible within your project is always better than shifting an unnecessary burden to the user.

If you don't use Try and solve the problem in your VB.NET source code, Visual Basic displays an error message to the user. You might want to provide your own runtime error messages (you'll see how in a moment). To most users, the kind of message displayed earlier in Figure 4-4 is obscure, confusing, and sometimes, frightening. VB.NET error messages are generally intended for you, the programmer, not for ordinary users.

Instead of displaying a forbidding system message, you might want to substitute your own, custom, user-friendly error message, like this:

```
Private Sub Form1_Load(ByVal sender As System.Object, ByVal e
    As System.EventArgs) Handles MyBase.Load

    Try

        Dim sr As New System.IO.StreamReader("c:\myfile.doc")

        Catch er As system.IO.FileNotFoundException

        MsgBox("No file named myfile.doc was found on Drive
    C:")

    End Try

End Sub
```

Notice that you put the `Try-End Try` structure around possible error-triggering code. In fact, in some situations, you surround *all* the code in a procedure with the `Try-End Try` envelope. Here's how the `Try-End Try` structure works:

```
Try
'watch the line(s) of code here for any problems
Catch a type of error
' insert line(s) of code here to handle that particular error
Catch another type of error
' insert line(s) of code here to handle that second error
Finally
'insert optional line(s) of code here that you want executed
    within the Try structure
End Try
```

It's pretty easy to understand the relationship between `Try` and `Catch`. The relationship is similar to the following:

' *Start of Try structure*

If **there was an error** Then '*Catch*

React in some way to this error

End If '*End of Catch code block*

If **there was a different error** Then '*Catch*

React in some way to this error

End If '*End of Catch code block*

' *End of Try structure*

(The purpose of that `Finally` zone in the `Try-End Try` block is mysterious at first. Why do you need it? Couldn't you just put the code *after* the `End Try`? I'll explain the `Finally` command soon.)

The term *exception* is used in C-like languages (and now in VB.NET) to mean *error*. Code between the `Try` and `End Try` commands is watched for errors. You can use the generic `exception` or merely trap a specific exception such as the following:

```
Catch er As DivideByZeroException
```

To see a list of all the specific exceptions, choose Debug⇨Exceptions and then expand the Common Language Runtime exceptions by clicking on the +. You may have to do a bit of hunting. For instance, the `FileNotFound` error is located two expansions down in the hierarchy: Common Language Runtime Exceptions⇨SystemIO. So you have to expand both (click the + next to each) to finally find `FileNotFoundException`. However, the Exceptions window does include a Find button that should help you locate the precise exception you're after. Also notice in the Exceptions window that you can make the program ignore any of the exceptions (click the Continue option in the Exceptions window). This is the equivalent of `On Error Resume Next` in VB 6.

You can include in your `Try-End Try` structure as many `Catch` phrases as you want, and you can respond individually to each of them. You can respond by notifying the user (as in the preceding example) or by quietly correcting the error in the source code following the `Catch`. You can also provide a brief error message:

`er.Message`

Or, as you did in the preceding example, you can provide a "fully qualified" (meaning "all the adjectives") error message:

`er.ToString`

The official syntax

Here's the full, official `Try-Catch-Finally` structure's syntax:

```
Try
    tryStatements
[Catch₁ [exception [As type]] [When expression]
    catchStatements₁
[Exit Try]
Catch₂ [exception [As type]] [When expression]
    catchStatements₂
[Exit Try]
...
Catchₙ [exception [As type]] [When expression]
    catchStatementsₙ]
[Exit Try]
[Finally
    finallyStatements]
End Try
```

Following the `Try` block, you list one or more `Catch` statements. A `Catch` statement requires a variable name and an `As` clause defining the type of exception (`er As Exception`). One Exception type is generic and therefore traps all exceptions, not just a specific one such as `FileNotFound`.

For example, here's how to trap *all* exceptions:

```
Try
```

```
      Dim sr As New System.IO.StreamReader("c:\xxxxx")

Catch er As Exception

   'Respond to any kind of error.

End Try
```

An optional `Exit Try` statement causes program flow to leap out of the `Try` structure and continue execution with whatever follows the `End Try` statement. If code is in the `Finally` block, however, it is executed.

Understanding Finally

The `Finally` statement contains any code that you want to be executed after error processing has been completed. Any code in `Finally` is *always* executed, whether or not any `Catch` blocks were executed. This is the primary reason you would use the `Finally` block: Your source code that follows the `End Try` line may never execute, depending on how things go in the `Try` structure.

How does this work in the real world? Suppose that a major disaster occurs, and your `Catch` block includes an `Exit Sub` or `Exit Function` command to leap out of your procedure in response. In either case, any code in that procedure that follows `End Try` is not executed. By contrast, code in the `Finally` block executes no matter what. The most common use for the `Finally` section is to free up resources that were acquired in the `Try` block, to close opened files, and the like.

Note that if you use the `Exit Try` command to get out of a `Try` block prematurely (before executing other `Catch` blocks or other nested `Try` blocks), the code in the `Finally` block will nonetheless execute.

For example, if you were to acquire a Mutex lock (don't ask!) in your `Try` block, you would want to release that lock when you were finished with it, regardless of whether or not the `Try` block exited with a successful completion or an exception (error). You typically use the following type of code in the `Finally` block:

```
        objMainKey.Close()
        objFileRead.Close()
        objFilename.Close()
'close a file
' close an object reference
'delete a bad file
'tie up other loose ends
```

Throwing exceptions

You can use a `Throw` command to generate your own error flags and attach
error messages. This is how you inform outside code that is using one of
your methods or procedures that an error occurred.

Both of these syntaxes work:

```
Dim e As Exception
e = New Exception("F problem")
Throw e
```

Or, more simply:

```
Throw New Exception("Problem in the Addition function")
```

I repeat: When you `Throw` an exception, you're telling an outsider (source
code that tried to execute your procedure, also called a *client*) that a
problem occurred. When you write a Web service or create a custom
control, you are building an object that can be used by a client.

Here's an example. Suppose that you write a function that wants to always
get the name *Bob* sent to it. If the client tries to send some other name, you
throw back an exception. The `Form_Load` event in this example is the
outsider that will call the `IsItBob` procedure:

```
Private Sub Form1_Load(ByVal sender As System.Object, ByVal e
    As System.EventArgs) Handles MyBase.Load

    Try
        IsItBob("Chris") 'call the procedure
    Catch er As Exception 'find out if there was an error
    thrown back at us
        MsgBox(er.ToString) 'if there was an error thrown,
    display it
    End Try

End Sub

Sub IsItBob(ByVal s As String)

    Dim er As Exception

If s <> "Bob" Then 'they sent the wrong name!
    er = New Exception("This Function needs the name Bob")
    'create an exception variable
    Throw er 'throw it back to the caller
End If

End Sub
```

Points to remember

Here are a few points to remember about the VB.NET Try-End Try
approach to error handling:

✦ If you want, you can nest Try-End Try blocks in other End-Try blocks.

✦ The new Try-End Try technique was written from scratch with .NET in
   mind. As a happy result, the Catch command can catch all errors that
   can happen in the .NET framework (in any method or property of all the
   zillions of objects in that framework).

✦ Some programmers might be tempted to enclose their entire project in
   a huge Try-End Try block, thereby ensuring that any and every possible runtime error will be caught. This would slow execution somewhat,
   but it sure would catch everything. It's rather clumsy, though, and you
   will likely want to trap errors in specific areas where you think they
   might actually potentially occur.

Book II

Tapping the Power of .NET Editor

The 5th Wave
By Rich Tennant

"We're here to clean the code."

Contents at a Glance

Chapter 1: Organizing Your Projects

In this chapter, you begin to explore what is probably the world's best programming environment: the Visual Studio .NET editor. Called the IDE (Integrated Development Environment), this set of programming tools is the result of over two decades of work by some of the most talented people in the computer industry. As you'll see, the .NET IDE is very thoughtfully designed and highly customizable.

But before getting into the details about ways to exploit the power of the IDE, let's first consider the overall organization of VB.NET projects and how you subdivide your programming into various containers.

Understanding Modules

The form is the primary Visual Basic organizational tool. It's a visual interface (onto which you put controls such as buttons and TextBoxes so that the user can interact with it) and also a container for your source code. Technically, while you're writing your source code (in design mode), a form is a *class*. Then, when you press F5 to run your code (at runtime), the form becomes an *object*. More on this in Book VII.

When you write a VB.NET program, you usually start with an empty form and then add a few buttons or other user-interface controls. Each of those buttons are supposed to *do* something if the user clicks them, so you write some programming in each button's `Click` event. Then, when the user clicks, that programming is executed and does whatever job the button is supposed to do. A form is essentially a *window*. Some projects have more than one form, because some applications require more than a single window.

There's a kind of natural relationship between the forms that the user sees in an application and the way that you, the programmer, organize the source code (lines of programming) in the application. For example, you might have an inventory program that is divided into two forms: one form to let the user view the current inventory and a second form to let the user add new products to the inventory. The user, then, has two different views of your program, each view offering different controls to accomplish distinct tasks. Quite naturally, your programming also divides along the same lines: the code that displays the existing inventory database and the separate code that accepts user input to modify the database. You write the code that handles database input in the same form that the user sees when performing that activity. Likewise, you put the code that handles searching in the second form.

It is possible to communicate between forms, so that code in one form can change another's properties or access its procedures. This technique is described later in this book, and also in the appendix. (Search the appendix for "Communication between forms.")

You may not even realize it, but this approach neatly subdivides your applications into logical units of source code, tied to the various purposes of the visible surfaces that the user interacts with. However, sometimes you need to write programming procedures that will be used in more than one form in your application. Or, more commonly, you need to store information in variables that can be accessed from various forms in the application.

Let's assume that you write a program to handle retail sales. You need to refer to the state sales tax in several different forms in your program. The best solution is to create a constant or variable named `SalesTax` and put it somewhere in your program where it can be accessed from anywhere in your program. (Then, when the sales tax goes up — it *never* goes down — you can just change that one constant and your program will be up to date.)

The place to put variables, constants, and procedures that can be used by an entire VB.NET program is in a *module*. Recall that a variable declared within a procedure is accessible only from within that same procedure. Moving further out, a variable declared outside a procedure in a form is accessible from anywhere within that form. However, to make a variable (or constant or procedure) accessible to all the forms in a project, you put it into a module.

What's a module? It's a faceless form. It's essentially a form without a user interface — no visible components. But a module also has the special feature that its contents are visible throughout the project — as long as you declare them using the `Public` keyword. The VB.NET module is therefore similar to the traditional VB module (although in earlier versions of VB, you would use the `Global` keyword, which is no longer part of the VB language).

Where are the modules? By default, VB.NET doesn't automatically create a module when you start a new VB.NET project. If you decide that you want to be able to access a procedure, constant, or variable from anywhere in your project, you must create a module, like this:

1. **Choose Project➪Add New Item.**

The Add New Item dialog box opens.

2. **Double-click the Module icon in the Add New Item dialog box.**

The dialog box closes and Module1.vb appears in the Solution Explorer. The Module is opened in the code window as well.

Unlike previous versions of VB, the module isn't empty. It contains `Module...End Module`, as shown in Figure 1-1.

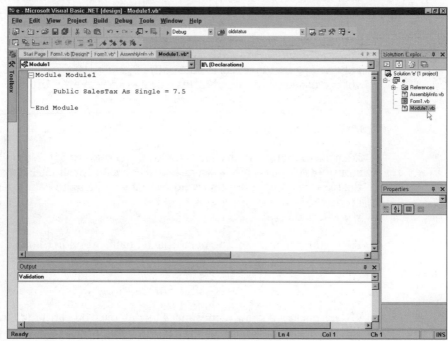

Figure 1-1:
VB.NET modules are defined by a couple of code lines, as shown here.

After you create the `Public SalesTax` variable in Module1, as shown in Figure 1-1, you can then use that value in any of your forms, like this:

```
Private Sub Form1_Load(ByVal sender As System.Object, ByVal e
    As System.EventArgs) Handles MyBase.Load
```

```
            MsgBox(SalesTax)

End Sub
```

Note that you need not qualify `SalesTax` by naming its module
(`Module1.SalesTax`). Instead, you can use it just as if it were a variable
defined in the form itself.

What Are Your References?

As you've seen, many functions are available to VB.NET directly (because
they are part of the core language, commands you can just type in, such as
`MsgBox` or +). Other functions, however, such as `Random`, are easier to use if
you use `Imports` to specify their namespace. These functions *can* be used
without the `Imports` command, but then you have to qualify them each
time you use them by describing their namespace, like this:

```
Dim r As System.IO.BinaryWriter
```

The `BinaryWriter` class is part of the `System.IO` namespace. If you leave
out the namespace, you get the error message `Type BinaryWriter is`
`not defined`.

```
Dim r As BinaryWriter
```

Instead of adding `System.IO` each time you refer to `BinaryWriter` (or other
input/output classes), it's usually easier to simply put an `Imports` statement
at the very top of your code window that specifies the namespace:

```
Imports System.IO
```

Then you can leave off the namespace qualification in the rest of your form's
code:

```
Dim r As BinaryWriter
```

VB.NET includes a few namespaces by default. You can see them listed in the
Solution Explorer (choose View⇨Solution Explorer). Click the References +
node. The default namespaces are `System`, `Data`, `Drawing`, `Forms`, and `XML`.
Given that you may rarely use the `XML` namespace but you may often use the
`IO` namespace, it's strange that `XML` is one of the defaults. In any case, you
need not use `Imports` for these few namespaces because they are already
referenced automatically whenever you start a new VB.NET project.

In addition to adding libraries (namespaces), you can also add controls to
your project. Lots of controls are available, including some of your old

favorites from VB 6, such as the `MSComm` control. I discuss how to add controls later in this chapter.

Using Components

Components, also known as *controls,* are pre-written objects that you can add to your forms. It would take you weeks to program all the things that the `TextBox` component can do. Fortunately, the work is already done and a TextBox icon is just sitting there on your Toolbox waiting for you to double-click it to add one to any form.

The Toolbox

If the Toolbox isn't visible, press Ctrl+Alt+X. Click the Form1.vb (Design) tab at the top of the IDE to switch to design mode.

Click the Windows Forms tab in the Toolbox to display the ordinary Windows controls.

Notice the down-arrow icon at the bottom of the Toolbox. Click it to scroll down and see additional controls.

The controls you'll likely use most often are clustered near the top of the Toolbox: `PictureBox`, `Label`, `TextBox`, `GroupBox` (formerly `Frame`), `Button` (formerly `CommandButton`), `CheckBox`, `RadioButton` (formerly `OptionButton`), `ComboBox`, and `ListBox`. By default, 46 controls are on the Toolbox, but you can add many other controls to the Toolbox.

Adding more controls to the Toolbox

Right-click the Toolbox and choose Customize Toolbox from the context menu. You should see the dialog box shown in Figure 1-2.

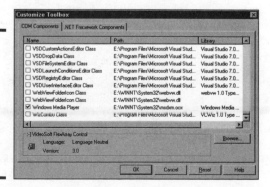

Figure 1-2:
Use this
Customize
Toolbox
dialog box
to add
controls to
your
Toolbox.

If you want to use any of the many additional controls listed in the Customize Toolbox dialog box in your VB project, go ahead and click the checkbox next to the control's name. When you close the dialog box, that control's icon will be added to the Toolbox. (You have to scroll the Toolbox down because your new control's icon is added at the bottom of the Toolbox.)

As you can see in Figure 1-2, I chose the Windows Media Player control.

Then I double-clicked its icon and — voila! — a fully functional Media Player is added to my VB project, as shown in Figure 1-3. Also, the Media Player's icon has been added to your Toolbox.

Figure 1-3:
Do you want to show movies in the VB application you're building? Just add Media Player to your Toolbox, and it's yours to use.

To make Media Player work, locate a movie file type that it can play (.MPG or .AVI) on your hard drive (or on the Internet) and then simply change the Media Player's `Filename` property either in the Properties window, or by assigning it in programming code (perhaps in response to the user's choice of file from the `OpenFileDialog` control).

Precisely which additional controls are available in the Components dialog box depends on which products you've installed on your system. (Some additional controls come with VB; others come with other applications.) You can buy commercial controls as well. For information on these third-party controls, take a look at one of the VB magazines, or try `http://searchvb.techtarget.com`.

From Project to Solution

This chapter is all about containers — the various ways that you subdivide and organize your source code when writing a program. So it's only fitting that the chapter concludes with the biggest container of all: the *solution*.

From smallest to largest, the VB.NET containers are as follows: procedures (subs or functions), classes, forms (or modules), projects, and solutions. These containers are nested within each other, like Russian eggs: Solutions contain one or more projects, projects contain one or more forms, forms contain one or more classes, and classes contain one or more procedures. Book VII covers classes and OOP programming in general.

If *project* is just another name for *application*, what, then, is a *solution?* It's a container big enough to hold more than a single project. Why would you put two applications together into a solution? Perhaps they are related. You might, for instance, have an application that helps you write press releases. You might decide to include, in the same solution, a utility that spell-checks. These two, independent projects, then, can be contained in a single solution.

Adding other files

You can freely add various kinds of files to a solution, and they will show up in the Solution Explorer along with any existing files. For instance, perhaps you want to add a little documentation that describes your solution. HTML files have lately become the standard way to display readme and other info to a user. To add an HTML file to your solution, follow these steps:

1. **Right-click the solution's name in the Solution Explorer.**

   A context menu appears.

2. **Choose Add⇨Add New Item from the context menu.**

3. **Click the Add New Item menu item.**

   The Add New Item dialog box appears.

4. **Double-click the HTML Page icon.**

   Your new HTML page appears, ready for you to type into it (and it also appears in the Solution Explorer).

When a user double-clicks on an .HTM file, it opens for viewing in the user's browser.

When you add a new file of any kind to your project, it is stored on the hard drive in the same directory as all the other files in that project. The directory name is the same as the name of your project (the boldface item in Solution Explorer). A typical path is `C:\Documents and Settings\`

`Richard Mansfield\My Documents\Visual Studio Projects\`
`WindowsApplication2`. However, you can put your VB.NET projects anywhere you want to put them. You can even move them to a different computer entirely. Just copy the entire folder and its subfolders.

Avoiding DLL hell

A few years ago, when computer memory and hard drive space were more
costly, somebody came up with the idea (a *terrible idea,* it turned out) to use
dynamic link libraries. DLLs are libraries of functions (like VB.NET assemblies), but they are generally stored in a common folder (System or System32)
on your hard drive and are shared between various programs that depend on
them. DLLs and similar libraries of functions are called *dependencies,* and
applications need them to be able to run. The problem is that older DLLs are
replaced with new, improved versions (faster, some bugs were fixed, and so
on). But what happens when an older application needs the *older* DLL version? Worse, what happens when an old and a new application are simultaneously running, and each wants to use a different version of the same DLL?

DLLs are loaded from disk into memory only as needed (hence their name
dynamic) in an effort to conserve RAM memory. However, the use of DLLs
has led to serious versioning problems, often referred to as "DLL hell."
VB.NET and the other .NET languages attempt to solve this problem in a
way that *does* waste space on the hard drive and in RAM, but it avoids hell,
which is always a good idea.

In .NET, dependency files are stored right there in the same folder as the
source code, the executable (runnable .exe) file, associated HTML files, and
whatever else is needed to run the solution. It's all in the solution folder
together — so it's all ready to be used.

Of course, this means that some code libraries will be stored in various
duplicated places around your hard drive in the various solution folders.
But, so what? That's better than having to share one copy of a DLL between
multiple applications, and having to wonder whether it's the right version
for each application.

As RAM and drive space become extremely cheap, we have to rethink some
of our old practices. Now that you can buy 700MB of storage space on a
writeable CD for less than a penny, everything from program design to
backup strategies should adjust to the new reality.

Easier deployment

The new .NET approach to code libraries and other dependencies greatly
simplifies deployment. You can give someone else your VB.NET application
merely by copying the application's files to the other person's hard drive.

Happily, all the necessary dependency files are right there in the application's folder.

No need to go through an elaborate setup and registration process. You can even upgrade a VB.NET application on the fly while it's running, without needing to reboot the server if you're on a network. In the past, the deployment problems of registration (putting information into the Registry), versioning, and such made life difficult for programmers and administrators alike. VB.NET completely abolishes DLL locking, XML configuration files, and component registration (applause! applause!).

To deploy your VB.NET application, you just copy a directory. Controls located in your application's subfolders are simply available to your application; you need not worry about registering them or worry that they are "locked." They're not locked and they're not registered — but they *work* just fine. That's the new model. Did you create a better version of a control that's part of an old project? Just copy the new control into the solution folder and replace the older version. It runs right away.

Note that executables (the actual primary application .exe file that executes a program) are located in the solution folder within a \Release subfolder. You won't see this folder until you've switched from debug mode (the default while writing and testing your application) to release mode.

To execute a VB.NET application outside the VB.NET IDE (without pressing F5 as you do when testing an application you're writing), you can compile it by choosing Build⇨Build Solution (which updates the executable by recompiling and taking into account any modified files), or choose Rebuild Solution (which recompiles all, not just changed, files). In any case, right-click the name of your solution (which is in boldface) in the Solution Explorer and then choose Properties.

You see the path to your project (labeled *Project folder*), so you can use Windows explorer to locate .exe files for your application in its \bin or \Debug subfolder. However, you don't want to use these file as your final executable.

When you are finished writing and testing an application, you want to switch it from the default *debug* form of the .exe to a *release* form (which contains no extra debugging code and thus executes faster). To do this, follow these steps:

1. **Choose Build⇨Configuration Manager.**

   The Configuration Manager dialog box appears.

2. **Drop the listbox at the top of the dialog box.**

   A drop-down list appears, giving you several options.

3. **Change the Configuration option from Debug to Release.**

4. **Click Close.**

   The Configuration Manager dialog box closes.

5. **Now recompile your solution by choosing Build⇨ReBuild Solution.**

6. **Use Windows Explorer to look at your solution's folder.**

   You see that a new subfolder named *release* has been added under the Obj folder. The .exe within this release folder is what you want to use or share with others.

Now when you look in your solution's folder, you see that a new \Release subfolder has been created and a release .exe file is within it. That .exe file is the one you should add to your Start menu or create as a shortcut on your desktop. It's the one to use when your project is finished.

You may notice in your solution's folder several dependency files that VB.NET creates for you when you write a VB.NET project. These files have extensions such as .vb, .suo, and .resx. No use frightening yourself by trying to figure out the purpose of most of these. VB.NET automatically handles those files for you, so they can usually remain behind the curtain. Here and there in this book, I describe the purpose of some of the dependency files, but for now, just allow VB.NET to do its housekeeping behind the scenes. The one file extension you might want to memorize is .sln. That's the solution file. So if you are browsing with Windows Explorer and you want to launch a solution within VB.NET, double-click its .sln file and off you go.

Chapter 2: Viewing Your Work

In This Chapter

✔ **Employing the great designer**

✔ **Exploring top-down programming**

✔ **Understanding code-behind programming**

✔ **Working with Web projects' multiple code windows**

*I*t's time to dive into the famous .NET IDE and see how to exploit it when creating programs for Windows or Internet environments. This chapter shows you why the IDE is justly considered the finest suite of tools yet created for programmers and developers.

As you doubtless guessed from the *.NET* in VB.NET, a major aspect of this new language is its many new features that expedite creating Web sites. Currently, computing is dividing into two great streams: local, Windows-based programming and *distributed,* Internet-based programming. VB.NET contains various tools that help you to create effective programs in either environment, programs that will be displayed in a browser or in a traditional window.

Using the Designer

VB.NET follows in the rapid application development tradition of its predecessor versions, splitting your job as a programmer between two primary windows: the design window and the code window.

Previous chapters spent a bit of time trying various programming examples in the code window, so this chapter shows you what you can do in the design window.

Choose File⇨New⇨Project and then double-click the Windows Application icon. You see an empty form, ready for you to design it, as shown in Figure 2-1.

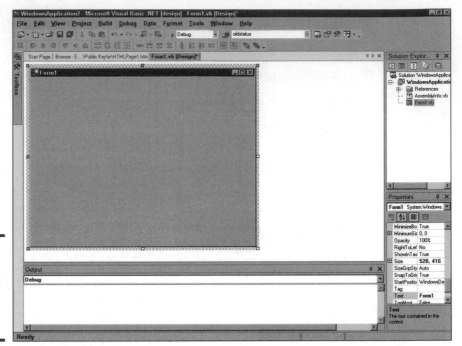

Figure 2-1:
An empty
form invites
you to build
a new
program.

One significant job that nearly all programmers must frequently face is creating an efficient and ergonomic user interface. VB.NET offers you lots of controls that you can place on your forms to permit the user to interact with your program.

Top-down design

Some programmers prefer to first design the user-interface and then to fill in the programming "underneath" the various controls (in their Click event or other events). This is known as the *top-down* approach. Other programmers like to first use paper and pencil to create an outline of the various functions and features of their program; then they decide which user-interface controls are most appropriate. *Bottoms up* is the name for that, or more formally, *bottom up*.

No matter which approach you use, you have to pick and choose user-interface components at some point in the process of building an application.

To illustrate the top-down approach (which I prefer), this section shows you how to create a visual interface first and then write the code that makes the interface controls actually do their jobs. The act of choosing various controls that the user will interact with leads naturally to an understanding of what programming you must write to make those controls useful. Let's create a little utility that will display graphics files.

Clearly, you need three things to make this program work: a container that will display the graphic files, a way for the user to locate which files to view on the hard drive, and a way for the user to signal the program that he or she is ready to change the graphic.

Usually, you have more than one way to achieve a given goal in VB.NET. One solution to the three user-interaction jobs just identified would be to add a `PictureBox` to display the graphic, a `Button` for users to click when they wanted to change the graphic, and an `OpenFileDialog` control.

However, to practice some new programming techniques, you could just as easily display the graphic on the form itself and also respond to a click on the form itself when the user wants to change the picture. This example shows how to do it that way. You use no controls at all — because you borrow the `OpenFileDialog` control's properties and methods by creating an object from the `OpenFileDialog` class without actually adding the control itself to your project.

To create this program, follow these steps:

1. **Double-click the form in the design window.**

   You are taken to the code window, and the most commonly used event for whatever you double-clicked is created for you. In the case of a form, that is the `Load` event; for a `Button`, it's the `Click` event; and so on.

   You want to put this program's code into the `Form_Click` event, however, so that when the users click the form, they are shown an `OpenFileDialog`.

2. **Go to the top of the code window and click the down-arrow symbol in the listbox on the left.**

   The list of available classes drops down, as shown in Figure 2-2.

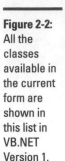
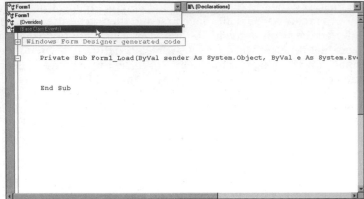

Figure 2-2:
All the
classes
available in
the current
form are
shown in
this list in
VB.NET
Version 1.

Unfortunately, VB.NET Version 1 makes life a little complicated when you want to select a new event for a form. You cannot use the `Form1` class in the listbox shown in Figure 2-2. Instead, you must select `(Base Class Events)`. This oddity is fixed in the new 2003 version of VB.NET. The `Base Class Events` entry has been replaced by `Form1 Events`.

3. **Click** `(Base Class Events)` **in the top left listbox.**

   The set of events available to your form now appears in the top right listbox, as shown in Figure 2-3.

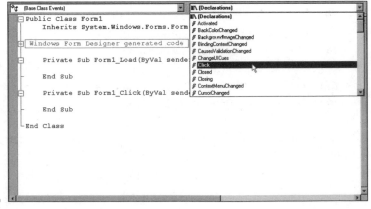

Figure 2-3:
Here are all
the events
that you can
use to
manage a
form's
behavior.

4. **Click the** `Click` **event in the top right listbox, as shown in Figure 2-3.**

A `Form1_Click` event sub is inserted into your code window, and the listbox closes.

5. **In the** `Click` **event, type this code:**

```
Private Sub Form1_Click(ByVal sender As Object,
ByVal e As System.EventArgs) Handles MyBase.Click


    Dim ofd As New OpenFileDialog()

    ofd.ShowDialog()

    Me.BackgroundImage =
Image.FromFile(ofd.FileName)

End Sub
```

6. **Press F5.**

The program runs.

7. **Click the form.**

The `OpenFileDialog` is displayed.

8. **Locate a graphic file on your hard drive and then double-click it.**

The dialog box closes, and the graphic file is displayed on your form, as shown in Figure 2-4.

Figure 2-4:
Your program works as expected, displaying an image on the form's background.

The programming is fairly straightforward. First, you create a new `OpenFile Dialog` object (which, as you see, can be done entirely within your source code, not requiring that you add that control from the Toolbox to your form):

```
Dim ofd As New OpenFileDialog()
```

Then you use the `ShowDialog` method of the `OpenFileDialog` object to display the user's hard drive:

```
ofd.ShowDialog()
```

Finally, you use the `FileName` property of the `OpenFileDialog` (which contains the user's selection after the dialog box closes). You load this file into the `BackgroundImage` property of the form.

```
Me.BackgroundImage = Image.FromFile(ofd.FileName)
```

Note that it would have been nice if VB had just called this property the `Image` property, as it does when you display a graphic file in a `PictureBox`:

```
PictureBox1.Image = Image.FromFile(ofd.FileName)
```

However, at this stage in the development of computer languages, complete consistency is still more a hope than a reality.

Using Multiple Code Windows

Now it's time for a preview of Web programming. VB.NET tries to make writing a Web application as easy as possible, and as similar as possible to writing a traditional Windows program. However, when you write for the Internet, you need to know about some additional code windows. Often, you need not *use* those code windows because VB.NET creates much of the necessary HTML and XML code for you, but you should know about that code if you ever need to examine it or make some changes yourself, by hand.

Your first VB.NET Web program

Okay, here we go. In this example, you see how to avoid firewalls, and you get a taste of Internet programming techniques:

1. **Choose File⇨New⇨Project.**

    You see the new project dialog box.

2. **Single-click the ASP.NET Web Application icon.**

   Your new project is named WebApplication1. If you previously created any ASP.NET projects, the new project will be named WebApplication2 or whatever. ASP.NET is the .NET technology that creates Web pages.

3. **Double-click the ASP.NET Web Application icon.**

   If you have firewall software running (and you should), you will be asked whether you want to allow Visual Studio .NET to act as a server.

   Firewalls alert you when outsiders attempt to get into your computer from the Internet, but they can also alert you when an application in your computer attempts to contact the Internet or attempts to behave like a server. In this case, you can see in Figure 2-5 that when you create a new Web project in VB.NET, the Visual Studio environment must pose as an Internet server. Without this capability, you couldn't test your Web applications in Visual Studio. Internet programming involves an interaction between at least two computers: the server that contains the programming (referred to as ASP.NET programming) and the browser (on a separate computer) that is interacting with the server. For testing purposes, Visual Studio .NET can imitate this interaction within a single computer — posing as a server on a kind of virtual "Internet" within your machine, and communicating with your browser.

**Book II
Chapter 2**

Viewing Your Work

Figure 2-5:
The excellent firewall software ZoneAlarm is detecting Visual Studio's attempt to act as a server.

4. **If you have firewall software, answer Yes, to say that you do give Visual Studio permission to act as a server.**

   The dialog box closes and VB.NET creates a new Internet-style (WebForm) VB.NET program for you, as shown in Figure 2-6.

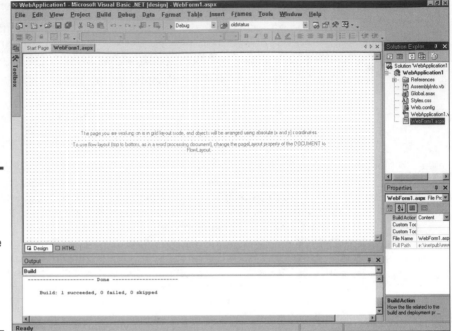

Figure 2-6:
This is the basic template that you see when you start a new WebForm project in VB.NET.

If you don't see the results shown in Figure 2-6 when you attempt to start a new ASP.NET Web Application, the most likely problem is that you have not installed all the necessary .NET elements. You must have IIS (Internet Information Services) running on your machine to test any ASP. NET projects, including the examples used in this book.

If you don't have IIS installed, I describe how to install these elements in Book IV, Chapter 1. You need to have IIS installed before you can run the following example.

A WebForm application is the same thing as an ASP.NET application: It means that the source code is executed on the server, and then the user's browser (located on the computer of the visitor to your Web site) is sent a *plain HTML* version of the Web page. Firewall software is designed to permit plain HTML to pass but also to block executable code (to prevent viruses). Therefore, no executable code is sent to a browser from ASP.NET (WebForm) applications.

Figure 2-6 illustrates how I like to organize the VB.NET editor. The main design window is dragged until it is rather large, and all the secondary windows (Solution Explorer, Toolbox, and others) are sent to the sides, merely visible as tabs. To make them tabs, right-click a window's (such as the Toolbox's)

title bar and select the useful *auto-hide* feature. Secondary windows that have their auto-hide feature activated are only a mouse-move away from becoming visible, but they don't clutter the screen when not needed. *Mouse-move* because you don't even have to click one of those tabs. Instead, you can just hover your mouse pointer on top of the tab for a half-second and the secondary window pops open.

Of course, you can get into much more detail about ASP.NET programming in Book IV. For now, just follow along — monkey-see, monkey-do — and you'll have your first .NET Internet program up and running in seconds.

In the Toolbox (with the Toolbox's Web Form tab selected), double-click the Button icon. That places a `Button` control on your WebForm. Drag the Button wherever you like on the WebForm. Click the Button to select it and press F4. The Properties window opens. Change its Text property to `Click me!`.

Now double-click the Button. You might be surprised to find yourself looking at the following VB.NET code:

```
Public Class WebForm1
    Inherits System.Web.UI.Page
    Protected WithEvents Button1 As
    System.Web.UI.WebControls.Button

Web Form Designer Generated Code

    Private Sub Page_Load(ByVal sender As System.Object,
    ByVal e As System.EventArgs) Handles MyBase.Load
        'Put user code to initialize the page here
    End Sub

    Private Sub Button1_Click(ByVal sender As System.Object,
    ByVal e As System.EventArgs) Handles Button1.Click

    End Sub
End Class
```

Code-behind programming

Don't worry about the details of this code (and don't open that *Web Form Designer Generated Code* section; no sense frightening yourself). All you need to understand at this point is that you are working with the full VB.NET language here, so this source code and this way of working is going to be familiar to you.

This page you're seeing is known as *code-behind*. It's not HTML; it's VB.NET, but it will be automatically translated into HTML before the WebForm page that it sits "behind" is sent to the visitor to your Web site. This process is pretty cool, and it provides the power to ASP.NET. It also makes life much,

much easier for you than Web programming was only a short time ago when you *didn't* have VB.NET as your Web language.

Your goal in this example is to let the user click the Button and see the current date and time. In plain HTML — a mere page-description language that cannot even add 2+2 — doing this would be impossible. But with ASP.NET, the entire VB.NET language can be used to provide generous computing features to your Web site pages. Type the following into the `Button1_Click` event:

```
Private Sub Button1_Click(ByVal sender As System.Object,
    ByVal e As System.EventArgs) Handles Button1.Click

Response.Write(Now)

End Sub
```

Press F5. If all goes well, VB.NET grinds away for a little while; then your Internet Explorer browser loads this ASP.NET Web page and displays the current date and time, as shown in Figure 2-7.

Figure 2-7:
Voila! Your
first .NET
Web
program
successfully
shows the
date and
time to a
visitor to
your
Web site.

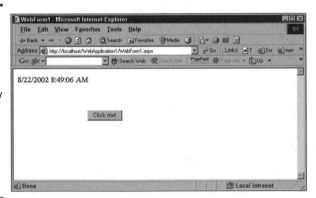

If all does *not* go well, be patient. In Book IV, you see how to shake down your Visual Studio .NET installation — to ensure that you can create and test the Internet (ASP.NET) examples throughout the book.

Understanding ASP.NET Code Windows

This chapter is all about the design and code windows that you use in the .NET IDE to create Windows or Web programs. Previous sections of this chapter cover the traditional Windows views. The traditional views had two primary windows: design (where you drop controls onto a form) and code (where you write your programming). Now consider the views available in ASP.NET programming. You still have a design window, but you have *several* code windows: HTML, XML (disco), Global.ASAX, Styles.CSS, Web.Config, and ASPX.VB. Yikes! Fortunately, often the only code window you have to deal with is that last one, the ASPX.VB (or *code-behind*) window. It contains the VB.NET source code that you're primarily interested in.

Nonetheless, in the interest of full disclosure and just so you know what's there if you need it, let's briefly tour the other busy little code windows that VB.NET automatically generates for you when you work on a Web project.

WebForm.ASPX

Click the WebForm1.ASPX tab at the top of the code/design window to open the design view. You see your Button sitting there saying `Click me!`. Now notice the two tabs on the *bottom* of the window; your current view, Design, is highlighted. But click the other tab labeled HTML.

You see the raw HTML code that describes your page, and you see the Button you've put on it. HTML is not really a computer language in the traditional sense because it cannot compute (can't do math, can't sort data, and so on). It's merely a page description language (how big is the text, where is it located, what color is it?). HTML is not the place where any information actually gets processed. The information is processed in ASP.NET by the code-behind programming language (which is VB.NET in your case, but it can also be one of the other .NET languages).

Precisely because it's harmless (big text, even if colored red, cannot attack your hard drive like a virus could), HTML slips right past firewalls and gets a free pass into everyone's network. Firewalls are designed to ignore HTML but block executable code.

You, too, can pretty much ignore HTML when programming for the Web in VB.NET. The Web Forms controls on the Toolbox can do most of what you want to do for the user interface part of your Web project, and when you drop one of those controls onto the design window, VB.NET automatically creates the necessary HTML to describe that control. Here's what VB.NET wrote in HTML to describe your button control:

```
<form id="Form1" method="post" runat="server">
<asp:Button id="Button1" style="Z-INDEX: 101;LEFT: 173px;
    POSITION: absolute; TOP: 96px" runat="server" Text="Click
    me!"></asp:Button>
```

Note that the `Top` and `Left` values may differ in your code because you may have dragged the button to a different location in the design window.

Global.ASAX

Double-click the Global.ASAX filename in the Solution Explorer. You see its design window, but click the hyperlink that reads `click here to switch to code view`. Now you're looking at yet another code window, but this one can sometimes be quite important to you, the programmer.

Applications usually need to have a central file or two that contains general settings, specifying behaviors, dependencies, and other *global* information. ASP.NET applications employ two such files: Global.ASAX and Web.Config.

Each ASP.NET application has a Global.ASAX file. The purpose of this file is to contain events and declarations that can be used across the entire ASP.NET application. The Global.ASAX file is similar to the VB traditional Sub Main or Modules (where you can write functions, define API calls, and declare variables if you want to make these items available to the entire application).

You can write code in the Global.ASAX events, but this code is usually not a user interface (it doesn't ordinarily generate HTML to send back to the visitor's browser), nor does this code usually execute each time a page is requested. The items that are typically stored in a Global.ASAX file are: Object Tag declarations; application or session event programming; application directives, and server-side includes. Book IV explores each of these items in detail.

Web.Config

Double-click the Web.Config file in the Solution Explorer. In this file, you can specify compilation options, tracing and error handling features, security settings, cookie specs, and so on for each Web project in your solution. (You can use multiple configuration files, each in a different folder — and the file will govern only its own folder's contents and subdirectories under it.)

Styles.CSS

Styles.CSS is a typical HTML cascading style sheet, which can be used as an efficient way of defining custom styles (appearance of text, and so on). To see how it works, double-click Styles.CSS in the Solution explorer, and you see a series of specifications. Normally, you can leave these defaults alone and just ignore this file.

XML (vsdisco)

Don't worry about the XML file until Book IV. If you don't see a `.vsdisco` file, don't worry about it at all. It can usually be ignored by the programmer anyway. It's a *discovery* file that contains *metadata,* which is supposed to make XML self-describing. See? You don't want to worry about it.

Chapter 3: Investigating the Toolbox

In This Chapter

✔ **Toolbox 101**

✔ **Understanding the TextBox**

✔ **Using COM and .NET framework components**

✔ **Choosing between HTML and Web controls**

This chapter is a tour of things you can do with the Toolbox, leading you through some of the most important controls on it. Although Visual C++ is only now getting some of the components that make programming more efficient, Visual Basic has had this functionality for over a decade.

The Toolbox is where the controls (also called *components*) sit, waiting for you to double-click one to place it on a form. For convenience, most of the controls you'll likely use often are available on the default view of the Toolbox: PictureBox, Label, TextBox, GroupBox, Button, CheckBox, RadioButton, ComboBox, and ListBox. Unfortunately, not *all* of the most common controls are on the default view. You must scroll (click the down-arrow icon at the bottom of the Toolbox) to access the six highly useful Dialog controls.

Also, some controls are a bit strange: The ScrollBar controls aren't of much use — because the TextBox, where you're most likely to need scroll bars, includes its own ScrollBars property. But for every dubious control, you find quite a few really useful ones.

Most controls save you quite a bit of programming time. For example, the DataGrid control is an excellent, full-featured, quick way to connect a database to your application. And you can add many, many other controls to the Toolbox; just right-click it and choose Customize Toolbox.

Working with the TextBox

Doubtless the TextBox is among the most used Visual Basic components — second only to the Button control, I would guess. The TextBox is so important that learning more about it is worth your time. A TextBox behaves like a simple word processor, but it does have its limitations. For instance, at any one time, it can display only a single font and a single type style (such as italics) for the entire contents. Also, it can display only one size of text at a time. You can change the font, style, and size by changing the TextBox's properties — but the entire contents of the TextBox will change. You cannot change a single word, for example, to italics. It's all or nothing.

The RichTextBox control on the Toolbox does not suffer from several of the ordinary TextBox's limitations. You might want to experiment with the RichTextBox if your project has special word-processing needs, or if you expect to exceed the TextBox's 65,535 character (about 10,000 words) limit.

TextBoxes can be used for both input and output: They can display text or accept the user's typed text. However, if you're merely identifying the purpose of, say, a CheckBox, use a Label instead. A TextBox would be overkill.

Adjusting TextBox Properties

The TextBox is such an important component that a good part of this chapter looks closely at it and its properties. Choose File⇨New⇨Project and double-click the Windows Application icon. If necessary, click the Windows Forms tab in the Toolbox (which should be selected automatically by default), and then double-click the TextBox icon in the Toolbox.

After that, you should take several steps to clean up some default property settings — which, at least with the TextBox component, aren't usually what you want. (At this point you *cannot* stretch the TextBox vertically to make it higher — that's forbidden right now. Be patient.)

Many Visual Basic components have quite a few properties — and the TextBox has more than most. However, you usually don't have to change very many of the default properties. In general, each property defaults to its most common value (exceptions include the TextBox's notorious default to MultiLine = False). All of the VB.NET controls' Visible properties default to True, rather than False, for instance. This is because you almost always want your components to be visible to the user. (Some controls, such as the Timer, are used internally by your program and are never made visible to the user. Those few controls have no Visible property at all, of course. Also, they are not displayed on your forms. Instead, they are placed on a new "tray" just below the form, visible to you, the programmer, only while designing your program.)

However, some default properties will be wrong for your project. And a few defaults are nearly *always* wrong for *any* project. One of these infamous defaults is the TextBox's Text property. It defaults to the name of the TextBox (TextBox1, for example), and I doubt that any programmer ever wanted to display that to a user. Most often, you want the user to see a blank TextBox, which users later fill in with text that they type.

Your first job is to get rid of that default text, which says TextBox1 in the Toolbox. The default should have been a blank, empty Text property, but unfortunately, you're stuck with always having to remove TextBox1 for each TextBox you create. (This has been going on for 10 years, since VB Version 1! There are an estimated 4 to 6 million VB programmers, and all of them use TextBoxes. With the hours wasted, we could have built a second Golden Gate Bridge.)

TIP

Sometimes you see a phrase such as, "You can't change this at runtime." *Runtime* means the same thing as run mode or execution (in other words, "while the application is running"). Likewise, sometimes you see a message that says, "Change the property at design time." *Design time* refers to design mode, meaning that you are typing code or dropping controls on a form. You are working on the application in the Visual Basic editor but the program is not running. You haven't pressed F5 to test the application, nor is the finished application being run as an executable by a user.

Some properties (such as the Name property) can be changed only at design time. Other properties (such as the Text property) can be changed either during design time or runtime. Yet other properties (such as the contents of a ListBox) can be changed *only* during runtime — by the programming you write. Every property you see in the Properties window can be set at design time, at least.

It's important to understand that components, such as TextBoxes, start out with all of their properties in one state or another. The Width property, for example, is set to *some* width, and the Text property contains (or doesn't contain) some text. In any case, the condition of the properties determines what the user first sees when the application runs, or how the component first behaves.

You don't want users to be greeted with TextBox1 (the default) sitting in your TextBox each time they run your application. So click the TextBox to select it. (Selecting a control during design time causes its properties to be displayed in the Properties window. If the Properties window isn't visible, press F4.)

Then click the Text property in the Properties window, and drag your mouse across the right column where you see Textbox1 so that you've selected it. Press Del. It disappears.

The second property that you usually have to change for the TextBox is the MultiLine property. By default, it's set to False, which forces all of your text onto a single line, no matter how high the TextBox actually is. Take a look at Figure 3-1.

Book II
Chapter 3

Investigating
the Toolbox

Figure 3-1:
With the
MultiLine
property set
to the
default,
there is no
word-wrap,
and
everything
typed
appears on
a single
line (as
illustrated in
the upper
TextBox).

Double-click the MultiLine property in the Properties window, which toggles it to True. Now, at last, you can adjust the height of the TextBox because you've made it MultiLine-capable. So, stretch and position the TextBox to make your form look the way you want.

After you've cleaned up the Text and MultiLine properties, you still probably want to fix the Font property — because it defaults to a small size. I generally change it to a more readable 11-point size. Click the Font property in the Properties window, and you see an ellipsis (. . .), indicating that there is more to see. Click the ellipsis button and you then see a dialog box where you can change several qualities of the font. Change it to 11 in the Size list, and then click OK. Notice that the size of the font in the Design window becomes larger. This instant visual response is one of the most widely imitated features that Visual Basic introduced to programming languages.

Now you've got a good, usable TextBox. If you're going to use more than one TextBox in a project, you can avoid having to adjust all these properties for each TextBox. Simply click the TextBox that you just finished cleaning up, and press Ctrl+C to copy it. Then click the Form, and press Ctrl+V to paste a new TextBox with all the same properties inherited from its parent.

Some important TextBox properties (and many that aren't)

Now you're ready to dive into the TextBox's properties. This section covers each major property in turn. Many of these properties are also properties of other components, as well as being properties of forms.

For example, the BackColor property is fairly universal — most components have this property so that you can change their color. But the main lesson I hope you learn from the following in-depth survey is that the majority of properties are of little use. I tell you which ones are valuable, and which ones you can usually just forget. I also mention properties that used to be part of VB but, in VB.NET, have been either renamed or eliminated.

The following sections cover the properties in alphabetical order, as you see them in the Properties window if you click the Alphabetic icon at the top of the Properties window.

DataBindings

Appearing first in the list of TextBox properties is the DataBindings property, which is used to attach a control to a database. Book V covers this property in more detail.

Dynamic Properties

The Dynamic Properties feature isn't a single property. It permits you to specify that certain properties can be changed during runtime. You can't know while writing your program, for example, the user's preference for the WordWrap property. Your program could allow the user to choose True or False for WordWrap from a menu; then it could store the user's answer in an external configuration file. Or a system administrator could efficiently adjust a database connection for all users by making a simple change to their .config files. This system is somewhat similar to the way that cookies store information outside the executable code. However, dynamic properties are a new, advanced technique and are probably of little use to the average programmer.

AcceptsReturn and AcceptsTab

The new AcceptsReturn and AcceptsTab properties describe how VB.NET reacts to the user pressing the Return or Tab keys. Normally, by default, pressing Return moves you down to the next line in a MultiLine-style TextBox. Set AcceptsReturn to False, and pressing Return causes a simulated mouse-click on the default button on the form. Set AcceptsTab to True, and a tab (move over five spaces) will be inserted into the text. Set it to False, and pressing Tab moves you to the next control on the form, according to the TabIndex property (described later in this section).

Accessibility

The three new Accessibility properties provide features for people with disabilities.

AllowDrop

`AllowDrop` determines whether or not this `TextBox` permits drag-and-drop operations.

Anchor

`Anchor` is a valuable new property. It determines whether and how a control stretches if the user stretches the form. The default for the `TextBox` is `Top`, `Left` — which means that the `TextBox` doesn't enlarge or shrink in size if the user drags the form to resize it. Click `Anchor` in the Properties window, drop the listbox by clicking the down-arrow icon, and click all four of the image map edges. You can then see the `TextBox` grow and shrink as the user adjusts the size of the form by pressing F5 to run the program and dragging the form to resize it.

AutoSize

`AutoSize` determines whether or not the size of the `TextBox` changes to accommodate any changes in the font or font size.

BackColor

If you want to, you can change a `TextBox`'s `BackColor` property to pink or blue or some other color (but it's best to leave it white in most applications). Similarly, you can change the text color by adjusting the `ForeColor` property. Again, you should probably leave well enough alone. The default black text on a white background is not only more legible — it's also more dignified.

BorderStyle

Leave the `BorderStyle` (formerly `Appearance`) property alone. It provides part of the 3D framing effect. If you try changing it to one alternative, `FixedSingle`, you turn back time so that the user interface looks like it was designed prior to Windows 95. If you set it to the third option, `None`, you go back even farther in time — regressing all the way to DOS.

CausesValidation

The `CausesValidation` property can remain set to `True`, with no harm done. When set to `True`, the `Validate` event is triggered when the focus shifts from the `TextBox` to the other component (when the user clicks it or tabs to it). This property comes in handy only with database work — forget about it for now.

CharacterCasing

The `CharacterCasing` property can be set to force all text to be lowercase, uppercase, or mixed.

ContextMenu

You can add context menu controls to your form from the Toolbox. A particular context menu control can be assigned to a control by specifying the context menu's name property in the `ContextMenu` property.

Controls

`Controls` is a new property that represents a collection of any child controls within the current control. `Controls` isn't listed in the Properties window, but it is in the Intellisense list.

Cursor

The new `Cursor` property is what used to be called the `MouseIcon` property, and it determines what the mouse pointer looks like when it is on top of the `TextBox` (should you want to change it from the default pointer). I advise against changing this property — unless you're sure you will not confuse the user.

Dock

`Dock` determines whether or not you want to cause the control to move to one of several positions within its container (the form). Changing this property also changes the size of the control.

DragIcon and DragMode

The former `DragIcon` and `DragMode` properties are no longer available in VB.NET.

Enabled

The `Enabled` property, if set to `False`, prevents users from typing anything into the `TextBox` (which is said to be *disabled*). Any text already in the `TextBox` appears light gray rather than the default black to indicate that the `TextBox` is disabled.

Components are disabled when it makes no sense for the user to try to use them. For example, suppose you have several `TextBoxes` on a form on which the user is supposed to fill in data about himself, and he fills in the TextBox for his age with 44 years. You could then disable a checkbox in which he is supposed to indicate whether or not he is a member of AARP. You have to be over 50 for AARP, so it makes no sense to leave that checkbox enabled. `Enabled` is often used in programming in response to situations like the one described in this AARP example. The code for this is `TextBox1.Enabled = False`.

Font and ForeColor

The Font and ForeColor properties were defined earlier in this chapter.

HideSelection

The HideSelection property is yet another highly esoteric option. Text can be selected within a TextBox — by programming (as is done by a spell-checker to signal a misspelled word) or by the user dragging the mouse over some text. In either case, the text is highlighted. HideSelection, when set to False, means that selected text in your TextBox remains highlighted, even if the TextBox loses the focus (meaning that the user clicks some other form to give it the focus).

I can't really think of a use for this HideSelection property, and, as you've seen in this chapter, many properties are just like it: highly specialized. I suggest that you not clutter your brain trying to memorize these rare birds. What you do need to remember is that VB contains hundreds of programming features, and if you want to do something highly specialized, you probably can. The way to find out how to accomplish your specific goal is to press F1, click the Search Tab in Help, and type in some words that describe your highly specialized job. Unlike the Help Index feature (which locates major topics), the Search feature reads through all of Help looking for specialized words or phrases.

Index

The former Index property is now gone. (It worked with control arrays, which are not supported in VB.NET — although in VB.NET you *can* imitate their ability to create controls at runtime, as well as respond with a single event to behaviors affecting an entire group of controls. This topic is covered in Book III, Chapter 4.)

Lines

The Lines property is a collection (an array) of the individual lines of text in the TextBox. Each line is distinct from the previous line because the user pressed the Enter key to move down. You can access the individual lines by using code like this:

```
Dim x as String
X = TextBox1.Lines(2)
```

This example code puts the third line down from the top of the TextBox into variable X. Note that (2) represents the *third* line and not the second — it's the old "zeroth" problem in computer language lists.

Location

The `Location` property, with its `X` (horizontal position) and `Y` (vertical position) attributes, replaces the previous `Left` and `Top` properties. However you can still use `Left` and `Top` in your code, but they inexplicably don't appear in the Properties window, consistency being the hobgoblin of little minds.

You can adjust these `X` and `Y` properties in the Properties window or in your programming code to move a control dynamically during runtime.

Locked

The `Locked` property is similar to, but less drastic than, setting the `Enabled` property to `False`. When set to `True`, `Locked` permits the `TextBox`'s text to be scrolled, and even highlighted, by the user. It also permits you, the programmer, to change the text: `TextBox1.Text = "This new text."` The text is not changed to a gray color. However, as when `Enabled` is set to `False`, the user cannot edit the text.

MaxLength

The `MaxLength` property enables you to specify that the user can enter only a particular number of characters into the `TextBox`. This is useful if you want users to enter information such as a zip code, the length of which you know in advance.

Modified

The `Modified` property tells you whether the text has been changed by the user (since the `TextBox` was created, or since you last set the `Modified` property to `False`). Modified doesn't appear in the Properties window, but you can use it in source code.

Modifiers

The `Modifiers` property simply drops down a list of the various scope declaration keywords: `friend`, `public`, and so on.

MouseIcon

The traditional `MouseIcon` property is now called `Cursor`, as discussed earlier in this chapter.

MultiLine

The `MultiLine` property was discussed earlier in this chapter.

OLE

The OLE properties are no longer available.

PasswordChar

The `PasswordChar` property enables you to specify which character should appear visible to the user when he or she types in a password. In other words, if you want to use a `TextBox` as a password-entry field for the user, you can type in a * symbol as the `PasswordChar`. If you type in any character as the `PasswordChar`, the `TextBox` displays only that character as users type their passwords (for example, **********). You know the routine. (I've always wondered whether this subterfuge is all that necessary — after all, do you have people hovering over your shoulder all the time, just waiting to see your password? I suppose it's better to hide it though — there are lurkers.) Note that the `MultiLine` property must be set to `False` for the password feature to work properly.

ReadOnly

The new `ReadOnly` property at first seems baffling. When set to `True`, the text in the `TextBox` can only be "read," not changed. `ReadOnly` seems rather unnecessary, given that the `Enabled` property does the same thing. The difference? With `Enabled True` and `ReadOnly False`, the text in the `TextBox` can at least be copied.

RightToLeft

For an English speaker, the `RightToLeft` property has no value and should be left at its default. However, some languages, such as Arabic and Hebrew, run text from right to left. You would set `RightToLeft` for those languages so that vertical scroll bars appear on the left side of a `TextBox`.

Scrollbars

The `Scrollbars` property enables you to add horizontal or vertical scroll bars to your `TextBox` so that the user can employ them as a way of moving through text that exceeds the size of the `TextBox`. However, even without them, the user can always press the arrow keys, the PgUp and PgDn keys, the spacebar, and so on to move around through text that's not shown within the visible opening of the `TextBox`.

Size

The traditional, classic, pre-VB.NET `Height` and `Width` properties are no longer available. They have been replaced with a `Size` property that includes — what shall we call them? — a pair of "subproperties" named `Height` and `Width`. The `TabIndex` property defines the order in which components get focus as the user repeatedly presses the Tab key to move among them.

The TabStop property, when set to False, removes the component from the TabIndex list. TabIndex is useful because it offers a quick way for the user to move among the input components (TextBoxes, CheckBoxes, and so forth) on a form — all without having to remove his or her hands from the keyboard and reach for the mouse to click a component into the focus. However, some components, such as a PictureBox, are not usually employed as user-input devices. So you can set their TabStop properties to False to eliminate them from the TabIndex group. Components such as Labels that can never be used as input devices simply have no TabIndex property in the first place, and are therefore never included in the tabbing.

Sometimes, though, you do want to permit a PictureBox to become part of the TabIndex list so that the user can interact with it. How can a PictureBox ever be used as an input device, you ask? A simple example is when the PictureBox is clicked at all, anywhere, something happens (because you put some programming into its Click event). You might display several small PictureBoxes, each containing a different image — perhaps a car, a bus, a train, or a plane. When you click one, a phone number where you can arrange for that kind of transportation is displayed.

Here's a more sophisticated example: Put a map of Italy into a PictureBox in a cookbook application, let users click on whatever location on the map they choose, and then display a list of recipes typical to the locale that was clicked. (The *x* and *y* coordinates for the MouseDown event tell you exactly where, on a graphic, the user clicked.)

Tag

The Tag property is a kind of Post-It note that you can attach to a component. You can type in some unique text as a way of identifying it when it is passed to a procedure. Sometimes, Tag is also used like a little cookie — holding some information that is supposed to stick with the control and always be available.

Text

This property is covered earlier in this chapter.

TextAlign

There's a new TextAlign (formerly Alignment) property, but it merely offers three alternatives to the traditional left-justify (default). You can center or right-justify the text, but such adjustments are rarely of any use (unless you specialize in wedding invitations, where the centering alignment is always the necessary style).

ToolTipText

A ToolTipText property used to be displayed in the Properties window, representing the small help phrase that pops up to inform the user about the purpose of a component when the user pauses the mouse pointer on top of the component. For mysterious reasons, this property has been promoted to become a full control, and now resides on the Toolbar rather than in the Properties window. Unique among all controls — and, indeed, unique compared to the way properties are typically handled — you must add a ToolTip control to your form, and *then* the other controls on the form have a ToolTip property in the Properties window.

Visible

The Visible property determines whether or not the user can see the TextBox. During design time, components are always visible. But during runtime, if you set the Visible property to False, the user cannot see the component. When would you want to make a component invisible? There are at least a couple of uses for this property.

Although it's not traditional, Microsoft and other developers recently started employing a new way of interacting with users. For example, if the user clicks a button that's labeled Additional Features, the button is set to Visible = False and is replaced with two or three RadioButtons from which the user can select additional preferences. Those RadioButtons were always sitting there, but their Visible property was False until (or if) the user clicked the button, revealing them.

A second use for Visible is when you want to use a feature of a component, but you don't want the user to see that component. The most frequent use of this trick is to employ an invisible ListBox. ListBoxes can alphabetize. You can assign a list of names to a ListBox, set its Sorted property to True, and it organizes the names for you. However, users never need to see this ListBox if they don't need to interact with it. You just wanted to borrow the alphabetizing capability of the ListBox control.

WhatsThisHelpID

The WhatsThisHelpID property is no longer available.

WordWrap

The new WordWrap property mystifies me. I cannot imagine why you would ever want to set it to False. Do so, and if users type a line longer than the width of the TextBox, instead of automatically moving to the line below, the text scrolls off to the left to accommodate the super-long line they're typing. This is the way a TextBox behaves if its MultiLine property is set to False. Why you would do it with MultiLine set to True (creating a

`TextBox` that *can* display multiple lines) is beyond me. One difference: If the user presses Enter, a new line of text does begin.

Using COM and .NET Components

Right-click the Toolbox and choose Customize Toolbox. Notice the two tabs in the Customize Toolbox dialog box. COM components are older controls (VBX, OCX, ActiveX, they were called, variously, over the years) that you might have available on your computer and might want to add to your projects. Remember, though, that most of these controls have been superceded by superior VB.NET controls and that you'll have some potential deployment problems if users who receive your applications don't have these controls available on their machines.

What controls you see listed in the COM components tab depends on which previous versions of VB were installed on your computer, and also on whether you purchased any third-party controls.

Click the other tab, named .NET Framework Controls, on the Customize Toolbox dialog box. You notice that most of these are checked (meaning they've been added to the Toolbox). However, you find a few legacy controls here, too, such as the `FileListBox`. If you should feel you have a use for these, just check them and they are placed at the bottom of the Toolbox when you close the Customize Toolbox dialog box.

The Data tab in the Toolbox is covered in Book V.

Internet Programming Components

VB.NET offers a whole set of Internet-site components when you're creating a WebForm project (a Web site). To start a brand new Web project, follow these steps:

1. **Choose File⇨New⇨Blank Solution.**

You get a clean start, with no programming or projects.

2. **Choose File⇨New⇨Project.**

You see the New Project dialog box.

3. **Click Visual Basic Projects in the Project Types pane.**

You see various templates for the various kinds of projects you can build in VB.NET.

4. **Double-click the ASP.NET Web Application icon.**

   A new Web Application, with a blank WebForm1, is displayed.

5. **Open the Toolbox.**

   You now see that a Web Forms tab (and an HTML tab) have been added to the Toolbox. The Web Forms tab is selected by default.

Notice all the controls that you can place on a Web page. Book V explores many of them. For now, just notice what's available. Considering the limitations that HTML and browsers place on user interaction over the Internet, the suite of Web Controls is pretty impressive.

The *Web Forms* controls are a set of server-side controls that you can place on WebForms. When someone visits your Web site, those controls are translated into HTML on your server computer and then sent to the visitor's browser as HTML.

Recall that plain HTML pages leap easily over firewalls and past browser security settings. HTML is all about appearance, so it cannot transmit a virus any more than you can catch a cold by watching someone sneeze on TV. However, HTML is a clumsy language to work with, particularly if you're trying to do anything more than specify display settings such as font size.

So, to give you the best of both worlds, Microsoft lets you use rich WebControls and the full VB.NET language when you're designing your Web pages (WebForms). Server-side, you have the rich set of components and a rich language to work with. Then, when the user (a visitor to your Web page) requests one of these rich WebForms, VB.NET (technically ASP.NET) automatically translates your VB.NET source code into HTML equivalents and then composes an HTML page to send to the user.

A WebForm is similar to the traditional VB form, and a WebControl is similar to the traditional VB control — so you're in a familiar environment inside an alien world. The alien world is the .NET framework, but the familiar environment is the Visual Basic paradigm and the .NET IDE.

When you work within the WebForm/WebControl model, if you've programmed VB before, you'll feel fairly at home. In many ways, this kind of programming is like traditional VB programming (events, the Property window, the form, the Toolbox and so on). But, do be aware, when you add a WebControl to a WebForm, VB.NET translates that control into HTML.

Some people say that HTML is a rather restrictive environment, that it limits what can be displayed. They are correct. Forcing a rich control like a `RichTextBox` into HTML is like shoving a wedding cake through a pipe.

Something gets lost in the translation. What comes out the other end isn't quite what was pushed into the pipe.

On the other hand, you're likely to be surprised at what Microsoft's busy programmers have been able to accomplish, given the restrictions imposed by browser architecture, security needs, and Internet bandwidth constraints.

HTML Controls

There is some overlap, some redundancy between the set of components available on the Web Forms controls and those on the HTML controls tab in the VB.NET Toolbox. My advice is to choose the Web Forms controls, when possible.

They have several advantages, most important of which is that you get to program using the tested and familiar VB language.

With Web Forms controls, you can use events, set properties within those events, and otherwise avoid the restrictive and often inefficient HTML language. (Inefficient from a programmer's point of view because to create a table, for example, you have to type in many, many repetitive <TD> codes and other tags.)

HTML also suffers from having only a single data type, the *string*. This prevents the computer from assisting you with type safety, as well as limiting your ability to compute. HTML cannot even add 2+2.

However, don't throw out HTML controls entirely. They can be useful if you must ever split your programming between your server and script you write that will run within the user's browser. Why is an HTML control useful in this specialized situation? The control will be exactly the same within both the server and the browser runtime environments, simplifying your job of writing the browser script.

HTML controls are also useful if you're merely updating an existing ASP or HTML page by transforming it into a WebForm. In this situation, by limiting yourself to HTML controls, you won't disturb the other elements on the original Web page. Nonetheless, when possible, use WebControls rather than the traditional HTML controls.

Chapter 4: Windows, Windows Everywhere

In This Chapter

✔ Exploiting the Properties window

✔ Working with the Task List window

✔ Understanding the Output and Command windows

This chapter explores several important windows that you are likely to use often when programming in the VB.NET editor. The Property window is where you change various elements of your forms and controls. The Solution Explorer window provides you with an abstract, overall view of the various files and projects in your current application (or applications — a *solution* can embrace more than a single application). The Task List window shows you what needs to be fixed or worked on — rather like a nagging assistant, but it knows what you need to pay attention to. Finally, the Output and Command windows are useful for debugging your applications.

Changing Property Values

Start a new VB.NET Windows-style project. Click the Form1.vb (Design) tab at the top of the editor design/code window to switch to Design mode.

Press F4. If the Properties window is not visible, F4 brings it up. Now double-click the Button icon in the Toolbox to add a button to your form. Notice in Figure 4-1 that the Properties window has two columns. On the left is the property name, and on the right are the values, the actual current status of that property.

Adjusting values

Double-clicking in the left pane usually changes the value of the property. For example, double-click the Visible property and it switches from its default True to False. Double-click it again, and it goes back to True. Properties with two possible values toggle like that. Properties with more than two possible values usually cycle through their various values as you double-click them.

When you single-click a property, sometimes a button appears in its right pane. A down-arrow button means that you can click it to drop down a list of values for that property. Try clicking the Forecolor property to see the down-arrow button. An ellipsis (...) button means that if you click it, a dialog box is displayed. Try clicking the Font property to see the ellipsis, as shown in Figure 4-2.

You may see several kinds of dialog boxes if you click an ellipsis button. When changing the BackGroundImage property of a Button control, for example, you see an Open File dialog box that you can use to locate a graphics file. The Font property is somewhat unusual because it actually defines several related properties: `Font`, `FontSize`, and `FontStyle` (italics and bold). If you click its ellipsis button, you see the dialog box shown in Figure 4-2, in which you can select the various font-related properties all at once.

Figure 4-2:
Dialog boxes, such as this Font dialog box, help you quickly adjust a complex property's value.

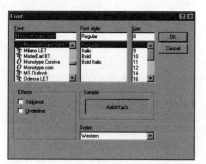

Changing several components at once

Occasionally, you may want to change the same property for several components at the same time. Imagine that you have two `RadioButtons`, three `Labels`, and a `TextBox` on a form. You want to enlarge all their fonts so that the user can more easily read them. You want to change all their Font properties from the default 8 to 11. You can do this in the following two ways:

✦ **Click the `Font` property for the** `TextBox`: Change it to 11. Then click a `RadioButton` to select it (so that its properties fill the Properties window). You see that VB has already selected the `Font` property for you. Whatever property was last selected for *any* control remains selected, even as you move from component to component. Sometimes, two components don't share a property; in those cases, the default property is selected.

✦ **Drag your mouse:** The fastest way to change a property simultaneously for multiple components is to drag your mouse around all the components. This selects all of them, and drag handles appear around all selected components as you can see in Figure 4-3. When you do this, the Properties window displays only those properties that all the selected components have in common (see Figure 4-3). When you change the `Font` property with several components selected, for example, that property changes for each of the selected components all at once.

The categorized view

I don't find the feature useful, but some programmers like to click the icon at the top of the Properties window (far left) that switches to Categories view. This rearranges the properties into (supposedly) logical groups: Behavior, Appearance, and so on. However, categorizing the highly varied set of properties is really impossible. To prove my point, the Design category contains the `Name`, `Locked`, and `Modifiers` properties, which, as far as I can tell, have nothing in common with each other, nor with "design." So, I prefer to leave the list displayed alphabetically. But the view you choose is, as usual, your decision. VB is marvelously flexible.

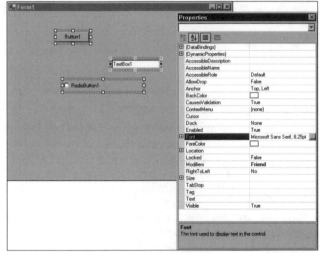

Figure 4-3:
When you select multiple components, the Properties window displays whatever properties they have in common.

Using the Task List Window

The Task List window is automatically filled with a list of any errors in your project. If you have an error in your source code (in some cases, even if you haven't yet pressed F5 to test the program) that error is listed and you can double-click the error message in the Task List window to be taken directly to the line in the source code where the error occurs. After you edit the line or otherwise fix the problem, the error message is removed from the Task List.

The Task List can also be used as a reminder or to-do list, where you add your own notes to yourself, Internet URLs of interest, or whatever. To add your own note, just click the top line in the Task List and start typing.

Now, to see the various options you can select among in the Task List, right-click somewhere within the Task List window other than on the title bar. In the context menu, you see several options.

The Previous View option switches you to whatever view (of those described next) that you had previously activated. The All option shows every possible type of Task List entry (*all* the choices described next). The Comment option shows only any links you have created in the code. In VB.NET, a comment begins with a single quote mark, but if you want the comment to be displayed in the Task List, you must follow it with one of the special words: todo, hack, or undone, like this:

```
'hack Dim ofd As New OpenFileDialog() Appears in Task List

'This comment won't appear in the Task list
```

Comment links can be removed from the task list by either deleting the entire comment in your source code or deleting only the special word. This comment feature doesn't work with XML or HTML source code.

The Build Errors option shows any errors that the compiler has detected in your source code. Actual errors are listed with a high priority (a red exclamation point), but mere warnings are listed with normal priority (no symbol). The User option displays anything that you have directly typed into the Task List window yourself. User reminders include a checkbox, and when you finish a task, you can click it to put a line through the text and gray it — indicating that you've done the job. User notes can also be deleted.

The Shortcut option displays bookmarks in your source code. You can add bookmarks (shortcuts) to any location in your code by clicking the line to put the insertion point there and then choosing Edit➪Bookmarks➪ Add Task List Shortcut. Like the other items in the Task List, to go to a particular bookmark in your source code, double-click that bookmark in the Task List. Deleting a Bookmark requires that you again position the insertion point in the line of source code and then choose Edit➪Bookmarks➪ Remove Task List Shortcut.

Choose the Current File option if you want to see only the entries in the file currently displayed in the code window. Choose Checked to see only the entries that have a check in their checkboxes, and choose Unchecked for the reverse.

In the same context menu where you can choose the various views, you can also specify that the Task List be sorted in various ways (by category, priority, description, file, or checked).

If you prefer that the Task List or Output windows don't automatically open as needed, change their default behavior by choosing Tools⇨Options⇨ Environment (in the left pane of the Options dialog box) and then clicking Projects and Solutions in the left pane. Uncheck the checkboxes.

Also, while you're looking at the Options dialog box, note that you can control how the Task List window behaves in a variety of ways. Choose Tools⇨Options⇨Environment (in the left pane of the Options dialog box) and then click Task List in the left pane. Here's where you can also add to or modify the special words that trigger a comment's inclusion in the Task List. And don't forget that you can shrink the Task List window like any other in the IDE by right-clicking its title bar and choosing Auto Hide.

A brief look at namespaces

Here's a typical example of the kind of problem that is brought to your attention in the Task List.

Namespaces are a new feature of VB.NET. They are designed to prevent confusion if two classes (stored in two different namespaces) share the same name.

For example, what happens if a class is named StrBreak in MyNameSpace1, and another class, also named StrBreak, is in a different namespace: MyNameSpace2? Then you use Imports to import both of these namespaces into the same project:

```
Imports MyNameSpace1
Imports MyNameSpace2
```

Now the problem occurs when somewhere lower in the code you try to use the StrBreak class. Which of the two StrBreak classes should be used?

Fortunately, Microsoft has thought of this problem. If you do try to use an ambiguous command — such as StrBreak in the preceding example — the VB.NET editor underlines StrBreak in your programming code, indicating that it is a problem. VB.NET also lists the problem in your Task List window, informing you that you need to "fully qualify" which namespace should be used. In other words, you would have to add the namespace's name to the function name, like this:

```
MyNameSpace2.StrBreak
```

Working with the Output and Command Windows

You generally use the Output and Command windows when debugging your programs, so I cover them in detail in Book III, Chapter 6. However, because you're currently touring the significant IDE windows, you can briefly consider their uses now.

The Command window for immediate queries

Suppose that you are testing a VB.NET program. You press F5 to run your program. If something seems wrong, you can begin debugging by pausing (breaking) the program by choosing Debug⇔Break All or by pressing Ctrl+Break. You then enter *break mode*. Technically, the program is still running (and it can be restarted from wherever it was when you broke into it, halting it, by pressing F5 again).

In break mode, you can test the contents of variables by typing their names directly in the Command window, as you see later in this section. However, I want to warn you of some naming confusion regarding this window. In all previous versions of VB, it was called the Immediate window. In the VB.NET Debug⇔Windows menu, it is also called the Immediate window. When the window is opened (as well as in some VB.NET documentation), however, it is called Command Window⇔Immediate. The reason for this confusion is that the Visual Studio editor is attempting to provide C programmers with their familiar tools, as well as VB and other programmers. So, now the traditional VB Immediate window is merged with the decades-old DOS-style window used by C programmers. The window defaults to Immediate mode, but to switch to Command mode, type **>cmd** and press Enter. In Command mode, you can type in some menu options, as well as certain options not available on menus. However, Command mode is a pretty clumsy way of doing things such as Edit-replace, involving escape characters, switches, and other long-abandoned, not mourned, input methods. Best ignore the Command mode. Switch back to Immediate mode by typing **>immed**.

Here's how you can use the Command window. When testing a program, one of your best tools is the *breakpoint.* You can specify one or more breakpoints in your program. While running, the program stops at a breakpoint just as if you had pressed Ctrl+Break (or if you've made the breakpoint *conditional,* such as $x > 4$, it breaks when that condition occurs).

When the IDE enters break mode, the code window pops up, showing you where the break occurred, so that you can see or change the code, you can single-step, or you can look at the Watch window or Command window to see the values in variables.

In the Command window, you can type **?** **i** and press Enter to see the current contents of the variable i. You can also type the names of functions (if they're within the scope of the current breakpoint) to test them, or type in expressions such as ? i * 2. The ? symbol is short for Print, and when you press Enter, the result is printed on the next line in the Command window.

You set a breakpoint by clicking the gray margin to the left of the line in the code window where you want the break. A red dot appears in the gray margin. The red dot alerts you that a line of code is a breakpoint. Execution halts on this line (or perhaps not if the breakpoint is conditional), and VB.NET enters break mode. Click the red dot a second time to delete the breakpoint.

Follow these steps to try it:

1. **Type this into the** Form_Load **event:**

```
Private Sub Form1_Load(ByVal sender As
System.Object, ByVal e As System.EventArgs) Handles
MyBase.Load

    Dim n As Integer = 9

    n -= 2

End Sub
```

2. **Click in the gray area on the left of the screen on the line** n -= 2 **(which means, in traditional VB,** n = n - 2**).**

   A red dot appears in the margin, indicating that this is now a breakpoint.

3. **Press F5 to run this program.**

   You see the program halt execution and display the Command window, as shown in Figure 4-4. If you don't see the Command window, choose View⇨Other Windows⇨Command Window, or click its tab in the bottom of the IDE.

4. **Press F8 to step through the next line of code that subtracts 2.**

   If you haven't switched to the traditional VB keyboard layout, you must press F11 to single step.

5. **Type ?n again on a new line in the Command window and press Enter.**

   This time you see that n now contains 7.

The Output window for multi-line results

The Output window appears when you press F5 to test an application; then the project ends (not breaks) because you stop it from running (you click the x in the upper right of a form, for example), or it has naturally completed its job and ends.

The Output window is somewhat DOS-like, but it has its uses. It is read-only, but you can control it (add panes, text, and so on) and do a few other fancy things via code. However, for most practical purposes, you'll limit yourself to simply reading what it displays. After all, *output* is its name, so that is its primary purpose.

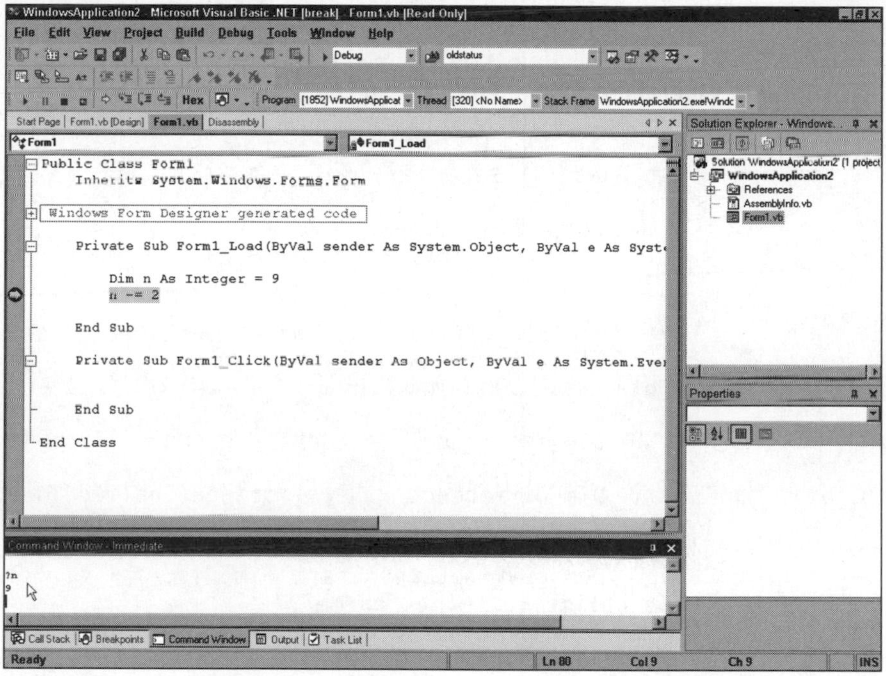

Figure 4-4:
Notice that the current value of variable *n* is displayed in the Command window, after you typed in *?n.*

The primary use for the Output window is during the testing process. Use the Output window to display some results that are too lengthy to put into a messagebox.

For example, displaying a messagebox when you have a short result to test is a common practice. You do it often in this book's examples, like this:

```
Private Sub Form1_Load(ByVal sender As System.Object, ByVal e
    As System.EventArgs) Handles MyBase.Load
        MsgBox(Now)
End Sub
```

When you press F5, some information is displayed in a messagebox. This is a generally more efficient alternative to using a breakpoint to see the contents of a variable at some location within your application (which is a common debugging technique).

However, sometimes, you want to see the contents of several variables or the results coming out of several functions. In that case, a messagebox is clumsy (because it doesn't automatically line wrap), and using the Command window is often preferable. Here's an example that displays multiple results in the Command window:

```
Private Sub Form1_Load(ByVal sender As System.Object, ByVal e
    As System.EventArgs) Handles MyBase.Load

        Dim hr As Integer = 2
        Dim mn As Integer = 13


        Dim StartTime As New DateTime(DateTime.Now.Ticks)
        Dim EndTime As New
DateTime(StartTime.AddHours(hr).Ticks)

        EndTime = EndTime.AddMinutes(mn)

        Dim Difference = New TimeSpan(EndTime.Ticks -
StartTime.Ticks)

        Debug.WriteLine("Start Time is: " +
StartTime.ToString("hh:mm"))
        Debug.WriteLine("Ending Time is: " +
EndTime.ToString("hh:mm"))
        Debug.WriteLine("Number of hours elapsed is: " +
Difference.Hours.ToString)
        Debug.WriteLine("Number of minutes elapsed is: " +
Difference.Minutes.ToString)

End Sub
```

Press F5 to run this example, and then stop the program (click the x in the form, or choose Debug⇨Stop Debugging). Now look in the Output window to see the results, part of which are shown in Figure 4-5.

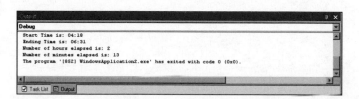

Notice the `Debug.WriteLine` commands. Those commands send information to the Output window. You can use the alternative syntax, which does exactly the same thing: `Console.WriteLine`. The `WriteLine` method displays its arguments and then automatically moves down one line. If you want to see all your information on the same line (with no line feed), just use `Console.Write` instead.

Chapter 5: Customization — Doing It Your Way

In This Chapter

↙ **Viewing your options**

↙ **Personalizing the IDE**

↙ **Saving your arrangement**

↙ **Customizing with macros**

I n this chapter, you see how to customize the IDE to make the process of writing and editing VB.NET projects as smooth as possible. The IDE is a highly flexible environment; you can personalize it in a variety of ways.

Exploring Tools⇨Options

There are several features in the Tools⇨Options menu that you should be aware of. First, you can consider whether or not you want the Output and Task List windows to automatically open when they are likely to be needed.

Automatic windows

Microsoft does extensive usability testing and spends quite a bit of time with focus groups, poring over user-submitted wish lists, and employing other tactics to ensure that their applications and utilities are easy to use and include the features people want. To my mind, this is why their products succeed — why, for example, people migrated to Microsoft Word and Internet Explorer from the initially more popular competitors WordPerfect and Netscape.

Another wise tactic Microsoft employs is to assume that it doesn't know everything. Therefore, even if people in focus groups vote overwhelmingly for a particular feature, Microsoft generally makes that feature the default but also allows you to turn it off if you prefer. That's what many of the items in the Tools⇨Options menu are: options with generally preferable defaults. But it's up to you if you want to change the default settings.

One example is that when you test a VB.NET project by pressing F5, the Output window automatically pops open to show you the progress of the compilation and any `console.writeline` output you've requested. Also, if build errors occurred, the Task List window automatically opens, describing the errors and their location in the source code. These are sensible defaults — most of us want the VB.NET IDE to work this way. But if you don't, you can change the defaults by choosing Tools⇨Options⇨Environment (in the left pane of the Options dialog box) and then clicking Projects and Solutions in the left pane. Uncheck the checkboxes and the Output and Task List windows will *not* automatically be displayed, you eccentric rebel, you.

Controlling your keyboard

As you know, .NET represents a grand unification scheme: an attempt to bring all computer languages (or most surviving languages anyway) into the same editor; to make their objects and components usable by any other language in the family; to make them work harmoniously within the same IDE; and to provide — as much as practical — common protocols, techniques, and tools.

Among the benefits of this drive toward unification is that the features of various applications are becoming standardized (and none too soon, either). For example, Word has offered users the capability of redefining the keyboard for years. I've always found it useful to redefine the default behavior of the F10 key. I like to make it save all opened files. It's a quick way to ensure that my work is safe from power outages, crashes, and other computer age annoyances. I just hit the F10 key now and then, and my work is saved.

All Microsoft applications ship with various default keyboard shortcuts. Ctrl+O, for example, usually displays the Open File dialog box. Collectively, a set of shortcuts is known as a *mapping scheme*. Clearly, life is easier if the same scheme can be used in all your applications. That's why I wanted to define the F10 key in the VB.NET IDE as Save all Files.

Redefining keys is easy; the process is similar to the way you do it in Word and other Microsoft applications:

1. **Choose Tools⇨Options.**

The Options dialog box opens.

2. **Click the Environment icon in the left pane to expand it.**

The various options available under the Environment heading are shown.

3. **Click the Keyboard option, as shown in Figure 5-1.**

4. **Scroll the list of actions until you find File.SaveAll; then click it.**

The File.SaveAll action is selected. Note that the menu items are listed in the format: *MenuTitle.Action*.

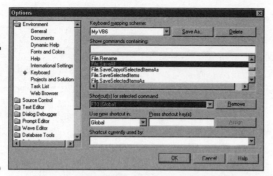

Figure 5-1:
Here's the
dialog box
that you use
to redefine
the .NET IDE
keyboard.

5. **Now click the Press shortcut key(s) textbox.**

   The textbox gets the focus (the insertion cursor blinks within the textbox).

6. **Press F10.**

   F10 appears within the Press shortcut key(s) textbox, and if it's already assigned to any other action, you see it listed in the Shortcut currently used by listbox.

7. **Click the Assign button.**

   Now whenever you press F10, all open files are saved.

8. **Click OK.**

   The dialog box closes.

Overloaded senses

You say: Wow! How can I remember the proper names for all the new .NET classes, functions, and arguments? You won't. However, VB.NET can help you figure out the proper programming syntax and diction in several ways. First, you can just type the source code in the VB.NET IDE and its Intellisense features (auto list members and parameter completion) kick in and provide you with suggestions in the form of lists that pop out while you type a line of code in the code window. Be sure that the Intellisense features are turned on (Tools⇨Options⇨Text Editor⇨All Languages). Be sure that the checkboxes next to Auto list members and Parameter information are checked.

Changing toolbars

VB.NET permits you to add or remove items from toolbars, as well as add and remove entire toolbars from the IDE. To do this, choose Tools⇨Customize, use the Commands tab to manage individual items within toolbars, and use the Toolbars tab to manage the entire toolbars.

Formatting controls

When you add controls to forms, they aren't automatically pretty. They aren't necessarily lined up vertically or horizontally, nor are they the same size. But they should be if you want your work to look polished. VB.NET provides some quick ways to format your controls.

When you first add several `Buttons` and a `TextBox` to a form and drag them around, they are haphazard, as shown in Figure 5-2.

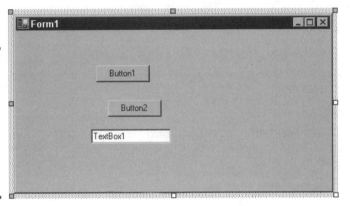

Figure 5-2: BEFORE: Controls should be positioned so that they align and are of some similar size.

Although the controls in Figure 5-2 look randomly positioned, a grid is actually underneath them to which they automatically align — like magnets jumping onto a refrigerator door. By default, this *snap to grid* feature is turned on in the IDE, and you should leave it on. It makes it easier for you to drag controls into alignment. To see whether the feature is on, choose Tools⇨Options⇨Windows Forms Designer. In this dialog box, you can also adjust the size of the grid and its visibility.

Another way to align controls is to drag your mouse around all the controls (which selects them as a group) and then choose Format⇨Align and Format⇨ Make Same Size. Yet another good way to align is to click one control to select it, and then press Ctrl⇨Arrow keys to move it or Shift⇨Arrow keys to resize it. When you finish fiddling with their size and position, the controls are neatly aligned, as you can see in Figure 5-3.

Of course, you can adjust many other specialized options in the Options dialog box. It may be worth your while to take a few minutes to open all the different dialog boxes (by clicking the various categories listed in the left pane) to see just what you can do with the IDE thanks to the Tools⇨Options menu.

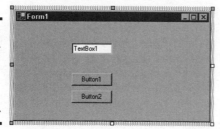

Figure 5-3:
AFTER: After alignment, the form looks more professional.

Your IDE, Your Way

Some programmers like to arrange the IDE as shown in Figure 5-4.

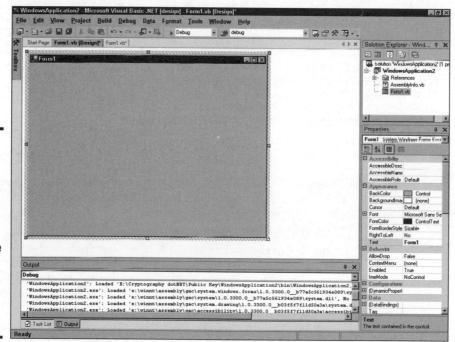

Figure 5-4:
This Is a popular layout, providing a large area for the design/code pane, and keeping the Toolbox available but tabbed.

The layout shown in Figure 5-4 is practical for many programmers, and it is the VB.NET default layout — so Microsoft focus groups must have indicated its popularity. This layout keeps only the Solution Explorer and Properties window always visible, and the Toolbox is tabbed so that you can quickly access it. However, I also like to select the Auto Hide option by right-clicking the title bar of the Solution Explorer, Properties window, and Output window. This hides them but exposes a tab, just like the Toolbox. In this way, you have the maximum screen space for your primary work areas: the design and code windows.

You can drag the various child windows around to different positions in the IDE, and you can "dock" them, meaning they attach to each other or to the frame of the IDE. (In Figure 5-4 the Solution Explorer and Properties windows are docked to each other and also to the right side of the IDE itself.) Sometimes you need to drag windows around and drop them in various ways to finally get them to dock where you want them — so you should experiment. Also, use the View menu to display other windows that you may want to see.

Going back to the default layout

You can manipulate the windows within the IDE and their behaviors in various ways by choosing options on the Windows menu. You can tab, tile, or dock various windows and position them in various ways. If you become hopelessly confused, you can reset the layout to the default VB.NET arrangement by clicking the Start Page tab in the code or design window and then choosing Visual Studio Default in the Window layout listbox. Also look at Tools⇨Options⇨Environment⇨General. In that dialog box, you can choose between tabbed or MDI style child windows. (MDI means multiple document interface, and there are no tabs involved; instead, you can tile various windows within the IDE.)

Making quick layout changes

Quickly switching between alternative IDE layouts and behaviors is easy. You can switch between layouts from the VB.NET Start Page. Here's how:

1. **To get to the VB.NET Start Page, click the Start Page tab on top of the design/code window (it may or may not be visible as a tab). Or choose View⇨Web Browser⇨Home (this does not work in the 2003 version of VB.NET).**

   If that doesn't work, restart VB.NET so that you see the Start Page. If you still don't see a page named Start when you fire up VB.NET, choose Tools⇨Options, and then under Environment, select General in the left pane of the Options dialog box. Locate the At Startup drop-down listbox and choose Show Start Page.

2. **On the left side of the Start Page, select the My Profile option. (This tab is on the top of the Start Page in VB.NET 2003.)**

   The Profile Editing options appear.

3. **Select whatever profile you like, or save a custom profile. Then click one of the tabs at the top of the design window (such as Form1.vb) to return to ordinary IDE editing mode.**

No matter which layout you choose as you work with the IDE, over time you are likely to make further adjustments to auto-hiding (I recommend it for all windows other than the design/code window) and other features. Visual

Studio .NET is smart enough to retain your changes between sessions. So, the next time you start VB.NET, you should see the same arrangement that was in effect when you last shut it down. (Note that switching layouts *does* cause your previous layout customizations to be lost.)

Creating Macros

Perhaps you've created macros (little programs) in an application such as Word. Macros can be a real timesaver, automating tasks that you perform frequently.

Finally, with macros available for years in every other major Microsoft application, Visual Basic .NET and the VS.NET IDE now have a macro facility. You can automate the IDE is several ways: assigning layout configurations to tabs, adding built-in shortcut keys, making custom add-ins, creating your own wizards, modifying toolbars, and even extending the existing Tools⇨Options menu with your own options.

For those of us who love to program, macros are among the most enjoyable of special features — easy, little utilities that can be quite simple to create but are also sometimes useful.

The VS.NET IDE macro facility permits you to record macros. For example, suppose that you frequently display the index for the help system. Instead of pressing F1, which by default displays the dynamic help feature (information about the currently selected control or code), you want to simply see the Help index immediately.

You could choose Help⇨Index menu or press Ctrl+Alt+F2, but that's a bit cumbersome. Instead, you want a fancy macro that allows you to press a single key to make the Index pop right up, right there, right now. You decide to redefine the F12 key, assigning it to your macro (because F12 defaults to Edit GoTo, which you never use). Follow these steps:

1. **Load a project or create a new Windows project.**

   Choose File⇨New⇨Project, and then double-click the Windows application icon.

2. **Click the Design tab at the top of the main VB.NET window.**

   You are in Design view.

3. **Choose Tools⇨Macros⇨Record Temporary Macro.**

   A toolbar appears.

4. **Choose Help⇨Index.**

5. **Stop the recording by clicking the middle icon on the macros toolbar.**

6. **Choose Tools⇨Macros⇨Save Temporary Macro and name the macro ShowIndex.**

   The new macro now appears in the Solution Explorer, where you can double-click it to activate it.

Now for another interesting trick. Choose View⇨Other Windows⇨ Macro Explorer. Right-click your new `ShowIndex` macro in the Macro Explorer (which should be visible next to the Solution Explorer), and choose Edit from the context menu. A new IDE appears, this one devoted to the art and science of macros. You see the following code; it's the source code of your macro:

```
Option Strict Off
Option Explicit Off
Imports EnvDTE
Imports System.Diagnostics

Public Module RecordingModule
    Sub ShowIndex()
    DTE.ExecuteCommand ("Help.Index")
    End Sub
End Module
```

Now you can assign the ShowIndex macro to F12 by following these steps:

1. **Choose Tools⇨Customize.**

2. **Click the Keyboard button at the bottom of the Customize dialog box.**

   An Options dialog box appears.

3. **In the Show Commands Containing field, type** ShowIndex.

   You see a list of any available macros, one of which is your new macro: `Macros.MyMacros.RecordingModule.ShowIndex`.

4. **Click your new macro to select it, click the Press Shortcut Keys field, and then press F12.**

5. **Click the Assign button to formally assign F12 to your macro.**

   You may see a message warning you that can't modify one of the default keyboard mapping schemes. If you don't, go to Step 7.

6. **When asked whether you want to make a copy of the scheme, click the Yes button and name it MyScheme.**

7. **Click the OK button and then the Close button.**

8. **Click the x at the top right of the Macro Explorer.**

   The Macro Explorer window closes.

9. **Press F12.**

   The Help Index appears, just as you wanted it to.

Book III

Advanced
Visual Basic .NET
Programming

The 5th Wave   By Rich Tennant

Re·al Pro·gram·mers

©RICHTENNANT

Real Programmers code in pen.

Contents at a Glance

Chapter 1: Understanding Variable Types

In This Chapter

✔ Understanding the main kinds of data

✔ Seeing all the types

✔ Chameleon tricks: Converting one type into another

✔ Working with expressions

✔ Learning about precedence

This chapter is all about variables in VB.NET. Variables are essential to computer programming, just as they are in many other aspects of life. Any container with a label is the real-world equivalent of a variable. And you're surrounded by named containers — they're fundamental to data processing. You also discover how to handle variables when they're grouped together into expressions.

Two Main Kinds of Data

It's called data processing, or information processing. But no matter how huge the database program or how sophisticated the graphics program, all computer programs process only two categories of information: strings or numbers.

Words

A *string* is characters strung together: `"Don Wilson"`, `"b"`, and `"454-5001 ext. 23"` are all strings. *Text* is another word for *string*. When you assign some literal text to a string variable, the text is enclosed in quotation marks:

```
Dim MyVariable As String
MyVariable = "This is Tuesday."
```

If there's enough memory in your computer and an application permits large strings, you can hold the entire phone book in a single string if you wish. By contrast, `""` is an empty string. Don't be fooled, because empty strings are sometimes useful.

A string can be a single character, really huge, empty, or anything in between. It can contain letters of the alphabet, symbols such as * or @, and even digits such as "2".

Note, however, that a *digit* is not the same as a true *number*. A digit is just a character (string) representation. You can't do math with strings.

You *can* concatenate strings: `Print "fluor" & "ide"` displays `fluoride`. `Print "2" & "3"` displays 23. But you can't multiply or subtract or do other math on strings. VB prefers that you use the & symbol to concatenate strings and reserves + for adding numbers. It usually accepts + with strings, but it doesn't like it. Besides, using + may confuse you into thinking that you are adding numeric variables:

```
Dim n As String = "5"
Dim m As String = "20"
Dim o As String
o = n + m
```

The final line of this code could be mistaken for addition, but no math is happening here. So, to make it absolutely clear that you are *concatenating* two strings, use the ampersand rather than the plus sign:

```
o = n & m
```

Numbers

You've seen how to work with strings. Numbers are the other kind of data, and they operate inside the computer just as they do in real life: You can do all kinds of math with them.

Remember the difference between true numbers and numbers-stored-as-strings (digits). Programmers sometimes store numbers as strings, though, if they don't expect that they'll be doing math with them. Your zip code ("27244") and phone number ("336-555-0123") make better sense stored as strings. You're never going to multiply them, are you?

What's more, some kinds of numeric information simply can't be stored as a numeric variable. You can't store a phone number as a numeric variable if you want to include those hyphens in it. Symbols such as hyphens must be stored in a string. If you leave the quotation marks off a phone number, such as 336-555-0123, Visual Basic thinks you want to subtract real numbers, and it calculates the value, -342.

Always remember to enclose strings in quotation marks. An integer is a numeric variable type. Here's how a phone number is misunderstood if you try to use it as an integer numeric type (the hyphens are thought to be minus signs):

```
Dim nAs Integer
        n= 336 - 555 - 123
msgbox(n)
```

Understanding Variables

Variables are a way of storing information — sometimes quite briefly (because the contents of a variable can *vary,* as the name implies). Nonetheless, you are talking about storing data when you discuss variables. Here's how it works. The computer asks you to type in how much you're willing to pay for a new TV. You oblige and type in **299**. What happens then? The computer must remember that information. It stores the information in a *variable*.

Does the programmer want to store this 299 as a string or a numeric variable? Probably numeric, because it may be necessary to do some math on it (comparing it to the cost of various models, calculating sales tax, adding it to other purchases, and so on).

Each variable has a name that the programmer gives it. Usually, programmers like to use memorable variable names — something easily recognized, such as UsersTopTvPrice. Underscore characters are allowed in variable names, so some programmers make the name even more readable this way: Users_Top_Tv_Price. After the user types in **299** (called a *value*), the program assigns the value to the variable. Assume that the user types the answer into TextBox1:

```
Dim TopTvPrice As Integer
TopTvPrice = TextBox1.Text
```

This source code assigns the value (whatever value the user types in) to the variable. The content of the TextBox, the value, is copied into the variable TopTvPrice.

A great debate is raging among programmers about just how much power a computer language should have to change a variable type all by itself. The TopTvPrice variable in this example started out being declared an Integer type, but when VB.NET saw that you wanted to assign *text* (a string type), it automatically changed the type to accommodate you (by definition, textbox contents are strings).

Some languages — such as C — forbid permitting languages to change type (only programmers can do it, and they must explicitly change the type by writing the necessary programming). If you prefer to be strict about data type conversions, type Option Strict On at the very top of the code window. With that option on, VB.NET displays an error message if you try to assign a string to a variable declared As Integer.

**Book III
Chapter 1**

**Understanding
Variable Types**

In other words, if the variable `TopTvPrice` has been declared as an Integer type, and you write the line of code `TopTvPrice = TextBox1.Text`, VB.NET flags this as an error and puts this message in the Task List for you: `Option Strict On disallows implicit conversions from ' 'String to 'Integer'`.

If you do want to leave `Option Strict On`, you must force conversions in your programming, and not simply trust that VB.NET does it for you. You see how to force conversions of variable types later in this chapter.

How to Name Variables

You must observe several rules when making up a name for a variable (otherwise, Visual Basic protests):

+ It must start with a letter, not a digit.

+ It can't be one of the Visual Basic command words, such as `For` or `Dim`.

+ It can't contain any punctuation marks or spaces.

How to Create a Variable

In previous versions of VB, when you needed to use a variable in a program, you could simply type in a name for it, and *voila,* the variable comes into existence. This is called *implicit declaration.* VB.NET frowns on this kind of thing. VB.NET wants all variables to be explicitly declared and wants their variable type to be specified in that variable declaration, like this:

```
Dim UsersAge as Integer
```

That's the VB.NET default. However, if you're a radical and want to use implicit declaration, you can type this at the very top (above any `Imports` statements) of your code window:

```
Option Explicit Off
```

Here's an example of implicit declaration. Perhaps your program displays an `InputBox` that asks the user how old he or she is. The variable in which you want to store his or her answer (the value) can be named `UsersAge` (I know, I know; it should be `User'sAge`, but you can't use punctuation in variable names):

```
UsersAge = InputBox ("How old are you?")
```

As soon as the user types **44**, or whatever, and closes the `InputBox`, the value 44 is assigned to the variable `UsersAge`. The value is stored. When your program later wants to process that data, it knows where to look. It merely uses the variable name. Say you want to find out if the user is eligible for AARP (the < symbol means less than):

```
If UsersAge < 50 Then MsgBox ("You're too young to join
    AARP, pup.")
```

Notice that you use the variable name as you use any other number in this programming. When the program executes, whatever number the user typed in is compared to 50.

Explicit declaration is a second, longer way to create a variable Many programmers swear by it and VB.NET defaults to it. You use the `Dim` command to explicitly declare the variable:

```
Dim UsersAge As Integer
UsersAge = InputBox ("How old are you?")
```

If you're going to use several variables in the procedure, `Dim` each of them:

```
Dim UsersAge, UsersHeight As Integer
Dim UsersName, Nickname As String
```

Notice that you can combine several declarations on a single line, as long as they are the same variable type. That's why the `As String` variable names are not declared in the same line as the `Integer` types in the preceding code example.

Or, if you use the `As` command, you can combine types on the same declaration line:

```
Dim UsersName As String, UsersHeight As Integer
```

VB.NET also permits you to declare a variable *and* assign a value to it on the same line:

```
Dim UsersAge As Integer = 21
```

If you are declaring multiple variables on a single line, you only need to use the `Dim` at the start of the line, and then just separate the variable names on the rest of the line by commas. Now do you see one reason why you can't use punctuation in variable names? Visual Basic uses various kinds of punctuation to mean various things in a line of code. Recall that the single-quote symbol (') means that you're making an annotation (a comment) and VB should ignore everything following the ' on that line. The * means multiply, & means concatenate text, and so on.

Notice that the line of code beginning with `Dim` ends with an `As` clause that specifies the variables' type.

One reason that using an explicit declaration is so highly regarded by many programmers is that when you look later at the code you wrote and you're trying to figure it out, you can see a list of all the variables right there at the top of the procedure or at the top of a class (if you want the variable to apply to the entire class — not just a single procedure). A second reason, avoiding certain kinds of bugs, is covered at the end of this chapter.

VB.NET has nine fundamental variable types, but thousands of objects that you can use as *types*. You'll get to know fundamental types later in this chapter. For now, just note that each declared variable must be explicitly typed (*typed* here means given a data type, not pressing keys on the keyboard).

`Dim` stands for *dimension,* an old computer term for "set aside some memory for this." Although `Dim` is the most commonly used, there are seven additional declaration commands: `Static`, `Public`, `Protected`, `Friend`, `Shared`, `Protected Friend`, and `Private`. Recall that these additional commands specify either *scope* (from how many locations in your program the variable can be accessed) or *lifetime* (how long the variable holds its value — only while the procedure within which it is declared is executing, or while the entire program is running).

Manipulating Variables

Variables hold only one value at a time. But the value can change as necessary (hence the name *variable*). For example, you could write the following code (although it makes no sense to do so):

```
Dim TVShow as String
TVShow = "Barney"
TVShow = "Five-O"
```

When this program executes, VB assigns the text `Barney` to the variable `TVShow`, but immediately dumps that value and replaces it with `Five-O`. When a new value is assigned to a variable, the previous value in that variable simply no longer exists.

You can assign *literal* values (`"Barney"` or 299, as illustrated previously), but you can also assign one variable's value to another. When you assign a variable to another variable, the variable on the left of the equals sign (=) gets the value held in the variable to the right of the =. At this point, both variables contain the same value. This is like making a copy of the value. In this next example, the contents (the value) in the variable PopularShow are copied into the variable MyTVShow:

```
MyTVShow = PopularShow
```

One practical and common use of copying one variable into another was illustrated earlier in this chapter with this line:

```
TopTvPrice = TextBox1.Text
```

Some more efficiencies

Sometimes you want to concatenate or otherwise combine two variables. Suppose that you want to personalize your program, so you first ask the user to type in his or her name, and then you use that variable along with another variable to create a complete sentence:

```
Dim Msg, Result As String
        Result = InputBox("Please type your first name.")
        Msg = "Thank you, " & Result
        MsgBox(Msg)
```

You have some ways to shorten code. If you're one of those people who is always looking to conserve variable names, you can reuse Result like this, without even needing that second variable Msg:

```
Dim Result As String
        Result = InputBox("Please type your first name.")
        Result = "Thank you, " & Result
        MsgBox(Result)
```

Or if you're one of those people who are really, really conservative and always want to save space and condense code, you can do it like this:

```
Dim Result As String
        Result = InputBox("Please type your first name.")
        Msgbox("Thank you, " & Result)
```

As the preceding code illustrates, a variable can be part of what's assigned to itself. One use for this technique is illustrated in the preceding code: You want to preserve the contents of the variable (Result), but you want to add something to the contents ("Thank you"). To demonstrate this same principle with a numeric variable, perform the following math equations using the variable name:

```
A = 233
A = A + 1
```

Now, A holds 234.

Saving time with +=

VB.NET introduces a new technique when you are adding a variable's current contents to some new value (as in the example in the previous section). You can avoid repeating the variable's name by combining + with = , for example. Here's how this trick works. Instead of the following code:

```
A = A + 1
```

you can now use:

```
A += 1
```

This condensation has several variations:

- ✦ A *= 4 (The value currently in variable A is multiplied by 4 and assigned to A.)

- ✦ A -= 1 (Decrement the value currently in variable A.)

Here's an example:

```
Dim Brother as String
Brother = "Tom"
Brother &= " and Bob"
```

Now Brother contains Tom and Bob. This technique, which avoids repeating the variable name (Brother = Brother & " and Bob" as in the traditional VB approach) is wildly popular with C and C-derivative language programmers. See if it appeals to you. It does come in handy to avoid repeating really lengthy variable (or object) names, which are sometimes necessary in VB.NET.

You usually can choose from several ways to code, and your personal style will emerge over time. Notice how I always seem to use Result or Response as the variable names with the InputBox command? It's just a little habit of mine; you can use Reaction, Retort, Reply, or Rejoinder, just as long as it begins with an *R*. Just kidding! Actually, you can use Answer, Users_Input, or whatever. You know the rules for thinking up variable names: You can use pretty much any word, or even a nonsense word like jaaaaakaa. But it's best to make your variable names descriptive of what the variable holds. And, it's helpful after a while to settle on some consistent way of naming frequently used variables, like those you assign the result of an InputBox user input. This consistency makes your programming easier to read. There is a whole set of naming conventions that you might want to consider using, such as prepending txt whenever naming a TextBox (as in txtPhoneNumber). To see a list of these conventions, look at this book's Cheat Sheet.

Understanding Data Types

Text variables (strings) are pretty simple. The string is the only fundamental text data type. Now let's look at numeric variables.

There are several fundamental types of numeric variables. The reason for these different numeric data types is to enable you to speed up your applications with some of them and achieve greater precision with others.

Previous versions of VB had a default variable type. By default, unless you specifically defined them as something else with Dim, VB made all variables the *variant* type. This was convenient because you didn't have to worry about saying: ThisVariable holds strings, but ThisOtherVariable holds only whole numbers (no fractions). Instead, you let VB decide which type to use based on the value you assigned to it or the context in which it was used. For example, if you assigned what was a numeric variable type to a TextBox, the variable type was automatically changed from numeric to string (because a TextBox can display only a string type).

Fatal flaws

However, the variant type, efficient though it often was, had two fatal flaws from the perspective of those who designed VB.NET. First, in some cases, VB had a hard time figuring out which type the variant should change to — resulting in an error. Second, the other languages in the .NET universe do not use variants — and the .NET philosophy requires conformity between its various languages (at least on the fundamental issues, such as variable typing). Therefore, the variant variable is no longer part of the VB language. It has been banished in VB.NET.

**Book III
Chapter 1**

**Understanding
Variable Types**

Here's an example that shows how variants achieved their chameleon changes:

```
A = 12
B = 12.4
```

When it assigns the 12 to A, VB figures that 12 can be an *integer* type, but when it assigns 12.4 to B, VB knows that this number has to be changed to the *floating-point* (has a decimal point) type because it is a fraction. So, VB types the variables for you. It can even convert some kinds of data:

```
A = "12"
B = 14
B = B + A
MsgBox (B)
```

In this example, you get the correct mathematical answer of 26 because when you assigned 14 to B, it automatically became an integer variable type, and then you assigned a string to it, which converted the string into an integer. However, don't take this too far. It's best not to mix types if you can avoid it.

The interpreting that VB must do when it works with variants was said to slow program execution down some, although I never noticed it. In any case, variants are no longer available. But (as I explain in the discussion of implicit conversions in the "Understanding Variables" section, earlier in this chapter) VB.NET can change an integer type into a string type, for example, so the integer can be properly displayed in a TextBox.

Important numeric types

The simplest numeric variable type is `Boolean`. It can hold only two states: `True` and `False` (it defaults to `False`). Use this when you want a toggle variable (something that switches off and on like a light switch). To create a Boolean variable, use the following code:

```
Dim MyToggle As Boolean
```

Another simple data type is the `Integer` and its larger sister, the `Long` type. Before VB.NET, the `Integer` data type was 16 bits large and the `Long` data type was 32 bits large. Now these types are twice as big as they used to be: `Integer` is 32 bits large and `Long` is 64 bits large (and `Long` is an `Integer` too — no fraction, no decimal point). If your program needs to use a 16-bit integer, use the new type `Short`.

So if you're translating pre-.NET VB code, you need to change any `As Integer` or `Cint` commands to `As Short` and `Cshort`, respectively. Similarly, `As Long` and `CLng` now must be changed to `As Integer` and `Cint`.

You'd be surprised at how often the only thing you need is an integer in programming that involves math. In most programming, the `Integer` is the most common numeric data type. (No fractions are allowed with an `Integer`.) If your non-fractional number is larger or smaller than an integer can hold, make it a `Long` data type.

```
Dim MyLittleNumber As Integer
Dim MyBigNumber As Long
```

The other major numeric type is called *floating point*. It has similar small and large versions called `Single` and `Double`, respectively. Use it when your program requires the precision of using fractions:

```
Dim MyFraction As Single, MyBiggerNumber As Double
```

Why division is bizarre

Computers calculate in different ways with different numeric variable types. They can do arithmetic faster with integer types than with floating-point types because floating-point suffers from the problem of decimal points, and the bothersome fractions to the right of decimal points.

Why are fractions such trouble? The simplest explanation is understandable if you recall that elementary school teachers have to spend much more time teaching *division* than teaching multiplication or other basic arithmetic techniques. Anyone who has written a list for Santa or made a stack of cookies understands addition. Subtraction, too, is clear enough — for example, when older brother steals some cookies from the stack. Multiplication is pretty easy to get once you understand the idea of addition. Multiplication is just addition repeated over and over.

But division is in a class by itself. Division can cause something to go below unity, below one, into the problematic world of fractions. Suddenly, two simple digits such as 3 and 1 can expand into a list of digits bigger than the universe, .3333333333333333333; you get an infinitely long result if you try to divide 1 by 3. Infinity is a disturbing result when you are used to getting neat, understandable results from adding and subtracting.

And there are those *remainders,* unsettling things left over after the arithmetic is supposedly finished. Plus, in the real world, if something becomes fractional, it dies. Few creatures, other than worms and some plants, can survive being "in half." All in all, division is a bizarre, dangerous, fantastic maneuver regardless of how you slice it.

Computers have exactly the same problems working with division that children do; they have more to consider and more to manipulate. Just like us, the computer must calculate more slowly when working with numeric variable types that can have fractions (the floating-point data types). If you want to speed up your programs, see if you can get away with merely using the integer data type. Integers don't involve fractions. If you don't need the precision that fractions offer — and most of the time you don't — use Integers. After all, the IRS lets you round off pennies to the nearest dollar, so be brave and, if possible, just ignore any fractional details in your calculations. (This advice does *not* apply to NASA scientists calculating the Mars Lander trajectory.)

However, the distinctions between numeric data types was more important in the past — when memory was small and expensive, and processing speed was relatively slow. Today, choosing conservative data types may not much matter unless you are writing a program with specialized, heavy-duty number crunching.

VB.NET also has a new `Char` type, which is an unsigned 16-bit type that is used to store Unicode characters. The new `Decimal` type is a 96-bit signed integer scaled by a variable power of 10.

Forcing Yourself to Declare Variables

Recall that you can turn off the requirement that all variables be explicitly declared (by using the `Option Explicit Off` command).

But be warned that many programming teachers insist that all variables be officially, explicitly declared. One reason they do this is so that you can easily see which variables are in use — without having to search the code for them. A second reason to require the declaration of variables is that it prevents a common source of error. Consider this code:

```
TempString = "Tex"
TempString = TemString & "as"
MsgBox (TempString)
```

You probably think that this code displays a message box with the word Texas in it. No, it only displays as. Can you see why? One of those variable names is misspelled, which is very easy to do. (TemString, the typo made when this code was typed in, contains nothing. So when you add nothing to "as", you're left with "as.") However, with `Option Strict` in force (the VB.NET default), VB alerts you if you make this common kind of mistake.

With `Option Explicit On`, if you try running the previous example code, VB.NET responds by highlighting the first instance of `TempString` and telling you "The name TempString is not declared." So go ahead and declare it:

```
Private Sub Form1_Load(ByVal sender As System.Object, ByVal e
    As System.EventArgs) Handles MyBase.Load

    Dim TempString As String

    TempString = "Tex"
    TempString = TemString & "as"
    MsgBox(TempString)

End Sub
```

When you first type this code, VB.NET underlines the error with squiggles and if you press F5 to run this code, VB shows you the typo, as you can see in Figure 1-1.

You never intended to have a variable named TemString, and with `Option Explicit` turned on, VB.NET shows you the typo. VB.NET flags any undeclared variables.

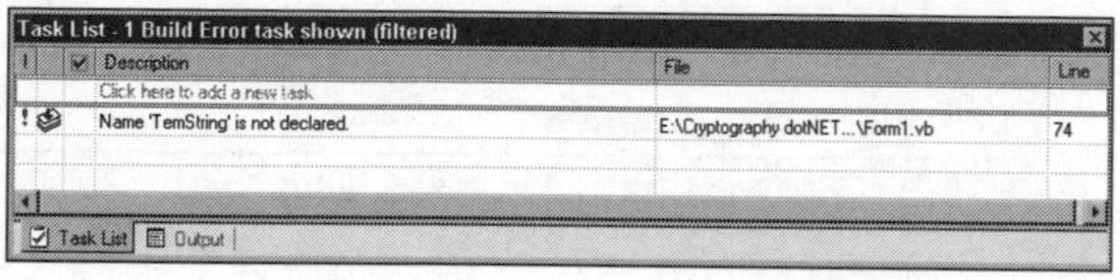

Figure 1-1:
When you
use the
`Option`
`Explicit`
feature,
VB.NET
points out
any typos in
variable
names.

```
Task List - 1 Build Error task shown (filtered)                                    [X]
|  ✓  Description                                    File                      Line
        Click here to add a new task.
!  ⬧  Name 'TemString' is not declared.             E:\Cryptography dotNET...\Form1.vb   74

[ ✓ Task List ] [ ⊞ Output ]
```

Converting Data Types

When you leave `Option Strict` turned on, you must *coerce* variables to
change type. You must explicitly program the change. VB.NET boasts four
ways to change one data type into another. The `.ToString` method is
designed to convert any numeric data type into a text string.

The second way to convert data is to use the familiar, traditional VB functions: `CStr()`, `CBool()`, `CByte()`, `CChar()`, `CShort()`, `CInt()`, `CLng()`,
`CDate()`, `CDbl()`, `CSng()`, `CDec()`, and `CObj()`, as in the following example:

```
Dim s As String
Dim i As Integer = 1551
s = CStr(i)
MessageBox.Show(s)
```

The third way is to use the `Convert` method, like this:

```
Dim s As String
Dim i As Integer = 1551
s = Convert.ToString(i)
MessageBox.Show(s)
```

The fourth way uses the `CType` function, with this syntax:

```
Dim s As String
Dim i As Integer = 1551
s = CType(i, String)
MessageBox.Show(s)
```

Take your pick.

**Book III
Chapter 1**

Understanding
Variable Types

Table 1-1 shows all the VB.NET data types.

Table 1-1	The VB.NET Data Types		
Traditional VB type	*New .NET type*	*Memory Size*	*Range*
Boolean	System.Boolean	4 bytes	True or False
Char	System.Char	2 bytes	0-65535 (unsigned)
Byte	System.Byte	1 byte	0-255 (unsigned)
Object	System.Object	4 bytes	Any Type
Date	System.DateTime	8 bytes	01-Jan-0001 to 31-Dec-9999
Double	System.Double	8 bytes	+/-1.797E308
Decimal	System.Decimal	12 bytes	28 digits
Integer	System.Int16	2 bytes	-32,768 to 32,767
	System.Int32	4 bytes	+/-2.147E9
Long	System.Int64	8 bytes	+/-9.223E18
Single	System.Single	4 bytes	+/-3.402E38
String	System.String	CharacterCount * 2 (plus 10 bytes)	2 billion characters

Understanding Expressions

Now you should consider *operators* — ways to take two or more elements (such as two variables) and combine, modify, compare, or otherwise manipulate them.

You need to know how you can compare numbers in various ways (such as greater-than or equal) or compare text in various ways (alphabetically, or find similarity with the Like command). There is also a set of arithmetic operators, such as +. Finally, you should know a bit about the logical operators such as And, Not, and Or, which you can use to create longer, more complex expressions. Finally, you learn how to use parentheses to specify the order in which the parts of a complex expression should be evaluated.

Operators are used in expressions to compare two elements (such as two variables), to do math on them, or to perform a "logical" operation on them. The plus sign (+), for example, is an operator in the following example: 2 + 4. The greater-than symbol (>) is an operator in this example that says n is greater than z: n > z.

Many expressions are a combination of programming elements that, taken together, can be evaluated as either *true* or *false*. For example, this is an expression: Mary is older than Sue. Although it's more complex, this, too, is an expression: Bob is smaller than Stan, but Stan is wealthier than Sondra. Even though expressions can get quite lengthy, if *any* of their assertions are false, the entire expression is evaluated as false. However, some expressions produce results other than simply true or false.

Expressions are not composed only of variables. Expressions can also be built out of literal numbers, literal strings, numeric variables, string variables, numeric variables in an array, a function that returns a number or string, a constant, or any combination of these.

An expression is looked at and evaluated by VB during runtime. This evaluation produces a result. It may be that the expression is True, or it may produce the number 6 or some other result that the expression yields, such as the expression "A" & "sk", which produces the result "Ask".

An expression must contain at least two elements, separated by an operator. For example, the expression "A" > "B" asks whether the literal letter A is greater alphabetically than the letter B, which is untrue, so this expression evaluates to False. The operator is the greater-than symbol: >.

Comparison Operators

Often, you need to compare two values, and then your program reacts based on the result of the comparison. Say, for example, that the user has typed in his or her age, and you want to respond to the age in your code:

```
Dim usersage As Integer

    Dim Msg As String

    If UsersAge < 50 Then
        Msg = "You "
    Else
        Msg = "You do not "
    End If

    Msg += "qualify for reduced term insurance."

    MsgBox(Msg)
```

The *expression* in this code is UsersAge < 50. This particular expression uses one of the comparison (also called *relational*) operators: the less-than symbol (<). The line of code means: *If the value in the UsersAge variable is less than 50, then show the "You qualify..." message. Otherwise (Else), show the "You do not qualify..." message.*

The eight comparison operators

Table 1-2 lists the eight comparison operators used in VB.NET.

Table 1-2	The VB.NET Comparison Operators
Operator	*Description*
<	Less than
<=	Less than or equal to
>	Greater than
>=	Greater than or equal to
<>	Not equal
=	Equal
Is	Do two object variables refer to the same object?
Like	Pattern matching

It's easy to remember the meaning of the < and > symbols. The large end of the symbol is greater, so A > B means A is greater than B. A < B means A is less than B.

You can use the comparison operators with text as well. When used with literal text (or text variables), the operators refer to the alphabetic qualities of the text, with the value of Andy being less than Anne.

The Is operator is highly specialized. It tells you if two object variable names refer to the same object. You can use it with arrays that keep track of controls or forms.

The Like operator lets you compare a string to a pattern, using wildcards. This operator is similar to the wildcards you can use when searching, using the symbols * or ?. In the Windows search utility or in Explorer, for example, you can see all files ending with .DOC by typing ***.DOC**.

Working with the Like operator

Use Like to compare strings, as follows:

```
Dim Msg, A As String
A = "Rudolpho"

If A Like "Ru*" Then Msg = "Close Enough"
MsgBox(Msg)
```

In the preceding example, the message is displayed. The Like operator can be used to forgive user typos. When testing for Pennsylvania, **you can** accept `Like Pen*` because no other state starts with those characters, so any misspellings the user makes farther on in this word can be ignored.

The following example uses the `Like` operator to compare against a single character in a particular position. (Notice that the two logical lines are placed on a single physical line here, separated by a colon. You can use a separate line for `MsgBox(A)`, but it's so short that I just stuck it onto the end of the other code. If you do put two or more logical lines together, remember that the colon is necessary to separate them.)

```
Dim A As Boolean
A = "Nora" Like "?ora" : MsgBox(A)
```

This results in `True`.

Recall that many expressions simply evaluate to `True` or `False`, and therefore the expression returns a Boolean answer. So, you can declare a Boolean variable to receive that answer, as in the previous example. Here's another example:

```
Dim A As Boolean
A = "Nora" Like "F?ora" : MsgBox(A)
```

This results in `False`, because the first letter in `Nora` isn't *F,* the third letter isn't *o,* and so on.

You can also use `Like` to compare when you don't care about a match between a series of characters, like this:

```
If "David" Like "*d" Then
```

This code results in `Match`. `"D*"` or `"**D*d"` or `"*i*"` all match `"David"`.

Or you can use the following to match a single character in the text against a single character or range of characters in the list enclosed by brackets:

```
If "Empire" Like "??[n-q]*" Then
```

This code results in `Match`, because the third character in `Empire`, *p,* falls within the range `n-q`. You can also use multiple ranges such as `"[n-r t-w]"`.

Or you can use the following to match if a single character in the text is not in the list:

```
If "Empire" Like "??[!n-q]*" Then
```

This code results in `No Match` (the ! symbol means "not").

Using Arithmetic Operators

Arithmetic operators work pretty much as you expect them to. They do some math and provide a result. Table 1-3 lists the arithmetic operators used in VB.NET.

Table 1-3	The VB.NET Arithmetic Operators
Operator	*Description*
^	Exponentiation — the number multiplied by itself (for example, 5 ^ 2 is 25 and 5 ^ 3 is 125)
–	Negation — negative numbers (such as –25)
*	Multiplication
/	Division
\	Integer division — division with no remainder, no fraction, no decimal point (for example 8 \ 6 results in the answer 1). Use this if you don't need the remainder.
Mod	Modulo arithmetic (explained in the text following this table)
+	Addition
–	Subtraction
&	String concatenation (This & is still supported in VB.NET, but is no longer necessary. It was used in previous versions of VB with variant variable types. VB.NET has no variants, so you can use + for numeric addition as well as concatenation.)

Use the arithmetic operators like this:

```
If B + A > 12 Then
```

The modulo (Mod) operator gives you any remainder after a division, but not the results of the division itself. You just get the remainder. This is useful when you want to know if some number divides evenly into another number. That way, you can do things at intervals. For example, suppose that you want to print the page number in bold on every fifth page. Here's how you can code that:

```
If PageNumber Mod 5 = 0 Then
   FontBold = True
Else
   FontBold = 0
End If
```

Here are some more Mod examples:

+ 15 Mod 5 results in 0.
+ 16 Mod 5 results in 1.
+ 17 Mod 5 results in 2.
+ 20 Mod 5 results in 0.

The Logical Operators

The logical operators are sometimes called *Boolean* operators because technically they operate on individual *bits* (and a bit can only be in two states: true or false, on or off). But whatever you call them, the logical operators are most often used to create a compound expression. The logical operators that you use frequently are And, Or, and Not. They allow you to construct expressions like this:

```
If BettysAge > 55 And JohnsAge > 50 Then
```

The And operator means that both comparisons must be true for the entire expression to be true.

Similarly, Or allows you to create an expression where only one comparison must be true for the entire expression to be true:

```
If TomsMother = Visiting Or SandysMothersAge > 78 Then
```

The Not operator is good for switching a toggle back and forth, like this:

```
Private Sub Button1_Click(ByVal sender As System.Object,
    ByVal e As System.EventArgs) Handles Button1.Click

        Static Toggle As Boolean

        Toggle = Not Toggle

        If Toggle Then MsgBox("See this message every other
    time you click")

    End Sub
```

The Static command preserves the contents of the variable Toggle (Dim does not). Remember the Static command; it comes in very handy when you need to retain a value in a local variable (a variable declared within a procedure, as in the preceding code). Typically, you use it with counters or toggles.

The Boolean variable type is the simplest one: It has only two states: `True` or `False`. It can be flipped back and forth like a light switch. This line, `Toggle = Not Toggle`, means: *If Toggle's value is False, make it now True. If it's True, make it False.* You'll be surprised at how often you use this technique in your programming.

Table 1-4 is a list of all the logical operators, some of which have esoteric uses in cryptography and such.

Table 1-4	The VB.NET Logical Operators
Operator	*Description*
`Not`	Logical negation
`And`	And
`Or`	Inclusive Or
`Xor`	Either but not Both

Here's an example of a logical operator at work:

```
If 5 + 2 = 4 Or 6 + 6 = 12 Then MsgBox("One of them is true.")
```

One of these expressions is true, so the `MsgBox` comment is displayed. Only one or the other needs to be true. Here's another example:

```
If 5 + 2 = 4 And 6 + 6 = 12 Then MsgBox ("Both of them are
    true.")
```

This is false, so nothing is displayed. *Both* expressions, the first and the second, must be true for the printing to take place.

VB.NET offers two new operators — `AndAlso` and `OrElse` — which differ technically from the way that the `And` and `Or` logical operators work, and differ in how expressions using them are evaluated. The purpose of this is to attempt to prevent some esoteric, yet possible, errors. If this is important to you, see the entry titled "AND, OR, XOR and NOT" in the appendix on this book's Web site at `dummies.com/extras`.

Operator Precedence

When you use more than one operator in an expression, which operator should be evaluated first? Simple expressions are usually unambiguous: 2 + 3 can only result in 5.

But sometimes a more complex expression can be solved in more than one way, like this one:

```
3 * 10 + 5
```

Does this mean *first multiply 3 times 10, resulting in 30, and then add 5 to the result?* Should VB evaluate this expression as 35? Or, does it mean *add 10 to 5, resulting in 15, and then multiply the result by 3?* This alternative evaluation results in 45.

Expressions are not necessarily evaluated by the computer from left to right. Left-to-right evaluation in the previous example results in 35, because 3 is multiplied by 10 before the 5 is added to that result. But remember that complex expressions can be evaluated backwards sometimes.

Visual Basic enforces an *order of precedence,* a hierarchy by which various relationships are resolved between numbers in an expression. For example, multiplication is always carried out before addition.

Fortunately, you don't have to memorize the order of precedence. Instead, to make sure that you get the results you intend when using more than one operator, just use parentheses to enclose the items that you want to be evaluated first. Using the previous example, if you want to multiply 3 * 10, and then add 5, write it like this:

```
(3 * 10) + 5
```

By enclosing an operator and its two surrounding values in parentheses, you tell VB that you want the enclosed items to be considered as a single value and to be evaluated before anything else happens.

If you intended to say add 10 + 5 and then multiply by 3, move the parentheses like this instead:

```
3 * (10 + 5)
```

In longer expressions, you can even nest parentheses to make clear which items are to be calculated in which order, like this:

```
3 * ((9 + 1) + 5)
```

If you work with these kinds of expressions a great deal, you may want to memorize Table 1-5. But most people just use parentheses and forget about this problem. If you're interested, the table lists the order in which VB evaluates an expression, from first evaluated to last.

Table 1-5	The VB.NET Arithmetic Operators in Order of Precedence
Operator	*Description*
^	Exponents (6 ^ 2 is 36. The number is multiplied by itself X number of times.)
-	Negation (negative numbers such as -33)
* /	Multiplication and division
\	Integer division (division with no remainder, no fraction)
Mod	Modulo arithmetic
+ -	Addition and subtraction
The relational operators	Evaluated left to right
The logical operators	Evaluated left to right

Given that multiplication has precedence over addition, the ambiguous example that started this discussion can be evaluated in the following way:

```
3 * 10 + 5
```

So, the result is 35.

A Note on Arrays

Recall that I said that a variable can hold only one value at a time. Sometimes, though, it's useful to collect a whole group of values together in one package. There's a special way to group values: You give them one "variable name," but you give each individual value a unique index number. This is similar to the way that all your neighbors share the same road name but are distinguished from each other by house numbers: 12 Elm, 13 Elm, 14 Elm, and so on.

A group of values, sharing the same name, but with different index numbers is called an *array*. Arrays are so important — and have been so enhanced in VB.NET from previous versions of VB — that all of the next chapter is devoted to them.

Chapter 2: Working with Arrays

In This Chapter

✔ Discovering initialization techniques

✔ Using object arrays

✔ Searching and sorting

✔ Do it your way: Using one array to sort another

✔ Tapping into the ArrayList powerhouse

✔ Data binding

✔ Employing enumerators

✔ Knowing when to use hashtables

A rrays are essential computing tools: They provide a way to efficiently store and retrieve related data. But if you think you know what arrays can do in VB, think again. VB.NET has taken arrays to a whole new level of usefulness.

Arrays boast a variety of new, special capabilities in VB.NET. They can contain objects, they can search and sort themselves, and the new ArrayList class is particularly valuable and flexible. In addition, you also want to explore the strong typing available from the new HashTable class. All these topics are covered in this chapter.

Boundaries versus Elements

Before exploring the various interesting new ways you can use arrays in VB.NET, I need to first point out that arrays are *always* zero-based in the .NET framework.

In previous versions of VB, you could use the Option Base statement to force arrays to start with element one instead of zero. The Option Base statement has now been removed from the VB language.

In practical terms, this means that you must always be aware that the dimension you declare for your array is not its actual capacity. This is a bit strange, but programmers have to live with it — like those apartment buildings where superstitious people insist on having no 13th floor, so the building has one fewer floor (total) than the highest floor listed in the elevator.

Just remember that in VB.NET an array can always contain one more value than the number you declare as its dimension.

For example, `Dim MyArray (10)` actually results in an array with 11 elements. Put another way, the index numbers to the elements in this array are 0, 1, 2, . . . 10. The array has 11 index numbers, 11 elements, and these elements can contain 11 values. However, the index numbers themselves range from 0 to 10.

This has several implications, particularly when you manipulate arrays in loop structures. You can use the `UBound` function of an array (or the `Count` property of an `ArrayList`) to find out the highest element number, like this:

```
UBound(myarray)
```

Or you can use the `Length` property to find out how many actual elements (its true capacity) are in the array, like this:

```
myarray.Length
```

In the following example, the `UBound` function returns `10`, but the `Length` property is `11`:

```
Dim MyArray(10) As String

Console.WriteLine("UBound is: " & UBound(MyArray))
Console.WriteLine("Length Property is: " & MyArray.Length)
```

Zero-based arrays and other types of zero-based lists have always bedeviled programmers. That's why the `Option Base 1` statement was made available in earlier versions of VB. Nonetheless, the .NET Common Language Specification requires zero-based arrays, for compatibility with other languages.

The zero-based array is one example of how .NET requires VB to conform to the way the C language and its offspring — C++, C#, Java, and so on — have always done things. In my view, it may have been better to add flexible lower boundaries (base) to the C-type languages than to remove the `Option Base` feature from VB.

However, a partial solution to this problem is available, if you're willing to go it pretty much alone.

A simple solution

For some programmers, perhaps the best way to avoid errors when working with arrays is to simply ignore the "zeroth" element entirely: Never write any value to it, and never try to read it either. This does no harm; it just wastes a tiny bit of memory, and memory today is very, very cheap. If you choose to use this tactic (and can convince programmers you work with of its virtues), you'll find that it offers several advantages.

If you consistently ignore the zeroth element in your arrays, you simplify several aspects of your programming. One advantage is that you can write loops for your arrays, knowing that the first index number is always 1 and the last index number is always correctly returned by the UBound function. Or you can just look to see what upper bound you gave the array in your code when you declared the array (the Dim statement).

Another advantage to avoiding the zeroth element is that some collections and other sets in VB.NET do start with an index of 1. All your programming that involves lists of items can therefore be made consistent, and you never have to think twice (or, as is usually the case, debug your programming after getting an "out of bounds" error message).

The final advantage you gain with this approach is that the index numbers actually refer to the item numbers. It makes sense; it's the way humans actually think and talk. Book(3) is truly the third book in the array of books. (If you use a zero-based array, Book(3) is the *fourth* book.)

Here's an example showing you how to ignore the zeroth element when writing values to an array and reading back those values:

```
Private Sub Form1_Load(ByVal sender As System.Object, ByVal e
    As System.EventArgs) Handles MyBase.Load

        Dim MyArray(3) As String
        Dim i As Integer

        For i = 1 To 3
            myArray(i) = i.tostring
        Next

        For i = 1 To 3
            Console.WriteLine(myArray(i))
        Next

End Sub
```

Group programming

A word of warning: If you work with groups of other programmers, you'll likely find resistance to this "avoid zero" idea. However, the majority of VB programmers are thought to work alone or in very small groups — parents writing a quick quiz program for their children's homework, a couple of accountants dashing off a little utility program to help them in their work, and so on. For programming like this — amateur and semi-professional — consistently using one-based indexes helps these programmers avoid one of the most frequent sources of annoying bugs in computer programming.

A second word of warning: Much database programming and some of the methods you find in classes such as the HashTable, Arrays, and ArrayLists expect you to specify ranges and other index-related code using zero-based indexing. So, in those cases, you can't avoid the zero-base problem.

Initialization

In VB.NET, you can assign values to variables on the same line that declares them. The same feature is available to arrays. If you want to use this same-line shortcut approach, you must use braces to enclose the array's values, like this:

```
Private Sub Form1_Load(ByVal sender As System.Object, ByVal e
    As System.EventArgs) Handles MyBase.Load

        Dim MyArray() As String = {"", "Lois Lane", "Jimmy"}
        Dim i As Integer


        For i = 1 To UBound(MyArray)
            Console.WriteLine(MyArray(i))
        Next

    End Sub
```

Notice that you can't specify an upper boundary when initializing values in this fashion. The ( ) must be left empty, as this example illustrates. Also notice that I left the zeroth string blank between the braces, in keeping with the suggestion that you can just ignore the zeroth element in all your arrays.

Arrays of Objects

You can create an array of objects in VB.NET that is, among other things, a way to store different data types within an array.

To create an object array, you first declare an object variable, and then you instantiate each object in the array. This example creates an array holding six book objects. Don't type (Windows Form Designer generated code). That is included here just to show you where to put the global array arrBook. Also, don't worry that you're creating a *class* here. You get to work with classes quite a bit in Book VII.

```
Public Class Form1

    Inherits System.Windows.Forms.Form

    Dim arrBook(6) As Book 'create the array object variable

(Windows Form Designer generated code)

    Private Sub Form1_Load(ByVal sender As System.Object,
    ByVal e As System.EventArgs) Handles MyBase.Load
        Dim i As Integer

        'instantiate each member of the array:
        For i = 1 To 6
            arrBook(i) = New Book()
        Next

        ' set the two properties of one of the array members
        arrBook(3).Title = "Babu"
        arrBook(3).Description = "This book is large."

        Dim s As String = arrBook(3).Title
        Console.WriteLine(s)

    End Sub

End Class

Public Class Book
    Private _Title As String
    Private _Description As String

    Public Property Title() As String
        Get
            Return _Title
        End Get
        Set(ByVal Value As String)
            _Title = Value
        End Set
    End Property

    Public Property Description() As String
        Get
            Return _Description
        End Get
        Set(ByVal Value As String)
            _Description = Value
        End Set
    End Property

End Class
```

Array Search and Sort Methods

In VB.NET, arrays have the capability to both sort and search themselves. By default, an array sorts alphabetically from A to Z. Also note that, when sorted, the index numbers of the array's elements will change.

Here's an example showing how to use both the sort and the search methods of the array object. The simplest syntax for these two methods is as follows:

```
Array.Sort(myArray)
```

and:

```
anIndex = Array.BinarySearch(myArray, "Penni Goetz")
```

To see these features in action, put a TextBox on a form, and change the TextBox's MultiLine property to True:

```
Private Sub Form1_Load(ByVal sender As System.Object, ByVal e
    As System.EventArgs) Handles MyBase.Load

    Dim myarray(4) As String

    myarray.SetValue("one", 1)
    myarray.SetValue("two", 2)
    myarray.SetValue("three", 3)
    myarray.SetValue("four", 4)

    Dim cr As String = vbCrLf 'carriage return
    Dim show As String

    Dim i As Integer

    For i = 1 To 4
        show = show & myarray(i) & cr
    Next

    TextBox1.Text = show & cr & cr & "SORTED:" & cr

    Array.Sort(myarray)

    show = ""
    For i = 1 To 4

        show = show & myarray(i) & cr

    Next

    Dim anIndex As Integer

    anIndex = Array.BinarySearch(myarray, "two")
```

```
    Dim r As String = CStr(anIndex)

    show += cr & "The word two was found at index number
" & r & " within the array"

    TextBox1.Text += show

    show = ""

    For i = 1 To 4

        show = show & myarray(i) & cr

    Next

    TextBox1.Select(0, 0) 'turn off selection

End Sub
```

If you are sorting an array of numbers rather than strings and you have a
negative number in the array (perhaps because you are looking at monthly
profit results, and you had a *bad* month), you can't use the "ignore the
zeroth index" suggestion that I made earlier in this chapter. Why? Because
the zeroth index in an integer array has a default value of 0, and thus it gets
sorted between your negative and positive numbers. Also, if you had only
one negative number, it would be at index 0; therefore, it would not show up
in a list generated by a counter going up from 1 to ubound list!).

Note the use of the SetValue method in this example. Its syntax enables
you to add or replace an item anywhere within an array by specifying the
index number:

```
myarray.SetValue("one", 2)
```

The Sort method is overloaded with eight variations, including one that
sorts only a subset of the array:

```
Array.Sort(myarray, StartIndex, LengthOfSubset)
```

Although I can't think of a use for this feature, here's an example that specifies that you want only the fifth through eighth items sorted:

```
Array.Sort(myarray, 4, 7)
```

(However, if you are using my suggestion and avoiding the zeroth item, this
example sorts the *fourth* through *seventh* items.)

Custom Sorting

You can even sort one array based on the elements in *another* array. You can use this interesting capability in creative ways because it allows you to devise your own custom sorting rules.

For example, suppose that the entries in a single-dimension array hold first names and last names separated simply by a space character: Mary Jones, Bob Smith, and so on. However, you need to sort them by their last names. You can create a second array that holds only the last names, alphabetize it, and simultaneously also sort the original array. This has the effect of rearranging the original array in sync with the second array. Note that the second array is *not* alphabetized. It merely gets sorted in parallel with the first array. The arguments of the Sort method look like this: myarray.Sort(firstarray, secondarray). Only firstarray here is alphabetized; secondarray merely goes along for the ride.

Here's an example:

```
Private Sub Form1_Load(ByVal sender As System.Object, ByVal e
    As System.EventArgs) Handles MyBase.Load
        Dim cr As String = vbCrLf 'carriage return

        Dim myarray(5) As String
        Dim lastnames(5) As String

        myarray(0) = "Monica Lewis"
        myarray(1) = "Georgio Apples"
        myarray(2) = "Sandy Shores"
        myarray(3) = "Dee Lighted"
        myarray(4) = "Andy Cane"
        myarray(5) = "Darva Slots"

        TextBox1.Clear()

        'create an array of the last names:

        Dim i As Integer
        Dim x As Integer
        Dim s As String

        For i = 0 To UBound(myarray)
            s = myarray(i)
            x = s.IndexOf(" ") 'find blank space
            lastnames(i) = myarray(i).Substring(x) 'get last
name
            TextBox1.Text += lastnames(i) & cr
        Next

        TextBox1.Text += cr & "Sorted by last name:" & cr
```

```
myarray.Sort(lastnames, myarray)

For i = 0 To UBound(myarray)
    TextBox1.Text += myarray(i) & cr
Next

TextBox1.Select(0, 0) 'turn off selection
End Sub
```

When you use the array `Sort` method in this way, the array that serves as the key (the array to alphabetize by) is the first argument, followed by the array to be sorted. In this example, the arguments are (`lastnames, myarray`). So `myarray` is sorted in sync with the alphabetization that takes place in the `lastnames` array.

Many Members

Like most objects in VB.NET, the array object has many members. In addition to properties and methods that most objects have (such as `ToString`), several members are unique to the array class (`reverse`, `GetUpperBound`, and so on).

The simplest syntax for the reverse method reverses all the items in an array, like this:

```
Array.Reverse(myarray)
```

Or you can reverse only a subset of items within the array. In this example, the reversing starts with the item at index number 1 and only reverses two items:

```
Array.Reverse(myarray, 1, 2)
```

Here is a list of all the public properties of the array class: `IsFixedSize`, `IsReadOnly`, `IsSynchronized`, `Length`, `Rank` (number of dimensions), `SyncRoot`.

Here are the public methods: `BinarySearch`, `Clear`, `Clone`, `Copy`, `CopyTo`, `CreateInstance`, `Equals`, `GetEnumerator`, `GetHashCode`, `GetLength`, `GetLowerBound`, `GetType`, `GetUpperBound`, `GetValue`, `IndexOf`, `Initialize`, `LastIndexOf`, `Reverse`, `SetValue`, `Sort`, `ToString`.

`LastIndexOf` searches an array (or a portion of an array) for a value and returns the index of the final (highest) occurrence of that value. The `GetLowerBound` method is rather odd, because every array in VB.NET must have a lower bound of zero. This method is a vestige left over from an original plan to permit us programmers to specify a lower bound other than zero. The .NET framework *does* permit lower bounds for arrays, but you are not supposed to create instances of the array class and then adjust the lower bound. As the VB.NET help says, "Users should use the array constructs provided by the language."

The ArrayList Powerhouse

The new VB.NET `ArrayList` is a powerful tool. Familiarize yourself with it if you expect to ever need to manipulate arrays in your programming and you want to take advantage of the many features of this new object. For one thing, it can dynamically resize itself, so you don't have to resort to `ReDim` and other techniques that an array requires.

The ArrayList had no real equivalent before VB.NET, but the rather simple `Array` function was available. For most of the VB 10-year history, no function was available that created an array and then allowed you to add some data to it directly within your source code. Then in VB 6, the `Array` function was added to do just that. (Those of you familiar with early, 1980s, versions of Basic may recall the similar `DATA` statement that was used to insert items of data into an executing program.)

You can use the `Array` command in VB 6 to stuff some data into an array, like this:

```
Private Sub Form_Load()

Arx = Array("key", "Name", "Address")
MsgBox (Arx(2))

End Sub
```

The `Array` function has been deleted from the language, presumably because it returns a variant variable type, and variants are disallowed in the .NET framework. What's more, in VB.NET you can directly insert values into an array. (See the "Initialization" section, earlier in this chapter, for an example.)

The new `ArrayList` object can do what the `Array` function used to do — and much, much more.

Here's a VB.NET equivalent to the old `Array` command:

```
Dim MyArray as new ArrayList

  myArray.Add ("key")
  myArray.Add ("Name")
  myArray.Add ("Address")

Msgbox (MyArray(2))
```

Why use an ArrayList?

Clearly, the `Array` class and the `ArrayList` class in VB.NET have some redundancy. Both classes can search, sort, reverse, and manipulate their data in various ways.

An `ArrayList`, however, has more features and is generally more capable than an `Array`. One serious drawback to arrays is that removing or inserting items is cumbersome. For example, if you want to remove the fifth item in an array, you must write some programming to loop through the array and move down by one all the values from the fifth element up to the final element. The `ArrayList`, by contrast, is more flexible because it's designed to be more dynamic — the ArrayList automatically handles any resizing necessitated when you insert or delete elements. (All arrays in .NET can be resized at any time with the `ReDim` statement or `ReDim Preserve`, but the latter extracts a performance hit.)

To see some of the capabilities of an `ArrayList` in action, start a new VB.NET Windows-style project and put a `ListBox` and a `Button` on the form. Then type in this code, which illustrates how you can remove an element by using the `RemoveAt` method and specifying an index number:

```
Public Class Form1

    Inherits System.Windows.Forms.Form

    Public arrList As New ArrayList()

    Private Sub Form1_Load(ByVal sender As System.Object, _
ByVal e As System.EventArgs) Handles MyBase.Load
        arrList.Add("ET")
        arrList.Add("Pearl Harbor")
        arrList.Add("Rain")

        ListBox1.Items.AddRange(arrList.ToArray)

    End Sub

    Private Sub Button1_Click(ByVal sender As System.Object, _
ByVal e As System.EventArgs) Handles Button1.Click

        arrList.RemoveAt(1)

        ListBox1.Items.Clear()
        ListBox1.Items.AddRange(arrList.ToArray)

    End Sub
End Class
```

Book III
Chapter 2

Working with Arrays

Notice that you don't have to use For...Next or other loop code to feed the data from an array to a ListBox. Instead, you can simply slap it in with the ListBox's AddRange method. Alternatively, you can bind the data in an array directly to a ListBox. (This technique is illustrated in the section "Data Binding," later in this chapter.)

Here's another example of the capabilities of the ArrayList class. To see how you can specify an element's *contents* as another way of removing it, replace the line in boldface in the previous example with the following line:

```
arrList.Remove("Pearl Harbor")
```

Working with ranges

Among other features, an ArrayList can manipulate a range of its elements by adding (to the end of the ArrayList), inserting, reading, or removing the range all at once. To see an example that reads a range, replace the code currently in the Button1_Click event with this:

```
Private Sub Button1_Click(ByVal sender As System.Object,
    ByVal e As System.EventArgs) Handles Button1.Click

        Dim RangeOfArrList As ArrayList = arrList.GetRange(0,
    2)

        ListBox1.Items.Clear()
        ListBox1.Items.AddRange(RangeOfArrList.ToArray)

End Sub
```

In this example, the two numbers in the GetRange method specify the start index and number of elements in range, respectively. Then that range is copied into a new ArrayList named RangeOfArrList.

A very useful type of collection is the SortedList, which is similar to an array. It always automatically maintains its contents in alphabetical order. Whenever you add a new item, it is inserted into the list in the proper alphabetic location. This handy class is covered in Book VII, Chapter 4.

Data Binding

Another new technique in .NET permits you to bind ListBoxes, DataGrids, and other list-type controls to an array, hashtable, or other collection. Data binding has been available in VB for several years now, but prior to .NET you could only bind to a database or a recordset derived from a database.

Using the same example with a `ListBox` and `Button`, replace the `Button`'s `Click` event with this code to see how to bind an `ArrayList` to a `ListBox`:

```
Private Sub Button1_Click(ByVal sender As System.Object,
    ByVal e As System.EventArgs) Handles Button1.Click

    Dim Monkey As New ArrayList()

    Monkey.Add("A")
    Monkey.Add("B")
    Monkey.Add("C")
    Monkey.Add("D")
    Monkey.Add("E")
    Monkey.Add("F")

    ListBox1.DataSource = Monkey

End Sub
```

Enumerators

Microsoft is encouraging us to use *enumerators* when looping through a collection class (such as an array). If you prefer this approach, here's an example that illustrates how you can rewrite the preceding example to display both elements in the `RangeOfArrList` `ArrayList`:

**Book III
Chapter 2**

**Working with
Arrays**

```
Dim RangeArrListEnumerator As System.Collections.IEnumerator
  = _

    RangeOfArrList.GetEnumerator()

    While RangeArrListEnumerator.MoveNext()
        Console.Write(RangeArrListEnumerator.Current)
        Console.WriteLine()
    End While
```

This is an alternative to the more traditional VB approach to coding loops, where you use `For...Next` and loop until you reach the final element:

```
    Dim i As Integer
    For i = 0 To RangeOfArrList.Count - 1
        Console.Write(RangeOfArrList(i))
        Console.WriteLine()
    Next
```

Also, remember that an `ArrayList` is *dynamic* — it reallocates memory as needed when you add items to the `ArrayList`. However, you can set the `Capacity` property explicitly if you wish. In fact, you can freely resize an

ArrayList at any time by changing the Capacity property. If you don't expect to add any more new elements to an ArrayList, you can free memory by using the TrimToSize method.

The Uses of Hashtables

The collection class called a *hashtable* is quite similar to the ArrayList in both design and features. However, a hashtable permits strong data typing: You can give each element a *name* in addition to its index number.

In some situations, working with a collection of data is easier when each element is labeled. For example, if you need a collection of data that holds the foods eaten by each animal in a zoo, manipulating the data may be easier — and may make your code more readable — if each element is named after a different animal:

```
Dim Food As New Hashtable()

    Food.Add("Lion", "Meat")
    Food.Add("Bear", "Meat")
    Food.Add("Penguin", "Fish")

    Console.WriteLine(Food.Item("Bear"))
```

In this example, the names of the animals are the keys you can use to access the elements rather than their index numbers. Each key must be unique, although the data can be duplicated as much as you wish ("meat" and "meat" in this example). Hashtables can also be used in encryption — to translate a password into a pseudo-random numeric key. This use is covered in Book III, Chapter 7.

Chapter 3: Serious Serialization and Streams

In This Chapter

✓ **Understanding streams**

✓ **Working with StreamWriter and StreamReader methods**

✓ **Little bits: Using binary readers and writers**

✓ **Internet and memory streaming**

✓ **Serializing and deserializing**

This chapter is all about streaming, the metaphor that .NET language designers use for sending or receiving data. In the past, VB programmers used a somewhat more restrictive metaphor: saving and opening files. But in the brave new Internet world, data can be stored in more places than you can imagine — not just in files on your local hard drive. New times demand new thinking, so get ready for the data stream and all that it implies.

Understanding Streams

Streams are flows of data, to or from your application. Streams now replace traditional VB communication techniques between applications and files on a hard drive. What mainly distinguishes the concept of streaming from traditional approaches is that it isn't limited to communication with disk files. In the new world of *distributed* programming (typical of Web programming), there is more than one place to store data. In addition to files, for example, collections of data are in memory. Recall that in VB.NET, you can bind an array to a `ListBox` — treating the array, which resides in memory, as if it were a database. The Internet might be another source of data streaming into your application. This, too, is a non-traditional source of data.

So, to take into account the various places where you might get or send data, the idea of streaming permits connections between all kinds of data sources (known as *data stores*). It's even possible to connect one data stream to another.

In sum, once you grasp the concept of streams and learn how to use them to send or receive data, you can then employ the same techniques no matter what data stores are involved. In theory, getting data from a remote computer in Beijing should be no different from getting data off your own hard drive. I say *in theory* because, as much as we might wish it were so, it's not possible to do everything the same way in all situations. For example, when you're working with a file on your local hard drive, you can ask the stream to tell you the length of that file — how much data is stored there. When working with a remote file coming in from Peking, there is no `Length` property that you can query. Nonetheless, streaming is an improvement over the havoc of previous data access technologies. Improved consistency is preferable to no consistency.

You can still use the traditional VB random-access files techniques in VB.NET if you must. (In VB.NET, the syntax for these techniques is *similar* but not identical to traditional VB.) But you're encouraged to move to streams because of the greater flexibility they offer. Also, programming is moving away from the random-access file as a way of storing and accessing data. Instead, contemporary programming prefers databases and XML as data store constructs. It's all really pretty similar, when you get down to it — just labeled pieces of information organized one way or another. But fashions change, and right now, you should probably move away from random-access files and their "record number" techniques. If nothing else, basing your data storage on databases or XML makes your information more compatible with other applications (at least for the next few years until the next fashion in data storage takes the programming world by storm).

The Basics of Streaming

Traditional Visual Basic file access assigns a file number to each opened file. The simplest traditional format is as follows:

```
Open filepath {For Mode}{options}As {#} filenumber {Len =
    recordlength}
```

For example:

```
Open "C:\Test.Txt" As 5
```

However, for reasons known only to those in charge of .NET, the actual syntax of the VB.NET version of the traditional VB isn't exactly the same as it used to be. `Open` becomes `FileOpen` and the order of the arguments shifts around. So, you might as well just move on to streaming.

If you do want to stick with the older style file I/O, though, here's the VB.NET version:

```
FileOpen(5, "C:\Test.Txt", OpenMode.Random)
```

Streaming is more flexible, but you pay a penalty for this flexibility: Streaming requires more programming. To see a simple example, follow these steps:

1. **Chose File⇨New⇨Project.**

   You see the New Project dialog box.

2. **Double-click the Windows Application icon.**

   A new Windows-style application opens in the IDE.

3. **Double-click the TextBox icon in the WinForms tab of the Toolbox.**

   A TextBox is added to your Form1.

4. **Double-click a Button icon to add it also.**

5. **Click the TextBox in the IDE so that you can see its properties in the Properties window. (Press F4 if the Properties window isn't visible.)**

6. **Change the TextBox's Multiline property to True by double-clicking it in the Properties window. Also delete TextBox1 from the Text property in the Properties window.**

7. **Double-click the Button.**

   The Button's Click event is displayed in the code window.

8. **Type this in at the top of the code window:**

   ```
   Imports System.IO
   ```

9. **To try the simplest example of VB.NET file streaming, type this into the Button's Click event:**

   ```
   Private Sub Button1_Click(ByVal sender As
       System.Object, ByVal e As System.EventArgs) Handles
   Button1.Click

           Dim a As String = "This works fine."
           Dim b As String

           Dim sw As New StreamWriter("c:\test.txt")
           sw.WriteLine(a)
           sw.Close()

           Dim sr As New StreamReader("c:\test.txt")
           b = sr.ReadLine
           MsgBox(b)
           sr.Close()

       End Sub
   ```

Press F5 to run this example and see that it creates a new file (or replaces an existing one if you already have *c:\test.txt* on your hard drive). Then it writes your test line of text and closes the streamwriter. Next it opens that same file, reads the line of text, displays it in a messagebox, and closes the file.

Whenever you are communicating with peripherals — such as the hard drive — you want to add error-trapping code. What if the file already exists? What if the requested hard drive letter isn't available? What if the medium is full? There are many possible problems when an application communicates with other devices. However, to keep the examples in this chapter as simple, easy-to-understand, and compact as possible, I eliminate error-trapping code. The new `Try...Catch` VB.NET error-trapping techniques are covered in Book I, Chapter 4.

Here's a more flexible version of streaming. Replace the code in the Button's `Click` event with this:

```
Private Sub Button1_Click(ByVal sender As System.Object,
    ByVal e As System.EventArgs) Handles Button1.Click

        Dim strFileName As String = TextBox1.Text

        Dim objFilename As FileStream = New
FileStream(strFileName, FileMode.Open, FileAccess.Read,
FileShare.Read)

        Dim objFileRead As StreamReader = New
StreamReader(objFilename)

        TextBox1.Text = ""

        While (objFileRead.Peek() > -1)
            TextBox1.Text += objFileRead.ReadLine()
            TextBox1.Text += ControlChars.CrLf
        End While

        objFileRead.Close()
        objFilename.Close()

    End Sub
```

If you run this example, be sure to type a complete disk file path and file-name into the TextBox (such as `C:\test.txt`).Notice that you first create a filestream object and then use it to create a new streamreader. Later, within the `While...End While` loop, you use the streamreader to control the duration of the loop (with the `Peek` method), as well as to read individual text lines, one by one, within the opened file (with the `ReadLine` method).

The `ControlChars.CrLf` command inserts a line feed (moves down one line in the `TextBox`) following each line that the `ReadLine` method retrieves from the file. However, if you don't need to examine the file's contents line by line, you can simply replace the entire `While...End While` structure with this simple line of code that brings in the entire file (including line feeds) in one big gulp:

```
TextBox1.Text += objFileRead.ReadToEnd()
```

The `ReadToEnd` method is worth remembering. It's fast and effective.

Understanding FileModes

Remember that you can define several `FileModes` when creating a FileStream, and each has its specialized purpose:

✦ `FileMode.Create`: Overwrites (replaces) a file if the file already exists (if the filename is identical to the one you specify for your new FileStream). Otherwise, it creates a new file.

✦ `FileMode.Append`: Adds data to existing data in the file. If no such file exists, it creates a new file.

✦ `FileMode.CreateNew`: Triggers an error message if the file already exists (or in VB.NET terminology, *throws an exception*). Otherwise, it creates a new file.

✦ `FileMode.Open`: Opens an existing file. If the file doesn't exist, it triggers an error.

✦ `FileMode.OpenOrCreate`: Opens an existing file. If the file doesn't exist, it creates a new one.

✦ `FileMode.Truncate`: Opens an existing file and then deletes all its contents so that the filesize is zero bytes.

Alternative syntaxes to show you're at the end

You can use the `Peek` method of the StreamReader object as a way of knowing that you're at the end of a file. Or you can use the `ReadToEnd` method. But VB.NET is nothing if not generous with alternative techniques. Here are some other ways to test for end-of-file.

When reading from a file, you have to know when you've reached the end. You can substitute the `PeekChar` method for the `Peek` method, like this:

```
While (objFileRead.PeekChar()<> -1)
```

Or you can find out the total length of the file and use it to halt a loop (although this is a rather clumsy technique):

```
Dim fs As FileStream = New FileStream("c:\test.txt",
    FileMode.Open, FileAccess.Read)
Dim nn As Integer

'Get the file length:
        nn = fs.Length / 2 ' change bytes to int16
```

Or, you can use yet another technique for reading (or writing, using the FilePut command). In this case, you use the traditional VB approach to file reading. You test for the end-of-file with the venerable EOF property, End Of File. Also, you use the FileGet command to read from a file; in this case, you read individual characters.

First, create a class that reads a file. Recall that Form1 itself is a *class* in the VB.NET code window. So, to add a new class of your own, you must scroll down in the code window to the very bottom, *below* the End Class that concludes Form1. Type this new class at the bottom of the code window:

```
Public Class ReadBytes

    Private strRead As String

    Public Function ReadAFile()
        strRead = ""

        Dim chrHolder As Char
        Dim filenumber As Int16

        filenumber = FreeFile() ' whatever filenumber
isn't already used

        FileOpen(filenumber, "C:\test.txt",
OpenMode.Binary)

        Do While Not EOF(filenumber)
            FileGet(filenumber, chrHolder)
            strRead = strRead & chrHolder
        Loop
        FileClose(1)

        Return strRead

    End Function

End Class
```

Now, in the Form_Load event, type this to create an instance of your ReadBytes class, and use its ReadAFile method:

```
Private Sub Form1_Load(ByVal sender As System.Object, ByVal e
    As System.EventArgs) Handles MyBase.Load

        Dim objN As New ReadBytes()

        TextBox1.Text = objN.ReadAFile


End Sub
```

Of course, in a real-world programming situation, you pass the name of the file that you want to read to the class — rather than "hard wiring" c:\test.txt within the class itself. Generally classes are supposed to be accommodating, adaptable, flexible, and not highly specific to a single job.

Writing to a File

Now that you know how to read from a text file, it's time to see how to write to a file, which is quite similar to the previous file-reading examples. Again, be sure that Imports System.IO is at the top of your code window before using the following techniques.

The simplest approach to saving data into a file is as follows:

```
Dim sw As New StreamWriter("c:\test.txt")
sw.WriteLine("My example line.")
sw.WriteLine("A second line.")
sw.Close()
```

For the more flexible technique, type in the following:

```
Private Sub Button1_Click(ByVal sender As System.Object,
    ByVal e As System.EventArgs) Handles Button1.Click

        Dim strText As String = TextBox1.Text

        If (strText.Length < 1) Then
            MsgBox("Please type something into the TextBox so
    we can save it.")
            Exit Sub
        Else
            Dim strFileName As String = "C:\test.txt"
            Dim objOpenFile As FileStream = New
    FileStream(strFileName, FileMode.Append,
    FileAccess.Write, FileShare.Read)
```

```
        Dim objStreamWriter As StreamWriter = New
StreamWriter(objOpenFile)

        objStreamWriter.WriteLine(strText)

        objStreamWriter.Close()
        objOpenFile.Close()
        TextBox1.Text = "Done. File saved."
    End If

End Sub
```

Appending

Notice that because you use the `FileMode.Append` property in this example, each time you run this program new text is added to any existing text in the file. If you want to overwrite an existing file, use `FileMode.Create` instead. `FileMode.Create` also creates a new file if one by that name doesn't currently exist.

Using the SaveFile or OpenFile dialog boxes

You may often want to use the `SaveFileDialog` class (or the `SaveFileDialog` control on the Toolbox) when saving and loading files from the hard drive.

```
Private Sub Button1_Click(ByVal sender As System.Object,
ByVal e As System.EventArgs) Handles Button1.Click


    Dim sfd As New SaveFileDialog()

    If sfd.ShowDialog() = DialogResult.OK Then

        'actually save the file:

        Dim strText As String = TextBox1.Text

        If (strText.Length < 1) Then
            MsgBox("Please type something into the
TextBox so we can save it.")
            Exit Sub
        Else
            Dim strFileName As String = sfd.FileName
            Dim objOpenFile As FileStream = New
FileStream(strFileName, FileMode.Append,
FileAccess.Write, FileShare.Read)
            Dim objStreamWriter As StreamWriter = New
StreamWriter(objOpenFile)
```

```
                    objStreamWriter.WriteLine(strText)

                    objStreamWriter.Close()
                    objOpenFile.Close()
               End If

          End If

     End Sub
```

You can, of course, likewise use the `OpenFileDialog` class.

Using the Binary Methods

Another way to use streams is to read and write *binary* pieces of data, rather than individual characters, whole text lines, or whole file-size strings. The size of these binary data packages is up to you. You specify the size when you define the variable used to write, or when you choose the read mode (as in `r.ReadByte()` versus `r.ReadBoolean` or `r.ReadInt32`, and so on).

This technique also requires `Imports System.IO`. Here's an example of how to create a file and store individual byte-size chunks of data into it:

```
Private Sub Form1_Load(ByVal sender As System.Object, ByVal e
     As System.EventArgs) Handles MyBase.Load

     Dim fs As FileStream = New FileStream("c:\test1.txt",
FileMode.Create)

     Dim w As BinaryWriter = New BinaryWriter(fs)

     Dim i As Byte

     ' store 14 integers in a file (as bytes)
     For i = 1 To 14
          w.Write(i)
     Next

     w.Close()
     fs.Close()

End Sub
```

Note that if you look at this file using Notepad, you won't see the numbers; they are not stored here as text (digits). Instead, they are stored as an actual numeric data type. This is sometimes referred to as a *binary* file.

And here's how you read individual bytes from the file you just created in the previous example:

```
Private Sub Form1_Load(ByVal sender As System.Object, ByVal e
    As System.EventArgs) Handles MyBase.Load

        ' Create the reader for this particular file:
        Dim fs As New FileStream("c:\test1.txt",
    FileMode.Open, FileAccess.Read)
        Dim r As New BinaryReader(fs)

        Dim i As Integer
        ' Read the data, in bytes, from the Test1.txt file:
        For i = 1 To 14
            Debug.Write(r.ReadByte() & ",  ")
        Next i
        r.Close()
        fs.Close()

End Sub
```

Choosing a data type

`BinaryReader` and `BinaryWriter` can read and write information in quite a few different data types. In the previous examples, the data was saved as bytes because the variable *i* was declared as a byte type. The `BinaryWriter` doesn't care what variable type it is saving — nor does it save any information describing the variable type. So you, the programmer, must remember to read the data back (with the `BinaryReader`) using the correct `Read` method. The method (such as `ReadByte`, `ReadChar`, `ReadSingle`, and so on) should match the data type that was originally stored. There is a `Read` method for each variable type.

Same size fits all?

The data in this example was read back as bytes because I use the `ReadByte` method. How can this be? If you spoon sugar into a bowl, do you have to take it back out with the same spoon? No, you can store things using units of one size and then retrieve them in units of another size. You may fill a sugar bowl using a teaspoon, but someone may get the sugar out of that bowl using a tablespoon. It's up to you to transfer the data in or out in whatever size chunks makes sense.

To see the various data types you can use, in the code window, just below the line `Dim r As New BinaryReader(fs)`, type in the following new line of code. When you type the . (period), you see the list of data types available to a `BinaryReader`:

```
Debug.WriteLine(r.
```

The BinaryWriter class has a write method (illustrated in the previous example) and, alternatively, a writeline method that adds a newline character to the stored data.

Many Kinds of Streams

You now have become familiar with the FileStream — probably still the most common type of stream that you'll be using. It has two flavors: text and binary. This chapter's examples focus on them. You use the FileStream when working with local hard drives. The StreamWriter (and Reader) offer you methods that are easiest to use with text. The BinaryWriter (and Reader) offer methods that are easiest to use with other data types.

However, you should be aware of the *other* kinds of streams. The *MemoryStream* allows you to treat a computer's RAM memory in ways similar to the way that the FileStream communicates with files on the hard drive. The NetworkStream permits streaming over a local network or the Internet. The CryptoStream is used when encrypting and decrypting (and its use is covered in Book III, Chapter 7). Finally, the BufferedStream permits buffering when you are using streams that, themselves, do not include buffering functionality.

The various types of streams are generally programmed similarly, but you'll find some differences. A stream working with a file on your local hard drive can provide more information — such as file length or your current position within the file — than a NetworkStream, for example.

Streaming over the Internet

This is *new*. Doubtless you are familiar with the idea of saving information into disk files and then later reading that information by "opening" the file with an application's File⇨Open menu option. Anyone who has used a computer has done that.

But how do you grab data from a remote server on the Internet? Normally, you use a browser to load Web sites. That's familiar, too.

However, as a programmer, you're likely to find yourself increasingly writing applications that use the Internet as a data storage site. You can't import data into your applications conveniently via a browser. You have to get the data in a way similar to the way you programmatically access disk files on the local hard drive. You have to know the programming that treats the Internet as a virtual "local drive."

Put another way, saving and retrieving data from a local hard drive is no longer the only game in town. The future of computing is distributed here and there. Parts of programs, data stores — scattered who knows how far apart on servers around the world — all come together to get a job done. Once again: Those program parts and data stores are not necessarily located together on the same physical hard drive.

You need to find out how to communicate with *remote* data stores. The following example shows how to read data from the Internet. You use the WebRequest class to interact with a StreamReader. In this way, you can stream data into your VB.NET application from a Web site. Book IV goes deeply into Web programming, but here's a taste. Many programmers are likely to be amazed that you can do so much with so few lines of code. Be prepared for a pleasant shock when you press F5 to run this next example.

Put a TextBox on a Form, and then type these Imports statements at the very top of your code window:

```
Imports System.IO
Imports System.Net
```

Now type the following into the Form_Load event:

```
Private Sub Form1_Load(ByVal sender As System.Object, ByVal e
    As System.EventArgs) Handles MyBase.Load

Dim R As WebRequest = WebRequest.Create("http://yahoo.com/")

Dim WR As WebResponse

        Try
            WR = R.GetResponse
        Catch ex As Exception
            MsgBox(ex.Message)
            Exit Sub
        End Try

Dim SR As StreamReader = New
    StreamReader(WR.GetResponseStream)

        TextBox1.Text = SR.ReadToEnd

        SR.Close()

End Sub
```

This example brings in HTML code, unless you can find a .TXT file on some Web site. Try surfing the Internet a little, substituting URLs that you find in your browser's Address field for the http://yahoo.com used here.

Press F5 to run this program (and if you don't have high-speed Internet access, be patient because it may take a little while to fill the TextBox). As you see, the ReadToEnd method of the StreamReader brings in all the HTML code on the Web page you are streaming from.

If you want to read the lines one by one, rather than ReadToEnd in one chunk, replace this line:

```
TextBox1.Text = SR.ReadToEnd
```

With this:

```
While (SR.Peek() > -1)
        TextBox1.Text += SR.ReadLine()
        TextBox1.Text += ControlChars.CrLf
End While
```

For more detailed manipulation of the incoming stream, you can suck individual characters in with the Read or ReadBlock methods of the StreamReader.

Experimenting with Memory Streams

A memory stream saves data into an unsigned byte array, within RAM memory. Here's a simple example, showing how to save a couple of characters, Hi, into a memory stream and then read them back:

```
Private Sub Form1_Load(ByVal sender As System.Object,
ByVal e As System.EventArgs) Handles MyBase.Load

    Dim mStr As New MemoryStream()
    mStr.WriteByte(CByte(Asc("H")))
    mStr.WriteByte(CByte(Asc("i")))

    'reset pointer
    mStr.Position = 0

    Dim b As Byte = mStr.ReadByte()
    Console.Write(Chr(b).ToString)
    b = mStr.ReadByte()
    Console.Write(Chr(b).ToString)
    mStr.Close()
End Sub
```

Notice that before reading back into the stream, you must reset the internal pointer (mStr.Position = 0). This pointer always shows where the last read or write operating took place within the byte array. Unless you reset it back to the beginning (position 0), you are attempting to read a byte *beyond* the byte array in memory.

Also note that you have to change the characters into numbers (with the `Asc` command) and then change those numbers into bytes (with the `CByte` command) before you can send them into the stream. Likewise, when read, the bytes must be translated back into text characters with `Chr` and `ToString`.

You may be saying: Well, so? Why not just use a variable to store this `Hi` text instead of going to all the trouble of creating a memory stream and then translating the text into bytes?

Good point. In fact, memory streams have rather esoteric uses, but you might want to know that they exist. In specialized situations, a memory stream can take the place of disk files or buffers for short-term storage needs (thus potentially speeding up your application).

Another use I've read about is using memory streams to create independent copies of objects. If you simply assign one object variable to another (`obj2 = obj1`), they are *not* two independent objects. Instead, both variable names simply point to the *same* object. (This isn't true of normal variables, such as strings; it's just true of object variables.) So, if you want to create an actual independent copy of an object, you can *serialize* an object and send it into a memory stream, and then turn around and *deserialize* it — sending it through a memory stream into a different variable. In this case, the result is two independent copies of the object: the original and the one that comes back out of the memory stream.

Serialization into a Stream

Simple variable types, such as the string or byte or integer, are easy enough to store and retrieve. You have only three things to store per variable: its name, its type, and its value (its contents, such as the number `12` or the characters `"Diane"`). Because of their simplicity, these simple variable types can be directly streamed, as the previous examples in this chapter illustrate.

However, other kinds of data need to be streamed — more complex data structures, such as arrays or objects. Increasingly, programmers have joined a trend toward grouping related data into packages — just as several pieces of data are grouped on your driver's license (age, license number, address, hair color, and so on).

These structures can have a fairly intricate internal organization. Information describing their organization must be stored when they are sent to a stream. And their structure is often user-defined. (You, the programmer, create the structure of an object you define.) So, VB.NET can't know in advance the structure, the way it knows all about integers and strings.

Therefore, something must be done to deconstruct a complex data structure before it is sent into a stream. This something is called *serialization*. Serialization is the process of breaking down a complicated structure into bytes that can be streamed. For example, an object can contain public and private properties and functions, can belong to a particular assembly (library of code), has a name, and so on. Each of these elements must be identified by name. Also, internal order within the structure, individual data type, scope, contents, and other details about the structure must all enter the stream and be saved.

The VB.NET serialization capabilities are extensive. You can, for example, choose not to use binary serialization (although usually you want it), or you can specify that only *some* fields in a class should be serialized (although usually you won't). The point is, if you do have rare, special needs, VB.NET serialization probably has the capability to satisfy those needs. If you want to exclude a particular field from serialization, use the following syntax:

```
<NonSerialized()> Public Budget As String
```

Serialization in action

To see how serialization can send an object (or an array, a rectangle, or any other complex data structure) into a stream, first add these Imports statements to the very top of your code window:

```
Imports System.IO
Imports System.Runtime.Serialization.Formatters
Imports System.Runtime.Serialization.Formatters.Binary
```

In this example, you create an object and display three of its properties in the output window. Then you change those properties, serialize the object, and stream it to a file. Finally, you read the object back, deserialize it, and display the new properties in the output window to demonstrate that everything went well. This example performs binary serialization. Later in this chapter, you see how to do XML serialization as well.

Now create a serializable class by typing this at the very bottom of your code window (below the line End Class, which concludes the Form1 class):

```
<Serializable()> Public Class MyObject

    Public a As String = "Now to disk"
    Public b As String = "...and back."
    Public c As Integer = 120

End Class
```

Finally, type this into the Form1_Load event:

```
Private Sub Form1_Load(ByVal sender As System.Object, ByVal e
    As System.EventArgs) Handles MyBase.Load

        Dim obj As New MyObject()

        Console.WriteLine(obj.a)
        Console.WriteLine(obj.b)
        Console.WriteLine(obj.c)
        Console.WriteLine()

        obj.a = "this test"
        obj.b = "is now over."
        obj.c = 44
        Dim fs As New FileStream("c:\test.txt",
    FileMode.Create, FileAccess.Write)
        Dim BF As New Binary.BinaryFormatter()

        BF.Serialize(fs, obj)
        fs.close()

        'read it back

        Dim BF1 As New Binary.BinaryFormatter()
        Dim fs1 As New FileStream("c:\test.txt",
    FileMode.Open, FileAccess.Read)

        obj = BF1.Deserialize(fs1)
        fs1.Close()

        Console.WriteLine(obj.a)
        Console.WriteLine(obj.b)
        Console.WriteLine(obj.c)

    End Sub
```

If you use Notepad to look at the file created by the preceding code, it looks like this:

```
'   ÿÿÿ'      ^    PWindowsApplication2,
Version=1.0.979.12598, Culture=neutral, PublicKeyToken=null˜'
WindowsApplication2.MyObject~  'a'b'c' ' ' ˙ ^  ˙ ~ this
test˙¯  is now over.,
```

But remember that this object was serialized into binary format, so you won't expect to be able to read some of the data as text.

XML serialization

The previous example uses the binary serializer, but you can also use an XML (SOAP) serializer that saves structures, of course, in text format. XML serialization also ignores any private fields (binary serialization saves both private and public fields).

To try an example of XML serialization, choose Project⇨Add Reference, and then scroll down the list of components and add `System.Runtime.Serialization.Formatters.Soap` to your project. Oddly, some namespaces must be added in this way (as a reference) to a project rather than adding the usual `Imports` statement. The distinction between which namespaces are imported and which are added as references escapes me.

You see the `System.Runtime.Serialization.Formatters.Soap` reference in the Solution Explorer.

Now change four lines in the previous example, to change it from binary serialization to XML serialization.

Change:

```
Dim BF As New Binary.BinaryFormatter()
```

To:

```
Dim XMLf As New Soap.SoapFormatter()
```

Change:

```
BF.Serialize(fs, obj)
```

To:

```
XMLf.Serialize(fs, obj)
```

Change:

```
Dim BF1 As New Binary.BinaryFormatter()
```

To:

```
Dim XMLf1 As New Soap.SoapFormatter()
```

Change:

```
obj = BF1.Deserialize(fs1)
```

To:

```
obj = XMLf1.Deserialize(fs1)
```

Press F5 to run this example. You should get the same results as you did with the previous example. But the interesting thing is to examine the `c:\test.txt` file created by this XML serialization. You see the usual, verbose, XML SOAP formatting. The file is entirely text, and there are tags aplenty:

```
<SOAP-ENV:Envelope
    xmlns:xsi="http://www.w3.org/2001/XMLSchema-instance"
    xmlns:xsd="http://www.w3.org/2001/XMLSchema" xmlns:SOAP-
    ENC="http://schemas.xmlsoap.org/soap/encoding/"
    xmlns:SOAP-
    ENV="http://schemas.xmlsoap.org/soap/envelope/"
    xmlns:clr="http://schemas.microsoft.com/soap/encoding/clr
    /1.0" SOAP-
    ENV:encodingStyle="http://schemas.xmlsoap.org/soap/
    encoding/">
<SOAP-ENV:Body>
<a1:MyObject id="ref-1"
    xmlns:a1="http://schemas.microsoft.com/clr/nsassem/
    WindowsApplication2/WindowsApplication2%2C%20Version%3D1.
    0.982.13724%2C%20Culture%3Dneutral%2C%20PublicKeyToken%3D
    null">
<a id="ref-3">this test</a>
<b id="ref-4">is now over.</b>
<c>44</c>
</a1:MyObject>
</SOAP-ENV:Body>
</SOAP-ENV:Envelope>
```

The binary formatter is best when you are working within the .NET framework — because it's faster and produces more compact files. But if you need to send data across the Internet or otherwise work outside the .NET world, SOAP-style formatting is probably your choice.

The serializable attribute is not inheritable, so if you derive a new class from a serializable class, you must also explicitly mark that new class as `<Serializable()>`.

Multiple Serialization

You can mix and match data in the same file. After you've started piping data into a stream, you can continue to use that stream to send in additional data, even of a different data type. In other words, you can fill your data store with all kinds of data and data collections, as long as you remember to read them back in the correct order. If you store a byte, a string array, and then an object, you must read back the items in the same order that you stored them: byte, array, object.

Mixing types into the same stream

Here's an example showing how to save a structure followed by an arraylist.
Type this at the very top of your code window:

```
Imports System.IO
Imports System.Runtime.Serialization.Formatters
```

Now type the following into the Form_Load event:

```
Private Sub Form1_Load(ByVal sender As System.Object, ByVal e
    As System.EventArgs) Handles MyBase.Load

        Dim d As New Donut()
        d.Name = "Glazed"
        d.Size = 4
        d.Price = 0.85

        Dim MyArray As New ArrayList()

        MyArray.Add("Johnstown")
        MyArray.Add("Hunan")
        MyArray.Add("Bang")

        Dim fs As New FileStream("c:\test.txt",
    FileMode.Create, FileAccess.Write)
        'be sure you have used Project⇨Add Reference to add
    the
        'System.Runtime.Serialization.Formatters.Soap
        Dim XMLf As New Soap.SoapFormatter()

        'do multiple serialization:
        XMLf.Serialize(fs, d)
        XMLf.Serialize(fs, MyArray)
        fs.Close()
    End Sub

End Class

<Serializable()> Public Structure Donut
    Dim Name As String
    Dim Size As Integer
    Dim Price As Decimal
End Structure
```

Press F5 and then use Windows Explorer to look at Test.txt. You see in
Text.txt the huge SOAP file full of XML explanations of the structures and
data that were saved.

Reading back mixed data

When you read back the data from the previous example, just remember to deserialize the data types in the *same order* in which you serialized them. In other words, pay attention to the data types. In this example, you serialized a Donut structure, followed by an ArrayList.

The deserialize method returns only object variables, so you have to *cast* each of them into the correct type. You cast by specifying the correct type with the CType command. In this example, the incoming data packages are cast into a Donut and then an ArrayList.

Here's an example that deserializes the SOAP file created in the previous example:

```
Private Sub Form1_Load(ByVal sender As System.Object, ByVal
    e As System.EventArgs) Handles MyBase.Load

        Dim d1 As New Donut()
        Dim ar As New ArrayList()

        Dim fs As New FileStream("c:\test.txt",
    FileMode.Open, FileAccess.Read)
        Dim XMLf As New Soap.SoapFormatter()

        d1 = CType(XMLf.Deserialize(fs), Donut)
        ar = CType(XMLf.Deserialize(fs), ArrayList)

        fs.Close()

        Console.WriteLine(d1.Price)
        Console.WriteLine(ar(2))

    End Sub

End Class

<Serializable()> Public Structure Donut
    Dim Name As String
    Dim Size As Integer
    Dim Price As Decimal
End Structure
```

Notice that in this example, you created a stream (fs) and then used it to deserialize *both* your Donut structure and the ArrayList. One stream can handle multiple serializations or deserializations.

If you're coming from previous versions of VB, a Structure is similar to the traditional Type.

Chapter 4: Creating Runtime Controls

In This Chapter

- ✔ **Instantiating controls as objects**
- ✔ **Handling with care**
- ✔ **Naming controls**
- ✔ **Using `WithEvents`**
- ✔ **Creating your own controls**

This chapter explores some techniques you can use to make Toolbox controls do some fancy tricks. Also, you see how to create your own custom-made controls.

Dept. of Obscure Bug Prevention

Before getting into how to add controls to your project at runtime, I want to tell you about a truly exasperating bug that can vex you for hours. This bug, new in VB.NET, can be very hard to track down. It happened to me, and it took me an afternoon to figure it out.

Each event procedure in VB.NET *must* end with a `Handles` clause, like this:

```
Handles Button1.Click
```

If this clause is missing, VB.NET thinks that no event handler exists for `Button1`. Even if you write some code inside the event, without that `Handles` clause, the event's code will never be executed.

In previous versions of VB, an event was very simple. It looked like this:

```
Sub Button1_Click()

End Sub
```

VB always knew that any code within this procedure was to be executed in response to a user clicking `Button1`.

Now, in VB.NET, the actual name of the event (`Button1_Click`) is irrelevant to the event handling. VB.NET looks at the `Handles` clauses to decide which event is handled by which procedure. If no `Handles` clause specifies `Button1`, `Button1`'s event still triggers, but no source code executes in response to that triggering.

You may be fooled by this new approach to events. I was. I couldn't figure out why the Click event was not executing my code. After hours of maddening searches trying to locate the problem, I finally noticed that while typing I had accidentally pressed Enter at some point and deleted the `Handles Button1.Click` clause. Restoring that clause solved the problem. Making this bug even more difficult to track down is the fact that the code window is usually not wide enough to even show `Handles Button1.Click`. It's off to the right side, so you get used to not seeing the `Handles` clause.

It gets worse. This bug can get into your code even if you don't clumsily erase the `Handles` clause like I did. This bug can occur all by itself in a WebForm (an Internet style VB.NET application).

Understanding events

Notice that each event in VB.NET includes two arguments: the object that triggered the event, called `sender`, and an *event object*, e, that provides information about the event, if there is any. The event object's argument is usually an `EventArgs` type, but it can be different for a few controls. Usually, you simply ignore the `sender` and the event arguments when you're programming, but these arguments must nonetheless be included in the argument list in parentheses following every event's `Sub`. VB.NET supplies these arguments automatically when you double-click a control on the design window, after which VB.NET takes you to the code window and creates an event for that control.

In general, events signal that *something has happened* to a control or other object — for example, when you type something into a TextBox, that triggers the `TextBox`'s `TextChanged` event. Even objects that are not visible to the user can have things happen to them, and can thus benefit from having events. Technically, an event signals a "state change" — an alert that something's different. To be truly useful, many objects (not just visible controls) should have some way of permitting a programmer to customize the response of the object to various changes that may occur (such as what should happen when the object is clicked by a user). Events are the solution to this problem: An event is a container in which a programmer can write code that reacts to a state change. So, when you create a new object, you sometimes provide events — permitting other programmers to later specify how that object responds to state changes.

I suggest that you follow this next set of steps so that the bug is burned into your memory and you will look for it if ever the source code in an event fails to execute for you:

1. **Choose File⇨New⇨Project.**

You see the New Project dialog box.

2. **Double-click the ASP.Net Web Application icon.**

You start a new WebForm application.

3. **Double-click the Button icon in the Toolbox.**

A Button control is placed on the WebForm.

4. **Double-click the Button.**

You see that a Click event has been created for it in the code-behind window. It looks just like the Click event for a button in a VB.NET Windows-style application:

```
Private Sub Button1_Click(ByVal sender As
    System.Object, ByVal e As System.EventArgs) Handles
    Button1.Click


    End Sub
```

5. **Click the tab at the top of the code window that says** WebForm1.aspx.

You go back to the Design view.

6. **Single-click the button to select it.**

7. **Press the Del key.**

The Button is deleted. You have no button left on this form.

8. **Go back to the code-behind window by clicking the tab at the top of the design window that says** WebForm1.aspx.vb.

You now see the code window again, but the Button_Click event has not been removed! Dangerously, the only change is that the button's Handles clause has been stripped off. The rest of the event remains behind as a source of confusion, and as a source of the bug I'm describing.

9. **Click the** WebForm1.aspx **tab to go back to the Design view.**

10. **Add another Button from the Toolbox as you did before.**

11. Click the `WebForm1.aspx.vb` tab to get to the code-behind window once again.

Notice that the `Handles` clause still is not there.

12. Type this into the `Button1_Click` event:

```
Private Sub Button1_Click(ByVal sender As
    System.Object, ByVal e As System.EventArgs)

Response.Write("HI")

End Sub
```

13. Press F5.

After a while, your browser appears with the button displayed.

14. Click the button.

Nothing happens. Your code in the `Button_Click` event fails to execute. There is a `Sub Button1_Click` procedure in the source code, but it has no `Handles` clause, so it fails to respond when `Button1`'s `Click` event triggers.

15. Go back and add the `Handles` clause, so that it looks like this:

```
Private Sub Button1_Click(ByVal sender As
    System.Object, ByVal e As System.EventArgs) Handles
Button1.Click

        Response.Write("hi")

End Sub
```

16. Press F5 to execute the program again.

This time, when you click the button, the event's code is executed and you see `hi` printed in your browser. (If you don't see `hi` printed, it's probably because the button is in the upper left corner, covering the `hi`. Go back to design view, drag the button to the middle of the design window, and press F5 again.)

Remember this: You'll face this problem sooner or later. You'll think that you have a working event procedure but, to VB.NET, it's not an event handler at all. Nothing ever triggers it.

Why this redundancy? Why the need to follow `Button1_Click` with a repetitive `Handles Button1.Click` in the same line of code?

The reason is that you are allowed to use multiple `Handles` clauses in the same event. The following is legal:

```
Private Sub cmd_Click(ByVal sender As System.Object, ByVal e
    As
```

```
System.EventArgs) Handles cmdOK.Click, cmdApply.Click,
   cmdCancel.Click

Select Case sender.Name

          Case "cmdOK"
               'Insert Code Here to deal with their
   clicking the OK button
          Case "cmdApply"
               'Insert Code Here for Apply button clicking
          Case "cmdCancel"
               'Insert Code Here for Cancel button clicks
End Select

End Sub
```

This is how VB.NET deals with what used to be called control arrays in previous versions of VB. See the "Understanding events" sidebar for more explanation about events in VB.NET.

Arrays of Controls

Arrays, and collections of various kinds, are very useful because you can handle multiple objects at the same time. Grouping objects not only serves a clerical function (making clear that grouped objects are somehow related), but it also permits more efficient programming. You can loop through the entire array, making wholesale adjustments to all the objects in the array within a single loop.

Suppose you need to figure your average electric bill for the year? You can go the cumbersome route, using an individual text variable name for each month:

```
JanElect = 90
FebElect = 122
MarElect = 125
AprElect = 78
MayElect = 144
JneElect = 89
JulyElect = 90
AugElect = 140
SeptElect = 167
OctElect = 123
NovElect = 133
DecElect = 125

YearElectBill = JanElect+FebElect+MarElect+AprElect+MayElect+
JneElect+JulyElect+AugElect+SeptElect+OctElect+
   NovElect+DecElect
```

However, if you create an array, `MonthElectBill()`, you can program the calculation more efficiently, like this:

```
For I = 1 to 12
Total = Total + MonthElectBill(I)
Next I
```

Traditional control arrays

Some years back, the VB designers thought: Why not have arrays of controls? When you have several controls of the same type performing similar functions, grouping them into a control array permits efficiencies typical of any array. Also, a control array is the only way to create a new control (such as a brand-new `TextBox`, or a new group of buttons) while a program is running. The VB designers realized that you don't have to add the TextBox to the form from the Toolbox while designing the program; instead, a TextBox could magically instantiate (come into existence) while the program was running. You could, in other words, create controls *programmatically*.

Also, as is true of all kinds of collections, grouping controls into an array lets you manipulate their collective properties quickly. Because arrayed controls are each identified with unique index numbers, instead of text names, you can manage them as a unit in loops and other structures (such as `Select Case`), easily changing the same property in each control by using a single loop, for example. (Loops can cycle through *numbered* items, but they can't cycle through *named* items.)

Traditional VB provided several ways to create a control array, but probably the most popular was to simply assign the index property of a control during design time. During runtime, you can use the `Load` and `Unload` commands to instantiate new members of this array.

Each control in a control array got its own unique index number, but in traditional VB they shared every event in common. In other words, one `Click` event, for example, was shared by the entire array of button controls. An `Index` parameter specified which particular button was, in fact, clicked. So you write a `Select Case` structure within the shared event to determine which of the buttons is clicked and to respond appropriately, as in the following example:

```
Sub Buttons_Click (Index as Integer)

Select Case Index
Case 1
    MsgBox ("HI, you clicked the OK Button!")
Case 2
    MsgBox ("Click the Other Button. This one says Don't
  Click Me!")
```

```
End Select

End Sub
```

Grouping controls in VB.NET

Fortunately, a technique in VB.NET resembles this all-in-one-event coding.

Although classic control arrays have been removed from the language, VB.NET still lets you do what control arrays did. You can instantiate controls during runtime and also manipulate them as a group.

To accomplish what control arrays used to do, you must now instantiate controls (as objects) during runtime, and then let them share events. Interestingly, in VB.NET even various different *types* of controls can share a single event. For example, a `Button` control and a `CheckBox` could share a single event.

Which control (or controls) is being handled by an event is specified in the line that declares the event (following the `Handles` statement). I call it the `Handles` clause.

Instead of using index numbers to determine what you want a control to do (when it triggers an event), as was the case with control arrays, you must now use an object reference.

Remember this: Each instantiated control should be given its own, unique name, but programmer-instantiated controls do not automatically get a `Name` property specified for them by default. The `Name` property can now be changed during runtime. Also, you, the programmer, are responsible for creating events for runtime-generated controls. The following examples deal with both these issues.

Here's an example showing how you can add new controls to a form while a program is running. Assume that the user clicked a button asking to search for some information. You then want to create and display a `TextBox` for the user to enter the search criteria, and you also want to create (instantiate) a label above the `TextBox`, describing its purpose.

Use the File➪New➪Project menu item to start a brand new Windows-style application. In the Toolbox, double-click the button icon to place `Button1` on your form. Now double-click `Button1` to get to the code window.

As usual, VB.NET creates an event `Sub` for `Button1` because you double-clicked it. Notice, however, that *you* must type in an event `Sub` for the button named `btnSearch`, because that button isn't yet in existence on the form. (You can't double-click it and have VB.NET create an event `Sub` for it.) Instead, `btnSearch` is only instantiated during runtime when the program executes.

Type in the following source code, shown in boldface:

```
Public Class Form1

    Inherits System.Windows.Forms.Form

    Dim WithEvents btnSearch As New Button()


Private Sub Button1_Click(ByVal sender As System.Object,
    ByVal e As System.EventArgs) Handles Button1.Click

        Dim textBox1 As New TextBox()
        Dim label1 As New Label()


        ' specify some properties:
        label1.Text = "Enter your search term here..."
        label1.Location = New Point(50, 55) 'left/top
        label1.Size = New Size(125, 20) ' width/height
        label1.AutoSize = True
        label1.Name = "label1"

        textBox1.Text = ""
        textBox1.Location = New Point(50, 70)
        textBox1.Size = New Size(125, 20)
        textBox1.Name = "TextBox1"

        btnSearch.Text = "Start Searching"
        btnSearch.Location = New Point(50, 95)
        btnSearch.Size = New Size(125, 20)
        btnSearch.Name = "btnSearch"


        ' Add them to the form's controls collection.
        Controls.Add(textBox1)
        Controls.Add(label1)
        Controls.Add(btnSearch)


'display all the current controls

        Dim i As Integer, n As Integer
        Dim s As String
        n = Controls.Count


        For i = 0 To n - 1

            s = Controls(i).Name

            Debug.Write(s)
```

```
         Debug.WriteLine("")

      Next


   End Sub

Private Sub btnSearch_Click(ByVal sender As System.Object,
   ByVal e As System.EventArgs) Handles btnSearch.Click

      MsgBox("clicked")

End Sub

End Class
```

When adding new controls at design time, you want to at least specify their
name, size, and position on the form — especially their Name property. If
you forget their Name property, you won't be able to distinguish them in
code or write code to handle their events.

Use the Add method to include new controls in the form's controls collection:

```
Controls.Add(textBox1)
Controls.Add(label1)
Controls.Add(btnSearch)
```

Programmers expect VB.NET to assign names to dynamically added controls. However, be warned that VB.NET does not automatically assign names
to new controls added at design time. A runtime instantiated control's Name
property remains blank unless you specifically define it, as I did in the preceding example (textBox1.Name = "TextBox1").

Mass changes

Here's how to go through the current set of controls on a form and change
them all at once. The following example turns them all red:

```
n = Controls.Count

For i = 0 To n - 1
   Controls(i).BackColor = Color.Red
Next
```

Adding events

Of course, a control without any events is often useless. To add events to
controls created at runtime, you must add two separate pieces of code.

First, up at the top (outside any procedure, because this declaration can't be *local*), you must declare the control as having events by using the `WithEvents` command, like this:

```
Dim WithEvents btnSearch As New Button()
```

Then, in the location where you want to provide the code that responds to an event, type in an event procedure, like this:

```
Private Sub btnSearch_Click(ByVal sender As System.Object,
    ByVal e As System.EventArgs) Handles btnSearch.Click

        MsgBox("clicked")

End Sub
```

This event code that you type is indistinguishable from any other "normal" (VB.NET-created) event in the code. Notice that unlike the traditional VB 6 and earlier all-in-one event shared by all the controls in the entire control array, VB.NET expects you to give each newly created control its own name and then use that name to define an event that performs the function of `"Handles" Name.Event`, as illustrated by the `Click` event for `btnSearch` in the preceding example.

Multiple handles

If you're interested in creating an all-in-one event — where several controls' behaviors are handled within a single event — you can use some techniques new in VB.NET to make it happen. Here's an example that handles the `Click` events for three different controls. You do this by listing their names following the `Handles` command:

```
Private Sub cmd_Click(ByVal sender As System.Object, ByVal e
    As
System.EventArgs) Handles cmdOK.Click, cmdApply.Click,
    cmdCancel.Click

        Select Case sender.Name
            Case "cmdOK"
                'Insert Code Here to deal with their
clicking the OK button
            Case "cmdApply"
                'Insert Code Here for Apply button clicking
            Case "cmdCancel"
                'Insert Code Here for Cancel button clicks
        End Select

    End Sub
```

In addition to the multiple objects listed after `Handles`, notice another interesting thing in this code. Finally, a use for the `sender` parameter appears in every event within VB.NET. It is used in combination with the `.NAME` property to identify which button was, in fact, clicked. This event handles three `Click` events. `Sender` tells you which control raised (triggered) this event at any given time. In most VB.NET code, the `Sender` object is the same as both the name of the event and the name following the `Handles`:

```
Private Sub Button1_Click(ByVal sender As System.Object,
    ByVal e As System.EventArgs) Handles Button1.Click

        MsgBox(sender.Name)

End Sub
```

VB.NET creates the event in the code window for you, if you wish. Your `btnSearch` in the previous example doesn't show up in the design window, so you can't double-click it there to force VB.NET to create a `Click` event for it. However, you can use the drop-down list at the top left of the code window. After you have declared a control `WithEvents` (as in `Dim WithEvents btnSearch As New Button()`), you can then drop the list and locate `btnSearch` in the listbox. Click it to select it. Then drop the list in the top right of the code window, and click the event you want VB.NET to create for you in the code window.

All the controls on a form belong to a collection. You access the collection, as illustrated previously, using `Me.Controls` or simply `Controls`. You can add to the collection, as shown in the previous example, or you can subtract from it during runtime as well:

```
Me.Controls.Remove(Button1)
```

Note, too, that the `Me.Controls` collection also has several other methods: `Clear`, `Equals`, `GetChildIndex`, `GetEnumerator`, `GetHashCode`, `GetType`, `SetChildIndex`, `ShouldPersistAll`, and `ToString`. Three properties are also available to `Me.Controls`: `All`, `Count`, and `Item`.

Building Your Own Controls

For several years, VB has permitted programmers to build their own controls. You can create visual interfaces, add existing controls to your custom control, and provide properties, methods, and events — just like any prebuilt control.

In previous versions of VB, these custom controls were called ActiveX controls, but that name seems to have passed into history. Now they are called UserControls.

Follow these steps to create a little clock control that you can then add to your Toolbox and reuse in any of your projects. That's the reason to create UserControls — because you can then freely reuse them in any project.

1. **Start a new Windows-style project by choosing File⇨New⇨Project and double-clicking the Windows Application icon.**

2. **Choose Project⇨Add User Control.**

   The Add New Item dialog box opens.

3. **Double-click the UserControl icon in the dialog box.**

   A new kind of design window opens, showing a blank user control, as shown in Figure 4-1.

4. **Double-click the label icon in the Toolbox.**

   You add a label control to your UserControl.

5. **Click the label to select it and change its** BorderStyle **property to** Fixed3D **in the Properties window.**

6. **Resize the label to make it fairly small.**

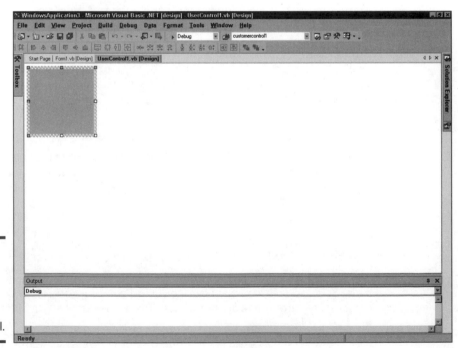

Figure 4-1:
Here's a
blank
template
for a
UserControl.

7. Resize the UserControl to make it just a little bit bigger than the border of the label (you need to move the label down and to the right a bit), as shown in Figure 4-2.

Figure 4-2:
A User-Control doesn't have a border, so you can borrow one from the label control.

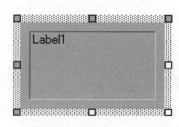

8. Double-click the timer control's icon in the Toolbox.

A timer is added to the UserControl (it's put in the tray at the bottom of the design window).

9. In the Properties window, change the Timer's Enabled **property to True.**

10. Double-click the timer in the tray.

The code window opens.

11. Type this programming into the Timer's Tick **event:**

```
Private Sub Timer1_Tick(ByVal sender As System.Object,
    ByVal e As System.EventArgs) Handles Timer1.Tick

    Label1.Text = TimeValue(Now)

End Sub
```

The timer now displays only the time, not the date. (If you type Label1.Text = Now, you get the date as well.)

Now test your UserControl on a Form. You can't simply press F5 and test a custom control.

However, keep in mind that the UserControl part can't be used until the solution is rebuilt (which is mentioned later for those switching right to the "Testing a UserControl" section).

Book III
Chapter 4

Creating Runtime Controls

Controls must have a container — a form, in this case — before they come to life and do their thing. Now you see one reason why you're allowed to have more than one project going on at the same time in a Solution. The container form must be available at the same time in the IDE to hold a UserControl for testing.

Testing a UserControl

To test the UserControl that you built in the previous example, follow these steps:

1. **Click the Form1.vb(Design) tab.**

You see the design window for Form1.

2. **Scroll the Toolbox by clicking the down-arrow icon at the bottom of the Toolbox.**

When you get to the very bottom of the Toolbox, you see your new UserControl! Convenient, isn't it?

Note that VB.NET 2003 doesn't behave this way. Instead of adding your UserControls to the bottom of the icons under the Toolbox's Windows Forms tab, it adds a new tab, coyly named *My User Controls.* Click that tab to find UserControl1.

3. **Double-click the UserControl icon on the Toolbox.**

It is added to Form1. Notice that it's already keeping time.

If you get an error message saying, in effect, that the UserControl can't be added, click the UserControl1.vb tab at the top of the design window. Choose Build⇨Build Solution. Click the Form1.vb(Design) tab to return to Form1.

4. **Drag the UserControl around and put it where you want it on the form.**

You see that it can be repositioned, just like any other control.

5. **With the UserControl selected (click it), make the Font property larger by using the Properties window.**

You see that the label's text becomes larger. You can change properties just as with any other control.

6. **Press F5.**

Your project runs, and the new timer UserControl displays the time, as shown in Figure 4-3.

Figure 4-3:
Your brand-
new
UserControl.

Reusing a UserControl

If you want to use your UserControl in other projects later, you can easily add it to the Toolbox.

Choose Tools⇨Customize Toolbox (or *Add/Remove Toolbox Items* in VB.NET 2003), click the .Net Framework Components tab, and then click the Browse button and locate your project on your hard drive. (It is in a folder named the same as your project's name, which is in boldface in Solution Explorer. The path to this folder is the following by default: `Documents and Settings\YourName\My Documents\Visual Studio Projects`. Look in the Bin subfolder for `YourProjectsName.dll` or `YourProjectsName.exe` and double-click it. The Customize Toolbox dialog box displays any UserControls and checks them so that they are now in your Toolbox. Click OK to close the dialog box. Now your UserControl is in the Toolbox. Your UserControls can be added to *any* project this way.

A second flavor of programmer-created control, called a CustomControl, allows you great freedom to specify precisely how it's drawn and other low-level coding. You can add a CustomControl to your project the same way you add a UserControl, but you're responsible for actually *painting* (making visible) a CustomControl. Also, a CustomControl isn't automatically added to your Toolbox the way a UserControl is. (Recall that when you first create a UserControl, VB.NET itself adds an icon for that control to the Toolbox, for use in the *current* project where the UserControl was created.)

Instead, to add a CustomControl, choose Tools⇨Customize Toolbox, click the .Net Framework Components tab, and then click the Browse button and follow the same instructions as for adding UserControls to new projects.

If you want to persist properties (meaning that you want to make sure that the properties' values are retained), VB 6 offered a feature called the `PropertyBag` to handle that task. `PropertyBag`s are gone in VB.NET, but you can use binary or SOAP serialization, as described in the previous chapter, to stream your control's state into a file. For more information on this topic, see "Property Bag Changes in Visual Basic .NET" at `http://msdn.microsoft.com/library/default.asp?url=/library/en-us/dv_vstechart/html/vbtchPropertyBagChangesInVisualBasicNET.asp`.

Chapter 5: Overloaded Functions and Parameters

In This Chapter

✔ **Sharing function names**

✔ **Using optional parameters**

✔ **Distinguishing by name, number, or type of parameters**

✔ **Replacing** as any

✔ **Dealing with missing parameters**

✔ **Understanding** ByVal **and** ByRef

One interesting new feature in VB.NET is called *overloading*. It sounds dubious, but the colorful name merely indicates a kind of efficiency: collapsing what used to be multiple functions into a single function.

As you doubtless noticed, VB.NET is overflowing with many thousands of built-in functions. Who can remember them all? Nobody. One way to reduce the overhead of so much functionality is to make a single function (or property or method) capable of doing various different things. That way, you only have to remember one function name and, thanks to the Intellisense that's built into VB.NET, you see all its variations when you type its name into the code window.

Under Tools⇨Options⇨Text Editor⇨All Languages⇨General, you want to select Auto List Members and Parameter Information — unless you have a photographic memory and have read through the entire .NET class documentation and know everything by heart. These two Intellisense features are, for most of us, essential: They display the properties and methods (with their arguments and their various alternative parameters) for each VB.NET function as you type in your source code.

This chapter shows you how to use overloaded functions, properties, and methods — and how to overload your own, as well.

Optional, the Old Pre-VB.NET Way

Sometimes you may want to use the same function name, but you want to accomplish different tasks with it. Traditionally, you can do this by using optional parameters. Here's a piece of VB 6 source code that illustrates the old way:

```
MyFunction (Optional SomeParam As Variant)

If IsMissing(SomeParam) Then

'Do one task because they didn't send SomeParam

Else

'Do a different task because they did send SomeParam

End If
```

In this code, the same MyFunction behaves differently based on what you pass to it. You can still use optional parameters, but their utility has been reduced in VB.NET. Among other things, the IsMissing command is no longer part of the VB language. This puts a slight crimp in things if you were to attempt to write code like the preceding example.

The traditional VB Variant data type could hold several special kinds of values: Null (not known), Empty (no value was ever assigned to this variable), and Missing (a variable was not sent, for example as part of procedures parameters). Null was sometimes used to identify fields in databases that were not available (or were unknown), while the Empty command could be used to represent something that didn't exist (as opposed to simply not being currently available).

Some programmers used the IsMissing command to see if an optional parameter had been passed to a procedure:

```
Sub SomeSub(Optional SomeParam As Variant)
    If IsMissing(SomeParam) Then
```

You can still use optional parameters with procedures, but you must declare them As *Type* and you must also supply a default value for them. More importantly, in VB.NET you can no longer write code that tells you whether or not a particular parameter has been passed.

The solution: If you need to test whether an optional parameter has been passed, overload the procedure. *Overloading* is a new technique where a function (or indeed a method, sub, property, or constructor) can be made to behave differently based on what data is passed to it. The data passed is technically called its *parameter signature*. This is similar to the way that a bank teller behaves differently depending on whether you hand her a deposit slip or a note saying "This is a holdup!"

In VB 6 and earlier, you could freely change a default value for parameters that you passed to a procedure. For example, if no parameter is passed to the following sub, it defaults to the value 101 for the Books parameter. Put another way, the variable Books contains the value 101.

```
Private Sub CountBooks(Optional Books As Integer = 101)
```

Because VB used to check parameters and employ any necessary default parameters that you had specified at *runtime,* it was possible to change a control to use a different default value, and VB respected that new value.

Also, you could simply declare a parameter as Optional and not provide any default whatsoever, if you wished:

```
Private Sub CountBooks(Optional Books As Integer)
```

And, if the optional parameter was a Variant type, you could have used the IsMissing command to determine whether or not the parameter was, in fact, passed at all.

But no more. VB.NET does things differently. VB.NET *compiles* any needed default values before runtime, so the default value becomes hard-wired into the compilation. The virtue of this approach is that it speeds things up at runtime.

So, instead of using the traditional optional parameters, you now accomplish the same thing by using overloading. In VB.NET, *every* optional parameter must declare a default value (which is passed to the procedure if the calling code does not supply that parameter). Note, too, that you must include the ByVal command in your parameter lists. Here's the VB.NET equivalent:

```
Private Sub CountBooks(Optional ByVal Books As Integer = 101)
```

Overloading in VB.NET

In VB.NET, you overload a function by writing several versions of that function. Each different version of the function uses the same function name but has a different argument list; in other words, different parameters are passed to each version.

Why bother? Why not create various different functions? Allowing various kinds of parameters to be passed is convenient sometimes. For example, say that you write a function to add two numbers together. You could overload it so that it accepted integers, long integers, or floating point variable types. You could even include a version that accepted strings, such as "12" rather than numeric types. In all these cases, you are simply adding two numbers, but your function is more useful if it can accept a variety of types.

Sharing the same name

Another benefit of overloading is that you have multiple procedures that do different things but share the same name. Typically, these various procedures do related but somewhat different variations on the same task.

The differences in the argument list can be different data types, a different order of parameters, or a different number of parameters — or two or three of these variations at once. The VB.NET compiler can then tell which version of this function should be used by examining the arguments passed to the function, the argument list. Technically, VB.NET creates unique *signatures* for overloaded functions. These signatures are based on the name of the function and the number, order, and types of the arguments.

As a side note, the signature is not affected by type modifiers (Shared or Private), parameter modifiers (ByVal or ByRef), the actual names of the parameters, the return type of the function, or the element type of a property. A function with three parameters — and two of those being optional — generates three signatures: one signature with all three parameters, one signature with one required parameter and one optional parameter, and one signature with just the required parameter.

VB.NET functions

VB.NET employs overloading quite extensively in the language itself. You can see it whenever VB.NET displays several argument lists that you can choose from. The MessageBox.Show method, for example, is really overloaded: It has 12 different argument lists. Try this. Type the following line into the code window within the Form_Load event:

```
messagebox.Show(
```

As soon as you type that left parenthesis, VB.NET pops up a gray box showing the first of the 12 different ways you can use the MessageBox object's Show method. The box says: 1 of 12. Use your keyboard's up- and down-arrow keys to see all the different ways that you can use this overloaded method, as shown in Figure 5-1.

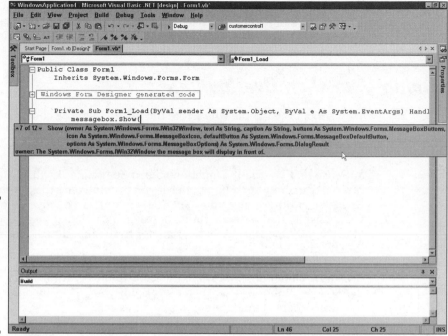

Figure 5-1:
The seventh variation on the Show method includes quite a few arguments.

Parameters, arguments, what's the difference? Programmers sometimes use these terms interchangeably, but there is a slight distinction. The various items in the parentheses in Figure 5-1 are technically *arguments,* because they are part of an *argument list* that tells the programmer which values can be used and lists their variable types. However, when a value is sent to a procedure, it is considered a *parameter,* as in the following example:

```
Private Sub Form1_Load(ByVal sender As System.Object, ByVal
    e As System.EventArgs) Handles MyBase.Load

    myfunction(2)

End Sub

Public Sub myfunction (ByVal passedvalue As Integer)

    MsgBox(passedvalue)

End Sub
```

In this source code, the (2) is a parameter that is being passed to myfunction. Passedvalue is an argument in the function's argument list:

(ByVal passedvalue As Integer). In a sense, both passedvalue and
(2) are the same thing, but as you can see, the shade of difference is based
on where in the source code you are located.

Doing Your Own Overloading

Why should the people who wrote the VB.NET source code have all the fun?
Here's an example of how you, too, can use overloading in your own VB.NET
source code when writing your own applications.

Suppose that you want a function named SearchBooks that gives you a list
of a particular author's book titles if you provide only the author's name.
However, at other times you want SearchBooks to behave differently: You
want a list limited to the author's books in a particular year if you also provide the year by passing that parameter to the function. Sounds like a job
for Overload Man!

Create two functions that share the same name (or think of it as a single
overloaded function — whatever works for you). The key point is that this
function accepts two different argument lists:

```
Public Overloads Function BookList(ByVal AuthorName As
    String) As Object

        ' write code to find all books by this author

End Function

Public Overloads Function BookList(ByVal AuthorName As
    String, ByVal YearNumber As Integer) As Object

' write code to find all books written in the particular year

End Function
```

Notice that you can use the Overloads keyword. It is optional. The compiler
will notice that you've written two identically named functions and assume
you want to overload them. However, if you use the keyword once, you must
use it for all the other functions.

Some programmers like to use the overloading technique to group a set of
identically named functions that, as this example illustrates, handle different jobs. This does have the potential of making source code harder to read
and harder to maintain. If you want to accomplish two unrelated jobs, you
should write two completely distinct functions (giving them different,
descriptive names so that you can tell what they do when you read the
source code), like this:

```
Public Function GetBooksByYear (ByVal YearNumber As Integer)
    As String
```

```
Public Function GetAllBooksByAuthor (ByVal AuthorName As
    String) As String
```

However, overloading is of value in various ways. Surely the designers of VB.NET itself consider it an essential technique, and they use overloading extensively. If you are careful to group related variations on a particular job within an overloaded function, the technique can be quite efficient.

Here's another line for you to type into the Form_Load event, pausing after typing the left parenthesis, to see the 18 variations:

```
console.WriteLine(
```

As Any Is Gone

One use for overloading is to replace the traditional VB As Any command. As Any has been deleted from the language, but you can use overloading to permit functions to return several different data types. However you can no longer declare a function As Any (meaning it can return any kind of data type):

```
Public MyFunction (parameters) As Any
```

When you declare a function, every parameter and the function's type (the return data type) must be specified.

In Visual Basic 6.0, you could specify As Any for the data type of any of the parameters of a function, and for its return type. The As Any keywords disable the compiler's type checking and allow variables of any data type to be passed to, or returned from, the function. The As Any command has been removed in VB.NET because As Any degrades type safety (increased type safety prevents certain kinds of bugs). So, if you want to permit more than one return type for a procedure in VB.NET, just use overloading.

Missing Parameters

Before VB.NET, when passing traditional parameters to a function, you could omit any parameters that you didn't want to specify by simply leaving them out of the parameter list. You did this by just leaving an empty space between the commas in the parameter list. (This is similar to the way overloading works in some cases, such as the various forms of the msgbox function in VB.NET where you can include or leave out a title for the message box, for example.)

The following example shows that if you wanted to specify only the first and third parameters for a MessageBox, you could just leave out the second parameter:

```
MsgBox("Your Name", , "Title")
```

VB understood that the empty area between commas in a parameter list meant that you wanted to use the default, or no parameter at all.

This tactic still works with many functions and methods in VB.NET, but not always! Sometimes, you must use the word Nothing instead.

For example, when you want to sort a DataRow, the first parameter specifies a filter (such as "all dates after 12/12/01"). The second parameter specifies the column to sort on, so you do want to specify that parameter.

However, if you want to avoid using a filter — if you want *all* the rows sorted, for example — you must use Nothing in the parameter list. Leaving the first parameter out in the following example raises an error message:

```
        Dim fx As String = "title"
'dt is a DataTable in a DataSet
        myRows = dt.Select(, fx)
```

Instead, you must use Nothing:

```
        Dim fx As String = "title"
        myRows = dt.Select(Nothing, fx)
```

Required Parameter Punctuation

The Call command is ancient. It has been used since the first versions of Basic more than 20 years ago. It means that you're calling a procedure. You can leave it out; Call is optional. But traditional VB has always required that if you *do* use it, you must enclose passed parameters within parentheses:

```
Call MySub (N)
```

If you omitted the Call command, you did not need to use parentheses:

```
MySub N
```

You could also add extra parentheses, which had the same effect as using the ByVal command (meaning that the called procedure couldn't then change any passed parameters):

```
Call MySub ((N))
MySub (N)
```

Now, however, VB.NET has changed the rules a bit. VB.NET requires parentheses in all cases, although the `Call` command remains optional:

```
Call MySub (N)
MySub (N)
```

To translate VB 6 and earlier code to VB.NET, you must go through and add parentheses to any procedure call that doesn't employ them.

ByVal Is the Default in VB.NET

You have two ways to pass parameters to a function: `ByRef` (by reference) or `ByVal` (by value). Traditionally, VB defaulted to the `ByRef` style, unless you specifically used the `ByVal` command.

Here's an example of how both `ByVal` and `ByRef` work. Normally, any of the variables passed to a function (or sub) can be changed by that function. However, you can prevent the function from being able to change the value in a variable if you use the `ByVal` command. Passing a value `ByVal` protects that variable's contents.

When you use `ByVal`, the passed variable can still be used for information (can be read by the function) and even changed temporarily for use within the function itself. But when you return to the place in your program from which you called the function, the value of the variable passed `ByVal` won't have been changed.

In the following example, X won't be changed, no matter what changes may happen to it while it's inside the function; Y, however, can be permanently changed by the function:

```
Public X, Y As Integer

Private Sub Form1_Load(ByVal sender As System.Object, ByVal e
    As System.EventArgs) Handles MyBase.Load

        X = 12
        Y = 12
        Newcost(X, Y)
        MsgBox("X = " & X & "  Y = " & Y)

End Sub

Function Newcost(ByVal X, ByRef Y)
        X = X + 1
        Y = Y + 1
End Function
```

This results in X = 12 Y = 13.

I defined X and Y as Public, thereby making them form-wide in scope. Both of these variables can therefore be changed within any procedure unless passed ByVal. I sent both X and Y to the function, but X is protected with the ByVal command. When the function adds 1 to each variable, a permanent change to Y occurs, but X remains unaffected by activities within the called function because I froze it with the ByVal command.

Although passed parameters traditionally have always defaulted to ByRef, in VB.NET most parameters now default to ByVal. In fact, if you leave out ByRef or ByVal in a parameter list, VB.NET inserts ByVal for you. VB.NET won't let the following kind of parameter list stand as is:

```
Function Newcost(X, Y)
```

As soon as you press the Enter key, that line is changed to the following:

```
Function Newcost(ByVal X, ByVal Y)
```

Some parameters still default to ByRef

Not *all* parameters in VB.NET default to ByVal (and this kind of inconsistency makes life *soooo* interesting for us programmers): References to classes, interfaces, arrays, and string variables all still default to ByRef.

The fact that ByVal is now the default may require considerable rewriting to older VB code — depending on how much the programmer relied on the use of public variables and the assumption that all variables were passed by default using the ByRef style.

And given that most parameters now default to ByVal but other items still default to ByRef, I suggest that you get used to specifying ByVal or ByRef for every argument in your argument list.

ParamArrays

Any procedure containing a ParamArray argument used to be able to accept any number of arguments in traditional VB, and it could also modify the value of any of those arguments. The calling routine used to be able to see any modifications. Now, in VB.NET, you can still use ParamArrays, but any modifications to the values won't be seen by the caller. This new approach is in keeping with the default to the ByVal style for most parameters.

Chapter 6: Smashing Bugs

In This Chapter

- ✔ **Understanding the problem**
- ✔ **Tracking down errors**
- ✔ **Handling logic errors**
- ✔ **Breaking in**
- ✔ **Step right up**
- ✔ **Where is** `On Error?`

*I*f you run into a puzzling problem while testing your VB.NET program, this is the chapter for you. Book I, Chapter 4 covered *error trapping* — the VB.NET techniques you use to prevent the user from getting into trouble while running your application. This chapter, however, explores the stratagems you use to eliminate bugs during the testing process.

No programming project of any significance simply comes to life error free. You always have to test your applications and then track down the inevitable problems that are revealed only during the testing phase. Then you must correct them.

Bugs usually aren't a result of negligence. Any sizable application is like a large office full of people: With such an enormous number of interacting behaviors, some unavoidably lead to trouble.

This chapter explores the more common types of errors you're likely to encounter and the VB.NET tools and techniques you can use to overcome them.

What's a Poor Debugger to Do?

What do you do when you press F5 to test your new application, and VB.NET throws up an error message? You can sit around and mope, or you can take steps. I suggest taking steps.

Fortunately, VB.NET offers an unquestionably excellent, powerful suite of debugging tools.

Options Strict and Explicit

Recall that in VB.NET — unlike earlier versions of VB — you must declare (Dim) all variables. (This is the default VB.NET behavior, but you can turn it off, as I describe in this section.) *Explicit declarations* mean that you must declare variables. You must declare X, for example, using Dim X as Integer or Dim X As Object (or whatever As data type you wish) before you can use the variable X. If you really want to avoid this necessity of declaring each variable, put the following line up at the top of your programming code window (above any procedures):

```
Option Explicit Off
```

Option Explicit is on by default in VB.NET and it's the Option that demands that each variable be explicitly declared.

A second option is off by default in VB.NET: Option Strict works with Option Explicit, but the Strict option prevents implicit conversion of data. For example, with Option Strict On, the following example (which forces the variable A to be converted to a string data type) fails to run:

```
Dim A as Integer
A = 1
TextBox1.Text = A
```

Although Option Strict is off by default, you can turn it on by typing this line at the top of your code window:

```
Option Strict On
```

I suggest that you leave the VB.NET default Option Explicit turned on. That way, you force yourself to get used to programming the new VB.NET way: All variables must be declared. This helps you decrease the number of bugs you have to track down. As for Option Strict, the jury is still out. It forces you to use .ToString rather often to convert numeric variable types into text (string) types before you can display them in TextBoxes or message boxes. You also may have to resort to such programming commands as CType, CInt, and others to *coerce* or *cast* variables from one type to another. Nonetheless, obscure bugs and mathematical imprecision can result from leaving Option Strict turned Off. My advice? While you're learning the basics of VB.NET, leave it turned Off. That way you have to worry less about variable types. But when you start to work on more sophisticated programs, consider turning Option Strict On.

In the next section, I show how to deal with bugs that get into your source code in spite of all your best efforts.

Using the Excellent VB.NET Facilities

Often, you can handle errors with the famous VB debugging facilities: the Command window (formerly the Immediate window), the Locals window, watches, breakpoints, single stepping, and other debugging features.

Start by finding out where the error happened

Debugging starts by finding out where the bug is located — which line or lines of source code are causing the problem. Alas, this isn't always a straightforward process, particularly when you're dealing with errors that occur outside traditional VB code, such as a database refusing to accept a `DataSet` that you are trying to `Update` into the database.

You begin your tour of the VB.NET debugging suite by looking at ways that VB.NET can help you locate a typical error. Type this function in the VB.NET code window:

```
Function Trythis As Integer

    Zum = Nara

End Function
```

As soon as you enter the `Zum=Nara` line of code, VB.NET does not like it. To demonstrate its displeasure, it underlines both `Zum` and `Nara`.

The VB.NET Auto Syntax Check feature watches as you type each line of code. As soon as you finish a line, it checks the line to see whether you mistyped anything or made some other kind of error such as leaving out something necessary. (VB knows you're finished with a line when you press the Enter key, use an arrow key to move off the line, or click the mouse pointer on another line.)

Book III
Chapter 6

Smashing Bugs

Beware the sawtooth blue line

If the syntax checker has a problem with a line of code, it underlines the error or errors with a sawtooth blue line (blue by default, anyway). In the preceding code example, you typed two variable names, neither of which you declared. VB.NET requires that all variables be declared (unless you add `Option Explicit Off` up at the top of your source code).

So you get jagged lines under each of the undeclared variable names. Figure 6-1 shows what happened when I pressed the Enter key after making these two errors.

Figure 6-1:
VB.NET
helpfully
flags errors
in your
source
code.

```
Function Trythis() As Integer

     Zum = Nara

End Function
```

Move your mouse pointer on top of one of the sawtoothed words in your code, and VB.NET provides an explanation of the error. Don't click; just slide the arrow onto the bad part, as shown in Figure 6-2.

Figure 6-2:
A brief error
message is
displayed
when you
pause your
pointer on
top of an
error in the
code.

```
Function Trythis() As Integer

     Zum = Nara
              Name 'Nara' is not declared.
End Function
```

The Auto Syntax Check feature is similar to the Microsoft Word *Check Spelling as You Type* feature. With this feature turned on, each word that you type in a Word document is spell-checked as you type it. If the word is misspelled, it is underlined with a sawtooth red line. This drives me crazy. I don't want to worry about spelling while I'm writing; I spell-check when I'm finished. Fortunately, you can turn off the constant spell-check in Word. Unfortunately, you can't turn off Auto Syntax Check — at least you can't in the current version of VB.NET. (In previous versions of VB, you could.) Although Auto Syntax Check doesn't bother me, it may bother some programmers. Perhaps it will be made optional at some future time.

If you are ever able to turn off Auto Syntax Checking, you'll still be warned about such errors when you press F5 to test and run your code.

Press F5 and a message appears, telling you that build errors occurred and asking whether you want to continue. After closing that message, you can look in the Task List window and see the errors described, as shown in Figure 6-3.

Figure 6-3:
The Task
List window
lists errors
in your
code.

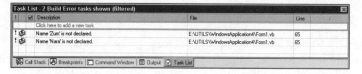

Double-click one of the errors in the Task List window to be taken to the line in the code window where the error occurred. The specific command that caused the problem is highlighted. To make the jagged blue lines go away in this example, declare the two variable names, like this:

```
Dim zum As String
Dim nara As String
```

If an error occurs outside traditional VB.NET code (if the error is generated server-side in script, for example), you often have to resort to inelegant methods of tracking it down. One of the more popular of these inelegant methods involves planting message box commands here and there in your source code, displaying the current state of variables. Then, periodically, the code halts and displays the message box, so you can see the status of suspect variables.

You can use the `msgbox` command in script and in objects embedded in a Web page (a VB.NET WebForm). If a message box appears before the error is generated, the line that contains the error is likely to follow the line with the message box in the source code, and vice versa. Note, however, that the `msgbox` technique is often undesirable. It stops execution each time, and it can be employed only in user services. Server-side components, more often than not, are compiled for unattended execution, which means message boxes won't be displayed at all.

Tracking Down Logic Errors

Logic errors are usually the most difficult of all to find and correct. VB.NET can't simply underline logic errors, as it can with syntax errors. Some logic errors can be so sinister, so well concealed, that you think you will be driven mad trying to find the source of the problem in your code. VB sensibly devotes the majority of its debugging features and resources to assisting you in locating logic errors.

A logic error occurs even though you have followed all the rules of syntax, made no typos, and otherwise satisfied VB.NET that your commands can be successfully carried out. You and VB think everything is ship-shape. When

**Book III
Chapter 6**

Smashing Bugs

you run the program, however, things go wrong. Perhaps the entire screen turns black, or every time the user enters $10, your program changes it into $1,000. That's just not right.

As with almost all programming errors, the key to correcting logic errors is finding out *where* in your program the problem is located. Which line of code (or multiple lines interacting) causes the problem?

Some computer languages have an elaborate debugging apparatus that sometimes even includes the use of two computer monitors: One shows the application just as the user sees it, and the other shows the lines of programming that match what the user is seeing. Using two computers is a good approach because when you are debugging logic errors, you often want to see the code that's currently causing the effects in the application. Unfortunately, most of us don't have the resources to dual-monitor debug.

It's not that you don't usually notice the symptoms of a logic error: Every time the user enters a number, the results are way, way off, for example. You know that somewhere your program is mangling these numbers, but until you X-ray the program, you often can't find out where the problem is located.

The voyeur technique

Many logic errors are best tracked down by watching the contents of a variable (or variables). You want to find out just where the variable's value changes and goes bad.

Four of the best VB.NET debugging tools help you keep an eye on the status of variables. The following examples demonstrate how to watch variables. Put a Button on your VB.NET form, double-click the Button, and then type this simple code:

```
Private Sub Button1_Click(ByVal sender As System.Object,
    ByVal e As System.EventArgs) Handles Button1.Click

    Dim a As Double, b As Double

    a = 112

    b = a / 2

    b = b + 6

End Sub
```

Click the gray margin to the left of the code window to add a red dot (a breakpoint) to the line a = 112.

Press F5 and then click the button on the form. You are now in break mode (the red dot changes to a yellow arrow and the line is highlighted in yellow). While you are in break mode, many debugging features are at your command. Make four of the debugging windows visible by choosing Debug⊃ Windows and selecting the Locals window. Also select the following three windows: Debug⊃Watch⊃Watch1, Debug⊃Autos, and View⊃Other Windows⊃ Command windows.

Drag the windows until they are on top of each other and their tabs are showing at the bottom of their common area, as shown in Figure 6-4.

First look at the Autos window. It displays the contents of all variables that have been declared in your entire project — and currently they are zero. Look at the Locals window, which displays the variables that have been declared in the currently executing procedure (as well as the parameters passed to this procedure and its object derivation).

Watch the variables in the Locals window change as you press F8 (if you're using the VB 6 keyboard scheme, or F11 for the default keyboard) to execute each line in the example code, as shown in Figure 6-4.

Change keyboard schemes by clicking Start Page⊃My Profile at the top of the Design Window.

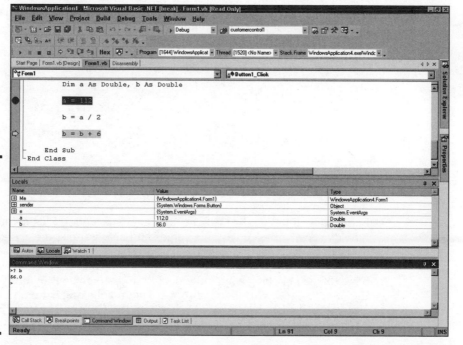

Figure 6-4:
The Locals window displays the contents of all local variables in the currently executing procedure.

Also look at the Command window. In this window, you can directly query or modify variables or expressions. To find out the value in variable b, for example, just type the following in the Command window and then press Enter (you must leave a space between the ? and the variable name):

```
? b
```

The answer — whatever value b currently holds — is displayed (printed) in the Command window. (The ? command is shorthand for the `Print` command.)

If you want to experiment by actually changing the value in a variable during break mode, double-click the number in the value column in the Locals or Watch window, and then type your new value.

Using Debug.WriteLine

Some programmers like to insert `Debug.WriteLine` (formerly `Debug.Print`) commands at different locations in their code to display the value of a variable. The `Debug.WriteLine` command displays its results in the Output window and then moves down a line. `Debug.Write` does the same thing, but without moving down a line in the Output window. You can also use the alternative `Console.Write` or `Writeline`.

In the following example, you insert some `Debug.Write` (*MyVariableName*) lines here and there in your source code, and then run the program and watch the results appear in the Output window:

```
Private Sub Button1_Click(ByVal sender As System.Object,
    ByVal e As System.EventArgs) Handles Button1.Click

    Dim a As Double

    a = 112
    Debug.WriteLine("Variable a now equals: " & a)

End Sub
```

This displays `Variable a now equals: 112` in the Output window.

Using several `Debug.WriteLine` commands is a good idea if you want to quickly see a series of variable values and also write some explanatory message about these values. You can do the same thing with a series of `MsgBox` commands, but for a group of several variables, it's annoying to have to keep clicking each individual `MsgBox` to close it before you can see the next `MsgBox`. With `Debug.WriteLine`, no clicking is involved; when the program runs, all the messages appear in the Output window.

The Command window responds

You can type in the Command window any executable commands that can be expressed on a single line, and then you can watch their effect. Note that you do this while the VB program is halted during a run; you can test conditions from within the program while it's in break (pause) mode.

You can get into break mode in several ways: by inserting a Stop command into your code, by setting a breakpoint in the code, by single-stepping (repeatedly pressing F8 or F11 to move through the source code line by line), by choosing Break in the Run menu (or the Toolbar), or by pressing Ctrl+Break.

The watch technique

The Locals window is fine for local variables, but what about form-wide or project-wide variables that have a larger scope in your source code? They don't show up in the Locals window.

In previous versions of VB, the Watch window permitted some highly useful debugging techniques, such as conditionally halting the program (throwing it into break mode so that you could examine variable values, see where the break occurred, and examine surrounding conditions). You could break when a condition became true and other tests. In VB.NET, the capability to break conditionally is now part of the Breakpoint debugging feature and is discussed in the "Setting conditional breakpoints" section later in this chapter.

An alternative way to use the Watch window is to keep an eye on the watches you've defined as you single-step through your code. The Watch window displays the value of all active watches.

Another tool in the Debug menu is the Quick Watch option. If you highlight (select) an expression or variable in the code window and then choose Debug⇨Quick Watch (or press Shift+F9), VB shows you the current contents or status of the highlighted expression or variable. VB also gives you the option of adding the item to the watched items in the Watch window.

Setting Breakpoints

Sometimes you have a strong suspicion about which form or module in your application contains an error. Or you may even think you know the specific procedure where the error can be found. Put a breakpoint inside that procedure by clicking the gray area to the left of the line where you want the break, or click the line to select it and then press F9.

Now, with the breakpoint, you can press F5 to execute the program at normal speed but VB.NET stops when execution enters the dubious form or procedure that contains the breakpoint. After halting the program in a suspect region, you can press F8 to single-step through the lines as you watch the values of suspect variables.

Breakpoints can be one of the most useful debugging aids. As you know, you can press Ctrl+Break and stop a running program in its tracks. But what if it's moving too fast to stop just where you want to look and check on things? What if it's rapidly alphabetizing a large list, for example, and you can't see what's happening?

While running, the program stops at a breakpoint just as if you had pressed Ctrl+Break. The code window pops up, showing you where the break occurred, so you can see or change the code, single-step, or look at the Watch window to see the values in variables.

A red dot appears in the gray margin to alert you that a line of code is a breakpoint. Click the red dot a second time to turn it off. You can set as many breakpoints as you want.

Another use for breakpoints is when you suspect that the program is never even executing some lines of code. Sometimes a logic error is caused because you think a subroutine, function, or event is getting executed but, in fact, the program never reaches that procedure for some reason. Whatever condition is supposed to activate that area of the program never occurs.

To find out whether a particular event is never executing, set a breakpoint on the first line of code in that procedure. Then, when you run your program, if the breakpoint never halts execution, you have proven that the procedure is never called.

Sometimes you set several breakpoints here and there in your code but then want to delete all of them. If you've set a lot of breakpoints, the Clear All Breakpoints (Ctrl+Shift+F9, or Debug⇨Clear All Breakpoints) feature allows you to get rid of all of them at once, without having to hunt them down and toggle them off individually by clicking their red dot.

Setting conditional breakpoints

Remember the example in which $10 grew to $1,000 for no good reason? To find out where that happened in your code, you could add breakpoints to stop the program when $10 grows larger than, say, $200 (that's your *condition*). Then, while the program is running and $10 is transformed into $1,000 (your logic error), VB halts the program and shows you exactly where the problem is located.

Type this code:

```
Private Sub Button1_Click(ByVal sender As System.Object,
    ByVal e As System.EventArgs) Handles Button1.Click

    Static moneyvariable = 55

    moneyvariable += 44

End Sub
```

To set a conditional breakpoint, follow these steps:

1. **Click the gray area to the left of the line of code where** `moneyvariable` **is increased by 44 (the second line).**

   Or you can click somewhere in the line of code to put your insertion cursor there, and then press F9. The red dot appears and the line of code itself changes to red as well.

2. **Right-click the red part of the line (not the red dot) and choose Breakpoint Properties.**

   The Breakpoint Properties dialog box appears.

3. **Click the Condition button.**

   The Breakpoint Condition dialog box appears, with the "is true" radio button selected by default.

4. **Type** `moneyvariable > 200`, **as shown in Figure 6-5, and then click OK.**

   The condition you've specified is `break if moneyvariable>200 is true`. The break is therefore triggered when this variable goes above 200.

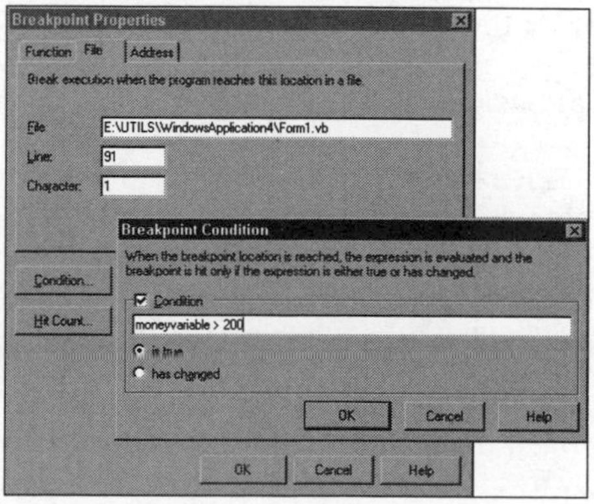

Figure 6-5:
Here's
where
you can
specify a
conditional
breakpoint.

5. **Press F5, and then click your button five times.**

   Your variable exceeds the conditional value and the editor enters break mode. Notice that this breakpoint, being *conditional,* did not automatically halt program execution when the breakpoint line was executed. Instead, it only halted when its condition was satisfied (in this example, when the value in the variable exceeded 200).

You can specify any kind of condition by using the `Is True`, `Has Changed`, or `Hit Count` options in the Breakpoint Properties dialog box and its Breakpoint Condition dialog box.

 A new Breakpoints Window lets you see and manipulate all your breakpoints at once. Open this window by choosing Debug➪Windows➪Breakpoints. You can also click the icon on the far right at the top of this window to open the Breakpoint Properties dialog box.

Global watches missing

The traditional VB Add Watch feature permitted you to create a *global* (project-wide) condition. You didn't have to set multiple conditional breakpoints; you simply set up a Watch condition that was project-wide in scope. (For example, your condition could tell you whether `moneyvariable > 200` for the entire project, not for a specific procedure or procedures.) Then, as soon as `moneyvariable` exceeded 200 anywhere in the project, VB went into break mode and showed you the line where this happened. I hope this useful debugging technique will be made available to VB.NET sometime soon.

In the code window, right-click a variable name and choose New Breakpoint. Click the Data tab. This is where C programmers — and only C programmers — can specify a break condition that is project-wide in scope (it breaks and displays the line *wherever* in the source code this condition becomes true). At the time of this writing, if a VB.NET (or C#) programmer attempts to set a condition in this tab and then clicks OK, an error message informs you that Basic does not support data breakpoints.

The only substitute — and it's not a complete substitute — is to set a *series* of conditional breakpoints here and there in your source code. You set a normal breakpoint by pressing F9 on a line of code. You can then edit the properties of that breakpoint to only break when `A > 90`, for example. You edit a breakpoint by right-clicking the code with the breakpoint and then choosing Breakpoint Properties from the context menu. Place a series of these conditional breakpoints in your code. This helps you find the offending line, but in a large project it doesn't help you nearly as much as a global expression watch. I've always found that global expression watches (such as break whenever and wherever `moneyvariable > 200`) are a major debugging tool, so I'm assuming that VB.NET will offer this feature in the future. For now, you must use the VB.NET Find (Edit➪Find) utility to locate all places in your code where `moneyvariable` is located, and then set up a conditional breakpoint on each of these lines of code.

Alternative Debugging Strategies

You likely noticed several other tools on the Debug menu. They're not as widely useful as breakpoints, single stepping, or watches, but when you need these lesser tools, you are glad they're available. Here's a brief survey of the minor debuggers.

Step Over (Shift+F10, or F10 for the default keyboard)

Step Over is the same as single stepping (F8), except that if you are about to single-step into a procedure, Step Over executes the procedure all at once, rather than step by step. No procedure calls are carried out, but all other commands are executed. So, if you are single-stepping (pressing F8 repeatedly) and you come upon a procedure that you know is not the location of the bug, press Shift+F10 on that line, and you step over the entire procedure. This option gets you past areas in your program that you know are free of bugs and can take a lot of single stepping to get through.

Step Out (Ctrl+Shift+F8, or Shift+F11 for the default keyboard)

The Step Out feature was introduced in VB 5. You must be in break mode for this to work. It executes the remaining lines of the procedure you're currently in but stops on the next line in the program (following the current procedure). Use this to quickly get past a procedure that you don't want to single-step through.

Run to Cursor (Ctrl+F10)

To use the Run to Cursor option, click somewhere else in your code (thereby moving the insertion cursor). VB remembers the original and new locations of the insertion cursor. Press Ctrl+F10, and the code between the original and new locations is executed.

This is a useful trick when you come upon a large For-Next loop. You want to get past the loop quickly rather than waste time completing the loop by pressing F8 over and over. Just click a program line past the loop, and then press Ctrl+F10. VB executes the loop at normal execution speed and then halts at the code following the loop. You can now resume stepping from there.

Set Next Statement (Ctrl+Shift+F10)

You must be in break mode to use Set Next Statement. With this feature, you can move anywhere in the current procedure and restart execution from there (it's the inverse of the Run To Cursor feature). While the program is in Break mode, go to the new location from which you want to start execution, and then click the new line of code where you want to resume execution. Now, pressing F8 single-steps from that new location forward in the program.

This is the way to skip over a line or lines of code. Suppose that you know that things are fine for several lines, but you suspect other lines farther down. Move down using Set Next Statement and start single stepping again.

The Call Stack

The Call Stack feature is on the Debug⇨Windows menu. The Call Stack provides a list of still-active procedures if the running VB program went into Break mode while it was in a procedure that had been called (invoked) by another procedure. Procedures can be nested (one can call on the services of another, which in turn calls yet another). The Call Stack option shows you the name of the procedure that called the current procedure. And if that calling procedure was itself called by yet another procedure, the Call Stack shows you the complete history of what is calling what.

On Error

VB 6 and earlier versions still contained the ancient, notorious GOTO command. It's been in disgrace since the mid '80s when professors of computing decried that it resulted in "spaghetti code" — the pathway of execution being difficult to follow because some programmers were jumping here and there in their source code. GOTO was banished from BASIC in the interest of "modular programming," which was — like today's object-oriented programming — thought to cure many of the ills of bad programming practices.

GOTO remained, however, for use with error trapping. It was used with the Error and Err objects. This technique is still supported in VB.NET. You can still use the following code:

```
On Error Goto HandleThis

HandleThis:
' take care of the error problem here.

or
On Error Resume Next
```

Nonetheless, there are compelling reasons to adapt to the new, more flexible, VB.NET Try-End Try technique, as you saw in Book I, Chapter 4.

Not least of these reasons is that the new technique was developed hand in hand with the development of VB.NET itself and can trap any VB.NET run-time error.

If you are trying to translate existing VB 6 or earlier projects into VB.NET, however, you may want to permit them to retain their already-tested On Error Goto code.

Chapter 7: No More Paranoia — Programmatic Encryption

In This Chapter

✔ On guard: The .NET security features

✔ Hashing it for a key

✔ Private places: Using symmetrical encryption

✔ Suggested further steps

✔ Public knowledge: Public key encryption

To me, encryption and other security topics are among the most interesting aspects of computing. There's something intriguing about the contest of intellects on either side — those cooking up new attacks versus those thinking up new defenses.

Oddly, though, while the importance of computer security is universally recognized, very few books even mention .NET security classes, much less provide examples. This chapter gives you the tools you need to protect your sensitive information. You find out how to employ the .NET security classes to thoroughly disguise data — making it as safe as possible from prying eyes. And there are plenty of code examples you can use.

The .NET security classes are too large to cover in a single chapter, so I concentrate here on demonstrating how to use the most important (and, I think, interesting) feature: encryption and decryption.

In addition, you build an application using the .NET DES encryption functions. It will likely prove quite useful to you once you've finished it: You can use it to securely hide your logon-password combinations, your private financial data, and so on. The fact that you've written it and that you have the source code means you can customize it to suit yourself. At the end of this chapter, I suggest some customizations you may find useful.

I enjoy programming in Visual Basic, and have enjoyed it for over a decade. However, if I were limited to creating one application for myself — if I could only write a single program in my life — it would probably be the one that you create in this chapter. Of all the programs you may write for yourself, it's likely that an encryption program to safeguard your information benefits the most from your intimate knowledge of how it works, how it can be made secure in your environment, and from your hands-on customization.

Do you have kids who use your computer? Do you have secrets you need to save in a particular way, for only a certain length of time, for example? Do you want a quick way to cut and paste your credit card numbers? Do you want a secure place to temporarily store order numbers and e-mail receipts when you buy something online or make a reservation?

Whatever your security needs are, they are highly specific to you. So being able to satisfy those needs by designing and maintaining your own personal security zone can be extremely useful.

The Two Tactics

Experts divide secret messaging into two broad categories. First, *steaganography* attempts to hide the fact that a secret message is, in fact, being sent. Invisible ink; microdots; shaving a runner's head, tattooing the message, and letting the hair grow out; burst radio transmissions posing as static — all these approaches involve pretending that nothing sly is going on. Recently, terrorists have been accused of using the Internet to communicate by concealing messages in graphics files. A picture of a rose can contain their information, if you know where to look.

More common, and generally more secure, is *cryptography,* which doesn't try to hide the fact that a message is being sent. Instead, the message is mangled, *encrypted,* transforming the original, called the *plaintext,* so that it can't be read. (After being encrypted, it's called *cyphertext.*)

Encryption can solve several computer security problems. For example, when you send something over the Internet, it can easily be intercepted. But if you encrypt the message, it can be impossible for the interceptor (the *intruder,* as he or she is called) to understand. Thus, an effectively encrypted message is useless to any intruder.

Cryptography can also protect information that isn't transmitted — information that merely sits on your hard drive but that you don't want others to see. Perhaps it's your diary, a list of all your ID/password combinations, your various investments, whatever. You can use the utility program that you build in this chapter to save a file to your hard drive that nobody but you can decipher.

Using the Great DES

The DES (Data Encryption Standard) encryption technology was created by IBM in the early '70s. Back then, IBM was one of the few games in town, and the government requested that the brilliant IBM R&D people come up with a way of protecting bank money transfers, government communications, and other sensitive information. In 1972, the National Bureau of Standards asked for a reliable, fast, inexpensive, standardized, very robust United States encryption system. They got what they wanted.

It was clear that computer communications would become increasingly essential in the modern world, and those communications had to be secured in some way. After all, the only difference between $1,000 and $1,000,000 in your savings account is three magnetic patterns on a hard drive somewhere.

DES was formally introduced in 1976, and to this day it is routinely used for the great majority of business and government encryption. With the DES technology built into .NET, you, too, can protect your secrets.

Making it public

Strangely, the DES algorithm was made public! In the past, the primary reason that people couldn't crack an encryption scheme was precisely because they didn't know how the scheme worked. If you decide to encrypt by spelling all the words backwards and also substituting x for e, you certainly don't tell people that's what you're doing.

The process used by the DES technique was published so that software could be written to automate the encryption process, and possibly for other more mysterious reasons. The inventors of DES said that knowledge of how a DES message was encrypted wouldn't provide an intruder with a way of decrypting it. Well . . .

IBM's DES system isn't really that tough to understand if you've done any bit-level programming. It's just that DES performs many, many transformations (such as rotation) of the key (password) against the plaintext.

Each individual transformation is simple. A typical rotation left of a 4-bit unit, for example, changes 0101 into 1010, or 1001 into 0011. However, DES does so *many* transformations, each one impacting the next one, that a cumulative distortion occurs, a sum-greater-than-the-parts effect. It's as if you started a rumor that was passed along through a million people. You certainly wouldn't recognize your original message when they finished with it.

Can it be cracked?

A dispute among cryptologists concerns whether or not the government (or amateur groups) has secretly cracked DES. (Some even claim that there was always a secret "trap door" built into the DES system right from the start — to permit government agencies access any time they wished. Like most conspiracy theories, this seems doubtful.)

However, if the government has subsequently cracked it, we wouldn't likely be told. Some experts claim that the fifteenth cycle, of the 16 cycles used by DES, has been successfully penetrated. Now and then an amateur group claims to have cracked DES completely. A 1999 attack on a DES message, during a contest, is said to have found a solution in a little more than 22 hours by testing 245 billion keys per second. This claim seems believable.

It does seem likely though that the basic, 56-bit version of DES is no longer secure from supercomputer (or massive parallel processing) brute force key searches. Therefore, if your diary contains information so exciting that you think someone is going to rent 24 hours on a supercomputer to crack your secret file, you should consider moving up to Triple-DES, which uses three times as many key bits (but runs three times slower, unfortunately). In this chapter, I show you how to use ordinary 56-bit DES and also 192-bit TripleDES. If you do decide to opt for TripleDES, be warned that you have to come up with a 24-character password, instead of the easier-to-remember 8-character DES password. And don't try to get clever: Simply repeating an 8-character password three times compromises the benefits of TripleDES.

If you do want to use TripleDES, simply change the following DES declare statement:

```
Dim des As New DESCryptoServiceProvider()
```

and replace it with the following TripleDES declaration:

```
Dim TripleDes As New TripleDESCryptoServiceProvider()
```

Also, you must adjust the source code to expand the key (and the initialization vector) three times larger than the DES key and vector pair (you expand from DES's 8-byte to TripleDES's 24-byte).

Choosing a good password

DES encryption — whatever size you use — requires a password. It's the password that DES uses to uniquely encrypt, and later decrypt, your file. You must be able to remember the password or you'll never be able to decrypt the file. The password should include digits (1 through 9) as well as alphabetic characters. What's more, you should choose the most random password that you will be able to remember. No matter how much encryption power you use, if people can guess your password, they're in! Your entire message rolls out for them to read.

Your dog's name is not a good password. Your address, your birthday, your favorite food — all of these would probably be tried by an even moderately motivated, semi-talented intruder. Don't write the password down and stick it in your desk. *Memorize it.*

Although computers make it possible to run millions of transformations on a message to encrypt it, computers are value-neutral. A computer doesn't know whether it's running an encryption program written by you (the innocent good person, trying to protect his personal information) or running an intruder's (the bad person trying to get into your bank account) key-testing hacking program that goes through entire dictionaries of possible passwords in a flash.

Encrypting in VB.NET

Now you can get down to cases. Here's a class, named `crypt`, that you can use to encrypt or decrypt a file on your hard drive. Before it encrypts (or decrypts) a file, you must provide this class with four pieces of information:

Book III
Chapter 7

No More Paranoia — Programmatic Encryption

✦ Tell it what file you want encrypted by setting its `filetoopen` property.

✦ Tell it the filename you want to give the new, encrypted version by setting its `filetosave` property.

✦ Tell it your password by setting its `password` property.

✦ Tell it whether you want to *encrypt* or *decrypt* by setting its `whichway` argument. You do this by setting a parameter when you create the `crypt` object. You may have noticed that when you create certain objects, you can provide them with *parameters,* just as you do when using a function. As you see in Book VII, when you write a class you can add this feature by using a *parameterized constructor.* It's just a `Sub New`, and that `New` tells VB.NET that you intend to receive a parameter when the object is instantiated (created) during runtime. These constructors are explained in detail in Book VII.

The `crypt` class requires three `Imports`, so start a new VB.NET Windows-style project and type the following at the very top of your code window:

```
Imports System.IO
Imports System.Text
Imports System.Security.Cryptography
```

Now, move your cursor to the very bottom of the code window, below the final line of code that says `End Class`, and type in the following new class:

```
Public Class crypt 'user must provide "whichway" (encrypt or
    decrypt) filetoopen, filetosave and key.

    Sub New(ByVal WhichWay As String) ' parameterized
constructor
        ' store their choice: encrypt or decrypt
        Way = WhichWay
    End Sub

    Private Way As String 'encrypt or decrypt
    Private pfname As String 'filename of incoming file
    Private efname As String 'filename of outgoing file
    Private pword As String ' the password the user enters


    Public WriteOnly Property password() As String
        Set(ByVal Value As String)
            pword = Value
        End Set
End Property

    Public WriteOnly Property filetoopen() As String
        Set(ByVal Value As String)
            pfname = Value
        End Set
End Property

    Public WriteOnly Property filetosave() As String
        Set(ByVal Value As String)
            efname = Value
        End Set
End Property

    Function cryptIt()

        If efname = "" Or pfname = "" Or pword = "" Then

            MsgBox("You must set the password, filetoopen,
and filetosave properties of this encrypt object before
using the CryptIt method.")
            Return ("error")

        End If

        'create the key from the password:

        Dim the_key(7) As Byte
        Dim doKey As New make_key(pword)

        the_key = doKey.MakeKey
```

```vb.net
    'random bytes for the initialization vector (see
description in text)
    Dim Vector() As Byte = {&H22, &HD1, &H11, &HA8, &H82,
&H62, &HDA, &H36}
    Dim buffer(4096) As Byte
    Dim tb As Long = 8 'Keeps track of number of bytes
written
    Dim packageSize As Integer 'Byte block size


    'Create the streams.
    Dim fileIn As New FileStream(pfname, FileMode.Open,
FileAccess.Read)
    Dim fileOut As New FileStream(efname,
FileMode.OpenOrCreate, FileAccess.Write)
    fileOut.SetLength(0)

    Dim tf As Long = fileIn.Length 'find out file size.

    Try
        'create the cryptography object
        Dim DES As New DESCryptoServiceProvider()

        'flow the streams

        If Way = "encrypt" Then

            Dim cryptStream As New CryptoStream(fileOut,
DES.CreateEncryptor(the_key, Vector),
CryptoStreamMode.Write)

            While tb < tf
                packageSize = fileIn.Read(buffer, 0,
4096)

                cryptStream.Write(buffer, 0, packageSize)
                tb = Convert.ToInt32(tb + packageSize /
DES.BlockSize * DES.BlockSize)
            End While

            cryptStream.Close()
            fileIn.Close()
            fileOut.Close()

        Else 'decrypt

            Dim decryptStream As New
CryptoStream(fileOut, DES.CreateDecryptor(the_key,
Vector), CryptoStreamMode.Write)

            While tb < tf
                packageSize = fileIn.Read(buffer, 0,
4096)
```

```
                    decryptStream.Write(buffer, 0,
     packageSize)
                    tb = Convert.ToInt32(tb + packageSize /
     DES.BlockSize * DES.BlockSize)
             End While

             decryptStream.Close()
             fileIn.Close()
             fileOut.Close()
        End If

    Catch e As Exception
        MsgBox(e.Message & "Perhaps you're using a bad
     password?")
        End Try

    End Function


End Class
```

At this point, you can't press F5 to see any results yet. You have to add some more elements to this project to be able to try this encryption class. Notice the squiggly line in your code window under `make_key`. That class has not been coded yet.

After the various properties are created at the top of this code, you come to `Function cryptIt()`, which is the method in this class that does the actual work. First, `cryptIt` checks to see if the user has set the necessary properties. If so, a key (a series of eight numbers) is created out of the user's password. The .NET DES encryption routine wants a byte array with eight bytes in it, so you first create the byte array, and then you instantiate a `doKey` object (which is created by the `MakeKey` class). `MakeKey` transforms the user's password into a random series of numbers (and I explain how this class does its job soon in this section):

```
Dim the_key(7) As Byte
Dim doKey As New make_key(pword)
the_key = doKey.MakeKey
```

Next in the `cryptIt` class, several necessary housekeeping variables are created. The initialization vector is required by the .NET DES encryption routine. Vectors are rather interesting, but you can skip the sidebar describing them if you're not interested. You can easily use the encryption code without understanding the vector.

Why use initialization vectors?

Intruders attempt to crack encrypted text in two primary ways: a brute force search for the key, or a search for repetitions in your text. These repetitions need not be obvious, such as the `abc` in `abc rana re iz abc`. Here's a repetition you may not immediately notice: `abc rana re iz bcd`. The `bcd` is a repetition of `abc`, although it has been shifted forward by one letter in the alphabet. A computer can test for such shifting quite easily and rapidly, noting any patterns it discovers. And I mean *any*. Intruders may also have several different encrypted messages, and they can look for repetitions within each message but also can compare the messages against each other, looking for repetitions across messages. For example, during the second world war, the English searched encrypted German messages for words like *Luftwaffe* and *Unterseeboot*.

The initialization vector's job is to prevent a particular kind of repetition that can plague DES-encrypted messages. The initialization vector is a byte array just like the key. In fact, you could require the user to enter an eight-character password that you then transform into an eight-byte array. To make life easier for the user, though, the `cryptIt` class instead just defines eight random byte values itself in the code.

DES is called a *block cipher* because the plaintext is broken down into eight-byte groups, which are each transformed independently. However, each resulting transformation is then, itself, used to help transform the next block.

For this reason, if you change a single letter in the message, all subsequent letters will be encrypted differently. A whiplash effect rattles all the links down the chain of blocks. Thus, even if your message is entirely repetitive —

such as `Hello Hello Hello Hello` — it will nonetheless never reveal this repetition in the ciphertext, which looks something like this: `a6iG=1h9&@-->gn)831#i/.`

This chain reaction is a significant aspect of the DES system. Not only is the key used to distort the plaintext, a mathematical quality of each block is also used to distort the next block down the chain. This works very well except for the first block. There's nothing to distort this block other than the password. That's a serious weakness if two messages are encrypted using the same password and if those messages both start with the same plaintext. It's more common than you may think for two messages to start the same way. Each letter you write your sister, for example, may start: *Dear Janice*. Repetitive greetings or introductions are actually rather common, even during wartime.

The vector's job is to provide another layer of protection by simulating a plaintext block that precedes the start of the message. Of course, to provide this protection, you should generate unique initialization vectors and/or unique passwords for each message. For your personal privacy needs, however, it's okay to hardwire the initialization vector because you probably will store only a single file on your hard drive (to contain your financial information, passwords, and so on). There won't be multiple messages with repetitive greetings for an intruder to compare. Nonetheless, there's an easy way to modify the example program in this chapter so that the password generates both the eight bytes for the key and also the eight bytes needed for the vector. The sidebar titled "Understanding hash," later in this chapter, explains this modification.

Streaming the encryption

After the initialization vector is defined in the `cryptIt` source code, a pair of filestreams are defined. They carry the data in from the plaintext file and out to the cyphertext file during the encryption process. (This class can also decrypt, so if that's what's going on, these same streams instead carry cyphertext in and send plaintext out.)

Finally, the actual encryption takes place, starting with the creation of a `DESCryptoServiceProvider()` object. After that object is instantiated, the code determines whether the user wants to encrypt or decrypt. The only difference between the two processes is that you use two different cryptostreams, one `CreateEncryptor` and the other `CreateDecryptor`. I put those declarations within the `If...End if` structure. Then, as long as tb < tf (the bytes written are less than the total bytes in the source file), the streams flow. The encryption process reads in a chunk from the `FileIn` stream; then it's encrypted and streamed out to `FileOut` (via the `cryptoStream`). Finally, the number of bytes written is updated into the variable tb.

When the process is complete, all three streams are closed. Interestingly, if someone provides the wrong password for decrypting a file, the DES crypto class *knows* that it is the wrong password. Many decryption schemes simply spew out nonsense text when given the wrong password (they simply go ahead and generate what results from grinding the bad password against the cyphertext). The .NET DES scheme, however, throws a `Bad Data` error message. This means that the correct password is somehow contained within the encrypted file (either somehow disguised, or in the form of a hash or checksum). In any case, if an exception is thrown, you can display a message to users asking whether they supplied the wrong password and asking them to try again, as I did in this example.

Generating a password

To actually use the `CryptIt` class, you must also have the class that generates the key out of the user's password, so type in the following class at the very bottom of your code window, below all the other existing lines of code:

```
Public Class make_key

    Sub New(ByVal TheirPassword As String) ' parameterized
    constructor
        ' store the password
        kpassword = TheirPassword
    End Sub

    Private kpassword As String 'the password string

    Public ReadOnly HashedKey(7) As Byte
```

```
Function MakeKey()
    ' Declare a byte array that will hold the key
    Dim arrByte(7) As Byte

    Dim AscEncod As New ASCIIEncoding()
    Dim i As Integer = 0
    AscEncod.GetBytes(kpassword, i, kpassword.Length,
arrByte, i)

    'Generate a hash value from the password
    Dim hashSha As New SHA1CryptoServiceProvider()
    Dim arrHash() As Byte = hashSha.ComputeHash(arrByte)

    'store the hash into the key array
    For i = 0 To 7
        HashedKey(i) = arrHash(i)
    Next i

    Return HashedKey

End Function


Function Create() 'method to transform password string
into a key

    ' Save the current value of the LastFile property to
the registry.
    Dim arrByte(7) As Byte

    'change the password string into a byte array:
    Dim AscEncod As New ASCIIEncoding()
    Dim i As Integer = 0
    AscEncod.GetBytes(kpassword, i, kpassword.Length,
arrByte, i)

    'Get the hash value of the password byte array:
    Dim hash As New SHA1CryptoServiceProvider()
    Dim arrHash(7) As Byte
    hash.ComputeHash(arrByte)

    'return the key:

    Return arrHash

End Function

End Class
```

This `Make_Key` class begins with a parameterized constructor (the `Sub New`), which requires that when clients using the class instantiate the class, they must provide a password as a parameter, like this:

```
Dim doKey As New make_key(pword)
```

Then the `MakeKey` method creates an 8-byte array, and the password is separated by the `ASCIIEncoding` class into individual bytes (each character's ASCII code value) and stored into the array. After that, the `SHA1CryptoServiceProvider` class generates a hash out of the array.

The user's password `strKey` is passed to this procedure; then the password is separated into individual ASCII values held in a byte array. This byte array is fed to the `ComputeHash` method of the `SHA1CryptoServiceProvider` class, which returns the hash value. I put the hash into my `TheKey` array, for later use in the encryption (or decryption) procedures.

What does the key do?

A key is used in encryption to provide a way of distorting the plaintext. Here's a simple example. Assume that you think up an encryption scheme. Your idea is to drop the password's characters into every other letter of the plaintext, like this:

Key: `Mike`

Plaintext: `Ring of fire.`

Encryption: `RMiinkge Moifk efMiirkee.`

Many times, as illustrated here, the key is repeated as often as necessary throughout the plaintext. For illustration purposes, I used alphabetic characters here. However, with the arrival of the computer, modern encryption generally involves mathematical transformations rather than the simple character substitutions or transpositions characteristic of classic encryption schemes. Computers are so good at math, compared to us, and so much faster at it as well. So, before being used mathematically in a modern encryption scheme like DES, the text password is transformed (hashed, for example) into a numeric value (the *key*) that can then be employed in the mathematical encryption. Remember, DES wants an 8-byte numeric array, not a password. That's the job of the `make_key` class in this chapter.

Understanding hash

Hashing is used in two main ways in computing: to speed up database searches, and in various security techniques such as digital signatures, encryption, and message integrity checking. A hash function calculates a mathematical value (a number) by looking at a string of characters and transforming them in some fashion according to repeatable rules. In this way, hashing is similar to, though usually simpler than, encryption algorithms. (In fact, hashing is usually *part* of what goes on in an encryption scheme.) Hashing, however, is faster than encryption, and the resulting hash value tends to be shorter than a ciphertext.

There are many different hash functions, so you won't get the same hash value when you feed a given string to two different hash functions. However, feed that string twice or 100 times to the *same* hash function and you *do* get a reliable, predictable, unvarying value.

Searching is fundamental to database applications. And searching through numbers is far faster than searching through words, such as people's names. That's why databases often use numeric keys (a field within each record that contains a *number* unique to that record). Why is it faster? Assume that you have a database that will always remain smaller than 10,000 entries. First, there are only 10 digits to try to match (0 to 9), and also a fixed length of four because of the 10,000-entry limit: 0000 to 9999. If you were to search through the *name* field, however, the length of the names *varies* (slowing down the matching process), but, worse, there are 26 possible alphabetic characters to deal with rather than only 10 digits. It's just much slower to try to match variable-length strings compared to fixed-length numbers.

In encryption, hashing also has its obvious uses. A hash function generates an apparently random numeric equivalent to any string. In the key-generating class make_key described earlier, the user's password is hashed, and this adds yet another layer of safety to the entire encryption process. Built into the .NET cryptography library is the SHA1CryptoServiceProvider class, which I use in the make_key class. SHA-1 is a hash function that was first made available in 1994, and it is considered quite effective against both kinds of brute force attacks (known as *collision* and *inversion* attacks). SHA-1 can handle a message as large as 2 to the 64th power, and it produces a 20-byte-long hash. You only need an 8-byte key for the DES encryption used in the cryptIt class example program, so you ignore all but the first eight bytes generated by SHA-1. However, if you want to see the complete hash value, temporarily change the loop in the make_key class to this:

```
For i = 0 To 19

Console.Write(arrHash(i) &
", ")
      'HashedKey(i) =
arrHash(i)
      Next i
```

If you're disinclined to waste things, you can use eight of the unused 12 bytes provided by SHA-1 in the make_key class for your initialization vector.

Finishing the Program

To complete the DES encryption application that's been developed in this chapter, you should add two buttons and two textboxes to the form. Ensure that TextBox2 is fairly small and drag it down near the bottom of the form; TextBox2 is where the user enters the password, so it needs to be only a single-line TextBox. But set TextBox1's MultiLine property to True, and stretch it to make it fairly large so that users can enter as much text as they like, as shown in Figure 7-1.

Figure 7-1:
Arrange your crypto program's user interface like this.

It's nice to show the user some mangled text from the resulting encryption. This chapter's example program, therefore, displays some of the encrypted text after users click the button captioned *Encrypt*. They type something into the textbox, type in a password, click the Encrypt button, and, voila, the transformed result appears in the textbox, as shown in Figure 7-1. Mangled text excites users. They think, "Wow! Nobody can figure *this* out!"

Displaying mangled text

Here's a function you should type into the Form1 class to display the encrypted result. The same function does a second job; it displays the decrypted plaintext if the user clicks the Decrypt button instead.

Move down through Public Class Form1 in your code window until your blinking insertion cursor is just above the line End Class. (Be sure that you're still in the Form1 class, not in the Crypt class or some other class beneath the Form1 class.) Now type the following function just above the line End Class:

```
Function showcrypt(ByVal fname As String) 'displays a file in
    the textbox

        Dim fs As FileStream = New FileStream(fname,
    FileMode.Open)

        Dim r As New StreamReader(fs)

        Dim x As Integer = fs.Length
        Dim i As Integer

        ' Read in all the data from the file:

        TextBox1.Text = r.ReadToEnd

        r.Close()
        fs.Close()

        'kill the temp file
        Dim fa As New FileInfo("c:\temp")
        fa.Delete()

    End Function
```

The CryptIt class creates a temporary file on the hard drive (named
C:\temp) to hold the intermediary results of encryption or decryption. This
file must be destroyed, however, or it would hold the plaintext after encryption had been performed on it. That would be bad: People could read all
your secrets if they could locate the temp file. So, at the end of this
ShowCrypt function, the temp file is deleted.

If you want to increase security, replace the plaintext filestream with a
memorystream. Even though the plaintext file is deleted, determined and
sophisticated spies can locate deleted data on a hard drive.

Now, all that remains to be done to complete this application is to respond
when the user clicks the two buttons. Type in the following code for the
button that encrypts:

```
Private Sub Button1_Click(ByVal sender As System.Object,
    ByVal e As System.EventArgs) Handles Button1.Click
        'encrypt the contents of the TextBox

        Dim sfd As New SaveFileDialog()
        sfd.ShowDialog()

        Dim objCrypt As New crypt("encrypt")
        objCrypt.filetoopen = "c:\temp"
        objCrypt.filetosave = sfd.FileName
        If Len(TextBox2.Text) <> 8 Then MsgBox("Your password
    must be eight characters long") : Exit Sub
```

```
objCrypt.password = TextBox2.Text.ToUpper

'save textbox1 to c:\temp

Dim strText As String = TextBox1.Text

If (strText.Length < 1) Then
    MsgBox("Please type something into the TextBox so
we can encrypt it.")
    Exit Sub
Else
    Dim strFileName As String = "C:\temp"
    Dim objOpenFile As FileStream = New
FileStream(strFileName, FileMode.Create,
FileAccess.Write, FileShare.None)
    Dim objStreamWriter As StreamWriter = New
StreamWriter(objOpenFile)
    objStreamWriter.WriteLine(strText)
    objStreamWriter.Close()
    objOpenFile.Close()
End If


Dim n As StringBuilder
n = objCrypt.cryptIt()
showcrypt(sfd.FileName)


'delete the password
TextBox2.Text = ""


End Sub
```

This button's click event first displays a Save File dialog box and asks the user to specify where on the hard drive to store the encrypted file and what name to give it. Then it streams the contents of the large TextBox1 to a temporary file in preparation for encrypting the text. Finally, the cryptIt method is invoked, and after the encryption is finished, the showcrypt function displays the results (mangled text like this :10!@09jd ()#JF&).

Finish the application by typing in the following code for Button2, which decrypts:

```
Private Sub Button2_Click(ByVal sender As System.Object,
ByVal e As System.EventArgs) Handles Button2.Click
    'decrypt a saved file

    Dim ofd As New OpenFileDialog()
    ofd.ShowDialog()
```

```
Dim objDecrypt As New crypt("decrypt")
objDecrypt.filetoopen = ofd.FileName
objDecrypt.filetosave = "c:\temp"
objDecrypt.password = TextBox2.Text
Dim n As StringBuilder
n = objDecrypt.cryptIt()
showcrypt("c:\temp")


'delete the password
TextBox2.Text = ""


   End Sub
```

Trying the program

Time to try out the program. Press F5 and type an eight-character password into the lower TextBox. In the future, you can use any password you want, but while experimenting in this chapter, use the password MYSTERY2. Later in this chapter, you will see why this is important.

Now copy and paste a few paragraphs of text into TextBox1, the upper TextBox. Click the Encrypt button. You see the Save As dialog box. Use the drop-down list at the top of the dialog box to move to your C: drive. Then type secrets as the filename for your encrypted file. Use C:\secrets as the filename.

Click the Save button. The dialog box closes and the upper textbox's text is replace with encrypted text. Now try going the other way: Type the password you used to encrypt the file, and click the Decrypt button. The Open dialog box appears. Double-click the filename you used when encrypting, and there you are: Your plaintext is restored.

Some Suggested Additions to the Crypt Program

You can use the project you created previously in this chapter as-is. It will calm the paranoiac in you by efficiently hiding your secrets. However, I want to suggest some exciting and sinister improvements to conclude this chapter. Read on, friend.

Fifty years ago, still struggling with their categories, psychologists came up with the delightful word *paranoiac* (combining *paranoia* with *maniac*). These days of political correctness have forced shrinks to rename many kinds of mental disturbances, in an effort to soften the insult by using words such as *borderline,* which suggests that with a little help, the person can come over the line to join the happy, smiling normal people, whoever they may be.

Whatever you call it, surely nothing is wrong with being moderately paranoiac about your personal information. After all, some of your secrets, if known, could be used against you in various ways.

Luckily, in this chapter you actually constructed encryption/decryption and key-making classes that make use of the sophisticated security classes built into .NET. Now I want to suggest some additions and customizations that can make your crypt utility even more useful to you as a way of protecting your private information.

For one thing, if only *you* are going to use it, and you're going to create only one file that holds all your private data, why not simplify things and hardwire the filename (put it into the source code rather than displaying OpenFile or SaveFile dialog boxes to have the user type it in)? That way, when you run the program, you only have to type in the password and the file is automatically opened, decrypted, and displayed. Then, when you've finished editing the information and want to store it encrypted, you simply click a button and it's all done for you automatically.

Remember that all the source code for these additions, as well as all the code for this book, is available for quick downloading from this book's Web site at dummies.com/extras.

Here's an example of code that you can type into the Form_Load event to automatically open, decrypt, and display plaintext:

```
Private Sub Form1_Load(ByVal sender As System.Object, ByVal e
    As System.EventArgs) Handles MyBase.Load


        'load and decrypt the encrypted file

        Dim objDecrypt As New crypt("decrypt")

        objDecrypt.filetoopen = "c:\secrets"
        objDecrypt.filetosave = "c:\tem"
        objDecrypt.password = passwordFromForm2
        Dim n As StringBuilder
        n = objDecrypt.cryptIt()

        showcrypt("c:\tem")

        'kill the temp file
        Dim fa As New FileInfo("c:\tem")
        fa.Delete()

    End Sub
```

Note that `filetoopen` is simply hardwired here (shown in boldface). Also note that the password comes from another Form, `Form2`. The variable `passwordFromForm2` is currently underlined with a squiggly line because it hasn't yet been declared. This is a clever trick that you may want to try. It adds one more layer of protection.

When people run your program, all they see is an empty `Form2`. There are no buttons on it, nothing to interact with. I set its `FormBorderStyle` property to `None`, its `BackGroundImage` property to some graphic file, and its `Opacity` property to `75%`, just to make it look spooky to someone who may stumble upon this utility. It just sits there.

However, it *is* waiting to accept any keystrokes users may type. Whatever they type becomes the *key* used to decrypt your secret file. They will probably never be able to figure this out, but if they do, they still don't know the key. You know the key, though, so when you run the program, and the spooky `Form2` shows up, you just type in your 8-character password and `Form2` disappears, `Form1` appears, and the decrypted file is displayed. All in a flash, but highly secure.

If I were you, I'd add a Timer to `Form2` and write code in its `Tick` event that gradually makes `Form2` disappear by slowly decreasing its `Opacity` property. How *spoooooky* for anyone trying to get to your secrets. They'll worry about what other tricks you may have up your sleeve.

Making it happen

Use Project⇨Add Windows Form to add `Form2` to your project, and use Project⇨Add Module to add `Module1`.

When this project runs, `Form2` is not supposed to do anything until the user types the number 2 above the keyboard, thereby making `Form2` disappear and `Form1` appear. (You can, of course, change this trigger character to suit yourself.)

Now, in the `Module1`, type the following variable. Putting it in a `Module` permits both `Form2` and `Form1` to access the variable. This is a way to communicate information between forms:

```
Module Module1
    'this variable can now be seen in both Form1 and Form2

    Public passwordFromForm2 As String

End Module
```

Now, switch to Form2's code window and type the following code into Form2's Form_KeyDown event. To create the KeyDown event, open the drop-down list on the top right of the code window and click KeyDown:

```
Public Class Form2
    Inherits System.Windows.Forms.Form

Windows Form Designer generated code

    Dim presses As String

Private Sub Form2_KeyDown(ByVal sender As Object, ByVal e As
    System.Windows.Forms.KeyEventArgs) Handles MyBase.KeyDown

    presses += e.KeyCode.ToString

        If e.KeyCode = Keys.D2 Then 'pressing the number 2
    triggers the end of the key input
            'form one is displayed and the user's key input
    is then sent as the password
            'to decrypt. If the wrong password was entered,
    the program will shut down in
            'form1--no text will be decrypted or displayed.

            'this will be in all uppercase
            passwordFromForm2 = presses.Substring(0, 7) & "2"


        Me.Hide()

        Dim n As New Form1
        n.Show()

        End If

    End Sub
End Class
```

Notice that just above the line Private Sub Form2_KeyDown..., you must add the following line to declare the variable presses:

```
Dim presses As String
```

For this key-detection feature to work, you must switch to design view and set Form2's KeyPreview property to True in the properties window.

One more thing. You have to change the Startup object from Form1 (the default) to Form2. That way, the code in Form2 is the first code executed when your project starts running. To make this change, follow these steps:

1. **Choose View⇨Solution Explorer.**

   Solution Explorer is displayed.

2. **Right-click the name of your project (which is the only line in boldface in Solution Explorer).**

   A context menu appears.

3. **Click Properties in the context menu.**

   Your project's Property Pages dialog box opens.

4. **Drop the listbox under *Startup object* by clicking its down-arrow button.**

   You see the forms and module listed as potential startup objects.

5. **Click** Form2 **in the drop-down listbox.**

   Form2 is now displayed as the new startup object.

6. **Click OK.**

   The dialog box closes.

Notice that the variable presses here continues to accumulate all the characters that the user types in, until the user types the digit 2. Then, all characters in presses (except the first 8) are discarded and the passwordFromForm2 is filled with those first 8 characters. Interestingly, the numbers are identified in the e.keycode with a D in addition to the digit, so if you press, for example, 3, e.keycode contains D3.

Here's what happens if your password is treatww2 and you type that in: As soon as you press the 2 key, the presses.Substring(0, 8) contains treatwwD because the variable presses contains treatwwD2, but only 8 of its characters are retained when you use the Substring method to strip off any extras.

Anyway, Form2 hides, Form1 is displayed, and Form1's Load event triggers, bringing in the entire decrypted text for you to view.

Also in Form1, you can change the process of encryption by hardwiring your filename and avoiding having to interact with a SaveFileDialog. Remember, too, that the password is already available for the encryption process in the variable passwordFromForm2.

Beyond paranoiac

Here's another feature I find useful. Sometimes I get distracted while computing. I make some changes to the decrypted data in the TextBox, but I forget to shut down the Crypt program. Or I switch to Internet Explorer for a little browsing or leave the computer to get something to drink. I've done this while the crypt program is running, leaving my entire private life gaping open there in the TextBox for anyone to read.

To prevent this problem, I like to add two Timers that shut down the Crypt program automatically if there have been no keypresses for one minute. Also, the following code adds a useful search feature, so that you can quickly locate passwords and so on in your TextBox.

First, remove the main, large TextBox (not the password TextBox) and add a RichTextBox from the Toolbox in its place. The document in a RichTextBox automatically scrolls to display a match if one is found when you're searching. Also, set Form1's KeyPreview property to True. Then type the following variable declarations at the top of the code window:

```
Dim freezer As Boolean

'these next variables are used by the Searchit routine
Dim searchstring As String, pos As Integer
Dim pressedonce As Boolean
Dim Search, Where    ' Declare variables as objects
(default).

Dim isdirty As Boolean 'has the user changed the textbox
at all?

Private Sub Form1_Load(ByVal sender As Object, ByVal e As
System.EventArgs) Handles MyBase.Load
        'load and decrypt the encrypted file
```

Search (press Ctrl+H) all references in your code to TextBox1 and Replace them with RichTextBox1.

Now add two Timer controls to Form1 and type in this code:

```
'These timers prevent you from forgetting to shut down
    'this application. If no keypresses are made for 1
minute,
    'the program is shut down:

    Private Sub Timer1_Tick(ByVal sender As System.Object,
ByVal e As System.EventArgs) Handles Timer1.Tick
        'Timer1's Interval should be set to 6000 (six
seconds)
        ' and it's enabled to true (in the Properties
window).

        Static Counter As Integer

        If freezer = True Then
            Counter = 0
            Me.Text = "        Frozen        "
```

```
        Exit Sub
    End If

    Counter = Counter + 1
    If Counter = 9 Then End 'Shutdown!

End Sub


 Private Sub Timer2_Tick(ByVal sender As System.Object,
 ByVal e As System.EventArgs) Handles Timer2.Tick

    'Timer2's Interval should be set to 60000 (one
 minute)
    ' and it's enabled to false (in the Properties
 window).


    '1 minute has elapsed so turn freezer off
    freezer = False
    Timer2.Enabled = False

End Sub
```

The Form's KeyDown event detects keypresses (affecting the freezer variable used by the timers) and also detects if the user presses F3 or CTRL+F, either of which triggers a search of the RichTextBox's contents.

```
Private Sub Form1_KeyDown(ByVal sender As Object, ByVal e As
    System.Windows.Forms.KeyEventArgs) Handles MyBase.KeyDown
        'For this to work, the Form's KEYPREVIEW PROPERTY
 MUST BE SET TO TRUE! (default=false)

    'This procedure searches through the TextBox
    'when the user presses F3 or Crlt+F...

    freezer = True 'a keypress, so stop the Timer
 countdown
    Timer2.Enabled = True 'watch to see if 1 minute
 passes
    'after last keypress and if so, turn freezer false


    If e.KeyCode = 114 Then ' pressed f3 to search

        searchit()

        Exit Sub

    End If

    If e.KeyCode = Keys.F And e.Control = True Then
```

```
                              'pressed CTRL+F to search

                              searchit()

                              Exit Sub

                      End If


              End Sub
```

Here's the procedure that searches the RichTextBox:

```
Private Sub searchit()


        Dim x As String, n As String
        x = LCase(RichTextBox1.Text)
        If pos = 0 Then pos = 1

        If pressedonce = True Then GoTo cont

        If searchstring <> "" Then n = searchstring

        Search = InputBox("Please enter your search text", , n)
        If Search = "" Then pressedonce = False : Exit Sub
    'they clicked the cancel button on the Search Input box
        pressedonce = True
        Search = LCase(Search)
        searchstring = Search

cont:

        Where = InStr(pos, x, Search) ' Find string in text.
        Dim ra = x.Length

        If Where Then    ' If found,
            RichTextBox1.SelectionStart = Where - 1 ' set
    selection start and
            RichTextBox1.SelectionLength = Len(Search)  ' set
    selection length.
            pos = Where + Len(Search)
        Else
            MsgBox("Search text not found.")  ' Notify user.
            pressedonce = False
            pos = 0
            Search = Nothing
            Where = Nothing
        End If

    End Sub
```

Finally, I sometimes make changes to the RichTextBox, but forget to press the button to actually encrypt and save those changes to the disk file. Instead, I go ahead and click the x in the top right of the form or press Alt+F4 to shut down the program.

Here's a way to alert the user that editing hasn't been saved when the program is about to shut down. You test the isdirty variable (which is set if any changes are made to the RichTextBox), and you also check the freezer variable:

```
Private Sub Form1_Closing(ByVal sender As Object, ByVal e As
    System.ComponentModel.CancelEventArgs) Handles
    MyBase.Closing

        If isdirty and freezer = True Then

            Dim r As Integer
            r = MsgBox("You have made changes in the TextBox.
Do you really want to quit without encrypting those
changes? Click Yes to END the program, click NO to return
to the program.", MsgBoxStyle.YesNo, "Do you really want
to quit?")

If r = 6 Then End
'OR
e.Cancel = True 'cancel the closing

            End If

End Sub
```

Recall that if Freezer is False, there has been one minute of activity. In that case, you don't want to halt the shutdown (you don't want the messagebox holding up shutdown).

Be very careful if you use the preceding technique. Messageboxes can be dangerous in a secret program like this one. If you were to shut down this program and walk away from your computer, it's possible that you wouldn't notice the messagebox. A messagebox will prevent the program from shutting down, allowing others to view your secrets if they come upon the computer while you're away. Rather than using a messagebox, a safer approach would be to add a form to the project and simply display it for 20 seconds or so (put a Timer control on it to keep track), informing users that they can click a button on that form to encrypt if they wish to. Then after 20 seconds elapses, End the program if the user has not clicked the button.

Public Key Encryption

Stronger than DES but slower, public key encryption is quite interesting in its own right. You employ *two* keys, one of which is not kept secret. Rather, it's made public.

In this chapter, you explored what is known as *symmetric* encryption. Both the encryption and decryption use the same single key and, functionally, the same algorithm. This technique is also known as *private key* encryption because you have to keep the key secret or the game is over and the cipher-text can be unlocked by anyone.

With *public key, asymmetric* encryption, anyone can know the public key, and the encryption process differs from the decryption process. Asymmetric encryption is fascinating but beyond the scope of this book. If you're interested in experimenting with it, take a look at the `RSACryptoServiceProvider` class in VB.NET.

Book IV

Programming for the Web

The 5th Wave   By Rich Tennant

©RICHTENNANT

VISUAL WEB DEVELOPMENT TEAM

"Give him air! Give him air! He'll be okay. He's just been exposed to some raw HTML code. It must have accidently flashed across his screen from the server."

Contents at a Glance

Chapter 1: Introduction to ASP.NET

In This Chapter

✔ **Understanding ASP.NET**

✔ **Discovering the advantages**

✔ **A quick look at HTML**

✔ **Installing IIS**

✔ **Trying your first ASP.NET program**

A SP.NET is the technology built into .NET that you use to create Web pages and other Internet-based applications. In fact, some say that programmers will have to migrate to VB.NET, in spite of the mature, tested technologies in VB 6. Why? Because in the future, if your applications don't access the Internet, they'll be as dated and inefficient as an application today that employs cassette tapes for storage. The Internet is quickly becoming a necessity.

ASP.NET offers significant benefits to programmers and developers, but it does grow out of an older technology. ASP (Active Server Pages) has been used the world over since early 1997. However useful and widespread it has become in the past four years, ASP nonetheless has some serious drawbacks.

ASP.NET avoids those drawbacks and also offers a variety of valuable new tools. ASP.NET is not merely the next version of ASP. ASP was thrown out and ASP.NET was written from the ground up. It's a brand new, object-oriented language.

This chapter offers an overview of the ASP.NET features that you may find useful as you expand your programming skills beyond the Windows/local hard drive platform and move into the brave new world of Internet programming.

ASP.NET involves two primary technologies: WebForms, which are user-interface controls with code behind them that together make a Web page for visitors to view in their browsers; and Web Services, which are a class or classes that provide functionality but no user interface. Web Services cannot be viewed in a browser; they are only used programmatically in a way similar to how a VB Windows form might use functions stored in a traditional VB Module. Web Services are covered in Book IV, Chapter 2.

Introducing ASP.NET

Programming for the Internet has been rather difficult and complex for quite a long time. ASP.NET to the rescue. In a white paper explaining the ASP.NET technology, Microsoft's Anthony Moore points out that ASP.NET and its Web Forms feature represent an important advance in programmer-friendly tools. He even compares these new tools to the vast improvement in traditional Windows programming efficiency that occurred when Visual Basic Version 1 was introduced more than 10 years ago.

Before VB came along, Windows applications were quite difficult to build — time-consuming, complex, and disagreeable. The C language, with all its syntactic convolutions and complicated, inverted phrasing, was all that was available to Windows programmers until VB 1 made its welcome appearance.

Similarly, programming to make Web sites interact with users was a nasty hassle. Now, though, ASP.NET, VB.NET, and improvements to the Visual Studio IDE bring VB-like efficiencies to what was tedious and cumbersome CGI and ASP programming. Mr. Moore puts it this way:

> As with creating Windows applications, creating a reliable and scalable Web application is extremely complicated. Our hope for ASP.NET is that it hides most of this complexity from you just as Visual Basic 1.0 did for Windows development. We also want to make the two experiences as similar to each other as possible so that you can "use the skills you already have."

I cover the advantages of ASP.NET later in this chapter, in the section "Multiple New Advantages."

The Purpose of ASP

The main idea of Active Server Pages is that people (or just one person) are surfing around the Internet (or a local intranet) and arrive at a page in your Web site. But instead of merely seeing static, canned content on that page (simple, pre-written HTML), you want to provide *dynamic* content. The best way to dynamically interact with a visitor is to generate the Web page on your server right then and there. Then you send the resulting fresh HTML to the visitor.

This is how you can make your Web site attractive, up-to-date, varying, and interesting to the visitor. Also note that a given Web page may be used by thousands of people simultaneously. This possibility requires some adjustments in how you program. For example, how can your program persist (remembers) global variables?

You explore Web application examples throughout this book and discover techniques you can use to address variable persistence and a variety of other Internet-programming related issues. Web page programming is not the same as writing a traditional Windows program where only one person at a time uses your application.

HTML's limitations

Web pages are programmed in a language called HTML, which browsers such as Internet Explorer understand and respond to. Pure HTML merely describes how text and graphics should *look* — size, location, color, and so on. You can do no significant computing with HTML. You cannot even add 2+2. By itself, HTML is as useless as an interior decorator at Desert Storm.

HTML merely specifies that a headline is relatively large, that some body text on the Web page is colored blue, that one graphic is lower on the page than another graphic, and so on. HTML also includes a few simple objects such as tables and listboxes. However, even the tables and listboxes are static, essentially lifeless, display objects.

To expand the capabilities of HTML, the idea of an *active server* was developed. It permits you to compute on your server; then the results of that computation are composed into a page of HTML. The HTML page is then sent off to the visitor's computer for viewing in his or her browser. This capability brings your Web pages alive.

ASP uses a script language (JavaScript or VBScript) to do its computing. Script languages are a subset of their parent language (Java or Visual Basic). However, with ASP, visitors don't need to have language features built into their computer. They get the *results* of your server-side computing, which is translated into ordinary HTML and then sent to them as a page that they can view. If they click a Submit button, for example, that fact is communicated back to your server, where further computing can take place and another HTML page is generated to be sent back to the visitor. This cycle can continue for as long as your visitor is interested.

ASP, therefore, permits you to do lots of useful things on your server that you could never do with HTML. You can access a database, insert prewritten components, revise your Web pages (include news about your company, today's date, and so on) so that visitors don't get bored seeing the same content each time they visit, and many other valuable techniques. The visitor sees the most recent product announcements, late-breaking information, and anything else you want to provide. Your Web pages become interactive, responsive, and timely.

Firewalls and other necessary evils

Because ASP sends standard HTML to the visitor, ASP overcomes a browser-compatibility problem. It doesn't matter if people are using Netscape, Internet Explorer (IE), or some other browser — they can view your standard HTML pages. In addition, firewalls — designed to keep hackers, whackers, viruses, worms, and other invaders out of your computer — are designed to permit HTML to pass unchallenged. Innocent, merely descriptive, merely visual HTML can do no damage to your computer, any more than a picture of a gun can fire.

You can insert scripting into an HTML page and, therefore, let the visitor's computer do some limited computing. This is called *client-side* scripting. It works fine if you're sure that all your visitors have the necessary language components installed on their machines, that their security settings permit scripting (many block scripts), and that they are all using the same browser (and that browser supports scripting). So, if you're merely running a site that is intended for use in-house on an intranet, and everybody in your company uses IE, and you're sure they all have the right components on their hard drives, go ahead and try some client-side computing. Intranets often permit scripting. However, you have many reasons to prefer server-side computing that sends HTML results to clients.

ASP, during its relatively brief life, served us well. It offered easy access to tools such as Excel or databases; it improved security; it permitted targeted data transmission (by sending only what a particular visitor requests) to speed up getting a page to the visitor; it allowed browser and component independence; and so on. However, ASP had its weaknesses (including clumsy validation, state management, and caching). ASP is now passing into history as an important first step in Internet programming. Its successor, ASP.NET, offers us major advantages over ASP. In sum, ASP.NET cures most of the weaknesses found in ASP.

Marching toward ASP.NET

Programmers wanted more than ASP offered, and now you can see file and Web page extensions named ASPX. That extension tells you that ASP.NET is being used. In fact, much ASP source code can run just fine without any serious modifications by using the ASP.NET engine. So, to force an ASP source code file to run under ASP.NET, just change its filename extension from .ASP to ASPX. In some cases, it can work without modification.

ASP.NET doesn't require that you jettison any existing ASP code you've written. In fact, ASP pages can run side by side, simultaneously with ASP.NET pages. You can keep your current ASP Web applications running on the same server as new ASP.NET Web applications you create.

The following list is an overview of the strengths and features you'll find when you begin using ASP.NET:

✦ ASP.NET code is easier to write, debug, and maintain than ASP, particularly for larger projects. ASP.NET provides you with a generous suite of debugging tools that were simply unavailable in ASP (including breakpoints, tracing, and extensive error messages). ASP.NET debugging techniques are covered in Book IV, Chapter 6.

✦ ASP.NET code can be written in the full Visual Basic.NET language, so you can leverage some of your existing programming knowledge, transferring your experience from the Windows OS platform to the browser intranet/Internet platform. Script languages — used in the past by ASP — offer most, but not all, of the commands and features of full languages. Programmers wanted full languages. ASP.NET allows you to program with the full power of languages such as Visual Basic .NET or C#.

✦ The Visual Studio .NET integrated design environment offers you all the support you've always enjoyed with mature, RAD (rapid application development) languages such as Visual Basic. In the past, RAD was not largely available to Web programmers.

✦ Often you need to write very little source code of your own. ASP.NET gives you a toolbox full of smart, rich server-side components that you can just drop right into your ASP.NET projects. (Maintain state, validate, cache — you'll find that many programming problems are now handled for you by components.)

✦ Legacy ActiveX components that you've written can be used with .NET languages.

✦ Powerful IDE debugging tools are available.

✦ You get WYSIWYG design and editing.

✦ Wizards can step you through tedious or complex tasks.

✦ The object-oriented foundation of ASP.NET programming can make it easier to read, reuse, maintain, and share code among groups of programmers who must work together on a single project.

✦ ASP.NET VB.NET source code is written in a separate window and saved in a separate file from the HTML. (HTML is also used to contribute to an ASP.NET Web page.) This *code-behind* feature makes life easier because you don't have to try to read through mixed HTML/VB.NET source code.

**Book IV
Chapter 1**

**Introduction to
ASP.NET**

Segregated source files

When writing ASP, you had to mix your programming (script source code) in with the HTML source code.

These script/HTML files used to grow large and unwieldy — including the mess that programmers have for decades called *spaghetti code* because the execution path (what happens when) was difficult to trace by merely reading through the code. ASP source code was a patchwork quilt of HTML and scripting (code). What's more, usually the person who is talented at designing the *look* of a Web site (using HTML) is not the best person to write scripting (using script or, now in ASP.NET, using VB.NET).

Here's the scenario in the past when ASP pages were written: A designer comes up with a nice-looking page. He hands this (purely HTML code) to a programmer who inserts his ASP scripting into the file. Next, the artist decides to make some changes to the page's appearance, so the .HTM file is passed back to the artist for some touching up. Pretty soon, the artist and the programmer are stepping on each other's toes and the source code is a mish-mash.

ASP.NET solves this problem by separating programming source code and visual design (HTML) source code into two different files. (You *can* segregate files in traditional ASP with Include files and style sheets — but this isn't as effective a solution as ASP.NET now offers.) With ASP.NET, programming code is stored in a code-behind file, separate from the HTML file that the designer works with.

Browser independence

The old bugaboo about whether users are using IE or Navigator/ Communicator is now easier to handle. ASP.NET includes components (prewritten controls that you just drop into your ASP.NET source code) that are sensitive and can detect the user's browser version. The component is smart enough to generate HTML best suited to the visitor's browser. So, you, the programmer, no longer have to write various If...Then structures to accommodate the 4 percent or so of people who've chosen not to use the latest version of IE.

Some people, though, still have older, less capable versions of IE, such as IE Version 3. When it detects a less-capable browser, the ASP.NET component "gracefully degrades" the Web page (making it look as good as the limited IE 3 resources can manage). These variations in browsers used to pose a serious problem for programmers; you had to write all the code yourself to handle this problem, and writing that code was *hard*. Also, the new client-container-sensitive ASP.NET components can even work with the new specialized devices such as handheld units. You really have to be graceful when you degrade a Web page from the typical 17-inch desktop monitor to a little 3-inch screen.

Runs faster

ASP.NET also runs faster than scripted (interpreted) code. ASP.NET is compiled so that it can offer various efficiencies such as just-in-time (JIT) compilation, optimization, early binding, and caching. You, the developer, can specify when compilation takes place. Source code is translated into an intermediate language (IL). Then, if you wish, the IL can be translated (compiled) into native code right away. Or, if you prefer, you can choose just-in-time compilation that occurs when the project is executed. The older ASP interpreted code means that every time a page was requested, the source code had to be re-read. Obviously, this can be a serious performance hit. Also, scalability suffers: Interpreted pages won't run, as-is, in a Web farm. (A Web farm is an Internet site that uses two or more server machines to handle the large amount of traffic from visitors to the site.)

The ASP.NET scalability makes it possible to permit many incoming requests to be handled at the same time, without slugging the servers into catatonia as a result.

Multiple New Advantages

The ASP.NET runtime has been built to take advantage of multiprocessor or clustered server structures. Also, the runtime ensures robust, continuous performance by keeping track of all running processes. If any process freezes or begins to leak, the runtime kills the process that is behaving badly and spawns a new process to take its place.

ASP.NET sits on top of the .NET runtime. .NET is designed from the ground up as an Internet-based platform (as opposed to a hard-drive–based platform like Windows). .NET will ultimately offer such interesting services as natural language processing, rich application development, a new user interface, and even a new file system.

The ASP.NET Page Framework handles events in a straightforward way that will be familiar to any Visual Basic programmer who has worked with VB forms.

Easier deployment

Deployment is simplified. You add an ASP.NET application to your server merely by copying the ASP.NET application's folder to the server's hard drive. No need to go through an elaborate setup and registration process. You can even upgrade an ASP.NET application on the fly while it's running, without needing to reboot the server (because the Registry is not involved). When you deployed small ASP applications, you didn't have too much of a hassle. But if you had larger, more complex ASP n-tier apps that used components, registration, versioning, and other problems (sometimes called "DLL Hell"), they made life difficult for programmers and administrators alike. ASP.NET completely abolishes DLL locking, XML configuration files, and component registration.

To deploy your ASP.NET Web app, just copy the main folder (which automatically copies its subfolders as well). Controls located in your application's BIN subfolder are simply available to your application; you need not worry about registering them or worry that they are locked. They're not locked and they're not registered — but they *work* just fine. That's the new model. Do you have a newer, better version of a control that you've written and now improved? Just copy it into the folder on the server. It runs right away.

Also, adjusting settings in an ASP.NET application is as simple as changing a text file. ASP.NET applications avoid Registry complexity by maintaining their customization and other configuration data in simple text files. No need to use special administrator utilities, such as the MMC, or to hand-edit the Registry itself.

You have some new terms to learn. For example, *WinForms* and *WebForms*. A VB.NET WinForm corresponds to the classic, familiar VB form. A WebForm is the name used in VB.NET to describe a Web page.

As you've seen in this chapter, ASP.NET isn't simply an incremental, modest upgrade of ASP. Instead, it has been completely rewritten to take full advantage of the .NET environment. Segregated source files, browser independence, a common IDE, language independence, improved security and deployment, and other features should make ASP.NET the language of choice for many new applications. If you want to get your hands on some ASP.NET code, look at the next section of this chapter, "Setting Up IIS for ASP.NET."

Setting Up IIS for ASP.NET

Before you can actually start experimenting with ASP.NET, you first must ensure that your computer has the necessary programs and utilities installed to support and debug ASP.NET. After you accomplish that, this section shows you how to build a simple program that demonstrates some of the power and potential of ASP.NET.

In the past couple of years, many people have had problems setting up a local ASP testing platform. By *local,* I mean that your single, desktop computer simulates both sides of an Internet conversation (the client browser communicating with a remote server's Web site, and vice versa).

In other words, you want to use a single desktop machine to write and debug ASP or ASP.NET applications. You don't want to have to put your code on a server and then run around to another machine and "visit" the Web page on that server, just to be able to test your ASP.NET code.

Instead, you set up a simulated "local server." To do that, you need to install Microsoft's "fake" server right there on your local hard drive. This allows you to test your ASP code by "deploying" it to the fake server (pretending to be a Web site) and then watching how it works on the "client" browser when you "visit" that Web site with your copy of Internet Explorer.

ASP and ASP.NET run on a server (*ASP* means Active *Server* Pages). When the Web page on which ASP.NET code resides is requested by a browser, ASP.NET composes HTML code that displays the results of any VB programming you've included in the page, adds that code to any other HTML in your source code for that page, and then sends the finished page back to the visitor's browser.

At this point, the results are displayed to the visitor. This behavior (because the computing is distributed across two machines) seems as if it requires two computers to test it: one computer acting as a server for the other client computer. However, for many developers, it is inconvenient to set up a two-machine, client-server system. They prefer to work on their single computer when developing and testing ASP.NET programs.

Recognizing that a two-machine testing system is often impractical, Microsoft came up with a cool way to simulate a client/server setup within a single computer. This simulation was called Personal Web Server in Windows 98 and Peer Web Services in NT 4. Now it's called the *Personal Tier* and *Personal Web Manager*. Don't ask. Microsoft has always been better at thinking up new terminology, than maintaining consistency.

The XP operating system comes with IIS, so you don't need a substitute. Also, XP users may want to consider Microsoft's impressive (and free) Web Matrix Project, which includes a development server. Read all about it at http://aspnetpro.com/features/2002/08/asp200208sm_f/asp200208sm_f.asp and http://asp.net/webmatrix/default.aspx?tabindex= 4&tabid=46.

Personal Tier applications run totally within the Internet Explorer process. Personal Tier, therefore, requires a different way of accessing files stored on your computer.

In this book, we're using Windows 2000. In Windows 2000, the client/server simulator is called Personal Web Manager and it is part of IIS, the Microsoft Internet Information Services. However, by default, IIS is not installed when Windows 2000 is installed.

Follow these steps

To be able to use Visual Basic .NET and test ASP.NET examples in Windows 2000, you need to install IIS and the Script Debugger. If IIS isn't properly set up on your computer, you'll get the error message shown in Figure 1-1 if you try, for example, to create a new Visual Basic .NET Web application project.

Figure 1-1:
Without IIS installed on your machine, Web server simulation isn't possible, and therefore you can't test ASP.NET code.

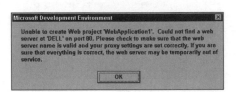

Alas, installing a "personal Web" on Windows 2000 (a Web server and server extensions) is neither automatic nor straightforward. Follow these steps:

1. **On a computer running Windows 2000, choose Start⇨Settings⇨ Control Panel.**

2. **Double-click the Add/Remove Programs icon in Control Panel.**

3. **In the Add/Remove Programs dialog box, click the Add/Remove Windows Components icon located on the left side. (If you are running Windows 2000 Server, you must click the Components button on the right side of this dialog box after clicking the Add/Remove Windows Components icon located on the left side.)**

The Windows Components Wizard opens.

4. **Click the check box next to Internet Information Services (IIS) and Script Debugger.**

5. **Click the Next button.**

After some preliminaries, you are asked to insert the Windows 2000 CD.

6. Click OK.

The wizard copies the necessary files from the CD. This can take quite a while. Don't lose heart if nothing seems to be happening.

7. Click Finish.

8. To see what you've accomplished, click Start⇨Programs⇨ Administrative Tools.

After you complete these steps, you see that three new utilities have been added to your Administrative tools:

✦ Internet Services Manager

✦ Personal Web Manager

✦ Server Extensions Administrator

Now you have a fake "Web" and fake "server" to work with. They *are* fake, but they do such a good imitation of a real server sitting somewhere out there on the Internet that neither your browser nor ASP.NET can tell the difference.

Trying out your first ASP.NET application

Okay, it's time to try some ASP.NET in action. Follow these steps to see how easy Web programming can be when you work with ASP.NET:

1. Choose File⇨New⇨Project in the VB.NET IDE.

The New Project dialog box opens.

2. In the Name field, type FirstWebApp.

3. Double-click the ASP.NET Web Application icon.

The IDE grinds away, setting things up. If you have a firewall installed, such as ZoneAlarm, it may pop up and ask "Do you want to allow Microsoft Visual Studio .NET to act as a server?" Say "Yes!" Indeed you do! That's the faux server trying to do its thing. You may also be asked "Do you want to access the Internet?" Again, that's what you want. Answer "Yes!" Your computer thinks that the IDE is accessing the Internet, which it's not but the simulation is working.

After the dust settles, you see the WebForm design window, shown in Figure 1-2.

**Book IV
Chapter 1**

**Introduction to
ASP.NET**

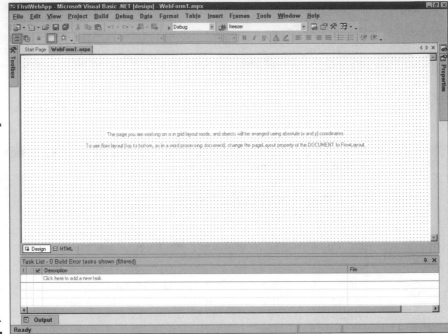

Figure 1-2:
Here's
where you
create Web
pages with
VB.NET.
It is similar,
but not
identical,
to the
Windows
form design
environment.

After VS.NET creates a new WebForm, you see a message that you are currently in grid layout mode in the Design window. In other words, any controls that you add to this page are located wherever you put them. This is also known as *absolute positioning* — meaning that you can move controls anywhere on the page. The alternative is called *flow layout,* which sounds good but isn't: All your controls (and other elements such as text) are stacked up one on top of each other, flush left against the left side of the page. This is traditional HTML positioning; it is restrictive and leads to pages that are visually out of balance, amateur, and disturbing. However, should you ever wish to use this mode, you can change the document's (the WebForm's) `PageLayout` property to `FlowLayout` in the Properties window.

4. **Using the Toolbox, add a Label, two TextBoxes, and a Button to your WebForm (and change the Label's `Text` property in the properties window), as shown in Figure 1-3.**

5. **Double-click the Button.**

   Just as in traditional VB, you are taken to a code window. This is the *code-behind* file, so called because it works behind the scenes to provide computing power to an associated HTML page.

Don't be distracted by the various "designer code" that's been inserted into the code window. You can ignore it. You are simply going to provide some source code in the button's Click event that adds together the numbers that the user enters into the two TextBoxes. Just for fun, you also display the current time. Repeatedly clicking the button updates the time, illustrating the ASP.NET cycle: The user's browser sends a Click message to the server, the page is dynamically refreshed at the server, and then the page is sent back to the browser where it's repainted.

6. Type the following into the Button_Click event:

```
Private Sub Button1_Click(ByVal sender As
    System.Object, ByVal e As System.EventArgs) Handles
    Button1.Click

        Dim firstnum, secondnum, totalnum As Integer

        firstnum = CInt(TextBox1.Text)
        secondnum = CInt(TextBox2.Text)

        totalnum = firstnum + secondnum
```

```
          Label1.Text = "The sum is: " & totalnum &
"<br/>" & _
          "The current time is: " & Format(Now, "h:mm")

      End Sub
```

7. **Press F5.**

   It takes a little while for the communication to be set up between the "server" and your browser, but pretty soon Internet Explorer should appear with the page loaded into it.

8. **Type in a number in each Textbox, and then click the button.**

   You see the response from the "server," as shown in Figure 1-4.

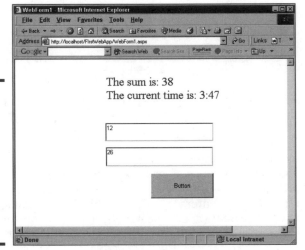

Figure 1-4:
Finally, communication between your simulated server and your browser.

This book's source code has been saved in plain-vanilla Notepad .TXT format. However, if you copy source code into the VB.NET IDE from a word processor such as WordPad or Word, you'll find that all sorts of extra formatting codes show up in addition to the simple text characters. For example, look at this simple source code line:

```
<p />       Enter first number: <input type="text"
    id="txtfirst" runat="server" NAME="txtfirst">
```

If you copy the preceding line from Word into the HTML view in the VB.NET IDE, that line inflates and ends up looking like the following pseudo-HTML:

```
<p />        Enter first number: <input type="text"
    id="txtfirst" runat="server" NAME="txtfirst">
<p class=GX>&lt;p /&gt;<span style='mso-tab-count:1'>
    </span>Enter first
number: &lt;input type=&quot;text&quot;
    id=&quot;txtfirst&quot;
runat=&quot;server&quot; NAME=&quot;txtfirst&quot;&gt;</p>
```

One solution — should you ever witness this kind of inflation — involves a two-stage copy and paste process. First, copy the source code from Word and paste it into Notepad. When you do that, Notepad automatically strips off all the formatting codes, leaving behind the plain text. Then you can copy the source code from Notepad and paste it into the VB.NET IDE successfully. Another solution is to copy it, but then choose Edit⇨Paste as HTML in the IDE.

Chapter 2: Everything's Eventual

In This Chapter

✔ Looking at ASP.NET source code

✔ Handling simple validation

✔ Preserving values within a page

✔ Preserving values across pages

✔ Using the `Session` property

✔ Alternative ways to preserve values

✔ Avoiding cookies

Throughout this book you find examples illustrating various aspects of ASP.NET and VB.NET. However, it's worth taking the time to consider several issues right here. There are interesting, novel facets to ASP.NET source code, facets you'll want to understand, such as splitting code between server and client, preserving the state of your variables, and understanding why you might want to avoid using cookies.

Understanding ASP.NET Source Code

Server-side controls is a new concept that you want to understand. Load the example ASP.NET program that appears at the end of Book IV, Chapter 1. Then click the tab at the top of the design window titled WebForm1.aspx. This tab can display the HTML code — so now click the HTML tab at the bottom of the design window.

Notice that when you added the textboxes, the label, and the button to the WebForm, VB.NET enclosed them within an HTML form:

```
<form id="Form1" method="post" runat="server">
```

Note that `runat="server"` attribute. ASP.NET sees this command and automatically forces the Value of server-side controls to be POSTed (sent) back to the page. Each control within the HTML form also includes the `runat="server"` command.

Having server-side controls is a great feature. It preserves the state of the controls and lets the server know the values that the user entered. (In the example program, the values POSTed back are the numbers that the user entered to be added together.) ASP.NET does this for you automatically.

The problem of persistence

When users fill in a form on your Web site, they don't like it at all if they come back to that form later and have to fill it in a second time! They expect stability and efficiency. They expect data to be durable, not to evaporate just because a button is clicked or the browser screen is redrawn. This durability is a quality known to programmers as *persistence*. Data or variables that survive various changes are said to *persist*.

How does ASP.NET manage to preserve *state* (the current status of something) and values? ASP.NET makes some changes to your source code when you use server-side controls. Press F5 to run the example program again in Internet Explorer, type in a couple of numbers, and then click the button. Now view the changes to your original source code by choosing View⇨ Source in IE. (The numbers I entered are shown here in boldface.)

```
<!DOCTYPE HTML PUBLIC "-//W3C//DTD HTML 4.0
    Transitional//EN">
<HTML>
        <HEAD>
              <title>WebForm1</title>
              <meta name="GENERATOR" content="Microsoft
    Visual Studio.NET 7.0">
              <meta name="CODE_LANGUAGE" content="Visual
    Basic 7.0">
              <meta name="vs_defaultClientScript"
    content="JavaScript">
              <meta name="vs_targetSchema"
    content="http://schemas.microsoft.com/intellisense/ie5">
        </HEAD>
        <body MS_POSITIONING="GridLayout">
              <form name="Form1" method="post"
    action="WebForm1.aspx" id="Form1">

<input type="hidden" name="__VIEWSTATE"
    value="dDwtMTM3MDk5MDcwNDs7Pp+nbdCOCxMLpKOSw13VDXMjYrZ/"
    />

                    <input name="TextBox1" type="text"
    value="345" id="TextBox1"
    style="height:42px;width:252px;Z-INDEX: 101; LEFT: 209px;
    POSITION: absolute; TOP: 148px" />
                    <input name="TextBox2" type="text"
    value="6" id="TextBox2" style="height:44px;width:250px;Z-
    INDEX: 102; LEFT: 210px; POSITION: absolute; TOP: 204px"
    />
```

```
                    <input type="submit" name="Button1"
value="Button" id="Button1"
style="height:57px;width:146px;Z-INDEX: 103; LEFT: 315px;
POSITION: absolute; TOP: 265px" />
                    <span id="Label1" style="font-
size:Large;height:29px;width:569px;Z-INDEX: 104; LEFT:
211px; POSITION: absolute; TOP: 37px">The sum is:
351<br/>The current time is: 7:02</span>
                </form>
        </body>
</HTML>
```

You see some surprises. ASP.NET has been a busy little bunny. This source code is the HTML, which ASP.NET composes in response to your clicking the button and then sends to the browser, containing the results of the addition and the current time.

ASP.NET looked at your source code, made some additions and adjustments, and then created the HTML you now see using IE's View⇨Source option. Compare this HTML to the HTML in the IDE. (Your source will look similar to this, not identical, because some elements must necessarily be unique to your code, such as the current time.)

Notice that the Value elements in the textboxes in browser HTML source code contain the numbers that you typed in before clicking the button. These values have *persisted* during the round trip from browser to server and back to browser.

Also notice that no VB.NET source code is in the browser source. The VB.NET *code-behind* sits "behind" the HTML and does any computing that's required. But the only reference to the VB.NET is action="WebForm1. aspx". The VB.NET code runs on the server and is never sent to the user's browser; only pure HTML is sent to the user (well, you can also send DHTML and other items if you wish, but VB is certainly never sent). But if you do try to send DHTML or executable objects, most firewalls scream bloody murder and do everything they can to block the transmitted page. Recall that security concerns (concerns that executables may be viruses) are the primary reason that code execution must take place server-side rather than in the visitor's computer.

Using ID to access controls

ASP.NET retained your form's and controls' NAME and also used those names for the ID attributes as well. Every server control is given a unique ID (and if you don't supply one yourself, ASP.NET will supply it). Unique IDs allow you to write programming for every server control (identifying a control by its ID). Note that this entire page in the browser is, in some abstract sense, an *object,* containing input and output features, behaviors (adding numbers), properties (values), and events (click). However, unlike an ordinary (encapsulated) control, it looks like ordinary HTML to a firewall — so it is permitted to pass over the firewall into a visitor's browser. In this way, computation within a Web page becomes possible.

Simple Validation

With ASP.NET, the full VB.NET language is available to you server-side. (You could also use other languages such as C#.) You can also do all kinds of computing with VB.NET. You can implement validation safeguards on the server, for example. Here's an example showing how to add some code to the example from Book IV, Chapter 1 that reacts if the user enters a larger number than you want in Textbox1 (the new source code you should type in is in boldface):

```
Private Sub Button1_Click(ByVal sender As System.Object,
    ByVal e As System.EventArgs) Handles Button1.Click

        If CInt(TextBox1.Text) > 999 Then

            Label1.Text = "You must provide a number lower
than 1000."

            Exit Sub

        End If

        Dim firstnum, secondnum, totalnum As Integer

        firstnum = CInt(TextBox1.Text)
        secondnum = CInt(TextBox2.Text)

        totalnum = firstnum + secondnum

        Label1.Text = "The sum is: " & totalnum & "<br/>" & _
        "The current time is: " & Format(Now, "h:mm")

    End Sub
```

Just as in Windows applications, you can refer in your code-behind module to the various properties of controls on your WebForm. In this example, you check to see what users have typed into their browsers in the top textbox, by looking at its text property. Then, if necessary, you put a message into the text property of the label to warn the user. Also, you refuse to add the numbers together (Exit Sub) until the user responds to your warning.

Notice the <br/> embedded in the string used for Label1.Text. It's HTML, not VB, but when you're writing for a Web page, special characters like that are necessary. In a Windows-style VB.NET program, you can use the carriage-return linefeed constant `vbCrLf` to force the text display to move down one line in the label, as in the following code:

```
Label1.Text = "The sum is: " & totalnum & vbCrLf & _
"The current time is: " & Format(Now, "h:mm")
```

However, when your text is being displayed in the HTML of a WebForm, you must use the HTML tag for line break: `<br/>`.

Managing State

Given the back-and-forth, client-server-client, divided nature of ASP.NET applications, you may well be wondering, just what can I, the programmer, do to manage and preserve variables and to know what is going on at any given time? For example, is this the first time visitors are seeing my Web page? Or have they been interacting with it for several minutes and have made several round trips between their browsers and my server? Perhaps they've clicked a button several times. How can you know?

You have a way to tell whether a form is about to make its first trip to the visitor's browser or whether it has been posted back (meaning that previous requests have occurred from this particular client — this visitor — at this particular time). You can use an `If...Then` construct in your ASP.NET source code to determine whether this is the first trip.

Why does this matter? For example, say that you need to fill a listbox only once (when the visitor first requests your page) with the names of the books you sell. You don't need to fill this listbox over and over, each time the visitor sends another request to view the page (by clicking a Submit button or whatever). Here's how to detect whether this is the first time:

```
Private Sub Page_Load(ByVal sender As System.Object, ByVal e
    As System.EventArgs) Handles MyBase.Load
        'Put user code to initialize the page here

    If Not Page.IsPostBack Then
            'make a connection to the database and fill a
ListBox with book title info.

        Response.Write("First Time")

    Else

        Response.Write("Not the first time...")
'make a connection to the database and fill a ListBox
with book title info.

        End If

End Sub
```

You don't need to access this database every time the user sends a postback. That's unnecessary and wastes time. Worse, it also destroys information you may need from the user. For example, suppose that the user clicked one of the items in your `ListBox`, so you need to know (for processing on the server in your VB.NET code) which item the visitor selected. If you refill the `ListBox` during the postback, you'll *destroy* the user's selection. You can no longer query the `SelectedItem.Text` property of the `ListBox` if you refill it.

The WebForm's `Page_Load` event is triggered every time the page gets loaded into your server, so you can use it to react to the first request, and then use it to react differently to subsequent requests. Query the `IsPostBack` property of the `Page` object to decide how your code should react.

Every time a Web page is requested or posted back (another kind of request), the server processes its events. First the `Page_Load` event is triggered, causing the page and any controls' ViewStates to be automatically restored. Any other triggered events on the page are processed next (although they are not triggered in any particular order that the server can detect). You can respond to these events in your code.

After all the controls' events have triggered, the `Page_Unload` event triggers. In that event, you can write code to terminate database connections, discard objects, and otherwise gracefully close down the page. You can also employ similar `Session_OnStart` and `Session_OnEnd` events.

Preserving values within a single page

Now consider how to preserve variables in the WebForm environment. In the wonderful world of the Web, objects blink in and out of existence faster than bubbles at a carwash. You, the programmer, must know how to make some information durable in this flickering, often transitory, world of Internet communication.

How do you force information to persist between round trips from the user's browser and your server?

Recall that given the high traffic possible on the Internet (many people potentially communicating all at once with your server), it is impossible to preserve controls, variables, and other information in the same way that this data is held in RAM memory when one person is using one machine, as is the case with traditional Windows applications.

Remember that the WebForm server composes a new HTML WebForm page each time it replies to the user's browser, and then it sends that page off to the browser and *throws away* its copy of what it just sent off. But perhaps you need data to persist. For example, what if you want to permit the user to click a button, and you want to increment a counter each time the button is clicked?

Although ASP.NET doesn't keep Web pages in memory on the server after it sends them off, it does preserve most states on a page between round trips from user to server. It preserves controls and their properties, for example, in the ViewState (and you can also use the ViewState object to store your data).

Variables aren't automatically preserved, though. There are several strategies you can use. You can, for example, use the ViewState object — a bag that you can dump information into and trust that the information survives the round trip from the user to the server and back to the user. Consider the ViewState object as behaving similarly to the traditional VB Static command, forcing data persistence within a procedure. The ViewState object is useful to store information for an individual visitor to your site. (To preserve data needed by *all* visitors to your site, use the Application object, described later in this section.)

A ViewState object can store more complex data than simple data types can store. A ViewState object can also hold hash tables, arraylists, and dataset objects. Here's how it works.

Put a Button control on a WebForm. Double-click that button to get to its Click event. Type this into the Button's click event:

```
Private Sub Button1_Click(ByVal sender As System.Object,
    ByVal e As System.EventArgs) Handles Button1.Click

        Dim counter As Integer
        counter = CInt(ViewState("counter"))
        counter += 1
        ViewState("counter") = counter   'save the value of
counter
        Response.Write(counter.ToString())

End Sub
```

Press F5 to run this Web application and then notice that each time you click the button, the variable counter increments and displays the new count in the browser. Remember that each click triggers a round trip to the server, and that the page is *discarded* by the server each time it sends that page back to the browser. Nonetheless, given that you dumped the counter's value into the State "bag," the value of counter is saved between those round trips.

Preserving values across pages

You can choose from a couple of good ways to pass data *between* pages in a Web site. The first one is simple, but it's not secure, so don't pass sensitive data using this technique. (You find out how to pass data securely later in this chapter, in the "Storing data with the Session property" section.)

Follow these steps to slyly add some data to the HTML that describes a hyperlink and then pass it using that hyperlink:

1. **Click the Design tab at the bottom of the WebForm1.aspx design window.**

You see the design mode for this WebForm.

2. **Click the WebForms tab in the Toolbox.**

You see all the WebForm controls.

3. **Double-click the HyperLink control icon.**

A HyperLink is added to your WebForm1.ASPX page.

4. **Choose Project⇨Add Web Form.**

You see the Add New Item dialog box.

5. **Double-click the WebForm icon in the Add New Item dialog box.**

A second Web page (named WebForm2.ASPX) is added to this project.

6. **Go back to WebForm1 and, if it's not selected, click the hyperlink control on WebForm1 to select it.**

7. **In the Properties window click the** NavigateUrl **property of the HyperLink control to select it.**

8. **Click the ... (ellipsis) button in the** NavigateUrl **property.**

The Select URL dialog box appears, as shown in Figure 2-1.

Figure 2-1:
Use this dialog box to direct a hyperlink on one Web page (WebForm) to target another Web page in your project.

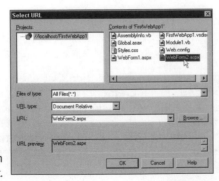

9. **Double-click WebForm2.ASPX in the Select URL dialog box.**

WebForm2 now becomes the target of the Hyperlink control and the dialog box closes.

10. **Change the HyperLink1 control's** Text **property to "Go to page 2 in My Site."**

You also want to add a little information to the Hyperlink control's HTML code. This is a way that you can pass data between Web pages. In this example, you pass data from WebPage1 to WebPage2. Follow these steps to create the code that passes data:

1. **Click the HTML tab on the bottom of the WebForm1.aspx design window.**

You see the HTML view.

2. **Locate the hyperlink control HTML code and modify its URL property by adding** ?MyString=3 **to the code, like this (shown in boldface):**

```
<asp:HyperLink id="HyperLink1" style="Z-INDEX: 105;
LEFT: 543px; POSITION: absolute; TOP: 159px"
runat="server" Height="46px" Width="198px"
NavigateUrl="WebForm2.aspx?MyString=3">Go to page
two in my site.</asp:HyperLink>
```

The absolute positioning values (such as TOP: 159px) will differ in your code, based on where you positioned your hyperlink on your page.

3. **Click the WebForm2.aspx tab at the top of the design window.**

The design window displays WebForm2.

4. **Double-click the Button control icon in the Toolbox.**

A Button is added to WebForm2.

5. **Double-click the Button on WebForm2.**

You are taken to the code window and the Button's Click event.

6. **Type the following code. It retrieves the value of** MyString **and makes it available to WebForm2's VB.NET code:**

```
Private Sub Button1_Click(ByVal sender As
    System.Object, ByVal e As System.EventArgs) Handles
    Button1.Click

    Dim MyString As String

    MyString =
CStr(Request.QueryString("MyString"))

    Response.Write("The data was passed and it is:
" & MyString)

End Sub
```

7. **Press F5 to test your project.**

    You see WebForm1, the startup page, in Internet Explorer.

8. **Click the hyperlink.**

    IE displays WebForm2.

9. **Click the Button control on WebForm2.**

    You see that the value of the variable `MyString`, which was 3, has been passed to WebForm2 from WebForm1.

Notice that double-clicking the button to add it to Webform2 puts it in the topmost/leftmost position on WebForm2. So, by default, the button covers up the text "The data."

Using the URL to store data is highly insecure. Not only is it easy for others to view the URL, but they can also make changes to it and send it back to your server with poison data. A better way to store data — if security is an issue — is to use the `Session` property, as I explain in the following section.

Storing data with the Session property

An alternative, more secure, and perhaps more elegant way to save information between round trips to the server is to employ the `Session` property of the `Page` object. Session variables do use up memory on the server (as opposed to client-side cookies, which are maintained on the visitors' individual hard drives).

Remember that the `ViewState` object described earlier in this chapter works only within a single Web page, but the session state has enough scope to embrace all the Web pages in a Web site. So you can use session state to pass data between a Web site's pages.

To see how this works, follow these steps:

1. **Start a new WebForm project, and then click the WebForm1.aspx tab in the design window.**

    WebForm1 is displayed in the design window.

2. **Double-click the Button control in the Toolbox twice.**

    You add two Button controls to WebForm1.

3. **Double-click Button1.**

    You are taken to the code window and the Button's `Click` event.

4. **Type in the following code that adds two items of data to the `Session` property:**

```
Private Sub Button1_Click(ByVal sender As
    System.Object, ByVal e As System.EventArgs) Handles
Button1.Click

    Session("Message") = "This information"
    Session("SecondMessage") = "comes from the
session property "

End Sub
```

Note that the name within the parentheses is equivalent to a variable name, and the data following the = sign is equivalent to a variable's value.

5. Click the WebForm1.aspx tab in the design window.

WebForm1 is displayed in the design window.

6. Double-click Button2.

You are taken to the code window and you see Button2's Click event.

7. Type this into Button2's Click event:

```
Private Sub Button2_Click(ByVal sender As
    System.Object, ByVal e As System.EventArgs) Handles
Button2.Click

    Dim firstinfo = Session("Message")
    Dim secondinfo = Session("SecondMessage")

    Response.Write(firstinfo.ToString & " " &
secondinfo.ToString)

End Sub
```

8. Press F5 to run the project and click Button1.

The data and its associated "variable names" are stored in the session property.

9. Click Button2.

Internet Explorer displays the information that's been retrieved from the Session property.

Alternatives to the Session Property

The Session property is one of several clever ways that you can store values in ASP.NET. This section covers other ways to save values in ASP.NET projects. Each has its advantages.

Book IV
Chapter 2

Everything's
Eventual

The Application object

Use this technique only for values that don't frequently change after your Web project has been instantiated; otherwise, you can slow things down. The Application object works similarly to the Session property, except you must lock and unlock Application objects:

```
'add a variable and provide a value to it:
        Application.Lock()
        Application.Add("namehold", "Rita Jones")
        Application.UnLock()
```

The Application object is best used to store values that your entire application needs, such as your company's current sale items or a database connection string.

Public variables

Put Public variables in a Module, and they remain preserved during the lifetime of the process:

```
Module MyVars

    Public counter As Integer

End Module

Public Sub Page_Load(ByVal sender As System.Object, ByVal e
    As System.EventArgs) Handles MyBase.Load

        counter += 1
        Response.Write(counter)

End Sub
```

Each time you press F5 to refresh this page in your browser, the next higher number is displayed — demonstrating that the value of counter has been preserved. Declaring counter in a Module makes it available to your entire project (and to as many Web Pages as you have in this project). You can add a Module by choosing Project⇨Add New Item and then double-clicking the module icon.

Why Bother?

Why all this concern over what would have simply been global Public variables in earlier versions of Visual Basic? Why, now that you're creating Web sites, should you have to be bothered with new, tricky ways of preserving variables' values?

The answer is that Web programming is necessarily different from traditional Windows programming. Put simply: When you write traditional VB Windows applications, you're working within a limited, predictable, stable, one-on-one environment. There's just the application's user and his or her hard drive. That's a predictable relationship, simplifying everything from security to communications.

But if you expose your server hard drive to the Internet when you create a Web page, you're permitting perhaps thousands of people to access your window/form/page at the same time. If your site is really popular, it may be hosting more than 10,000 simultaneous visitors. Can your source code embrace one person, but then suddenly embrace 10,000 people? Can your source code expand its reach? (The term *scalability* describes your code's capability to handle large numbers of visitors.) Also, what do you do about the proven fact that out of 10,000 people, a small minority are either crazy or evil? Suddenly, what was a private, relatively safe Windows application environment becomes a public nightmare. You've now got some of the problems facing celebrities: stalkers, peepers, and other bothersome folk.

Also, do you see the memory problems? How can your server store 23,456 separate WebForms at the same time (to preserve the variables for each visitor to your site)? The answer is that your server — even a monster server farm — would struggle to store this much constantly changing data. So you, working in partnership with ASP.NET, must use various strategies to preserve *state* (the properties of controls, the values in variables, and so on). And, as you see in the rest of this book, you must use other tricks, too. But to be professional about all this, I'll call them *techniques* rather than tricks.

Why Not Cookies?

You may wonder why you wouldn't use cookies to persist data. If you want to store information between sessions — so that visitors can return to your Web site and not have to retype their phone number and address, for example — client-side cookies are one way to do it. Here's an example that stores and then retrieves a cookie on the visitor's hard drive:

```
Public Sub Page_Load(ByVal sender As System.Object, ByVal e
    As System.EventArgs) Handles MyBase.Load


    Dim PhoneCookie As New
HttpCookie("VisitorsPhoneNumber", "434 777-8900")
    PhoneCookie.Expires = Now.AddMonths(4) 'destroy it 4
months from now
    Response.Cookies.Add(PhoneCookie)

    ' get the cookie back from the client:
```

```
        Dim s As String
        Dim CookieName As String = "PhoneCookie"


        For Each CookieName In Request.Cookies.AllKeys 'keys
are similar to variable names
            Dim cookie As HttpCookie =
Request.Cookies(CookieName)
            s = cookie.Value & "</br>"
            Response.Write(s)
        Next

End Sub
```

Lately, though, using client-side cookies is being discouraged for two reasons. First, some users turn off the cookie feature in their computer. Second, some devices, particularly mobile devices, don't allow cookies at all. However, in a stable, predictable environment such as a corporation's intranet, cookies do remain a useful way to persist data.

Chapter 3: Using ASP.NET Controls

In This Chapter

✔ Displaying images

✔ Containing with a panel

✔ Using the table control

✔ Understanding the calendar control

✔ Getting the most from AdRotator

✔ Using styles

This chapter explores various controls that you can use in your WebForms. I assume that you're familiar with the classic Windows controls — such as the TextBox — that I cover in earlier chapters of this book. Here, I explain special behaviors of various useful controls when you use them for Internet programming.

Displaying Images

Use the Image control to show graphics (.GIF, .JPG, .JPEG, .BMP, .WMF, or .PNG). You can assign the graphics file during either design time or runtime, by providing a URL to the `ImageURL` property or by binding the Image control's `ImageURL` property to a database containing graphics.

The Image control is unusual among WebControls in that it has no events. You can't respond if the user clicks the image, for example. If you want to display a map of Europe and let the user click one of the countries in the map to, say, ask for a list of olive oil brands from that country, you must use the `ImageButton` WebControl. It not only has a `Click` event, but it also provides the X/Y coordinates to tell you where, within the graphic, the user's mouse pointer was when the click occurred.

Containing with the Panel Container

The new Panel WebControl is somewhat similar to earlier VB container controls (such as the Frame). The Panel defines a zone — a subdivision of the Web page within which you can define a look (change the Panel's `BackColor`, for example), add controls at runtime, or manipulate a group of controls simultaneously (such as a set of RadioButtons that work together).

For example, you can set the Panel's `Visible` property to `False`, and *all* controls contained within the Panel also become invisible at the same time. You can also type text into a Panel.

The Panel must be selected for you to add other controls within it by double-clicking them in the Toolbox. Add a Panel control from the Toolbox, and then click the Panel to select it in the design window. Now, in the Toolbox, double-click other controls that you want to place within the Panel.

You can also add controls to a Panel by dragging the controls on the WebForm in Design view and then dropping them into a Panel.

The Table Control

You can build a typical HTML table using the WebForm Table Control. Add a Table control to the design window, and then click the Rows collection in the Properties window. Use the TableRow Collection Editor to add new rows, as shown in Figure 3-1.

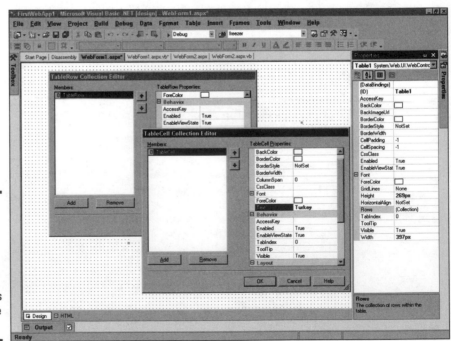

Figure 3-1: Use these dialog boxes to manually add rows and columns to your table control.

Click on the Cells collection ellipsis button inside the TableRow Collection Editor dialog box to bring up the TableCell Collection editor, where you can add columns, type in data, and otherwise manipulate the columns (fields). Of course, you can also bind the Table control to a database, as I explain in Book IV, Chapter 4.

The Rich Calendar

Taking HTML to its limits, the clever Calendar WebControl provides a valuable addition to your bag of Web-programming tricks.

The Calendar control is based on a nice set of date/time functions built into the .NET framework. It has many members, such as `GetDayOfYear`, `GetDaysInMonth`, `GetDaysInYear`, `GetEra` and so on. All this functionality replaces the somewhat smaller set of date/time functions in traditional VB.

The Calendar control permits users to view or navigate between dates, as well as to send (post back) their choice of day or days back to your server for processing. This would be an improvement over many hotel reservation Web pages, which require that you search through four ListBoxes (arrival day and month, departure day and month). With the calendar control, visitors could simply highlight and select the days they will be staying.

The calendar is rendered as an HTML table, of course, but plenty of JavaScript is in there as well. You can't see much of the actual HTML source code by clicking the HTML tab in the design window. Instead, press F5 and then use the browser's View⇨Source option. You might be startled at the massive redundancy so typical of HTML. A `<TD>` element is included for each day in the entire calendar, including JavaScript postback events that trigger when the user clicks any of the days.

If you're programming for an intranet, you could also use the Calendar control to display scheduled meetings, appointments, tasks, or other information related to scheduling.

Users can move between months by clicking the arrows at the top corners of the Calendar, or you can provide them with additional navigation methods (such as TextBoxes where they type in a date, Buttons, ListBoxes, and so on). Then you can change the month displayed programmatically, like this:

```
Private Sub Calendar1_SelectionChanged(ByVal sender As
    System.Object, ByVal e As System.EventArgs) Handles
    Calendar1.SelectionChanged

        Calendar1.VisibleDate = CDate("12/16/2002")

End Sub
```

Press F5, click any date within the calendar, and December 2002 is displayed.

Detecting user selections

The `VisibleDate` property represents which month is viewed, but the `SelectedDate` property represents the date, or range of dates, that the user chooses in the Calendar. If the user selects more than one date, the dates must be contiguous. Also, without additional programming on your part, the user's selections are limited to day, week, or month ranges. You detect a user selection (the click on a date) with this event:

```
Response.write(Calendar1.SelectedDate.ToString())
```

To permit the user to select more than one day, change the `SelectionMode` property. You determine how many dates the user selected in this way:

```
Calendar1.SelectedDates.Count
```

Getting the specific range of dates that the user may have selected is not quite as simple:

```
If Calendar1.SelectedDates.Count > 1 Then

  Dim FirstDate as DateTime
  Dim LastDate as DateTime

  FirstDate = SelectedDates(0)
  LastDate = SelectedDates(Calendar1.SelectedDates.Count -
1)

  Response.Write (FirstDate.ToString)
  Response.Write (LastDate.ToString)

End If
```

Programmatic date selection

You can programmatically select noncontiguous dates or any size range of dates. So if this is something you need, give the user additional controls, such as two Calendars — one they click to select dates, and the other that is read-only and displays their selection.

Programmatic selection of dates does not trigger the `SelectionChanged` event; only user-clicks raise the event.

Use the Properties window to change the `SelectedDayStyle.Backcolor` property to blue or something other than the default white, so that the user can see the selections. Also you can highlight today's date by adjusting the `BackColor`, `BorderColor`, `BorderStyle`, or other properties of the `TodayDayStyle` property, as shown in Figure 3-2.

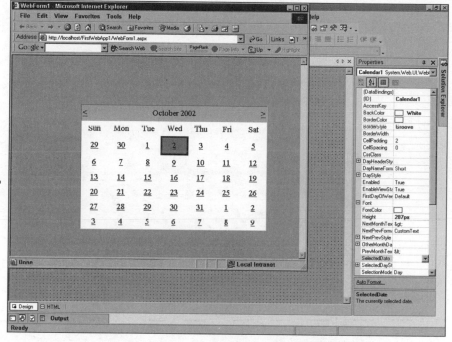

Figure 3-2:
The
Calendar
control is
among
the most
feature-rich
of the new
WebControls.

Older browsers won't be able to render all the appearance-related proper-ties available to the Calendar control, but they are gracefully degraded auto-matically for the lesser browser — a benefit automatically offered to all WebControls.

If you're interested in displaying data from a database in the calendar, note that you can't directly bind the entire calendar to a DataSet, as you can, for example, with a DataGrid control. Instead, you use the Calendar's DayRender event. It gets triggered as each day in the current month is being displayed. Write programming within this event that adds data to the information being sent to the user.

Here's an example of how you can use the DayRender event:

```
Private Sub Calendar1_DayRender(ByVal sender As Object, ByVal
    e As System.Web.UI.WebControls.DayRenderEventArgs)
    Handles Calendar1.DayRender

        Dim c As Color
        Dim n As Integer

        n = CInt(e.Day.DayNumberText)
```

```
If Not e.Day.IsOtherMonth And (n Mod 2 = 0) Then

     e.Cell.BackColor = c.AliceBlue
Else
     e.Cell.BackColor = c.Orchid
End If

End Sub
```

The result of this program is shown in Figure 3-3.

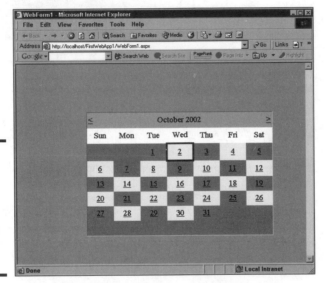

Figure 3-3:
You can define colors for any cell (day) in the Calendar control.

The DayRender event triggers as ASP.NET is creating the HTML to send *each day* to the user's browser. This way, you can add information about holidays and upcoming meetings, or you can otherwise modify the appearance and data in each day's cell.

One important argument used by the DayRender event is the DayRender EventArgs object (ByVal e As DayRenderEventArgs). (Some people refer to this as a *property;* others consider it an object in itself. Take your choice.)

The DayRenderEventArgs object contains two important objects (which are also sometimes referred to as *properties* rather than *objects*). The Cell object allows you to specify the appearance of each day, as you did in the previous example with the following code:

```
e.Cell.BackColor = c.AliceBlue
```

And the Day object allows you to prevent the day from being selected or query (read) information about the day, as you did in the previous example with the following code:

```
If Not e.Day.IsOtherMonth
```

The Day object has a variety of properties for you to query, such as IsToday and IsSelected.

Adding controls to the calendar

You can also use the *Controls* collection of the Cell object to add text, HTML code such as
 (line break), controls, or other objects to a given day. The following code demonstrates how to add a Label control to identify your birthday on the calendar:

```
Public Sub Calendar1_DayRender(ByVal s As Object, ByVal e As
    DayRenderEventArgs) Handles Calendar1.DayRender

        Dim c As Color
        Dim myBirthday As DateTime
        Dim labelBirthday As New Label()

        myBirthday = New DateTime(2003, 9, 30)
        If e.Day.Date = myBirthday Then
            labelBirthday.Text = "<br>" & "RICHARD'S
BIRTHDAY"
            e.Cell.Controls.Add(labelBirthday)
            e.Cell.BackColor = c.SlateBlue
        End If


    End Sub
```

With this code, you get the results shown in Figure 3-4. Note that this example and the following example require the user to scroll the calendar. The birth-day defined in the previous code requires that you scroll to September, 2003 to see the effect.

Notice that the layout of a Calendar can be distorted when you add a Label control, as shown in Figure 3-4. To avoid this, you can change the Calendar's Height and Width properties to be large enough to embrace added controls without distortion, you can limit yourself to small symbols, or you can just change the backcolor in the individual cells that you want to add text to. Then put a TextBox or Label outside the Calendar where you describe the special day, without affecting the size of the Calendar's cells.

**Book IV
Chapter 3**

**Using ASP.NET
Controls**

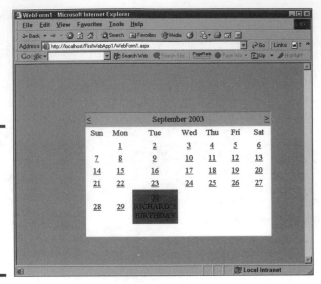

Figure 3-4:
You can add Labels or other controls to any day (cell) in the Calendar control.

Protecting days

Assume that it makes no sense to you to permit users to select days in the Calendar when your store is closed. If you want to prevent the user from being able to select particular days, use the `IsSelectable` property of the `Day` object. The following code prevents the user from selecting my birthday:

```
Public Sub Calendar1_DayRender(ByVal s As Object, ByVal e As
    DayRenderEventArgs) Handles Calendar1.DayRender
Dim myBirthday As DateTime

    myBirthday = New DateTime(2001, 9, 30)

    If e.Day.Date = myBirthday Then

    e.Day.IsSelectable = False

    End If
End Sub
```

The AdRotator

Th AdRotator WebControl displays an advertisement on your WebForm. It requires an .XML file whose URL you specify in the AdRotator's `AdvertisementFile` property.

There are some restrictions: The XML file must be stored with "the application's domain" as they say. In plain English, just save it to the hard drive in the same folder with the .aspx, .vsdisco, and other support files for your current application. Also, save the advertisement graphic .GIF (or .JPG, or whatever) file in that folder.

Here's how to use the AdRotator. Use Notepad to create the following XML file, and save it as `MyAd.XML` into the `C:\Inetput\wwwroot\` *whateveryoursolutionnameis* folder. Locate the folder on your hard drive with the same name as your solution (the name that's boldface in Solution Explorer). Then save a .GIF or other graphic file for the ad. Here's the XML file to use for this example:

```
<Advertisements>
    <Ad>
        <ImageUrl>button.gif</ImageUrl>
        <NavigateUrl>http://dell.</NavigateUrl>
        <AlternateText>Cannot display</AlternateText>
        <Keyword>Take 1</Keyword>
        <Impressions>100</Impressions>
    </Ad>
</Advertisements>
```

Substitute the name of a .GIF, .JPG, or other graphics file for the `button.gif` used in the `ImageUrl` (which can be a relative URL, as in the preceding example, or an absolute URL — meaning that the full path is spelled out). Also, instead of `dell.`, use the name of your computer. (XP users can find the name of their computer by choosing Start⇨Control Panel⇨ Performance and Maintenance⇨See basic information about your computer⇨Computer Name.) Note that the `NavigateUrl` property points to the URL of the page to be displayed if the user clicks your AdRotator.

This little project requires care: Make a single mistake in your XML file and it may not work. Also ensure that the .gif file has the same name in the folder as in the XML code, and that your computer name is correct.

Put an AdRotator control on your WebForm, and in the Properties window change its `AdvertisementFile` property to `MyAd.XML`. Press F5 and you see your ad displayed, as shown in Figure 3-5.

**Book IV
Chapter 3**

**Using ASP.NET
Controls**

Figure 3-5:
Create an
ad banner
with the
AdRotator
control.

Your XML file must be well formed. So, if you're in the habit of writing *badly formed* XML, get with the program! The XML file must conform to this format:

```
<Advertisements>
<Ad>
    <ImageUrl>Filename of the graphic to display</ImageUrl>
    <NavigateUrl>URL of the path to the page the used sees if
    the user clicks your ad</NavigateUrl>
    <AlternateText>Text to display if image can't be displayed
    </AlternateText>
    <Keyword>Keyword to filter ads</Keyword>
    <Impressions>relative weight of ad<Impressions>
</Ad>
</Advertisements>
```

However, of all these properties, only the ImageURL is absolutely required. The AlternativeText property is displayed as a ToolTip in Internet Explorer, if the graphic is successfully displayed. You can use the Impressions property to define how often the ad is displayed. You can fill the XML file with as many <Ad> sections as you want. Give them relative weight by setting the <Impressions> property. If one of the <Ad> sections has 1000 as its weight, and the only other <Ad> section has a weight of 100, the second <Ad> is displayed only one tenth as often as the first ad.

Using Style Objects with WebControls

As you saw in the preceding section, you can either define the properties of an AdRotator in an event (AdCreated), or you can reference a separate .XML file to define those properties. This is how ASP.NET segregates the work of designers who manipulate the appearance of a Web page (HTML) from the work of a programmer who manipulates the behavior of that page (using VB.NET). They can both work on different files. Similarly, cascading style sheets (.css files) and other techniques permit two files to define one object.

You can employ a level of abstraction with WebControls. Some ASP.NET WebControls permit you to use *style objects* to specify properties. The DataList WebControl, for example, has a BorderStyle property, and SelectedDayStyle is part of the Calendar control. The Button control has a ControlStyle property that works much the same way.

You can, of course, use the Property window to specify styles, or do it programmatically in an event (or by modifying the HTML). A third way is to use a style object.

To see how this works, put a Button control on your WebForm and then double-click that Button to get to the code-behind code window (the VB.NET code window). You see the empty `Button1 Click` event. Type this into the event:

```
Private Sub Button1_Click(ByVal sender As System.Object,
    ByVal e As System.EventArgs) Handles Button1.Click
        Dim stl As New Style()

        stl.BackColor = Color.MintCream
        stl.BorderColor = Color.MistyRose

        Button1.ControlStyle.CopyFrom(stl)
End Sub
```

When you employ the `CopyFrom` method, as illustrated in the preceding code, *all* the style object's settings are applied to the Button (or whatever WebControl is being used). This includes nulls. Try a different tactic, using the `MergeWith` method. Replace the `CopyFrom` method in the previous code with the following code:

```
Button1.ControlStyle.MergeWith(stl)
```

`MergeWith` sets only the properties already defined in the style object and does not change any properties undefined in the style object.

Inheritance and precedence in style objects

In some sophisticated WebControls, style objects can inherit properties from other style objects. The Calendar WebControl, for example, bases `SelectedDayStyle` property on its `DayStyle` object. If you don't specify properties for `SelectedDayStyle`, it inherits its properties from the `DayStyle` property. Put another way, if you do specify one of these properties, your choice wins (has precedence).

WebControls expose two properties that let you manipulate CSS styles: `CSSStyle` and `CSSClass`. If you set the `CSSStyle` property, you can set a string of style attributes to be applied to the control. The `CSSStyle` property specifies style attributes that are not exposed through other properties; it allows you to assign a stylesheet class to the control.

Don't confuse templates with styles

You can easily get templates and styles mixed up because they do almost the same things and operate in almost the same ways. Here's how to tell them apart.

Templates are used only by the DataList, DataGrid, and Repeater controls, and templates focus on adding other WebControls (such as a Label) to a cell within these lists. In fact, the Repeater won't work *unless* you give it a template.

However, you can use a style with a template to define the appearance of elements that you specify within your templates. Templates are HTML, but they can also include embedded Web Forms controls. The template's features are rendered instead of the default HTML that was used to render that control.

Wouldn't it be nice if only a single tool could do this abstraction job, rather than two tools: templates and styles? And, just to make things even more interesting for all of us programmers, as the VB.NET Help feature puts it: "Each control supports a slightly different set of templates that specify layouts for different portions of the control, such as the header, footer, item, and selected item."

Chapter 4: Making Database Connections on WebForms

In This Chapter

✔ **Installing SQL Server**

✔ **Installing sample databases**

✔ **Creating connections**

✔ **Binding to arrays**

✔ **Connecting a database to a Web page**

✔ **Solving security problems**

*I*n this chapter, you prepare your computer to provide access to databases. After you've installed SQL Server and some sample databases, you see how to bind an array of data to a control, and also how to connect a database to a Web page. Finally, it's likely that you need to adjust the security settings in SQL Server to actually be able to connect to databases — and that's the subject of the final section of this chapter.

Take a look down in your Windows tray, near the clock on your desktop. Do you see an icon that looks like a vertical computer with a triangle on it, like the one circled in Figure 4-1?

Figure 4-1:
If this icon is visible, SQL Server is available on your machine.

If you don't have SQL Server running — the icon is missing or the arrow is red — you do need SQL Server for this chapter and for Book V, which focuses on .NET database programming.

If the arrow on the icon is red, it means that SQL Server is installed but not currently running. Try double-clicking the icon and then starting SQL Server from the SQL Server Service Manager dialog box that pops up. If you cannot start it, you need to reinstall SQL Server, as described in the first section of this chapter.

Installing SQL Server

Not all versions of Visual Studio include SQL Server. All versions (including Professional, Enterprise Developer, Enterprise Architect, and Academic) *do* include the Microsoft SQL Server 2000 Desktop Engine (MSDE 2000). Only the Enterprise version of Visual Studio.NET actually comes with SQL Server 2000, and even that is a development version. To see the features of each version of VB.NET, look at this Web address:
```
http://msdn.microsoft.com/library/default.asp?url=/library/
en-us/vsintro7/html/vxoriVisualStudioEditions.asp.
```

SQL Server does for database programming something similar to what the Personal Web Server (along with IIS) does for Internet WebForm programming.

SQL Server is a set of utilities from Microsoft that perform a variety of useful jobs. Among other things, SQL Server helps simulate a server computer holding a database with which your "client" computer (your VB.NET Windows or WebForm application) communicates.

Recall that in Book IV, Chapter 1, you installed IIS so that you could test your ASP.NET pages. Now, to manage and test database connections, you need to install SQL Server (if you don't have it already). *SQL* (Structured Query Language) is the best way to ask for data from a data store. For example, give me only the phone numbers of people with overdue bills, or give me the names of all publishers located in California and Nevada.

Try it now

If you haven't installed SQL Server 2000 or MSDE 2000 when you installed VB.NET itself, install it now. (If you've already installed it, but it's not working — perhaps it has a logon failure or whatever — first uninstall it using Control Panel's Add/Remove Programs utility, and then reinstall it.)

To install SQL Server, put your VB.NET CD Disk 1 in the CD drive, and then use Control Panel's Add/Remove Programs utility. When the Add/Remove Programs dialog box opens, click the Add New Programs icon on the left side of the dialog box. Now click the CD or Floppy button and follow the instructions to install SQL Server from the VB.NET CDs.

Installing SQL Server or MSDE can be tricky, partly because so many possible computer configurations exist: people with new XP machines, people with old 2000 machines, people who were on the .NET technical beta list and have some legacy registrations or code libraries floating around, people using VS.NET 2003, and so on.

After you run Visual Studio .NET Setup, a menu comes up that asks whether you want Windows Component Update, Visual Studio .NET, or Service Releases. SQL Server Desktop Edition is actually listed as a Visual Studio .NET feature. Note also that you may see that SQL Server Desktop Engine is already checked! However, the Feature Description says that you have to "manually launch setup.exe from the ..\Setup\MSDE subfolder under the main Visual Studio .NET installation folder."

Installation agony

You might see various mystery error messages during MSDE installation, such as `Problem with Named Instance` after a regular setup. Then MSDE may never seem to install. You reboot the computer several times. Suddenly, to your great joy, even though you still get that same error message, you reboot and something wonderful happens: Dame Fortune smiles down; the stars align. Things mysteriously go right this time, and the server's icon appears in your tray! It's working at last, although nobody can explain why.

Some users report success by taking the following step after running Visual Studio setup and installing MSDE. Manually launch Setup.exe from the `SETUP\MSDE` folder after the Visual Studio installation is complete. Find the MSDE setup.exe file on your computer by locating the following path (or a similar path, because yours won't say 2003, for example, if you are using the earlier version of VS.NET):

```
Program Files\...\Microsoft Visual Studio .NET 2003\Setup\
    MSDE\Setup.exe
```

Then run this Setup.exe file by double-clicking it in Windows Explorer. In the same folder with the Setup.exe file, you can find a Readme.Txt file that looks scary but might assist you. However, I suggest that you use Google instead if you still don't see the server icon (indicating success) on the right side of your Taskbar.

If you face problems installing MSDE or SQL Server — and many people do — try the suggestions in this chapter and be prepared to reboot several times. If you are still having problems, someone else has probably had similar difficulties because their machine history and configuration resemble yours. Go to Google Groups (`http://www.google.com/grphp`) and search for `MSDE Setup`. You'll see many messages with solutions.

Also, if you have solved an MSDE, SQL Server, or sample database installation problem not described in this chapter, please e-mail me at richardm52@ hotmail.com so that I can put your solution on this book's Web site for others to see.

Installing the Sample Databases

In order to follow the database-related examples in this book, you need to have the same sample databases on your computer that I have. VB.NET supplies several sample databases for you to play around with, most notably sample databases named Northwind and pubs.

Are these databases on your computer? To find out, choose View⇨ Server Explorer in the VB.NET IDE. You should see a list similar to the one shown in Figure 4-2.

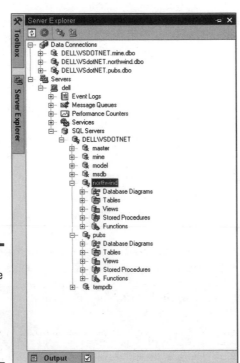

Figure 4-2:
Do you have any SQL Servers listed in your Server Explorer?

If you don't see SQL Server or MSDE 2000, reboot your computer. The installer may not tell you to reboot, but as far as I can tell, you must reboot.

You just installed it, so it should show up. Now open the SQL Server listings in Server Explorer (click the +) so that you can see what databases, if any, are available. If you don't see Pubs and Northwind listed (as shown in Figure 4-2), you need to install the Samples that come with VB.NET. To install the sample databases, follow these steps:

1. **Close Visual Studio.NET and then choose Start⇨ Programs⇨ Microsoft .NET Framework SDK⇨ Samples and Quickstart Tutorials.**

A file named StartSamples is displayed to you in Internet Explorer.

2. **Click "Step 1: Install the .NET Framework Samples Database" in Internet Explorer.**

3. **Follow the instructions to save two files to a temporary directory.**

You don't see a prompt that specifically says "Save two files to a temporary directory." You see a "file download" dialog box that says, cryptically, "Some files can harm your computer," "This type of file could harm your computer if it contains malicious code," and so on. The dialog box asks whether you want to open the file or save it to the computer. When you pick Save, it only saves INSTMSDE.EXE.

You might prefer to choose "Set up the QuickStarts" and then choose Open when you see the file download prompt.

4. **Use Windows Explorer to locate the temporary directory where you saved those two files.**

5. **Double-click the InstMSDE.exe file to install the samples.**

If this file fails to install, double-click the SQL Server icon on your tray, and then click the red button to stop SQL Server from running. Rerun InstMSDE.exe. Then reboot your computer to restart SQL Server.

6. **Double-click the ConfigSamples.exe in your temporary directory.**

The samples are configured and you should now see the Northwind and GrocerToGo database connections in your Server Explorer. If not, try rebooting.

Note that in Figure 4-2, the Northwind database is shown under VSDOTNET, and GrocerToGo isn't shown at all. In your install, you may see both VSDOTNET and NETSDK listed, with both GrocerToGo and Northwind listed under VSDOTNET.

Making Connections to Databases

The last housekeeping job to do before getting into database programming in VB.NET is to make a couple of connections to databases. Click the + next to Data Connections in the Server Explorer. Do you see connections to Northwind.dbo and Pubs.dbo? If not, make those connections right now by following these steps:

1. **Right-click Data Connections in the Server Explorer.**

   A context menu appears.

2. **Choose Add Connection from the context menu.**

   The Data Link Properties dialog box appears.

3. **Click the Provider tab.**

   You see a list of data providers (connection utilities).

4. **Click Microsoft OLE DB Provider for SQL Server in the listbox to select it.**

5. **Click the Next button.**

6. **Open the list under "Select or enter a server name" and choose your SQL Server's name. (Your server's name will be your computer's name, plus** VSDOTNET **or** NETSDK.**)**

7. **Click the radio button next to Use Windows NT Integrated security.**

8. **Drop the list under "Select the database on the server".**

9. **Choose Northwind (or whatever database you want to create a connection for).**

10. **Click the Test Connection button.**

11. **Click the OK button to close the dialog box.**

    Now, with these data connections established, you can use them to quickly bind controls to the databases or to write source code to access the databases programmatically.

It's quite easy to create a brand new SQL Server database of your own. Just right-click the Data Connections entry in Server Explorer, and then fill in the server name. (If your SQL Server is listed as, for example, Dell\VsDotNet in Server Explorer, use that as the server name.) Then provide a name for your new database.

Choose Windows security (because it's simpler). When the dialog box closes, you see your new database listed in Server Explorer. Click the + to open it up, right-click Tables, and choose New Table from the context menu to begin the process of defining the structure of your new database. More on this in Book V, Chapter 6.

Simple Binding

If you're experienced with VB 6 and earlier versions, you know that some controls, such as TextBoxes, can be bound (connected) to databases. This way, they display data from the database and also automatically update what they show when you "move" to a different record in the database.

Good news: VB.NET permits you to bind *any* control to a database (even those that may seem to make no sense, such as a button control). Not only that, but you can even bind collections such as arrays and hashtables! I have much more to say about databases and data binding in Book V, but now you can discover at least how to bind various objects and controls to a database and display the results in the visitor's browser using ASP.NET.

To see how to bind an ordinary array to a ListBox on a WebForm, first place a ListBox control from the Toolbox onto an empty WebForm. Notice that the ListBox says *unbound.* You knew that.

Now double-click the WebForm background to get to the code window where you can type the following code into the Page_Load event:

```
Public Sub Page_Load(ByVal sender As System.Object, ByVal e
    As System.EventArgs) Handles MyBase.Load

    If Not Page.IsPostBack Then
        Dim clora() As String = {"aphas", "Rora", "Snad"}
        ListBox1.DataSource = clora
        Me.DataBind()
    End If

End Sub
```

Recall that you can fill an array with values by enclosing the list of values in brackets, as shown in the preceding code. Notice that all you have to do to fill the ListBox with the array is to set its DataSource to the array's name, and then use the Page object's DataBind method (which simultaneously binds all controls on the page). Press F5 and be prepared to gasp when you see how stunningly simple, yet powerful, these new features are.

TIP

If you don't need to fill a ListBox or other bound control repeatedly (if you only want to fill it when the visitor first views your Web page), surround the source code with an If...Then structure that queries the IsPostBack method, as shown in the preceding code example. This can speed things up considerably if your data source is large or complicated.

Binding to Databases

Before ASP, connecting a Web page to a database was a real wrestling match. Now, with ASP.NET, you may find the job almost trivial. The source code is brief and quite elegant in its brevity. However, as you know, there's no free lunch. As programming has become increasingly user-friendly, security has gone in the other direction. You can even view object oriented programming primarily as an effort to solve security issues — to help programmers work together without gaining access to each other's inner code (encapsulation).

In any case, it's time to step up to bat and try a real database connection. Be warned, though: The first time you run the following example, you may get an error message. You may receive the `Access is Denied` message. You are not allowed into a database that is on your own computer!

Perhaps you know enough about SQL and Windows security to have anticipated this problem. Or, perhaps you're like me, not an expert in the security permissions issues on your own personal computer. After all, most of us don't have to protect ourselves from ourselves.

Why not find out? Try the next example. Then, later in this chapter in the "Dealing with Security Denials" section, I'll show you how to give yourself the necessary permissions to use the sample databases Pubs and Northwind.

Start a new WebForm project by choosing File➪New➪Project and then double-clicking the ASP.NET Web Application icon in the New Project dialog box.

Double-click the ListBox icon in the WebForms tab of the Toolbox to add a ListBox to your WebForm. Double-click the WebForm in the design window to get to the code window.

At the very top of your code window, import these three namespaces by typing these lines:

```
Imports System.Data
Imports System.Data.SqlClient
Imports System.Data.OleDb
```

Now, type the following into the `Form_Load` event:

```
Public Sub Page_Load(ByVal sender As System.Object, ByVal e
    As System.EventArgs) Handles MyBase.Load

Dim SqlConnString As String = "Initial
    Catalog=pubs;Integrated Security=SSPI"
```

```
        If Not Page.IsPostBack Then

            Dim conn As New SqlConnection(SqlConnString)
            Dim sql As String = "SELECT * FROM Authors"

            Dim SQLcmd As New SqlCommand(sql, conn)
            Dim dr As SqlDataReader

            Try
                conn.Open()
            Catch ex As Exception
                Response.Write(ex.Message) 'was there a
problem?
            End Try


            ' Read data into the DataReader
            dr =
SQLcmd.ExecuteReader(CommandBehavior.CloseConnection)


            ' Show all the records in the ListBox
            Do While dr.Read

                Dim total As Integer = dr.FieldCount - 1

                ' Get the entire set of data at once.
                Dim AllData(total) As Object
                dr.GetValues(AllData)

                Dim i As Integer
                Dim n As String

                For i = 0 To total 'show one record
                    n = dr.GetName(i)
                    ListBox1.Items.Add(n & ": " &
AllData(i).ToString)
                Next i

                ListBox1.Items.Add("_____") ' line to
divide records

            Loop 'move to next record

        End If
    End Sub
End Class
```

I explain all of these methods and objects in Book V. They work essentially the same way whether you're accessing a database for a Web page or for a traditional Windows application. For now, I want you to see that, indeed, you can quickly and easily manipulate the contents of databases on Web pages. Press F5. If you *do* get an `Access Denied` error message, follow the steps in the rest of this chapter to solve the problem. If you don't get any error messages, happy you! You see the result shown in Figure 4-3.

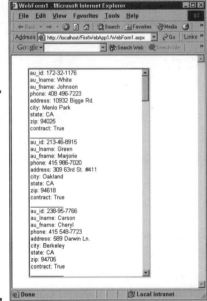

Figure 4-3:
If you don't have any security problems, accessing a database from within a Web page is quite quick and easy using ASP.NET.

Dealing with Security Denials

When you press F5 to run the code example in the preceding section, you may get an error message explaining that you don't have permission to connect to the database. Join the group.

Or you may see a different error message: `ExecuteReader requires an open and available Connection. The connection's current state is Closed.` The `ExecuteReader` method doesn't work because the connection is never actually opened.

If you get one of these `Permission Denied`, `ExecuteReader`, or `Access Denied` error messages, it means that you (or your Web page) are trying to read a database that is defined as off limits to you. Perhaps it requires a password, and your connection string doesn't include a password. That's one reason why I suggest you choose "Windows Integrated Security" when creating database connections. No password or login name is then required. Another reason for denial of access is that you haven't let SQL server know that you want permission. By default, you, or Web pages, are *not* given permission. The following suggestions apply to users with full SQL Server (not the MSDE version).

Before taking any further steps to cure the `Access Denied` problem, you should ensure that you are logged onto your computer as an Administrator. Belonging to this group allows you to adjust permission levels, change passwords, and otherwise control your computer's security defenses. To see what's going on, double-click Administrative Tools in Control Panel. (In Windows XP, choose Performance and Maintenance in Control Panel, and then choose Administrative Tools.) Then double-click Computer Management.

In the left pane of the Computer Management dialog box, click the + next to Local Users and Groups to expand it; then click Users. In the right pane, find the listing for your name (the name you log on with when Windows starts up). Right-click your name and choose Properties. Click the Member Of tab, and you see the list of groups that you belong to, something like the list shown in Figure 4-4.

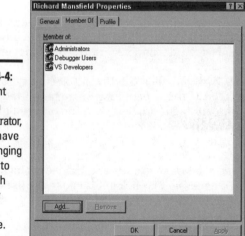

Figure 4-4:
You want to be an Administrator, so you have wide-ranging powers to deal with security on your machine.

Book IV
Chapter 4

Making Database Connections on WebForms

Try to click the Add button if necessary to give yourself Administrator status. If you can't get this far, you *don't* have enough status and need to find out how to be added to the Administrators group. Essentially, this means that you need to find someone who *is* an Administrator on this computer and convince him or her to give you that same status.

Now, when you're sure you're an administrator, you can go ahead and grant access permissions. Choose Start⇨Programs⇨Microsoft SQL Server⇨ Enterprise Manager. If you don't see this utility on your computer, it likely means that the SQL Server set of utilities failed to install along with it.

This happened to me, and it has happened to others. In that case, the only solution I've found is to get your copy of the actual full SQL Server CD, or to download the 120-day trial version of SQL Server, both of which successfully install Enterprise Manager and the other SQL Server utilities. The trial version is available from `http://www.microsoft.com/sql/evaluation/trial`.

Perhaps by the time this book is written, a solution to this problem will have been announced. Doubtless a Windows Registry entry is hanging things up and needs to be removed. Try searching the Microsoft MSDN site for Enterprise Manager (or try searching the Google News search engine).

To grant yourself permission to use the sample databases, run Enterprise Manager. Don't worry about which permissions you should or shouldn't grant. Grant them all, willy-nilly. After all, these are sample databases and there's nothing in them that you need to try to protect. You'll be surprised at how many different kinds and levels of permissions SQL Server offers.

Choose Start⇨Programs⇨Microsoft SQL Server⇨Enterprise Manager. Your first job is to make sure that you can log in to SQL Server. Each person who uses a Windows computer (recent operating systems, anyway) can have a separate login/password combination. Each of these people can have separate desktops, separate e-mail accounts, and separate security levels.

In the left pane of Enterprise Manager, click the + next to Security to expand it. Click Logins and you see a list of those people who are permitted to log in to SQL Server (which is a different login process than the one you use when logging into your Windows session). See if your login name is in the right pane. If it isn't, right-click Logins in the left pane, and then choose New Login. Click the ... button next to Name in the *SQL Server Login Properties — New Login* dialog box. You see a list of all groups and individual logins. Click Add to add Administrators (if necessary). Click OK to close the list of names dialog box and return to the *SQL Server Login Properties — New Login* dialog box. Now click the Windows Authentication radio button.

Click the Server Roles tab and check all the checkboxes so that every possible behavior is permitted to this person or group. Your dialog box should look like the one shown in Figure 4-5.

If you have doubts about giving wide permissions to a person or group, you want to consult with others in your organization and decide how to implement a security policy that makes sense in your company. The advice I'm giving here is for people working on a desktop computer alone, who don't want to be bothered with security hangups while learning .NET.

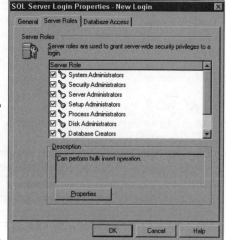

Figure 4-5:
This is what
it looks like
when you
give total
permission
to a person
or group.

Now click the Database Access tab and repeat your previous tactic: Give permission to access every database listed. Also click all the checkboxes in the Database Roles for Northwind (as shown in Figure 4-6) and for each other database listed in this page. Again, you are avoiding mysterious error messages when working with these sample databases. Click OK to close the dialog box and apply the changes.

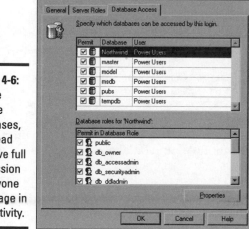

Figure 4-6:
For the
sample
databases,
go ahead
and give full
permission
for anyone
to engage in
any activity.

Now reopen the *SQL Server Login Properties — New Login* dialog box. Click the ... button next to Name and locate your own login name. Repeat all the previous steps to add your personal login name to the various activities listed in the checkboxes on the Server Roles and Database Access tabs of this dialog box.

Allowing Web page access

Finally, you also have to give the same permissions to your Web pages. When you are accessing one of these databases via a WebForm (as you did in the previous example source code in this chapter), the Web page itself (named ASPNET) must have permission to access the databases! It's not enough that you, or Administrators in general, have all kinds of permissions. When you try to get through to a database from a Windows form, your group or personal login governs access. But when you run a simulated Internet-client contact via a WebForm, ASPNET must itself have permission. To give ASPNET permission, reopen the *SQL Server Login Properties — New Login* dialog box. Click the ... button next to Name and locate ASPNET, as shown in Figure 4-7.

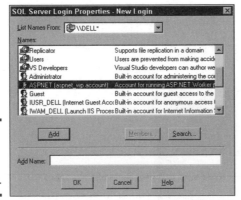

Figure 4-7:
Even ASP
must have
permissions.

Repeat all the previous steps to add ASPNET to the various activities listed in the checkboxes on the Server Roles and Database Access tabs of this dialog box.

Chapter 5: Creating a Web Service

In This Chapter

✔ **What are Web Services?**

✔ **No fear: Creating your first Web Service**

✔ **Connecting to a database**

✔ **Testing and debugging**

✔ **Discovering and consuming**

They're always thinking up new names for old ideas. A Web Service has a relationship to a WebForm that is similar to the relationship between a Module and a VB.NET Form.

A Module contains a class or classes but has no user interface. It's just a repository — maybe some global variables and a collection of procedures (like a DLL, namespace, or assembly) — that does a job or a set of related jobs.

Perhaps you write a series of functions that translate one currency into another. You then choose to put those functions together in a Module for use with Windows programs. If you move that Module to the Web, making it available to other programs to access over the Internet, it's no longer a Module (or DLL). Instead, it is called a *Web Service*.

Web Service is just the latest name for a function or set of functions that do a job for a program. You *call* (or nowadays, they like to say *consume*) the service by providing some data — the parameters that you *pass* to the service, such as $125 to be translated into another currency.

Then, the programming in the function(s) of the Web Service figures out what that equals in German marks and returns the answer to your application by sending back `249.697 deutsche marks`. Your program can make use of this information. Why use Web Services? Well, the ratio of $ to `marks` changes minute by minute. You can't define it in your source code. So, your program consumes a $ to `DEM` Web Service that always provides current, accurate results, thanks to the Internet.

The main difference between a Web Service and a function in a Module, DLL, namespace, or assembly is that a Web Service isn't located on your computer's hard drive. It's on the Internet. And, because it's on the Web, it must communicate with the caller in a special way to avoid firewall rejection. That special way is XML, an offshoot of HTML.

Why Web Services Matter

Web Services could prove to be an important programming technology in the coming years. Simply put, Web Services are the latest effort to bridge the communication gap between applications, operating systems, and platforms. Sometimes called *platform independence,* this communication problem has proven surprisingly difficult to solve. But unlike previous attempts that have all more or less failed, Web Services may actually succeed.

Web Services are stateless (which solves several communication and timing problems) and also communicate via ordinary text (which obviously simplifies searching, programming, and just plain *understanding* the messages).

Being stateless and text-based also makes Web Services fundamentally platform-independent. In theory — and usually in practice — Web Services freely communicate between Macs and PCs, between contemporary data formats and legacy structures, between local processes and remote ones, between *your* database format and *mine*.

A Web Service, however, involves more than just sending a message from one computer, requesting that a remote computer perform a job (process some data).

Distributed computing

Some very important implications arise when you divide data and processing between more than one machine. Think of it as the adjustment you must make when you get married. It's like figuring out how to manage your money jointly with your new spouse. A joint checking account forces you to behave differently than you did when you were single. It's more complicated.

You have to share data and synchronize your deposits and withdrawals to avoid bouncing checks. You may even have to figure out some security measures, ways to communicate about your finances without letting others in on your secrets. What was once merely a computation job within your single checkbook now also becomes a *communication* problem between two checkbooks.

Likewise, in traditional computing, a programmer wrote procedures knowing various facts about the environment in which the procedures operate: which operating system is used, the language in which other procedures are written, and the location and structure of any data used by the procedures. In other words, the programmer was working within a predictable, stable, fundamentally *local* environment.

Distributed computing does not offer the programmer that kind of predictability. The data may reside in Des Moines, on a machine running Linux, but the procedure that processes that data may sit on a computer in London running Windows. Web Services exchange information between distributed computers.

Web Services employ XML and other technologies to solve the communication and security problems associated with today's Internet-based computing.

Visual Studio to the rescue

Although Web Services themselves are designed to be platform-independent, programmers must depend on a particular platform and, usually, a single language during the process of creating the Web Services. Programmers and developers need to work within an environment that offers them a rich set of useful and familiar tools: debugging features, pop-up lists of methods, an effective help system, and so on.

Web Services make a special demand on the programmer. Exchanged information must be translated into XML and communicated via SOAP (Simple Object Access Protocol) calls, a subset of XML. (Don't be fooled by the hopeful, but often misleading, use of the word *simple* here.)

Fortunately, Visual Studio .NET provides an answer to the verbosity and complexity of XML and SOAP. It's likely that the majority of Web Services programmers will choose the Microsoft VS .NET as their programming environment. It isn't the only Web Services programming environment, but it appears destined to be the dominant one. What's more, it features many useful tools, including the capability to automatically generate SOAP envelopes — lifting that significant burden from the programmer.

VS.NET includes other important tools. For example, ADO.NET brings database programming up to speed with its support for disconnected DataSets and the capability to automatically translate data into XML for transmission to a remote computer. In sum, VS.NET boasts a powerful set of tools to assist programmers and developers in creating and maintaining Web Services.

An Overview of Web Services

The following list covers the main points to remember about Web Services:

✦ **They are free of physical (geographical) and computer language constraints.** Web Services are made available on the Internet (but you also have the option of keeping some of them on your local hard drive), so they can be accessed from *anywhere:* from within your local intranet, from Zambia, or from anywhere else.

**Book IV
Chapter 5**

**Creating a
Web Service**

✦ **They are essentially a set of functions (or a collection of functions).** Therefore, they do not include a user interface — no textboxes, buttons, and so on for people to interact with. Think of a Web Service as a utility that sits there and responds to requests coming in from the Internet (or intranet).

✦ **They communicate with applications and with one another using the XML-based technology SOAP.** This eliminates the difficulties that have traditionally hampered computer-to-computer communications. In the past, proprietary database structures, unique object models, and incompatible computer languages have made life very difficult for programmers trying to reach out and touch a computer beyond the one they are working on. All too often, even the various applications on the same computer's hard drive could not efficiently communicate.

✦ **They can't transmit viruses.** Because a Web Service merely sends text (XML) over the Internet (rather than an executable), there is no possibility that a Web Service can transmit a virus. Firewalls are designed to block executables but to permit text to pass right through — so firewalls do not block Web Service communications.

✦ **They are based on a universal standardized language: XML.** Because they are written in XML, any application that is able to deal with XML can access any Web Service.

✦ **They permit applications to consume (use) the functions that the Web Service exposes (makes available).** In this way, Web Services are just like traditional classes. However, unlike traditional classes, Web Services do not require that the consumer application employ the same object model as the Web Service. Both the Web Service and its consumers rely instead on XML as their shared protocol. Traditional objects are said to be tightly coupled to specific object models. Web Services are not.

✦ **They decrease inefficiencies.** Perhaps most important in the long run, Web Services can circumvent traditional inefficiencies within organizations. A salesman in Santa Barbara should be able to pretty easily access the data and software at the home office in Des Moines, thanks to the relative simplicity and universality offered by the Web Services communication model. This, anyway, is the hope. We'll see how it plays out in practice.

Why worry?

Most programmers now face a daunting task: migrating from traditional Windows-based programming to Internet-based programming. For many programmers, this migration is as challenging as anything they will face in their entire career. Not only must they cope with a new platform — the Internet — but they must also learn to employ novel technologies to ensure the stability and security of their applications.

And, ideally — but perhaps too *idealistically,* only time will tell — Web Services may permit many of today's non-programmers to join in the fun. Web Service programming can be quite high-level and relatively easy to use — particularly for people using Visual Basic.NET. Web Services can be assembled as objects into modular applications that, hopefully, many business people will be able fashion themselves rather than relying on over-worked, understaffed, chronically behind IT staffs. After all, who is in a better position to know what's needed and to update a business or e-business utility than the business people who use it daily?

Perhaps IT staff can generate sufficiently well-designed and clearly described Web Service objects so that the actual applications employing those objects can be put together by business people. Salespeople, department managers, analysts, and so on could then join in the effort to improve a company's efficiency. In the Internet Age, most businesses must try to be as agile as possible — and Web Services offer great agility to a company transitioning to e-business.

The solution at last?

Whatever way things eventually turn out, many experts believe that Web Services may just be, at long last, the solution to one of computing's most serious problems. And if Web Services *do* solve the backward compatibility, messaging security, and cross-platform communication difficulties — the Tower of Babel that has plagued programmers and developers for decades — you'll certainly want to be among the early adopters who start converting to this new technology relatively soon. Remember, in the fast-moving information economy, only agile companies survive. Until quite recently Polaroid was among the bluest of the blue chip stocks. Nothing was ever supposed to happen to it. Then, of course, along came the digital camera.

Creating Your First Web Service

To see how Web Services are created, choose File⇨New⇨Project; then in the New Project dialog box, double-click the ASP.NET Web Service icon. A new project is created. (If the new project can't be created, see the information about setting up IIS for ASP.NET in Book IV, Chapter 1).

You first see a design window, and you can add controls to this window. But remember that a Web Service doesn't display any user interface, so it would be rather eccentric of you to add a button that no one will ever see. However, you may want to use some non-visible controls, such as the data connection controls.

**Book IV
Chapter 5**

Creating a
Web Service

Click the "Click here to switch to code view" link in the center of the design window. You now see the template. When VB.NET first creates a Web Service template for you, it provides this source code in the code window:

```
Imports System.Web.Services

<WebService(Namespace := "http://tempuri.org/")> _
Public Class Service1
    Inherits System.Web.Services.WebService

" Web Services Designer Generated Code "

    ' WEB SERVICE EXAMPLE
    ' The HelloWorld() example service returns the string
Hello World.
    ' To build, uncomment the following lines then save and
build the project.
    ' To test this web service, ensure that the .asmx file is
the start page
    ' and press F5.
    '
    '<WebMethod()> Public Function HelloWorld() As String
    '       HelloWorld = "Hello World"
    ' End Function

End Class
```

To write your own Web Service, replace the WEB SERVICE EXAMPLE (all those commented lines that begin with the ' character) with your own code.

To see how you write a Web Service and then test it, try creating a new Web Service that provides the current time and date. Delete the commented lines and then type the following source code, shown in boldface:

```
Imports System.Web.Services

Imports System

<WebService(Namespace := "http://tempuri.org/")> _
Public Class Service1

    Inherits System.Web.Services.WebService

" Web Services Designer Generated Code "

<WebMethod()> Public Function WhatTimeIsIt() As String

        Dim s As String
```

```
        s = Now.ToString

        Return s

    End Function

End Class
```

The `<WebService(Namespace:="http://tempuri.org/")>` element specifies that this is a special kind of class, a Web Service. Notice the `< >` symbols, which traditionally enclose an element in HTML. This `WebService` element can be omitted because ASP.NET understands that you are writing a Web Service (its file extension is .ASMX, which makes that clear). However, the element has its uses. It can include various attributes, including the namespace and also a `Description` attribute, like this:

```
<WebService(Description:="Provides the current date and
    time", Namespace:="http://tempuri.org/")> Public Class
    Service1
```

Also, you use the `<WebMethod()>` element to make it clear that the function is part of a Web Service. (You can include a `Description` attribute in this element, too.) The `<WebMethod()>` element is *not* optional. You must include it because it's the only way that a remote client can see and access your function (method) from the outside.

This mingling of HTML-style source code (elements, attributes) with VB.NET code may seem a bit awkward at first. But you get used to it. Aside from those elements, the source code in this function is typical, familiar VB.NET.

Now press F5 to test this Web Service. You should see your browser fire up and display the information shown in Figure 5-1. (You can ignore the information about tempuri and changing the default namespace for now. That's information you must deal with when deploying a real Web Service on the Internet.)

The name of your Web Service is displayed as a hyperlink, as shown in Figure 5-1. (If you provide a `Description` attribute for your WebMethod, it is displayed just below the link.) Click the link and you see the Invoke button, as shown in Figure 5-2.

Click the Invoke button to imitate a request to your Web service — as if someone had sent the request over the Internet — and your service responds. You see the result shown in Figure 5-3.

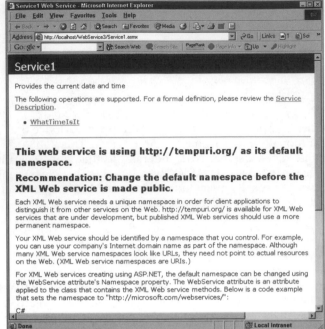

Figure 5-1:
Notice that
if you've
included a
`Descrip-`
`tion`
attribute,
it will be
displayed at
the top of
this page.

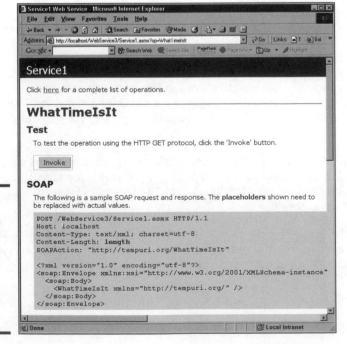

Figure 5-2:
Here's
where you
can click
an Invoke
button
to run
your Web
Service.

Figure 5-3:
There you are! Your Web Service "sent back" the date and time as a string in XML format to the remote client.

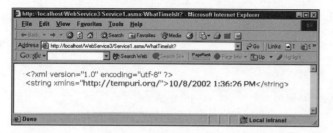

```
<?xml version="1.0" encoding="utf-8" ?>
<string xmlns="http://tempuri.org/">10/8/2002 1:36:26 PM</string>
```

Connecting a Web Service to a Database

As usual, it's important to know how to connect your VB.NET projects — of whatever type — to databases. The next example shows how it can be done. (If you have problems getting this example to work, see Book IV, Chapter 4, to see how to install SQL Server, install the sample databases, and make database connections.)

First, you must add a couple of database-related Imports statements; then you can create your database connection function and send back information from your database to the remote client requesting it.

Add the Imports statements (in boldface) to your existing Imports:

```
Imports System.Web.Services
Imports System

Imports System.Data
Imports System.Data.SqlClient
```

Now delete your WhatTimeIsIt Web Service from the previous example, and replace it with the following code:

```
<WebService(Description:="Sends back a list of jobs from our
    database", Namespace:="http://tempuri.org/")> Public
    Class Service1

    Inherits System.Web.Services.WebService

    <WebMethod()> Public Function ShowJobs() As DataSet
```

```
    Dim connPubs As New
SqlConnection("server=localhost;Initial
Catalog=pubs;Integrated Security=SSPI")
    Dim Datacmd As New SqlDataAdapter("select * from
Jobs", connPubs)
    Dim ds As New DataSet()
    Datacmd.Fill(ds, "Jobs")

    Return ds

  End Function

End Class
```

Possibly, when you installed the MSDE server (during VB.NET installation or in the previous chapter), *two* named instances of MSDE were installed. If so, you must specify the server name in the previous code. Just substitute your server name for `localhost` in the connection string where it says `server= localhost`.

If you tried the example titled "Binding to Databases" in Book IV, Chapter 4, you find nothing startling here in this code. You use the same VB.NET source code to connect to a database and return a dataset whether you're doing it from within a Windows form, a WebForm, or a Web Service. That's pretty cool.

Press F5 and then click the link and click the Invoke button to see the results, as shown in Figure 5-4.

Briefly examine the XML message that results when the data is retrieved and displayed in the browser (part of which is shown in Figure 5-4). Notice that it is divided into two primary sections. First, the *schema* (structure) describes each field and some details about it, such as its data type. Second comes the dataset itself, with the records and actual values. XML is, as you see, extremely verbose, just like its parent HTML. Be grateful that ASP.NET generates HTML and XML for you when you work with ASP.NET WebForms and Web Services.

When real clients access your Web Service, they get back only the XML result (partly shown in Figure 5-4). It's up to the client, then, to "discover" what information is available in that result, and to make use of it programmatically. The two browser views that you interact with when testing a Web Service in the VB.NET editor (shown in Figures 5-1 and 5-2) are merely for your convenience when working on a Web Service and testing it.

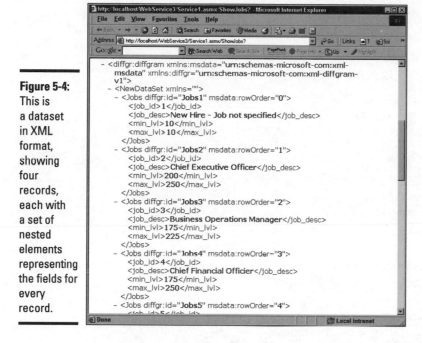

Figure 5-4:
This is a dataset in XML format, showing four records, each with a set of nested elements representing the fields for every record.

Testing Multiple Methods and Passing Parameters

So far you've seen examples of Web Services that have a single method and don't have any arguments (meaning that they don't receive passed data — parameters). Of course, you can expose multiple methods and accept passed parameters. The next example shows you how to test this type of Web Service, "passing" parameters by posing as the remote client.

This example exposes two methods: One accepts a string and responds to the caller by sending back the length of the string. The other method accepts two strings and then concatenates them and returns the result. Erase your code in the code window, and type the following into the code window:

```
Imports System.Web.Services
Imports System

<WebService(Description:="Counts characters, or concatenates
    two strings", Namespace:="http://tempuri.org/")> Public
    Class Service1
```

```
      Inherits System.Web.Services.WebService

<WebMethod(Description:="Please supply a string")> Public
    Function CountChars(ByVal s As String) As Integer

        Return s.Length

End Function

<WebMethod(Description:="Please supply two strings")> Public
    Function Concat(ByVal s As String, ByVal s1 As String) As
    String

        Return s & s1

End Function

End Class
```

Press F5 to test this Web Service. As shown in Figure 5-5, there are now two links, one for each exposed method.

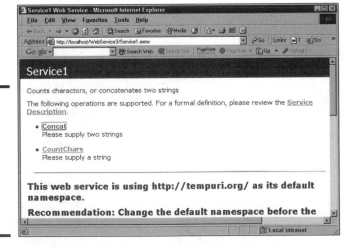

Figure 5-5:
In this example, your Web Service exposes two functions to clients.

Click the Concat link. You now see that in addition to the Invoke button, two Textboxes appear, where you can provide the two strings required by the Concat method, as shown in Figure 5-6. Notice that by providing a Description attribute, you are describing what parameter(s) each method requires.

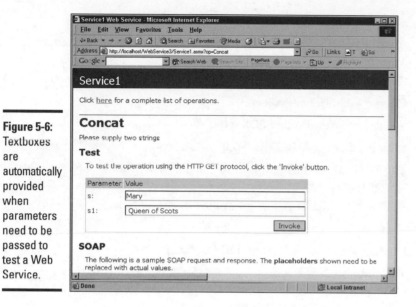

Figure 5-6:
Textboxes
are
automatically
provided
when
parameters
need to be
passed to
test a Web
Service.

Type in two strings, click the Invoke button, and see the XML response that
is sent back to the client:

```
<?xml version="1.0" encoding="utf-8" ?>
<string xmlns="http://tempuri.org/">Mary Queen of
    Scots</string>
```

You may have noticed in the various Web Service browser testing pages the
SOAP code and links you can click to see "a complete list of operators" and
a "service description." These XML files are essential to the communication
process between a client and your Web Service. Fortunately, though, you
can generally ignore them and let ASP.NET translate your VB.NET source
code into the necessary XML.

How to Call a Web Service

Now that you've seen how to create and test a Web Service, it's useful to go
to the other side of the connection and see how you can use (*consume*) a
Web Service from within VB.NET.

The idea is that more and more organizations will make Web Services available for various purposes. You need to know how to write source code that
takes advantage of those services. Follow these steps to add a Web reference to a Windows project:

1. **Shut down VB.**

2. **Answer *yes* if you are asked whether you want to save changes to your Web Service project.**

3. **Restart VB.NET.**

4. **Choose File⇨New⇨Project.**

   You see the New Project dialog box.

5. **Double-click the Windows Application icon.**

   The New Project dialog box closes, and a new Windows-style application is available to you.

6. **Double-click the TextBox icon in the Toolbox twice.**

   Two TextBoxes are added to your form.

7. **Double-click the background of the form.**

   The code window opens and your insertion cursor is in the Form_Load event.

8. **Choose Project⇨Add Web Reference.**

   The Add Web Reference dialog box opens, as shown in Figure 5-7.

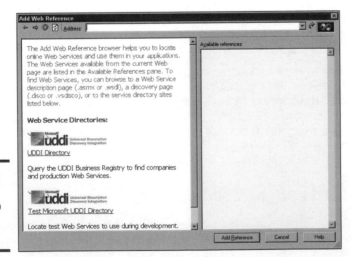

Figure 5-7:
Use this browser to test Web Services.

The dialog box shown in Figure 5-7 is actually a pared down browser window, featuring a URL address Textbox, plus Back and Forward buttons.

9. **Into the Address Textbox shown in Figure 5-7, type the path to your "local host" (simulated Web site) Web Service. The address will be something like this (depending on what you named your Web Service project and your Web Service). If you let VB.NET automatically name your project, it is probably named** WebService1 **and the actual WebService is named** Service1. **In that case, you can type this into the Address TextBox:**

```
http://localhost/WebService1/Service1.asmx
```

10. **Click the arrow icon to the right of the Address Textbox.**

You see the result shown in Figure 5-8.

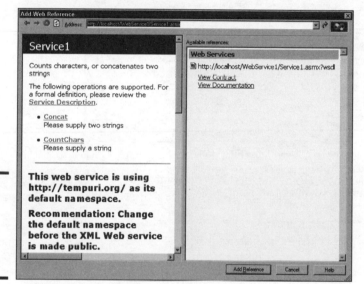

Figure 5-8:
Add this
Web
Reference
to your
project.

11. **Click the Add Reference button.**

The Add Reference browser window closes, a reference to this Web Service is added to your project, and you are returned to the code window. By adding this reference, you simulate a location on the Internet. However, in this case, the Web Service is located on your computer, on the *local* host.

Now you want to write code that connects your Windows project to the Web Service, uses its methods, and displays the results that are returned from the Web Service.

Type the following line into the `Form_Load` event, noticing that as you type the period after `localhost`, the .NET Intellisense feature lists for you any Web Services available at that site (as shown in Figure 5-9). In this case, the only service is named `Service1`:

```
dim WebServiceAnswer as New localhost.Service1
```

Figure 5-9:
The excellent auto-list-members Intellisense feature shows you the Web Service's name.

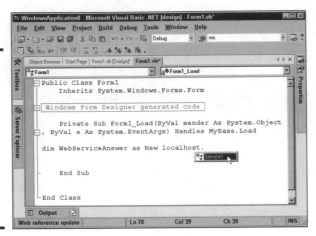

Now finish typing the following code into the `Form_Load` event to complete the Web Service access:

```
Private Sub Form1_Load(ByVal sender As System.Object, ByVal e
    As System.EventArgs) Handles MyBase.Load

    Dim WebServiceAnswer As New localhost.Service1()

    Dim param As String = TextBox1.Text

    TextBox2.Text = WebServiceAnswer.CountChars(param)

End Sub
```

Press F5 and notice that `Textbox1` contains the default `Text` value: `Text Box1`. `Textbox2` contains 8, the character count of the text in `TextBox1`. The Web Service did its job. (If you have a firewall running on your machine, it might put up a notice when you press F5 to run this example. It might want to know if you will grant permission for this service to connect to local host port 80. Go ahead and give permission. You know what's going on.)

Readers who are super alert, or who have had way too much coffee, may notice that the `CountChars` method sends back an Integer rather than the string that TextBoxes use to display text. Sometimes you must use a type conversion function, such as `.ToString` or `CStr` to transform a numeric data type into a string. Sometimes when you're testing a program, VB.NET throws up an error message saying that "type x cannot be changed into type y." Other times, VB.NET automatically transforms smaller numeric types into larger types or changes numbers into strings when you are displaying them in a TextBox. Just be aware that the conversion functions exist so that you can use them when error messages appear. For more information, see "Type Conversion Functions" in VB.NET Help.

If you make any changes to a Web Service, you must rebuild it for the client before you can retest it. (In the previous example, you added a Web Reference for a Windows-style client application, so you would have to rebuild in that situation.) To do this, right-click localhost in the Solution Explorer. Choose Update Web Reference in the context menu.

Chapter 6: Bugs in the Web

In This Chapter

✓ ASP.NET debugging

✓ Tracing

✓ Web page error handling

✓ Avoiding mistakes with validation controls

ASP.NET programs can reside in various computers. A client application here can use a Web Service there, and both of them can update a database over in Hong Kong. Such programs are called *distributed*.

As you may expect, debugging distributed programming is somewhat more complicated than ordinary application debugging. It's not easy, for example, to see inside someone else's Web Service code. You have to depend on their documentation and any error messages they may send back.

This chapter explores two primary topics: techniques you can use to debug ASP.NET programming, and the new set of validation controls that you can insert into your projects to trap incorrect user input.

Limitations on Traditional Debugging Tools

You can use breakpoints, single-stepping, watches, and other debugging features built into the Visual Studio .NET IDE, but they work only within your code window. Your code halts. Then you just switch to your browser to check what's happening visually. ASP.NET doesn't send its HTML results to the browser until your code is *finished* with its job. So, by putting a breakpoint in your code, for example, you prevent the HTML from being sent when the breakpoint halts execution.

To see how this works, start an ASP.NET application and then type the following into the Form_Load event of WebForm1:

```
Public Sub Page_Load(ByVal sender As System.Object, ByVal e
    As System.EventArgs) Handles MyBase.Load

        Dim i, j As Integer
        For i = 1 To 21
            j += i
        Next

End Sub
```

Put a breakpoint on the j += I line (by clicking the gray panel to the left of the code window until a red dot appears). Press F5. The execution indeed stops on the breakpoint. Now switch over to the browser window that ASP.NET opened to display this page. You see that Internet Explorer displays a message at the bottom of its window, saying "Web site found. Waiting for reply . . . " Indeed. Your HTML page hasn't been composed and sent to the browser because your VB.NET code-behind is in break mode — it hasn't yet built the HTML.

To get a feel for another debugging technique, you can try stepping through the code here (pressing F11), or you can repeatedly press F5 to watch the value of j increase in the Locals window. To display the Locals window, choose Debug⇨Windows⇨Locals.

Click the red dot to remove it, and then press F5 again. Now the browser displays (a blank page, in this case), but at least the HTML has been sent.

Response.Write to the rescue

You can resort to the old MsgBox technique to display variables during a program run. In traditional Windows programming, programmers often insert lines like the following in their source code:

```
MsgBox ("The variables j = " & j)
```

However, if you insert this line in your ASP.NET program, when you press F5, you get the helpful, lengthy error message shown in Figure 6-1.

In addition to what you can see in Figure 6-1, you also get the following stack trace (which I explain later in this section):

```
[InvalidOperationException: It is invalid to show a modal
    dialog or form when the application is not running in
    UserInteractive mode. Specify the ServiceNotification or
    DefaultDesktopOnly style to display a notification from a
    service application.]
```

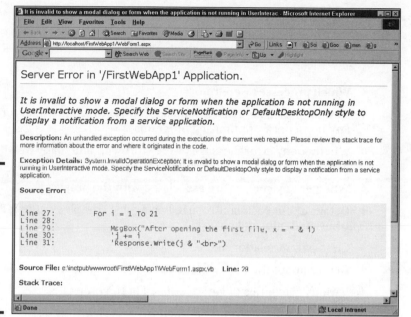

Figure 6-1:
ASP.NET
provides
huge
runtime
error
messages,
right in the
browser.

Instead of viewing variables in a message box, you can print them on the browser window with `response.write`, like this:

```
For i - 1 To 21
          j += i
          Response.Write("Variable J = " & j & "<br>")
Next
```

The `<br>` is HTML for line break, forcing the next `.Write` to go down one line.

There are better ways

This technique is good, but if you forget to remove one of these items, it can be embarrassing or even crash the program later when others are using your application. ASP.NET, however, offers a nice, new set of tracing features that you may want to experiment with. For one thing, the results of a trace are appended to the end of the browser page, whereas `response.write` comments are contained within the page — which can be messy.

Tracing in ASP.NET

Tracing provides *lots* of information. Among other things, tracing tells you the following:

✦ Which processes were run.

✦ How long each step takes in milliseconds (which is useful for locating any bottlenecks, optimizing programs).

✦ Whether any error messages were "thrown," and many details about them.

✦ Whether any cookies are associated with the project.

✦ Details about each control used on a page (the size of the HTML it's translated into, and so on).

✦ Child-parent relationships.

✦ Details about the request (such as when it happened).

✦ Various categories of variables used in the project.

To see how tracing works in an ASP.NET project, type the following into the Page_Load event:

```
Public Sub Page_Load(ByVal sender As System.Object, ByVal e
    As System.EventArgs) Handles MyBase.Load
        Trace.Warn("WARNING: Load Function starting")

        Dim result As String = Compare(5, -3)
        Trace.Write("In result in Page_Load is:", result)

    Trace.Warn("WARNING: Load Function finished")
End Sub

    Public Function Compare(ByVal a As Integer, ByVal b As
    Integer) As String

        'show category, value
        Trace.Write("Value of a in the Compare Function: ",
    a)
        Trace.Write("Value of b in the Compare Function: ",
    b)

        Dim answer As String

        If a > b Then
            answer = a & " is greater than " & b
```

```
Else
    answer = b & " is greater than " & a
End If

Return answer

End Function
```

Now enable tracing for the current page by switching to design view. (Click the WebForm1.aspx tab at the top of the code window.) In the properties window, double-click the Trace property to turn it to True.

There's also a TraceMode property, but you should normally leave it to the default SortByTime. This shows you the steps in the order that they were carried out by ASP.NET in the process of executing your source code and then building the resulting HTML code to send to the browser.

Press F5 and you should see quite a bit of information in the browser, including the trace information shown in Table 6-1.

Table 6-1	Trace Data Can Be Very Informative		
Trace Information			
Category	*Message*	*From First (s)*	*From Last (s)*
aspx.page	Begin Init		
aspx.page	End Init	0.037178	0.037178
	WARNING: Load Function starting	0.063165	0.025987
Value of a in the Compare Function:	5	0.100825	0.037660
Value of b in the Compare Function:	-3	0.101059	0.000235
In result in Page_Load is:	5 is greater than -3	0.101216	0.000157
	WARNING: Load Function finished	0.101353	0.000137
aspx.page	Begin PreRender	0.101498	0.000146
aspx.page	End PreRender	0.105913	0.004414
aspx.page	Begin SaveViewState	0.140197	0.034284
aspx.page	End SaveViewState	0.188640	0.048444
aspx.page	Begin Render	0.188840	0.000199
aspx.page	End Render	0.554962	0.366123

The trace data tells you what steps were carried out, in what order, and how long each step took. Notice that the information in the trace from the third through the seventh row is there because you used the Trace object's warn and write methods to show the values of variables and the starting and stopping of your source code.

Note that the warn method displays its results in red (as do any exceptions — error messages).

Understanding the trace sections

A trace displays six major sections, of which the Trace Information section is usually the most valuable for debugging purposes (as shown in Table 6-1). However, you should know at least the meaning of the other sections.

The *Request Details* section at the top identifies the HTTP request type and other information about the request, such as when it was made, the type of character encoding (usually Unicode), and so on.

The *Control Tree* describes any server controls you've placed on your WebForm, and it also specifies which controls are contained by other objects. For example, all controls are contained within the WebForm itself.

The *Cookies Collection* includes the Session ID, as well as any cookies provided to your application by the client.

The *Headers Collection* displays Http headers sent by the client to your server. Notice that this also includes cookie information.

The *Server Variables* section identifies quite a bit about the state of your server, including its name, URL (Internet address), the type of connection, and so on.

Throwing an exception

If you want to see how to throw an exception of your own that is displayed in the browser, add the following lines (in boldface) at the top of the Compare function in the code for the previous example in this chapter:

```
Public Function Compare(ByVal a As Integer, ByVal b As
Integer) As String

    If b < 0 Or a < 0 Then

        Throw New ArgumentOutOfRangeException("variable a
or b", "You can't use negative numbers. Why not? Just
because.")

    End If
```

Now when you press F5, the program halts at the line where the `Throw` occurs. The error is displayed, along with any information you supplied to describe the error.

If you don't need to see a trace of some of your code, you can turn tracing off (by putting the following line in your code):

```
Trace.IsEnabled = False
```

Then later turn it back on by setting it to `True`.

Application-Wide Tracing

The preceding examples demonstrate how to use tracing within a single Web page, but Web sites are often made up of multiple pages — and sometimes those pages interact with each other. Therefore, it's useful to be able to trace the entire application. To do that, you have to manually change a configuration file.

In the solution explorer, double-click the `Web.Config` entry to open the configuration file. Scroll down that code until you locate this entry:

```
<!-- APPLICATION-LEVEL TRACE LOGGING
        Application-level tracing enables trace log output
  for every page within an application.
        Set trace enabled="true" to enable application
trace logging.  If pageOutput="true", the
        trace information is displayed at the bottom of
each page.  Otherwise, you can view the
        application trace log by browsing the "trace.axd"
page from your web application
        root.
  -->
<trace enabled="false" requestLimit="10" pageOutput="false"
  traceMode="SortByTime" localOnly="true" />
```

As you can see, application-wide tracing is turned off by default. However, you can simply change `"false"` to `"true"` to turn it on. Application-wide tracing is not appended to the end of the HTML displayed in a browser. Instead, it is placed in a file named `trace.axd`. You can view this file in your browser by going to your Web application's root directory. In this example, you type the following into Internet Explorer's Address Textbox, and then click the Go button to the right of the Textbox:

```
http://localhost/firstwebapp/trace.axd
```

In the preceding code line, replace the term `firstwebapp` with your project's name.

You see something like the result shown in Figure 6-2.

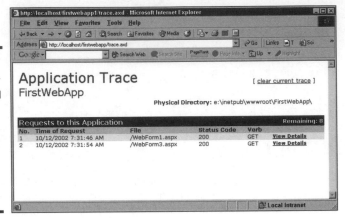

Figure 6-2:
Application-level tracing shows you which Web pages were requested and when they were requested.

I added a Web page named WebForm3 to this project to demonstrate application-level tracing. To make a request for that page, I put a hyperlink control on WebForm1 and then set its NavigateURL property to point to WebForm3. Running the application and clicking the link generated a request for WebForm3, as shown in Figure 6-2.

The .axd file contains an expandable list of the various pages that were requested. To see the trace details for any particular page, click the View Details hyperlink to the right.

The reqestlimit attribute specifies the number of trace requests to hold in memory. The pageoutput attribute — which isn't working at the time of this writing — is supposed to permit you to view tracing application-wide, but it prevents the appendage of tracing details to each page. LocalOnly specifies whether or not the .axd file is viewable only on the host Web server.

Tracing does slow things down, so you should not enable it when you release your Web Application for public use. However, you can leave the individual Trace.Write or Trace.Warn statements located in various places in your code because they are ignored after tracing is disabled in the release version.

Using Validation Controls

The old saying "garbage in, garbage out" is the truth. Most so-called "computer" errors are not actually made by the computer at all. The computer still knows how to add and subtract, and it simply never makes calculation mistakes.

"Computer" errors are actually "people" errors: either programming or data entry mess-ups. Data validation attempts to ensure that a user enters accurate data. I use the phrase "attempts to ensure" because no amount of data validation can prevent someone from entering, say, Nggg as his or her name.

Data validation, however, can take a look at the numbers entered by a tired teller at the end of the day and make sure he doesn't deduct a $400 million withdrawal from your account.

Validating user input at the source

ASP.NET offers a new set of five *validators*, controls on the Web Forms tab of the Toolbox that can make your life easier. To try one of these new validation controls and see how it works, follow these steps:

1. **Start VB.NET and choose Create New Project.**

The New Project dialog box appears.

2. **Double-click the ASP.NET Web Application icon.**

The dialog box closes and you see the WebForm design window for your new project.

3. **Open the Toolbox and use the down-arrow icon to scroll through the controls available on the Web Forms tab.**

Eventually, you come upon a set of validation controls, symbolized by checkbox icons, as shown in Figure 6-3. The validation controls help you avoid writing some code because they test the user's input for you.

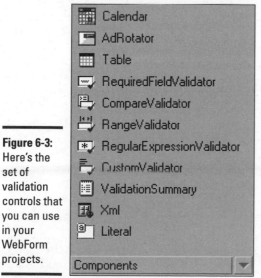

Figure 6-3:
Here's the set of validation controls that you can use in your WebForm projects.

4. **Click the tab at the top of the design window that says WebForm1.aspx. (You're probably still in this view anyway.)**

   This is your design file.

5. **Also click the Design tab at the bottom of the design window. (You're probably still in this view anyway, too.)**

   Now you're allowed to place controls onto the WebForm.

6. **Double-click the RangeValidator control to place it on your WebForm. Then double-click a TextBox, a Label control, and a Button control to place them on your WebForm.**

   Each of these controls overlaps each other in the upper left corner, so you want to drag them with your mouse so that you can easily see them and work with them.

7. **Click the RangeValidator control in the design window to select it, and then press F4 to display the Properties window.**

8. **In the RangeValidator's Properties window, enter the following values:**

   Maximum Value: 39

   Minimum Value: 3

   ErrorMessage: Your number must be between 3 and 39

   ControlToValidate: TextBox1

   (When the user types a number in the TextBox, the number is automatically checked for validity by the RangeValidator.)

   Type: Integer

   (A numeric type, rather than the default text string.)

9. **Change the Button's** Text **property to** ClickThis.

10. **Double-click the Button to open the code window.**

11. **Type the following code into the** Button_Click **event:**

```
Public Sub Button1_Click(ByVal sender As Object, ByVal
    e As System.EventArgs) Handles Button1.Click

    RangeValidator1.Validate()

    If Page.IsValid = True Then
    Label1.Text = "Your entry is valid"
    End If

End Sub
```

    The Validate method of the RangeValidator control is first fired, and then the Page object's IsValid property is tested. If it's True (the user entered a valid number), you display a `valid` message in the label. If the user types in a number that's out of range (such as 2 or 55, in this case), the RangeValidator's `ErrorMessage` property is displayed in the browser.

It's not strictly necessary to type the `RangeValidator1.Validate()` code. When the user clicks the button, the form is sent back to the server (submitted, or posted back, as they say). The validation controls automatically test (validate) whenever a postback occurs.

Now you can test your project. Press F5. Type 2 into the Textbox, which is an invalid number, and then click the button. You see the result shown in Figure 6-4.

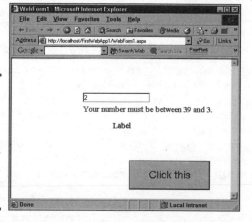

Figure 6-4: The Range-Validator control won't permit the user to enter the number 2.

Notice that the RangeValidator displays its error message wherever it is located on the WebForm. For this reason, you should move the RangeValidator so that it's located near the TextBox that it works with.

If you click the button with nothing in the TextBox, the RangeValidator doesn't think that an error has occurred. Having no input isn't always an error. For example, you may want to leave some fields optional. If you want to insist that the user enter a value, you can employ a RequiredFieldValidator (which I discuss soon in this section) in addition to the RangeValidator for that TextBox.

You might ask: "Why not just write the following code in the `Click` event, rather than using the RangeValidator?"

```
If CInt(TextBox1.Text) < 3 or CInt(TextBox1.Text) > 39 Then
    Response.write ("Must be between 3 and 39")
End If
```

(CInt forces the Text property to change from its default String data type to an Int.)

Programmatic validation, of course, works. But the validation controls offer you more flexibility. Also, if you have several controls on a page that you need to validate, the validation controls are probably your best route (because the ValidationSummary control can manage all validation on an entire WebPage).

Advantages of validation controls

With validation controls, you can write less code — or even in some cases just set a few properties. Beyond that, validation controls give you the ability to check either individual data (individual TextBox entries, for example, using RangeValidator1.IsValid) or the validity of the entire page at once (using Page.IsValid). You can also specify the text, location, and appearance of error messages generated by the validation controls.

One final point: The validation controls attempt to do their job efficiently within the visitor's browser (client-side, in other words), without requiring a round trip to your server (which slows things down). However, this only works client-side if the visitor's browser is set to permit scripts to run (some people disable this feature). If the job can't be done client-side, the validation job is done on the server. All this happens automatically, but you can disable the client-side behavior if you wish, by setting the Enable ClientScript property to false. I'm not sure why you'd want to do this, though.

Be grateful. With ASP.NET, you can set a couple of properties and the validation scripts are generated for you and are sent to the server automatically if necessary. Anyone who has wrestled with ASP in the past — dealing with crazy cross-browser compatibility scripting, hoping it might work, and writing some of this code essentially in the dark — is appreciative of the simplicity and efficiency of the .NET approach to these problems.

Understanding the Validation Controls

For each input control you want to validate, you add a separate validation control. In the preceding example, you wanted to validate the TextBox, so you dedicated a RangeValidator control to that job. When the Web page is sent back to the server (in the example, when the user clicks the Button to submit the contents of the TextBox back to the server), the page object sends the text to the validation control that has its ControlToValidate property set to the TextBox.

You can attach more than a one-validation control to a single TextBox (or any control). For example, if you need to check for a range of numbers and make sure that the user didn't leave the TextBox empty, you can set the `ControlToValidate` properties of both the RangeValidator and Required FieldValidator controls to point to that TextBox. However, if you are permitting the user to enter more than one valid pattern (for example, either `24456` or `24456-2242` may be a permissible, valid zip code pattern), you should not use multiple validation controls. In this situation, use the pattern-matching validation control (the RegularExpressionValidator, as it's called), and specify that two valid patterns are permitted.

When the page object sends data to a validation control for testing, the validation control sets a property that specifies whether or not the test was passed. For example, in the preceding example, the `IsValid` property of the `Page` object is set to either `True` or `False`. So you can test the condition of `Page.IsValid` and respond appropriately in your programming.

Note that if you have several validation controls active on a given page and any one of them fails some data, the `Page.IsValid` property is set to `False`. So, you should normally test the `Page.IsValid` property first. Then, if the property is `True`, your programming can safely go ahead and, for example, save the user's input to a database:

```
If Page.IsValid = True Then
```

`True` means that you can be assured that the user has correctly entered the necessary data. If the `Page.IsValid` property tests `False`, you probably want to figure out which validation control or controls are individually set to False. To do that, you can test their `IsValid` properties:

```
If RangeValidator1.IsValid = False Then
```

Alternatively, you can use a loop structure to test all the validators, using the `Page.Validators` collection, like this:

```
x = page.validators(0).IsValid
```

After you know which data is bad, you can display a message, asking the user to try again.

However, you have a simpler way to test a group of validation controls. Use the ValidationSummary control, which collects all the error messages from active validation controls on your WebPage. More on that in the "Using ValidationSummary" section, later in this chapter.

**Book IV
Chapter 6**

Bugs in the Web

Some validation controls test more than one factor at a time. For example, the RangeValidator can test for a range and also test that the data type is an integer if you set its Type value to Integer.

A summary of uses

Here is a summary of the uses of the six validation controls:

✦ **RequiredFieldValidator:** Makes sure that the user fills in a required entry.

✦ **RangeValidator:** You specify an upper and lower boundary, and data outside that range is invalid. In the preceding example, you used a range of numbers, but you can also specify a range of dates or an alphabetic range (*a* through *f,* for example). It can also check for data type.

✦ **CompareValidator:** Checks the user's entry against a property value in a different control on the page, against a value from a database, against another control, or against a literal value ("this" and 3 are literal values, as opposed to variables). You use comparison operators for this test: > for greater than, = for equals, and so on.

✦ **RegularExpressionValidator:** This control is a pattern-matcher. VB.NET includes a feature called regular expressions (from Unix via C). Use it to compare what the user entered against a specified sequence of characters or digits. This works well when ensuring that the user entered a valid e-mail address (must have an @ symbol), social security number, credit card number, zip code, phone number, and the like). Recall that you can specify two or more acceptable patterns simultaneously — such as two patterns of zip code numbers, one five digits long and a second style nine digits long with a hyphen. And, with regular expressions, you can be highly specific about your requirements. If you are interested in regular expressions (which can be used to search and replace), you can find lots of examples in VB.NET Help.

✦ **CustomValidator:** Allows you to define the validation by writing custom code. Use this if you are getting information about the correct pattern at runtime. For example, if the user clicks a CheckBox indicating that he or she is Canadian, you can have code that changes your validation from zip code to the Canadian postal code pattern, which uses alphabetic characters.

✦ **ValidationSummary:** Collects all error messages from all validation controls on the page.

Using ValidationSummary

Sometimes you don't want your Validation control to display its error message in the user's browser. Perhaps you want to send a different message, or perhaps you can adjust the user's input on the server without bothering the visitor. To do this, set the control's `Display` property to `false`.

And if the visitor is supposed to fill in several TextBoxes or other data-entry controls, you may want to suppress the individual validation controls' error messages and summarize all errors on the page in a single message. To do that, you use the ValidationSummary control.

To try the ValidationSummary control (and also see examples of using a regular expression validation and a compare validation), put two TextBoxes on a WebForm. Add a button (when it is clicked — even with no code in its `Click` event — it still triggers a request to the server and causes the validation process to execute).

Add a RegularExpressionValidator control and set its `ControlToValidate` property to `TextBox1`. Set its `ValidationExpression` property to the following:

```
((\(\d{3}\) ?)@  >(\d{3}-))?\d{3}-\d{4}
```

Can you remember that? No? Luckily, VB.NET gives you a little help with these not-so-regular expressions. The easy way to do this is to click the ... button in the `ValidationExpression` property in the Properties window. You then see the Regular Expression Editor dialog box, as shown in Figure 6-5.

Figure 6-5:
Use this editor to quickly generate common regular expressions for validation.

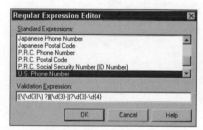

Set the `ErrorMessage` property to `Please use (nnn)nnn-nnnn format to enter this phone number`. Now, to suppress the RegularExpression Validator's error message, set its `Display` property to `None`.

Add a CompareValidator control to the form and set its `ControlToValidate` property to `TextBox2`. Set its `ValueToCompare` property to `1880` (because you're asking the visitors to enter their birth year, and you'll test for greater-than 1880). Set its `Operator` property to `GreaterThan`. Set its `ErrorMessage` property to `You must have been born after 1880, please re-enter your birth year...` Finally, set its `Display` property to `None`.

Add a ValidationSummary control to the form and set its `HeaderText` property to `The following errors must be fixed before you can submit this information...`

Now press F5 and enter an incorrect phone number format, and in TextBox2 enter 1777. Click the button. You see the resulting summary of the problems on this page, as shown in Figure 6-6.

Figure 6-6:
The Validation-Summary control can really save you some programming time, because it gathers and reports validation failures for the entire page.

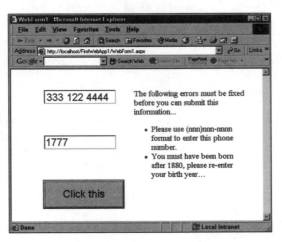

Book V

Visual Basic .NET Database Programming

The 5th Wave   By Rich Tennant

"You know how cats love to play with strings... Mittens would rather write them."

Contents at a Glance

Chapter 1: The Basics of Databases

In This Chapter

✔ Understanding the client-server model

✔ ADO.NET and scalability

✔ Working with connection, adapter, and DataSet objects

✔ Introducing the DataAdapter

✔ Using tables, columns, and records

✔ Understanding the value of indexes

✔ Creating a DataSet with the DataSet control

✔ Adding a table to a DataSet

✔ Viewing DataSet code

*E*xperts estimate that 80 percent of all computer programming involves databases. Fortunately, VB.NET has many tools to help you create, revise, manage, and otherwise deal with databases efficiently. This book shows you how easy it is to use those tools.

Nevertheless, in spite of the many VB.NET RAD (Rapid Application Development) tools, a programmer also has to *program,* to write source code by hand — without the assistance of wizards, prewritten code, built-in components, add-ins, and the many other helpful features that VB.NET offers. When you find yourself wondering how to solve a database-related task in VB.NET, you're likely to find example source code in this book that shows you how to do the job.

In this chapter, I explain the meaning of the current buzzwords in database programming: the client-server relationship, n-tier applications, distributed programming, and scalability, along with traditional database programming concepts, such as the table.

At the end of this chapter is a short example that shows you how to connect a VB.NET application to a server database in seven quick steps. This example should prove to you beyond any doubt that you made a wise choice when deciding to use Visual Basic to do your database programming.

Servers and Their Clients

VB.NET is designed to build client-server database applications. You can certainly use VB.NET tools to create a database that resides only in your local computer. But this is "The Age of the Internet." Confining yourself to your private little hard drive is, well, old fashioned at best.

A client-server database application creates a one-to-many relationship: one database that resides on a server computer and can be accessed through your VB.NET database application from many client computers on a network or on the Internet.

You can test this client-server communication by simulating it in your personal computer. No actual network or server is needed. In Book IV, Chapter 4, you see how to install Microsoft SQL Server and use it as a virtual server for testing your VB.NET database applications. You also install the sample databases that are used throughout this book. If you haven't installed SQL Server or the sample databases yet, make sure to do that now before proceeding any further.

In a client-server application, the VB.NET client-side database application does most of the work. Specifically, the client application does the following:

✦ Establishes communication between the client and server machines

✦ Defines the connection to the database

✦ Specifies what particular type of data it wants to see

✦ Displays the data to the user

✦ Optionally permits the user to modify the data

✦ Optionally validates the data (checks it for errors)

✦ Optionally does other data processing, such as totaling monthly expenses

✦ Returns the data to the server asking for permission to update the database with any changes the client made

The server's job

"Well," you might ask, "What does the *server* do?" It holds the database (which may be very large and require lots of storage space). The server also has the job of accessing the data directly from the database and sending it to the clients. Finally, a server may also have the responsibility of performing some validation checks of its own on the data that clients submit to it or of making some security decisions about whether the client has permission to make the request.

Dividing a database application between a pair of client and server computers is known as a *two-tier application.* It is also common to find *three-tier applications:* a user computer (running the part of the application that displays a visible user-interface, data entry forms, and such), a second computer holding the business logic (determining what data is needed from the database and how to contact the database), and a third computer holding the database itself (along with programming that answers requests for data and handles updates to the database). The idea of breaking an application into separate parts and spreading those parts among different machines on a network is known as *distributed computing.* Some database programs — called *n-tier* applications — are divided among even more than three machines.

Is the onus on you?

Now that you've seen the relationship between client and server, you no doubt fear that the onus is on you. You're the one who is writing the client application that does all the jobs necessary to manage data. I don't know about you, but I've never liked having onuses on me.

You're in luck. You chose VB.NET as your programming language. Fortunately, VB.NET comes with a set of components and wizards that do most of the work for you. Visual Basic was the first Rapid Application Development language — and most people think it continues to be the best. And after you've worked a bit with VB, you'll understand just how rapidly you can get from idea to application with the world's most popular computer language. Because VB.NET comes with so many built-in, prewritten solutions to common programming problems, you can sometimes create sophisticated behaviors just by dragging and dropping controls onto a VB.NET form (as in the example in the "Viewing a DataSet's Code" section of this chapter). By taking full advantage of VB.NET features, you, the database programmer, can pass the onus to VB.NET. And computers are so much more patient when dealing with an onus than people are.

ADO.NET: It's about Scalability

You find out about ADO.NET throughout this book. ADO.NET is the database technology built into VB.NET. In this chapter, you get a preview of what is probably the main reason to learn to use ADO.NET: It makes database management highly *scalable.*

Briefly, the problem is large local area networks and the Internet. For most of the history of personal computing, your database application could establish a connection to a database and keep that connection open until the user was finished reading or modifying the data.

This approach works okay if you have a few people — perhaps 10 or so — who need a connection with the database at the same time. But hundreds or possibly thousands of people on the Internet can't be simultaneously looking through your wonderful new catalog of Irish Flannel Sweaters. They simply can't all be connected at once. Figuring out how to ramp up to handle ever larger demands is one aspect of the concept referred to as *scalability*.

Can your application handle five clients and then grow gracefully to 5,000? Or will it — like the Microsoft Access database system and others — grind to a halt and smolder as soon as more than 10 connections are open?

A few people can sit close together on a couch and read the same book at the same time. It can work if they like each other and all have exacting hygienic practices. But you can see that this group-read idea can't be expanded much. Ten people can find it difficult; more than 10 can find it impossible no matter how often they wash themselves.

So the solution to this problem is a "library" model, albeit a library that can make as many copies of a popular book as are requested. Each person who wants one can check out his or her own copy and return it later.

In ADO.NET, you use *disconnected DataSets,* which are copies of data from the database. Actually, a DataSet is sort of like a free-floating little database all its own.

Here's what happens: A brief connection to the server's database is made while a DataSet is "checked out." Then the connection is broken. The DataSet is sent to the requesting client application. The client can keep the DataSet as long as necessary and manipulate the data as much as desired. If the client wants to update the database, a new (and brief) connection is established with the server database. The DataSet is submitted to the server, which decides whether or not to merge the changes into the database.

Using this library model, your database system is quite scalable. The server database has been uncoupled from sustained connections to clients. So thousands of DataSets can be copied and sent out and the server doesn't suffer overload.

ADO, the VB 6 database technology and the predecessor of ADO.NET, did feature a *recordset,* which could be disconnected from a database. But the ADO.NET DataSet, which replaces the recordset, is more capable and more robust. In fact, you really should visualize a DataSet as a small, portable database in itself. The recordset was a far more limited object.

The Big Three: Connection, Adapter, and DataSet Objects

The VB.NET Toolbox contains three controls that can work together to simplify creating a database-related application. These controls are the DataSet, the Connection object, and the DataAdapter object.

The *DataSet* is a mini-database that sits in your local (client) computer until you have finished with it. It is detached from the primary database. Throughout this book, I have much more to say about the DataSet object, and you put it through its paces in many examples.

The *Connection object* is uncomplicated. It merely holds a `Connection String` property that usually looks something like this:

```
myConnection.ConnectionString =
    "Provider=SQLOLEDB.1;Integrated Security=SSPI;Persist
    Security Info=False;Initial Catalog=pubs;Data
    Source=DELL"
```

The `Catalog` name, however, may be `Northwind` or whatever database connection you want to establish from VB.NET. `Data Source` is the name of your computer. (You see how to figure out that name in Book V, Chapter 3.) My computer's name is `DELL`. While testing your VB.NET applications, you specify the name of your computer as the `Data Source` because your own computer poses as a remote server. When you are ready to deploy your application in a real-world situation, the `Data Source` is a path (or Internet address) to a remote server that holds the database that you want to access.

The Connection object's other property of interest specifies how many seconds the Connection object should spend attempting to connect to a database before giving up and generating an error message. The default is 15 seconds; you can set it to any value between 10 and 30 seconds for a *WinForm* (Windows style application) and somewhat longer for a *WebForm* (Internet-style application). Here's how you can add this property to ConnectionString:

```
myConnection.ConnectionString = "user
    id=sa;password=ra24X;initial catalog=northwind;data
    source=DELL;Connect Timeout=30"
```

As you can see by comparing the two `ConnectionStrings` you've looked at in this section, you can specify security for a connection between a client application and a server database in different ways (`Integrated`, `password`, `user id`, `Persist Security Info`). To keep things simple, I suggest that you stick with Windows Integrated Security rather than having to worry about `ID` and `Password` attributes. Instead, when defining a connection, use `Integrated Security=SSPI`.

Even though the Connection object is fairly simple, it does have a lot of possible parameters. Fortunately, VB.NET happily helps you define new connections using a wizard (more on that next).

The *DataAdapter object* is the workhorse of the DataSet support controls. Adding a DataAdapter control to a VB.NET form launches the Data Adapter Configuration Wizard. This wizard steps you through the process of creating a connection to a database and defining a query (such as "send me the names of all customers in Boston"). It also writes lots of source code for you. When the wizard closes, you can use the DataAdapter to create a DataSet object. In fact, the only source code you have to write is this:

```
SqlDataAdapter1.Fill(DataSetName, "tablename")
```

Your DataSet is automatically loaded with the data you requested in your query. Imagine, connecting to a remote server's database and then getting back a DataSet based on your query specifications — and only having to write one line of source code. But I'm getting ahead of myself.

Two primary database types are accessed in VB.NET: OLE and SQL. OLE is the older technology and is the one you use with Access-style databases and others. SQL works with SQL Server and is the one I focus on in this book. To service these two types of databases, VB.NET includes two sets of connector controls and two sets of adapter controls: the OleDbDataAdaper and OleDbConnection controls, and the SqlDataAdaper and SqlConnection controls. VB.NET has two separate Command controls as well.

Getting Results in Seven Easy Steps

In this section, you see how quickly you can connect to a server database with VB.NET tools. In seven quick steps, you'll watch as a big table of data travels from its server database and is displayed in your client grid before your very eyes. You'll be "slap speechless," as they say down here in the South. You'll be dancing like a bug on a barbeque.

You get to do hands-on programming soon enough. Elsewhere in this book, you work with the powerful DataAdapter control that I'm illustrating here. But it can't hurt to give it a go right now, just to amaze yourself.

It's time to see how much VB.NET can do to help you with your database programming. You are about to see VB.NET make a connection, define a query, access the data, and display the DataSet it created. Follow these steps:

1. After starting a new VB.NET Windows-style project, open Server Explorer (choose View⇨Server Explorer), as shown in Figure 1-1.

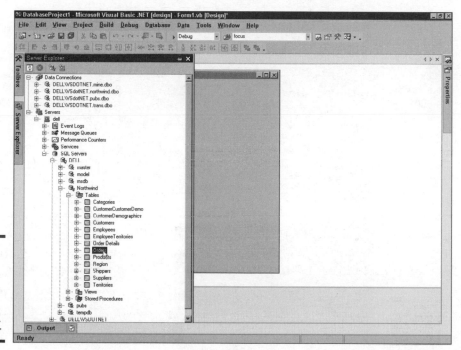

Figure 1-1:
Server
Explorer
is new
in Visual
Studio .NET.

You can do lots of things with Server Explorer, including adding, editing, and deleting tables and columns. You can even *create* a database. Later in this book, you see how.

2. Drag a table (named Orders) and drop it onto the VB.NET form, as shown in Figure 1-2.

This table is from the Northwind database, one of the sample databases you install in Book IV, Chapter 4. As soon as the Orders table is dropped onto your form, a Connection control and DataAdapter control are added to your project. They are placed in the tray below the form.

3. To create a DataSet that contains the Orders table, right-click the SqlDataAdapter1 icon in the tray and choose Generate Dataset, as shown in Figure 1-3.

The Generate Dataset dialog box appears.

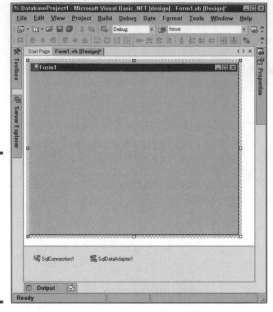

Figure 1-2:
Adding
tables from
an SQL
database is
as easy as
dragging
and
dropping.

Figure 1-3:
A Data-
Adapter can
generate
as many
DataSets as
you want.

4. **Your only job is to give this new DataSet a name.**

   Type **dsMaxie** (the **ds** to remind you that this is a DataSet).

5. **Click OK, and your new DataSet appears in the tray, as you can see in Figure 1-4.**

   Your new DataSet was created for you courtesy of the DataAdapter control.

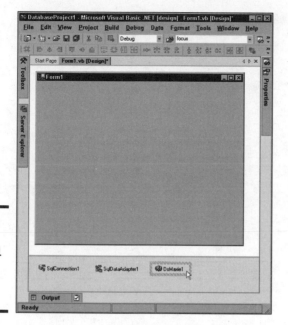

Figure 1-4:
You see
`dsMaxie1`
sitting
proudly in
the tray.

6. **Right-click the SqlDataAdapter1 icon again, but this time choose Preview Data.**

The Data Adapter Preview utility opens.

7. **Click the Fill DataSet button.**

All the data in the Orders table rolls into view, as you can see in Figure 1-5. That didn't take long, did it? (Well, try doing something like that a couple of years ago in the C language — we're talking *days!*)

You discover much more about DataSets in the coming chapters. Perhaps you'll come to consider the ASP.NET DataSet your new friend. But before getting too deep into creating database programs, you need to understand some basic concepts about their structure.

A *database* is a collection of information organized in some fashion and stored in a computer. If you have a little address book in your desk or purse, it's *almost* a database. All it needs to get formal recognition as a proper database is for you to copy its information into a computer and save it — in some orderly way — in a file. But consider what happens when you take the names, addresses, and phone numbers of all your friends and relatives and copy that data into the computer. Just randomly typing data isn't going to result in an organized store of information. You must first define a database structure, perhaps a structure similar to that in your address book, with alphabetical order and permitting one entry per page.

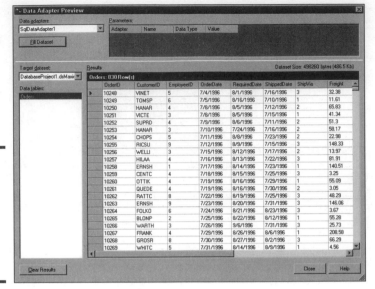

Figure 1-5:
The Orders table is extracted from the server and sent to the DataSet.

Understanding Rows, Columns, Tables, and All the Rest

There are various types of databases, but this book concentrates on the type that is currently by far the most popular: the relational database. A *relational database* has three primary qualities:

✦ **Data is stored in tables (which are subdivided into *columns* or, as they used to be called, *fields*).** For example, your personal address book could be a table with columns such as LastName, FirstName, Street, City, State, ZipCode, and PhoneNumber. The columns are the categories into which the data is subdivided.

✦ **You can join tables (in a *relationship*) so that you can later extract data from more than one table at a time.** For example, suppose you have a table that you've named *Gift*, which contains a PhoneNumber column (as a unique identifier of each person in your database) along with the price of the gift you received last Christmas from the person identified with that column. You can join the PhoneNumber column in the Gift table with the PhoneNumber column in an AddressBook table.

Then you can get information from both tables at once. (Both of these tables must include that same PhoneNumber column for this *joining* to work.) The term *relational database* derives from the relationships you can create by joining tables.

✦ **You can query tables, getting back DataSets (subsets of a table or tables).** A DataSet is a query (or request) for a list of, for example, the FirstName and GiftPrice columns of each row.

Read on. Look at Figures 1-6, 1-7, and 1-8 for examples to help you understand the terms *table, row,* and *column*.

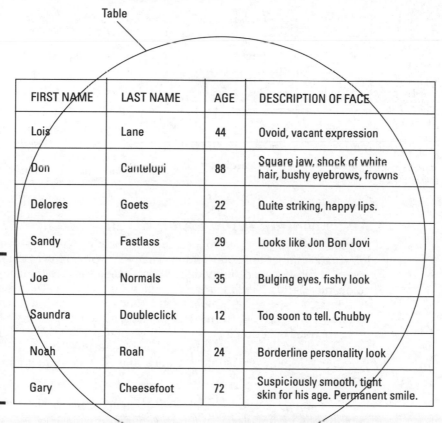

Table

FIRST NAME	LAST NAME	AGE	DESCRIPTION OF FACE
Lois	Lane	44	Ovoid, vacant expression
Don	Cantelupi	88	Square jaw, shock of white hair, bushy eyebrows, frowns
Delores	Goets	22	Quite striking, happy lips.
Sandy	Fastlass	29	Looks like Jon Bon Jovi
Joe	Normals	35	Bulging eyes, fishy look
Saundra	Doubleclick	12	Too soon to tell. Chubby
Noah	Roah	24	Borderline personality look
Gary	Cheesefoot	72	Suspiciously smooth, tight skin for his age. Permanent smile.

Figure 1-6:
A table is a relatively large-scale set of data; it includes multiple rows and columns.

Column

FIRST NAME	LAST NAME	AGE	DESCRIPTION OF FACE
Lois	Lane	44	Ovoid, vacant expression
Don	Cantelopi	88	Square jaw, shock of white hair, bushy eyebrows, frowns
Delores	Goets	22	Quite striking, happy lips.
Sandy	Fastlass	29	Looks like Jon Bon Jovi
Joe	Normals	35	Bulging eyes, fishy look
Saundra	Doubleclick	12	Too soon to tell. Chubby
Noah	Roah	24	Borderline personality look
Gary	Cheesefoot	72	Suspiciously smooth, tight skin for his age. Permanent smile.

Figure 1-7: A column is a *vertical* category of data, described by a title such as Age, Name, Address, or whatever category name you want to use.

Rows contain information about a single entry

Suppose that on each page of your personal address book, you always write information about only one person. That way, you don't get confused; each page describes a single individual. In database terms, each page, after it has some information filled in, is a *row* (which used to be called a *record*).

As shown in Figure 1-6, the top line on each page in the address book is a group of titles describing characteristics such as Name, Age, and so on. You can see where the term *columns* comes from. Reading down a column tells you the same category of information about all the different entries (rows) in the table.

Each column has its own name, or *label,* such as DescriptionOfFace. A row contains the information that fills the column, such as `quite striking, happy lips`. Rows do not have label names.

Each row usually contains several columns. In the address book example, each row has four columns: FirstName, LastName, Age, and Description OfFace. Here's an example of a single row in this database:

```
Joe          Normals    35    Bulging eyes, fishy look
```

One way to think of the relationship between rows and columns is to think of a baseball scoreboard. Many scoreboards put three labels across the top: Runs, Hits, and Errors. These are the column names, and they describe the meaning of the columns of data below them. The rows contain the data about the two individual teams. Remember that a row contains a set of information about an individual entity. There are two rows: Guest and Violent Toads (or whatever fauna or warrior the local team is named after). The data for Guest might be 4, 6, and 3; for the Violent Toads, the data might be 74, 63, and 1. With 74 runs, you know this is either high school baseball or a ballgame on Mars.

Some databases allow you to use more than one word for column names, such as Description of Face. However, other database styles require you to enclose multiple-word names in brackets or single quotes: [Description of Face] or 'Description of Face'. Some databases forbid two words (by forbidding the use of spaces).

Row

FIRST NAME	LAST NAME	AGE	DESCRIPTION OF FACE
Lois	Lane	44	Ovoid, vacant expression
Don	Cantelopi	88	Square jaw, shock of white hair, bushy eyebrows, frowns
Delores	Goets	22	Quite striking, happy lips.
Sandy	Fastlass	29	Looks like Jon Bon Jovi
Joe	Normals	35	Bulging eyes, fishy look
Saundra	Doubleclick	12	Too soon to tell. Chubby
Noah	Roah	24	Borderline personality look
Gary	Cheesefoot	72	Suspiciously smooth, tight skin for his age. Permanent smile.

Figure 1-8:
A row is a *horizontal* set of data describing a single person or thing — all the columns taken together as "adjectives" about the subject of this unique row.

If you're having trouble with two-word column names when programming, try enclosing the name in brackets or single quotes. Although Microsoft Access-style databases permit spaces in column names, most relational databases do not permit spaces. If the database does not permit you to use spaces, you must resort to using an underscore character to separate words (such as Description_of_Face) or slamming the words together (such as DescriptionOfFace).

Tables are made up of columns

Back to the address book example. Suppose that you decide to create a database, and at first all you have in it is the information from your address book. This small, simple database has only one table, which you name Addresses. (Tables are relatively large-scale collections of data, but a database can be even larger; it can contain multiple tables, representing, say, all the information about the employees, products, sales, and other data for a huge corporation.) You define the contents of a database when you create it, so you determine how many tables it has, the column names, and other organizational details.

Say that you've already marked the birthdays of all your friends and relatives on your calendar, and now you decide to put this data into a second table in your database. You name the table Gifts and define five columns for it: LastName, Birthday, FavoriteColor, ShoeSize, and Comments.

Notice that both your Addresses table and your Gifts table have a LastName column in common. These two LastName columns contain the same data in both tables. This common column enables you to *join* the tables. You can then *query* (ask for information from) both of these tables at once. You can use a query such as, "What is Normals's address and birthday?" His address information is held only in the Addresses table, and his birthday is listed in the Gifts table. But because both tables contain Normals in a LastName column that is identical in both tables, they can provide their respective additional information about Joe: his address from the Addresses table and his birthday from the Gifts table. The *result* of this query (the information you get back) is made available in what's called a DataSet. It contains only the data that you need for a particular purpose — in this example, mailing a birthday gift.

If you are particularly sharp right now, you may say, "What happens if *two* people share the same last name, *Normals?*" Very good point. Now sit down! That is a problem, because at least one column must contain unique data for each record. This problem is solved with keys and indexes, which I cover later in this chapter in the section whimsically titled "Indexes — a Key to Success."

Why use multiple tables?

Why have two tables: Addresses and Gifts? Why not just put all the data into one big table? Bulging, single-table databases are less flexible and less efficient than multiple, smaller tables — both when used by average people and when manipulated by a programmer.

You separate data into tables and then you separate it further into columns for the same reason that most people use labeled folders in their filing cabinets. Storing, retrieving, and managing the contents of an organized filing cabinet with many thin, alphabetized folders is much easier than using a few huge folders bursting with papers.

If the database is small, however, its organization doesn't matter much. You don't have to worry about dividing your little address book database into several tables because it doesn't have that many entries. You're not *that* popular, are you?

But if you're designing a multiuser database with 250,000 rows, every little efficiency matters when searching and sorting such a large amount of data. By creating several tables, you can improve the organization of the database, write programming code for it more easily, and generally retrieve rows faster when querying. Why? Primarily because putting everything into one big database can result in dreadful redundancies.

To understand how and why this redundancy occurs, and why it's sometimes good to use several tables rather than one big one, consider a database that lists 100 book publishers and 8,000 books. The database is divided into four tables: Authors, Publishers, TitleAuthor, and Titles. If all this information were stored in a single table, duplicated data would be all over the place.

Why? You would have to repeat the publishers' names, addresses, and phone numbers many times for each of the 8,000 books. It would be better to store each Publisher only once and store their data (name, address, and phone number) only once.

When you look up a title in the Titles table, the publisher's name is part of each title's row (so you do have to provide the publisher's name 8,000 times). But if you want the publisher's address, phone number, and other details, no problem — because the Publisher's table and the Titles table both contain a PublishersName column. That way, you can get the other details about a publisher by matching the PublishersName column in the two tables. You store each publisher's address and phone number only once because you have separate tables. What's more, if you need to change the publisher's phone number later because they move to new offices, a single change in the Publishers table is the only change you have to make in the entire database.

Tangled relationships: Using unique data to tie tables together

When you specify a relationship between tables while designing a database, you're saying, "I may need additional information about this fellow, and if I do, it can be found in this other table using a column that is identical in both tables — the *primary key.*"

Suppose that you have several tables in a database, and all have a column named ID. In each of these tables, John Jones has an ID number of 242522. The database may have several people named John Jones, so name columns are not going to provide you with a unique key to a unique row (record) about a particular Mr. Jones. To be specific about which Mr. Jones, I look up the ID number in the second table.

A key is a column in a table that guarantees each entry in the column is unique to the row it resides in. Sometimes called the primary key, a key column prevents confusion. You can't use the FirstName column as a key because you may have six or more Joes in your organization. You can't use the LastName column because you could have more than one person named Smith. Phone numbers *seem* good, but no. You can't use the home phone number column because your office may suffer from raging nepotism and all four of the boss's wretched offspring work for Daddy. Because these slackers also still live at home, they all share the same phone number. Maybe they don't *yet* work at the office, but when designing a database, you don't want the whole thing to become broken if one of Daddy's angels comes to work in the future. What's a puzzled database designer to do? Well, don't sit there wringing your hands and moaning. Figure out a column that must always be unique. A Social Security number column, for example, makes a good key column. Or, as I explain in the next section of this chapter, you can generate a series of unique ID numbers within a table automatically. You can let the computer assign serial numbers, like the sequential, never-repeated, numbers on a roll of movie tickets.

Let the database do it for you: AutoNumber columns

You can let the database generate a unique ID number for each row. These serial numbers start with 1 when you add the first row and go up by 1 for each new row entered into the database. (Some database programmers insist that every table should have a column with a unique serial number so that you can ensure that every row is unique.)

Such database-generated serial numbers are put into an *AutoNumber* column. The AutoNumber column acts as a unique key, and its main function is to permit tables to be linked. How? When designing the database, you specify that the AutoNumber column be included in more than one table as a way of joining those tables.

Indexes — a Key to Success

Information in a relational database is not automatically stored alphabetically (or by numeric order, if the column is numeric). In a Name column, *Anderware* can follow *Zimbare*. Or maybe not. Whatever. At first, this seems surprising because you certainly don't expect a "filing system" to permit folders to be stored in any order.

However, rows in a relational database aren't sorted. When someone adds a row to a database, it's just put at the end of a table. No attempt is made to place it in some particular position, such as alphabetical order. When a row is deleted, who cares? A relational database has a real "la-ti-dah" attitude about alphabetization. When designing a database, however, you should specify one or more of its columns as *indexes*. That's the key to the organization of a relational database.

Imagine nonalphabetic yellow pages

Many columns are not indexed (sorted). If you want to search for a particular row in a column that's not indexed, the database software must search down through every row until it finds the right one. How would you like it if the Yellow Pages in the phone book were not alphabetized like that? You'd be turning pages all night, looking for a plumber, hoping to stumble on the right page.

An index in a relational database is the one exception to the blithe, uncaring order I've just described. An indexed column solves the problem of finding a particular row in the jumble of data. The database software can quickly locate a specific row if a column is indexed.

So, when you're designing a database, you need to decide which column or columns should be indexed. (Unindexed data *can* be searched; it just takes longer.) Indexing doesn't, of course, speed things up in some kinds of queries. If the query is, "Give me a list of all people over 50," and the Age column isn't indexed, each record still must be searched.

Here's the general rule: You should index any columns that are likely to be searched. In the example address book database (remember it had two tables, one for Gifts), you are far more likely to search some columns than others. You'd probably search the Name and Birthday columns, but you would not likely search the [Favorite Color], [Shoe Size], or Comments columns. The purpose of the Gift table is to help you buy gifts for people, so it's unlikely that you'd ever query it like this: "Give me a list of everyone whose favorite color is green." But it's quite likely that you would query like this: "List everyone who has a birthday in August."

So, for the Gift table, you may specify that the Name and Birthday columns should be indexed and that the others should be left unindexed. But what happens if you later buy some size 8 blue shoes on sale and want to search the database to see whether any of your friends or relatives wear that size and like blue? No problemo. Remember, you can always still conduct searches on unindexed columns; finding the information you need just takes longer. You are simply optimizing the average execution speed of your database when you decide which columns to index.

The database software automatically creates and maintains the indexes you specify. You need to do nothing more than specify which columns should be indexed.

Hey, let's index every column!

Some of you are probably thinking, "Why not index all the columns? That would be super-efficient." Wrong. When publishers create an index for a book, they don't index all the words in the book, do they? They include the words likely to be searched for, not words such as "the" or "twelve."

An index of all the words would suffer from several drawbacks. First of all, it would be bigger than the book. Second, most of the index would be of little use to anyone; it would be inefficient precisely because it was so big. A quick scan of the book itself may be faster than slogging through a massively bloated, highly repetitive index.

You don't index every column in a table for a similar reason: Too much of a good thing is a bad thing. Efficiencies start to degrade, storage space gets tight, multiuser traffic jams can occur, and other bugaboos arise.

Building Your First DataSet

But enough theory. Time to get your hands out of your pockets and build a DataSet. In the process, you get real-world experience with the meaning of the terms you've read about: column, row, table, key, and DataSet.

A DataSet can contain all the basic elements of a database: tables, keys, indexes, and even relations between tables. So by creating a DataSet, you'll be discovering the structure of a database at the same time. The fundamental differences between a DataSet and a database are that a database generally resides on a hard drive in one or more files and is usually larger. A DataSet usually holds a subset of the data in a full database.

A DataSet can be stored on a hard drive, but it can also simply be pulled out of an existing database — and therefore may merely reside in the computer's memory while someone manipulates or views it. Then, if changes are made, the DataSet can be merged back into the database from which it was extracted.

Creating a DataSet

In the following example, you create a DataSet and then find out how to add rows to it and read those rows. You can create and manipulate DataSets using VB.NET data controls and Server Explorer in many ways. However, to get off to a good start, you use the simplest approach of all: dropping a DataSet control from the Toolbox onto a form. In this example, you are not extracting a DataSet by extracting a subset of an existing database (technically, a *subset* is referred to as a *query* or *result*). Instead, you create a DataSet yourself, defining its structure (technically, *schema*). This is virtually identical to the way that you would create an actual database, but a DataSet is simply smaller than an ordinary database.

Follow these steps:

1. **Choose File⇔New⇔Project.**

The New Project dialog box appears.

2. **In the Name column, type** AddressBook.

Did you know that it's very easy to put your Windows-style projects in any directory that you want? Just click the Browse button in the New Project dialog box and choose a directory. You can even type in the name of a directory that doesn't exist, and VB.NET creates it for you.

3. **Double-click the Windows Application icon.**

The dialog box closes and you see an empty form.

4. **Open the Toolbox (press Ctrl+Alt+X or click its tab).**

5. **Click the Data tab in the Toolbox.**

You see a set of database-related controls.

6. **Double-click the DataSet icon in the Toolbox.**

The Add Dataset dialog box appears, as shown in Figure 1-9.

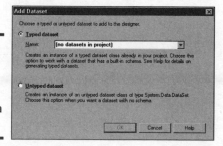

Figure 1-9:
Use this wizard to add a DataSet to a project.

7. **Choose the Untyped Dataset option by clicking that radio button.**

   You have no DataSet in this project yet, so you can't use the Typed Dataset option.

8. **Click OK.**

   The dialog box closes and a new DataSet object icon appears in the tray below your form. The tray is where VB.NET puts controls that are never made visible to the user, such as a Timer.

Adding a table to a DataSet

Now it's time to define the structure, or *schema,* of your new DataSet. It's time to add a table to it.

Inside that table, define three columns: one for the last name of each person in your address book, the second for the first name, and the third for an autoincrementing primary key.

1. **Right-click the DataSet1 icon from the previous example in the tray, and choose Properties.**

   The Properties window is displayed, showing the properties of DataSet1.

2. **In the Properties window, change the** Name **property (*not* the** DataSetName **property) of DataSet1 to** dsAddresses.

   The DataSet icon in the tray changes to display its new name. (Behind the scenes, VB.NET also changes the name in the source code that it writes automatically to define the contents of your form.)

3. **In the Properties window, click the Tables property and then click the ellipsis (...).**

   The Tables Collection Editor appears.

4. **In the Tables Collection Editor, click the Add button.**

   The table's properties are displayed, as shown in Figure 1-10.

Figure 1-10:
Here's where you can define or edit tables and their properties.

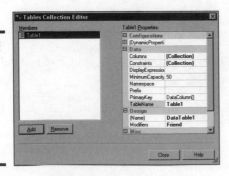

5. **Change the** Name **property (***not* **the** TableName **property) to** Friends.

   VB.NET again changes the source code behind the scenes. You don't have to worry about these details. Just relax and know that VB.NET knows how to write the code that defines your new DataSet's schema.

6. **In the Properties list of the Tables Collection Editor, click Columns and then click the ellipsis.**

   The Columns Collection Editor dialog box appears.

7. **In the Columns Collection Editor, click the Add button.**

   You can now define a new column and its properties, as shown in Figure 1-11. Note that the DataType property for all columns defaults to the string (text) type, although you can change it. This is the data type that you want for the LastName and FirstName columns.

Figure 1-11:
Use this dialog box to add columns to a table and edit the properties of those columns.

8. **Change the** Name **property (***not* **the** ColumnName **property) to** LastName. **(The name defaults to** DataColumn1.**)**

9. **Click the Add button.**

   Column2 is now created.

10. **Change this column's** Name **property to** FirstName.

11. **Click the Add button.**

    Column3 is now created.

12. **Change this column's** Name **property to** Key, **and its** ReadOnly **property to** True.

    With the ReadOnly property True, nobody can *write* (change) any of the data in this column. That's what you want; it's supposed to be looked at (read) only.

13. **Double-click the** `Unique` **property.**

It changes from `False` to `True`. Now the DataSet refuses to permit two rows to contain identical data in the Key column. In addition, as long as this property is `True`, you can't use the Remove button in the Columns Collection Editor dialog box to delete the column.

14. **Double-click the** `AutoIncrement` **property.**

It changes from `False` to `True`. Now the DataSet automatically increments (increases) the number in this column by one for each row. Notice that when you double-clicked this property, VB.NET was wise enough to change this column's `DataType` property from String to Integer. After all, you want ordinary numbers (1, 2, 3, 4, and so on) in this column, not text. Text can't be incremented. Also notice that you can change the `AutoIncrementSeed` (starting number) property and the `AutoIncrementSeedStep` (amount of increase in each step) property. However, the defaults are what you want: start from zero and go up by one each time. This way, the first record you add to this table is automatically given a 0 in the Key column, the next record you add is given a 1, and so on up.

15. **Click the Close button twice.**

The Columns Collection Editor and the Tables Collection Editor close.

There is no actual data in your dataset, but you have created its schema.

Viewing a DataSet's Code

While you've been sitting on your fancy perch using dialog boxes and controls to create a DataSet, VB.NET has been busy in the code window doing all the grunt work to write the programming. Just for a good scare, open the code window by double-clicking Form1 in the design window. Now click the + symbol next to *Windows Form Designer generated code* to reveal the tons of code that VB.NET doesn't think you need to bother your pretty head about.

Behind the scenes in a Region

Essentially, some of the code that you see when you click the + symbol next to a Region in the code window is housekeeping. In previous versions of VB, you would not have seen the code that specified, for example, the Name and Text (title bar caption) properties of your form. However, VB.NET lets you view and, if you really want to live dangerously, modify housekeeping code, such as this:

```
Me.Name = "Form1"
Me.Text = "Form1"
```

You're better off using the Properties window in design mode to make changes to the properties of forms and controls. And you're better off using the Toolbox to add controls to your form. Generally speaking, you should simply ignore this Region (called *Windows Form Designer generated code*, and called Region after you click the +). Leave it alone.

Some will ignore this advice and prefer to do the hard way in source code what they could do the easy way with the Toolbox. But be warned. You aren't really supposed to modify most of the code in the Region areas. VB.NET warns you with the following comment in the code itself:

```
'NOTE: The following procedure
is required by the Windows
Form Designer

'It can be modified using
the Windows Form Designer.

'Do not modify it using
the code editor.
```

So, you've been warned. You *are* allowed to insert initialization (startup housekeeping) code here in Sub New. However, most VB programmers prefer to use the Form_Load event for initialization code instead:

```
Public Sub New()
        MyBase.New()

        'This call is required
by the Windows Form
Designer.

        InitializeComponent()

        'Add any initialization
after the
InitializeComponent() call
End Sub
```

Chapter 2: User Interface Techniques

In This Chapter

- ✔ Working with the Data Form Wizard
- ✔ Modifying DataSets
- ✔ Using the single-row style
- ✔ Looking at the BindingContext object
- ✔ Using classic components
- ✔ Attaching a data-aware control
- ✔ Moving through rows
- ✔ Using the DataGrid

Few things in this life gladden a VB.NET database programmer's heart more than finding out about new productivity tools to make coding easier. This chapter focuses on several such wizards and utilities. When you know how to use the Data Form Wizard, the SQL Query Builder, and other helpers, creating a database application — a visual interface through which a user can interact with a database — is pretty easy.

Using the Data Form Wizard

In VB.NET, you can display data to the user in many ways. One of the best ways is to use the Data Form Wizard to add a *grid* view of a DataSet. The user can then easily read, navigate, or edit the data. You begin this chapter by seeing how to use this most excellent wizard. Big fun for you!

I'm assuming that you've already followed the instructions in Book IV, Chapter 4 to create an SQL Server connection to the *pubs* sample database. Such a connection lives outside your VB.NET projects, so the connection still exists even when you start a new VB.NET project.

To see what the Data Form Wizard can do for you, follow these steps:

1. **Choose File➪New Project to create a new project in VB.NET.**

The New Project dialog box appears.

2. **Name your new project datWiz.**

3. **Double-click the Windows Application icon.**

   VB.NET builds the default components of a WinForm project.

4. **Choose Project⇨Add New Item, and then double-click the Data Form Wizard icon.**

   The wizard is displayed.

5. **Click Next.**

   You are asked which DataSet you want to use.

6. **Type** dsAuthors **in the "Create a new dataset named" box. This is the name of your new DataSet. Then click Next.**

   You're asked to choose a connection to a database.

7. **Click the down-arrow button and select the pubs.dbo connection.**

   Your computer's name is listed as the first part of the pubs.dbo name.

8. **Click Next.**

   You see the tables in this database.

9. **Double-click the Authors table.**

   This table moves from the left pane to the Selected Item(s) pane on the right side, as shown in Figure 2-1.

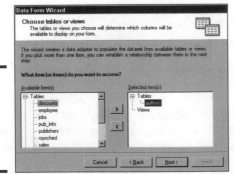

Figure 2-1: Select which tables you want to access.

10. **Click Next.**

    As a side note, here's a tale that teaches us that sometimes programming is a mystery within an enigma: This book's technical editor followed the previous steps, and a message box popped up at this point, saying The following error occurred: 'Value cannot be null. Parameter name: type'. He went back and started over from Step 1, and then he

saw the following message (in a Generate Dataset messagebox): The
schema file "C:\documents and settings\mlerch\my documents\
visual studio projects\datwiz\dsauthors.xsd" already
exists. Do you want to replace it?

He clicked Yes, but he got the same error as earlier. When he clicked No,
he got this message: The following error occurred: '' At this
point, he was getting a little steamed. He viewed the authors table in
enterprise manager, and it looked just fine. The connection was live and
all the data was there. He then whipped up a little command-line utility
(remember he's a tech editor, and he can do this kind of thing) that
queried the authors table from pubs, and it worked fine too! After all of
this hassle, he walked away in a snit. He later came back to his computer to try again — this time with a sandwich (because a sandwich
always helps). After starting the wizard again, the "use the following
dataset" drop-down was filled. Noting that but ignoring it, he followed
the previous instructions from Steps 1 to 10. This time, they worked!
What gives? It's definitely elves. The moral of this story is: In programming, you just never know what will happen.

You can now specify which columns in the Authors table you want to
display in the DataForm grid.

11. **Leave all columns selected (the default) in the Authors table, and
then click Next.**

You're now asked which of the two types of Data Form Wizard displays
you want to use, as shown in Figure 2-2.

12. **Leave the default All Records in a Grid radio button selected.**

The user now sees multiple rows when this grid is displayed.

13. **Click Finish.**

The Data Form Wizard closes.

Figure 2-2:
The Data
Form
Wizard
can display
either a
grid or a
series of
TextBoxes.

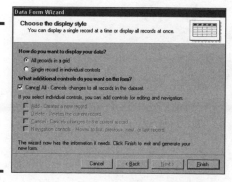

You now see the DataForm, complete with a DataGrid control that already has all the column names from the Authors table filled in, as shown in Figure 2-3. Notice, too, that connection and data adapter controls have been added to the tray beneath the form.

Locate the dsAuthors.XSD file in Solution Explorer. An additional file (currently hidden) also supports your DataSet. By default, the Solution Explorer hides some files. To see them, click the name of your project (the line in boldface in the Solution Explorer, such as WindowsApplication1) to reveal the icons in the Solution Explorer title bar (these icons are always visible in VB.NET 2003).

Then click the Show All Files icon (which looks like a collection of files and folders). Now click all the + symbols in Solution Explorer to reveal the hidden files.

Click the + symbol next to the dsAuthors.XSD file in Solution Explorer, and there it is — the hidden VB.NET code file, dsAuthors.VB. Right-click dsAuthors.VB and choose View Code. You see a hair-raising chunk of 657 lines of code that you didn't write: classes within classes, imported namespaces, overridden functions, and members without end. Your best move is to close this window and not tamper with it. VB.NET does lots of things for you behind the scenes. In cases like this, the less you know, the better. That's my advice. Perhaps Solution Explorer was wise to hide this file.

Before you press F5 to see the DataForm in action, you must make VB.NET display the DataForm. By default, Form1 is the Startup object. This means that only Form1 is automatically displayed when the project executes. The DataForm is a separate form, not simply a control placed on Form1.

Figure 2-3:
After a DataSet object has been created, a DataGrid bound to that DataSet displays column names (the DataSet table's basic structure).

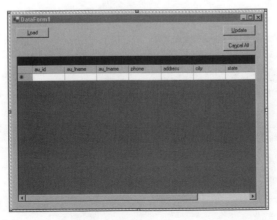

Displaying an alternate form

To display the DataForm, you can write some code for the `Form1_Load` event, like this:

```
Private Sub Form1_Load(ByVal sender As System.Object, ByVal e
     As System.EventArgs) Handles MyBase.Load

        Dim df As New DataForm1()
        df.Show()

End Sub
```

Setting the Startup object

Or, more in line with your wishes for this project, you can simply make DataForm1 the default Startup object. Follow these steps:

1. **Open the Solution Explorer window (press Ctrl+R).**

2. **Right-click the name of this project (which is the entry in boldface) in the Solution Explorer window, and choose Properties.**

   The dialog box shown in Figure 2-4 appears.

3. **Change the Startup object to DataForm1, and then click OK.**

4. **Press F5, and then click the Load button when the DataForm is displayed, as shown in Figure 2-5.**

Figure 2-4:
Make the
DataForm
the startup
object here.

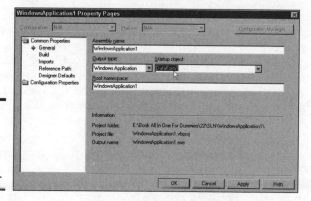

Figure 2-5:
The
DataForm's
DataGrid is
filled with
your
DataSet.

	au_id	au_lname	au_fname	phone	address	city	state
▶	172-32-1176	White	Johnson	408 496-7223	10932 Bigge	Menlo Park	CA
	213-46-8915	Green	Marjorie	415 986-7020	309 63rd St.	Oakland	CA
	238-95-7766	Carson	Cheryl	415 548-7723	589 Darwin L	Berkeley	CA
	267-41-2394	O'Leary	Michael	408 286-2428	22 Cleveland	San Jose	CA
	274-80-9391	Straight	Dean	415 834-2919	5420 College	Oakland	CA
	341-22-1782	Smith	Meander	913 843-0462	10 Mississipp	Lawrence	KS
	409-56-7008	Bennet	Abraham	415 658-9932	6223 Batema	Berkeley	CA
	427-17-2319	Dull	Ann	415 836-7128	3410 Blonde	Palo Alto	CA
	472-27-2349	Gringlesby	Burt	707 938-6445	PO Box 792	Covelo	CA
	486-29-1786	Locksley	Charlene	415 585-4620	18 Broadway	San Francisc	CA
	527-72-3246	Greene	Morningstar	615 297-2723	22 Graybar H	Nashville	TN
	648-92-1872	Blotchet-Halls	Reginald	503 745-6402	55 Hillsdale B	Corvallis	OR
	672-71-3249	Yokomoto	Akiko	415 935-4228	3 Silver Ct.	Walnut Creek	CA
	712-45-1867	del Castillo	Innes	615 996-8275	2286 Cram Pl	Ann Arbor	MI
	722-51-5454	DeFrance	Michel	219 547-9982	3 Balding Pl.	Gary	IN
	724-08-9931	Stringer	Dirk	415 843-2991	5420 Telegra	Oakland	CA
	724-80-9391	MacFeather	Stearns	415 354-7128	44 Upland Ht	Oakland	CA

If you're experimenting while learning VB.NET, it's sometimes useful to start with a blank slate — an empty form that has no leftover source code from a previous experiment to confuse things. In this book, I often tell you to start a new VB.NET project to ensure that you won't see any side effects. However, you can save time by simply choosing Project➪Add Windows Form (or another item) and making that new form the Startup object. Then, when you press F5, the new form is displayed. Note that if you are working on an Internet-style VB.NET project (a WebForm), you can right-click the WebForm's name in Solution Explorer and set that form as the Startup object directly in the context menu. No need to open the project's Property dialog box (shown earlier in Figure 2-4).

As you can see in the tray below your design window, the Data Form Wizard added your dsAuthors DataSet automatically. However, the wizard renamed it objdsAuthors from your original name, dsAuthors, for reasons only a wizard knows. Technically, dsAuthors is the *class* name, and objdsAuthors, dsAuthors1, or some other slightly modified name is the *object* that has been instantiated (brought into existence) from that class during program execution. Got that? It's a subtle distinction in some situations, but one that object-oriented programming theorists are quite serious about. For more about this, see Book VII.

Modifying a DataSet

In addition to the Data Form Wizard, VB.NET offers another wizard you can use to modify or generate DataSet objects such as objdsAuthors. This wizard is known as the Data Adapter Configuration Wizard. When it creates a new DataSet object, it automatically renames the DataSet by appending 1 to the first DataSet's name, 2 to the second DataSet's name, and so on (like the default names given to controls when you add them to a form).

In this section, you see how to modify a DataSet using the Data Adapter Configuration Wizard. You already have a DataSet object, so now you can modify it so that it displays the results from a different SQL query than the query in the previous example: Show all data in the Authors table. Follow these steps:

1. **Click the DataForm1.vb [Design] tab at the top of the design window.**

   The DataForm is displayed.

2. **Right-click OleDbDataAdapter1 in the tray below the form and choose Configure Data Adapter.**

   The Data Adapter Configuration Wizard appears.

3. **Click Next three times.**

4. **Click the Query Builder button.**

   Query Builder opens and you see the existing SQL query specifying the current DataSet (show all data in Authors).

5. **Right-click the title bar of the Authors table box in the top pane and choose Remove.**

   The Authors table box is annihilated, as well as the SQL query associated with it, leaving behind an empty query (SELECT *nothing* FROM *nothing*). The actual Authors table itself isn't deleted from the DataSet, merely the SQL query that displayed it in the DataGrid. In fact, as you see shortly, a single DataSet can contain more than one table. Indeed, it can contain various kinds of data from all kinds of sources, including simple text files, XML incoming from Internet sources, and so on. (DataSets are extremely flexible about what kinds of data stores they can accept information from.)

6. **Right-click the top pane (where the Authors table used to be) and choose Add Table.**

   The Add Table dialog box appears.

7. **Double-click the Jobs table.**

   A box is created displaying the Jobs table in the top pane of Query Builder.

8. **Click the Close button.**

   The Add Table dialog box closes.

9. **In the Jobs box, click the All Columns option.**

   Now the SQL statement changes to the following:

   ```
   SELECT   jobs.*
   FROM     jobs
   ```

   This code tells SQL to put all columns (*) in this table into the DataSet.

10. **Click OK to close Query Builder, and then click Next.**

    The wizard generates various functions and mappings and performs other wizard-type activities behind the scenes. Pay no attention to the man behind the curtain.

11. **Click Finish.**

    The wizard closes.

12. **Right-click the OleDbDataAdapter1 icon in the tray and choose Generate DateSet.**

    You see the Generate Dataset dialog box.

13. **Click OK.**

    The DataSet is *regenerated*. The Jobs table is added to the existing Authors table in the DataSet object.

    From time to time, you may see the error message `C:\documents and settings\mlerch\my documents\visual studio projects\ datwiz\dsauthors.xsd. This file has been modified outside the source editor. Do you want to reload it?` This is a security warning and, unless you have reason to believe that something is awry, just ignore it.

14. **To prove to yourself that a single DataSet can contain more than one table, right-click the objdsAuthors icon in the tray and choose View Schema.**

    The structure of the DataSet is displayed. Now two tables are in this DataSet, as shown in Figure 2-6.

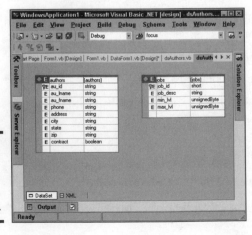

Figure 2-6:
A DataSet can contain more than a single table.

TIP

During design time, while you (or a wizard) are writing the programming for your DataSet, you specify the connection (the pubs database, in this case) and the structure (the tables and columns) of the DataSet. However, the data itself isn't loaded into the DataSet object until you run the program.

15. **Click the DataForm1.vb [Design] tab at the top of the design window.**

The DataForm is displayed.

16. **You now want to bind this DataGrid to the Jobs table, so click the DataGrid in the design window and press F4.**

The Properties window opens, displaying the DataGrid's properties.

17. **Click the DataSource property, and then click the down arrow and select objdsAuthors.Jobs as the DataSource.**

The headers in the DataGrid change to reflect the column names of the Jobs table.

18. **Press F5 to run the program, and then click the Load button on the form.**

The DataGrid fills with this new set of data, as shown in Figure 2-7.

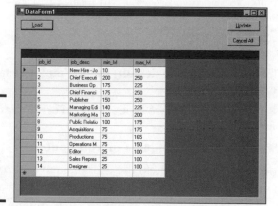

Figure 2-7:
Your
modified
DataGrid
displays its
contents.

The Single-Row DataForm Style

The wizard constructed some interesting source code for the Load, Update, and Clear buttons, but you explore that later. In this section, you turn your attention to the alternative DataForm style, the one that uses TextBoxes instead of a DataGrid. Follow these steps:

1. **Choose Project⇨Add New Item, and then double-click the Data Form Wizard icon.**

   The wizard is displayed, and DataForm2 is added to your project. You're creating a new DataForm so that you can start with a clean slate and not worry about any code left over from the wizard's activities in DataForm1.

2. **Click Next.**

   You are asked which DataSet you want to use.

3. **Click the Create a New DataSet Named option, type** dsEmployee **as the name of your new DataSet, and then click Next.**

   You're asked to choose a connection to a database.

4. **Click the down-arrow button, select the pubs.dbo connection, and then click Next.**

   Recall that you see your computer's name prepended to the name *pubs.dbo.*

   The tables in the pubs database appear.

5. **Double-click the Employee table.**

   The table moves from the left pane to the Selected Item(s) pane on the right.

6. **Click Next.**

   You can now specify the columns you want to display.

7. **Leave all columns selected (the default) in the Employee table, and then click Next.**

   You're now asked which of the two types of Data Form Wizard displays you want to use.

8. **Choose the Single Row in Individual Controls option.**

   You see a series of buttons that help the user maneuver through the DataSet.

9. **Leave all the checkboxes selected, and then click Finish.**

   The Data Form Wizard closes. The wizard put a slew of controls on the form — including lots of buttons permitting the user to do various things with the DataSet, as shown in Figure 2-8.

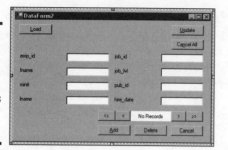

Figure 2-8:
The busy
wizard has
put quite a
few controls
on this form
for you.

Next, make DataForm2 the Startup object:

1. Right-click the project name (in boldface) in Solution Explorer, and choose Properties.

The Project Property Pages dialog box appears.

2. Change the startup object to DataForm2, and then click OK.

3. Press F5 to see the results of the wizard's labors.

4. Click the Load button.

The DataSet, and consequently the DataForm, are filled with rows of data, as shown in Figure 2-9.

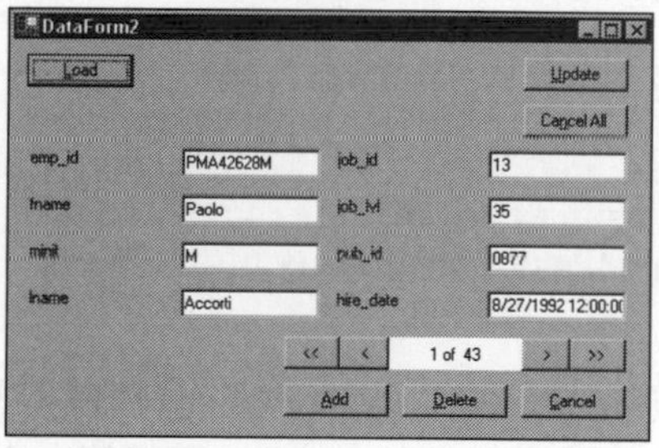

Figure 2-9:
The
alternative
DataForm
style
displays one
row of data
at a time.

A Brief Tour of Some Interesting Code

The wizard has written source code that you can learn from in this form, as well as in DataForm1. You see how to determine which row is the current row, how to move "up" to the next row, how to delete a row, and other useful techniques.

The Count property

Here's the code that the wizard wrote to calculate which row is the current row:

```
Me.BindingContext(objdsEmployee, "employee").Count.ToString
```

The key item here is the `Count` property of the `employee` table object. You explore the sometimes useful BindingContext object later.

The ToString method

Remember that `ToString` method? VB.NET can be strict about data types, unlike classic VB.

VB.NET doesn't like to treat numeric objects (such as the `Count` property) as if they were text (string) data. The `ToString` method (which zillions of objects have as one of their methods) *casts,* or changes, a numeric or other data type into a string that you can then assign to a Label or TextBox, or you can otherwise use as a string. Sometimes, though, VB.NET automatically does numeric-to-string conversion for you when you assign a numeric variable to the `Text` property of a TextBox.

However, do remember that if you ever get a `SystemInvalidCastException` error message when you're testing a project, you're attempting to cast one variable into a type that it can't be changed into. *Exception* in VB.NET means *error.* But *exception* sounds nicer than *error,* doesn't it? Try it next time you take a driver's license test. Tell them that you made no errors, just a few exceptions.

If you have a casting error, adding `.ToString` following the problem data usually solves the problem, as in `Count.ToString`. Some programmers use `ToString` all the time, even if it's not strictly required.

The Position property of the BindingContext object

The button on DataForm2 with the > symbol on it moves the user up one row in the DataSet. Here's a portion of the code you see when you double-click that button:

```
Me.BindingContext(objdsEmployee, "employee").Position =
    (Me.BindingContext(objdsEmployee, "employee").Position + 1)

Me.objdsEmployee_PositionChanged()
```

Me means the current form (DataForm2, in this example). The BindingContext object of this form contains a DataSet object named `objdsEmployee` that you're currently using. That DataSet object contains a table named `employee`. The BindingContext object maintains a `Position` property that specifies the current location. By "current location," I mean which row is currently displayed: Is it row 3? Or the first row? Or the last row? You can read or change the current position. Using the new += operator, you can simplify the preceding code so that you don't have to repeat the entire object definition:

```
Me.BindingContext(objdsEmployee, "employee").Position += 1
```

Deleting a row

The essential code to delete the current row follows:

```
Me.BindingContext(objdsEmployee,
    "employee").RemoveAt(Me.BindingContext(objdsEmployee,
    "employee").Position)
```

Another way to delete a row is to use the `Remove` method of a DataTable's Rows collection, like this (`dt` has previously been declared with the `Dim` command as a DataTable object in a DataSet):

```
dt.Rows.Remove(dt.Rows(CurrentRow))
```

Adding a row

The essential code to add a new row to the DataSet uses the `AddNew` method:

```
Me.BindingContext(objdsEmployee, "employee").AddNew()
```

If you want, continue this tour of the source code that the wizard has written under the Update, Cancel, Cancel All, MoveToLast (>>), and Load buttons on your own. You need not understand it all right now. Taking little tours of wizard code is one of the best ways to begin to familiarize yourself with VB.NET database programming technique. After all, the wizards really know how to get things done.

But more on this programmatic, no-wizard-involved database-programming-by-hand in future chapters. This is just a taste of things to come. It's time to continue the tour of ways to display data to a user.

Using the Classic Components

Visual Basic classic components are the controls that old hands at VB have seen for years: Labels, TextBoxes, ListBoxes, and the like. In VB 6, of the 20 classic VB components, 7 were *data-aware* — capable of being linked to a data control or a DataSet. The data-aware classic controls were TextBox, Label, CheckBox, PictureBox, Image, ComboBox, and ListBox.

Recall that in VB.NET, these controls are all still data-aware (the Image control has been dropped from the language), but so are *all other* visible controls. Even the Scrollbar and Button can be bound to a database, although they are seemingly unrelated to database interfaces.

In VB.NET all visible controls have a DataBindings collection (found at the very top of the Properties window), which means that they can be bound to a data source. Controls with no visible surface, such as Timers, are the exception. They have no DataBindings collection.

Technically, DataBindings is called a collection (not a property) because several properties and objects can be contained under the name DataBindings. However, call it a property if you wish. Microsoft, other language purveyors, even professors of OOP, aren't very consistent about their use of terms such as *property* or *object*. For example, several properties are contained under the name Font, but Font itself is still considered a property, not a collection. My advice is to relax and not ask for too much consistency in computer language grammar and diction.

Interestingly, all the properties of each control can be bound to the data source — not just the obvious properties such as Text, but also bizarre ones (at least bizarre in the context of data binding) such as BorderStyle. This is a bit mind-boggling, but it could be of use. It means that you can take charge of the control's appearance and some of its behavior from data in a data source, such as a database or a DataSet. This raises some interesting possibilities.

Attaching a Data-Aware Control

The TextBox is one of the VB workhorses. It's a mini word processor, enabling users to view or edit text. You now find out how to bind TextBoxes to a DataSet, and how to move through the DataSet, displaying data from each row in turn in the TextBoxes.

To attach a TextBox to a DataSet, follow these steps:

1. **Create a new project in VB.NET by choosing File⇨New ⇨ Project.**

   The New Project dialog box appears.

2. **Name your new project whatever you want.**

3. **Double-click the Windows Application icon.**

   VB.NET builds the default components of a WinForm project.

4. **Open VB.NET Server Explorer (choose View⇨Server Explorer).**

5. **Click + next to Servers, click + next to your computer's name, and then click + next to SQL Servers.**

   You see a list of the SQL Server connections.

6. **Click + next to your computer's name (\NETSDK, VSDOTNET, or VSDOTNET2003), click + next to the Pubs database, and finally click + next to Tables underneath Pubs.**

   You see the tables in the Pubs database.

7. **Drag the Jobs table from Server Explorer and drop it onto your VB.NET form.**

   VB.NET adds an SqlConnection1 control and an SqlDataAdapter1 control to your tray.

8. **Right-click the SqlDataAdapter1 control in the tray and choose Generate DataSet.**

   The Generate DataSet Class dialog box appears. (You may have to click on the Form and then the SQLDataAdapter1 a couple of times before the correct context menu appears. Or try clicking the adapter first, and then right-click the adapter to see the context menu. This is a little bug.)

9. **Leave the New radio button selected, and name your new dataset dsJobs.**

10. **Choose the Add This DataSet to the Designer option.**

    You want to add a DataSet named dsJobs1 to this project. You bind your TextBoxes to dsJobs1 so that you can display various columns of data (one column per TextBox) to the user.

11. **Click OK.**

    The dialog box closes and the DsJobs1 DataSet object appears in your tray.

You're now ready to create the user interface so that people can view (and edit if you permit them to) the data in your DataSet.

Binding controls and properties to a DataSet

Here's one way to attach, or *bind*, VB.NET controls to a DataSet. Recall that some controls (such as the DataGrid) have their own wizard. When you add one of those controls to a form, the wizard pops up, takes over, and does the binding for you by asking you to fill in some information.

This example, however, shows you how to bind by hand. And it works for any control that you want to display data in. To see how to bind controls and their properties to a data source, follow these steps:

1. **Add three TextBoxes to your form.**

2. **Click TextBox1 and then press F4 to display the Properties window for TextBox1.**

3. **Click the small + next to the DataBindings collection (which is at the very top of the Properties window).**

The DataBindings collection expands. Notice that for a TextBox, VB.NET assumes you probably want to bind data to the Text property. That's sensible. You deal with the Advanced option shortly.

4. **Click the Text property in the Properties window and click the down-arrow button that appears. Note that you should click the Text property within the DataBindings collection,** *not* **the other Text property farther down in the Properties window.**

A list displays all the data sources currently in your project. In this case, the only data source is your DataSet, dsJobs1.

5. **Click the + next to Jobs to expand it.**

You see all the available columns in the Jobs table, as shown in Figure 2-10.

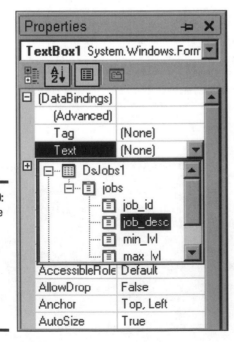

Figure 2-10:
You choose which column of data you want to display in this TextBox.

6. **Double-click jobs.job_desc.**

The job description column is attached to TextBox1.

It took me a while to realize that I had to click the words *jobs.job_desc* rather than the icon to its left in the Properties window. Perhaps this will be corrected sometime, and you can click either the icon or the words (which is typical Windows behavior).

7. **Click TextBox2 to select it (don't double-click) and repeat Steps 5 through 7, but this time choose jobs.min_lvl.**

The minimum annual salary level is attached to TextBox2.

8. **Click TextBox3 to select it and repeat Steps 5 through 7, but choose jobs.max_lvl.**

The maximum annual salary level is attached to TextBox3.

At this point, you may think you're finished and ready to press F5 to test your bindings. Not so fast! There's one more little job. You have to tell your project to fill the DataSet when the program runs. The three controls on the tray already know what table and columns in that table you want. In fact, a DataSet schema (structure) is already in place in the DataSet object (DsJobs1) on the tray. The actual data, however, must be pulled out of the database and poured into that schema when the program runs. You must write some new code in the Form_Load event to do this pouring:

1. **Double-click the form in the design window to get to the code window.**

To fill the DataSet object with the data from the Jobs table in the Pubs database, you must use the Fill method of the SqlDataAdapter1 object.

2. **Type the following into the Form_Load event:**

```
Private Sub Form1_Load(ByVal sender As System.Object,
    ByVal e As System.EventArgs) Handles MyBase.Load

    SqlDataAdapter1.Fill(DsJobs1)

End Sub
```

3. **Now go ahead and press F5.**

Three columns from the first row in the DataSet are displayed in the three TextBoxes, as shown in Figure 2-11.

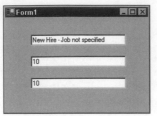

Figure 2-11:
This
"unspeci-
fied" job
pays $10,000
a year.

Notice that when you press F5 to fill the three TextBoxes in Step 3, the first Textbox's text is selected (which you can tell because it's white text on a black background). This is rather odd behavior, although there is a kind of logic to it in some situations. If the user presses any key on the keyboard to type something into that TextBox, the current selected contents are automatically deleted to make room for the user's new input. This may or may not be the behavior you want. If you want to deselect it before the user sees it, type this as the second line in your Form_Load event:

```
TextBox1.SelectionLength = 0
```

Binding to other properties

As promised, you can bind virtually any properties to a database or to any source of data. Remember that in ADO.NET, a database is only one potential source.

To see for yourself, follow these steps:

1. **Click any TextBox in your form in Design view to select it, and then press F4 to display the Properties window.**

2. **Click the + next to the DataBindings collection.**

3. **Click the Advanced property to select it.**

4. **Click the ... (ellipsis) button at the right side of the Advanced property.**

   The Advanced Binding dialog box appears, as shown in Figure 2-12.

Binding the ForeColor property of the TextBox to the job_id number in the data source may produce some colorful text, but it would be unpredictable and, honestly, peculiar. However, storing specifications for properties in a data source could come in handy. For example, you may want to turn the text color (ForeColor) property red if someone misses a rent payment. That way, you can look down the list of all your tenants and instantly see which were in arrears.

Figure 2-12:
This isn't
your father's
Visual
Basic. You
can bind
almost any
property to
a data
source.

Moving through a DataSet's Rows

The user wants to be able to see various rows and conveniently navigate
through the information in the DataSet. In previous versions of VB, you can
move forward and back through data using commands such as these:

```
Data1.Rowset.MoveNext
Data1.Rowset.MovePrevious
Data1.Rowset.MoveLast
```

No more. A DataSet can reside in a cache, in RAM, not necessarily in a database on a hard drive. ADO.NET can be used in both connected and disconnected modes, but we're focusing on the disconnected DataSet.

One way to think of a DataSet is as an intelligent array. That is, a DataSet, like
an array, is an ordered collection of information. To move "through" the data
sequentially, you code the process yourself (no MovePrevious, MoveNext, or
similar commands are available). To "MoveNext," you can establish a global
variable and increment it to keep track of where you are in the DataSet.

In your code window, just above Form_Load, declare a public variable
named Pointer. (As with any variable, you can choose whatever name
you wish to give the variable. But to follow this example, you should name
it Pointer):

```
Public Pointer As Integer
```

Then add a Button to your form. Use the Properties window to change the
Button's Text property to Next. Each time the user clicks this button, you

display data from the next row in the DataSet. Double-click the button to get to its `Click` event, and then type the following:

```
Private Sub Button1_Click(ByVal sender As System.Object,
    ByVal e As System.EventArgs) Handles Button1.Click

    Pointer += 1

    Dim r1 As String
    Dim r2, r3 As Byte

    Try
        r1 = dsJobs1.Jobs(Pointer).job_desc
        r2 = dsJobs1.Jobs(Pointer).min_lvl
        r3 = dsJobs1.Jobs(Pointer).max_lvl

        textbox1.Text = r1
        textbox2.Text = CStr(r2)
        textbox3.Text = CStr(r3)
    Catch er As Exception
        MessageBox.Show("Error" & er.ToString)
    Finally
    End Try

End Sub
```

The first thing that happens is that the index (`Pointer`) to the DataSet's array is incremented. `Pointer += 1` is the VB.NET equivalent to the traditional VB `Pointer = Pointer + 1`.

Next, you declare three variables to hold data from each column in the row. Then you assign the data to each variable. The first assignment line looks like this:

```
r1 = dsJobs1.Jobs(Pointer).job_desc
```

`dsJobs1` is the name of the DataSet; `Jobs` is the name of the table in that DataSet that you're interested in; `pointer` is the index to the `dsJobs1.Jobs` array; and `job_desc` is the column of data you are retrieving.

Note that the job description column is a string variable type in the DataSet, but both the minimum and maximum salary columns are byte (numeric) types. I didn't know that in advance when I wrote this program. I thought all three may be strings, so I originally wrote the following:

```
Dim r1, r2, r3 As String
```

But the VB.NET compiler didn't like this and displayed the following error message:

```
Option strict disallows implicit conversions from System.Byte
   to System.String.
```

Finally, the `Try-Catch-Finally-End Try` structure replaces the VB traditional `On Error Resume` technique for trapping runtime errors. In general,
you should always surround code that interacts with a database or DataSet
by the `Try...End Try` structure, in case things go wrong.

Press F5, and then click the Next button repeatedly to move through the
entire set of rows in this DataSet.

If you click the button 14 times, you see an error message (and a long one at
that) informing you that there is no row at position 14. This is a clear, high-
quality (because specific) error message. Error messages in general in VB.NET
are improved over previous versions of VB. Nonetheless, this kind of message
can frighten a user. You should add the following code to the button to
prevent this awkward message from ever being displayed to the user:

```
Private Sub Button1_Click(ByVal sender As System.Object,
   ByVal e As System.EventArgs) Handles Button1.Click


   If Pointer > DsJobs1.jobs.Rows.Count Then

      Pointer -= 1
      MsgBox ("You are at the end of the data.")
   Exit Sub
End If

Pointer += 1


Dim r1 As String
Dim r2, r3 As Byte
```

You can also use a `BindingContext` object to maintain a pointer to the
current row in a DataSet. In a Button object designed to move to the next
row in the DataSet, you can use code like the following in the Button's
`Click` event:

```
Private Sub Button1_Click(ByVal sender As System.Object,
   ByVal e As System.EventArgs) Handles Button1.Click

   Me.BindingContext(DsJobs1, "jobs").Position() += 1

End Sub
```

Or you can move in the other direction one row:

```
Private Sub Button1_Click(ByVal sender As System.Object,
    ByVal e As System.EventArgs) Handles Button1.Click

    Me.BindingContext(DsJobs1, "jobs").Position() -= 1

End Sub
```

The BindingContext object does keep track of the first and last row positions, so you don't have to worry about going outside the bounds of the available rows. This is a simpler, easier way to maintain a pointer to the current position in the rows collection in a DataSet, as well as to move displayed data in the bound controls as the user (or some other agent) changes the current row. I showed you how to manage the job yourself because it's often useful to know how to do important programming tasks.

A Few More Words about the DataSet

Recall that you can think of a DataSet as a mini-database detached from the parent database(s) from which it was extracted. A DataSet has one or more tables, columns, rows, constraints, and relations. You can write programming that reads or changes the elements of a DataSet (either its structure or its data). A DataSet has properties and methods. It has several collections (similar to traditional arrays). There are collections of tables, relations, rows, and columns.

A DataSet created by using the Generate DataSet option on a DataAdapter control's context menu is *strongly typed*. You can tell by double-clicking the schema file, which has an .XSD extension, in the Solution Explorer. The schema file specifies the names of the tables and columns, along with the data type used in each column. Whenever you create a DataSet using a VB.NET tool (such as the OleDbCommand control), an .XSD file is created automatically. Strongly typed data is related to XML structures; things are carefully described by text tags, not simply by their position in the structure (their index number, for example).

Programs don't execute faster with a strongly typed DataSet, but it can be easier to write programming code for typed DataSets because the lines are slightly less verbose, although perhaps a bit less readable and less descriptive. Also, you can open the Class View window (View⇨Class View) and see a huge amount of detail about the schema of your DataSet. In fact, a strongly typed dataset is simply a particular kind of class, where its tables are actually manipulated as if they were properties.

A strongly typed DataSet permits this kind of coding:

```
r1 = dsJobs1.Jobs(Pointer).job_desc
```

An untyped DataSet does the same thing with this longer line of code:

```
r1 = dsJobs1.Tables("Jobs")(Pointer).Columns("job_desc")
```

A strongly typed DataSet also includes automatic type checking, which makes it easy to ensure that data of the wrong type does not get stored in the DataSet.

The Splendid DataGrid

Now it's time to move back up to a higher-level, VB.NET rapid application development feature — the DataGrid control.

The DataGrid is one of the best controls for displaying large amounts of data to the user or displaying data from more than one table. It's highly efficient, flexible, easy for the user to work with, and offers several different styles.

To see how to use the DataGrid, follow these steps:

1. **Remove the three TextBoxes and the Button you used in the preceding example.**

Leave the SqlDataAdapter, SqlConnection, and DataSet objects on the tray as they were (connected to the Jobs table).

2. **Double-click the form to go to the code window. Delete the entire** Button_Click **event and replace the source code inside the** Form_Load **event with this line:**

```
SqlDataAdapter1.Fill(DsJobs1)
```

If you don't already have an SQLDataAdapter, an SQLConnection, and a DataSet on your form, follow the steps for the example earlier in this chapter, in the section titled, "Attaching a Data-Aware Control."

3. **On your clean, uncluttered form, add a DataGrid from the Toolbox.**

The DataGrid is on the Windows Forms tab in the Toolbox.

4. **Press F4 to display the Properties window.**

5. **Locate the DataGrid's** DataSource **(not** DataBindings**) property, click the down-arrow button to display the list of data sources that VB.NET knows about, and then click** dsJobs1.jobs**. (You could use** DataBindings**, but this example illustrates an alternative approach.)**

6. **Press F5 to run the program.**

A filled DataGrid is displayed. If you stretch the form and also stretch the DataGrid, it looks as shown in Figure 2-13.

Figure 2-13:
The
DataGrid
control is
a highly
efficient
way to
display a
table of
information.

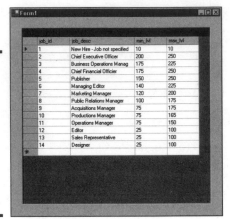

Note that you can't simply drop a DataGrid onto a form, add the three database-related objects on the tray (the SqlDataAdapter, SqlConnection, and DataSet objects), and then press F5. You must type in that line of code in the Form_Load event to *fill* the DataSet before any bound control can display the data.

You can also change the format of the DataGrid. To do so, stop the project from running, and then follow these steps:

1. **Back in the VB.NET design window, right-click the DataGrid and choose Auto Format.**

The AutoFormat dialog box appears, as shown in Figure 2-14.

Figure 2-14:
Use this
dialog box
to select
from a
variety of
DataGrid
formats.

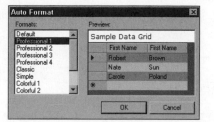

2. **Chose Colorful1 and then click OK.**

3. **Press F5.**

You see a nice, well-designed variant of the default DataGrid appearance.

You can also customize the fonts, colors, and other elements of any DataGrid format, using the Properties window. You work again with the DataGrid in Book V, Chapter 4, when you create relations between tables.

Chapter 3: Managing DataSets

The key to understanding the ADO.NET technology is the DataSet. In this chapter, you focus on how to create, save, and load a DataSet. To better understand the DataSet concept — and to give yourself maximum flexibility — you go through these various tasks *programmatically.* That means you write the code rather than leave it up to a wizard.

Actually, in addition to learning your way around the DataSet, you actually create a database management program that can be useful to you. It can manage whatever you collect — coins, recipes, old fishing lures, whatever. And, as always when you create an application, you can easily modify it to suit your every whim. However, the version of this program provided here is merely intended to demonstrate how to work with DataSets. You build a more elegant database management application in Book VII, Chapter 4.

More about DataSets

A brief review: A DataSet is a copy of some data (containing as many tables as you want) that is held in memory or stored as two XML files on a hard drive. To simplify the contents of each XML file, the structure (the names of the tables, columns, and other features) of the DataSet is stored in one file (the *schema file*), while the actual *data* (the rows of information) is stored in a separate file.

A DataSet does not require an active connection to a database. A DataSet object is fairly self-sufficient, and it behaves rather like a typical object, in that it contains a variety of commands (methods) and properties you can employ to manage its data.

Typically, you connect to a large database and then extract a DataSet from that database. This way, you need not maintain a constant connection between your machine and the database (which may be on the Internet somewhere else in the world, and may be very busy providing DataSets to other people besides you). Instead, you can work all you want with the DataSet in your computer and then return the DataSet for merging with the big database. Recall that this kind of *disconnectedness* (also known as *distributed applications* or *distributed programming*) is perhaps the primary distinction between traditional programming and programming designed to work on the Internet. Disconnected DataSets permit lots of people to get to the data store without causing traffic jams. Good manners make for good reunions; that's our motto.

Building a DataSet

DataSets are stored in XML files, so they are especially useful for transmitting data over networks and across firewalls. DataSets can be extracted from existing databases, or you can just create a brand new DataSet that isn't derived from a larger database. Next, you see how to create an independent DataSet that isn't extracted from some larger database.

The programming techniques illustrated here serve you well when you use a DataSet with existing databases. And, when you think about it, creating a DataSet from scratch isn't all that different from creating a database — DataSets are, remember, essentially small databases themselves.

In the next section, you create a little DataSet that mimics a cookbook. It has one table (named Recipes). This table is equivalent to an entire cookbook. The table has two columns (named Title and Recipes). In this DataSet, each row holds a single recipe in your cookbook, and each row is therefore divided into two sections: the title section holding the recipe's title, and the recipes section holding the recipe itself. You also see how to save and open a DataSet stored on your hard drive in XML format. Let's get cooking.

Some global variables and namespaces

First off, you want to import some namespaces (to make referring to database objects and their members easier and less verbose). Follow these steps:

1. **Start a new VB.NET project (File⇨New⇨Project).**

2. **Name the project** Ds **for DataSet.**

3. **Double-click the Windows Application icon in the New Project dialog box.**

4. **Double-click the form in the design window to get to the code window.**

5. **Go to the very top of the code window, and press Enter several times to give yourself some white space. Put the following** Imports **statements at the very top of the code window (and I mean up above *all* code, including** Public Class Form**):**

```
Imports System.Data
Imports System.Data.OleDb
Imports System.Data.SqlClient
Imports System.Data.SqlTypes
Imports System.Data.SqlDbType
```

You don't always need all these Imports statements when working with DataSets, but it doesn't hurt anything to have them up there.

You also want to declare some of your own global variables. In VB.NET, global variables can be placed in a module (Project⇨Add Module) and thus be made available to the entire project (all the forms and other containers in the project). Or, if you just need to make the variables global to an individual form, you can do what I describe in the following steps.

6. **A few lines down, just below the line** Inherits System.Windows. Forms.Form, **type the lines that appear here in boldface:**

```
Public Class Form1
     Inherits System.Windows.Forms.Form

     Dim ds As New DataSet(), dr As DataRow, dt As
     DataTable

     'holds a deleted record
     Dim titlehold As String, recipehold As String

     'holds the current filenames
     Dim schemafilepath As String, datafilepath As
     String

     'holds the total records and current record number
     Dim TotalRows As Integer, CurrentRow As Integer
```

You've just created your formwide global variables.

These variables are used by more than one procedure (subroutine) in your form, so you want them to be global to the form — to retain their contents even when the program isn't executing within any particular procedure. If they were declared (with the `Dim` command) *inside* a procedure, they would be local to the procedure. Other procedures couldn't access them in that case. Solution? Declare them *outside* any particular procedure, to make them global to the form. (And if you want them to be global to the entire project — to be accessible from all the forms — you need to declare them with the `Public` keyword, and put them in a module. Choose Project⇨ Add Module.)

Put a form's global variables between the `Inherits` line and the `Sub Form_Load` line (or the first `Sub`, whatever it is) in `Class Form`.

Building a DataSet in code

Now it's time to create the DataSet. Although, as you've seen, you can create a DataSet using the database controls in VB.NET (the OldDbDataAdapter and SQLDataAdaper controls, among others), sometimes you may want to let the user create his or her own DataSet files from scratch. This is one of those times. To do that, you need to create the DataSet not with controls during program design, but within your source code during program execution. You take the user's specifications about the tables and columns, and you write programming that translates those specs into a DataSet schema.

Scroll all the way down to the bottom of the code window and just above the `End Class` line. Type the following `Test` subroutine:

```
Sub Test()

	'TEST THE DATASET OBJECT:

	'Create a new table named Recipes with title and
recipes (the description of the actual recipe) columns.

	dt = New DataTable("Recipes")
	dt.Columns.Add("title", GetType(String))
	dt.Columns.Add("recipes", GetType(String))
	ds.Tables.Add(dt)

	' stick some data into the first row's two columns
	dr = dt.NewRow()
	dr!title = "First Test Recipe"
	dr!recipes = "Instructions on making popular pies..."
	dt.Rows.Add(dr)

	'save the structure (schema) of this dataset
	ds.WriteXmlSchema("c:\RecipesDataSet.xml")
	'save the actual data that's currently in this
dataset
	ds.WriteXml("c:\RecipesData.xml")
```

```
        Debug.WriteLine("DataSet Loaded. ")
        Debug.WriteLine("Number of Tables: " &
ds.Tables.Count)

        Dim s As String

        s = ds.Tables(0).Columns.Count.ToString

        Debug.WriteLine("Table 1 has " & s & " columns")


        s = ds.Tables(0).Rows.Count.ToString()

        Debug.WriteLine("Table 1 currently has " & s & "
rows" & "(" & s & " records of data)")


        dt = ds.Tables(0)
        For Each dr In dt.Rows

            Debug.WriteLine("ColumnName: " &
dt.Columns(0).ColumnName & "  Data: " & dr(0).ToString)
            'Debug.WriteLine(" ")

            Debug.WriteLine("ColumnName: " &
dt.Columns(1).ColumnName & "  Data: " & dr(1).ToString)
        Next

    End Sub
```

This subroutine will be removed from your project later; you're merely using
it now to see how to work with a DataSet.

Now scroll back up in the code window, locate the Form1_Load event, and
type the following boldface line so that it's the first thing that happens when
you run the application:

```
Private Sub Form1_Load(ByVal sender As System.Object, ByVal e
    As System.EventArgs) Handles MyBase.Load

        Test() : End

End Sub
```

The : in the preceding code is the way that you tell VB.NET to deal with
two logical (or virtual) "lines" of code, even though those "lines" are on the
same physical line in the editor. You can just as easily write code like the
following:

```
Test()
End
```

Press F5. The test runs and the program stops by itself (thanks to that End command).

To see the results of your experiment, follow these steps:

1. **Open the VB.NET Output window by choosing View⇨ Other Windows⇨Output.**

2. **Make sure the Debug option appears in the drop-down box in the Output window. (If you don't see Debug just under the title bar in the Output window, click the down-arrow button at the top right of the Output window and select Debug.)**

   You should see the following results at the bottom of the Output window. You have to scroll down in the Output window to see this:

   ```
   DataSet Loaded.
   Number of Tables: 1
   Table 1 has 2 columns
   Table 1 currently has 1 rows(1 records of data)
   ColumnName: title  Data: First Test Recipe
   ColumnName: recipes  Data: Instructions on making
       popular pies...
   The program '[1256] ds.exe' has exited with code 0
       (0x0).
   ```

Creating global object variables

In this example, you've seen how to create a new DataSet and define a table and columns within it. Also included is the code necessary to read information from and store information in a DataSet's rows. Each of the various tasks that were accomplished in this code is described by comments within the code. However, consider some of the highlights:

```
Dim ds As New DataSet(), dr As DataRow, dt As DataTable
```

With this line, you created global object variables for a DataSet object (ds), a DataRow object (dr), and a DataTable object (dt). The DataRow object contains a collection of all the individual rows (or what used to be called *records*) of data, however many there may be. The number of rows can grow or shrink — depending on whether new data units (rows) are added or deleted from the DataSet.

Defining the schema

You began by creating a table named recipes (and so far, this is just a table object, because it hasn't been made part of the DataSet yet):

```
dt = New DataTable("Recipes")
```

Note that you can create as many tables as you want for your DataSet, but you're going to use only one in this DataSet.

Then you created two columns (formerly known as *fields*). These are named `title` and `recipes`, but you could have named them anything you wanted to. At the same time you created them, you added them to the Columns collection of the `Recipes` table object:

```
dt.Columns.Add("title", GetType(String))
dt.Columns.Add("recipes", GetType(String))
```

You can add as many columns as you want to your table, but you're going to use only two in your recipe DataSet: the title of each recipe and the description (the recipe itself). So, given that you have two categories of information in this table, you should just use two columns.

Then, pleased with yourself, you added the `recipes` table to the Tables collection of the DataSet named `ds`:

```
ds.Tables.Add(dt)
```

Only at this point in the code does `dt` become part of `ds`.

Adding some rows (the actual data)

You specified the tables and columns in your DataSet. In other words, you've defined a structure for the DataSet. (It's as if you had a book full of blank pages, wrote RECIPES on the cover, and drew a vertical line from top to bottom on each page, dividing each page into two zones. Then you labeled the two zones Title and Recipe.)

Then you stored an actual row in the DataSet. A DataSet contains both structures (tables and, within tables, columns) as well as rows (actual records of data). You created a new row:

```
dr = dt.NewRow()
```

Then you added some data to each of the two columns in that row:

```
dr!title = "First Test Recipe"
dr!recipes = "Instructions on making pies..."
```

And finally, you added the new row to the Rows collection of the table (which already resides in the DataSet, so this row becomes part of the DataSet):

```
dt.Rows.Add(dr)
```

Then you used the `WriteXMLSchema` command to save the structure into one file:

```
ds.WriteXmlSchema("c:\RecipesDataSet.xml")
```

And you used the `WriteXML` command to save the data (the rows) in a separate file:

```
ds.WriteXml("c:\RecipesData.xml")
```

Note that a DataSet need not be saved to the hard drive as files. Indeed, it's more common to simply keep the DataSet in the computer's memory while the user reads it or modifies it. Then, when the user is through, any changes can be merged back into the original database and the DataSet itself can be simply discarded. However, to give you a good idea how you can manipulate independent DataSets, in this example you are storing them to disk. I simply chose the location and filenames for convenience. You can change `c:\RecipesData.xml`, for example, to whatever path and filename you wish. There is no special place where you must store a DataSet, nor is there a special filename that you must give it.

The following code finds out how many columns and rows (individual records of data) are in a DataSet:

```
Dim s As String

s = ds.Tables(0).Columns.Count.ToString
s = ds.Tables(0).Rows.Count.ToString()
```

Finally, you used a technique that extracts all the data in your table:

```
For Each dr In dt.Rows

    Debug.Write("ColumnName: " & dt.Columns(0).ColumnName & "
   Data: " & dr(0).ToString)
    Debug.WriteLine(" ")

    Debug.Write("ColumnName: " & dt.Columns(1).ColumnName & "
   Data: " & dr(1).ToString)
    Debug.WriteLine(" ")
Next
```

This is the kind of code you can use to fill a ListBox with all the titles — `dr(0)` — in the DataSet. Then the user can click one of those titles to choose that particular row, and you can display both the title and the description in a pair of TextBoxes, for example.

By the way, to add more rows, you just repeat the code that created the first record, changing only the actual data that you're putting into the new rows:

```
dr = dt.NewRow()

dr!title = "2nd Test Recipe"
dr!recipes = "All about fish"
dt.Rows.Add(dr)
```

Playing around

Perhaps you feel like playing around with this example a little (adding a second table, for example) and working with the `Debug.WriteLine` command to find out how to generate mass quantities of debugging information. You can see the results in the Output window.

When you've finished playing around, delete the entire `Sub Test` from your source code, and also remove this line from the `Form1_Load` event:

```
Test() : End
```

The `Test Sub` was for experimentation only. You're going to create new code for this project. Now that you understand the basics of DataSets, it's time to move on to some real-world examples that make use of DataSets.

Use the Toolbox to put a button control on your form. Change the Button's `Name` property to `btnAdd` and its `Text` property to `Add Record`.

Creating a DataSet

Now you're closer to giving the user of your application the capability to create a new DataSet (and save it to the hard drive) or to open an existing DataSet (located on the hard drive). But hold your horses; you first need to provide the user with a way to initiate those tasks.

Creating menus

Typically, New, Save, and Open options are located on a File menu. So go ahead and add a MainMenu control to your form. Now you should add a File main menu, with New, Open, and Save submenus under it. (Add these menus in the order specified so that their default names will be correct when you add code in the next steps.) If you don't know how to use the MainMenu control, see Book I, Chapter 2.

The user must first create a new DataSet and save it to the hard drive, or at least open an existing DataSet, so type this warning into the `Form_Load` event:

```
Private Sub Form1_Load(ByVal sender As System.Object, ByVal e
    As System.EventArgs) Handles MyBase.Load

    MsgBox("Before you can add records, you must first
use the New or Open options on the menu")
    btnAdd.Enabled = False

End Sub
```

In this example, you write programming that lets users create a new
DataSet any time they want, as many times as they want. You first want to
add a SaveFileDialog from the Toolbox to the form. And while you're at it, go
ahead and add an OpenFileDialog as well. (You use it later when you give the
user the capability to Open an existing DataSet.) These dialog boxes' icons
are not visible on the upper part of the Toolbox; click the small down-arrow
icon on the bottom right of the Toolbox to scroll it.

Type the following in the Click event for MenuItem2 in the code window.
Drop the listbox on the top left of the code window, and then double-click
MenuItem2:

```
Private Sub MenuItem2_Click(ByVal sender As System.Object,
    ByVal e As System.EventArgs) Handles MenuItem2.Click

    'NEW: Creates a DataSet

    'Create a new DataSet with a table named Recipes that
includes a title and a desc column.
    'first get user's name for the new DataSet
    Dim userFilePath As String

    SaveFileDialog1.FileName = "MyData"
    SaveFileDialog1.InitialDirectory = "C:\"
    SaveFileDialog1.RestoreDirectory = True
    SaveFileDialog1.Title = "Create a New PDM DataSet"
    SaveFileDialog1.Filter = "mailto:PDM|*.PDM"
    SaveFileDialog1.ShowDialog()
    userFilePath = SaveFileDialog1.FileName

    Dim n As Integer = userFilePath.IndexOf(".")
    If n <> -1 Then
        'there's an extension, so remove it
        userFilePath = userFilePath.Substring(0, n)
    End If


    dt = New DataTable("Recipes")
    dt.Columns.Add("title", GetType(String))
    dt.Columns.Add("desc", GetType(String))

    'Specify titles as primary key
```

```
        Dim colArray(1) As DataColumn
        colArray(0) = dt.Columns("title")
        dt.PrimaryKey = colArray


        ds.Tables.Add(dt)

        Try
            'save the structure (schema) of this dataset
            ds.WriteXmlSchema(userFilePath & "schm.xml")
            'save data that's currently in this dataset
            ds.WriteXml(userFilePath & "data.xml")

            'store these filenames in global variables for
saving later
            schemafilepath = userFilePath & "schm.xml"
            datafilepath = userFilePath & "data.xml"

            'save a file to display their filename:
            ds.WriteXml(userFilePath & ".PDM")

        Catch er As Exception 'if there was a problem opening
this file
            Throw (er)

        Finally

        End Try

        dt = ds.Tables!Recipes ' set dt to point to this
table
        btnAdd.Enabled = True

    End Sub
```

All you want to do here is establish a new (empty) DataSet and save its structure (one table, two columns) to the hard drive. You use the names `Recipes`, `title`, and `recipes` for the structure, but that's okay because the user never sees these internal labels any more than they see your variable names.

Notice that before you use the Tables collection's `Add` method to put your Recipes table into the DataSet, you define a primary key. This ensures that your Recipes table won't have duplicate titles:

```
Dim colArray(1) As DataColumn
        colArray(0) = dt.Columns("title")
        dt.PrimaryKey = colArray
```

An alternative syntax to the previous three lines is this:

```
        dt.PrimaryKey = New DataColumn() {dt.Columns("title")}
```

Now, all you need to get from users is their choice of a filename. XML DataSets are stored in two different files, the schema file and the data file. Having to deal with two files may be baffling to users, so you devise a way to ask the user for only a single filename when opening, creating, or saving a DataSet XML file. You put the burden of managing two filenames on the computer, by writing code to handle it.

You use the filename that the user supplies twice: First, you append `schm.xml` for the schema file; second, you append `data.xml` for a separate file that holds the data. Finally, to make things less confusing for the users (when they go to open one of their DataSets on the hard drive), you create a third file with the extension PDM. This last file has no other purpose than to provide users with an easily recognizable, single filename when they use the Open menu option. *PDM* stands for *Personal Data Manager*.

You use the SaveFile dialog box to get the user's choice of directory and file-name. It's a straightforward request, but you always need to anticipate ways that users may foul things up. In this case, they may get excited and add a file extension such as TXT to their filename. You don't want that. You're actually creating three files to which you'll add special extensions. So, if the user adds an extension, you remove it in code, like this:

```
Dim n As Integer = userFilePath.IndexOf(".")
If n <> -1 Then
    'there's an extension, so remove it
    userFilePath = userFilePath.Substring(0, n)
End If
```

After the users give you a valid filename and file path, you create their new DataSet using the WriteXmlSchema method and save a separate .XML file that holds the data.

Understanding Collections' Syntax

Note that many objects contain collections. *Collections* are similar to arrays. A DataSet contains a tables collection. In turn, each table has a columns collection, which tells you how that table is subdivided, and a rows collection, which contains the actual items of data in the collection.

You can usually query or edit individual elements in a collection in two ways. You can refer to them by index number (starting with zero) or by their name:

```
dt = ds.Tables!Recipes 'by name
dt = ds.Tables("Recipes") 'same, but an alternative
    punctuation
dt = ds.Tables(0) 'same, but here you use the table's index
    number rather than its name.
```

Whichever of these options you use, the global `dt` variable now points to the particular DataSet and table that the user created with the `MenuItem2_Click` event. I chose to use this version in the previous code:

```
dt = ds.Tables!Recipes ' set dt to point to this table
```

It's easy to read because it's one of the styles that includes the name of the table.

Opening an Existing DataSet

What if the user wants to open an existing PDM DataSet located on the hard drive? Begin by putting two TextBoxes on your form:

1. **Click the Form1.vb [Design] tab on top of the code window to get to the design window.**

2. **Use the ToolBox to add two TextBoxes, one above the other.**

3. **Set the `MultiLine` property of the lower TextBox to `True`. Then change the `Name` property of the lower TextBox to `txtDesc` and the `Name` property of the upper TextBox to `txtTitle`.**

4. **Delete the value `TextBox1` from the `Text` properties of both TextBoxes. You want the TextBoxes to be blank. (To delete these values, click a TextBox to select it, and press F4 to display the Properties window. Then select `TextBox1` in the `Text` property by dragging your mouse across `TextBox1`. Press the Del key to remove it. Then press Enter.)**

5. **Locate the Open menu's click event by clicking the Form1.vb [Design] tab on top of the code window and then double-clicking the Open item in the menu structure. It's MenuItem3.**

6. **Type the code that opens existing DataSet files:**

```
Private Sub MenuItem3_Click(ByVal sender As
   System.Object, ByVal e As System.EventArgs) Handles
   MenuItem3.Click
      'OPEN

      Dim userFilePath As String
      Dim userfilenameonly As String, userpathonly As
String

      OpenFileDialog1.FileName = "PDM"
      OpenFileDialog1.Filter = "PDM Files|*.PDM⇨All
files (*.*)|*.*"

      OpenFileDialog1.InitialDirectory = "C:\"
      OpenFileDialog1.RestoreDirectory = True
```

```
            OpenFileDialog1.Title = "Open a PDM DataSet"

        If OpenFileDialog1.ShowDialog() =
DialogResult.OK Then
            userFilePath = OpenFileDialog1.FileName

            'extract path and filename
            Dim l As Integer, m As Integer

            Dim position As Integer

            Do
                position = m
                m = InStr(m + 1, userFilePath, "\")
            Loop Until m = 0

            l = Len(userFilePath)


            userfilenameonly =
Microsoft.VisualBasic.Right(userFilePath, l -
position)
            userpathonly =
Microsoft.VisualBasic.Left(userFilePath, position)

            'strip any extension from filename:
            Dim n As Integer =
userfilenameonly.IndexOf(".")
            If n <> -1 Then
                'there's an extension, so remove it
                userfilenameonly =
userfilenameonly.Substring(0, n)
            End If
        End If


        Try
            'get the structure file
            ds.ReadXmlSchema(userpathonly &
userfilenameonly & "schm.xml")
            'get the data file
            ds.ReadXml(userpathonly & userfilenameonly
& "data.xml")

            schemafilepath = userpathonly &
userfilenameonly & "schm.xml"
            datafilepath = userpathonly &
userfilenameonly & "data.xml"

        Catch er As Exception 'if there was a problem
opening this file
```

```
        Throw (er)

    Finally

        dt = ds.Tables!Recipes ' set dt to point to
this table

    End Try


    TotalRows = dt.Rows.Count
    If TotalRows = 0 Then Exit Sub 'file contains
no rows to display

    CurrentRow = 0

    txtTitle.Text = dt.Rows(CurrentRow).Item(0)
    txtDesc.Text = dt.Rows(CurrentRow).Item(1)

    btnAdd.Enabled = True



    End Sub
```

In this procedure, you first show the users an OpenFile dialog box and allow them to double-click a filename (ending in .PDM). You get their choice of DataSet: It may be COOKBOOK.PDM or ADDRESSBOOK.PDM or COINCOLLECTION.PDM or whatever DataSet they've previously created. Their choice is returned to your program as the `FileName` property of the FileOpen dialog box:

```
userFilePath = OpenFileDialog1.FileName
```

After you have the filename (which actually includes the entire path — the disk name\directory name\filename, such as: `C:\MyCoins.PDM`), you have to separate the path from the filename (`C:\` from `MyCoins.PDM`s in this example). You need these separate strings because you must open two XML files: the schema (structure definition) file (`MyCoinsSchm.XML` in the example) and the data file (`MyCoinsData.XML`).

This code finds where the path ends and the filename begins by searching for the \ symbol in `C:\MyCoins.PDM`:

```
'extract path and filename
Dim l As Integer, m As Integer
Dim position As Integer

Do
    position = m
```

```
        m = InStr(m + 1, userFilePath, "\")
Loop Until m = 0
```

When this loop is finished, the variable named `position` contains the location of the rightmost \. Why look for more than one \? Because if users stored their database in a subdirectory, more than one \ is in the file path, like this: `C:\MyData\PDM\MyCoins.PDM`.

When you exit this loop, you can then extract the file path and put it in a variable named `userpathonly`, like this:

```
userpathonly = Microsoft.VisualBasic.Left(userFilePath,
    position)
```

This code illustrates how to employ the classic VB `Left` function. However, if you want to use the VB.NET equivalent, use the new `Substring` method.

So, for example, you extract the following:

```
C:\MyData\PDM\
```

And you can extract the file name, getting the following:

```
MyCoins.PDM
```

Now you're ready to open your schema and data files by appending your special extensions to the filename, like this:

```
'get the structure file
ds.ReadXmlSchema(userpathonly & userfilenameonly &
    "schm.xml")
'get the data file
 ds.ReadXml(userpathonly & userfilenameonly & "data.xml")
```

And, as you did in the `mnuNew` code, you must save the filenames in global variables so that you can save the data back to these files when the user chooses the Save option in the File menu or clicks the Exit button to shut down the program:

```
schemafilepath = userpathonly & userfilenameonly & "schm.xml"
datafilepath = userpathonly & userfilenameonly & "data.xml"
```

Technically, you need to keep saving the structure file (scmn.xml). The PDM doesn't contain any features for adjusting the structure by adding new tables or columns. However, saving doesn't hurt anything — and the capability is in place if you ever decide to expand the PDM and let users add tables.

Next, you point the datatable variable (dt) to your newly opened DataSet:

```
dt = ds.Tables!Recipes ' set dt to point to this table
```

Then you put the total number of records into the global variable
TotalRows, and set the CurrentRow pointer to 0 (the first record):

```
TotalRows = dt.Rows.Count
CurrentRow = 0
```

Then you display the current record in your two TextBoxes:

```
txtTitle.Text = dt.Rows(CurrentRow).Item(0)
txtDesc.Text = dt.Rows(CurrentRow).Item(1)
```

Adding and Removing Data

You've finished the New and Open code, so now you can figure out how
to add records to and remove records from a DataSet.

Adding data to a DataSet

To add data to your DataSet, double-click the Button on your form to get to
its Click event and type in this code:

```
Private Sub btnAdd_Click(ByVal sender As System.Object,
    ByVal e As System.EventArgs) Handles btnAdd.Click

    'if they have no active DataSet, refuse to
allow a new record:
    If datafilepath = "" Then
        MsgBox("Please Open a DataSet, or create
one using the New option in the File menu--before
attempting to add a new record.")
        txtTitle.Text = ""
        txtDesc.Text = ""
        Exit Sub
    End If

    'if they have an incomplete record, refuse:
    If txtTitle Is "" Or txtDesc Is "" Then
MsgBox("One of your TextBoxes has no data. You must
enter something for the title and something for the
description.") : Exit Sub

    ' stick the new data into the first row's two
columns

    Try
```

```
                         dr = dt.NewRow()
                Catch er As Exception 'maybe there is no active
DataSet?
                    ' if not, build a DataSet

                    dt = New DataTable("Recipes")
                    dt.Columns.Add("title", GetType(String))
                    dt.Columns.Add("desc", GetType(String))
                    ds.Tables.Add(dt)
                    dr = dt.NewRow()
                End Try

                dr!title = txtTitle.Text
                dr!desc = txtDesc.Text
                dt.Rows.Add(dr)
                TotalRows = TotalRows + 1
                CurrentRow = CurrentRow + 1

                Me.Text = "Record Added...Total records: " &
TotalRows


        End Sub
```

The first line tests to see if the user has some data in both TextBoxes. You don't want an incomplete record. However, if the users do have a new record (text in the TextBoxes) that they want to save to the DataSet (*committing it,* as the saying is), you let them.

You use the NewRow method to notify your DataSet that a new row of data is coming. Then you fill the new row's two columns (title and desc) with the data in the TextBoxes. Then the Add method commits the data to the DataSet. You increment your total records counter and your current row pointer.

And, because users don't like to click a button and see *nothing* happen, you place a reassuring message in the form's title bar, telling them that the record has been added.

Removing data from a DataSet

Users must be able to delete, as well as add, records from your DataSet. Here's code that you can use to remove the "current" record:

```
dt.Rows.Remove(dt.Rows(CurrentRow))
```

If you look in VB.NET Help, you may think that there are two methods for deleting a row in a DataSet: Delete and Remove. However, the Delete method doesn't actually get rid of a row; it simply marks the row for later deletion when (or if) the programmer uses the AcceptChanges method. Marking a row is useful for such jobs as permitting an Undo option and restoring the row. In this example, however, you use the `Remove` method, which gets rid of the row completely, right then and there.

Saving a DataSet

The Save feature stores the DataSet to a file on the hard drive. Double-click the Save menu item to get to its `Click` event in the code window (which is MenuItem4). Then type the following into the `MenuItem4_Click` event:

```
Private Sub MenuItem4_Click(ByVal sender As System.Object,
    ByVal e As System.EventArgs) Handles MenuItem4.Click

    'SAVE

    If ds.Tables.Count = 0 Then MsgBox("Please use the
New option to first create a new DataSet") : Exit Sub
'nothing to save

    'otherwise, save the dataset
    Try

        ds.WriteXmlSchema(schemafilepath)
        ds.WriteXml(datafilepath)
    Catch ex As Exception

        MsgBox("There was a problem writing this data.
There is no file path. You must first use the New option
to create a disk file.  " & ex.ToString)


    End Try

    Me.Text = "Saved..."

End Sub
```

If the DataSet has no tables, the users don't have any data to save yet, so you just quit this subroutine. However, if there is a DataSet, you use the two `WriteXML` methods to save the DataSet's structure and its data.

Testing . . . Testing

Now you can test your project to make sure that the XML files are being created on the hard drive. In addition, you can see the interesting way that a DataSet's schema and data are saved. Follow these steps:

1. **Press F5.**

A dialog box appears, telling you that you cannot add records until you've created a new database.

2. **Click OK.**

The dialog box closes.

3. **Choose File⇨New.**

The file saving dialog box appears.

4. **Click the Save button.**

The file saving dialog box closes and the default filename MyData is created on your hard drive. Recall that this program creates three files for the price of one. Now you have an active DataSet in your project. In the next step, you add a few records to it.

5. **In the Title TextBox (on top) in your form, type a title. In the lower TextBox, type a description.**

6. **Click the Add Record button.**

Notice that your message, Record Added..., appears in the title bar of the form.

7. **Now replace the Title field with another title and change the description TextBox as well.**

8. **Click the Add Record button again.**

9. **Choose File⇨Save to store these two records on the hard drive.**

10. **Stop the application.**

Now take a look at the files to see how a DataSet is saved in XML. Use Windows Notepad to open the MyDatadata.XML file on your hard drive (Start⇨Programs⇨Accessories⇨Notepad.) This XML file is where the DataSet's actual rows (records) were stored.

The data should look something like this in Notepad:

```
<?xml version="1.0" standalone="yes"?>
<NewDataSet>
  <Recipes>
    <title>Coin One</title>
    <desc>Original Authentic Coin with Claudvius's Portrait
    on it</desc>
  </Recipes>
  <Recipes>
    <title>Second Coin</title>
    <desc>Of unknown origin, but looks just like Livia</desc>
  </Recipes>
</NewDataSet>
```

Then use Notepad to open the schema XML file (MyDataschm.XML). You see the DataSet defined in a kind of nesting process, with the two rows nested inside the Recipes table, which itself is nested in the DataSet.

Moving through a DataSet

Users often want to scroll up or down through a set of data. When working with an older ADO Recordset, you could use the MoveNext, MovePrevious, MoveFirst, and MoveLast methods to maneuver users through their records. The newer ADO.NET DataSet, however, has no such methods. It's up to you, the programmer, to organize and navigate the data "rows" inside the DataSet. That's why you created TotalRows and CurrentRow global variables — to keep track of where the user is located in the set of rows. (Technically, TotalRows isn't necessary; the DataSet *does* know that and you could ask it any time with ds.Tables(0).Rows.Count. However, in some situations, you want to keep track of your total data units, so no harm is done in looking at how to do it.)

Put two more Buttons on the form and change their Name properties to btnNext and btnPrevious. Change their Text properties to Next and Previous, respectively.

The btnNext and btnPrevious buttons allow the user to move forward or backward through the currently loaded DataSet. Set the btnPrevious Click event:

```
Private Sub btnPrevious_Click(ByVal sender As System.Object,
    ByVal e As System.EventArgs) Handles btnPrevious.Click

        If CurrentRow = 0 Then Exit Sub

        CurrentRow = CurrentRow - 1

        txtTitle.Text = dt.Rows(CurrentRow).Item(0)
        txtDesc.Text = dt.Rows(CurrentRow).Item(1)

        Me.Text = CurrentRow + 1.ToString

    End Sub
```

You first must check to see whether the users are viewing the "lowest" record. If CurrentRow = 0, no additional records are available to be viewed "below" the currently displayed one. So, if that's the case, you merely exit the subroutine.

I put the word "lowest" in quotes because in a *relational* set of data, there is no "lower" or "higher" any more than in relativistic astrophysics there is a "lower" or "higher" planet or star. It all depends on your point of view. A DataSet, which is relational, has no particular order. The records (rows) are added and deleted from the DataSet without regard to their alphabetical order.

If you want to present an alphabetized DataSet to the user, you must take special programmatic steps yourself. You see how to sort a DataSet later (the DataSet has no built-in sort method).

So, back to your code: If there is a record to display (you're not at the "lowest" record in the DataSet), you adjust the CurrentRow variable, grab the text from the DataSet, and assign it to the two TextBoxes. Again, you display something to the user in the form's title bar; in this case, you show them the record number.

Moving forward (or "up," if you prefer) through the records is accomplished in the btnNext procedure:

```
Private Sub btnNext_Click(ByVal sender As System.Object,
    ByVal e As System.EventArgs) Handles btnNext.Click

        If CurrentRow = TotalRows - 1 Then Exit Sub

        CurrentRow = CurrentRow + 1

        txtTitle.Text = dt.Rows(CurrentRow).Item(0)
        txtDesc.Text = dt.Rows(CurrentRow).Item(1)

        Me.Text = CurrentRow + 1.ToString

    End Sub
```

Just as in the btnPrevious code, you must first see whether the user is asking to see a record that doesn't exist. If the CurrentRow isn't the "highest" row, you proceed to adjust CurrentRow up by 1 and then display that record. The rest of the code is identical to the btnPrevious code.

Why must you subtract 1 when getting information from the TotalRows global variable in the PDM's code? Why can't you just hold the actual total number of rows in your TotalRows variable? That's because of the "zeroth" problem in computer programming languages: Some arrays and collections start with an index of 1 and others start with an index of 0. As the PDM program illustrates, you have to deal with both ways of counting when using a DataSet. The Count property of a DataSet's Tables().Rows collection begins with 1 but the DataRecords collection of a DataSet begins with 0. So, to keep things working correctly — to keep the TotalRows and CurrentRow variables in sync — you must subtract 1 from TotalRows each time you use it.

Try testing these new buttons. Press F5 and use your project's File⇨Open feature to load the DataSet named `MyData` that you created previously. It has two rows, so click the Previous and Next buttons to test them.

Searching a DataSet

Any good database program permits users to search through the entire group of records and return those that match a specific criterion. The PDM must offer this feature, too. The user can type a string (text) of any length. A ListBox then displays all records that contain that text anywhere in their description (desc) field. Then the users can click the title of the record that they want to display in the TextBoxes. Follow these steps:

1. **Put a ListBox on your form.**

   It's okay if the ListBox partially covers the TextBoxes.

2. **Change the ListBox's** `Name` **property to** `lstResults` **and its** `Visible` **property to** `False`.

3. **Put a Button on the form, too, and change its** `Name` **property to** `btnSearch` **and its** `Text` **property to** `Search`.

4. **Type this code into the** `btnSearch Click` **event:**

```
Private Sub btnSearch_Click(ByVal sender As
    System.Object, ByVal e As System.EventArgs) Handles
    btnSearch.Click
        'SEARCH

        'if they have no active DataSet, refuse:

        If ds.Tables.Count = 0 Then
            MsgBox("Please use the File menu to Open a
    DataSet, or create a New one first.")
            Exit Sub
        End If

        'search for the target in both columns, then
    display it

        Dim searchfor As String = InputBox("Enter Your
    Search Term", "Search")

        searchfor = searchfor.ToLower
        lstResults.Items.Clear()

        Dim i, x, y, count As Integer

        For i = 0 To TotalRows - 1
```

```
        x =
ds.Tables(0).Rows(i).Item(0).ToString.ToLower.Index
Of(searchfor)  ' see if title column matches
        y =
ds.Tables(0).Rows(i).Item(1).ToString.ToLower.Index
Of(searchfor)  ' see about desc column too

        If x <> -1 Or y <> -1 Then 'match

lstResults.Items.Add(ds.Tables(0).Rows(i).Item(0))
'add title field to listbox
            count += 1
        End If
    Next i


    If count = 0 Then 'no matches found
        MsgBox("No match for " & searchfor & " was
found...")
    Else
        lstResults.Visible = True
    End If

End Sub
```

First, you see whether the table contains anything and, if not, exit the sub. You let the users know that they can't search until they've created or opened a DataSet.

Now you want to make the search ignore capitalization (either in the user's search string or in the records being searched). So you use the `ToLower` method to reduce both the user's string and, later, the records as well, to all-lowercase characters. This means, for example, that `ROMAN` matches Roman, `roman`, `RoMaN`, and so on. The characters themselves, not their capitalization, trigger hits.

You empty any contents in the lstResults ListBox with the `Clear` method (in case some records are still listed from a previous search).

A loop is then used to search from `0` to `TotalRows -1` (the entire set of records). You use the `IndexOf` (character location within the string) method to see if `searchfor` (the string the user typed in) is found in any of the records in the entire DataSet. If so, you've found a match as you store the Title field of that record in the ListBox.

A `count` variable keeps track of any hits. If `count` is `0` when you finish with the loop, you display a message to the user that no matches were found, and you exit the subroutine at that point.

Otherwise, the lstResults ListBox is displayed so that the users can choose the record they want to see (by clicking its title in the ListBox, which you code next).

Go ahead and test this. You can load the MyData test file by choosing File⇨Open and then clicking the Search button.

You have a couple of other ways to search a DataSet, involving the DataTable object's `Select` method or a DataView object's `RowFiler` property. However, both of them search only for entire strings, not substrings, which is what you want. Come again? A search for entire strings requires that you enter precisely the entire phrase. For example, to trigger a match on the title "Duck a L'orange," you have to type all that in. However, you want to be able to search the entire recipe book and get a list of all recipes with, for example, the word "orange" in their title or their description. So, instead of using one of the search techniques built into the DataTable or DataView objects, you used the `IndexOf` method, which triggers a match on substrings.

Selecting a Search Hit

For mysterious reasons, the ListBox no longer has a `Click` event. Instead, the `SelectedIndexChanged` event is the default event. Fortunately, it's similar to `Click`.

Double-click the ListBox on the form to get to its `SeletedIndexChanged` event. Then type the following code into the event to permit the user to click a title and view the entire record in the TextBoxes:

```
Private Sub lstResults_SelectedIndexChanged(ByVal sender As
    System.Object, ByVal e As System.EventArgs) Handles
    lstResults.SelectedIndexChanged

        lstResults.Visible = False

        Dim i As Integer
        Dim s As String

        s = lstResults.SelectedItem.ToString    'which item
    did they click?

        'find their choice

        For Each dr In dt.Rows  'search the DataSet to find
    the correct Description
            i = i + 1
```

```
                    If dr(0).ToString = s Then
                        txtTitle.Text = dr(0).ToString
                        txtDesc.Text = dr(1).ToString
                        CurrentRow = i
                        Exit For
                    End If
            Next

        End Sub
```

First, you make the ListBox invisible, and then you put the user's choice
(the Title field that the user selected in the ListBox) into the variable s.
Then you go through all the records until you find a match in the Title field
(dr(0)). When the match is found, you put the text from that record into
the two TextBoxes. You also update the CurrentRow variable.

Adding Extra Features

Of course, as it stands, the application built in this chapter can use some
additional features to make it work smoothly. Here are some suggestions if
you want to improve it on your own:

✦ Sort the rows by the Title column, so that they are listed alphabetically
  in the lstResults ListBox.

✦ Add a second visible ListBox that displays all the titles in the entire
  DataSet, so that the user can click any of them to see the associated
  description in the Recipes column.

✦ Add code to prevent the user from entering identical titles.

✦ Expand the features of the Add New Record function to test for identical
  titles when the user attempts to add the record, and also to permit the
  user to cancel the process of adding a new record.

✦ Add a Delete button.

✦ Add an Undo button to reverse the most recent Delete.

✦ Add a feature that prints the currently viewed record.

However, my advice is to wait and use the database management program
that you build in Book VII, Chapter 4. It relies on the SortedList class to
solve the alphabetization problem in a highly effective way.

Chapter 4: Migrating to ADO.NET

In This Chapter

✔ **Filtering**

✔ **Working with the DataView**

✔ **Creating relations**

✔ **Communicating with a database**

✔ **Using the XML Designer**

Arrays, ArrayLists, DataViews, DataTables — all of these objects have a built-in sorting method. Oddly, the DataSet does not. You can, of course, specify that a particular column be indexed (and if it's a primary key column, its values are forced to be unique). However, although indexing a column makes searching more efficient, it does not maintain the rows in alphabetical order.

Precisely how indexing works varies among the different database types. Typically, databases include a primary key (also known as a primary key index). Some databases also feature a "clustered" index in which the rows are maintained in the same order as the index. In other words, when you add a new record, it is inserted into its alphabetical location within the set of existing rows (rather than simply appended to the end of the set). This kind of indexing is not available, however, to DataSets.

When you first create an SQL query to extract a DataSet from a database, you can specify that the result be ordered (alphabetized) in a particular way (ascending or, more rarely, descending). You can also specify that the DataSet be ordered by whatever column you want (alphabetically by title column in the recipe book, for example).

This is all well and good, but what happens after the DataSet gets into the user's computer and the user starts adding new rows of information? There's the problem. Each new row is not inserted alphabetically. So, if you permit the user to go to the next or previous row by clicking buttons to maneuver through the DataSet, or if you display the entire list of titles (for example, in a ListBox), some of the rows (at the bottom of the ListBox) will be out of alphabetical order. That's bad. You have to figure out a way around that problem. You want your DataSet to always be in alphabetical order, even when the user adds a new record or changes a title so that the recipe must now be listed elsewhere in the alphabetized list.

Providing an ordered list is such a common user-interface issue that it's surprising that the DataSet doesn't have a sort method.

Your first thought may be to just set the ListBox's `Sorted` property to `True`. That way, when you display all the titles, they are displayed in alphabetical order. True, but it doesn't solve the following two problems:

✦ When users add some recipes to the collection and then click the Next button to move up to the end of the rows, they go past recipes titled X, Y, and Z and find a mixture of S, R, A, Q, N, or whatever (the added recipes are just sitting at the end in no particular order).

✦ The order of the titles displayed in the ListBox becomes out of sync with the recipes column. For example, if the user clicks the third title in the ListBox, it may or may not represent the third record in the DataSet. Why? Because perhaps the user has added a new row and its title begins with `A`. That record shows up at the beginning (top) of the ListBox and bumps all lower titles down one in the ListBox (but not in the DataSet's table). When users click in the ListBox, they expect to see the recipe for that title displayed in a TextBox. How do you, the programmer, figure out which row in the DataSet to display? You can't use the `SelectedIndex` property of the ListBox. It tells you which title the user clicked, but not which row in the DataSet to display. The `SelectedIndex` number doesn't necessarily sync with the DataSet's item number (`Tables(0).Rows(i).Item(1)`).

You have several ways to deal with this. You could search the DataSet for the title that matches the one the user clicked and then display the recipe. As long as the title column contains unique entries (is a primary key), this works. (There is also such a thing as a unique index that is not the primary key.)

You can choose from two approaches to query and sort the records in a DataSet: the `Select` method, and the DataView object. These two techniques are worth knowing about because sorting and searching are quite common database-related jobs. However, as you see, they don't solve the problem outlined in the preceding paragraphs. They do not permit you a way of sorting the DataSet itself.

I suspect that in the drive toward scalability (another word for one size fits all), some features that are useful to small- or medium-size applications have been left out. Clearly, a huge database with 10,000 records isn't going to be interacted with by clicking Next and Previous buttons. Nor is it practical to display a huge ListBox with 10,000 titles. There are other, better ways to interact with monster databases. But many of us work with smaller projects, such as a small office's inventory or personnel file. Creating utilities on this scale with a DataSet becomes problematic when you attempt to use a DataSet and find you can't sort it. However, probably the best solution is to simply search on your primary key field for a match to the string that the user clicked in the ListBox. This doesn't solve the Next and Previous button navigation method, though.

Filtering

When you use the `Select` method of the DataTable object to get a list of data, the process is called *filtering,* which is essentially the same process as what's called *querying,* when you use SQL to extract a subset of the data in a database. You say, give me a list, ordered by age, of all the kids on the swim team who are still in the "minnows" class. This process involves both searching and sorting simultaneously.

To experiment with the `Select` method, start a new VB.NET Windows style project, and add a ListBox to the form.

Type these `Imports` statements at the very top of the code window:

```
Imports System.Data
Imports System.Data.OleDb
Imports System.Data.SqlClient
Imports System.Data.SqlTypes
Imports System.Data.SqlDbType
```

Now type these declarations just above the `Private Sub Form_Load` line:

```
Dim ds As New DataSet(), dr As DataRow, dt As DataTable

' Used to create a new table, and an array of DataRow objects
Dim newRows() As DataRow
Dim newTable As DataTable
```

The `newRows` and `newTable` objects are used in later examples in this chapter.

Now, in the `Form_Load` event, you define the schema of a DataSet and populate it with some rows of names. For simplicity, in this example you use the same schema as in the example in the previous chapter. However, you let the computer generate a list of 30 rows that you can experiment with. Type the following code into the `Form_Load` event:

```
Private Sub Form1_Load(ByVal sender As System.Object, ByVal e
    As System.EventArgs) Handles MyBase.Load

        'define the dataset:
        dt = New DataTable("Recipes")
        dt.Columns.Add("title", GetType(String))
        dt.Columns.Add("desc", GetType(String))
```

```
Dim colArray(1) As DataColumn
colArray(0) = dt.Columns("title")
dt.PrimaryKey = colArray

ds.Tables.Add(dt)

'create 30 random titles and descriptions, and add
them to the DataSet:
makeupnames()

'display the random title and description columns in
the listbox
Dim i As Integer, n As String
For i = 0 To dt.Rows.Count - 1
    n = ds.Tables(0).Rows(i).Item(0) & "..." &
ds.Tables(0).Rows(i).Item(1)
    ListBox1.Items.Add(n)
Next i

End Sub
```

Just below the End Sub that ends the Form_Load event, add this subroutine, which makes up 30 fake, random titles and recipes and adds them to the DataSet. They are out of alphabetical order. (They're just random nonsense until you later alphabetize them using the Select method.) Type in this Sub:

```
Sub makeupnames()
    'create ten fake names
    Dim rndGenerator As New System.Random(1)
    Dim i, j, x As Integer
    Dim word As String

    For i = 1 To 30
        For j = 1 To 6
            x = rndGenerator.Next(97, 123) 'limit it to
lowercase letters
            word += Chr(x) 'add a character (from the
ASCII code value) to the word
        Next
        dr = dt.NewRow()
        dr!title = word.ToUpper 'make the titles
uppercase to distinguish them
        dr!desc = word
        dt.Rows.Add(dr)
        word = ""
    Next

End Sub
```

Book V
Chapter 4

Migrating to
ADO.NET

Notice that by seeding the random number generator with an integer —
(1) in this example — you force it to provide the same list of random names
each time the program runs. I chose this approach so that you can
repeatedly test various aspects of these examples and tell at a glance
how the records have been selected or ordered.

Now press F5 to see your DataSet's titles column displayed. Notice that they
are not in alphabetical order, as shown in Figure 4-1. (Also, I stretched the
form and ListBox to make them larger while designing this project.)

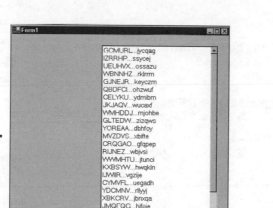

Figure 4-1:
An
unorganized
list is
difficult to
use.

At this point, you decide to display an alphabetized list by creating a new
array (of DataRow objects), and by specifying that the Select method
should order them alphabetically (which is the default behavior of the
Select method).

Add a button control to the form and change its Text property to Order by
Select Method. Double-click the button and type this into its Click event:

```
Private Sub Button1_Click(ByVal sender As System.Object,
    ByVal e As System.EventArgs) Handles Button1.Click

Dim i As Integer
        ListBox1.Items.Clear()

        ' Create a new table, and an array of DataRow objects
        Dim newRows() As DataRow
        Dim newTable As DataTable
        Dim n As String

        ' Get the DataTable of a DataSet.
        newTable = ds.Tables("Recipes")
```

```
newRows = newTable.Select()


' Display the values in both columns of each DataRow.
For i = 0 To newRows.GetUpperBound(0)
     n = newRows(i)("Title") & "..." &
newRows(i)("Desc")
     ListBox1.Items.Add(n)
Next i
```

```
End Sub
```

Press F5 and click the button. The titles are now alphabetized within the ListBox, as shown in Figure 4-2.

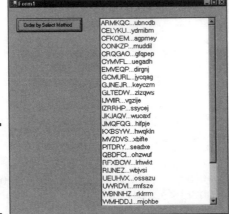

Figure 4-2:
A sorted list
created by
the Select
method.

Interestingly, in this array of DataRows (`newRows`), the Titles and Desc columns remain synchronized. This is what you wanted to happen to your DataSet, but you had to create a new array and use the Select method of the DataTable to accomplish it. The DataSet doesn't have a Select method, or any other way of sorting itself.

One is sorted, the other isn't

Even after creating this new array, notice that the DataSet itself isn't alphabetized, just the new array. As you see in a moment, to alphabetize the DataSet, you can try to replace the rows in the DataSet by deleting the current DataSet's rows and then dumping this `newRows` array into the DataSet. That sorts the DataSet, albeit in a rather roundabout way.

If you do try to replace the existing DataRows with the new array, you run into all kinds of permissions problems: `Primary key row already exists, can't be duplicated;` `Row does not exist;` `Column Title does not allow nulls;` and other problems. The following code shows a way to replace the rows in the DataSet with the rows in the array. (This solution was discovered by this book's technical editor, Mike Lerch.)

```
Private Sub Button2_Click(ByVal sender As System.Object,
    ByVal e As System.EventArgs) Handles Button2.Click
        Dim i As Integer
        Dim newRows() As DataRow
        Dim newTable As DataTable
        Dim n As String

        ListBox1.Items.Clear()

        newTable = ds.Tables(0).Copy()

        ds.Tables(0).Rows.Clear()

        newRows = newTable.Select()

        For i = 0 To newRows.GetUpperBound(0)
            ds.Tables(0).ImportRow(newRows(i))
        Next

        For i = 0 To dt.Rows.Count - 1
            n = ds.Tables(0).Rows(i).Item(0) & "..." &
    ds.Tables(0).Rows(i).Item(1)
            ListBox1.Items.Add(n)
        Next i
    End Sub
```

The overloaded Select method

When you use the `Select` method with no parameters (just empty parentheses), it automatically puts the result in alphabetical order by the primary key field. In this example, you specified that the Titles column is the primary key field. So you can simply use the no-parameter form to get the results you want:

```
newRows = newTable.Select()
```

However, there are three other forms of this method (which means that it is *overloaded*). You can specify a `Criterion`, which is an SQL-like string that defines how you want the rows to be filtered (queried). Here's an example that doesn't display any titles starting with A through E:

```
'find all rows matching the filter: (greater than F in the
    alphabet)
Dim Criterion = "Title > 'F'"
newRows = newTable.Select(Criterion)
```

This result is still sorted because the Title column is the primary key. But no rows beginning with letters lower than F in the alphabet are placed into the newRows array. The list of possible expressions (filters or criteria) is extensive and involves various special characters and punctuation rules. To see how to define a criterion to use with the Select method, open the VB.NET Help feature (choose Help⇨Index). Type **DataColumn.Expression** into the *Look for* textbox, and double-click the DataColumn.Expression property in the left pane of the Help window.

Yet another variation of the Select method permits sorting in descending order (backward from Z to A). The final Select method enables you to specify that only rows matching a particular DataViewRowState property are to be placed into the array. DataViewRowState includes added, modified, deleted, unchanged, and so on.

Which version is it?

Frequently, it's useful to employ a filter to see the current version of the DataTable, as opposed to the original version that was loaded into the DataSet at the start. Use code like this:

```
dv.RowStateFilter=DataViewRowState.Deleted
```

You can also test the status of individual rows in a DataTable by querying the RowState property. The following results are returned on these various rows when you run this code: Detached, Added, Unchanged, Modified, Deleted.

```
Private Sub Form1_Load(ByVal sender As System.Object, ByVal e
    As System.EventArgs) Handles MyBase.Load

    Dim dTable As New DataTable("dTable")
    Dim dCol As New DataColumn("Title",
Type.GetType("System.String"))
    dTable.Columns.Add(dCol)
    Dim dRow As DataRow

    ' Make a new DataRow.
    dRow = dTable.NewRow()
    Console.WriteLine(dRow.RowState.ToString())

    dTable.Rows.Add(dRow)
    Console.WriteLine(dRow.RowState.ToString())
```

```
        dRow("Title") = "Moby Dick" 'edit the row
        Console.WriteLine(dRow.RowState.ToString())

        dTable.AcceptChanges() 'this makes the rowstate
"unchanged"
        Console.WriteLine(dRow.RowState.ToString())

        dRow.Delete()
        Console.WriteLine(dRow.RowState.ToString())
    End Sub
```

When using the Select method, you can set the third parameter to specify which version of the rows you want to see, as in this pseudocode example:

```
newRows = newTable.Select(filter expression, sort mode,
    DataViewRowState)
```

Pseudocode uses descriptive names to illustrate the elements of source code, but the code isn't actually runnable.

You have to replace the italicized parameters in the preceding sample line of code with actual VB.NET expressions or enumerations (various built-in constants). For example, before you can run this line, you must replace DataViewRowState with one of the enumerations shown in Figure 4-3.

Enumerations are lists of constants. These sets of constants are built into .NET, or you can create your own with the Enum statement.

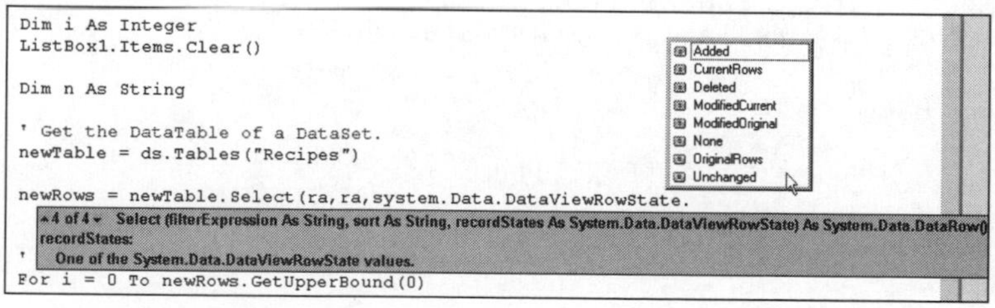

Figure 4-3:
Built-in .NET enumerations include the set of colors that can be used for the BackColor property or these choices of RowState parameters.

If you are using a DataView object, set its RowStateFilter property to specify which version of the rows you want to see:

```
Dim drView As DataRowView
dv.RowFilter = "Title LIKE '*q*'"
dv.Sort = "Title"
dv.RowStateFilter = DataViewRowState.Deleted
```

Using the DataView Object

Using the DataView feature is not too hard. You have to create a few objects and use For Each to iterate through them to display them. Add a button to the form used in the previous example, and change its Text property to Display Dataview Q.

Then double-click that button and type this into its Click event:

```
Private Sub Button2_Click(ByVal sender As System.Object,
    ByVal e As System.EventArgs) Handles Button2.Click
        'Create a DataView and display it

        ' Get a reference to the Recipes table.
        Dim dtNew As DataTable = ds.Tables("Recipes")
        ' Create a dataview
        Dim dv As New DataView(dtNew)
        Dim drView As DataRowView
        ' Set the criterion filter and sort on title.
        ' This criterion says: list all records with a Q in
    the title field
        dv.RowFilter = "Title LIKE '*q*'"
        dv.Sort = "Title"

        'display the DataSet

        Dim i As Integer, s As String
        ListBox1.Items.Clear()
        Me.Text = "From DataView"

        For Each drView In dv
            s = drView(i)
            ListBox1.Items.Add(s)
        Next

    End Sub
```

Close Relations

One of the prime virtues of a DataSet is that it permits you to create relations, just like a real database. After all, the kind of database that's most popular these days — and that includes SQL Server and DataSets — is called a *relational* database. So, just what are relations, and why are they so popular?

A relation is a connection between two tables that both share a common, primary key (a column in which each row contains unique data). The fact that they identify their rows uniquely, and both do it the same way, permits you to access data simultaneously from both rows but in sync. This can be useful when one table contains details not available in the other table. Recall that you sometimes use two tables to prevent redundancy.

Master-detail, parent-child

Data coming from multiple yet related tables is often referred to as master-detail. This points to the fact that the master table (the *parent*) may contain a list of publishers and their addresses, phone numbers, and other information. However, because each publisher puts out many books, you don't want to have to repeat the publisher's address, phone number, and so on for each book. That's the redundancy that multiple tables solves. You simply put the main information about each publisher in one table, and you link (make a relation or join) that table to a different detail table (the *child*) that lists all the books for each publisher. The child table doesn't contain the publisher's address, phone number, and so on; rather, it contains details about each book.

This master-detail relationship between tables is quite common. In a dentist's office, they put your name, phone number, and so on in one table; then they link it to a second table containing, for example, details about your payment history.

In the following sections, you first see how to create a relation between two tables programmatically, and then you see how to use wizards and the excellent, graphic XML Designer, which shows you a visual diagram of tables and any relations between them.

Programmatic relations

Start a new VB.NET Windows-style project. Double-click the form to get to the Form1_Load event in the code window. Type the following code above the Private Sub Form1_Load line:

```
Dim ds As New DataSet(), dr As DataRow, dt, dt1 As DataTable
```

Add a second form to the project (Project⇨Add Windows Form). You create two tables, dt and dt1, and then you define a relationship between them. Type the following code into the Form2_Load event (in this example, the explanation of the various parts of the source code is provided by comments within the code itself):

```
Private Sub Form2_Load(ByVal sender As System.Object, ByVal e
    As System.EventArgs) Handles MyBase.Load


        'define two new datasets:
        dt = New DataTable("Recipes")
        dt.Columns.Add("title", GetType(String))
        dt.Columns.Add("desc", GetType(String))

        Dim colArray(1) As DataColumn 'make title primary key
(unique)
        colArray(0) = dt.Columns("title")
        dt.PrimaryKey = colArray


        dt1 = New DataTable("Calories")
        dt1.Columns.Add("title", GetType(String))
        dt1.Columns.Add("CalorieCount", GetType(Integer))

        'make title primary key (unique) for this table, too.
        colArray(0) = dt1.Columns("title")
        dt1.PrimaryKey = colArray

        'add both tables to the dataset
        ds.Tables.Add(dt)
        ds.Tables.Add(dt1)


        'add three rows to the two tables:
        dr = dt.NewRow()
        dr!title = "First Title"
        dr!desc = "Description of first title"
        dt.Rows.Add(dr)

        dr = dt.NewRow()
        dr!title = "Second Title"
        dr!desc = "Description of second title"
        dt.Rows.Add(dr)

        dr = dt.NewRow()
        dr!title = "Third Title"
        dr!desc = "Description of third title"
        dt.Rows.Add(dr)

        'second table:

        dr = dt1.NewRow()
        dr!title = "First Title"
        dr!CalorieCount = 130
        dt1.Rows.Add(dr)

        dr = dt1.NewRow()
```

```
        dr!title = "Second Title"
        dr!CalorieCount = 220
        dt1.Rows.Add(dr)

        dr = dt1.NewRow()
        dr!title = "Third Title"
        dr!CalorieCount = 30
        dt1.Rows.Add(dr)

        'now create a relation between these two tables

        'This next line of code creates a new relation object
named
        ' "CalRel" and specifies that the first column
        ' (Recipes.Title) is the parent and the second column
        ' (Calories.Title) is the child (the parent/child
relation is
        ' based on the order that you specify the two columns
in the
        ' parameter list).

        ds.Relations.Add("CalRel",
ds.Tables("Recipes").Columns("Title"), _

ds.Tables("Calories").Columns("Title"))

        ' Now, loop through each row in the parent table's
rows collection
        ' (it has three rows), and then loop through each row
in the relation
        ' object (there is only one row), displaying the
"count"
        ' (the parent table's row number), and both columns
in the child.
        ' Note that you are not accessing dt1 directly (the
child table)
        ' instead, you are accessing the relation object

        Dim da As DataRow
        Dim count As Integer

        For Each dr In dt.Rows
            For Each da In dr.GetChildRows("CalRel")
                count += 1
                Console.WriteLine(count & "." & da("Title") &
" " & da("CalorieCount"))
            Next
        Next

    End Sub
```

Creating a DataSet with Relations

As you doubtless know by now, VB.NET offers you many interesting *auto-coding* features — wizards, designers, parsers, add-ins, and other helpers that let you drag-and-drop or answer a series of questions before they write source code for you. Sometimes you can get hundreds of lines of source code based on a three-minute little quiz from a wizard.

In the next example, you see how to connect to two different tables in the Pubs sample database and how to create a relation between the ID column that they have in common. You use both a wizard and a designer. You also see how to bind a DataGrid and a ListBox to the database connection. If you haven't yet installed SQL Server and the sample databases, see Book IV, Chapter 4 before continuing with this example.

Relations, via wizards and designers

You need to know how to summon wizards and designers to make your life as a programmer easier than you thought possible. To create a connection between a DataBase and a DataSet, follow these steps:

1. **Start a new Windows-style VB.NET project.**

2. **On the form, place a ListBox and a DataGrid from the Windows Forms tab of the Toolbox.**

3. **Double-click the OleDbDataAdapter icon in the Data tab of the Toolbox.**

   An OleDbDataAdapter is added to your form, and the Data Adapter Configuration Wizard opens. You can use either this OleDbDataAdapter (which is slower but more versatile because it connects to more databases) or the SqlDataAdapter you've been using in most examples in this book. For variety, you use the OleDbDataAdapter in this example.

4. **Click Next.**

5. **Choose the Pubs database in the drop-down list.**

6. **Click Next.**

7. **Leave the "Use SQL statements" radio button selected.**

8. **Click Next.**

9. **Click the Query Builder button.**

10. **Double-click Publishers in the Add Table dialog box.**

    The publishers table is added to the Query Builder dialog box.

11. **Click Close to close the Add Table dialog box.**

12. **Click pub_id and pub_name in the top pane.**

This SQL query is constructed for you:

```
SELECT      pub_id, pub_name
FROM        publishers
```

The pub_id column is the one on which a relation is created to link this table with another table in the Pubs database.

13. **Click OK, and then click Finish.**

An OleDataAdapter1 and an OleDbConnection1 are added to your form. You need only this one connection to the database, but to add a new table you should now add a second OleDataAdapter to your form. This new adapter also employs the existing OleDbConnection.

14. **Double-click the OleDataAdapter icon in the Toolbox.**

The Data Adapter Configuration Wizard dialog box opens again.

15. **Select the Pubs database and click Next.**

16. **Leave the "Use SQL statements" radio button selected. Click Next.**

17. **Click the Query Builder button.**

18. **Double-click Employee in the Add Table dialog box.**

The employee table is added to the Query Builder dialog box.

19. **Click Close to close the Add Table dialog box.**

20. **Click lname, job_lvl, pub_id, hire_date, and emp_id in the top pane to specify that you want to access the data in these columns.**

This SQL query is constructed:

```
SELECT      lname, job_lvl, pub_id, hire_date, emp_id
FROM        employee
```

21. **Click OK, and then click Finish.**

Now you need to build a DataSet that includes both of these tables. Right-click either of the OleDataAdapter icons in the tray beneath your form. Choose Generate DataSet from the context menu. Click the box next to both pub_info and publishers. Name this DataSet dsPubs in the New TextBox on the dialog box. Click OK. You now see a new DataSet icon in your tray.

Using the XML Designer

At this point, you open the XML Designer to create your relation, so follow these steps:

1. **Double-click the dsPubs.xsd filename in Solution Explorer.**

The XML Designer opens, as shown in Figure 4-4. Notice the two little key symbols next to the primary key fields in both tables. Pub_id is a unique field, and you create your relation based on it. At this point, however, the primary key field in the Employee table is emp_id.

Figure 4-4:
This designer helps you graphically study and edit relations between tables.

If you don't see dsTitles.xsd in Solution Explorer, click the name of your project (which is in boldface in the Solution Explorer) to highlight it, and then click the icon in the Solution Explorer title bar to Show All Files.

2. **Open the Toolbox and notice that when the XML Designer is open, you see a number of XML Schema icons that you can use to create a structure.**

3. **The employee table is your child (details) table in this relationship, so drag a relation icon from the Toolbox and drop it on the employee table.**

The Edit Relation dialog box opens, as shown in Figure 4-5. (You may see the employee table on the left in your version.)

4. **In the Name field, the designer has provided a name for your relation:** employeeemployee.

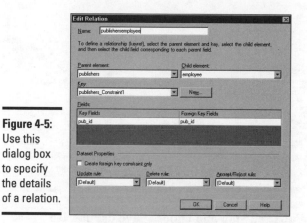

Figure 4-5:
Use this
dialog box
to specify
the details
of a relation.

5. Ensure that the Parent element is publishers **and the Child element
is** employee.

Now the name changes to publishersemployee. You want to remember this name so that you can use it in a minute when you bind the ListBox and DataGrid to the relation.

Note the use of the term *element* here for what you normally call a *table*. *Element* is a term used in XML to refer to an item enclosed by <> </> symbols, as in the following line:

```
<H1>This is a headline</H1>
```

The reason for using *element* here is that VB.NET has actually translated your DataSet (the tables, their schema, their relation, and eventually even their data) into XML. This way they can be communicated over firewalls on the Internet. To see the XML source code that VB.NET has so thoughtfully generated for you, right-click either table in the designer and choose View XML Source.

6. Ensure that the Key Fields and Foreign Key Fields both say pub_id.

7. Click OK.

The dialog box closes and you see something that looks like a necklace appear in the XML Designer, connecting the two tables graphically and symbolizing their relation, as shown in Figure 4-6.

Figure 4-6:
This
necklace
symbolizes
the relation
now
established
between
these two
tables.

8. **Right-click the dsPubs.xsd* tab and choose Save dsPubs.xsd.**

9. **Click Form1.vb(Design).**

You see your form, almost ready to display this relation.

Binding the controls

You now need to bind the ListBox to the Publishers master (parent) table
and bind the DataGrid to the details (child) table, pub_info. To do that,
follow these steps:

1. **Click the ListBox to select it.**

2. **Press F4.**

The Properties window opens.

3. **Select the DataSource property and click the down-arrow icon next
to that property.**

You see a list of possible data sources.

4. **Click dsPubs1, your DataSet.**

5. **Select the DisplayMember property and click the down-arrow icon
next to that property.**

You see a list of columns (fields) within the table you chose as your data
source.

6. **Choose pub_name, under the Publishers node.**

A *node* is an entry with a - or + symbol next to it in a list, indicating that
other items are listed underneath it and subordinate to it.

The property should now read publishers.pub_name.

7. **Click the DataGrid to select it.**

8. **Click the** `DataSource` **property in the Properties window, and click the down-arrow icon next to that property.**

   You see a list of possible data sources.

9. **Click dsPubs1, your DataSet's name.**

10. **Click the** `DataMember` **property in the Properties window, and click the down-arrow icon next to that property.**

11. **Click publishers to open the node.**

   You see the relation.

12. **Double-click publishersemployee. Note that the relation is a property of the publishers table.**

   The entry `publishers.publishersemployee` is now listed as your `DisplayMember`, and the DataGrid control displays the five fields (the schema) of the child table in the DataSet.

At this point, your DataGrid is now able to display all child rows in the child table whenever the user clicks on a publisher's name in the parent table (displayed in the ListBox). By selecting the relation object as the DataMember for the DataGrid, you make it possible to see the details (child) fields.

One more detail

Most people assume that with the DataSet created and the controls bound, you can just press F5 and see the data in the controls. Not so fast. You do have to write just a little source code to complete the process. Double-click the form to get to the code window, and type this into the `Form_Load` event:

```
Private Sub Form1_Load(ByVal sender As System.Object, ByVal e
    As System.EventArgs) Handles MyBase.Load
        DsPubs1.Clear()
        OleDbDataAdapter1.Fill(DsPubs1)
        OleDbDataAdapter2.Fill(DsPubs1)
End Sub
```

Using the `Clear` method isn't strictly necessary here because this is the first time that this DataSet is being used in this application. Nonetheless, it's a good habit to empty a DataSet of all its contents prior to filling it with new data. The `Fill` method of a DataAdapter object dumps the data from the database connection into the DataSet.

Press F5. You should see the results shown in Figure 4-7.

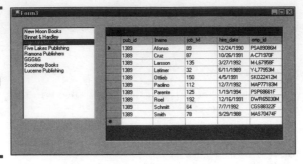

Figure 4-7:
Your
reward, a
working
parent-child
DataSet
relation,
comes into
view.

Try clicking various publishers' names in the ListBox to see the details
about their employees in the DataGrid. Notice, too, that the pub_id is identical in each row in the DataGrid. This is the only redundancy, however,
because the child (detail) table shown in the DataGrid does not have to
duplicate all information about each publisher (its address and so on). The
only necessary duplication is the primary key field's data.

Chapter 5: Deeper into ADO.NET

his chapter ties up some database-related loose ends. You see how to write code to connect to databases, how to specify alternative names when working with imported tables, and how to speed up data access if all you need to do is see, rather than modify, the data. Also, you deal with the problem of more than one person wanting to update the same data with their differently edited versions. Finally, you see why you can pretty much leave the XML heavy lifting up to VB.NET.

Creating a DataSet Programmatically

You know how to use an ADO or SQL DataAdapter to populate a DataSet from a data source.

Now you discover how to do the job programmatically. Even though wizards and other assistants are generally quite useful, it's also helpful to understand how to write source code yourself. Sometimes you have to do things the old-fashioned way.

To see how to create a connection, create a command, and then carry out that command to pump data from a database into a DataSet, follow these steps:

1. **Start a new VB.NET Windows-style application by choosing File⇨New⇨Project.**

2. **Give the application a name.**

3. **Double-click the Windows Application icon.**

4. **Put a DataGrid (from the Windows Forms tab on the Toolbox) onto Form1.**

Get ready to type some code. But, first, you need to import the usual data-related namespaces.

5. **Double-click the form to open the code window. At the top, above the first line (above** Public Class Form1**), type these five lines:**

```
Imports System.Data
Imports System.Data.OleDb
Imports System.Data.SqlTypes
Imports System.Data.SqlDbType
Imports System.Data.SqlClient
```

6. **Locate the** Form_Load **event.**

Recall that this event is where initialization — things you want to do before displaying a form to the user — usually takes place in your code.

7. **Just above the** Form_Load **event, type this:**

```
Dim ds As DataSet = New DataSet()
```

This code makes ds a global variable, usable by all procedures in the form. I generally like to make the DataSet variable global to a form because I often need to use it in several procedures, but doing that isn't strictly necessary in this example.

8. **In the** Form_Load **event, type the following:**

```
Private Sub Form1_Load(ByVal sender As System.Object,
    ByVal e As System.EventArgs) Handles MyBase.Load

Dim nwindConn As OleDbConnection = New
    OleDbConnection("Provider=SQLOLEDB;Data
    Source=localhost;Integrated Security=SSPI;Initial
    Catalog=northwind")

Dim selectCMD As OleDbCommand = New
    OleDbCommand("SELECT * FROM Customers", nwindConn)

selectCMD.CommandTimeout = 30

Dim dataAdapter As OleDbDataAdapter = New
    OleDbDataAdapter()
dataAdapter.SelectCommand = selectCMD

nwindConn.Open()

dataAdapter.Fill(ds, "Customers")

nwindConn.Close()

DataGrid1.DataSource = ds

End Sub
```

If you have problems using *localhost* in the connection string in the preceding code and the program won't work, substitute your computer's name plus the SQL server name. For example,
`Source=`*YourComputersName*`\NETSDK` or
`Source=`*YourComputersName*`\VSDOTNET`.

Beginning programmers often come across a long line of code in a book and don't realize that VB.NET looks at lines as *logical units* (something like sentences). In the code you just typed for this example, you see one such line — starting with `Dim` and ending with `northwind")`. It must be all on a *single* line in the code window, so don't press Enter until you type the entire line. You won't be able to see the entire line all at once in the IDE, but you can use the right-arrow key to scroll to the right to view the line.

9. **Press F5 to run this program.**

10. **Click the + button in the grid, and then click Customers.**

Your DataGrid fills with loads of data from the Northwind sample database that comes with VB.NET, as shown in Figure 5-1.

Figure 5-1:
This grid fills with columns of data without the help of a wizard.

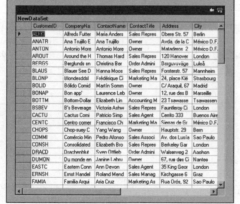

Note that the `Imports` statements in Step 5 are not strictly necessary. You could omit them, but then you'd have to specify the namespaces (`System.Data`, `System.Data.ADO`, and the rest of the items following the `Imports` command) for each class that required these libraries. For example, you would have to use the longer, fully qualified version (`System.Data.OldeDb.OleDbConnection`) rather than the simpler form `OleDbConnection`. After you import a namespace, you can leave its name off any references in your code to objects within that namespace.

The multiple namespaces mystery

Few people, including myself, are privy to the secret reason why you need *five* `System.Data Imports` statements for the various database-related programming classes. Few people know why they can't be combined into a single big `System.Data` library. It must have something to do with the way the people who wrote ADO.NET wanted to organize things. They have their containers and their idea of the proper granularity, so that's what we programmers get.

One little problem for us: It's impossible to memorize all the locations of the items we need — which namespaces hold which functions. So programmers have lots of trial-and-error work, deciding which namespaces to import and how to *qualify* functions that we need to use. (*Qualify* here means which namespaces must be spelled out to specify a particular language element in your programming code and which can be left out.)

To avoid this problem, I suggest that whenever you work with data, you just add all five namespaces and don't worry about it. In the example you're building right now, only two namespaces are truly necessary:

```
Imports System.Data
Imports System.Data.OleDb
```

But go ahead and include them all. Why worry? Importing a namespace doesn't add anything to the size of your final executable program. The libraries of code represented by namespaces are not added to your program's .exe file.

More about namespaces

Recall that namespaces are a new feature of VB.NET. They are designed to prevent confusion if two classes (in two different namespaces) share the same name.

For example, suppose you have a `StrBreak` function in `MyNameSpace1` and a `StrBreak` function in `MyNameSpace2`, a different namespace. You import both of these namespaces into the same project:

```
Imports MyNameSpace1
Imports MyNameSpace2
```

Now suppose that somewhere lower in the code, you try to use the `StrBreak` function.

Which of the two `StrBreak` functions is selected?

Fortunately, Microsoft has thought through this problem. If you try to use an ambiguous command — such as `StrBreak` in the preceding example — the VB.NET editor underlines `StrBreak` in your programming code, indicating that it is a problem. VB.NET also lists the problem in your Task List window, informing you that you need to "fully qualify" which namespace should be used. In other words, you have to add the namespace's name to the function name, like this:

```
MyNameSpace2.StrBreak
```

Understanding the code

In this section, you look at the rest of the source code in the example to see what's happening. After the OLEdb connection is made, an SQL query is defined in this line:

```
Dim selectCMD As OleDbCommand = New OleDbCommand("SELECT *
    FROM Customers", nwindConn)
```

This line says to get all data from the Customers table in the Northwind database, defined in the nwindConn connection. * means *all* in SQL, the query language often used to get subsets — DataSets — of information from data sources. Book V, Chapter 6 covers the most important SQL statements.

You tell the SQL command to spend no more than 30 seconds trying to get its DataSet with the CommandTimeout method. Next, you define a dataAdapter. Finally, the connection is opened to the database and the dataAdapter is used to fill ds, the previously defined global DataSet variable, with the Customers table.

Note that you can use an alternative line to fill the DataSet:

```
dataAdapter.Fill(ds)
```

But if you do, when the DataGrid is displayed, the + node (the icon you click to reveal the data) displays *Table* to the user, rather than the more informative *Customers*.

After closing the connection, you fill the DataGrid with the contents of your DataSet:

```
nwindConn.Close()
DataGrid1.DataSource = ds
```

The ADO.NET code in the preceding example shouldn't seem alien if you've used ADO. But you must get accustomed to a few changes. The Set command isn't used *anywhere* in VB.NET! For a comprehensive tutorial on the changes made to the VB language between VB 6 and VB.NET, see the appendix on this book's Web site at dummies.com/extras.

The ADO version of this line is as follows:

```
Set myRecordset = myCommand.Execute
```

In ADO.NET, this becomes the following:

```
dataAdapter.SelectCommand = selectCMD
```

Substituting Names (Mapping)

When you first load data from a database into a DataSet, the names of the tables and columns in the DataSet are the same as those used in the database. If you prefer to use different names while working with the DataSet, just create your new names in the DataSet command, and then *map* your names to the ones used in the original database. Both OleDbCommand and SqlCommand use their TableMappings collections to map custom names to database names. When you return the data to the database, all is well. Any edited data flows into the correct columns and tables as named originally in their database.

Why would you want to map, or rename, tables and columns? Perhaps the database is written in a foreign language, and you find it easier to work with mapped aliases rather than foreign words. Or maybe you have an in-house naming scheme for your databases, but you are working with DataSets from some other organization. You want to maintain the custom naming scheme in your programming. So map. Here's an example showing how to map a table named Employees to XcorpEmployees:

```
Dim dataAdapter As OleDbDataAdapter = New OleDbDataAdapter()
dataAdapter.TableMappings.Add("Employees", "XcorpEmployees")
```

You can add as many mappings as you wish to the TableMappings collection. To map a column name, use .ColumnMappings.Add("MapName", "OriginalName").

Read-Only Sequential

If your application merely needs a read-only version of a DataSet, it's easy. Just create an OleDbDataReader (or SQLDataReader), both of which have properties and methods that can assist you in scanning the query result. Also, they retrieve data faster than a typical DataSet. You can use methods such as NextResult (the equivalent of the ADO MoveNext command). And, instead of the ADO EOF (end-of-file) delimiter, you get the ADO.NET HasMoreRows property to see whether you've reached the last of the records.

EOF is an ancient command, used for more than 20 years to indicate that a file or recordset has reached its end:

```
Do While (Not myRecordset.EOF)
```

However, those in charge of naming things (or should I say *renaming* things) at Microsoft have decided that you can use the new Read property in VB.NET to detect the end of a set of data:

```
While (drDataReader.Read)
```

Suppose that you want to instantiate an OleDbDataReader or SqlDataReader object. In the following example, I assume that you have added an SqlConnection object named SqlConnection1 from the Toolbox to your form and that you have added a ListBox to your form. I also assume that you have right-clicked the SqlConnection1 icon, chosen Properties, and selected `Pubs.Dbo` as the `ConnectionString` property in the Properties window.

Make sure that this `Imports` statement is at the top of your code window:

```
Imports System.Data.SqlClient
```

Then type this into the `Form_Load` event:

```
Private Sub Form1_Load(ByVal sender As System.Object, ByVal e
    As System.EventArgs) Handles MyBase.Load


    Dim dReader As SqlDataReader
    Dim dQuery As String = "SELECT Au_lName, Au FName FROM
Authors"
    Dim dCommand As New SqlCommand(dQuery, SqlConnection1)

    SqlConnection1.Open()

    dReader = dCommand.ExecuteReader

    While dReader.Read()
ListBox1.Items.Add(dReader.GetString(0) & ", " &
    dReader.GetString(1))

    End While

    dReader.Close()
    SqlConnection1.Close()

End Sub
```

Notice that after the usual set of `Dim` statements, you must invoke the `ExecuteReader` method of the SqlDataReader object before you start reading the data from the database.

Sometimes an existing connection — one that's listed as a `ConnectionString` property in the Properties window — fails. You chose pubs.dbo as your `ConnectionString` in this example. Nevertheless, it's possible that VB.NET halts on this line when you press F5:

```
SqlConnection1.Open()
```

Then VB.NET displays an error message saying that it "can't open a connection without specifying a data source or server." If that happens to you, choose the New Connection option as SQLConnection1's `ConnectionString` in the Properties window. Then follow the instructions described in Book V, Chapter 4, in the section that covers making connections to databases.

What If Someone Else Modifies the Database in the Meantime?

Consider this scenario: While your DataSet has been disconnected from its database, someone else has also been working with some or all of that same data in his or her separate DataSet.

Maybe the other person modified some of that same data and updated the database by restoring his DataSet's contents to the database. What if the person edited a record that you also edited? Should you now overwrite the other person's changes with your changes? Or vice versa?

Unfortunately, the ADO.NET DataSet commands can't handle this problem automatically. What current technology could? ADO.NET is not artificially intelligent, after all. ADO.NET won't automatically lock a record in the database and warn others that they must wait because the record is being edited.

It's up to you to write programming to solve a potential problem when new versions of a record conflict. If this is a possible problem for the database you're working with, you have to find a solution and write the source code implementing that solution yourself.

The problem of two or more users in conflict during their attempts to flush back disconnected data into a database is sometimes called the *problem of concurrency.* Other people call it *a tough gig.* Whatever you call it, the question remains: When two or more users try to update a given record, should the changes made by the last person to update that record win? Should that be the rule? Or is there another rule, such as "The author of the book's version is always the one that is stored."

Optimism versus pessimism

You can approach the concurrency problem in two fundamental ways: pessimistic concurrency and optimistic concurrency. *Optimistic concurrency* prevents outsiders from changing a record (row) only while another person is updating that record. The updating usually takes very little time, so the lockout is brief.

Pessimistic concurrency, by contrast, locks out others for a longer time. The lock starts when one user accesses a record (which that user may potentially edit or delete) and remains in effect until the original user sends the record back to the database. (This is similar to the older style of database programming that maintained an open connection between an application and a database.)

Pessimism

Pessimistic concurrency is useful if you need to freeze a record while, for example, making arrangements for a customer. If an Amtrak agent is talking to someone about booking a sleeping car room on the train for a popular holiday, pessimistic locking prevents two agents in two different stations from contending for the same room (and thereby angering a customer). In that kind of situation, you want to lock the record for that room until the first customer makes up his or her mind and either reserves that room or decides not to reserve it.

The problem is that when you're using a DataSet, you can't use pessimistic concurrency. It's not practical in a disconnected architecture, and it's not scalable for the same reason that maintaining an open connection between an application and a DataSet isn't scalable.

Optimism

Optimistic concurrency locks a record only briefly, during the save to a hard drive. This prevents a nasty collision if two different records are simultaneously sent to the same record location in a database.

When a user attempts to update a record under optimistic concurrency, the updated data is compared to the existing record in the database. If there is any difference between them, the update is rejected. An exception is raised (an error message is generated). You, the programmer, must handle such errors in ADO.NET. You must write programming that responds to this type of error (using the `Try-Catch` error handling system in VB.NET) and decides what to do about the changed record. Do you accept it? Or do you have some criteria that can reconcile a data clash?

One version of optimistic concurrency is known as "last-in wins." This version doesn't compare the updated record to the original record. It merely lets each new update replace the previous version of the record. The "last-in wins" approach is the most scalable approach you can employ.

Comparing versions with optimistic concurrency

When deciding which record gets saved, classic optimistic concurrency compares versions by checking their version number (or, in some cases, their time and date stamps) or by saving all the values (all the data in the DataSet is saved when the data is initially read).

If the version number approach is used, each record must have a version number (or datestamp) column. This special column is saved on the client computer when the record is first read. Then if that client has modified a record, the database is checked to see whether the stored version number matches the version number currently in the database. If they match, it proves that no other person has modified that record since it was "checked out" for use by the client. Therefore, it is safe to update the record with the client's edited version. You can use an SQL statement like the following to conduct this test:

```
UPDATE myTable SET Field1 = ChangedValue1, Field2 =
    ChangedValue2
WHERE ClientStoredStamp = OriginalStampInDatabase
```

If this SQL is attempted, but the `ClientStoredStamp` doesn't match the `OriginalStampInDatabase`, an error is returned and you can write programming to make a decision about what to do. (You can store the client's editing and thereby replace the current record, extract the current record to compare it to the client's edited record, or save both versions and ask a human to make the decision. The latter is the slowest, but most finely tuned, approach.) It's also your responsibility to write the programming that updates the version or datetime column whenever a record is modified.

The other primary approach to managing optimistic concurrency is to save a copy of a record when it's first read. This means your DataSet has two copies of any record that's read: the one from the database, and the one the user modified. Using this approach, when the user attempts to update a record, the original version that came from the database is compared to whatever is now in that database. If they match, there's no problem. It proves that no one has messed with the record while it's been "checked out" of your DataSet, so you can go ahead and save the updated version (containing the user's modifications) to the database without worrying about overwriting someone else's work. Alternatively, you can query the DataSet's `DataViewRowState` property, which includes `added`, `modified`, `deleted`, `unchanged` conditions, as described in the previous chapter.

Every DataSet command includes four parameter collections, one for each of the four commands: `Select`, `Update`, `Insert`, `Delete`. Each parameter corresponds to a placeholder (? in an SQL statement) in the command text. The properties of a parameter specify both the column with which the parameter is associated and whether the parameter represents the edited version or the original version. These parameter collections make it possible for the DataSet command to generate dynamic SQL (or provide parameters to a stored procedure).

Building optimistic concurrency parameters

Fortunately, VB.NET builds the necessary DataSet parameters for you to implement optimistic concurrency using the SQL or stored procedure approach. Here's how:

1. **Create a VB.NET project that includes a data connection using an SqlDataAdapter object.**

2. **In the design window tray, right-click the SqlDataAdapter icon and choose Configure DataAdapter.**

The Data Adapter Configuration Wizard opens.

3. **Click Next.**

4. **In the Which Data Connection list, choose the *computername*pubs.dbo data connection, and then click Next.**

Substitute your computer's name for *computername*. If the pubs.dbo connection is not listed, follow the steps for installing SQL Server in Book IV, Chapter 4.

5. **Choose the Use SQL Statements option, and then click Next.**

6. **Click the Query Builder button.**

7. **If the Add Table dialog box appears automatically, go to Step 9. If the Add Table dialog box does not appear, right-click the background in the top pane of the Query Builder dialog box.**

A context menu pops out.

8. **Choose Add Table from the context menu.**

The Add Table dialog box appears.

9. **Choose Authors in the Add Table dialog box, and then click the Add button.**

10. **Click Close to close the Add Table dialog box.**

11. **In the Authors table, choose the All Columns option, and then click OK.**

This SQL statement is accepted and displayed.

12. **Click the Advanced Options button.**

13. **Choose the Use Optimistic Concurrency option (which is selected by default), and then click OK.**

14. **Click Finish.**

The wizard closes.

Now look at the code in the editor.

You need to write whatever programming you feel is necessary to ensure that the records that were supposed to be updated were, in fact, updated. (*Updated* means that records were changed in the database.) What programming you write depends on how you want to determine which version is stored in the database and which is discarded. Put this programming in the RowUpdated event. You can get to this event by selecting SQLAdapter1 in the drop-down list on the top left of the code window and then clicking RowUpdated in the drop-down list on the top right of the code window.

A lengthy discussion of handling concurrency is beyond the scope of this book. If you are deeply into .NET database programming, see the entries in VB.NET Help for RowUpdated, Optimistic Currency, and related topics for tutorials and code examples.

A Brief Look at XML

This book is not the place to dive into XML theory and practice. Just be aware that XML is automatically created by VB.NET for you when your program builds a DataSet, and in various other situations as well. XML also underlies other VB.NET elements, but it's mostly done behind the scenes and you need not write the code, nor even understand it. Thank goodness.

In this section, I briefly consider the nature of XML, the data storage and message-sending format used by ADO.NET. (In fact, much of the entire .NET technology relies on XML for various tasks.)

When you create a DataSet in VB.NET, it is translated into XML. For example, if you create a DataSet based on the Authors table in the Pubs sample database, you can then look over in the VB.NET Solution Explorer window and find an .XSD file (the schema of the DataSet written in XML). You didn't create this schema; VB.NET built it when you created your DataSet. Here's an example of an XML schema file that describes the structure of a DataSet:

```
<xsd:schema id="dsAuthors"
    targetNamespace="http://www.tempuri.org/dsAuthors.xsd"
    xmlns="http://www.tempuri.org/dsAuthors.xsd"
    xmlns:xsd="http://www.w3.org/1999/XMLSchema"
    xmlns:msdata="urn:schemas-microsoft-com:xml-msdata">
  <xsd:element name="authors">
    <xsd:complexType content="elementOnly">
      <xsd:all>
        <xsd:element name="au_id" type="xsd:string"/>
        <xsd:element name="au_lname" type="xsd:string"/>
        <xsd:element name="au_fname" type="xsd:string"/>
        <xsd:element name="phone" type="xsd:string"/>
        <xsd:element name="address" minOccurs="0"
    type="xsd:string"/>
```

```
      <xsd:element name="city" minOccurs="0"
  type="xsd:string"/>
      <xsd:element name="state" minOccurs="0"
  type="xsd:string"/>
      <xsd:element name="zip" minOccurs="0"
  type="xsd:string"/>
      <xsd:element name="contract" type="xsd:boolean"/>
    </xsd:all>
  </xsd:complexType>
  <xsd:key name="Constraint1" msdata:PrimaryKey="True">
    <xsd:selector>.</xsd:selector>
    <xsd:field>au_id</xsd:field>
  </xsd:key>
</xsd:element>
<xsd:element name="dsAuthors" msdata:IsDataSet="True">
  <xsd:complexType>
    <xsd:choice maxOccurs="unbounded">
      <xsd:element ref="authors"/>
    </xsd:choice>
  </xsd:complexType>
</xsd:element>
</xsd:schema>
```

As you can see, XML is often rather verbose and, in places, actually redundant. Let's just shudder and move on.

If you ever find yourself in the mood to actually work with XML source code, well, what can I say? To each his own. If this mood does come over you, VB.NET offers an XML Designer. You first write a DataSet schema in XML, and then you let the VB.NET XML Designer translate it into a DataSet. If you want to explore the XML Designer, choose Project⇨Add New Item, and double-click the XML Schema icon in the right pane of the Add New Item dialog box. Right-click the designer window, and choose Add to place elements (tables) or attributes (columns) into the Schema window. When you finish, right-click the designer window, and choose Generate DataSet.

Chapter 6: Querying Data

In This Chapter

↙ **Working with Query Builder**

↙ **Doing SQL queries the easy way**

↙ **Sorting rows with the ORDER BY clause**

↙ **Including queries in Visual Basic applications**

↙ **Joining tables into a relationship**

↙ **Adding user-input to an SQL query**

↙ **A brief dictionary of SQL**

↙ **Understanding action queries**

*W*hen you open a connection to a database or other data store, you generally want to get information out of it. But in most cases, you don't want *all* the information in it, just some. That's where queries come into play. This chapter shows you how to use SQL and some tools built into VB.NET to get exactly what you want out of databases and other data sources.

Automatic SQL: Using Query Builder

A *query* is usually a request for only a subset, only a portion, of the information in a database. "Show me a list of all accounts that are past due more than three months." When you run that query, you can put the results into a DataSet.

The data you get back in a DataSet can be extracted from more than one table in the source data, grouped according to specific criteria, and sorted in many useful ways.

Narrowing down data by using a query is one option, but you can also simply load in complete tables as well. Nonetheless, queries are frequently used because usually you just do not need the whole table.

Queries help you to create smaller, faster, more efficient DataSets. There's no reason to download the name of every person living in Iowa City, if all you need is a list of those who owe you money. In that case, write a query that fills a DataSet with only people who have negative balances in the database's table of customers.

Over the years, SQL (Structured Query Language) has become the standard way of querying databases. Using SQL, you can specify your queries using understandable, English-like phrases. You ask a query similar to the following English: "Give me a list of all publishers located in California, and alphabetize the list by the publishers' names." In return, you get a DataSet containing that data, arranged the way you requested. Any publisher whose State column contains anything other than `CA` is ignored and does not become part of the DataSet.

Here's the SQL query that builds this California-publishers-only DataSet:

```
SELECT * FROM Publishers WHERE State = 'CA' ORDER BY
    'PubName'
```

This chapter explores the uses of Query Builder, a VB.NET tool that makes creating even complex SQL queries easy. You work briefly with Query Builder in previous chapters, but here you find out how to take full advantage of this valuable tool.

In this chapter, you first explore the kind of SQL query that returns a set of data. However, you can use SQL also to change or delete database information and even to create tables. SQL statements that change a database are called *action queries*. For examples of action queries, see the section "SQL action queries: Changing a database," later in this chapter.

Using Query Builder

Query Builder is part of a wizard that appears when you add an SqlDataAdapter or OleDbDataAdapter control to a Windows project in VB.NET. If you already have one of these controls on a form, you can fire up the Query Builder by right-clicking one of the controls and choosing Configure Data Adapter.

Variously called Query Builder, Query Designer, SQL Builder, and so on, this useful VB.NET tool makes creating and modifying SQL queries easier. I use the term *Query Builder* because it appears more often than the other terms in the Microsoft documentation. Whatever it's called, this tool is the fastest way to create an SQL query (without having to write it yourself).

If you haven't yet installed IIS or defined a connection to the pubs sample database, follow the instructions in Book IV, Chapter 4, before attempting the examples in this chapter.

To see how to use Query Builder, start a new VB Windows application and attach a database to it, as shown in the following steps:

1. **Start a new project in VB.NET (choose File⇨New⇨Project).**

   The New Project dialog box appears.

2. **Name this project** *Queries.*

3. **Double-click the Windows Application icon.**

4. **Click the Data tab in the VB.NET Toolbox.**

5. **Double-click the SqlDataAdapter control.**

   The Data Adapter Configuration Wizard appears.

6. **Click Next.**

7. **On the second page of the wizard, click the down arrow and choose the YourComputerName\VSDOTNET.pubs.dbo data connection.**

8. **Click Next.**

9. **Click the Use SQL Statements option, and then click Next.**

10. **Click the Query Builder button.**

    The useful Query Builder utility appears.

Building an SQL query

To build an SQL query using the VB.NET Query Builder, follow these steps:

1. **Open Query Builder, as described in the preceding section.**

   Note that the following examples build on the example query described in the preceding section.

2. **In the top pane of the Query Builder window, right-click the background and choose Add Table (if the Add Table dialog box isn't already visible).**

   The Add Table dialog box appears.

3. **Double-click the Publishers table.**

   The Publishers table is added to Query Builder.

4. **Click Close.**

   The Add Table dialog box closes.

   An SQL query is generated automatically for you:

   ```
   SELECT
   FROM          publishers
   ```

5. **In the Publishers table, select the All Columns option.**

Until Step 5, your query doesn't specify any columns from this table yet. To do that, you must click the boxes next to the column names, or if you want to get all the columns, click the first box next to the * symbol. Go ahead and click the top box with the *. You see the Query Builder create this SQL query:

```
SELECT      publishers.*
FROM        publishers
```

Note that *if* you only select the city and state columns, you see this SQL instead:

```
SELECT      city, state
FROM        publishers
```

It's customary (though not required) to put SQL commands such as `SELECT FROM` in all caps and the rest of the SQL statement, such as `Authors`, in initial caps. However, the Query Builder, in its wisdom, chooses to lowercase table, column, and other data in a statement.

6. **In the Diagram pane (the top pane in the Query Builder window), right-click in the background and choose Run.**

Your query, `SELECT publishers.*`, is executed against the Publishers database. The Results pane, at the bottom of the Query Builder window, displays the results of the query, as you can see in Figure 6-1. You get a complete list of all publishers in this database.

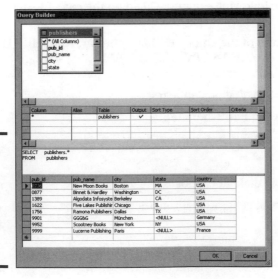

Figure 6-1:
You can view and edit a database's rows using the Query Builder.

The four window panes

The Query Builder window has four panes, named (from top to bottom) Diagram, Grid, SQL, and Results, as shown in Figure 6-2.

Grid   Diagram

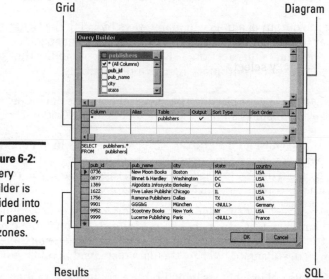

Figure 6-2:
Query
Builder is
divided into
four panes,
or zones.

Results   SQL

Here's what the various panes of the Query Builder window do for you:

✦ **Diagram pane:** Shows the contents of your data structures (usually tables), as well as any relationships between the structures.

✦ **Grid pane:** Enables you to create new relationships and specify a variety of qualities that define your query.

✦ **SQL pane:** Allows you to type an SQL query (or just observe an automatically generated SQL query).

✦ **Results pane:** Shows you the DataSet that results from executing the current query.

Using ORDER BY to Sort Rows

Recall that a typical table in a relational database doesn't maintain its rows in alphabetical (or any other) order. Earlier in this chapter, in Figure 6-1, you see that the only ordered column in that table is the pub_id column.

But what if you want the publishers ordered alphabetically by their names? That's perhaps a more useful order for your DataSet than listing them by an ID number. Remember that unique ID numbers are useful as a primary key in a database — speeding data retrieval (such as your query) or creating relations. But the results of a query, a DataSet, are sometimes intended for human consumption. And we humans often prefer to have a list alphabetized.

You can adjust the output of a query in many ways by using the Grid pane in Query Builder to request a sorting order or other kinds of specifications that govern the output. In this section, I show you how to modify the Query Builder's Grid pane to sort your query results alphabetically.

As you see in Figure 6-1, Query Builder has several columns, including Sort Type and Sort Order. You can modify these elements in the Grid pane:

✦ **Output:** With the Output checkboxes, you can specify which columns you want to display in the final result. Each column can contain a particular table. In the examples I describe in this chapter, you're working with only one table: the Publishers table.

You rarely need to show all columns in your query, but every column with a checkmark in its Output checkbox is shown. If you choose not to display output for a particular column, that column can nevertheless be used as a way of sorting or filtering the data displayed in other columns.

✦ **Table:** The Table column shows which table a column is attached to (so you know which tables' data are displayed in the column).

✦ **Criteria:** These are grouping criteria, including aggregate functions that you use when generating summary reports. The SQL language is extensive and flexible, and it offers many ways to filter and organize data. You can specify complicated queries, such as "Find all authors whose first name begins with *L* and who published all their works between 1880 and 1889."

After you create some query results (such as the publishers query results in the example described in the preceding section), you can sort the output by following these steps:

1. **In the Grid pane in Query Builder, under the Column heading, click the cell where the * is displayed (refer to Figure 6-2). (Don't click the gray title bar, or you select the entire column. Click the cell.) A down-arrow button appears in that cell. Click the button, and you see a list of the columns in the publishers table. Select pub_name from the list.**

Your SQL query automatically changes to the following:

```
SELECT      pub_name
FROM        publishers
```

2. **Click the first *cell* in the Sort Type column in the Grid pane, and then click the down-arrow button that appears.**

   A list appears, with two options: Ascending and Descending.

3. **Choose Ascending (for an *A* to *Z* ordering), rather than Descending (for *Z* to *A* ordering).**

   Query Builder automatically adds the appropriate line to your SQL statement (in this case, ORDER BY pub_name). Also, an A-Z icon is added to the table representation in the top pane.

   Note that making this change also turns the list of all columns (except the ID column) in the Results pane from black to gray.

   The gray color tells you that changes have been made to the query that are not yet shown in the results. The result is displayed in gray because it is now an old set that no longer represents the current SQL statement. You have to use the Run command again to create an updated result set if you want to see what the current SQL statement produces.

4. **Right-click the background in the top pane (the Diagram pane) of Query Builder, and choose Run from the context menu.**

   The results of your current SQL statement are displayed in the Results pane. The list of publishers' names is now displayed alphabetically, as shown in Figure 6-3.

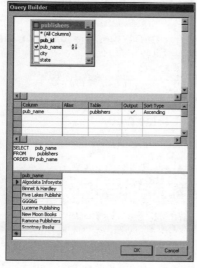

Figure 6-3:
Now just the publishers are displayed, and they are alphabetized.

You can sort by more than one column, too. Why would you do that? Perhaps you want a list of all your contacts sorted first by city and then in alphabetical order by last name within each city. Later in this chapter, you create a multiple column sort. People sorted by Last Name and then First Name can also be useful.

Choosing from 73.2 Million Possible Results, Give or Take a Few

SQL enables you to create requests for information in millions of ways. SQL statements can filter and configure data in highly complicated arrangements. Before you go too far, however, try constructing a few common filters, as described in this section. Note that the following examples build on the example query described in the preceding section.

You try the following filters by adjusting the Criteria column in Query Builder. This way, you get a feel for what the Criteria column does. (You may have to stretch the Query Builder window wider to reveal the Criteria column.)

You want a table with lots of rows to experiment with now, so begin by switching to the Authors table. There are many more authors than there are publishers (believe me, I know):

1. **Right-click the title bar of the Publishers(dbo) box (in the Diagram pane), and choose Remove.**

   This gets rid of the Publishers(dbo) table. The Results pane's data goes gray.

2. **Right-click the Diagram pane, and choose Add Table.**

3. **Double-click the Authors table.**

4. **Click Close to close the Add Table dialog box.**

5. **Click au_lname to add the author last name column to your query.**

6. **Type > 'P' in the Criteria cell on the same row where au_lname is listed. The Criteria column is the seventh one to the right, so you may have to stretch the Query Builder to see it.**

   After you move out of the criteria cell, a symbol that looks like a funnel appears in the top pane, next to the column for which you specified a criterion. A criterion is also known as a *filter*.

   If anyone has a last name that is simply P, it won't display. Only records starting with Pa and above are displayed. To include P, you use >=, which means greater than or equal to. Never underestimate the possibilities.

7. Right-click the Diagram pane, and choose Run.

The WHERE clause in the SQL statement in the SQL pane reads like this: WHERE (au_lname > 'P'). And in the Results pane, the list begins with authors whose names start with P, and the list ends with the Z names, just as you'd hoped.

How about seeing only names beginning with P and Q? Change the Criteria cell to > 'P' AND < 'R'. The SQL statement changes to WHERE (au_lname > 'P' AND au_lname < 'R'). Choose the Run option, and you see that only author names beginning with P and Q are displayed.

If you want to experiment with some of the 73.2 million possible SQL filters, be patient. This chapter ends with a small dictionary of the most common, useful SQL terms. The possibilities are not endless, but there are more ways to filter data than you'll ever use in your lifetime, dude.

From Separate Tables: Doing a Join

Sometimes, you want to get data from more than one table at a time. In the pubs sample database that you've been using in this book, for example, the Authors table includes all the names of the authors, but to see the titles of these authors' books, you have to look in a different table named Titles. What if you want to retrieve both the names and the book titles into a DataSet? You can create a join. (The term *join* is also known as a relationship — hence the term *relational database*.) Joins are quite similar to *relations* I describe in the previous chapter.

To join two tables, they must each contain the same key column. In the pubs database, the key in the Authors table is named au_id, but the key in the Titles table is named title_id. So these tables do not have a key in common. What to do? Fortunately (actually, this was intentional on the part of the database designer), a *third* table includes both au_id and title_id. This table can serve as a way to link (or sync, you may say) the rows in the Authors table to the rows in the Titles table. (Technically you can also construct a *cross join*. Query Builder will make one of those if you drop two tables in that don't have any common keys.)

If that third table did not exist, the person who designed this database has to add it. You are not likely to be given a database to work with that has the fatal structural flaw of floating tables that should be joinable but are not.

To see how to create a join, follow these steps:

1. **Open Query Builder, and add the Authors table to the Query Builder. (If you still have the previous example active, the author's table will already be there.)**

   Follow the steps in the "Building an SQL query" section, earlier in this chapter.

2. **Right-click the Diagram pane, and choose Add Table.**

3. **Double-click the TitleAuthor table.**

   Two things happened when you added that second table into Query Builder. First, a symbol that looks like hydraulic piping with a key joins the two tables. Notice that this pipe attaches at the locations of the key columns that they have in common (in this example, Au_ID). Second, Query Builder automatically modifies its SQL statement to specify the joined columns.

4. **Now add a third table, Titles, to Query Builder.**

   A second join symbol appears, connecting the title_id key column that these two tables have in common, as shown in Figure 6-4.

Figure 6-4:
When two tables have a key column in common, Query Builder can create joins for you.

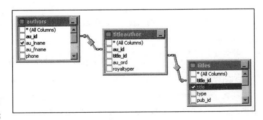

5. **Click Close to close the Add Table dialog box.**

6. **In the Diagram pane, click the au_lname and title options (as shown in Figure 6-4) next to the two columns that you want to display in your query results.**

   To follow my example, you want to display the Author (au_lname) from the Authors table and the title from the Titles table.

7. **Right-click the Diagram pane, and choose Run.**

   The author names and the titles of their books are displayed. Now your DataSet displays data from two different, joined tables.

Notice that one author name may be repeated several times in this example. That happens if an author has written more than one book. Similarly, if a title is repeated, it means that the book was co-authored. The join requires that the DataSet must include each row in which the key columns (the Au_ID columns) match. Note, though, that the parent key (the primary key) and the foreign key (the key in the second table) are not required to have the same name; they simply need to be defined as a relationship in the database. Even small database applications usually require joins. You need to understand this important feature, particularly how to work with what are called left or right outer joins. More about these later in this chapter.

Dynamic SQL

In the examples in this chapter, you've seen various ways to use SQL queries to create a DataSet. However, these queries were hard-wired into your source code. You, the programmer, specified these queries. But what if you want to permit your user to specify the SQL query?

In the following example, you let the user type a letter or letters, such as s. Then, in your program, you use the LIKE command to show the user all the names that begin with s. Follow these steps:

1. **For each of the three tables used in the preceding example, right-click them and choose Remove.**

2. **Click OK to close the Query Builder window.**

3. **Click Cancel to close the Data Adapter Configuration Wizard that hosts Query Builder.**

   You're going to abandon Query Builder in this example; it's a programmer's tool, an excellent one, but it can't be shown to users.

You're going to allow the user to specify which data should be displayed in a list of authors (lastname, firstname) that match the user's input. Here's the SQL statement that you embed in your source code to match the user's request:

```
"Select * from authors WHERE au_lname LIKE '" & n & "%'"
```

The LIKE operator lets you specify a pattern that must be matched. The % symbol means "and anything else." (It's very similar to the * symbol.) For example, 'S%' means "retrieve all records that begin with S and end with anything in addition to that character."

In this SQL statement, if the user types s, your DataSet is filled with the rows of any author with a last name beginning with S. Follow these steps:

1. **Click the (Form1.vb Design) tab at the top of the VB.NET design window to display your form.**

2. **From the Toolbox's Windows Forms tab, add a Button, a ListBox, and a TextBox to your form.**

3. **Double-click the form to get to the code window. At the top of the code window, add this** Imports **statement:**

   ```
   Imports System.Data.SqlClient
   ```

   You can also include the other System.Data namespaces by using Imports for them too, if you choose. For this example, .SqlClient is the only necessary namespace. (In recent versions of VB.NET, the System.Data namespace is *always* available because it's listed in Solution Explorer as one of the default references for any VB.NET project.)

4. **Double-click the button to get to its** Click **event in the code window, and then type the following in the event:**

   ```
   Private Sub Button1_Click(ByVal sender As System.Object,
       ByVal e As System.EventArgs) Handles Button1.Click

       ListBox1.Items.Clear()

       Dim dReader As SqlDataReader

       Dim n As String
       n = TextBox1.Text

       Dim dQuery As String = "Select * from authors WHERE
       au_lname LIKE '" & n & "%'"

       Dim dCommand As New SqlCommand(dQuery,
       SqlConnection1)

       SqlConnection1.Open()

       dReader = dCommand.ExecuteReader

       Dim t As String
       While dReader.Read()
           t = dReader.GetString(1) & ", " &
       dReader.GetString(2)
           ListBox1.Items.Add(t)
       End While

       dReader.Close()
       SqlConnection1.Close()
       Exit Sub

   End Sub
   ```

If you see a squiggly blue line underneath the references in this code to SQLConnection1, that means you've removed this control from your form (it was used in a previous example in this chapter and may still be available on your form's tray).

If the SQLDataAdapter1 control is not on your tray in the design window, go to the Toolbox, click the Data tab, and then double-click the SqlConnection control to put one back on your tray. Then use the Properties window to specify that its ConnectionString property points to the pubs sample database.

5. Press F5 to run the program, and then type the letter s.

You should see three hits displayed in the ListBox, as shown in Figure 6-5.

Figure 6-5:
The user gets to specify the SQL query in this example.

The heart of this program is the line in the code where you specify your query:

```
Dim dQuery As String = "Select * from authors WHERE au_lname
    LIKE '" & n & "%'"
```

Note that when you use the LIKE command, the variable data (the variable n in this code) must be enclosed in single quotes. This forces you to use double quotes around single quotes:

```
'" & n & "%'"
```

(Recall that the % symbol means "plus anything else." For example, 'La%' means "show all rows that begin with La and end with anything in addition to those characters.") When this program runs, if the user types s in the TextBox, the SQL query looks like the following in VB.NET:

```
Select * from authors WHERE au_lname LIKE 's%'
```

Notice the single quotes surrounding the variables in this SQL query example from earlier in this chapter:

```
SELECT * FROM Publishers WHERE State LIKE 'CA' ORDER BY
    'PubName'
```

In this example, I use a DataReader object, which is read-only and can't be edited. It works faster than creating a full (modifiable) DataSet.

In addition to the queries you can create using the Query Builder's Diagram and Grid panes, you can also type any SQL statement you want into the SQL pane. However, if you type one that the Query Builder can't illustrate in its Diagram or Grid panes — or one that it simply can't understand — when you click the OK button to close the Query Builder, it informs you that it can't *parse* (figure out) the query. Then you have the option of returning to the Query Builder to fix an error, or ignoring the message and continuing to work.

A Brief Dictionary of SQL

Use the rest of this chapter as a quick reference when you want to know how to use the Structured Query Language to extract particular data from a database. Each heading names an SQL term and describes its purpose, so you can quickly scan these heads to find just the technique you need.

You can experiment with the SQL clauses in this chapter by using the Run command in Query Builder and seeing what data comes out of the database. (An SQL clause is a combination of SQL terms such as SELECT and LIKE, along with database-specific terms such as table and column names.) The examples in this chapter are all SQL clauses.

Microsoft Terminology Shift Alert: I feel I must repeat this warning. Microsoft decided to change two key database-related words: record and field. Some players in computer programming (notably IBM) have long used the term *row* to represent an individual record of data, and the term *column* to represent a *category* of data (such as a Social Security Number column). In the past, Microsoft and others have used the term *record* rather than *row*, and the term *field* rather than *column*. In this book, I have adopted the new terminology — row and column — but now and then also use the older terms.

Alas, many flavors of SQL exist (standard ANSI SQL, Microsoft SQL Server Transact SQL, Oracle PL/SQL, ODBC SQL, and the version I explain here: Access SQL). Fortunately, these flavors of SQL are similar. However, because there are some differences between them, this little dictionary can't be generic (or as Microsoft likes to call it "agnostic"); this dictionary demonstrates Microsoft Access SQL because it remains the most widely used variant in the world.

The commands in the SQL language are referred to as *clauses* (such as ORDER BY), *keywords* (such as TOP), or *operators* (such as LIKE or BETWEEN). Some people find these distinctions — an attempt at a primitive grammar — less than useful. For example, in English grammar a *clause* means a group of words containing a subject and verb. The term *clause* is used similarly in SQL (SELECT Author, for example, is a valid clause in both English and SQL). Unfortunately, though, the single word SELECT is also sometimes called a clause in SQL. Puzzling.

In spite of these confusions, when I refer to the words used in the SQL language (such as SELECT or ORDER BY), I interchangeably use *clause, keyword, function,* and *operator* because all of these terms are, by now, conventions. I also follow the convention of capitalizing SQL commands, which helps to distinguish them from arguments (such as tables and columns).

SELECT: The main SQL clause to retrieve data

The SELECT clause, which is undoubtedly one of the more important SQL clauses, appears at the start of each SQL statement that retrieves data from a database.

Here's the required format for SELECT:

```
SELECT column(s) FROM table(s)
```

And here's an example:

```
SELECT      au_lname
FROM        dbo.authors
```

If you want to retrieve all columns from a table, use the * command, as in this example:

```
SELECT      dbo.authors.*
FROM        dbo.authors
```

The following example demonstrates the correct syntax for specifying two columns:

```
SELECT      phone, address
FROM        dbo.authors
```

SQL includes the following optional clauses for use in a SELECT clause (and I further explain each of these clauses in its own section):

✦ JOIN: Specifies the key columns used to connect two tables when getting data from those tables.

✦ GROUP BY: Specifies the column you want to use to combine rows (records) with the same values when you're summarizing using aggregate functions. For example, if you want a list of total sales by region, you use GROUP BY Region. The new DataSet lists each region only once and includes the tally of the number of sales in each region. The tally (which uses the SUM function described later in this chapter) is called an aggregate function.

✦ HAVING: Part of an aggregate function that enables you to specify criteria, such as "Show me only those results in which the name of the region begins with the letter C." The HAVING clause must be used with GROUPS, described later in this chapter. It is not identical to the WHERE clause, which is not used with GROUPS.

✦ ORDER BY: Specifies how to sort the DataSet.

The following example alphabetizes the results, based on the data in the Author column:

```
SELECT     au_lname
FROM       dbo.authors
ORDER BY   au_lname
```

The following example sorts on two columns, alphabetizing the last names. And if rows have identical last names, those rows are ordered alphabetically by the first name:

```
SELECT     au_lname, au_fname, phone
FROM       dbo.authors
ORDER BY   au_lname, au_fname
```

WHERE: Narrowing the field

After you specify the column(s) and table(s) by using the SELECT clause and its required partner, the FROM clause, you may want to further limit the data. You use the WHERE clause to provide criteria that limits (or filters) data, just as in English you may say, "Show me only the magazine subscriptions that cost less than $12 a year."

Here's the required format for WHERE:

```
WHERE column operator criteria
```

The following example shows how you use the WHERE clause:

```
SELECT      au_lname
FROM        dbo.authors
WHERE       (Au_lname LIKE 'S%')
```

In this example, the LIKE operator enables you to specify a pattern that must be matched. The % symbol says, "and anything else." For example, 'S%' means "Show all rows that begin with S and end with anything in addition to that character."

When you use the WHERE clause, you can use various operators to specify a relationship. Table 6-1 describes the meaning of each operator.

Table 6-1	Operators You Can Use with WHERE
Operator	*Meaning*
<	Less than. For example, the following shows all authors whose last name begins with A or B: `WHERE au_lname< 'C%'`
<=	Less than or equal to. For example, the following shows all author ID numbers less than or equal to 300: `WHERE au_id <= 300`
>	Greater than. For example, the following shows all author ID numbers above 300: `WHERE au_id > 300`
>=	Greater than or equal to. For example, the following shows all author ID numbers above 299: `WHERE au_id >= 300`
=	Equal to. For example, the following shows au_id 300 only, if it exists: `WHERE au_id = 300`
<>	Not equal to. For example, the following shows all author ID numbers other than 300: `WHERE au_id <> 300`
BETWEEN	Within a range. For example, the following shows all authors whose name begins with A, B, C, or D: `WHERE au_lname BETWEEN 'A' AND 'D'`
LIKE	Matches a pattern. For example, the following shows all authors whose name begins with the characters Adam: `WHERE au_lname LIKE 'Adam%'`
IN	Matches items in a list. For example, the following shows all authors whose name is either Andrews or Brown: `WHERE au_lname IN ('Andrews', 'Brown')` This syntax does not permit pattern matching (where you use the %, *, _, or ? symbols). Notice that the term IN here is used to mean "in this list." It does not mean *between*.

BETWEEN: Specifying a range

The BETWEEN operator enables you to specify a range, such as between two dates or two zip codes. This example shows how you use the BETWEEN operator:

```
SELECT      zip
FROM        dbo.authors
WHERE       (zip BETWEEN '20000' AND '40000')
```

Figure 6-6 shows the resulting DataSet when you run this example.

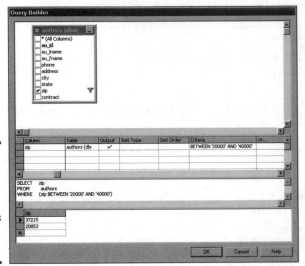

Figure 6-6:
This is your DataSet, showing only two hits for this query.

The zip code data is stored in a column that uses the Integer data type. If this column were a Date data type, you would have to surround the criteria with # symbols, like this:

```
BETWEEN #1993# AND #1995#
```

LIKE: Using a pattern match

The LIKE operator enables you to use wildcards when asking for data. For example, if you want to see all the rows that begin with the letters ab, you use this operator in your SQL query:

```
WHERE (au_lname LIKE 'ab%')
```

The % means "plus anything else." In other words, all author names beginning with ab are returned.

You can also use an underscore character to represent a single character. For example, you can match any Author name that begins with a and ends in c by using WHERE (au_lname LIKE 'a_c'). To match any Author name that begins with a and has a c in the third character position, use LIKE 'a_c%'.

Alas, you specify wildcards in SQL in two ways. It's one of those oddities in computer languages that you just have to live with (like the fact that some kinds of lists start counting from 0, but others count from 1).

ANSI SQL (the version of SQL used by Query Builder) uses % to mean "and any number of other characters." For example, Ma% displays Max, Max Headroom, and Maximillian, among whatever other rows contain text that begins with the letters ma. On the other hand, Microsoft Access SQL uses a * symbol rather than %.

Likewise, to specify a single character, ANSI uses _ (underline) but Jet uses ? (as in Ma?, which matches May, but not Mayo). If one kind of pattern-matching symbol isn't working for you, try the other. These variations are one reason for the famous programmer's warning: "Know your data source." You should always be careful to avoid making assumptions about the nature of data sources. Someday, you may have to write a program that accesses two or three data sources, requiring two or three distinct SQL variants. So, always double-check the rules that govern any data source that you deal with.

ORDER BY: Sorting the results

The ORDER BY clause enables you to specify how you want data to be sorted: numerically or alphabetically, ascending (from a to z) or descending (from z to a). Here's an example:

```
SELECT     au_lname
FROM       dbo.authors
ORDER BY   au_lname
```

This example orders the Authors table, based on the contents of the Author column, alphabetically from a to z (ascending). To reverse the order (descending from z to a), use this clause:

```
ORDER BY   au_lname DESC
```

You can also order by multiple columns. If a table has separate LastName and FirstName columns, for example, you could alphabetize the names first by the last names and then by the first names within any duplicate last names, like this:

```
ORDER BY   LastName, FirstName
```

To create a descending order by last name, but ascending by first name, use this code:

```
ORDER BY   LastName DESC, FirstName
```

To sort both columns in descending order, use this code:

```
ORDER BY   LastName DESC, FirstName DESC
```

TOP: Limiting a range

If you have a large database with thousands of rows and someone wants to see only the 25 best-performing products, you can use the ORDER BY DESC clause to make a list of the products in order of total sales (from most to least sales, thanks to DESC). Then, instead of stuffing the DataSet with this list of all 2,000 products, you can lop off the bottom 1975 by using the TOP keyword, like this:

```
SELECT TOP 25 *
FROM tblSales
ORDER BY TotalSales DESC
```

If any of these products sold the same number, you get more than 25 rows when you run this example. Ties count as a single result, thereby inflating the list.

You can also request a percentage of the total number of rows, rather than a specific number of rows (as in the preceding example). To see the top 5 percent of the TotalSales column, use this code:

```
SELECT TOP 5 PERCENT *
FROM tblSales
ORDER BY TotalSales DESC
```

JOIN: Getting data from more than one table at a time

To create a DataSet that includes data from more than a single table, you use the JOIN feature, introduced earlier in this chapter.

To create a join, you use an equal sign to connect identical columns in two tables, as in the following example:

```
SELECT     dbo.authors.au_lname, dbo.titleauthor.royaltyper
FROM       dbo.authors INNER JOIN
           dbo.titleauthor ON dbo.authors.au_id =
    dbo.titleauthor.au_id
```

The `INNER JOIN` command specifies that the details in the third line represent the join. The third line specifies that the Authors table is joined to the titleauthor table. (They both share a column named `au_id`, so they can join using that column.) The first line says, "Display the `au_lname` column (their names are in this column) from the Author table, and display the `royaltyper` column from the titleauthor table."

AS: Renaming columns (aliasing)

In some cases, you want a column to have a different name. Perhaps the column's real name (its name in the database) is misleading or overly complicated, and it confuses folks if displayed in a report.

Or perhaps you're building a calculated or aggregate column, and you must give the new column a name. (For an example showing how you use AS with an aggregate, see the "Calculating with aggregate functions" section, later in this chapter.)

You use the AS clause to name or rename a column. (This technique — inventing synonyms — is also sometimes called *mapping* in computer lingo.) The following example shows how you use the AS clause when a database uses the unclear field name `au_lname`:

```
SELECT     au_lname AS [Authors' Last Names]
FROM       dbo.authors
```

This example renames the obscure `au_lname` column from the Authors table to `Authors' Last Names`. Figure 6-7 shows the result.

DISTINCT: Eliminating duplicates

Sometimes, you get extraneous information when you do a query. For example, if you ask for a DataSet that includes the City column in a Publishers' address table, you get lots of New York entries in the DataSet. To avoid duplicates, you can use the `DISTINCT` keyword, as in this example. It returns only one entry from any given city:

```
SELECT DISTINCT City
FROM Publishers
```

Using `DISTINCT` can hinder performance in a large database such as the BIBLIO.MDB sample database. When I ran this example in the Query Builder, my hard drive thrashed away for several minutes, I was notified that I was running low on virtual memory, and I finally had to reset the computer. You've been warned.

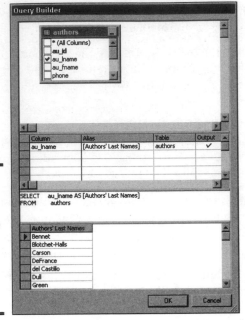

Figure 6-7:
With an AS clause, you can rename this database's confusing au_1name column.

COUNT, SUM, AVG, MAX, and MIN: *Calculating with aggregate functions*

You can use the five aggregate functions to figure out the number of rows (COUNT), the sum total of numeric rows (SUM), the average value of numeric rows (AVG), and the highest (MAX) or lowest (MIN) numeric row. Only the COUNT function can be used with text rows. An aggregate function can *calculate* things for you.

To try constructing an aggregate function using Query Builder, you can create an SQL query that tells you how many author names the Authors table contains. To see how to construct an aggregate function, follow these steps:

1. **Open Query Builder, and then add the Authors table to it.**

For details on how to add the table, see the section titled "Using Query Builder" earlier in this chapter.

2. **In the Authors window, click the check box next to au_1name.**

The SQL statement changes to the following:

```
SELECT     au_1name
FROM       dbo.authors
```

3. **Right-click anywhere in the background of the Diagram pane (at the top of the Query Builder window), and choose Group By.**

   A Group By option appears in the Grid pane, and a strange icon appears in the table diagram next to au_lname.

4. **Click the cell in the au_lname row where it says "Group By."**

   A down-arrow button appears. Click the down-arrow button to display a list of options. Select Count from this list.

   Now, the SQL statement looks like this:

   ```
   SELECT      COUNT(au_lname) AS Expr1
   FROM        dbo.authors
   ```

   The AS clause has created an alias named Expr1. That's not too descriptive of what you're doing.

5. **In the Alias column of the Grid Pane, change Expr1 to [Total Authors] surrounded by brackets, as shown in the following code:**

   Here's what the SQL statement looks like:

   ```
   SELECT      COUNT(au_lname) AS [Total Authors]
   FROM        dbo.authors
   ```

   Notice that because you're using two words for the alias, they've been enclosed in brackets.

6. **Right-click the Diagram pane and choose Run.**

   You see the total number of authors displayed in the Author column, as shown in Figure 6-8.

Figure 6-8:
The result of your aggregate function count.

GROUP BY: Summarizing

Use the GROUP BY clause if you want to collapse more than one row into a single row. For example, you can ask for a count of the number of publishers in each city. The following SQL query lists each city and the total number of publishers in that city:

```
SELECT COUNT(City) AS Total, City
FROM Publishers
GROUP BY City
```

HAVING: Narrowing criteria

The example in the preceding section shows how you can display all the cities stored in the table and, at the same time, list the number of times each city appears in the table.

If you want to narrow the number of cities, use the HAVING clause. (HAVING is similar to the WHERE clause, which I describe earlier in the chapter. However, you must use HAVING with the GROUP BY clause.)

I don't know of any sample tables that allow me to illustrate the concept of HAVING, but HAVING is really useful and largely misunderstood. Imagine a table called OrderSummary with OrderNumber, Quantity, City, and State columns. Imagine that you have the following entries:

OrderNumber	Quantity	City	State
1234	3	Albany	NY
2345	5	Los Angeles	CA
3456	3	Albany	NY
5678	4	Appleton	WI
6789	2	Springfield	IL

If your goal is to see cities where you've sold more than three total items city-wide, you might think you could run the following query:

```
SELECT SUM(Quantity) AS TotalItems, city, state FROM
    OrderSummary WHERE Quantity >3  GROUP BY city, state.
```

This query would show you that you've had five orders in Los Angeles and four orders in Appleton. But, of course, that's not telling you the whole story! You want to use the following query instead:

```
SELECT SUM(Quantity) AS TotalItems, city, state FROM
    OrderSummary GROUP BY city, state HAVING Quantity >3 .
```

With this HAVING query, you actually see that Albany, which wasn't listed at all in the first query, has more total item sales than any other city.

SQL action queries: Changing a database

SQL usually simply returns data from a data source, but you can also use SQL to *modify* the data in a database or other source. You can even use SQL to append new rows with the INSERT clause or add new tables with the SELECT INTO clause.

Using SQL statements to modify databases or their data is called an action query — but surely the word *query* isn't quite right here because nothing is being questioned. Nonetheless, you can do a lot to a database with this technique.

DELETE: Removing rows

Using SQL's DELETE query can be a dangerous business because you can wipe out an entire database with very little SQL code. To see what I mean, take a look at the next section.

The following SQL statement (don't do it!) destroys the entire Authors table in the BIBLIO.MDB database:

```
DELETE * FROM   dbo.authors
```

When you use DELETE, all data that has been returned by the SELECT clause vanishes — poof! You've been warned. Don't experiment with this clause unless you've backed up the database first.

You can use all the usual filters when defining what you want to delete. For example, the following code wipes out any author whose last name begins with A:

```
DELETE     au_lname
FROM       dbo.authors
WHERE      (au_lname LIKE 'A%')
```

Some versions of SQL leave out that first au_lname between the DELETE and FROM, but Microsoft Access SQL uses it.

The Microsoft Access database system prefers this syntax:

```
DELETE     *
FROM       dbo.authors
WHERE      (au_lname LIKE 'A%')
```

A DELETE query removes entire rows from a table. It doesn't simply empty the rows leaving them with nulls. It actually blows the rows away. If you want to delete data from individual columns, use an UPDATE query (as shown in the next section).

Additional action queries

You can create the following additional types of queries in the Diagram and Grid panes of Query Builder:

+ **Insert into query:** Adds a new row (record) and inserts its data into specified columns. This query creates an SQL `INSERT INTO-VALUES` statement.

+ **Insert from query:** Copies existing rows from one table to another, or within the same table; this process creates new rows. It uses an SQL `INSERT-SELECT` statement.

+ **Update query:** Changes the data of individual columns (fields) in one or more existing rows in a table. It uses an SQL `UPDATE` statement.

+ **Make table query:** Creates a new table. It uses the SQL `SELECT...INTO` statement.

Book VI

Fun and Games with Graphics

The 5th Wave   By Rich Tennant

History was about to repeat itself as Charlie van Gogh, Visual Basic .NET programmer and great-nephew of Vincent van Gogh is assigned the job of designing a user interface for his company's new database program.

"Sorry Chuck-management is still rejecting your latest designs."

Contents at a Glance

Chapter 1: You Be Picasso

In This Chapter

✔ Simplifying drawing

✔ Displaying shapes

✔ Using splines and polygons

✔ Understanding pens and brushes

✔ Working with paths, regions, and path gradients

✔ Handling transparency

*1*f you're like me, the pain of having to figure out new syntax and other .NET adjustments is more than offset by the almost total control you get over the language. A whole world is in there. The .NET framework is loaded with many thousands of classes and their multiple methods, properties, and events.

The GDI+ (Graphic Design Interface) is the library of classes that you can tap into for many kinds of visual effects. It is subdivided into three fundamental technologies:

✦ **Drawing (mainly in the** `System.Drawing` **and** `System.Drawing.2D` **namespaces).** These namespaces deal with all kinds of rendering: lines, circles, color fills, gradients, complicated curves, and so on. Drawing involves vector graphics, which are cartoon-like renderings that are calculated mathematically and, as a result, are entirely scalable: You can enlarge them at will without losing any resolution.

✦ **Imaging (**`System.Drawing.Imaging`**).** This technology manipulates images such as photographs and other images normally stored in graphics files (such as .bmp files). With these classes, you can do many jobs typical of photo editing software, including using alpha channels to create degrees of transparency, rotation, smoothing, and so on. Imaging works with bitmap graphics, which are photographic-quality renderings that are not truly scalable: Enlarge them too much and they lose resolution, becoming mosaic. When you take a digital photo, the result is a bitmap graphic.

✦ **Typography (**`System.Drawing.Text`**).** These classes manage the various colors, sizes, fonts, and other qualities of text.

This chapter focuses on the drawing features of the GDI+.

Drawing

You don't need the following namespaces for most of the examples in this chapter, but for some examples they are necessary. Rather than get into the tedious, inexplicable problem of which namespace must be imported for which particular drawing activity, just put these four lines at the top of your code window and then forget about it:

```
Imports System.Drawing
Imports System.Drawing.Drawing2D
Imports System.Drawing.Imaging
Imports System.Drawing.Text
```

To draw something, you must first make several decisions: the surface that you want to draw on, the "pen" (lines) or "brush" (fills and textures) that you use to draw, what kind of shape you want, where and how big the shape should be, and the color that you want to use.

The drawing surface, roughly the same as the *device context* in previous versions of VB, is an object — and it need not be a visible object. You get this object from an event's arguments, or by using a form's or control's CreateGraphics method.

Here's a simple example that paints the background red and then draws a blue rectangle and two white lines. Start a new VB.NET Windows-style program and double-click Form1 to get to the code window. Then select Form1 Events in the drop-down list at the top left of the code window (or Base Class Events for users of the original version of VB.NET). Now click Paint in the drop-down list at the top right of the code window to create the Form1_Paint event. Type the following code into the Paint event:

```
Private Sub Form1_Paint(ByVal sender As Object, ByVal e As
    System.Windows.Forms.PaintEventArgs) Handles MyBase.Paint

        ' Create a Graphics object.
        Dim g As Graphics = Me.CreateGraphics

        g.Clear(Color.Crimson)

        ' A blue rectangle starting at coordinates (50, 40)
    with 200-pixel width, 100-pixel height)
        g.DrawRectangle(Pens.LightSkyBlue, New Rectangle(50,
    40, 200, 100))

        ' A tan line starting at coordinates (30,80) and
    ending at coordinates (90, 300).
        g.DrawLine(Pens.BlanchedAlmond, 30, 80, 90, 300)

        ' A tan line starting at coordinates (30,80) and
    ending at coordinates (90, 300).
```

```
        g.DrawLine(Pens.BlanchedAlmond, 30, 80, 190, 300)

        ' Kill the graphics object
        g.Dispose()

    End Sub
```

You should notice several things about this source code. First, it's located in the form's `Paint` event, which causes the drawing to be reproduced as necessary, whenever the form is covered and then uncovered by another form, moved, or resized. To get to the paint event, drop the list on the left top of the code window and select (Base class events) rather than Form1. Drop the other listbox in the upper right and click Paint.

You first create the graphics object, based on this form's (me) `CreateGraphics` method. Then you use the `clear` method, which erases anything drawn on the object and then fills the object with whatever color you specify. VB.NET comes with a load of great, predefined colors. You see the list of them when you use the `Color` structure or the `Color` property of the Pens object. To see the list, just type the period following `Color.` and the list pops out.

To understand how to draw lines, circles, arcs, squares, and other objects, you must understand pixels and coordinates. Pixels are the default unit of measurement for a monitor screen. They are the tiniest individual dots you can see if you get up right next to the screen. Although it varies somewhat, figure roughly 100 pixels per inch. To see the precise dots-per-inch measurement for a particular monitor, query the `DpiY` or `DpiX` properties:

```
Dim g As Graphics = Me.CreateGraphics
MsgBox(g.DpiY)
```

The computer monitor is made up of many rows of pixels. You specify the location of drawn lines by providing a starting coordinate and an ending coordinate. For example, the starting coordinate for this line is 30 pixels over from the left side of the form and 80 pixels down from the top:

```
        ' A tan line starting at coordinates (30,80) and
    ending at coordinates (90, 300).
        g.DrawLine(Pens.BlanchedAlmond, 30, 80, 90, 300)
```

Coordinates are expressed in X,Y format, with X representing the horizontal measurement, and Y representing the vertical measurement. Similarly, the end point of this line is 90 pixels over from the left side and 300 pixels (about 3 inches) down from the top. See if you can identify which line this one is in Figure 1-1.

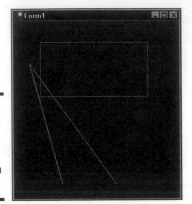

Figure 1-1:
Draw lines, boxes, and many other shapes with the GDI+.

The coordinate position 0,0 is the left, top of the drawing surface.

As you may expect, drawing different shapes requires different syntax. Notice the `DrawRectangle` method. It involves a rectangle object (`New Rectangle`), and its coordinates must be specified differently. The first two are the same (the starting point), but the final two coordinates specify the `width, height` values. Notice that the `width, height` values are different from the other coordinates described so far. The starting point is an absolute coordinate — a specific position within the drawing space (the form, in this case). However, the `width` and `height` measurements are *relative* to the starting point, not to the form's side or top. If you want a square that's about 1 inch by 1 inch in size, use 100,100 as the `width, height` values.

Finally, after drawing, you use `Dispose` to destroy the graphics object. This isn't strictly necessary, because VB.NET automatically conducts a garbage collection periodically. Garbage collection means freeing up memory (and other resources) by figuring out what objects are no longer used by the application and destroying them. However, you can potentially speed up your applications if you specifically dispose of a graphics object when you know you no longer need it.

The alternative way to get a graphics object is to grab it from the `Paint` event's argument list:

```
Dim g As Graphics = e.Graphics
```

Changing measurement units

If you prefer not to use the default pixel measurements, you can change to other available measuring schemes. This example uses inches:

```
Private Sub Form1_Paint(ByVal sender As Object, ByVal e As
    System.Windows.Forms.PaintEventArgs) Handles MyBase.Paint
```

```
Dim g As Graphics = Me.CreateGraphics
g.Clear(Color.White)

'measure by inches rather than pixels
g.PageUnit = GraphicsUnit.Inch

'draw--down two inches from top, and over two inches
from side--a 1" square:
    g.DrawRectangle(Pens.Moccasin, New Rectangle(2, 2, 1,
1))
```

End Sub

The available `GraphicsUnit` settings are `pixel`, `inch`, `display`, `document`, `millimeter`, `point`, and `word`. (Note that the *inch* setting does not necessarily translate into physical inches on your screen. Actual results depend on your screen resolution settings.)

Similarly, you can adjust the `PageScale` property to quickly shrink or blow up your graphics. For example, to adjust the scale to 50 percent of the current size, use the following code:

```
g.PageScale = .5
```

Add that line of code to the previous example and a half-inch square is drawn 1 inch from the top and sides. Notice that the `PageUnit` and `PageScale` properties affect both the size and position of your drawings.

When you change the `PageUnit`, you also change the size of pen objects. (In the preceding example, the pen is no longer the default 1 pixel wide; it's 1 inch, which is rather too fat to draw an outline around the square.) To make the pen 1 pixel large under these conditions, use the dots-per-inch `X` property of the graphics object, like this:

```
Dim p As New Pen(Color.Blue, 1 / g.DpiX)
g.DrawRectangle(p, New Rectangle(2, 2, 1, 1))
```

Resizing

Perhaps you want your drawing to enlarge or reduce in size when a user resizes a form. To make a drawing respond in this way, you specify its size in terms of the form's `ClientSize` properties, and you also put your drawing code in the form's `Resize` event, like this:

```
Private Sub Form1_Resize(ByVal sender As Object, ByVal e
As System.EventArgs) Handles MyBase.Resize

    Dim g As Graphics = Me.CreateGraphics
```

```
        g.Clear(Color.LightGray)

        ' A blue rectangle 1/2 inch less than the size of the
    form itself:
        g.DrawRectangle(Pens.MintCream, New Rectangle(50, 50,
    Me.ClientSize.Width - 100, Me.ClientSize.Height - 100))

        ' Destroy the Graphics object.
        g.Dispose()

    End Sub
```

When you press F5 to run this program, nothing happens until you drag the form to resize it. To make the rectangle appear when the program first executes, you would have to copy this code into the `Form_Paint` event as well.

Ellipses and Arcs

Just as a square is a certain kind of rectangle, a circle is one kind of ellipse — the perfect kind, you may say. You create ellipses — round shapes — by creating an invisible rectangle object and then "fitting" the ellipse within it. If your rectangle is square, the ellipse is a circle. If not, the ellipse looks a bit squashed.

Here's an example that creates both a circle and an ellipsoid shape:

```
Private Sub Form1_Paint(ByVal sender As Object, ByVal e As
    System.Windows.Forms.PaintEventArgs) Handles MyBase.Paint

        Dim g As Graphics = Me.CreateGraphics

        g.Clear(Color.WhiteSmoke)

        Dim rec As Rectangle = New Rectangle(30, 30, 150,
    150) 'square
        Dim rec1 As Rectangle = New Rectangle(30, 30, 150,
    250)

        g.DrawEllipse(New Pen(Color.DarkBlue), rec)
        g.DrawEllipse(New Pen(Color.DodgerBlue), rec1)

        ' Destroy the Graphics object.
        g.Dispose()

    End Sub
```

Here I assign the rectangles to variables (`rec` and `rec1`) rather than simply declaring them inline as literal values, like this:

```
g.DrawEllipse(New Pen(Color.DarkBlue), New Rectangle(30, 30,
     150, 150))
```

In most programming situations, you can use either technique — variables or inline literals — when filling in argument lists. It's your choice.

Notice that after you create the rectangle objects, you use them to define the boundaries when using the `DrawEllipse` method. The results are shown in Figure 1-2.

Book VI Chapter 1

You Be Picasso

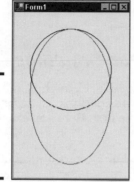

Figure 1-2: Use rectangle objects to bound ellipses.

An arc is a part of an ellipse. So, to draw an arc, you can use the rectangle boundaries, but you must also specify the starting position of the arc and its *sweep angle* (which is how far around the ellipse it should draw counter-clockwise). Both of these specs are in *degrees,* of which an ellipse is divided into 360. The starting position (0 degrees) is on the middle-right of the ellipse. So if you want your arc to start at the bottom of the ellipse, specify 90 — one quarter of the way around the ellipse from 0. And if you want the arc to draw halfway around, specify 180 as the sweep angle. Here's an example that draws one quarter around a circle and one half around an ellipsoid shape (as shown in Figure 1-3):

```
Dim rec As Rectangle = New Rectangle(30, 30, 150, 150)
     'square
Dim rec1 As Rectangle = New Rectangle(30, 30, 150, 250)

       g.DrawArc(New Pen(Color.DarkCyan), rec, 90, 90)
     'start at the bottom, go one-fourth around
       g.DrawArc(New Pen(Color.DarkOrchid), rec1, 0, 180)
     'start on the right, go half around
```

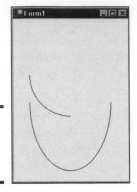

Figure 1-3:
Arcs are
partial
ellipses.

Polygons and Miscellaneous Linear Drawings

Polygons are multisided shapes. The `DrawPolygon` method automatically finishes a shape by drawing all the lines you specify in an array and then connecting the last point you specify to the first. Here's an example, with the outcome shown in Figure 1-4:

```
Private Sub Form1_Paint(ByVal sender As Object, ByVal e As
    System.Windows.Forms.PaintEventArgs) Handles MyBase.Paint

    Dim g As Graphics = Me.CreateGraphics

    g.Clear(Color.WhiteSmoke)

    Dim points() As Point = {New Point(12, 12), New
    Point(212, 22), New Point(34, 29), New Point(53, 23), New
    Point(38, 90), New Point(132, 152)}

    g.DrawPolygon(Pens.BlueViolet, points)

End Sub
```

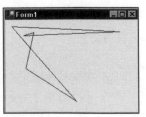

Figure 1-4:
Polygons
are drawn
from an
array of
points.

If you don't want a closed polygon, use the `DrawLine` method, instead of `DrawPolygon`, like this:

```
      g.DrawLines(Pens.BlueViolet, points)
```

A DrawRectangles method does for rectangles what the DrawLines method does for an array of lines. They both rely on arrays to do the job:

```
Dim recs() As Rectangle = {New Rectangle(12, 12, 43, 32), New
      Rectangle(212, 22, 44, 266), New Rectangle(34, 29, 53,
      450), New Rectangle(53, 23, 122, 366), New Rectangle(38,
      90, 233, 499), New Rectangle(132, 152, 12, 77)}
```

```
      g.DrawRectangles(Pens.BlueViolet, recs)
```

This rectangle array results in Figure 1-5.

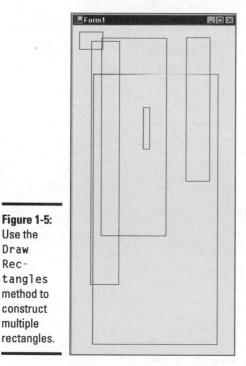

Figure 1-5:
Use the
Draw
Rec-
tangles
method to
construct
multiple
rectangles.

Splines, Cardinal, and Bezier

As you know, you can shake a whip as hard as you want and it never bends at angles or makes straight lines. It's always curved — sometimes tightly curved — but never straight. A material that can pass through points without creating sharp angles and lines is called a *spline*. This effect (smooth curves through points) can be generated mathematically, and VB.NET knows how.

Stiff whips

One formula produces what are known as *cardinal splines*. You specify an array of points and then use the DrawCurve method to produce the curves through those points. The following example shows four curves going through the same array of points, but the curves differ because the tension parameter is increased from 4 to 9, which causes different extremities of curvature (as if you were snapping increasingly stiff whips):

```
Dim g As Graphics = Me.CreateGraphics
g.Clear(Color.WhiteSmoke)

        Dim points() As Point = {New Point(54, 12), New
    Point(212, 122), New Point(134, 129), New Point(153,
    123), New Point(138, 190), New Point(132, 100)}

    g.DrawCurve(Pens.BlueViolet, points, 4)
    g.DrawCurve(Pens.BlueViolet, points, 3)
    g.DrawCurve(Pens.BlueViolet, points, 6)
    g.DrawCurve(Pens.DarkRed, points, 9)
```

The results are shown in Figure 1-6.

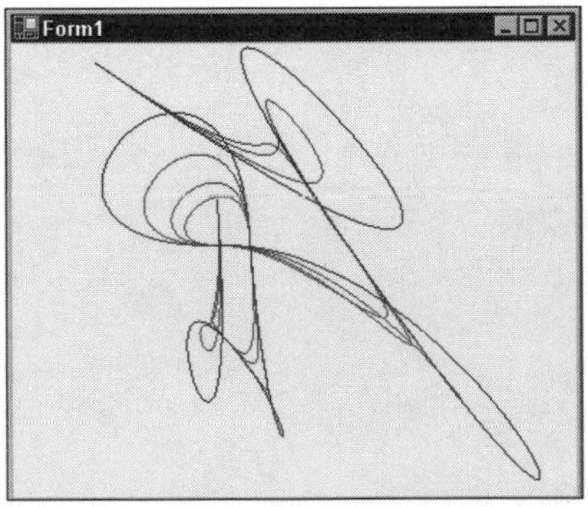

Figure 1-6: Specify various tensions to get differing cardinal curves.

A tension of zero results in a limp noodle of a whip. It stretches between each point in a straight line, producing no curves at all. Increasing tension, however, increasingly stiffens the whip, causing ever more extreme curves because the line is less flexible.

One of the overloaded parameter lists permits you to include offset and segments parameters — specifying where within a points array to start, and how many points in the array to use, respectively. You can also force a closed spline using the DrawClosedCurve method.

Kittens on the whip

A *Bezier spline* is a bit more elegant, more artistic usually. You specify four points: start point, two *influence* points, and end point. Those middle two points are interesting: The curve doesn't attempt to go through them, but it is drawn toward them as if by successive approximation, until the influence of the next point takes over and redirects the line. You may think of this "influencing" as kittens weakly tugging on a whip.

In the following example, a loop is used to show the effects of increasingly distant influence (or *control*) points. As you can see in this example (and in Figure 1-7), the horizontal X coordinate for the end point is increased by 100 pixels each time through the loop — gently and gracefully pulling the line away from the influence points:

```
Private Sub Form1_Paint(ByVal sender As Object, ByVal e As
    System.Windows.Forms.PaintEventArgs) Handles MyBase.Paint
        Dim i As Integer
        Dim g As Graphics = Me.CreateGraphics

        g.Clear(Color.WhiteSmoke)

        Dim p1 As New Point(54, 12)
        Dim p2 As New Point(212, 122)
        Dim p3 As New Point(134, 129)

        For i = 100 To 400 Step 100
            g.DrawBezier(Pens.BlueViolet, p1, p2, p3, New
    Point(i, 400))
        Next i

    End Sub
```

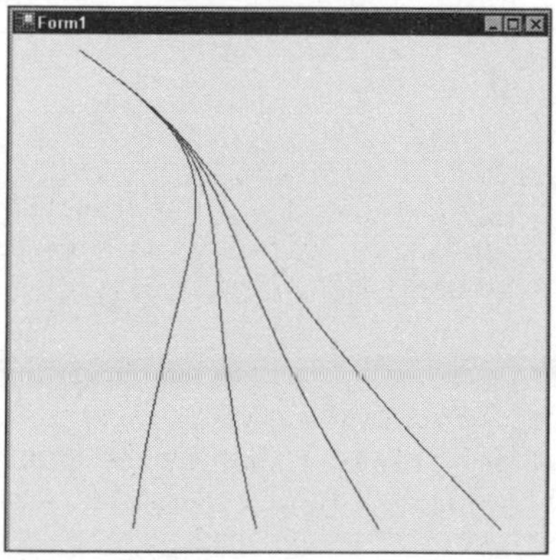

Figure 1-7:
The Bezier formula often produces the most graceful curves.

Smoothing via anti-aliasing

If you look closely at Figure 1-7, you see that the lines are graceful in shape but rather ragged as they attempt an analog curve through the digital universe of your computer's monitor. What you see is the sawtooth or stairstep effect caused as a curved line attempts to navigate down through what is a mosaic. It is a very *tiny* mosaic of pixels, true, but its essentially digital, quantum nature is revealed by the stairstep effect. The semi-cure for this problem is called *anti-aliasing* and has been used for years to refine the curves in text displayed on monitors. Try an experiment with the code that produced the curve shown in Figure 1-7. Add this new line of code (shown in boldface) following the line that paints the background with the `Clear` method:

```
Dim i As Integer
Dim g As Graphics = Me.CreateGraphics

g.Clear(Color.WhiteSmoke)
g.SmoothingMode = Drawing.Drawing2D.SmoothingMode.HighQuality

Dim p1 As New Point(54, 12)
Dim p2 As New Point(212, 122)
Dim p3 As New Point(134, 129)

For i = 100 To 400 Step 100
g.DrawBezier(Pens.BlueViolet, p1, p2, p3, New Point(i, 400))
Next i
```

The smoothing technology blends the edges of a line into the background using extra pixels that create a brief gradient into the background. The same line is shown twice in Figure 1-8, but the version on the left has been smoothed with the `HighQuality` version of the `SmoothingMode`.

Figure 1-8:
Smoothing sacrifices some sharpness in the line on the left, in exchange for avoiding the jaggies visible in the line on the right.

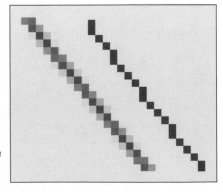

Pens and Brushes

You use pens and brushes to specify line, color, and texture for your graphics. As you may expect, there are many variations in the ways you can use pens and brushes.

Enlarging the pen

So far you've used the pen object in this chapter's examples. You've specified various colors to use with it. The pen defaults to a width of one-pixel, but you can make it larger (as shown in Figure 1-9) by using the following code:

```
Private Sub Form1_Paint(ByVal sender As Object, ByVal e As
    System.Windows.Forms.PaintEventArgs) Handles MyBase.Paint

        Dim g As Graphics = Me.CreateGraphics
        g.Clear(Color.White)

        g.SmoothingMode =
Drawing.Drawing2D.SmoothingMode.HighQuality

        Dim p1 As New Point(54, 12)
        Dim p2 As New Point(212, 122)
        Dim p3 As New Point(134, 129)

        Dim i, w As Integer
        Dim p As Pen
        For i = 100 To 400 Step 30
            w += 1
            p = New Pen(Color.Maroon, w)
            g.DrawBezier(p, p1, p2, p3, New Point(i, 400))
        Next i

    End Sub
```

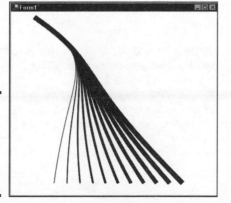

Figure 1-9:
In addition to its color, you can adjust a pen's width.

In this example, the variable w is increased by 1 each time through the loop, resulting in ever thicker pen lines.

Lines drawn with a pen need not be solid. You can use the DashStyle enumeration (an enumeration is a list of built-in constants such as DashDot, DashDotDot, Dot, and so on). This permits you to draw with various kinds of dotted or dashed lines. Beyond that, the StartCap and EndCap properties can be set to describe various shapes — arrows, balls, diamonds, and so on — that are attached to either end of a line.

The following code produces the result shown in Figure 1-10:

```
Dim g As Graphics = Me.CreateGraphics
    g.Clear(Color.White)

    Dim p As New Pen(Color.Blue, 5)
    p.DashStyle = Drawing.Drawing2D.DashStyle.Dot
    p.StartCap = Drawing.Drawing2D.LineCap.RoundAnchor
    p.EndCap = Drawing.Drawing2D.LineCap.ArrowAnchor
    g.DrawLine(p, 10, 10, 260, 10)
```

Figure 1-10:
Add graphics to the ends of your lines to "cap" them.

Using a brush to fill

You use the brush object to fill areas. You can fill with solid colors, textures, gradients (gradual changes from one color to another), and even bitmap photographs.

The simplest way to fill a shape is to use the Fill methods that include a set of predefined shapes. The following code creates a filled ellipse and two filled pie shapes (which are shown in Figure 1-11):

The following example code and other examples that follow assume that you first declare the graphics object within a form's Paint event, like this:

```
Dim g As Graphics = Me.CreateGraphics
g.Clear(Color.White)
```

Then you follow that declaration with the example code, such as this:

```
g.FillEllipse(Brushes.RoyalBlue, 10, 10, 190, 90)

g.FillPie(Brushes.RoyalBlue, 10, 100, 190, 90, 30, 200)

g.FillPie(Brushes.RoyalBlue, 100, 80, 160, 90, -50, 100)
```

Figure 1-11:
Various predefined shapes are available, including the ellipse and pie.

Hatches and Other Primitive Patterns

You can also fill with a set of crosshatch patterns (bricks, checkerboard, herringbone, and so on). Alas, they're rather dreary and smack of yard sale flyer design. If you do want to use them, here's how:

```
Dim brush As New HatchBrush(HatchStyle.Sphere, Color.Yellow,
    Color.Blue)

g.FillRectangle(brus, 10, 10, 190, 90)
```

These repetitive little designs are similar to the effect you can get by right-clicking your desktop, choosing Properties, and then clicking the Pattern button to specify a background pattern rather than wallpaper for your Windows desktop. Nobody uses these patterns, though. Which is quite sensible. They're usually annoying. If you do want to experiment with hatch fills, you can see the various patterns in the list that pops out when you type the period following HatchStyle.

Gradients

Gradients, on the other hand, create an excellent metallic effect and can be used to make your applications look more polished and professional. Using gold or silver gradients, you can achieve a bank-vault-like look that is quite superior to the default battleship gray paint job that most Windows applications have featured for more than a decade now.

Back in 1991 when I wrote my first book on Visual Basic, *The Visual Guide to Visual Basic,* I demonstrated how to create the metallic effect by designing a gradient in a separate drawing application and then saving the bitmap and importing it into a form or picturebox control. In those days, these were the only two objects with a `Picture` property that you could use to import bitmaps. However, I showed how to take a print-screen image of a button, import it into a drawing program, put a gradient on it, and then save it as a bitmap. This "button" could then be loaded into the `Picture` property of a `PictureBox`. When the user clicked the faux button, code in the `PictureBox`'s `Click` event responded as if a real button had been clicked. It worked well. Figure 1-12 shows an example of metallic gradients that frame two textboxes, and it also shows gradients on each of the buttons.

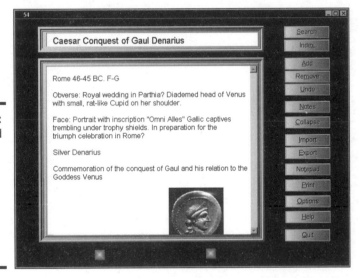

Figure 1-12: The tasteful use of gradients can add considerable visual appeal to your projects.

In Figure 1-12, the frames around the TextBoxes and the backgrounds of the buttons are gradients — subtle gradients in gold-tones, but gradients nonetheless. To achieve the chiseled lettering in the button's text, however, it was necessary to use a separate drawing program, and do the lettering off-sets for shadow and highlight in that program. VB.NET doesn't have facilities for that kind of thing — yet. All the buttons in Figure 1-12 have their `Text` property values deleted and their `Image` properties set to a gold gradient .BMP file with the appropriate, engraved caption for that button's function.

You can create gradients on the fly in the backgrounds of many controls, though, using various gradient features built into GDI+. The following example defines a rectangle object and uses it twice. First, it builds a `LinearGradientBrush` of the same size as that rectangle; second, with the `FillRectangle` method, it draws a rectangle the same size as the brush:

```
Dim rect As New Rectangle(10, 10, 300, 100)

Dim b As New LinearGradientBrush(rect, Color.Gold,
    Color.DarkGoldenrod, LinearGradientMode.ForwardDiagonal)

g.FillRectangle(b, rect)
```

Creating custom colors

The code in the previous example produces the quite-acceptable gold metal effects, if a bit dark. You can however, design your own custom colors — to generate precisely the light-to-medium metal gradient that looks best — by building a custom pen or brush. Here's how to specify a custom RGB color all your own, using color values for light gold and dark gold that produce excellent results:

```
    Dim pen1 As New Pen(Color.FromArgb(255, 224, 200), 1)
'light gold
    Dim pen2 As New Pen(Color.FromArgb(168, 128, 40), 1)
'dark gold

    g.DrawRectangle(pen2, 11, 11, 301, 101) 'do dark one
first
    g.DrawRectangle(pen1, 10, 10, 300, 100)
```

The order in which the two colored rectangles are drawn is important, as described a little later in this chapter.

You can use a pen thickness of 5 pixels or more for large frames, but for frames around TextBoxes or other objects, you likely want to use 1- or 2-pixel brush sizes. Placing several of these frames with slightly different thicknesses and colors around a TextBox can look quite nice, as Figure 1-12 demonstrated earlier.

To create a gradient with custom colors, write similar code using the same .FromArgb method. (ARGB is similar to RGB, but it includes an alpha channel specification, which you must try to forget about until later in this chapter.) The following code produces an excellent gold-metal gradient, only a hint of which you can see in the black-and-white reproduction in Figure 1-13. Try running it on your monitor to see the effect in all its color and glory.

```
Private Sub Form1_Paint(ByVal sender As Object, ByVal e As
    System.Windows.Forms.PaintEventArgs) Handles MyBase.Paint

    Dim g As Graphics = Me.CreateGraphics
    g.Clear(Color.White)

    Dim rect As New Rectangle(10, 10, 300, 100)
```

```
    Dim b As New LinearGradientBrush(rect,
Color.FromArgb(255, 224, 200), Color.FromArgb(168, 128,
40), LinearGradientMode.ForwardDiagonal)

    g.FillRectangle(b, rect)

    'now draw a frame around the metal panel:

    Dim pen1 As New Pen(Color.FromArgb(255, 224, 200), 1)
'light gold
    Dim pen2 As New Pen(Color.FromArgb(168, 128, 40), 2)
'dark gold

    g.DrawRectangle(pen2, 11, 11, 300, 100) 'do dark one
first
    g.DrawRectangle(pen1, 10, 10, 300, 100) ' move one
pixel offset from pen2

    End Sub
```

Figure 1-13:
Use
gradients
to add
sophistica-
tion to your
VB.NET
projects.

In general, light sources originate from the top left of objects seen on a
monitor. If you look carefully at a button or other Microsoft controls, you
can see that the top and left of the control are highlighted, and the right and
bottom are in shadow. That's why when using gradients, it's good to choose
LinearGradientMode.ForwardDiagonal, as I did in the previous example.
It's also good to create gradient frames, but with a pen that's impossible. If
you want a gradient frame, you should create a brush, draw its rectangle,
and then superimpose another rectangle on top of it (by simply drawing it
on the next code line or later). Make the superimposed rectangle only 1 or
2 pixels smaller than the framing rectangle. Or you can draw your rectangle
under a TextBox or other control. Drawing on the form won't cover up controls; they are "on top" of the drawn background.

Paths, Regions, and Path Gradients

Complex drawings, including specialized gradients, can be defined using *paths*. A path is a way to manipulate several graphics tools at once. It can contain whatever elements you wish: lines, ellipses, rectangles, and so on. You first instantiate a path object (As New GraphicsPath), and then you use the path's Add methods to add the various graphics elements to the path. The end of each element is automatically connected to the start of the next, unless you use the path's StartFigure method to prevent this joining.

Here's an example (and the results are shown in Figure 1-14):

```
Private Sub Form1_Paint(ByVal sender As Object, ByVal e As
    System.Windows.Forms.PaintEventArgs) Handles MyBase.Paint

        Dim g As Graphics = Me.CreateGraphics
        g.Clear(Color.White)
        g.SmoothingMode =
Drawing.Drawing2D.SmoothingMode.HighQuality
        Dim pa As New GraphicsPath()

        pa.StartFigure()
        pa.AddRectangle(New Rectangle(10, 10, 300, 100))
        pa.AddLine(215, 10, 400, 200)
        pa.AddLine(124, 24, 250, 250)

        pa.StartFigure() 'prevent previous and next lines
    from being automatically connected

        pa.AddLine(444, 44, 330, 330)

        Dim pen1 As New Pen(Color.Red, 4)
        g.DrawPath(pen1, pa)

End Sub
```

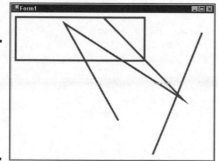

Figure 1-14: Paths group several drawing tools into a single object.

Regions

The *region* is sort of a super-path; it can contain other shapes, as well as containing various paths. It can be used to *clip* (remove parts of) drawn graphics. You can merge shapes with a region using five different methods:

✦ **Union:** All points in the region and the added shape are now part of the region.

✦ **Intersect:** After this method is finished, the only points left in the region are those that were in both the added shape and the original region.

✦ **Complement:** Only the points in the added shape that were *not* in the original region survive.

✦ **Exclude:** Only points in the original region that are *not* in the added shape survive.

✦ **XOR:** Only points in the original or the added shape, but not points that appear in both of them, survive.

Here's an example that uses the `Exclude` method to create an empty space within a region:

```
Dim r As New Region(New Rectangle(30, 40, 300, 300))
        Dim pa As New GraphicsPath()
        pa.AddRectangle(New Rectangle(120, 120, 190, 190))
        r.Exclude(pa) 'subtract this path's square from the
region
        g.FillRegion(Brushes.Black, r)
```

The PathGradientBrush

A PathGradientBrush object can build gradients with complicated colors and shapes. The following code creates a button-like shape with shading that highlights the center (and the results are shown in Figure 1-15):

```
Dim pa As New GraphicsPath()
pa.AddEllipse(30, 30, 50, 50) 'make a circle

Dim gbrush As New PathGradientBrush(pa)

Dim ArrColor() As Color = {Color.Gold} 'the "surround
colors" must be an array, even with only 1 color
gbrush.SurroundColors = ArrColor

gbrush.CenterColor = Color.Beige

g.FillPath(gbrush, pa)
```

Figure 1-15:
Use a Path-
Gradient-
Brush to
build
complex
gradients.

You can use various points and various surround colors by filling the surround color array.

Texture Brushes

Texture brushes may be a bit redundant, because you can use the `BackGroundImage` property of forms and controls to tile a bitmap across the drawing surface. However, the `TextureBrush` does give you a little more flexibility if you want to limit the area that's painted or flip the image (using the brush's `WrapMode` property).

The following code creates the results shown in Figure 1-16:

```
Dim tbrush As New TextureBrush(PictureBox1.Image)
g.FillEllipse(tbrush, 100, 100, 300, 300)
```

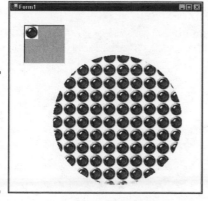

Figure 1-16:
Use the
Texture-
Brush to tile
a bitmap
within a
shape.

Notice that you have to first load a bitmap (.BMP or other graphic file) into a PictureBox or some other control with an `Image` property. You can't specify a file path as a `TextureBrush` argument. You can, of course, set the PictureBox's `Visible` property to `false` to hide it.

TIP

If you or someone you know knows how to use a graphics application such as PhotoShop, you can do many cool things with the visual design of your applications. Large programming outfits have a design department, but the millions of small business and home programmers who use Visual Basic can make their utilities and applications look elegant as well. You can customize buttons, textures, backgrounds, and other elements with the built-in textures, button-creators, drop-shadow wizards, and dozens of other tools. It's easy to put a bitmap into a VB.NET button or PictureBox using the `Image` property. (Refer to Figure 1-16 for a PictureBox example.)

Then, press the PrintScreen key, paste the screen into your graphics program, sample the gray of the background, and fill the white area around the button with the gray so that the white square disappears, as shown in Figure 1-17.

Turn off the PictureBox's `BorderStyle` property, and you have excellent buttons that the user can click, and they're round. (Button controls don't have a `BorderStyle` property that you can suppress, so PictureBoxes are more useful for this technique.) When the user clicks your PictureBox (as long as the `MouseDown` event is triggering), replace the original button image with one that's slightly darker, turned upside-down, and with the highlight suppressed. This creates a look like the button has been pushed in, as you can see in the bottom button shown in Figure 1-17.

Figure 1-17:
A light, darker, and (on the bottom) inverted button. These look better than the standard, battleship-gray VB.NET buttons.

Visibility Variations

VB.NET offers two interesting new properties that you can use to create cool effects with forms. You can make parts of them invisible (whatever is behind the form shows through in places), or you can specify how opaque (to what degree — from 0 to 100% — the form covers whatever is behind it).

Opacity is specified in fractions

For mysterious reasons, the opacity of a form ranges between 0 and 1, using fractions such as `.2` for 20 percent. You may have thought they'd use integers 0 to 100 instead, but it just goes to show that you never know. Perhaps someone thought floating point numbers were somehow more reminiscent of how you express percentages in calculations. It's a mystery, but the opacity feature can be interesting.

One startling and effective technique is to use a timer to make a form appear as if from a mist. You cause it to adjust the form's opacity property from 0 to 1 over time, so that it fades into view (or fades away):

```
Private Sub Timer1_Tick(ByVal sender As System.Object, ByVal
    e As System.EventArgs) Handles Timer1.Tick

'Set this timer's interval property to 3 or 4—really fast.

        Static x As Single
        x += 0.04 'raise the visibility a little

        If x >= 1 Then Timer1.Enabled = False 'once it
reaches full visibility (1), stop this process

        Me.Opacity = x

    End Sub
```

Understanding opacity and alpha blends

VB.NET pens and brushes have an optional opacity feature that specifies how much the drawing covers up anything underneath it. In other words, you specify how opaque the new drawing should be, from 0 (totally invisible, the new drawing doesn't show up at all) to 255 (totally opaque, the original background doesn't show through at all). Anything between these two figures results in degrees of show-through. The opacity argument is the first argument in the `FromArgb` method of the color object's four arguments. (Recall that you can also leave out the alpha specification, only specifying three arguments for the `FromArgb` method: the relative amounts of red, green, and blue.)

The following example superimposes a semi-transparent salmon-colored square on top of a solid square (and the results are shown in Figure 1-18):

```
Private Sub Form1_Paint(ByVal sender As Object, ByVal e As
    System.Windows.Forms.PaintEventArgs) Handles MyBase.Paint
```

```
Dim g As Graphics = Me.CreateGraphics
g.Clear(Color.White)

        g.FillRectangle(Brushes.HotPink, 10, 10, 100, 100)

        Dim br As New SolidBrush(Color.FromArgb(100, 243,
    165, 165))
        g.FillRectangle(br, 50, 50, 200, 200)

End Sub
```

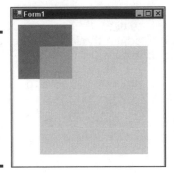

Figure 1-18:
Use alpha
blending
to super-
impose
semi-
transparent
graphics.

How can you figure out which blend of red, green, and blue produces salmon?
To create custom colors as I did in the previous example, you need to know
three numbers for the RGB specification. The easiest way to figure out which
numbers to use is to use a graphics application. I use the excellent Micrografx
Picture Publisher, whose color picker utility (shown in Figure 1-19) allows you
to drag your mouse around and select colors and shades of those colors quite
easily. Then you read the RGB numbers right there on screen:

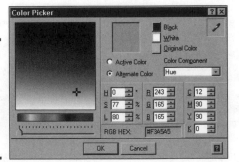

Figure 1-19:
Get RGB
values for
any custom
color using
a graphics
application.

Using the TransparencyKey Property

One final way to create transparency effects is to selectively make parts of a form vanish. The example shown in Figure 1-20 was created by simply setting the form's `BackColor` property to `red` and then setting the form's `TransparencyKey` property to `red` as well. (Click a form to select it; then set this property in the Properties window.) As you can see, the desktop wallpaper shows through wherever on the form the red color has been assigned. In other words, VB.NET simply does not paint any areas containing the special key color. I can't think of any uses for this, but remember that it's available in case something should occur to you. Notice the panel on the left. I set its `BorderStyle` property to `3-D`, but if you leave it flat, you could use panels (or labels) to cause selected areas to remain opaque within the otherwise translucent form background.

Figure 1-20:
Using the
Trans-
parency-
Key
property,
you can
make areas
in your
forms
disappear.

Chapter 2: The Creative Photographer

In This Chapter

- ✔ Handling images
- ✔ Learning to clip, rotate, and shear
- ✔ Resizing
- ✔ Displaying thumbnails
- ✔ Managing transparency
- ✔ Employing the Clipboard
- ✔ Loading and saving
- ✔ Manipulating text

This chapter explores the various ways that you can manipulate bitmaps in VB.NET. A bitmap is capable of displaying a photographic-quality image. Contrast that to the subject covered in the previous chapter: rendered drawings, which are highly scalable, but can never achieve realism much beyond the level of a cartoon. If Book VI, Chapter 1 is about drawings, this chapter is about photographs.

Transforming bitmaps is the specialty of such photo-editing graphics applications as PhotoShop and Picture Publisher. They include many dozens of effects such as camera filters, textures, unsharp masking (subtle sharpening), warps, and many other ways to play around with images. VB.NET comes nowhere close to the capabilities of photo-editing applications. If you want to create great-looking buttons or form backgrounds, you should become (or make friends with someone who is) adept at using a graphics application.

If you want to permit users of your projects to manipulate graphics, you should know something of the capabilities built into the .NET libraries. This chapter offers a brief survey of these capabilities. Perhaps you want to allow the user to choose the background images for the forms in your project. You can display graphics in thumbnail samples from which the user can choose, as described later in this chapter.

As usual, you must use Imports statements. For the examples in this chapter, add these Imports to the top of your code window:

```
Imports System.Drawing
Imports System.Drawing.Imaging
Imports System.IO
Imports System.Drawing.Drawing2D
Imports System.Drawing.Text
```

The following code shows you how to get an image from your hard drive using a bitmap object. Replace "c:\tut.bmp" with the location and name of a graphic file on your hard drive; you're sure to find some .BMP files in your C:\Windows\ folder:

```
Private Sub Form1_Paint(ByVal sender As Object, ByVal e As
    System.Windows.Forms.PaintEventArgs) Handles MyBase.Paint

    Dim g As Graphics = Me.CreateGraphics

    Dim bit As New Bitmap("c:\tut.bmp")
    g.DrawImage(bit, 0, 0)

End Sub
```

Using 0,0 and the X,Y coordinates for the location of the graphic puts it up against the upper left corner of the form, as shown in Figure 2-1.

Figure 2-1:
Use the
DrawImage
method to
display a
bitmap
graphic.

Clipping, Rotating, and Shearing

The .NET GDI+ libraries offer many ways to manage a graphic. The next example clips (removes a part), rotates, and shears (skews into a parallelogram shape). Replace `"c:\bird house.bmp"` with the location of a graphic file on your hard drive.

The following code produces the effects shown in Figure 2-2:

```
Private Sub Form1_Paint(ByVal sender As Object, ByVal e As
    System.Windows.Forms.PaintEventArgs) Handles MyBase.Paint

        Dim g As Graphics = Me.CreateGraphics

        Dim bit As New Bitmap("c:\bird house.bmp")

        'show top half
        g.DrawImage(bit, 20, 20, New Rectangle(0, 0,
bit.Width, bit.Height / 2), GraphicsUnit.Pixel)


        'rotate
        bit.RotateFlip(RotateFlipType.Rotate90FlipNone)
        g.DrawImage(bit, 340, 20)


        'skew, rotate and shrink
        Dim sk(2) As Point
        sk(0) = New Point(150, 220)
        sk(1) = New Point(270, 280)
        sk(2) = New Point(150, 330)

        g.DrawImage(bit, sk)

End Sub
```

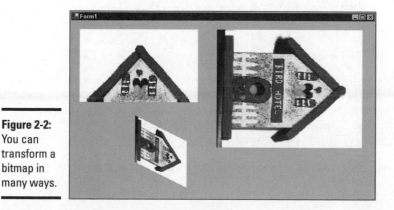

Figure 2-2: You can transform a bitmap in many ways.

The first transformation merely chops off the bottom half of the little bird hotel by specifying that the Height property be divided by 2. What do you suppose happens if you divide both the Height and Width properties by 2?

The second picture uses the RotateFlip property of the bitmap object to specify one of the built-in rotation and flipping options. These are rather limited (to quarter-turn rotations), so if you want finer control, use the point structure shown in the third transformation.

When you specify three points, you are telling VB.NET where to move the image's top-left, top-right, and bottom left corners, respectively. To picture this, imagine that your image is printed on a highly flexible rubber sheet, and you are allowed to move the top two corners and the bottom left corner to any position on the drawing surface. (The bottom right corner stays stuck and can't be moved, so all distortions are relative to that corner.)

Moving any of the three movable points closer to the right bottom point causes the image to shrink. Moving around the axis described by the fixed corner rotates the image. Moving the top points, but preserving the distance between the bottom points, skews the image. In the previous example, all three effects are achieved. First, you create an array of three points; then, you specify the X,Y coordinates for each point and draw the image.

Expansion and Contraction

Another way to magnify or shrink a graphic is to simply multiply the Height and Width properties by some factor. To expand a graphic by 50 percent, use this code:

```
Dim r As New Rectangle(10, 10, bit.Width * 1.5, bit.Height *
    1.5)
g.DrawImage(bit, r)
```

What happens if you use Width * 1.5, but Height * 3?

Thumbnails

You can use a GetThumbNailImage method of the Image object to display small versions of graphics files. However, it's just as easy to shrink graphics yourself. In the next example, I specify that I want to see thumbnail versions of all the files in the c:\photos directory, and that I want them displayed at a size of 75×75 pixels (as shown in Figure 2-3).

All you have to do is define a rectangle with whatever dimensions you wish, and then throw that rectangle into a DrawImage method, like this:

```
Private Sub Form1_Paint(ByVal sender As Object, ByVal e As
    System.Windows.Forms.PaintEventArgs) Handles MyBase.Paint

    Dim fname As String, finfo As FileInfo
    Dim x As Integer = 10, y As Integer = 10

    Dim g As Graphics = Me.CreateGraphics

    For Each fname In Directory.GetFiles("c:\photos")
        finfo = New FileInfo(fname)
        If finfo.Extension = ".bmp" Then 'display a
thumbnail on the form:

            Dim bit As New Bitmap(finfo.FullName)
            Dim r As New Rectangle(x, y, 75, 75) 'shrink
it

            g.DrawImage(bit, r)

            x += 85 'move over 1 thumbnail
            If x >= Me.Width - 75 Then y += 85 : x = 10
'start new row

        End If

    Next

End Sub
```

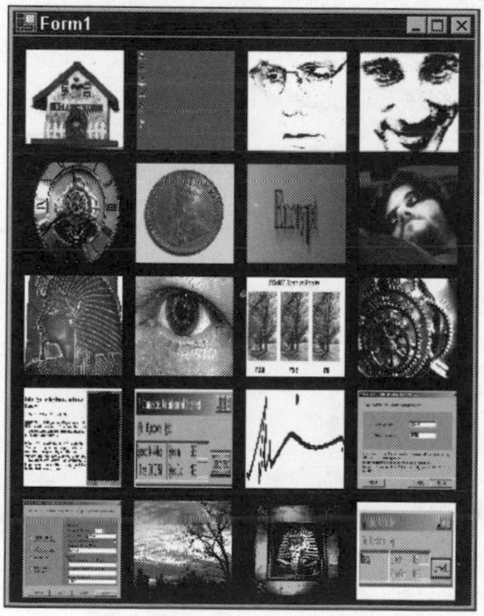

Figure 2-3:
Create your
own
thumbnails
using a
rectangle
object.

Image Transparency

Floating translucent graphics on your forms can be a startling and involving effect. Users generally react well to such efforts on the part of a programmer. One approach involves masking parts of an image. In other words, you create a masking color so that anywhere in the image where that color appears, the background shows through.

Avoiding unnecessary frames

In the following example, I defined black as the transparent color (as shown in Figure 2-4). Notice that in the lower clock, wherever black appears, the crosshatch background shows through — even in a few places behind the gears inside the clock. To make the clock entirely opaque, you can use a graphics program to adjust the contrast only within the clock, or you can simply replace the black background with some other color that's not in the clock itself (such as pink). Replace `"c:\clock 1.bmp"` with the location of a graphic file on your hard drive.

You must admit that a round clock floating against the background is better looking than the one bounded by the unnecessary square frame:

```
Private Sub Form1_Paint(ByVal sender As Object, ByVal e As
    System.Windows.Forms.PaintEventArgs) Handles MyBase.Paint

    'generate background pattern
    Dim g As Graphics = Me.CreateGraphics
    Dim brus As New HatchBrush(HatchStyle.LargeGrid,
Color.Black, Color.White)
    g.FillRectangle(brus, 0, 0, Me.Width, Me.Height)

    Dim bit As New Bitmap("c:\clock 1.bmp")

    'display clock twice
    g.DrawImage(bit, 10, 10)

    'show again, this time with black (0,0,0)
transparent:
    bit.MakeTransparent(Color.FromArgb(0, 0, 0))
    g.DrawImage(bit, 10, 355)

End Sub
```

As you can see in Figure 2-4, drawing (the hatch pattern) and imaging (the photo of a clock) can be combined on a single graphic. How do you know whether a drawing appears on top of the bitmap, or vice versa? How do you know whether the hatch pattern shows up under, or on top of, the clock? It all depends on which comes first in the code. To partially cover a drawn line with a bitmap graphic, use this code:

```
g.DrawLine(Pens.Blue, 0, 0, 100, 300)
g.DrawImage(bit, 10, 10)
```

Figure 2-4:
You can
specify a
particular
color as
"trans-
parent."

But to draw the line on top of the graphic, simply draw it after first displaying the bitmap, by reversing these lines of code:

```
g.DrawImage(bit, 10, 10)
g.DrawLine(Pens.Blue, 0, 0, 100, 300)
```

Opacity and fade-in

There is a way to specify the opacity of an entire bitmap, but you must go
through a bit of coding. Don't try to figure out the "array of arrays" business
in the following example. You can just cut and paste this into your code if
you need it, and adjust the opacity value from 0 to 1 as you wish.

The `For...Next` loop in the following code gradually increases the visibility
of the image by repeatedly repainting it, creating a fade-in effect.
Unfortunately, it seems to trigger an auto-immune response in the `Paint`
event, triggering it several times. I've not been able to figure out how to
make it fade the image in one time only. If you simply want to display an
image at a particular opacity, just eliminate the loop and set the `Opacity`
variable to whatever level (between 0 and 1) that you wish. Replace
`"c:\c.bmp"` with the location of a graphic file on your hard drive.

```
Private Sub Form1_Paint(ByVal sender As Object, ByVal e As
    System.Windows.Forms.PaintEventArgs) Handles MyBase.Paint

    Dim g As Graphics = Me.CreateGraphics
    Dim bit As New Bitmap("c:\c.bmp")

    ' Specify initial translucence factor.
    Dim opacity As Single = 0.02 'almost totally
invisible

    ' The opacity factor goes into location 4,4.
    Dim matrix()() As Single = {New Single() {1, 0, 0, 0,
0}, _
        New Single() {0, 1, 0, 0, 0}, _
        New Single() {0, 0, 1, 0, 0}, _
        New Single() {0, 0, 0, opacity, 0}, _
        New Single() {0, 0, 0, 0, 1}}

    Dim imageAt As New ImageAttributes()
    Dim cMatrix As New ColorMatrix(matrix)

    Dim i As Single
    For i = 0 To 100 Step 5
        imageAt.SetColorMatrix(cMatrix,
ColorMatrixFlag.Default, ColorAdjustType.Bitmap)
        g.DrawImage(bit, New Rectangle(10, 10, bit.Width,
bit.Height), 0, 0, bit.Width, bit.Height,
GraphicsUnit.Pixel, imageAt)
    Next i

End Sub
```

Adjust the Step size in the preceding code to make the fade look good on
your computer. How fast this fades in depends on your processor's speed
and the speed of your video card.

Using the Clipboard

To transfer graphics to and from other applications, the Windows Clipboard
is usually the easiest way. The following code copies the image on a form to
the Clipboard:

```
PictureBox1.Image = Image.FromFile("e:\c.bmp")
Clipboard.SetDataObject(PictureBox1.Image)
```

The following code imports a graphic from the Clipboard:

```
PictureBox1.Image =
    Clipboard.GetDataObject.GetData(DataFormats.Bitmap)
```

If you want to ensure that a bitmap is in the Clipboard before attempting to load it, here's how to test:

```
If Clipboard.GetDataObject.GetDataPresent(DataFormats.Bitmap)
    Then
```

Loading and Saving Graphics

You saw in the previous example how the `FromFile` method of the Image object can load a graphic from a file.

To save a graphic, you use the following code:

```
PictureBox1.Image.Save("e:\temp.bmp", ImageFormat.Bmp)
```

You can load or save images using other file formats, such as .GIF, .JPEG, and .TIFF. However, when using compressed formats such as .JPEG, you must also specify additional information, such as the compression ratio you want to use.

Using Type

You can "paint" type onto your graphics surfaces, using a brush. This means that you can fill the type with gradients, textures, and anything else that a brush can hold. Here's an example showing how to create text using a texture stored in a file on your hard drive:

```
Private Sub Form1_Paint(ByVal sender As Object, ByVal e As
    System.Windows.Forms.PaintEventArgs) Handles MyBase.Paint

        Dim g As Graphics = Me.CreateGraphics
        g.Clear(Color.White)

        Dim b As New
TextureBrush(Image.FromFile("c:\weave.bmp"))

        Dim f As New Font("serpentine", 260,
FontStyle.Regular, GraphicsUnit.Pixel)

        g.DrawString("B", f, b, 10, 10)

        Dim f1 As New Font("serpentine", 60,
FontStyle.Regular, GraphicsUnit.Pixel)

        g.DrawString("askets", f1, b, 240, 170)

        Dim p = New Pen(Color.Brown, 3)
```

```
        g.DrawLine(p, 253, 228, 495, 228)

End Sub
```

You can specify which measurement system you want to use with your font, including the familiar *point* typically used with fonts. However, because I am using pixels for all the drawing and imaging in these chapters, I decided to stick with `GraphicsUnit.Pixel` in this example.

Where to find a texture? Most graphics programs have a set of them, or you can just search Google for, say, "marble texture." You can find lots of great art on the Internet. Be aware, though, that if you are planning to distribute or sell your application, much of the art on the Internet is copyrighted.

You can torment text in many of the same ways that you can manipulate images and drawings: rotate it, use color, fill it with crosshatches, and other maneuvers too tiresome to contemplate. As with images, it's probably best to get creative with text only in a dedicated graphics application. You have far more control over the final result and lots of special effects at your disposal, such as lens flairs (the brilliant star glint that you see in diamond ads), beveling, and many others. You can easily display text on a form after you've created it in a graphics program and then saved it in a .bmp file. Just load the file into a button's `Image` property, and delete its existing `Text` property. Or use label controls with their `Image` properties.

Chapter 3: Mastering .NET Printing (It's Complicated Until You Know How)

In This Chapter

- ✓ **Introducing the printing objects**
- ✓ **Handling the bottom margin**
- ✓ **Using PrintDocument**
- ✓ **Determining printable page size**
- ✓ **Working with PrintPreview**
- ✓ **Printing bitmaps**
- ✓ **Understanding** `With...End With`

In previous versions of Visual Basic, printing was fairly straightforward. To print the contents of a TextBox to the printer, you needed only the following line of code:

```
Printer.Print Text1
```

To print a string, you needed the following line of code:

```
Printer.Print "This."
```

To print a whole form (in its graphic appearance), you needed the following line of code:

```
PrintForm
```

In VB.NET, you have much greater control over what gets printed, but there *is* a cost. You have to muster a fair amount of information (such as brush color, the height of each line of text, the margins, and so on), and you have to manage several other aspects of the printing process as well.

I want to thank my friend Evangelos Petroutsos for his valuable suggestions about how best to deal with a line cut-off problem; he made some important observations about printing in VB.NET that I've seen nowhere else. The examples in most books, and in VB.NET Help itself, cut the last line on a page in half. The programming in this chapter avoids that unhappy but all-too-common error.

Working with the Printer Objects

In VB.NET, you are in charge of how everything looks when you send data to the printer. You have great freedom to mix fonts, graphics, and other visual elements. In fact, you can control pretty much everything about the printed page. Technically, you are dumping text as a graphic into a drawing rectangle.

The flip side of this freedom is that you have to keep track of what you are printing and where it's going. To put it briefly, when printing text, you must ensure that you don't print off the page's right or bottom margins, or the printer renders only portions of some of the lines of text. Some characters may be cut off on the right side, a word may be divided awkwardly (*awk* on one line, and *wardly* on the next), or the bottom of the final line on a page may be chopped off (so that a "g" looks like an "a" and so on).

For most of us, printing text is more common than printing graphics, so I tackle text first in this chapter.

To understand how this all works in VB.NET — and to see how to prevent your text from being mangled at the bottom or right margins — follow these steps:

1. **Start a new Windows-style VB.NET project by choosing File⇨New⇨ Project and then double-clicking the Windows Application icon.**

2. **Double-click the form in the Design window.**

You now see the code window.

3. **Before getting started with the actual programming, type the following** Imports **statements at the top of your form:**

```
Imports System.Drawing
Imports System.Drawing.Drawing2D
Imports System.Drawing.Imaging
Imports System.IO
Imports System.Drawing.Text
Imports System.Drawing.Printing
```

4. **Add a TextBox and a Button to your form. Set the TextBox's** MultiLine **property to** True **in the Properties window.**

5. **With the Windows Forms tab selected in the Toolbox, scroll the toolbox until you see the printer-related controls' icons (which are near the bottom of the Toolbox icons).**

6. **Add a PrintDocument control to your form by double-clicking its icon in the Toolbox.**

7. **Double-click the PrintDocument1 icon in the tray beneath Form1 in design view.**

A `PrintDocument1_PrintPage` event is created in the code window.

8. **Move below the line `End Sub` that concludes the `PrintPage` event, and type in the following function (you fill in the programming for the `PrintPage` event later in this chapter):**

```
Function ParseWord() As String 'get the next word from
    the lext, and return it.

    'use Static to retain the cursor position value
between calls to this function
    Static CurPos As Integer
    Dim Word As String

    'Return an empty string if we've reached the
end of the Text.
    If CurPos >= TextBox1.Text.Length Then Return
""

    'find first non-space character
    While Not
System.Char.IsLetterOrDigit(TextBox1.Text.Chars(Cur
Pos))
        Word = Word & TextBox1.Text.Chars(CurPos)
        CurPos = CurPos + 1
        If CurPos >= TextBox1.Text.Length Then
Return Word 'end of Text
    End While

    'build a word from the characters until you hit
a space (IsWhiteSpace)
    While Not
(System.Char.IsWhiteSpace(TextBox1.Text.Chars(CurPo
s)))
        Word = Word & TextBox1.Text.Chars(CurPos)
        CurPos = CurPos + 1
        If CurPos >= TextBox1.Text.Length Then
Return Word 'end of Text
    End While

    Return Word

End Function
```

This function looks through all the text in TextBox1, character by character. It keeps track as it moves down through the text by using the variable CurPos (for *cursor position*), which keeps counting until it's greater than the length of the text:

Book VI
Chapter 3

Mastering .NET
Printing (It's
Complicated Until
You Know How)

```
If CurPos >= TextBox1.Text.Length Then
```

This `ParseWord` function's purpose is to return each word in the TextBox. It simply finds the next word and sends it back. The function knows when it has read a word because it comes upon a space character. This line means "as long as the current character (`CurPos`) is not `WhiteSpace`":

```
While Not
    (System.Char.IsWhiteSpace(TextBox1.Text.Chars(CurPos)))
```

The following line adds the current character to the word that's being built:

```
Word = Word & TextBox1.Text.Chars(CurPos)
```

The `While` loop that encloses these two lines ends when it reaches the end of the `Text` or when it finds a space character.

Above this `While` loop is another, similar loop that does its job first each time the function runs. It moves the cursor through white space or other non-printing characters. In other words, it gathers characters that are `Not System.Char.IsLetterOrDigit`. But as soon as it hits a letter or digit (a text character), this loop is exited and the second loop begins adding characters to build the word that is returned to the caller. The caller is the `PrintDocument1_PrintPage` event.

Using the PrintPage event

In the previous section, you saw how to parse a TextBox's `Text` property, extracting each word, one at a time, until you reach the end of the text. Now you see how to actually print by setting up the necessary preconditions. You define a rectangle based on the boundaries of the printable space (the paper size, minus the margins). You see how to use the important `MeasureString` method of the `Graphics` object and how to use `DrawString` to print each page.

In the `PrintDocument1_PrintPage` event created in the previous section, type the following code:

```
Private Sub PrintDocument1_PrintPage(ByVal sender As
    System.Object, ByVal e As
    System.Drawing.Printing.PrintPageEventArgs) Handles
    PrintDocument1.PrintPage

        Dim printerFont As New Font("Arial", 10)
        Dim LeftMargin As Integer =
    PrintDocument1.DefaultPageSettings.Margins.Left
        Dim TopMargin As Integer =
    PrintDocument1.DefaultPageSettings.Margins.Top
```

```
    Dim txtHeight As Integer = _

PrintDocument1.DefaultPageSettings.PaperSize.Height - _
        PrintDocument1.DefaultPageSettings.Margins.Top - _
        PrintDocument1.DefaultPageSettings.Margins.Bottom
    Dim txtWidth As Integer = _
        PrintDocument1.DefaultPageSettings.PaperSize.Width
- _

        PrintDocument1.DefaultPageSettings.Margins.Left -
_

        PrintDocument1.DefaultPageSettings.Margins.Right

    Dim linesPerPage As Integer = _
        e.MarginBounds.Height /
printerFont.GetHeight(e.Graphics)

    Dim R As New RectangleF(LeftMargin, TopMargin,
txtWidth, txtHeight)

    Static line As String
    Dim Words As String
    Dim columns, lines As Integer

    Words = ParseWord() 'get the first word

    ' build a single page of text
    ' if "" then we've reached the end of the
TextBox.Text
    ' if lines > linesPerPage then skip this and use
DrawString to print the page
    While Words <> "" And lines < linesPerPage
        line = line & Words
        Words = ParseWord()
        e.Graphics.MeasureString(line & Words,
printerFont, New SizeF(txtWidth, txtHeight), _
                                  New StringFormat,
columns, lines)
    End While

    If Words = "" And Trim(line) <> "" Then 'finished
        'print the last page

        e.Graphics.DrawString(line, printerFont,
Brushes.Black, R, _
                                  New StringFormat)
        e.HasMorePages = False
        Exit Sub 'quit because there are no more pages to
print
    End If

    'print page
```

Book VI
Chapter 3

Mastering .NET
Printing (It's
Complicated Until
You Know How)

```
          e.Graphics.DrawString(line, printerFont,
       Brushes.Black, R, New StringFormat)
          e.HasMorePages = True
          line = Words
End Sub
```

This is quite a bit of code to type in, and you're bound to make some errors if you try. It's best to copy and paste all this source code, and you can download it from this book's Web site at `dummies.com/extras`.

This `PrintPage` source code begins by declaring a few housekeeping variables. The first line merely specifies the font and font size, and the next two lines simply read the margin settings.

Now you need to figure out where on the page you can print. Many printers don't permit you to print all the way to the edges of the paper, and it usually looks pretty bad even if you were allowed to do it. So, there is normally a *printable* area, which is smaller than the physical page size.

Sometimes the user is permitted to adjust the margins in the `PageSetupDialog` control, for example. After the user has made this choice (or if the user simply leaves the margins set to their default size), your program must work within these measurements (the printable page, as opposed to the physical page).

Determining printable page size

The following code finds out how much room you have to print by accessing the `PaperSize` and `Margins` properties of the `PrintDocument` object's `DefaultPageSettings`:

```
Dim txtHeight As Integer = _

    PrintDocument1.DefaultPageSettings.PaperSize.Height - _
        PrintDocument1.DefaultPageSettings.Margins.Top - _
        PrintDocument1.DefaultPageSettings.Margins.Bottom
```

By subtracting the top and bottom margins from the physical height of the paper (which is usually 11 inches, but not always), you get the vertical measurement of the printable page. For example, the variable `txtHeight` here is 9 inches if the top and bottom margins are both 1 inch and the paper is 8×11 inches.

Printer measurements are by default expressed in 100ths of an inch, although you can change those units. So you can just use Integer variables to manage the printing process. A typical page is 8,500 units wide and 11,000 units high.

The following line of code calculates the horizontal free space by subtracting the left and right margins from the paper's width:

```
Dim txtWidth As Integer = _
        PrintDocument1.DefaultPageSettings.PaperSize.Width
    - _
        PrintDocument1.DefaultPageSettings.Margins.Left -
    _
        PrintDocument1.DefaultPageSettings.Margins.Right
```

You can determine the printable space on a page in two ways. Both are illustrated in this chapter's example code. The first way involves doing a little math with the `PrintDocument` object's `DefaultPageSettings`, as demonstrated in the previous code. The second method, described next, is simpler. It uses the `e` parameter — in this case, `e.MarginBounds.Height`.

**Book VI
Chapter 3**

**Mastering .NET
Printing (It's
Complicated Until
You Know How)**

After you figure out the printable space using `DefaultPageSettings`, you calculate how many lines of text you can print on this page by dividing the total height (within the margins) by the height of the font being used. Notice that `e.MarginBounds.Height` holds the same value that you calculated previously and stored in the `txtHeight` variable. You can use either technique to figure out printable space. The following line of code uses the `MarginBounds` object:

```
Dim linesPerPage As Integer = _
    e.MarginBounds.Height / printerFont.GetHeight(e.Graphics)
```

As you see, this project employs the relatively rarely used `e` parameter, which is passed to all events in VB.NET but is usually ignored. In this case, the `PrintPage` event gets important information from this parameter (`ByVal e As System.Drawing.Printing.PrintPageEventArgs`).

Next in this project, you define a graphic rectangle as your frame, based on the left and top margins and the width and height of the available printable space on the page:

```
Dim R As New RectangleF(LeftMargin, TopMargin, txtWidth,
    txtHeight)
```

Then you declare a couple of variables to hold the current line and word. You declare two more variables, `columns` and `lines`. The `MeasureString` method wants a couple of integers at the end of its argument list. And `lines` is also used to prevent the `While` loop from miscounting the lines.

Looping through the text

Now it's time to look at the loop that actually does the work of building each printable page. This `While` loop uses the `ParseWord` function to get each word in the TextBox and add it to the variable line. Then it uses MeasureString to see if an entire page has been created. When the program exits this loop, the variable line holds a full printer-page of text:

```
While Words <> "" And lines < linesPerPage
            line = line & Words
            Words = ParseWord()

            e.Graphics.MeasureString(line & Words,
    printerFont, New SizeF(txtWidth, txtHeight), _
                            New StringFormat, columns, lines)

End While
```

Next an If...Then structure tests to see whether the job is done. If the variable words contains no text ("") and the variable line (with leading and trailing spaces removed) isn't empty, that means line contains the final page that needs to be printed. So you print the page with the DrawString method, set the HasMorePages method to false, and leave the subroutine:

```
If Words = "" And Trim(line) <> "" Then 'if this is true,
    then we're finished
            'print the last page
            e.Graphics.DrawString(line, printerFont,
    Brushes.Black, R, _
                            New StringFormat)
            e.HasMorePages = False
            Exit Sub 'quit because there are no more pages to
    print
End If
```

However, if more pages need to print, you print the current page and then inform the PrintPageEventArgs parameter that there are more pages to print. This causes the PrintPage subroutine to begin execution again.

Triggering PrintPage with the Button control

To complete this text-printing utility, switch to design view by clicking the Form1.vb(Design) tab at the top of the code window. Now double-click the Button on your form to create a Button1_Click event. Type this into the Click event to trigger the printing process. When the PrintDocument object finishes printing, your program returns to this Click event to End the entire project and stop it from running:

```
Private Sub Button1_Click(ByVal sender As System.Object,
    ByVal e As System.EventArgs) Handles Button1.Click
        PrintDocument1.Print()
        End
End Sub
```

Press F5 to run this utility. Then paste a fairly large amount of text into the TextBox so that you can see that the right and bottom margins are being correctly calculated and printed. Example code in many books, and in VB.NET Help itself, lops off part of the final printed line on a page (not on *every* page, but on some pages).

Some very long lines are in this program's `PrintDocument1_PrintPage` event source code, but each must be preserved as a single long line in the code window. So, if you see all kinds of error messages (such as `Expected an expression`) in the Task List in the code window when you press F5 to test this, you probably have some broken lines. It's hard to fix these in the code window without introducing errors. Instead, try going back and copying the source code from this book's Web site, and this time run Windows Notepad and choose the Notepad Edit➪Word Wrap feature to turn off word wrap. Paste the source code into Notepad. Then select all the source code in Notepad and copy it. Finally, paste this code into the empty VB.NET code window. That should eliminate any broken lines.

As you can see, communication with peripherals like a printer is not as simple and direct in VB.NET as it was in previous versions of VB. You have to write more code, and it's the kind of code where you have to employ properties and methods in ways that are not always intuitive. Nonetheless, it's not *that* complex. You can always just copy the code you see in this book (and in Appendix A online) so that managing most peripheral jobs should work fine for you.

As you saw earlier by building the preceding project, you use the `PrintDocument` control to hold the actual text or graphics that are printed.

`PrintDocument1.Printersettings` has many properties that you can read and often change to manage the printer: `CanDuplex`, `Collate`, `Copies`, `DefaultPageSettings`, `Duplex`, `FromPage`, `IsDefaultPrinter`, `IsPlotter`, `IsValid`, `LandscapeAngle`, `MaximumCopies`, `MaximumPage`, `MinimumPage`, `PaperSizes`, `PaperSources`, `PrinterName`, `PrinterResolutions`, `PrintRange`, `PrintToFile`, `SupportsColor`, and `ToPage`.

`PrintDocument PageSettings` has these properties: `Bounds`, `Color`, `Landscape`, `Margins`, `PaperSize`, `PaperSource`, `PrinterResolution`, and `PrinterSettings`.

Using the Printer Dialog Controls

If you want to permit the user to specify elements such as margins, page orientation, paper size, and paper feeder, you can display the `PageSetupDialog` control (after adding it from the Toolbox to your form):

```
PageSetupDialog1.PageSettings =
    PrintDocument1.DefaultPageSettings()

If PageSetupDialog1.ShowDialog() = DialogResult.OK Then
      PrintDocument1.DefaultPageSettings =
    PageSetupDialog1.PageSettings
End If
```

Also, the user can choose the printer, page range, and number of copies using the `PrintDialog` control. Neither of these controls are illustrated in the previous example.

Using the PrintPreview Control

Using the `PrintPreview` control is not difficult. This is a new control in VB, and it is sometimes helpful. You can display to users how their output appears when printed (so that they don't waste paper to print pages that are not formatted to their liking). And they can click a Print button within the `PrintPreviewDialog` to initiate printing.

Use the following code to display the `PrintPreview`, showing users a sample of their output:

```
PrintPreviewDialog1.Document = PrintDocument1
PrintPreviewDialog1.ShowDialog()
```

In the example project at the start of this chapter, you put the line `PrintDocument1.Print()` in a `Button_Click` event so that the user could initiate the printing process. If you use `PrintPreviewDialog`, however, be sure *not* to include that line in your program. Why? Because the PrintPreview dialog box itself displays a Print button and a Close button to the user. If the user clicks the Print button, the document printing is initiated from there, automatically, by the `PrintPreviewDialog` itself.

If the user clicks the Close button without printing, it means that the user decided not to print. Perhaps you should display the `PrintDialog` and `PageSetupDialog` controls again to allow the user to make modifications, and then display the PrintPreview dialog box again.

Printing Graphics

You may want to be able to print graphics. It's not difficult, but you probably need to manipulate the graphic to make it look right on the paper in the printer. As is so often the case with graphics, your primary job is to manage size and position. In the following example, you calculate and adjust the position to fit the graphic on the paper.

Start a new VB.NET project and put a PictureBox and a Button on the form. Set the PictureBox's `SizeMode` to `AutoSize`. This forces the PictureBox to adjust its size to whatever graphic you assign to it. Use the PictureBox's `Image` property (click its ... button) to find a graphic file on your hard drive to load into the PictureBox.

At the top of the code window, add these `Imports` statements:

```
Imports System.Drawing
Imports System.Drawing.Drawing2D
Imports System.Drawing.Imaging
Imports System.IO
Imports System.Drawing.Text
Imports System.Drawing.Printing
```

Book VI
Chapter 3

Mastering .NET
Printing (It's
Complicated Until
You Know How)

Type the following code into the `Document1_PrintPage` event:

```
Private Sub PrintDocument1_PrintPage(ByVal sender As
    System.Object, ByVal e As
    System.Drawing.Printing.PrintPageEventArgs) Handles
    PrintDocument1.PrintPage

        With PrintDocument1.DefaultPageSettings.PaperSize

            If PictureBox1.Width < .Width Then
                PictureBox1.Left = (.Width -
PictureBox1.Width) / 2
            Else
                PictureBox1.Left = 0
            End If

        End With


        With PrintDocument1.DefaultPageSettings.PaperSize

            If PictureBox1.Height < .Height Then
                PictureBox1.Top = (.Height -
PictureBox1.Height) / 2
            Else
                PictureBox1.Top = 0
            End If

        End With

        Dim r As Rectangle = New Rectangle(PictureBox1.Left,
    PictureBox1.Top, PictureBox1.Width, PictureBox1.Height)

        e.Graphics.DrawImage(PictureBox1.Image, r)

End Sub
```

Type the following brief code into the Button's `Click` event:

```
Private Sub Button1_Click(ByVal sender As System.Object,
    ByVal e As System.EventArgs) Handles Button1.Click

        PrintDocument1.Print()

        End

End Sub
```

Understanding With . . . End With

The code in this `PrintPage` event determines the coordinates (the top and left position on the paper) that display the graphic in the center of the page. First, you use the `With` structure. Any property or method between `With` and `End With` that begins with a `.` (period) is assumed to belong to the object defined in the line that begins the structure. This way, you can avoid repeating the "full qualification" (the entire object name) each time you refer to one of its properties or methods.

In this example, you start the first `With` structure like this:

```
With PrintDocument1.DefaultPageSettings.PaperSize
```

So all words within this structure that begin with `.` are part of the `PrintDocument1.DefaultPageSettings.PaperSize` object. (This `With...End With` technique is similar to using the `Imports` statement to add a namespace at the top of a code window. Both techniques save you a little work by relieving you of having to fully qualify in your code all the members of a particular class.)

Notice how these two lines leave out the object qualifier, simply using `.Width` when referring to the width property of the `PrintDocument1.DefaultPageSettings.PaperSize` object:

```
If PictureBox1.Width < .Width Then
    PictureBox1.Left = (.Width - PictureBox1.Width) / 2
```

If you decide not to use this `With...End With` structure, you have to write these lines with fully qualified object references, like this:

```
If PictureBox1.Width <
    PrintDocument1.DefaultPageSettings.PaperSize.Width Then
    PictureBox1.Left =
    (PrintDocument1.DefaultPageSettings.PaperSize.Width -
    PictureBox1.Width) / 2
```

The first line asks: Is the PictureBox less wide than the paper? If so, you center the graphic horizontally on the paper by finding out how much less wide it is (subtracting the PictureBox width from the paper width) and then dividing that by two (to provide an equal left and right margin, thereby centering the graphic).

If the PictureBox is not less wide than the paper, you assign 0 to its position, pushing it as far to the left as possible. Similarly, the second With...End With structure calculates the Top position in order to attempt to center the graphic vertically on the paper.

Then you define a rectangle to hold the graphic and draw the image in the rectangle. The DrawImage method also prints your graphic (because it is in the PrintPage event):

```
Dim r As Rectangle = New Rectangle(PictureBox1.Left,
    PictureBox1.Top, PictureBox1.Width, PictureBox1.Height)

e.Graphics.DrawImage(PictureBox1.Image, r)
```

If you're brave

This is a bare-bones graphic printing routine. You may want to improve it by adding code that zooms or reduces the graphic or allows the user to specify the position on the paper where the graphic should be placed. Also, moving the PictureBox's Top and Left position is a rather simplified and, to be honest, vulgar way of specifying the printer coordinates. Nonetheless, be warned: Manipulating the coordinates of both the PictureBox and the paper is harder than it at first seems. You have to ensure that the graphic isn't positioned or expanded off the paper's physical size, and you have to avoid distorting the image by changing its aspect ratio (the ratio of height to width) if you stretch or shrink it.

Book VI
Chapter 3

Mastering .NET
Printing (It's
Complicated Until
You Know How)

Chapter 4: Constructing Wolfram Diagrams

In This Chapter

🖛 Understanding cellular automata

🖛 Working with bits and binary

🖛 Trying variations

🖛 A little about LIFE

🖛 One final variation

Most graphics jobs that you may tackle in the .NET world are calculated for you. You just provide four coordinates, for example, and a rectangle is drawn at the specified size and in the specified position. The DrawRectangle method is built into the .NET Framework.

Nonetheless, you may find yourself wanting or needing to do calculations yourself and display the results graphically. In this chapter, you see how to draw onscreen dynamically and how to manipulate individual bits. This chapter explores an intriguing aspect of graphical computing: *digital physics* and *cellular automata* — a discipline where art and science conjoin.

Cellular Automata

A fundamental concept in digital physics is called *cellular automata,* which is using a computer to create a world that follows certain rules. This little world can be brought to life on a two-dimensional grid, like a large checkerboard with thousands of squares. To implement automata on your computer, you use each pixel onscreen as if it were a square on the checkerboard. Each pixel is called a *cell.* Depending on your monitor's resolution, this chapter's example program allows you to paint as many as 700,000 cells.

The main idea underlying cellular automata is that you specify a rule, such as "Paint the next cell down black only if the cell above it is black." Then, you run a computer program that enforces that rule to see what patterns, if any, emerge. Of course, the result from a rule that simple is easily imagined: If a black cell is on the first horizontal line, it is propagated down through all subsequently drawn lines, resulting merely in a vertical line.

However, other rules, though only a little less simple, produce results that can't be visualized — indeed, can't even be imagined — without a computer.

Some of the most fascinating cellular automata behave like fractals, walking the line between complete chaos (just a gray blur of noise) and too much order (boring, repetitive patterns).

A pioneer in this field, Stephen Wolfram, spent more than a decade writing a book that explores the uses of the computer in producing intriguingly complex systems from quite simple rules. His recent book, *A New Kind of Science,* goes into the subject at length. And, the book is written so that any intelligent person can understand it. He makes it his job to write clearly.

In this chapter, you create a VB.NET program to reproduce the results of Wolfram's first 255 Rules. As you can see in Figure 4-1, which starts with a single black cell, this Wolfram diagram truly walks the line between chaos and order. Figures 4-2 and 4-3 zoom in on other details of the diagram. As Wolfram says, "its behavior seems neither highly regular, nor completely random."

Wolfram, at age 21, was the youngest member of the first group of MacArthur genius award winners, and he went on to create a stir in particle physics and the study of complex systems. He wrote Mathematica, a popular computer language for advanced math — and became immensely wealthy from it. Then he dropped out and little was heard from him during the past decade, while he experimented with cellular automata, wrote his book, and concluded that all science should be revised. Rather than relying only on rules based on mathematics as traditional science does, he believes that natural systems arise from very simple "programs" and that these simple beginnings can result in the complexity we see around us. He asserts that natural systems don't themselves do math; instead, they perform computational "work." In other words, they run simple programs that lead to everything from the branching structure of a leaf to the patterns of the shape of continents.

Figure 4-1:
Wolfram's
Rule #110, a
pattern
that's
neither
random, nor
orderly, but
somewhere
in between.

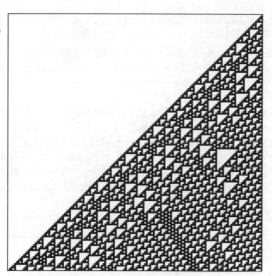

Figure 4-2:
Detail of the top of the pattern shown in Figure 4-1, magnified 400 percent. You can see the game of tag here between regularity and randomness.

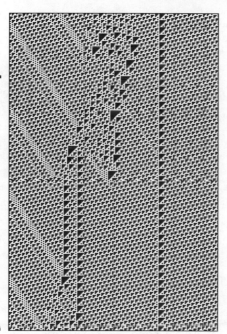

Figure 4-3:
200 percent magnification farther down in the dangling structure shown in Figure 4-1. This version is reversed, with white cells becoming black and vice versa.

The Automata Program

Before going farther, it's time to build the VB.NET program so that you can see Wolfram diagrams displayed on your screen and you can customize the program if you wish.

The bit-shifting operators used in this program were added to VB.NET in Version 2003. If you have the original version of VB.NET, the program used in this chapter will not work. However, upgrading to VB.NET 2003 is supposed to cost very little, so you might want to invest in it. VB.NET includes a few improvements to the VB.NET language, to the speed of the underlying .NET engine, to the Help system (more example code), and to the IDE.

Start a new VB.NET Windows-style program and type in these `Imports` statements at the very top of the code window:

```
Imports System.Drawing
Imports System.Drawing.Drawing2D
Imports System.Drawing.Design
```

Then type in the following code:

```
'specify the Wolfram diagram rule here (from 0 to 255):
Dim rule As Integer = 110

Dim endline As Integer = 900 'how many lines to draw

Dim i As Integer 'used as counter

Dim toLeft, Same, toRight, result As Integer 'the three
possible rule cells

Dim w As Integer
Dim BlackBrush As New SolidBrush(Color.Black)

Dim g As Graphics

Dim ycount As Integer 'specifies which line you're on

Dim arrPreviousLine() As Integer
Dim holdarray() As Integer
Dim blankarray() As Integer

Private Sub Form1_Load(ByVal sender As System.Object, ByVal e
    As System.EventArgs) Handles MyBase.Load

        g = Me.CreateGraphics 'do this earlier and it's wrong
        w = Me.Width - 1 'do this earlier and it's wrong
```

```
        ReDim arrPreviousLine(w + 1)   'set the array to
width of the form
        ReDim holdarray(w + 1) 'temporarily records all new
cell positions
        ReDim blankarray(w + 1) 'used to empty the holdarray
each iteration


        Show()

        'seed the first position

        Dim w2 As Integer = w / 2 'put a dark cell in the
middle of first line on screen
        arrPreviousLine(w2) = 1
        g.FillRectangle(BlackBrush, w2, 0, 1, 1)
        ycount += 1 'move down one line


        runit()

    End Sub

    Sub runit()

        Dim i, lines As Integer

        For lines = 1 To endline

            updatearray() 'draw the result onscreen
            ycount += 1 ' move down one line

        Next

    End Sub

    Sub updatearray() 'run through the array and draw in next
line

        Dim x As Integer

        For i = 1 To w

            x = analyze(i) 'figure out whether or not to
paint a cell

            If x <> 0 Then
                g.FillRectangle(BlackBrush, i, ycount, 1, 1)
                holdarray(i) = 1 'remember it was black
            End If

        Next i
```

```
      Array.Copy(holdarray, arrPreviousLine, w) 'put this
line into arrPreviousLine
      Array.Copy(blankarray, holdarray, w) 'fill holdarray
with zeros

 End Sub

 Function analyze(ByVal i As Integer) As Integer 'should a
cell be blank or not?

      'i (position within arrPreviousLine) is passed to
this function

      toLeft = arrPreviousLine(i - 1) 'cell to the left
      Same = arrPreviousLine(i) 'same cell
      toRight = arrPreviousLine(i + 1) 'cell to the right

      result = (toLeft * 4) + (Same * 2) + (toRight * 1)

If (rule >> result) And 1 Then


          Return 1
      Else
          Return 0
End If

End Function
```

Now, use the Properties Window to change the form's BackColor to White. Then drag the form in the design window to make it as large as possible. Press F5 and watch the rule play out. Try changing the line of code that specifies the Rule from 110 to other values to see how various rules create different patterns.

I explain how this code works later in this chapter.

Understanding the Rules

Wolfram's exploration into cellular automata in his book *A New Kind of Science* begins with a simple set of rules based on the state of the three cells in the row above the *target cell*. Each cell (each pixel in the example program in this chapter) is considered in turn. Should it be filled in or left blank?

To decide whether to fill in a cell, you look at the cell in the row directly above the target cell. Is the cell directly above filled in or blank? Then you look at the neighbor cells in the row directly above: Is the cell above and one-to-the-left filled in? Is the cell above and one-to-the-right filled in?

After you've answered these questions, you can then follow the rule as to whether or not to fill in the cell in question. Take a look at Figure 4-4. It shows the eight possible variations of three cells. A black cell is filled; a white cell is blank.

Figure 4-4:
There are eight possible combinations of three cells.

**Book VI
Chapter 4**

**Constructing
Wolfram Diagrams**

The rules, which range from Rule 0 to Rule 255, can be visualized as eight boxes, as shown below the three-cell combinations in Figure 4-5.

Figure 4-5:
Here are Rules 2, 3, and 255.

The way to interpret the rules is to compare the first row (of threes) with the second row (the rule). For example, Rule 2 in Figure 4-5 means that you fill the target cell only if the cell to the right in the row above is also filled. For all other combinations of the three cells, you leave the target cell blank. Rule 255 states that you fill the target cell no matter what the previous three cells' states are. In all eight possible states, you fill the target cell.

Experienced programmers will realize that this set of rules involves binary (base 2) arithmetic, and that the set of eight possible three-cell combinations can be expressed in a single byte (eight bits). Likewise, the 256 rules can also be expressed using a single byte, because eight bits in various combinations can represent the numbers 0 to 255.

A bit about binary

Programming is not mathematics; it's not even a science in the traditional sense. Programming falls somewhere between art and science. In fact, some of the most talented programmers were English or music majors in college. However, over the past couple of decades, professors of computer "science" have generally demanded that their students have a mathematical background, and computer studies have often been subsumed into math departments.

To me, this linkage between math and programming is as bogus as the requirement — which lasted 1,000 years — that only the few people who knew Latin were permitted to read or interpret the Bible.

There is no underlying relationship between Latin and scripture, any more than there is a fundamental link between math and programming. Some programming can involve math, just as some Bibles are in Latin. The attempt, though, to make mathematics a prerequisite for communicating with computers is probably more about job-preservation than practicality.

That said, math does enter the picture now and then, just as it does in real life. Be aware that VB.NET includes several *binary arithmetic* operators that can come in handy in specialized situations (such as when programming Wolfram rules).

You could create a huge 2048-case `Select Case` or `If Then` structure to decide how to fill in each target cell:

```
Select Case Rule 45
Select Case ThreeCells
Case  NoThreeCellsFilled
Case  OnlyTheRightCellFilled
Case OnlyTheMiddleCellFilled
Case TheTwoRightCellsFilled
'And so on for all 8 possibilities
End Select
'And so on for all 256 possible rules
End Select
```

But in programming, as in most intellectual activities, concision is a virtue. Plus, concise programs run faster. So, you think to yourself: This calls for binary math. When doing binary math, you are manipulating bits, and you can use some special operators beyond the familiar arithmetic operators (`+ - * /`). You can use `Or`, `And`, `Not`, `XOR`, and even some shift operators that bump the bits to the left or right. (Recall that the bit shifting operators were added to VB.NET in version 2003, and they are not available in the original version of VB.NET.)

But which binary operator does the job when deciding on a Wolfram rule? My first thought was to use the `And` operator, which tells you whether *both* bits in two compared numbers are true (for our purposes, *true* means the target cell should be filled in).

In binary math, numbers are expressed as groups of bits. A bit can be in only two states: either on (`true` or 1) or off (`false` or 0), so that's convenient with the Wolfram rules because each pixel (cell) can also be in only one of two states: filled in, or blank.

The number 3, for example, looks like this in binary: 11. That's because in binary, the rightmost bit is the 1's column, and the next bit to the left is the 2's column. Over one column farther left is the 4's, the 8's, and so on up to the leftmost bit position in a byte, which is the 128's column.

Thus, the binary number 101 means 4 + 1, for a total of 5. And 1111 means 8 + 4 + 2 + 1, for a total of 15. 10000 is 16, and so on.

When you And two binary numbers, you get a 1 (true) if both bits in the two numbers are true. Otherwise, you get a 0 in the result:

```
10010
11000 AND
10000 result
```

However, after messing around with this approach, I couldn't get the right results. AND wasn't doing the trick. So I tried OR (where you get true if *either* bit in two numbers is true). This resulted in the cells almost always being filled in. It was wrong, too. So was XOR.

I knew that a binary math solution to the problem had to exist, but hours of experimenting didn't produce the right result. I'm not one of those people who are gifted with great mathematical prowess — or whatever skill it is that instantly tells you how to compare three-cell permutations against 256 binary numbers to solve a Wolfram Rule.

So, after several hours of failed experiments, just trying things to see if they got results, I resorted to what every programmer sometimes must do. I used Google — specifically, Google Groups, which searches newsgroups. There I found examples of code written in Java and C# that showed binary techniques to test Wolfram rules. I don't find it difficult to translate Java or C# into VB, so I saw that the answer I was looking for is binary shifting:

```
If (rule >> result) And 1 Then
        Return 1
    Else
        Return 0
End If
```

This code returns 0 if the Wolfram rule requires you to leave the target cell blank.

To understand how this works, break it down into two steps:

```
Dim answer As Integer = rule >> result
If answer And 1 Then
```

First, you figure out the status of the three cells in the preceding line:

```
toLeft = arrPreviousLine(i - 1) 'cell to the left
Same = arrPreviousLine(i) 'same cell
toRight = arrPreviousLine(i + 1) 'cell to the right

result = (toLeft * 4) + (Same * 2) + (toRight * 1)
```

You put the information stored in the previous line's array into the variable `toLeft` (for the cell directly above the target, `-1`) and so on until you have the status of all three cells. Then you create a binary representation of these three cells by multiplying them by their binary column and then adding them together.

For example, if only the leftmost of the three cells in the row above is filled in, you get 100 in binary. If the leftmost and middle cells are filled in, you get 110. If the two outer cells are filled in, you get 101. As you can see, the binary representation is identical to the various possible combinations shown earlier in Figure 4-4. Now the variable `result` contains the status of the three cells.

Then you shift the value in the variable `rule` to the right by the amount contained in the variable `result`. This shift can range from no shift (000) all the way up to 7 (111) shifts. The bits in the `rule` are bumped to the right with each shift, falling off the right side (being discarded). On the left side, a zero is introduced for each shift. Shifting 10101010 by two results in 00101010. The rightmost 10 falls off and is lost, and two zeros are shoved into the left side. Shift Rule 5 (00001001) by 111 and you bump all the 1's off to the right.

After you do the shift, you check to see whether a 1 or 0 is in the rightmost bit position by using this code: `If answer And 1 Then`. Using `AND` this way is called *masking;* you can test to see whether any bits are 1 this way. `AND` with 00001000, for example, enables you to test the fourth bit.

It turns out that by shifting and then using the `AND` operator to test the rightmost bit, you get the correct answer to the Rule.

```
rule = 1 : result = 2 'shift two positions:
00000001 >> 2
answer = 00000000
```

```
rule = 2 : result = 1 'shift one position:
00000010 >> 1
answer = 00000001
```

If this mystifies you

Sometimes a monkey-see, monkey-do approach is just fine. After all, a primary virtue of Visual Basic has always been its high-level application development. You don't have to know exactly *how* a form's BackColor property is implemented. You can just change the color. And if this bit-shifting doesn't quite ring a bell for you, just use it and don't worry about it. It works, and sometimes that's enough.

How the Automata Program Works

The rest of the code is fairly straightforward. There are three arrays:

✦ arrPreviousLine contains the status (1 or 0) of each cell in the previous line.

✦ holdarray is filled with the status of the cells in the current line.

✦ blankarray is always filled with zeros.

When you finish a line and prepare to move down to the next line, the contents of holdarray are copied into arrPreviousLine. Then the zeros in blankarray are copied into holdarray, cleaning it out so that it can again be filled with each cell's status as that status is determined by the Analyze function.

In the Form_Load event, you set things up by sizing the arrays to the width (in pixels) of your form. You also determine how many lines down (also in pixels) you draw, and you put this value into the variable endline. Finally, you paint the center cell in line one black.

The runit sub governs the painting of the entire form, line by line. Its job is to decide when to end (loop from 1 to endline), and it also moves you down one line each time through that loop.

The updatearray sub draws each line. It loops from 1 to w (the form's width in pixels). For each pixel (or cell), the analyze function is called. The cell's position in the line (variable i) is passed to the function. The analyze function reports the results after examining the rule and the status of the three cells above the current cell held in arrPreviousLine. After the result comes back, if it's not zero, you paint the current cell. And you also store a 1 in the holdarray for later testing when you decide how to paint the cells in the line below it.

Variations

Sometimes it's interesting to continue drawing a Rule past the first screen. You get to see whether repeating patterns break up into randomness, or whether what looks chaotic eventually settles into some kind of organization.

It's no problem to continue following a Rule as long as you wish. For 3 screens or 3000, VB.NET and the computer are happy to oblige. Leave it running all night if you wish. All the Rules I've tried, though, have resolved into stasis within three or four screens. Perhaps you may be lucky and stumble on a Rule that goes on for hundreds of screens and then displays a picture of King Tut or something.

Multicolor superimposition with Rule 57

This variation to the original Wolfram automata program (that you constructed at the start of this chapter) draws Rule 57 three times, superimposing the results to create a cumulative drawing. It also shifts brush colors so that you can watch, mouth agape, as the architectural shapes build before your eyes.

Add these declarations to the original program (shown in boldface):

```
    Dim rule As Integer = 57

Dim BlackBrush As New SolidBrush(Color.Black)

    Dim BlueBrush As New SolidBrush(Color.LightSkyBlue)
    Dim GreenBrush As New SolidBrush(Color.LimeGreen)
    Dim drawcount As Integer
```

Then make the following changes to the Runit procedure (in boldface):

```
Sub runit()

    Dim i, lines As Integer

    For drawcount = 1 To 4 'do four redraws of entire
form

        For lines = 1 To endline

            updatearray() 'draw the result onscreen
            ycount += 1 ' move down one line

        Next

        ycount = 0 'go back to top line in form

    Next drawcount
```

```
End Sub
```

And, finally, change the `UpdateArray` procedure by adding these lines (in boldface):

```
If x <> 0 Then

    Select Case drawcount
        Case 1
            g.FillRectangle(BlackBrush, i, ycount, 1, 1)
        Case 2
            g.FillRectangle(GreenBrush, i, ycount, 1, 1)
        Case 3
            g.FillRectangle(BlueBrush, i, ycount, 1, 1)
    End Select

    holdarray(i) = 1 'remember it was painted
End If

Next i
```

Now press F5, and you get to watch an interesting structure being built, as shown in Figure 4-6.

Figure 4-6:
This is the result of three super-imposed screens of Rule 57.

No superimposition

If you want to watch a rule unfold without superimposing the new screens on top of previous screens, just add this line to the `Runit` procedure:

```
ycount = 0 'go back to top line in form
        g.Clear(Color.White)
```

The Game of LIFE

One of the earliest uses of computers to model natural behaviors was a program called LIFE, published in *Scientific American* in 1970. It had three rules, and they were somewhat more elaborate than the Wolfram Rules described earlier in this chapter. LIFE rules involve not only the status of cells in the previous row, but also the current row, and even the *following* row. Therefore, you had to draw the entire screen before applying these rules:

1. Any "living" cell (one that's filled in) with one living neighbor or none dies (turns blank) from loneliness.

2. Any living cell with four or more living neighbors dies from overcrowding.

3. If a dead cell has three living neighbors (no more, no less), it comes alive.

These rules can be enforced in a VB.NET program using a two-dimensional array (`oldarray`) that contains the results (0 for blank, 1 for "alive"):

```
Dim status As Integer = 0
'check 8 neighbor cells to find out how many neighbors a cell
    (i) has

                status += oldarray(i - 1, j - 1)
                status += oldarray(i - 1, j)
                status += oldarray(i - 1, j + 1)
                status += oldarray(i, j - 1)
                status += oldarray(i, j + 1)
                status += oldarray(i + 1, j - 1)
                status += oldarray(i + 1, j)
                status += oldarray(i + 1, j + 1)
```

The variables i and j are used to explore all eight neighbor cells around the target cell. The target cell is represented by the variable i here, and the eight cells that surround it are represented by j. As the program executes these lines of code, it accumulates data about each of the eight surrounding cells, simply *adding* to the variable status each time it finds a value (not zero) in a surrounding cell. After executing this code, status contains a number from 0 to 8, which is the information you need to decide whether to "turn on" or "turn off" the target cell.

After you calculate the status of the current cell, you can then use the rules to see whether the cell should be killed (blanked), brought alive (filled with color), or left alone. Here, for example, is code that tests for Rule 3:

```
'Rule #3: Is the current cell dead, but has three living
    neighbors?
If (status = 3 And oldarray(i, j) <> 1) Then 'it is born
End If
```

If you want to pursue implementing LIFE in VB.NET, you can find a good discussion on it and a complete example including source code at the following Web address:

```
http://msdn.microsoft.com/library/default.asp?url=/library/
    en-us/dnguinet/html/drguinet7_update.asp
```

A New Kind of Science

Wolfram's book goes on past the 256 Rules that I illustrate in this chapter's program. It includes exploration of more complex rules, such as averaging the colors of neighbor cells, updating cells more frequently than line by line, and substitution systems (where the number of cells can change, as opposed to the fixed grid of cells used in this chapter's example program).

In his book, *A New Kind of Science,* Wolfram proposes that rather than relying on equations to describe the universe and its contents, we would do far better if we explored the simple computer programs (algorithms) that he believes underlie the complexity of the universe. He asks: What if computation had been invented before calculus? The book is full of other intriguing ideas, too, such as the notion that when systems reach a modest degree of complexity, they are all equivalently complex, including human thought.

Several traditional academic physicists, and some other mainstream scientists, have denounced Wolfram's book. Conventional scientists — loyal to their fields' received ideas and to their training — are particularly suspicious of the notion that "true" science can result from computer experiments. Nonetheless, anyone familiar with academe understands that while professors pride themselves on their nonconformity to the general culture, they usually conform fiercely to the theories and intellectual fads within the academic community itself. True, professors often have strong disagreements among themselves, but the arguments are often over a point so vanishingly insignificant as to be almost pointless.

In the past, astronomy, encryption, biology, mathematics, and many other fields have enjoyed some of their greatest advances from gifted amateurs. Today's sciences often require considerable formal technical knowledge, not to mention a talent or interest in mathematics — the "language" of today's science.

What Wolfram is doing, in part, is restoring science and experimentation to the rest of us. He explicitly invites all of us to explore the simple computations that he believes will generate future science. Earlier in this chapter, I pointed out that programming is not mathematics. Wolfram is saying the same thing about science in general: that important new science can come from the language of computer programs (and simple language, at that).

One Final Variation

Another kind of experimenting you may want to try with the program in this chapter is to vary the initial condition. In all the examples so far, the experiment begins by painting the center cell in the first line. What happens, though, if you paint additional cells in that first row? If, in other words, the seed were different?

Try a random seed (with around 50 percent black cells) by commenting out the three original seed lines in the Form_Load event. Put a single-quote symbol in front of each of those lines in Form_Load, so that they won't execute. Then add the following new lines (in boldface):

```
Show()
'seed the first position

Dim rndGenerator As New System.Random(Now.Millisecond)
Dim r As Integer

For i = 0 To w - 1 'randomly seed the first line
    r = rndGenerator.Next(1, 3)
    If r = 1 Then
        arrPreviousLine(i) = 1
        g.FillRectangle(BlackBrush, i, 0, 1, 1)
    Else
    End If
Next

'          Dim w2 As Integer = w / 2 'put a dark cell in the
    middle of first line on screen
'          arrPreviousLine(w2) = 1
'        g.FillRectangle(BlackBrush, w2, 0, 1, 1)

ycount += 1 'move down one line
```

When you run the automata program now, Rule 90 gives you a wonderfully randomized — yet also recognizably rule-based — result. Your result will differ somewhat from the one shown in Figure 4-7 because when you run the program, the millisecond value that seeds the random number generator will, of course, differ from the millisecond that I used.

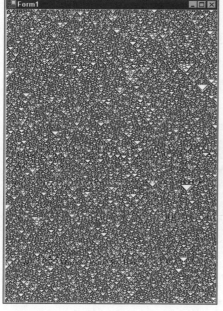

Figure 4-7:
This
dinosaur
skin texture
comes from
Rule 90.

Change to Rule 184 to get the nested, architectural slabs shown in Figure 4-8.

If this kind of thing interests you, keep experimenting. Some valuable science may be inside your machine, just waiting for you to discover it.

Figure 4-8:
This result
from Rule
184 is
random, yet
nested.

Book VII

Visual Basic .NET Object-Oriented Programming

The 5th Wave   By Rich Tennant

WANDA HAD THE DISTINCT FEELING HER HUSBAND'S NEW SOFTWARE PROGRAM WAS ABOUT TO BECOME INTERACTIVE.

Contents at a Glance

Chapter 1: Introduction to OOP

In This Chapter

✔ Understanding the main components of an object

✔ Discovering encapsulation

✔ Classes versus objects

✔ Seeing members

✔ Inheritance rules

✔ Polymorphing

What, you may ask, is an *object?* Answer: pretty much everything.

The items on the VB Toolbox are objects. Put a Button on a form, and you have a Button object. Lots of other things are called objects, too, as you'll soon see. Truth be told, everything in VB.NET is an object — even a lowly integer.

If everything is an object, is there any meaning to the concept *object?* Does the term *object* have any value in categorizing things? Has it become as descriptive as the word *thing?*

Very good points. You're right. In one sense, the word *object* has actually become nearly meaningless. In another sense, though, it's the key to unlocking the .NET universe. But we're getting ahead of ourselves.

Understanding Objects

To try to get a sense of what an object is, ask this question first: How does an object differ from a traditional variable or procedure? The answer is that an object is a container for *both* variables and procedures.

To put it another way, an object contains information (data) and also programming (functions and, sometimes, subs) that manipulates that information. So, in a way, an object is like a mini-program. (I'm generalizing here.)

Think of the objects on the Toolbox. (Yes, controls are objects, too.) For example, a Label control has qualities (variables) such as its Text property.

It also has behaviors (functions) such as its `Hide`, `SelectAll`, or `Paste` methods. (Notice that when they are enclosed within an object, a variable is called a *property* and a function is called a *method*.)

Usually, an object contains several pieces of data, known as its properties. For example, a TextBox control has a `ForeColor` property, which specifies the color of its text. Another piece of data, its `Size` property, specifies how high and wide the TextBox is.

In addition to its data, an object also usually includes some *data processing* (also known as *programming*), which describes the things it knows how to do with its data (or data passed to it). One example of this internal programming is a TextBox's `DataBind` method, which knows how to connect the TextBox to a database or other source of data. Programming within an object is known as the object's *methods*.

Finally, objects can (but often don't) have *events* — a place for a programmer who uses the object to define how the object behaves if some outside action (such as a mouse click) happens to that object.

To summarize: An object can have properties (qualities), methods (behaviors), and events (responses that programmers can fill in later). Together, these three features are known as the object's *members*.

Also, an object can (but doesn't necessarily) have a visible user interface. A Button object does have a visible user interface, but a Timer object does not. Some objects just count time, do math, search for a particular name in a database, or some other service that doesn't require direct, visual user input/output. Other objects do offer a visual interface, displaying results of a math calculation, or inviting the user to modify the object's data.

As you discover in this book, you can create objects that are intended to be used only within a single program. This kind of object isn't compiled into a control (such as a UserControl) or a library (such as an assembly). You don't add it to the Toolbox or save the code to a DLL file. Instead, objects can merely be a useful way of organizing your source code. Or not.

Using objects in your own source code remains optional. Many programs simply don't benefit much from object programming (known as OOP, Object-Oriented Programming). If you are writing a program just for your own use, or for your small business, OOP may be of no value to you. And millions of Visual Basic programmers are just such occasional, amateur, small business programmers. These programmers merely want to write a little state capitol quiz program for Sonny, or create a short state tax calculator for their small store. Jobs like this simply do not need OOP. Just write subs and functions and variables as you always have in previous versions of VB.

Whither Object-Oriented Programming?

OOP wafted up out of academe, just like other theoretical notions (usually French) such as post-structuralism, semiotics, existentialism, deconstruction, and so on. As far as I can tell, OOP isn't French, but it definitely originated within the ivy-covered walls. A generation of programmers have studied — and believe in — OOP theory.

Some programmers insist that all Visual Basic programs — indeed, all programs period — should be written using OOP. I'm not one of them. I feel that OOP is most useful when you're writing a program with other programmers as a group effort, or when you're attempting to create a large, complex program. In that situation, clerical problems require that people avoid stepping on each other's toes, or that one part of a program not cause unintended side-effects in another part.

OOP is fundamentally a solution to clerical problems that only arise when programming reaches a certain size and, therefore, a certain level of complexity.

Some people also advocate OOP because they claim that it permits you to more easily and safely reuse objects in future programs. In some cases (such as controls like the TextBox), this reuse feature is certainly true. In other cases, such as a small tax calculator, OOP's reuse features are sometimes less important.

Programming with objects forces you to follow some strict rules that can help avoid problems commonly encountered when group-programming, working with complex applications, or reusing complex code. Smaller, simpler applications often don't benefit from OOP techniques, for the same reason that walking to your car requires a lot less planning, organization, and equipment than does a skiing trip to Switzerland.

If you've never been exposed to OOP, you may find this chapter helpful. I outline for you what I think is the fundamental nature of OOP. (Nobody is absolutely sure about some elements of OOP because it includes conflicting theories, an evolving paradigm, and more than one set of rules to follow.)

I also explore some of the benefits of OOP, so that you can decide whether or not you want to learn more about it. Many VB programmers have resisted learning OOP, even though some OOP features have been available in VB for several years (since VB Version 4) and some basic OOP has been behind the scenes in VB from the very beginning in 1990. However, with VB.NET, Visual Basic now contains all the elements of a true, fully OOP-capable, language.

If you're experienced with VB.NET OOP, you may want to skip to the next chapter where I begin exploring more sophisticated OOP features and their implementation in VB.NET.

Encapsulation

A primary benefit of OOP is known as *encapsulation*. This means that an object doesn't permit outside programming to directly manipulate its data. You can compare it to how you count out your money and hand it to the salesclerk. You don't hand the salesclerk your wallet.

To me, encapsulation is the most impressive aspect of OOP. It's often useful to seal off a class after it has been tested and you know that it works. This prevents others (or perhaps you, later, when you revisit this object) from messing around with tested, effective code.

To achieve encapsulation, none of an object's variables should be declared `Public`; they're all declared with `Private`, `Dim`, `Friend`, or some other self-only scope. (`Friend` access makes a property or method available to other objects in your project, but not to outside objects.) The following `Private` declaration encapsulates the `m_EmployeeFirstName` variable:

```
Private m_EmployeeFirstName as String
```

The `m_` is a customary way to begin the name of this kind of private variable.

Any properties that you want to permit outsiders to access should be "exposed" to the outside code (another program) in a special way, using `Public` property procedures.

To get information about a property or change a property, outside (client) code must contact the property procedure that guards the `Private` property. Then the property procedure — not the client — accesses the object's `Private` property. The client doesn't get to manipulate an object's actual data directly. Again, it's like the salesclerk telling you that you owe $12, which prompts *you* to find those bills in your wallet and hand them over.

Here's how this combination property procedure/`Private` property looks in code:

```
Public Property LastName() As String

        Get
            Return m_lname
        End Get

        Set(ByVal Value As String)
            m_lname = Value
        End Set
```

```
End Property

Private m_lname As String  'the actual, hidden property
```

So far, I've been talking only about objects. Before going any farther, you need to nail down the difference between objects and classes.

Classes give birth to objects

When you first start a new VB.NET Windows-style project, a class is automatically created. The source code that defines the `Form1` class is automatically added to your code window.

In the code window, between the lines `Public Class Form1` and `End Class` sits the definition of this class. (Some of the class's source code is hidden within a Region section of the code window, but you can see it by clicking the + next to *Windows Form Designer generated code*). The point to understand is that the source code called `Class Form1` is the description that is used by VB.NET to create an actual `Form1` object. When is this object created? When the project is executed (runtime). When you press F5, the class becomes the object. In a sense, a class and its object are the same entity, but the class is like the DNA in a fertilized egg: It contains the complete description of what will later become the living thing.

You see the relationship. The source code is the *class*, but when that class's source code executes, an object is created based on whatever the code describes. The relationship between class and object has been compared to the relationship between blueprint and building, or recipe and cake.

Recall the distinction between design time and runtime? Design time is when you are typing in code or arranging controls on a form. Runtime is when you press F5 to actually execute your code (or when the user runs your final .EXE application).

The word *class* refers to the design-time work: writing code that defines an object (all the code between `Class` and `End Class`). Later, when the program runs, the information in the class code can be used to create an actual object. An object is said to be *instantiated* (an *instance* of it comes into existence) during runtime.

Also, just as a single blueprint can be used to build many houses, a class can be used to stamp out as many identical objects as you wish. Objects instantiated from the same class start out as identical (but they are independent of each other), just as cookie-cutter houses in some housing projects all look exactly alike. However, after instantiation, identical objects usually begin to differentiate. At that point, they can become less and less identical if their properties are changed, just as people all over Levittown — despairing of their indistinguishable houses — frantically began painting them different colors and planting different kinds of trees. Anything to distinguish their house from the neighbors' houses. Likewise, various TextBoxes on your form may have different sizes, different fonts, different positions, and so on. They began as identical TextBox objects when first born, but you rearranged them to suit your purposes as time went on.

Viewing Members

You can see the members of a class in various ways, but Intellisense offers one useful window into a class's *exposed* (public) property procedures and methods. Start a new VB.NET Windows-style program, and then double-click a button control in the Toolbox to put a button on the form. Double-click the button to see the code window, and in the button's `Click` event, type `button1`. As soon as you type the .(period), the Intellisense window drops down, showing you all the exposed (public) methods and properties of the button object. The properties have next to them an icon of a hand holding a videotape; the methods have an icon of a flying purple eraser, as you can see in Figure 1-1.

Figure 1-1:
Intellisense
lists display
all the
members of
an object.

Now choose View⇨Class View, and you open a window that shows you the classes in your current project, as you can see in Figure 1-2. When you pause the mouse pointer on top of any item listed in the Class View, you see its declaration and, therefore, its scope. In Figure 1-2, you can see that any object outside of this class (the `Form1` class) can't access the `Button1_Click` event because it's declared `Private`. Notice that any private member has a small lock icon next to it in Class View. Methods have the purple eraser icon next to them, and classes have a turquoise block icon.

Figure 1-2:
Class View
is a useful
way to see
how the
classes in
your
projects are
organized
and to see
the scope of
the class's
methods.

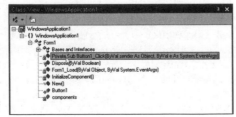

`Button1` is a class within a class. Yes, classes can contain other classes. The `Button1` class is within the `Form1` class. (`Form1` is the button's container.)

The `New` method is `Public` in scope (it has no lock icon next to it); therefore, other classes such as `Form2` can use the `New` method to instantiate new instances of `Form1`. Try putting this code into the button's `Click` event:

```
Private Sub Button1_Click(ByVal sender As System.Object,
    ByVal e As System.EventArgs) Handles Button1.Click

        Dim objForm1Clone As New Form1
        objForm1Clone.Text = "I'm a new Form1 object"
        objForm1Clone.Show()

End Sub
```

Now press F5 and click the button. There it is, a total clone of `Form1`, including the button and everything. The only difference is the `Text` property because you adjusted it. That's how objects start out as identical but then drift.

Automatic for the People

As you know, a form and all the VB.NET controls on the Toolbox contain quite a few built-in members you can use. When you start a VB.NET project, quite a few lines of default source code are written for you, but they are hidden a little in a Region. You can look in the region, but you're not supposed to touch most of that code.

Take a peek. Look in the VB.NET code window until you find the line `Windows Form Designer Generated Code`. Click the + next to it to open the node.

The `New` method is special in a class: It's called the *constructor* because it constructs the new object. The `New` method *always* executes when the class is first instantiated. (Remember how you usually write any initialization code for your programs — any startup conditions — in the `Form_Load` event? The `New` method is used somewhat similarly for classes: It takes care of necessary housekeeping to get the class up and running.) Not all classes have a constructor, but many do.

The line `MyBase.New` appears first within a `New` method, if the class inherits from a base (parent) class. More about this later. For now, just realize that your `Form1` class doesn't simply materialize out of thin air. It is *based* on a parent class from which it inherits lots of methods, properties, and events. A base class is the starting point for any child classes. The `System.Windows.Forms.Form` class is the base class for all VB.NET forms. This base class includes all the original programming that tells forms how to change

`BackColor`, resize themselves, draw their borders, and everything else forms can do. Your `Form1` inherits these capabilities.

The next line in `Public Sub New` is `InitializeComponent()`. It triggers a method by the same name in the `Form1` class, which you can see if you scroll down lower in the code window. This method was written for you by the Windows Form Designer, so you don't have to take the trouble. It's where any controls on the form, such as your button control, are given an object reference:

```
Me.Button1 = New System.Windows.Forms.Button
```

Remember that `Me` means the current object — in this case, `Form1`. Then some necessary properties are defined, such as the location of the button on the form. Next, the form's size and a couple of other properties are specified, and any controls are added to the controls collection of the container form.

How automatic is all this? Pretty automatic. Click the Form1.vb(Design) tab at the top of the code window, and stretch the button to make it larger. Also, change the button's `BackColor` in the Properties window to `blue` or something. Now click the Form1.vb tab to see the code again. Notice that two lines of code have automatically been added to describe the `Size` and `BackColor` properties of this button — because they are no longer the default properties as defined in the button base class:

```
    Me.Button1.BackColor =
System.Drawing.Color.FromArgb(CType(255, Byte),
CType(128, Byte), CType(128, Byte))
    Me.Button1.Size = New System.Drawing.Size(112, 64)
```

The `Sub Dispose` method is the opposite of the `New` constructor. `Dispose` describes the steps to be taken to destroy the object. In the case of a form, the main job is to go through the controls collection and make sure buttons or any other controls on the form are all killed off.

Inheriting

Another major feature of OOP is called *inheritance* — which occurs when one class inherits members from another class. You've already witnessed inheritance in this chapter when `Form1` inherited lots of methods and properties from the form base class. Simply starting a new VB.NET project triggers inheritance from the form base class. Likewise, dropping a button onto a form causes a new button class to inherit from the button base class (automatically coded by the Windows Designer in your code window's "region" hidden by default).

You also saw a slightly different kind of inheritance when you cloned Form1. This was a multiple inheritance: First, the original Form1 inherited from the form base class, and then the clone of Form1 inherited from Form1 (complete with inheriting the button that was on Form1). Note that any class that *doesn't* inherit is itself a base class. Any class that *does* inherit is called a *derived* class.

Inheritance includes various rules describing what can and can't be inherited and how it can be inherited. In fact, many times OOP isn't so much about how you program, as it is about a set of rules governing how you *organize* a program.

Polymorphism

I may as well introduce the third, and last, primary abstract pillar supporting OOP theory. *Polymorphism* means "having multiple shapes or forms." (The term *polymorphism* is itself polymorphic, because *polymorphism* has multiple meanings in computer programming. As Inga, the Swedish exchange student, says, "Big American fun!")

In general, polymorphism means that a variable, function, or method behaves differently, depending on conditions.

Variants for variety

One example of polymorphism is the behavior of the variant variable, familiar to VB 6 programmers. It isn't a numeric variable, nor is it a string variable.

If you add two variants holding 12 together with the + operator, you get a numeric result: 24. However, if you add two variants derived from TextBox.Text properties, you get a text result 1212. Although the variant has been eliminated in VB.NET, some of its polymorphic behavior still remains behind, like the scent of roasted turkey after Thanksgiving.

In VB.NET, you can find polymorphism in many places. Look at the behavior of numeric variables. They can morph into a string variable under certain circumstances. For example, you don't have to explicitly convert (coerce) the following numeric variable into a string variable to display it in a message box:

```
Dim n As Integer = 12
      n += 12        'add 12
      MsgBox(n)
```

MessageBoxes display strings, but here VB.NET made the necessary adjustment, morphing *n* temporarily into a string. If you ever get an error message saying that a particular variable cannot be converted to a string, add the `.ToString` method (`n.ToString`) to the variable.

Overloaded

A second kind of polymorphism occurs when a function behaves differently based on what parameters are passed to it. This is called *overloading,* and Book III, Chapter 5 covers this concept in depth.

What, not how

A third kind of polymorphism is related to inheritance, and this is the polymorphism most closely associated with OOP. A derived class has the ability to redefine the methods it inherits from the parent class. For example, if you have a parent class named `Employee`, it may have a method named `Overtime` that multiplies an hourly employee's salary by `1.5`. If you derive two classes from the base `Employee` class, the one named `HourlyEmployee` uses the `Overtime` method just as it was inherited. But perhaps the `PartTimeEmployee` and `SalariedEmployee` derived classes simply display a message: `This employee doesn't qualify for overtime. He is expected to slave away as necessary for the greater good.` Methods can thus be tailored to the different needs of various derived classes.

OOP polymorphism is a complicated way of simplifying. Another programmer who uses your classes may feel that the way that the same method (`Overtime`) works differently in the `HourlyEmployee` class than it does in the `SalariedEmployee` class is some kind of magic — given that both are derived from the same `Employee` base class.

You, however, created these derived classes and decided to sometimes override the original code that was in the base class. You built in the functionality using polymorphism and inheritance — rather than something simpler such as an `If...Then` or `Select...Case` structure.

Someone who uses your objects (some other programmer or yourself at a later date) need not understand precisely how the methods are polymorphic; he or she needs to understand only what the result is. Read more about messing around with inherited methods in the chapters to come.

Chapter 2: Creating Classes

In This Chapter

✔ **Understanding the main components of an object**

✔ **Instantiation**

✔ **Clients modifying properties**

✔ **More encapsulation**

I n this chapter, you see how to create new classes. You can create your own base classes, inherit from them, and morph them — willy nilly. Creating a class is actually not much more trouble than creating a function or sub. Just type **Class** in the code window, and there's your class. Then you fill in any methods or properties that you want that class to have. All of this may not be quite as straightforward as writing a function, though.

Defining Your First Class

To start off this chapter, try creating a class now. Start a new project in VB.NET (make it a traditional Windows style project by double-clicking the Windows Application icon in the New Project dialog box). Double-click the form to get to the code window, and scroll down to the very bottom of the code window.

You see the following line of code, which concludes the Form1 class definition:

```
End Class
```

You are going to create a namespace (just another container, which can hold multiple classes); then, within that namespace, you define a class. It's not necessary to add a new namespace. (You can use the one in which Class Form1 resides, if you wish.)

Namespaces are practical if you have a group of related classes that you want to "contain" within that namespace for convenience. Just to illustrate how it works, though, go ahead and use the Namespace (MySpecialLibrary) in this example.

At the very bottom of the code window, type in the following new class, which I named `BookCollection`. Just as you can name a function whatever name you want to give it, you can also give a class any name that you want, but it can't be a name you've already used (or a term that is in use by VB.NET, such as `End`):

```
Namespace MySpecialLibrary

    Public Class BookCollection

        Private Books(5) As String

        Public Sub New()
            Books(0) = "A Farewell to Arms"
            Books(1) = "The Corrections"
            Books(2) = "Kill, Kill, My Darling"
            Books(3) = "The Once and Future King"
            Books(4) = "The Story of My Times"
            Books(5) = "The Golden Bowl"
        End Sub

        Public Function GetBook(ByVal index As Integer) As
String

            If ((index < 0) Or (index >= Count)) Then
                Throw New IndexOutOfRangeException()
            End If
            Return Books(index)
        End Function

        ReadOnly Property Count() As Long
            Get
                Return Books.Length
            End Get
        End Property

    End Class

End Namespace
```

In VB.NET, you can actually use a language keyword for a variable, procedure, or class name if you like, but you must enclose it within brackets, like this: `[end]`.

Understanding the class members

Now take a look at the various components of this class. First, there are several *scoping* commands: `Public`, `Private`, and `ReadOnly`.

`Public Class` means that this class can be instantiated (brought into existence and used) by *any source code* located anywhere in this application or any outside application (a client application that is using your object).

Similarly, `Public Function` and `Public Sub` also mean that these two procedures can be used by code located anywhere. `Private`, by contrast, means that this array named `Books` can only be accessed from within this particular class.

The `ReadOnly` command means what it says: The `Count` property (which tells how many strings are available) can be *read* (queried), but not *written to* (changed), by any code.

The `Public Sub New....End Sub` code is optional. You can use it if you want to execute some code when the class is instantiated. It is called a *class constructor,* and it is always named `Sub New`.

Within the `Public Sub New`, you write any initialization code. In this example, you assign the data (the books in your library) to the five cells in your string array. (Of course, there are faster ways to fill an array, but this works fine for small amounts of data.) `Public Function GetString` is the *method* that this class exposes to the outside world.

The outside code (the "caller" that calls this class) that instantiates this class provides an integer to the `GetString` function (to tell it the index number of the string in the array that is wanted). Then the function returns the correct string to the outside caller.

The index number provided by outside code is tested (*validated*) to see if it is lower than zero or higher than the total number of available strings. For example, if the outside caller requests an index number 8 (s = strc.GetBook (8)), the error is thrown because there is no book number 8 in the array.

Validation is often cited as one of the primary advantages of OOP. Objects can verify the accuracy of data sent to their property procedures. If the incoming information isn't valid, the object can display an error message and refuse to send back bad data to the client. That's just what your object does:

```
If ((index < 0) Or (index >= Count)) Then
    Throw New IndexOutOfRangeException()
End If
```

The `Throw New` command means, "Create a new error object of the `Index OutOfRangeException` type." The error message displayed by this technique is for programmers, many of whom understand what it means. The `Index OutOfRangeException` is built into the .NET framework, and if you run the

**Book VII
Chapter 2**

Creating Classes

previous code, an error message is displayed unless the variable `index` is between 0 and the variable `count`.

If you want to provide a useful message for ordinary users of an object, substitute this:

```
If ((index < 0) Or (index >= Count)) Then
            MsgBox("You are using an index number that
    outside the range for his collection of books. Please use
    an index from 0 to " & Count - 1)
            End
End If
```

In either case, your `BookCollection` object's `GetString` method handles problems all by itself, without shifting that responsibility to the outside calling code. (The preceding example code does not provide an error message to a client application in most cases. You may want to use the `Return` method to send an error message to a client.)

Of course, validation code isn't exclusive to OOP. You can easily write code in an ordinary function to validate data passed to that function.

Finally, notice that the `Count` property is sort of half-public; it permits any outsider to read the count, but never to change it:

```
ReadOnly Property Count() As Long
    Get
        Count = Books.Length
    End Get
End Property
```

A `Public` or `Friend` property includes this `Get` structure (for reading), but also a `Set` structure (for changing the `Count`).The `Books` array (like all arrays in VB.NET) has a `length` property that provides the information you're after.

Instantiation

How does outside code (client code) instantiate this `BooksCollection` object and use its members, methods, and properties? Type the following code into the `Form_Load` event to instantiate your class and use two of its members:

```
Private Sub Form1_Load(ByVal sender As System.Object, ByVal e
    As System.EventArgs) Handles MyBase.Load

        Dim s As String
        Dim n As Long

        Dim strc As New MySpecialLibrary.BookCollection()
```

```
        n = strc.Count
        MsgBox(n)

        s = strc.GetBook(2)
        MsgBox(s)


    End Sub
```

If you were creating this example in a WebForm project, you would have to replace those MsgBox lines with the following, because message boxes don't pop out of Web pages:

```
Response.Write(n)
Response.Write(s)
```

Note that you used a namespace, so you instantiate a new BookCollection object by first specifying its namespace and then using a period (.) before specifying its actual name (BookCollection):

```
Dim strc As New MySpecialLibrary.BookCollection()
```

Technically, strc is called an *object variable* (or *object reference*) because it "holds" (or stands for) an object. In this case, strc stands for the MySpecialLibrary object.

How can you avoid having to specifically name the namespace? Use the Imports command, just as you do for other examples elsewhere in this book. The Imports command permits you to avoid having to specify ("fully qualify") the namespace for every class from within that namespace each time you reference one of those classes in your code.

When the strc variable contains the object reference after you've declared it as a new instance of your BookCollection object, you can use strc to access the members (properties and methods) of that object.

First, you get the ReadOnly Count property:

```
n = strc.Count
```

Next, you use the GetString method to get one of the strings:

```
s = strc.GetBook(2)
```

Now you know how to create a namespace, add a class to it, and add properties and methods. You also know how to access the members of the class from outside code.

Modifying class properties

How do you permit the user to change a property? Make it `Public` and also add a `Set` structure. To see how this works, go to the bottom of the class in the previous example — between the `End Property` line and the `End Class` line. Now type in this new property:

```
Private m_MoneyAmount As Decimal = 1400 'Hold the value

        Public Property Money() As Decimal

            Get 'outsider is querying
                Money = m_MoneyAmount
            End Get

            Set(ByVal Value As Decimal) 'outsider is changing
        the value
                If Value < 1 Then
                    Msgbox("Can't be less than $1")
                ElseIf Value > 1000000 Then
                    Msgbox("Don't kid yourself. You don't
        have a million!")
                Else
                    m_MoneyAmount = Value
                End If
            End Set

End Property
```

Note that you declare a private variable (`Private MoneyAmount`, in this example) to actually hold the value. You can optionally give private variables a default value, as I did here with `1400`.

You won't permit any outside code to directly modify the private variable. Also notice the validation code in the `Set` structure that tests whatever the outside code attempts to store into this property. The `Value` argument contains what the user is attempting to store into this property.

The `Currency` variable type has been dropped from VB.NET, so use the `Decimal` type whenever dealing with money.

To test this new property, change the code in the `Form_Load` event to the following:

```
Private Sub Form1_Load(ByVal sender As System.Object, ByVal e
        As System.EventArgs) Handles MyBase.Load

        Dim strc As New MySpecialLibrary.BookCollection()
        Dim n As Decimal
```

```
        n = strc.Money
        MsgBox(n)

        strc.Money = 12300

        n = strc.Money
        MsgBox(n)

End Sub
```

As you can see, the caller queries an object's property by assigning the `objectname.property` to a variable (n, in this example). A messagebox displays the default 1400 amount in the object's variable. Then the client modifies the object's property by assigning a value (12300 here) to the `objectname.property`. Another messagebox shows that the object now has a new value in its Money property.

Black boxes

Recall that another benefit of using OOP is that classes are "black boxes." They are sealed off like circuit boards inside stereo equipment. Users don't get to adjust anything on those boards except what the designer has permitted them to adjust by wiring the black boxes inside to knobs on the outside front panel interface.

A stereo receiver has publicly exposed members: properties (such as the loudness or tone knobs) and methods (such as a button that scans for the next FM station). It also performs a kind of validation: It doesn't permit you to turn the volume knob below 0 or up to 1,400. You are allowed a range of 1 to 10 for the loudness. (Although, as Spinal Tap famously revealed, some really expensive audio equipment goes up to 11.)

Additionally, the receiver doesn't let you see — or, worse, adjust — the internal programming that executes its Scan method. Put another way, a receiver is a black box with some public properties and events that you can mess around with — and lots of private stuff inside that you can't get to. That's just as well.

No outsiders allowed

Encapsulation means that other programmers (writing client "outside code" that uses your object) don't need to know the details of how the code in your object works.

Indeed, they can't usually even see any details you don't make public, because most classes are put into binary libraries (which are now called *assemblies*). When you put your source code into an assembly, outside users can't see it at all. All they can see — via your documentation and Intellisense member lists and parameter lists — is the public interface that you expose to them. An assembly can contain many namespaces, a namespace can contain many classes, and a class can contain many members (properties, subs, and functions). These are various, nested levels of *organization* — ways to structure your code so that related pieces are grouped sensibly together.

In addition to encapsulation, using classes can also simplify code maintenance. Programmers often have to go back and make adjustments to a program, perhaps a year after they wrote it. Maybe you want to add new features or improve the user interface. Unless you have a perfect memory, you become the outsider to your own code when you go back and look at it a year later.

You may then be glad that encapsulation relieves you of having to interpret the programming inside an object, and you may also be glad that validation helps you avoid feeding bad data to the object. Reusing a class also avoids your having to search throughout an entire application's source code to see whether BookCollection members, for example, are located at other places in the code. They're always encapsulated within the class to which they belong. In this way, the rules of OOP help enforce neatness and organization in your code. Encapsulation is practically essential if you are working on a large, complex program with other developers and programmers. You want to give them tested, proven, *encapsulated* classes that they can't rewrite or mess around with. All they get to adjust is the public members you permit them to see — like the volume and balance knobs.

Classes are more easily reused than traditional source code by other programmers, or by you in your future programs. If you create a class, for example, that accepts passwords, you can reuse it in future projects as often as you wish. As you've seen, objects are self-contained and self-validating. Therefore, you can usually add them to other projects quite quickly, without worrying that a constant, variable, or codependency exists somewhere outside the object. OOP often minimizes side effects, and it can also be an excellent way of organizing your source code to make it more understandable.

But what if you *inherit* a class, and then *polymorph* it by making changes to the way that object's methods or properties behave? Aha! If you use inheritance, all bets are off. Inheritance degrades the black box concept by permitting outsiders to modify all or parts of your class.

Nonetheless, emboldened by your success at creating your first class, you can now step into the more dangerous territory of class inheritance, in the next chapter.

Chapter 3: Inheritance

In This Chapter

✔ Is inheritance useful for you?

✔ Overriding existing members

✔ Using new VB.NET inheritance commands

✔ Understanding protected scope

✔ Using interfaces

*N*ew in VB.NET is a cornerstone of OOP called *inheritance*. It's similar to copying and pasting, enabling you to build a new class upon an already existing class. First you inherit the existing class, and then you can modify that class in your code.

Should You Inherit?

Be warned: Many people consider inheritance a dangerous technique and rarely worth the trouble it can cause. I rarely use it, but perhaps more from lack of experience than actual fear.

Other experts, however, swear by it. They claim that it improves productivity because you don't have to reinvent the wheel when you need a modified version of a wheel. I'm sure there's room enough in this world for people of both persuasions, so why don't you make up your own mind?

You can use the `Inherits` command to create a new class based on an existing class. Such secondary classes are called *derived* classes. A derived class starts off as identical to its parent. However, you then modify the members. Maybe you add new members or change existing members.

The idea is that you need not spend the time to write a brand new class from scratch if you already have an existing class that does most or some of what you need done in your new class. Just inherit the older class.

Overriding for Polymorphism

When programmers write a class, they can ward off some of the dangers of inheritance in several ways. For one, they can declare an entire class off limits by using the `NotInheritable` keyword. That defines a *sealed class*.

When only some members can be inherited

Or, if you permit only *some* of the members of a class to be modified during inheritance, you can mark those members `Overridable`. Only members specifically tagged with the `Overridable` keyword can be modified in a derived class. If the author of a class fears that unhappy consequences may occur if an inherited class messes around with a particular member, the author can simply leave out the `Overridable` keyword. Although overriding a method is more common, you can also override properties and events, too.

To see how to use inheritance, try this. Using the example class constructed in Book VII, Chapter 2, locate the following line:

```
Public Function GetBook(ByVal index As Integer) As String
```

Now add the term `Overridable` to the line, thereby giving any class that inherits the `BookCollection` class permission to modify how this method works. Recall that, by default, members are not overridable:

```
Public Overridable Function GetBook(ByVal index As Integer)
    As String
```

To see how to inherit, you now add a new class that inherits the `BookCollection` class. Move down in the code window to the bottom and click your mouse just above the final line (`End Namespace`). You want to be below the `End Class` line that concludes the `BookCollection` class, but just above `End Namespace`. Now type in the following new, derived, class:

```
Class InheritanceExample

Inherits BookCollection

Overrides Function GetBook(ByVal index As Integer) As String
    Return "This is the derived class and we don't have
  any strings to return."
End Function

End Class
```

To test this new class and see that it has indeed inherited, but morphed, the `GetBook` method, change the calling code so that it instantiates the derived class:

```
Private Sub Form1_Load(ByVal sender As System.Object, ByVal e
    As System.EventArgs) Handles MyBase.Load

    Dim strc As New MySpecialLibrary.InheritanceExample()

    Dim s As String
    Dim n As Long

    n = 12

    s = strc.GetBook(12)
    MsgBox(s)

End Sub
```

Notice that when you press F5 to run this example, the `GetString` method behaves quite differently in the derived class. Also, you may have observed that Intellisense provides lists of the members of each class that you create when you instantiate them in your code, as you can see in Figure 3-1.

**Book VII
Chapter 3**

Inheritance

Figure 3-1:
VB.NET
Intellisense
lists the
members of
your classes
when you
access them
in the code
window.

New inheritance commands

Several new VB.NET commands can be used with inheritance:

✦ `NotInheritable`: Declare a class with this command, and it simply can't be inherited by any other class:

```
NotInheritable Class MyClassName

End Class
```

✦ `MustInherit`: Sometimes you want to prevent people from using your class as-is. In other words, you want to force them to inherit the class and modify at least parts of it before it's used as an object. Classes marked `MustInherit` are called *virtual* or *abstract* classes.

```
MustInherit Class MyClassName

End Class
```

Think of an abstract class as a template. Perhaps you are building an application to manage your stamp collection. You notice that there are several categories of stamps: block, sheet, postcard, envelope, individual. Each category requires different methods to print reports, alphabetize, search, and sort. For example, you need to handle the report printing differently for stamps still on envelopes than you do for stamps in sheets.

You can sketch in the general behaviors and other members in an abstract class that you name, perhaps, `MustInherit Class Stamps`. However, the application is not intended to ever actually create a Stamps object because the members need to be tailored to the various categories of stamps. So a derived class for each stamp category must be created out of the abstract `Stamp` class.

✦ `NotOverridable`: When a method overrides a method in the derived class, you use the `Overrides` keyword, as in the example earlier in this chapter. And when you do use this `Overrides` keyword, the method in the derived class is by default overridable (if you derive yet another class from this derived class). So, if you want to prevent the method from being modified, you must use the `NotOverridable` keyword, like this:

```
NotOverridable Overrides Function MyMethodName()

End Function
```

As you see, inheritance can get pretty strange. Abstraction is fine up to a point, but this `NotOverridable Overrides` business is perhaps stretching things. It's positively French.

✦ `MustOverride`: When derived classes are created out of a `MustInherit` class, some of the code in the `MustInherit` class can be used in the derived classes as-is. However, you can force derived classes to revise a method by using the `MustOverride` keyword:

```
MustOverride Sub MyMethodName()

End Sub
```

✦ **MyBase:** Use `MyBase` to access a member in the parent (base) class from the derived class. It's considered good practice to reuse the code in the base class whenever possible. This prevents problems if the author of the base class should revise the code in the base class. Also, the base class may contain many lines of code in a given method, so why should you rewrite all that code if it's not necessary?

Protected Scope

As you've seen, VB.NET includes several *scope qualifiers,* which are keywords that you use to define how widely accessible elements of your program are. You use scope qualifiers to hide or expose various members of a class (or ordinary functions, subs, and variables). To review, `Public` exposes a class or one of its members to any caller — inside or outside the class or assembly (the code library) in which the `Public` item exists. The `Private` qualifier makes a class usable only within its own application, but not to outside applications. `Private` makes a member only usable within its own class. `Friend` makes a class or a member usable within its assembly.

Now it's time to introduce two new scope qualifiers. They are both related to inheritance. The `Protected` qualifier makes a member usable to all classes derived from its class. A protected member is private, but it's inherited. You use it like this:

```
Protected Uncirculated As Boolean

Protected Overridable Function AddValueForUncirculated
```

The second new qualifier is `Protected Friend`, which does what it says: It makes a member usable by any code in its assembly and also by any inherited classes.

Is Inheritance Worth the Risk?

If you think that some aspects of inheritance discussed in this chapter are baffling, you probably don't want to go farther into this arcane science. I haven't even touched on some of the really puzzling techniques involved when you inherit classes.

I've avoided discussing some quite subtle and bewildering aspects of inheritance because you, dear reader, are *my* protected friend. Classes can be nested within other classes. The `MyClass` keyword can be used as a way of dealing with the problem of calling a method in an inherited class that actually runs in the base class. Members in a derived class can *shadow* members in a base class, if both classes have the same name. Don't ask.

**Book VII
Chapter 3**

Inheritance

I'm afraid that I agree with those who say that inheritance can be confusing and is often just more trouble than it's worth. In many cases, if you need to reuse code, you can just copy it from the base class, paste it into your new class, and then modify it to suit your needs. To me, that's often a less complicated, less confusing process, and it is likely to prevent certain kinds of bugs.

Nevertheless, many intelligent people disagree with this view. Certainly, if you are working with a large program, tools such as inheritance can make the job easier and make such a program easier to maintain later. Some benefits of OOP — notably its modularity, reusability, and extensibility — become more significant and valuable as projects grow larger, and in proportion to the number of people working on the projects.

If you program alone and create small applications, you may have infrequent need to use OOP in general, and surely much less need to use inheritance in particular. So make up your own mind about the value of inheritance in programming. It may suit you just fine.

Working with Interfaces

A class exposes some or all of its members — its subs, functions, and properties — to the outside world. These exposed members are a class's public *interface*.

You can also create separate interfaces that are not part of a class. An interface that stands alone has no code in its methods, events, or properties — just the names (and parameters) of the members. It's a class that is stripped down. It's like a form you fill out the first time you visit a new dentist: a list of main topics such as "Allergic to Novocain?" and "Want gas, honey?" But the actual answers under each topic are left empty for you to fill in. I guess my dentist didn't actually use the word *honey*.

Interfaces are primarily used when you want to provide a way for several classes to implement a particular job, following a standardized way of accomplishing that job.

For example, say that you have a project that involves manipulating text and also manipulating numbers. You want to save the text into a file named `text` and save the numbers into a file named `numbers`. In other words, they *both* should have the ability to save their data to the hard drive, but they can actually implement the saving process in unique ways useful just to them. However, you want them to expose a standard interface so that outside callers see a `Save` method, and only a `Save` method, in all the classes that have the ability to save their contents.

Using interfaces simplifies things for the caller. The caller simply invokes the Save method in any of these classes, without having to worry about variations on the method's name (SaveText, OpenFile, or whatever, if each class had unique names). Nor does the caller have to worry about variations in behaviors.

By convention, interface names start with the letter I. For this example, type in the following interface outside the Form1 class so that it's available to all classes in your project. Click your mouse at the top of the code window, above the line Public Class Form1, and then type in the following interface:

```
Interface ISaveResults
    Sub Save(ByVal s As String)
End Interface
```

Notice that there's no code to actually implement the Save method, nor even any End Sub. It's just the name of the method and the parameter that the method wants to be passed to it — a string in this case.

Each class that uses this interface *must* follow the rules. It must create a Sub named Save, and it must take a string variable. Also, you don't need to use the Public qualifier in front of the Sub because in an interface, all members are always public. In fact, you can't use access modifiers with an interface's members.

Now create two classes, which do different things. What they have in common, though, is the interface that requires them to provide a Save method:

```
Public Class text
    Implements ISaveResults

    Sub save(ByVal s As String) Implements ISaveResults.Save
        Dim f As System.IO.StreamWriter =
    System.IO.File.AppendText("C:\text.txt")
        f.Write(s)
        f.Close()
    End Sub

End Class

Public Class numbers
    Implements ISaveResults

    Sub save(ByVal s As String) Implements ISaveResults.Save
```

```
        Dim f As System.IO.StreamWriter =
    System.IO.File.AppendText("C:\numbers.txt")
        f.Write(s)
        f.Close()
    End Sub

End Class
```

As you see, each class uses the template specified in the interface, providing a `Save` method and a string argument for it. Also notice that the `Implements` keyword must be used to declare the interface, and then it must also be used each time you fill in one of the members.

What happens if you don't include, in your class, all the members in the interface? VB.NET shows you an error message like this: `WindowsApplication1. Text must implement Sub Save (s as string) for interface WindowsApplication1.IsaveResults.`

Now test the interfaces for your classes by typing the following into the `Form_Load` event:

```
Private Sub Form1_Load(ByVal sender As System.Object, ByVal e
    As System.EventArgs) Handles MyBase.Load
        Dim t As New text()
        t.save("Mary")

        Dim n As New numbers()
        n.save("1233")
    End Sub
End Class
```

Press F5 and look in your `C:\` directory to see that two files have been created, just as expected.

Here's another example, where you can see how to deal with functions and properties when using an interface. Assume that you distribute fruit and that bananas are taxed at 5 percent, but apples are taxed at only 3 percent because the mayor's family raises apples and the fix is in.

Your program needs to keep track of the inventory, provide reports on spoilage ratios, and lots of other things. These jobs are handled within separate `Bananas` and `Apples` classes. However, one of the things that must be done in both classes is to accept a net sale price and send back the gross price after the tax has been added. This also requires a public property that holds the tax (which may be changed at some point if they vote the mayor out of office). As you will see, a property in an interface is handled essentially the same way as a method.

Erase the two classes from the previous example, and erase the code in the Form_Load event. Now type in the following interface above the line `Public Class Form1`:

```
Public Interface GrossSale
    Function CalcSale(ByVal n As Decimal) As Decimal
    Property tax() As Decimal
End Interface
```

Notice that this function and property are both simply declared, but they have no structure (no End) and no internal code — just their names, arguments, and variable types. Now type in the two classes that implement this interface:

```
Public Class Bananas

    Implements GrossSale

    Function CalcSale(ByVal n As Decimal) As Decimal
Implements GrossSale.CalcSale
        Return (1 + tax) * n
    End Function

    Private m_pTax

    Public Property tax() As Decimal Implements GrossSale.tax
        Get
            Return m_pTax
        End Get
        Set(ByVal Value As Decimal)
            m_pTax = Value
        End Set
    End Property

End Class

Public Class Apples
    Implements GrossSale

    Function CalcSale(ByVal n As Decimal) As Decimal
Implements GrossSale.CalcSale
        Return (1 + tax) * n
    End Function

    Private m_pTax

    Public Property tax() As Decimal Implements GrossSale.tax
        Get
            Return m_pTax
```

```
            End Get
            Set(ByVal Value As Decimal)
                m_pTax = Value
            End Set
        End Property

    End Class
```

These are ordinary class methods and properties, with the exception of the Implements "contract" added on to the end of their declaration lines. Finally, type in the following code to test the interfaces:

```
Private Sub Form1_Load(ByVal sender As System.Object, ByVal e
    As System.EventArgs) Handles MyBase.Load

        Dim a As New Apples()
        a.tax = 0.03
        Dim result As Decimal = a.CalcSale(140.22)

        Dim b As New Bananas()
        b.tax = 0.05
        Dim result1 As Decimal = b.CalcSale(20.16)

        MsgBox("Apples $" & result & "  Bananas $" & result1)

    End Sub
```

To use these classes, you instantiate them, provide the value for the tax property, and then call the CalcSale method. Each class does its own calculations and returns the results.

As you may have noticed, interfaces are similar to base (parent) classes: They define a structure that can be passed on to other classes and morphed. However, all the members of an interface are sketches — mere shells with no code of their own. The interface simply defines the "contract" — the members that each class using the interface must implement and fill in code for.

To conclude this discussion of inheritance, I have to ask you this: Do you feel that this chapter has convincingly demonstrated why you would want to use inheritance? Your answer is probably, "No!" And that's the point I'm trying to make. In most situations, you really *don't* want to use inheritance.

Chapter 4: Your First OOP Project

In This Chapter

✔ **Structuring classes with simple grammar**

✔ **Specifying a simple object**

✔ **Creating an object collection**

✔ **Building a client**

✔ **Fixing the** `Object reference not set` **error**

*1*n this chapter, you plunge in and create your first true OOP project. As you can see while you build this project, OOP has interesting capabilities and — perhaps you'll agree — can contribute to the efficiency of some kinds of programming.

Visualizing Classes

Working with OOP often raises some questions: How do I know what to make into a class? How do I organize a project so that it's object-oriented?

These can indeed be difficult decisions — and experts disagree on the best approach. Some advocate sitting down and figuring out the underlying grammar by writing a description of the problem that your application is designed to solve (which is an approach that I cover later in this chapter).

Other experts have worked up techniques such as UML (the Unified Modeling Language), which is visual modeling where you diagram your project (or, more commonly, a group of interworking projects known, hopefully, as a *solution*). Some people swear by older modeling languages with names like Booch, OMT, and OOSE.

The latest techniques involve the use of design patterns, with names such as *Singleton, Decorator, Chain of Responsibility,* and *Chain Reaction Crash.* You pick one of these patterns that best matches the job you're trying to accomplish; then you follow the rules that describe how to design your application so that it ends up resembling the pattern. (Okay, I made up *Chain Reaction Crash.*)

Actually, here in the real world, modeling languages, design patterns, and such are — like OOP itself — increasingly less useful as you go down the slope from mega-projects (such as the software that drives Bank of America or the software that makes .NET work) to medium-size or small-size applications.

If you are writing small personal programs for home or small office, you may be better off simply ignoring the entire OOP technology and just writing all your source code within Form1 (in other words, within a single class). This avoids lots of security (scoping) issues and other problems that arise when you begin to focus on the communication between different parts of your program rather than the communication between your program and its user.

Earlier in this book I suggest that one good way to design smaller projects is to first put various controls on a form (or a few forms). By designing the surface of your project that the user works with, you simultaneously see what kinds of code you are going to need to solve your project's problems. This approach is sometimes condemned by OOP theorists on the grounds that you must ignore user interaction until later, after you've described the internal structure of your project. I've seen books on OOP, though, where this advice is given in Chapter 4 and violated in Chapter 9, where the first thing they do is construct the user interface. Oh well.

For people intending to program in groups or construct larger, more complex software, OOP is indeed valuable. If you decide that you want to employ some OOP techniques, the rest of this chapter illustrates one way to go about structuring an OOP application.

Where Are the Nouns and the Verbs?

In this section, I use the recipe book example project that's familiar from earlier chapters in this book. In this example, you use the SortedList class from the .NET Framework, which neatly solves the alphabetization problem you face in Book V, Chapter 4. In that chapter, a workaround is used to force a DataSet to maintain its two columns in alphabetical order. In this example, you see how the SortedList handles this for you by always keeping its key and value pairs in sorted order.

A technique frequently used to figure out how to design an application using OOP is to write a narrative statement of the problem you're trying to solve. Then you analyze its grammar to find out which are the classes and which are the members of those classes.

Here's a very simplified problem statement for this application:

I have collected various recipes on my hard drive. Each recipe has a title and a description portion. I want to be able to choose one recipe by seeing a list of the titles, and I want to read the recipe on screen. I also want to be able to add or delete recipes from my collection.

Okay. OOP theory says that you should first locate the classes inherent in your project because the *nouns* in the problem statement suggest classes. Here are the nouns:

*I have collected various **recipes** on my **hard drive**. Each **recipe** has a **title** and a **description**. I want to be able to choose one recipe by seeing a **list** of the titles, and I want to read the recipe on **screen**. I also want to be able to add or delete recipes from my **collection**.*

OOP theory says you should now whittle down the list of nouns by throwing out those that "are irrelevant" (easy to say!). However, in this case, you consider hardware irrelevant, so get rid of *hard drive* and *screen*. They won't be classes in the program; they exist in the real world.

You also discard any nouns that seem too finite to be a class (those that have only one property, for example, and no methods at all). *Title* and *description* should be properties of a class rather than individual classes all their own.

The *list* is just another way of describing the collection of titles, so out goes *list*. Similarly, *collection* is just another way of describing *recipes,* so out goes *collection*.

You're left with `recipe` and `recipes` as your classes. Here's a new idea: One object can contain a *collection* of another object. In this project, it's useful to design the `recipes` object as containing a collection of recipe objects. To keep things straight, call the container class `RecipeCollection` and the individual recipe class `Recipe`. But do keep in mind their relationship: One is the container, and the other is the collection of objects it contains. Title and description can be properties of the `Recipe` class. Name them `Text` and `Title`. These properties are given their values within the *constructor* — a `Sub New` in the `Recipe` class that forces the outside caller to provide this information as parameters whenever the caller instantiates a new recipe object.

Okay, you now have to figure out the methods for these classes, so you look for the *verbs* in the description (ignoring the little verb forms such as *is* or *has*):

*I have **collected** various recipes on my hard drive. Each recipe has a title and a description portion. I want to be able to **choose** one recipe by **seeing** a list of the titles, and I want to **read** the recipe on screen. I also want to be able to **add** or **delete** recipes from my collection.*

Again, you must go through and discard "unwanted" verbs that don't seem as if they apply to the project. *Collected* has no relationship to what the software should do. It has already happened. *Choose* sounds like a `Click` event for a ListBox: You put the code in that event to display whichever title the user clicks. That *choose* causes the selected recipe to be displayed in a TextBox where it can be *read*.

Seeing a list involves filling a ListBox with the titles. The `RecipeCollection` class should therefore have a method that passes its entire collection of data to any caller (client code). You can call this the `SendList` method. When the user clicks on a single recipe in the ListBox, you get the title of that requested recipe from the ListBox's `SelectedItem` property, and you need a method in the `RecipeCollection` that receives a title and passes back the correct `Recipe` object represented by that title. Call this the `SendOneRecipe` method. `Add` and `delete` should be methods of the `RecipeCollection` class, too.

After this whittling process, you have the following:

`Recipe` **class with two properties:** `Title` **and** `Text`**.**

`RecipeCollection` **class with four methods:** `SendList`**,** `SendOneRecipe`**,** `Add`**, and** `Delete`**.**

The Simplest Object

It's time to write the classes. Choose File⇨New⇨Project, and double-click the Windows Application icon to start a new VB.NET Windows-style project.

You may or may not need the following line, but put it at the top of the Form1 code window, above `Public Class Form1`:

```
Imports System.Collections
```

Now choose Project⇨Add Class. Name this class `Recipe`. If you prefer, you can put your VB.NET classes in separate files with this Project⇨Add Class approach. Things work just the same as if you had added your new class below Form1's class in the Form1.vb code window. Using Project⇨Add Class simply organizes the project differently — segregating the classes into individual tabs on the top of the code window, and into separate files in the Solution Explorer.

This new `Recipe` class is a very simple class that holds an individual recipe. Each new recipe requires that you instantiate a new `Recipe` class — a technique that many OOP programs use for quite finite objects (individual employees each getting their own object, for example). The Recipe object has only two members. Type the following code into the Recipe class code window:

```
Public Class Recipe

    Public Sub New(ByVal title As String, ByVal text As
    String) 'the constructor
        m_title = title
        m_text = text
    End Sub

    Private m_title As String 'this is the key field
    Private m_text As String

    Public Property title() As String
        Get
            Return m_title
        End Get
        Set(ByVal Value As String)
            m_title = Value
        End Set
    End Property

    Public Property text() As String
        Get
            Return m_text
        End Get
        Set(ByVal Value As String)
            m_text = Value
        End Set
    End Property

End Class
```

This code should be familiar to you. There are two private variables starting with m_ (for "member data"). Technically, OOP programmers call these *fields* rather than variables. These two fields are used by the Public properties (which OOP programmers sometimes call *accessors* because they provide access to data but hold no data themselves).

VB.NET knows whether you mean to Set or Get with an accessor by how client code calls it.

Client code using the format X = MyClass.MyProperty triggers the get behavior in your class.

Client code using the format Dim aClassName(SomeDataToStore) triggers the set behavior in your class.

The Collection Object

In OOP programming, you often run across a situation where you have a set of related objects that you need to manipulate as a group. In this project, it is helpful to create a container class, `RecipeCollection`, that can provide any caller with the entire sorted list of recipes.

Just as arrays are convenient when you want to manipulate a set of related variables, so too are other kinds of collections. Lists, dictionaries, hashtables, arraylists, collections, queues, and stacks are other types of collections available in VB.NET for your use.

To keep the collection of recipes always sorted alphabetically while the user is working with them, you can use the handy `SortedList` class. The `Recipe Collection` object uses a `SortedList` to keep the collection of recipes in order.

A `SortedList` always keeps its items in alphabetical order. In fact, it maintains two internal arrays to store the two "columns" of elements in its list. One array holds the key; the other holds the value associated with the key.

Add a recipe to the sorted list and its Title/Text pair of data is inserted at the proper alphabetical place — based on the Title column. This is a *key-value* pair. You can get an item from a `SortedList` either by providing the key string (such as `"Rellenos"`) or by using the index number for the item: Give me item 3.

So far, I've been using the term *item,* but it's time to whip the cloth off the statue and reveal what's been previously concealed. These key-value pair items are actually *objects.* In this example, they are `Recipe` objects.

It's hard for people used to the traditional VB programming model to realize that you can throw objects around just as easily as you've always sent variables around in your programs. You're used to passing data as parameters and receiving them as arguments. First, you pass some data to a function:

```
Dim Result As String = switchnames("Doris", "Duke")
```

Then the function sends a result back to you, having manipulated that data:

```
Function switchnames(ByVal Name1 As String, ByVal Name2 As
    String) As String
        Return Name2 & "," & Name1
End Function
```

What you now need to realize is that you can manipulate objects in pretty much the same ways that you always manipulated ordinary data — send an object to a function, create an array of objects, and so on. It's counter-intuitive at first, but you soon get used to flinging objects around as if they were simple variables.

The several code examples that follow are simply for illustration. You won't use them in the project that you build in the section "The working example code," later in this chapter.

A `Recipe` object can be passed as a parameter. Here's how you can add a new recipe object to the `RecipeCollection`:

```
Dim r As New Recipe("Rosas Rellenos", "Buy from Rosa.
    Reheat.")
m_rcoll.add(r) 'add Recipe object to the RecipeCollection
```

And the `Add` method that accepts the `Recipe` object as an argument looks like this:

```
Public Sub add(ByVal aRecipe As Recipe)
            myColl.Add(aRecipe.title, aRecipe)
End Sub
```

The thing to notice here is that the argument being accepted by this method is an object, a `Recipe` object. It's almost as if, in creating your Recipe class, you had defined a new variable type `Recipe` to go along with the traditional `Integer`, `String`, `Long`, and other built-in types.

To review, you can declare an ordinary variable like this:

```
Dim S as String = "Data you want in to put into this
    variable"
```

You instantiate a new object like this:

```
Dim R as New Object("Any Data the object wants")
```

There are other ways to instantiate objects, but this is a convenient way if the object has a `New` constructor.

The working example code

Okay, enough theory. Now you can write some real code. Choose Project➪ Add Class. Name this class `RecipeCollection`. Type the following code into `RecipeCollection`'s code window:

```
Public Class RecipeCollection
    Private myColl As New SortedList

    Public Sub New() 'in a finished app, this constructor
loads the collection from the hard drive
    End Sub

    Public Sub add(ByVal aRecipe As Recipe) ' put a recipe
object into the sorted list
        'use try...catch...finally...end try to deal with
duplicate titles problem on key field in sortedlist.

        Try
            myColl.Add(aRecipe.title, aRecipe) 'this
determines the key (we want a sort on title)
        Catch ex As Exception
            Dim r As String = aRecipe.title & " is already a
title in the collection. This recipe has been renamed " &
aRecipe.title & "2"

            MsgBox(r)
            aRecipe.title &= "2"
            myColl.Add(aRecipe.title, aRecipe)

        End Try

    End Sub

    Public Sub delete(ByVal title As String)
        myColl.Remove(title)
    End Sub

    Public Function SendList() As SortedList
        'return the sorted list
        Return myColl
    End Function

    Public Function sendOneRecipe(ByVal title As String) As
Recipe
        Dim theRecipe As Recipe
        theRecipe - CType(myColl(title), Recipe)
        Return theRecipe
    End Function


End Class
```

First, you declare a new object variable to allow you to use the `SortedList` class. All its Public members are now at your disposal, but you need only the `Add` and `Delete` members in this project. Recall that you can see the members by typing the name of the object variable followed by a period(.) as shown in Figure 4-1.

Figure 4-1:
Good old
Intellisense
shows you
all the public
members
of the
Sorted-
List object.

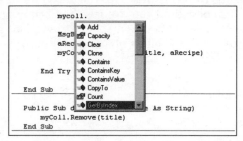

Now back to the `RecipeCollection` class. After creating your `myColl`
`SortedList`, you add a constructor. It's always named `New`, and if you want to
permit outside code to instantiate your object using the constructor, it must
be `Public`. You can create as many different constructors as you wish. They
are overloaded (meaning that they all share the name `New`, but have different
argument lists). Therefore, they offer users various ways to instantiate by
passing different parameters. The `RecipeCollection` in this example simply
offers up an empty constructor, so no parameters are passed to it.

The `Add` method of your collection class accepts a recipe object and stuffs it
into the existing `SortedList`. A `SortedList` permits duplicate values, but
not duplicate keys. The first argument, `aRecipe.title`, accepted by the
`Add` method of the `SortedList` is the key. (The second argument, `aRecipe`,
is an object in this case.) The key object must be unique or an exception
(error) is thrown. I catch any exception here and rename the key to solve
the problem:

```
Public Sub add(ByVal aRecipe As Recipe)

    Try
        myColl.Add(aRecipe.title, aRecipe) 'this
determines the key (we want a sort on title)

    Catch ex As Exception
        Dim r As String = aRecipe.title & " is already a
title in the collection. This recipe has been renamed " &
aRecipe.title & "2"
        MsgBox(r)
        aRecipe.title &= "2"
        myColl.Add(aRecipe.title, aRecipe)
    End Try

End Sub
```

The `Delete` method of your `RecipeCollection` object is simple. It just provides the key to the `SortedList`'s `Remove` method, and the `SortedList`
object handles the job for you. No problems here.

If client code (code outside the class that uses the class) wants to see an individual recipe from the collection, you expose a public method to do that. Notice that this method is defined as a SortedList. That permits you to send a SortedList object to the client. In this program, you simply send the entire SortedList that you named myColl.

```
Public Function SendList() As SortedList
        Return myColl
End Function
```

Finally, clients may want you to send them a single recipe object. How do you do that? Define a method as a Recipe, like this:

```
Public Function sendOneRecipe(ByVal title As String) As
    Recipe
        Dim theRecipe As Recipe
        theRecipe = CType(myColl(title), Recipe)
        Return theRecipe
End Function
```

Memorize this

This code includes a line you should memorize. The CType command is a cast (coercion), which forces one variable type into another. In this case, you are forcing (or casting) the myColl(title) expression into a Recipe object. Note that myColl(title) is a key/value pair from your SortedList.

myColl(title) is *not* merely the title field or merely a title property. When you say myColl(title), you are saying, in effect, "Give me the *pair* represented by this key." In other words, you get back an *object* out of the SortedList, and, here, cast it into a Recipe object type.

If this seems confusing to you, please re-read it and mess around with the code to see what's happening. It's important to understand that you can transform expressions like myColl(title) into objects.

In this example, you could alternatively get a recipe object like this, without casting:

```
Dim theRecipe As Recipe = myColl(title)
```

If you take that approach, you can then leave out the line with CType in it. However, I want to illustrate here the technique of casting. If you ever get an error message relating to casting, you'll know that you should try CType. You can cast an expression into a data type, object, structure, class, or interface.

Creating the Client

Finally, to test any OOP project, you should submit your classes to a client. In this case, you can use the `Form1` class to instantiate and employ your `Recipe` and `RecipeCollection` classes. Click the Form1.vb(Design) tab in the code window; then from the Toolbox put two TextBoxes, a ListBox, and a Button control on your form.

Change TextBox2's `MultiLine` property to `True` in the Properties window. The upper TextBox displays the `Title` property of each recipe object, and the lower TextBox displays the `Text` property of the same recipe object. The ListBox displays all the `Titles` in the entire `RecipeCollection`. The user clicks the ListBox to see a different recipe in the TextBoxes. The user clicks the button to add a recipe to the collection. See Figure 4-2.

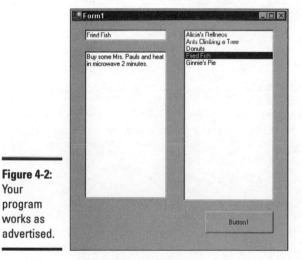

Book VII
Chapter 4

Your First OOP
Project

Figure 4-2:
Your program works as advertised.

Click the Form1.vb tab at the top of the code window, and type the following code into the code window:

```
Imports System.Collections

Public Class Form1
    Inherits System.Windows.Forms.Form

    'make these two objects available to all members of Form1
    class
    Private m_ListToDisplay As SortedList
    Private m_rcoll As RecipeCollection
```

```
 Private Sub Form1_Load(ByVal sender As System.Object,
ByVal e As System.EventArgs) Handles MyBase.Load
     'this "New" instantiates these objects, but since
they are up there in General Dec
     'all the members of this form1 class can use these
objects without having reinstantiate New versions.
     m_ListToDisplay = New SortedList
     m_rcoll = New RecipeCollection

     'these recipes are added out of alphabetical order,
but they are later sorted by the SortedList
     Dim r As New Recipe("Fried Fish", "Buy some Mrs.
Pauls and heat in microwave 2 minutes.")
     m_rcoll.add(r)

     Dim r1 As New Recipe("Donuts", "xBuy some Krispy
Kreme and heat in microwave 10 seconds.")
     m_rcoll.add(r1)

     Dim r2 As New Recipe("Ants Climbing a Tree", "Push
meat to side of pan and fry 2 sliced green onions and 1
t. minced ginger 30 sec.")
     m_rcoll.add(r2)

     Dim r3 As New Recipe("Ginnie's Pie", "Lemon and
meat.")
     m_rcoll.add(r3)

     FillListBox()

 End Sub

 Private Sub FillListBox()
     ListBox1.Items.Clear()
     m_ListToDisplay = m_rcoll.SendList 'get the
collection's list

     Dim i As Integer
     For i = 0 To m_ListToDisplay.Count - 1
         ListBox1.Items.Add(m_ListToDisplay.GetKey(i))
     Next i
 End Sub

 Private Sub ListBox1_SelectedIndexChanged(ByVal sender As
System.Object, ByVal e As System.EventArgs) Handles
ListBox1.SelectedIndexChanged

     Dim title As String = ListBox1.SelectedItem.ToString
     Dim theRecipe As Recipe =
m_rcoll.sendOneRecipe(title)
     TextBox1.Text = theRecipe.title
```

```
        TextBox2.Text = theRecipe.text

    End Sub

Private Sub Button1_Click(ByVal sender As System.Object,
    ByVal e As System.EventArgs) Handles Button1.Click
        'add new recipe

        Dim r As New Recipe("Alicia's Rellneos", "Buy from
    Alicia. Reheat.")
        m_rcoll.add(r) 'add to RecipeCollection
        FillListBox()

    End Sub
End Class
```

Your first job here is to declare a couple of object variables that are declared *outside* any of the procedures here in Form1. These objects, then, are scoped so they are not usable by clients:

```
Private m_ListToDisplay As SortedList
Private m_rcoll As RecipeCollection
```

You declare a `SortedList` object that is to be instantiated in `Form_Load` and later requests, and is passed, the `SortedList` maintained in the `RecipeCollection` class. You also declare an object variable to permit you to instantiate a `RecipeCollection` object here in Form1. This is important to remember: You can separate the declaration of an object from its instantiation — and you must often do it this way. Put the declaration up where it offers you a wider scope; then actually instantiate the object within an initialization procedure (such as `Form_Load`).

Recall that you *can* declare and instantiate an object all at once on the same line, like this:

```
Dim r As New Recipe("Fried Fish", "Buy some Mrs. Pauls and
    heat in microwave 2 minutes.")
```

But this limits this object's scope to the procedure in which it is declared.

Understanding the object reference not set to an instance of an object error

Using the `New` keyword actually creates (instantiates) an object. If you merely declare an object variable, however, an object is *not* created; the object variable contains `null`. Thus, the line `Private m_rcoll As RecipeCollection` simply declares `m_rcoll` as an object variable. It declares what kind of object it's going to be (but isn't yet).

It does not point to any instantiated object. Beginning (and not-so-new) VB.NET programmers find themselves frequently seeing the error message shown in Figure 4-3:

This notorious `NullReferenceException` may be a familiar friend to you. Here's code that triggers this error message when you press F5 to run the following code sample:

```
Public anObj As Object

Private Sub Form1_Load(ByVal sender As System.Object, ByVal e
    As System.EventArgs) Handles MyBase.Load

    MsgBox(anobj.ToString)

End Sub
```

You have declared a variable but have not instantiated the variable. It contains a `null` (nothing), which all object variables automatically contain until you actually assign a value to them. So, you solve the `NullReference` problem by instantiating a real object:

```
anObj = New String("c")
MsgBox(anObj.ToString)
```

Of course, string variables are rarely instantiated this way; it's much simpler to use the shortcut: `Dim MyString As String` (which instantiates the string and fills it with an `""` empty string, rather than a `null`). Likewise, when you declare other simple variables, such as integers, they are instantiated and given default (not `null`) values: `Dim MyInt As Integer` automatically provides this variable with the value 0 (which is quite different from `null`).

Just remember this, a kiss is not a kiss. Whoops. I mean, just remember that when you see the `NullReferenceException` error message, you need to instantiate the object that the object variable references. That usually means using the `New` keyword to bring this object into existence.

In the example program, it's important that the RecipeCollection and SortedList objects be available to several of the procedures here in Form1, so you declare them with a wide scope (by declaring them at the top, outside of any procedure), and then later you instantiate them in the initialization code (whatever event triggers first in the object, such as the Form_Load event). These two objects are instantiated with this code:

```
m_ListToDisplay = New SortedList
m_rcoll = New RecipeCollection
```

After instantiating your RecipeCollection and SortedList objects in the Form_Load event with the New command, you then add four recipe objects to the RecipeCollection object. In a finished application, you stream these objects in from a disk file. But to test this project, you just stuff a few sample recipe objects into the collection.

Then you call the FillListBox procedure:

```
ListBox1.Items.Clear()

m_ListToDisplay = m_rcoll.SendList 'get the collection's list

Dim i As Integer
For i = 0 To m_ListToDisplay.Count - 1
    ListBox1.Items.Add(m_ListToDisplay.GetKey(i))
Next i
```

Two points to notice here: After clearing any previous contents of the ListBox, you use the SendList method of your RecipeCollection class to transfer from that class a SortedList object to the SortedList object (m_ListTo Display) that resides here in your Form1 class.

Again, remember that you can send objects from class to class just as easily as you used to pass variables around in traditional programming.

Next you fill the ListBox with the titles (the various titles in the key array within the SortedList). To get these keys, surprise, you use the SortedList object's GetKey method.

Choosing from a ListBox

To display whatever recipe the user chooses from the ListBox's display of recipe titles, you get the title string (SelectedItem) that he or she clicked, and then you create a recipe object that receives a single recipe from the RecipeCollection (m_rcoll). You use the RecipeCollection's Send OneRecipe method to accomplish this transfer of information. After you have the object, you can display its .Title and .Text properties in the TextBoxes on your form. The following code gives you an example:

```
Dim title As String = ListBox1.SelectedItem.ToString
    Dim theRecipe As Recipe = m_rcoll.sendOneRecipe(title)
    TextBox1.Text = theRecipe.title
    TextBox2.Text = theRecipe.text
```

Adding to the collection

The final job in Form1 is to permit the user to add a new recipe to the
RecipeCollection:

```
Dim r As New Recipe("Alicia's Rellneos", "Buy from Alicia.
    Reheat.") .

m_rcoll.add(r) 'add to RecipeCollection

FillListBox()
```

Here you simulate a new recipe object. In the finished application, the user
types in this information, but you're just testing the Add method now. Then
you pass the Recipe object to the RecipeCollection's Add method for
inclusion in the collection. Then you refresh the ListBox so that it shows the
newly added recipe. This recipe's title begins with the letter A, and it is
properly displayed as the first item in the ListBox. The SortedList object
has done its job of maintaining the alphabetic order of the Recipe objects
that it contains.

Chapter 5: Exploiting the .NET Framework

In This Chapter

✔ Learning more about .NET

✔ Using the .NET Framework

✔ Searching techniques

✔ Employing the Internet

✔ Becoming comfortable with the Framework

✔ Getting help from Help

✔ Working with WinCV

✔ Examining a new class

*T*his chapter gives you some tools to best take advantage of the many built-in capabilities of the VB.NET language. I won't go so far as to call this chapter "The Magic Key to .NET," but it does include some pointers and ideas that I think you can find of value.

You see how to use VB.NET Help efficiently, how to find useful answers on the Internet when you are stumped, how to see entire classes laid out in the WinCV utility, and how to choose the best strategy when trying to understand new classes.

I wrestled with the idea of putting this chapter at the very start of the book, but I decided that it should probably appear only *after* you understand the OOP concepts explained in Book VII. In the past few chapters, you learned the fundamentals of OOP. Now you're better prepared to explore and exploit the huge collections of classes that make up the .NET framework.

Some of the examples and figures in this chapter may differ a bit from the results you get in your version of VB.NET when you try the techniques described here. I'm using VB.NET 2003, the latest version. If you have not upgraded and are using the first version of VB.NET, you can still use these techniques, but your results will differ in minor ways from those of people using VB.NET 2003. Most noticeable is the fact that VB.NET 2003 has a more complete Help system, with more frequent, less buggy, source code examples. In tips here and there in this chapter, I explain how results can differ for users of the older version of VB.NET.

Errors Can Trap You

Wrestling with the framework is no easy task at first. You sometimes find yourself getting inexplicable error messages when you try to use the classes in the VB.NET framework. For example, you can violate the many *scoping* rules imposed by OOP in countless ways. Here are two examples:

```
Error #97: Cannot call friend function on object that is not
    an instance of defining class.
```

```
Error #98: A property or method call cannot include a
    reference to a private object, either as an argument or
    as a return value.
```

Or you may get tripped up when trying to turn one kind of variable into another (usually trying to turn a numeric type into a string): `Wrong cast (data type conversion fails)`.

Related to conversion problems is the fact that some objects provide you with strings and other data directly — or at least you can use the `.ToString` method to convert the data. Other objects contain internal objects of their own or require that you query an `Item` or `Value` property to get at the data inside. To figure out how to use .NET Framework objects, you have to pay attention to how their classes are defined.

There are many possibilities for failure, but once you grasp some OOP and .NET fundamentals, your success rate ramps up and you feel happier and more comfortable in this huge collection of functions. You may find yourself even becoming far too happy, like the local TV weatherwoman. But even giddiness is better than the alternative gloom, right?

How to Use the .NET Framework

VB.NET Help has been getting stronger over the years. At first, it offered few code examples, but now it includes far more. Help also displays a brief description of a class along with the syntax you use to employ that class.

Here's a typical scenario: You want to offer the user of your project the ability to search a TextBox for a given word or phrase. Does the TextBox class have a search capability built-in?

Start a new VB.NET Windows-style project, put a TextBox on a form, and then choose Help⇨Index.

Type **textbox** in the Look for field of the Help dialog box, as shown in Figure 5-1.

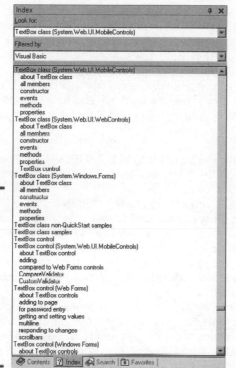

Figure 5-1:
Begin your
search for
help by
ensuring
that you're
looking at
the correct
Windows
or Web
version.

Users of the older version of VB.NET will see *TextBox Control (Web Forms)*
here because the MobileControls TextBox had not yet been added to
VB.NET in the older version.

As Figure 5-1 illustrates, often multiple classes are related to your search
term. In this case, you want the *Windows* style TextBox, but the first TextBox
class displayed in the Help window is a `System.Web` mobile version. Locate
TextBox Class (System.Windows.Forms), and click the *about* TextBox class.
The *about* entry gives you a general overview of a class, including some of
its more useful members (and it is available only in VB.NET 2003).

Always use all lowercase letters when searching for help. The Visual Studio
IDE isn't case-sensitive — it always assumes lowercase. However, many
other help engines *are* case-sensitive, and so are Internet searches.

Unfortunately, there's no mention in the *about* section describing the TextBox
of a search method. Click the *methods* entry in the left pane. Scroll the right
pane to see all the public methods you can use with a TextBox. Again, no
search feature.

At this point, you hum to yourself, perhaps even swaying a little back and forth in your chair. A TextBox's `Text` property is just one long string, so you should be able to search it using a `String` search method. In VB 6 and earlier, you used the `InStr` function. But what's available here in .NET?

You can find the answer most quickly by searching this book's Dictionary of VB 6/VB.NET Equivalents, found on this book's Web Site at `dummies.com/extras`. Just search for *InStr*. You can also find this appendix at the back of this book.

Or you can type `instr` into the Look for field in VB.NET Help. This returns a couple of results. (Users of the older version of VB.NET see only one result.)

The second result, InStr, tells you how to use the traditional InStr function, but also reminds you that you must use the backward-compatibility namespace to use this function: `Imports Microsoft.VisualBasic`. You don't want to be *backward*. You're supposed to be moving forward into .NET. The old functions won't all necessarily always be available in the years to come. Plus, .NET is generally faster and more flexible than the old-style way of doing things.

At the bottom of the InStr entry in Help are some suggested "See Also" entries. Click the general topic *String Manipulation*. You find a discussion of various .NET methods. Scroll down until you locate the section titled "Searching for Strings Within Your Strings." This sounds useful! The first example describes searching for a character, but the second is exactly what you want: an overloaded method (it does more than one kind of search). Double-click the *String.IndexOf Method* link in this Help window to get to that method's description, as shown in Figure 5-2. (Users of the older version of VB.NET won't see a result as complete as the one shown in Figure 5-2, which displays various languages' syntax.)

Figure 5-2:
Narrowing your search, you find the IndexOf method.

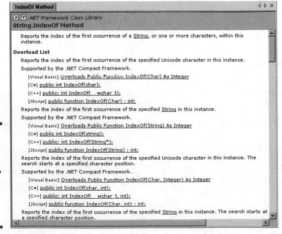

The Overload list displayed for the `IndexOf` method shows you several alternative string search methods available: by character, by string, starting searches from an index location within the target string, and searching only a substring in the target. Wow.

All you need for this job is to look for the first instance of the search string. Scroll to the bottom of the pane shown in Figure 5-2 to see sample code. Sample code is often the best way to find out the required syntax and punctuation for a command.

However, don't be confused by some of the strange punctuation and other odd qualities of this and many other examples you find in Help. Although nominally Visual Basic source code, some Help examples contain strange features. They generally *do* run in VB.NET, but they are somewhat alien in several particulars, as you can see in this sample code:

```
Imports System
Class Sample

    Public Shared Sub Main()

        Dim br1 As String = "0----+----1----+----2----+----3---
-+----4---+----5----+----6----+-"
        Dim br2 As String =
"0123456789012345678901234567890123456789012345678901234567890123456"
67890123456"
        Dim str As String = "Now is the time for all good men
to come to the aid of their party."
        Dim start As Integer
        Dim at As Integer
        Dim [end] As Integer
        Dim count As Integer

        [end] = str.Length
        start = [end] / 2
        Console.WriteLine()
        Console.WriteLine("All occurences of 'he' from position
{0} to {1}.", start, [end] - 1)
        Console.WriteLine("{1}{0}{2}{0}{3}{0}",
Environment.NewLine, br1, br2, str)
        Console.Write("The string 'he' occurs at position(s):
")

        count = 0
        at = 0
        While start <= [end] AndAlso at > - 1
            ' start+count must be a position within -str-.
            count = [end] - start
            at = str.IndexOf("he", start, count)
            If at = - 1 Then
```

```
            Exit While
          End If
          Console.Write("{0} ", at)
          start = at + 1
        End While
        Console.WriteLine()
    End Sub 'Main
End Class 'Sample
```

In this case, the example code was written by a C programmer. There are several giveaways. First is the use of `Sub Main`, which Visual Basic programmers almost never use. `Sub Main` is the equivalent of `Form_Load`, but is employed by programmers using languages that are not form-based. There is no default `Form1` in C, so C programmers are accustomed to starting their programs in `Sub Main` (which is where they put initialization code, and also where they test short code samples).

Another giveaway is the line `Imports System`. VB.NET programmers know that by default the `System` namespace is always available and need not be imported. Also, VB.NET programmers do not use the brace `{}` symbols to fill in fields when displaying results, nor do we use the word `end` as a variable name, requiring that it be enclosed in brackets `[]`. In fact, until VB.NET, the Visual Basic language didn't even permit the use of braces, semicolons, or brackets. Blessed simplicity, including the avoidance of extraneous junk punctuation, has always been the hallmark of Visual Basic.

In any case, you can quickly eliminate the C-flavored elements from example code, as long as you recognize them for what they are. Here's a simplified, and pure-VB.NET, translation of this same sample:

```
Private Sub Form1_Load(ByVal sender As System.Object, ByVal e
    As System.EventArgs) Handles MyBase.Load

    Dim s As String = "Now is the time for all good men
  to come to the aid of their party."
    Dim found As Integer = s.IndexOf("men")
    Console.Write(found)
End Sub
```

Class.Member Pair Searches

Try typing some `class.member` pairs. That's a good way to narrow down a search. For example, in the Help index *Look for* field, type `String.search`. No matches, as you suspected. There is no search method for the `String` object. How about `TextBox.Search`? Nope. How about `RichTextBox.Search`? No. Try `RichTextBox.Find`. Zowie! You struck gold. (Only VB.NET 2003 users see all the results.) Double-click the `RichTextBox.Find` item in the left pane of the Help window, and you see a heavily overloaded `Find` method and an excellent piece of sample code showing how it can be used.

+ Searches

This section covers several techniques that many programmers don't know about, but that can really narrow down a search. As you've doubtless discovered, clicking the Search tab at the bottom of the Help dialog box allows you to conduct a deep search. Where the Index only provides a search of major topics (titles of the help "articles"), the Search utility looks through the titles and the article text for *every* occurrence. It usually returns the maximum results: 500, which isn't too helpful. Suddenly, you're like Scarlet on the porch at Tara: *way* too many candidates.

For example, click the Search tab and then type **search** in the *Look for* field. Click the Search button, and you get 500 hits. So does **Search for string**. To require that the exact phrase be found (all words in their exact order), put quotes around it: **"Search for string"**. This produces 72 topics, which is still too many. (72 topics for VB.NET 2003 users; people using the older version of VB.NET get only 16 topics.)

Textbox search (without quotes) produces 15 (or 6 in the older version of VB.NET), which is a more useful list.

Scroll down the results topic until you locate the `TextBoxBase.Select Method` (VB.NET 2003 only).

Double-click it. The example code for this one is quite good. It demonstrates how to highlight a search hit within the text.

If you want to make the search utility show you only help pages that contain both the word *textbox* and *search*, put a + in front of the words: *+textbox +search*. You can also use *textbox OR search*. Or *textbox AND search*.

Never Forget the Internet

Yes, .NET is vast and, especially when you first work with it, complex. Nonetheless, you have important resources at your disposal. Always remember that the .NET programming community is huge and is growing daily. If you find yourself confused — and this or other books' indexes don't lead you to the answer you're looking for — you always have the Internet: the greatest research engine ever invented.

If VB.NET Help doesn't give you the results you're looking for, experts out on the Web are often quite willing to tell you the solution to your problem.

Searching newsgroups the efficient way

Your first stop on the Internet is Google Groups (`www.google.com/grphp`). This justly famous search engine now gives you ranked results instantly from all the Web newsgroups. Try looking in Groups for *search a textbox,* and you'll likely see a couple of useful code examples in the hits on just the first page. And remember that sometimes it's best to further narrow your search. If *search a textbox* gets 10,900 hits, you can narrow the hits considerably by looking for *search a textbox VB.NET.*

Don't ignore Google

Also take note of the newsgroup links shown at the bottom of each hit in Google Groups. Some of those newsgroups should perhaps be added to your copy of Outlook Express (Tools⇨Newsgroups — search in "newsgroups which contain" for *microsoft public dotnet* or *vb* or *lang basic*). Groups such as `microsoft.public.dotnet.languages.vb` and `comp.lang.basic.visual.misc` are the places to go with questions that experts may respond to. And don't be shy about posting a message to these groups if you can't find an answer to your question or if you know the answer to someone else's query.

Check out Safari

Publisher O'Reilly offers an online subscription to multiple reference books (at `Safari.Com`). This searchable online virtual library can be a help, particularly if you're working in esoteric areas of .NET, such as the security namespaces.

Observing the Framework

You find yourself trying to figure out how to accomplish something in VB.NET, and you wonder where, within the millions of possible .NET syntaxes, the answer lies.

Fortunately, the .NET Framework is hierarchical; it's organized so that you can go from general namespaces to classes to individual methods, and then go down into those method's various overloaded arguments.

Start with Help

So, if you're working with a project that requires file I/O. You can start looking in Help. Open VB.NET Help and click the Contents tab at the bottom of the Help left pane; then open the following subitems in the left pane: Visual Studio .NET⇨.NET Framework⇨Reference⇨Class Library.

You must be using the full-window, external version of VB.NET Help to see the Contents tab described in the preceding paragraph. Your VB.NET Help screen may appear within your IDE, rather than as the separate window shown in Figure 5-3. I prefer the separate window because you get more information at your fingertips all at once. To change from the internal (docked) version to the external Help window, choose Tools⇨Options. Then under the Environment folder in the left pane, choose Help. Click the External help option button.

Users of the older version of VB.NET may not be able to choose Visual Studio .NET⇨.NET Framework⇨Reference⇨Class Library. You may not have a *.NET Framework* subtree. Instead, you see Introducing Visual Studio .NET, Getting Assistance, Samples and Walkthroughs, Developing with Visual Studio .NET, and Visual Basic and Visual C#.

You now see a list of all the major, top-level categories. Most of them are in the System assembly, so when you import one of their namespaces, you begin with the word System. (as in Imports System.Data). See Figure 5-3.

Book VII Chapter 5

Exploiting the .NET Framework

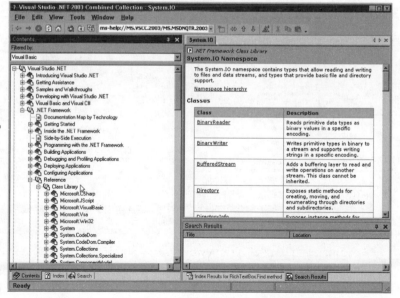

Figure 5-3: Here's a great place to start a search of the .NET Framework, in Help's Reference book.

The location shown in Figure 5-3 is so important that you may want to bookmark it for future reference. Click the icon (with the file folder and small +) on the right side of the toolbar at the top of the Help window. Now add this location to your Favorites, so that you can return here whenever you aren't sure which namespace to look in for a particular task. Click any of the `System.` namespaces listed beneath Reference⇨Class Library in Figure 5-3, and the right pane displays a brief summary of what category of jobs that namespace does. For example, `Drawing.Text` is described like this:

> *The System.Drawing.Text namespace provides advanced GDI+ typography functionality. Basic graphics functionality is provided by the namespace. The classes in this namespace allow users to create and use collections of fonts.*

You want to find how to do file I/O, so scroll down until you locate `System.IO`. Click the + to open `System.IO`, and then locate the File class under the `System.IO` node, as shown in Figure 5-4.

Figure 5-4:
Now you can see the various file management methods and links to examples of how to write code for them.

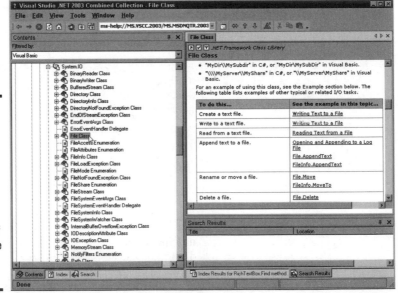

Although the .NET Framework is huge — bigger than the traditional VB runtime by far — it is manageable because it is largely consistent. Once you learn the ropes, you can handle most classes the same way.

Trying WinCV

Another excellent tool can assist you in navigating and exploiting the classes in the .NET Framework. Help is a big help, of course, but now consider this additional utility: WinCV.

Installing WinCV

.NET includes a great utility called WinCV (for Windows Class Viewer). You can use this great tool to see *all* the details about a class in the .NET Framework, as shown in Figure 5-5.

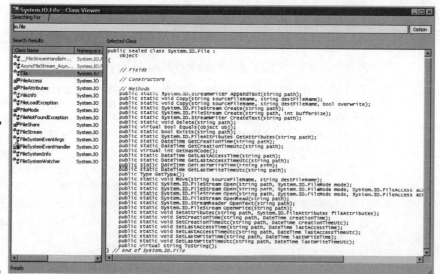

Figure 5-5:
Use the WinCV utility to get a detailed report on any class in the Framework.

Before going any farther, add this useful tool to your IDE. Microsoft includes many utilities in the Tools menu (and other menus) of the IDE by default, but it includes other tools you may like using. You can add favorite utilities to your IDE's Tool menu by hand. Right now, you want to add the WinCV utility, so follow these steps:

1. **Choose Tools⇨External Tools.**

You see the External Tools dialog box, as shown in Figure 5-6. (With your version of VB.NET, you may see a list of external tools that differs from those shown in Figure 5-6.).

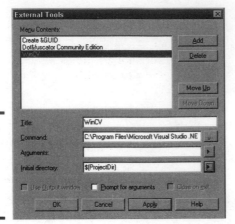

Figure 5-6:
Use this
dialog box
to add
utilities to
your editor.

2. **Type** WinCV **into the Title field, as shown in Figure 5-6.**

3. **Click the ellipsis ... button next to the Command field and locate WinCV.exe on your hard drive. It is in the path** `C:\Program Files\ Microsoft Visual Studio .NET 2003\SDK\v1.1\Bin\WinCV.exe`. **You must double-click WinCV.exe (or single-click it, and then click Open) before going to the next step.**

   (Your path may be `.NET 2002` if you've not upgraded to the latest version of Visual Studio .NET. Or your path may be `C:\program files\Microsoft visual Studio .NET\FrameworkSDK\Bin`.)

4. **Finally, choose Project Directory in the Initial Directory field (click the button with the right-arrow icon).**

5. **Click OK.**

   The dialog window closes and you now have WinCV on your Tools menu. Note that this is not the same tool as the Class View built into the View menu of VB.NET. That's also a useful tool, but it resembles Solution Explorer: It only shows the classes and members which are instantiated in your project, not details about .NET Framework classes.

Using WinCV

Now use WinCV to take a gander at the entire `File` class. You see all the methods lined up, in all their overloaded glory, and you see the variable types that they take as arguments. Just type **io.** (don't omit the period at the end), or better, type **io.file.** (You can leave off the *system* if you wish, because VB assumes it.) Refer to Figure 5-5 for an example of what you see.

When looking for a way to read and write files, you can simply type in the word **file** and scroll down the list that WinCV offers. However, it's helpful to know that typing **io** provides a more useful list of results. I mentioned the following point earlier, but it deserves repeating: Click any of the System. namespaces listed beneath Reference⇨Class Library (refer to Figure 5-3) and you see in the right pane a brief summary of the category of jobs that namespace performs. That location in Help can often be your starting point, showing you what to type into WinCV.

What's Void?

You may wonder what some of those methods shown in Figure 5-5 mean when declared Void. If you see Public Static Void, don't be alarmed. Void is just C# code that means "nothing is returned from this operation" (so it's like a Sub, where you need not provide a variable that accepts some returned value). A Void method requires less code because nothing is returned:

```
public static void Delete(string path)
```

The preceding code translates into this:

```
File.Delete("C:\Ftest.Txt")
```

How to Understand a New Class

You want to create a new file on your hard drive. You look in Help under the Reference⇨Class Library (refer to Figure 5-3) and locate *System.io*. So in WinCV, you type **system.io.** or just **io.** (with the dot). Following dozens of other items, you find the *File* entry displayed in the list of classes in WinCV.

This entry begins with these lines, which are very useful if you know how to interpret them:

```
// from module
    'c:\windows\microsoft.net\framework\v1.1.4322\mscorlib.dl
    l'
public sealed class System.IO.File :
    object
{
    // Fields

    // Constructors

    // Methods
    public static System.IO.StreamWriter AppendText(string
    path);
    public static void Copy(string sourceFileName, string
    destFileName);
```

```
public static void Copy(string sourceFileName, string
destFileName, bool overwrite);
 public static System.IO.FileStream Create(string path);
 public static System.IO.FileStream Create(string path,
int bufferSize);
 public static System.IO.StreamWriter CreateText(string
path);
 public static void Delete(string path);
```

First, notice that this class is `public` but `sealed`. *Sealed* means that you can't inherit this class, so that's not a technique you can use to borrow the methods of the file class. (Also, if you're interested, a class declaration followed by a colon tells you what the class is inherited from. In this case: `Object`.)

Because it is `public`, this class can be used by your VB.NET programming. Any of its methods marked `public` can be used. It does not contain any fields (private variables) nor any constructors. Without constructors, you can't use the `New` keyword to instantiate this class. Not to worry, though, when a method is declared `Static`, that means it can be used by any location in your project — it has great scope. All you have to do to use any of these `File.methods` is to add the `Imports`.

Now look at the line (the *signature*) that creates a file. Pay close attention to the various elements of this line:

```
public static System.IO.FileStream Create(string path);
```

This line (and the first line at the top of the WinCV window) tells you that a `FileStream` object is created when you use the `File` class. The `Create` method specifies how you write the source code to accomplish this job. It's public (you can use it) and static (you just use it as-is, without instantiating it). You just declare it.

Because it returns a variable of the `System.IO.FileStream` type, you must first create a variable of the `FileStream` type and then assign the return value of the `Create` method to this `FileStream` variable:

```
Dim fStream as FileStream = File.Create ....
```

To complete this line, you have to fill in (`string path`). This means that you must provide a string literal (or variable) that contains the path on the hard drive where you want the file to go:

```
Dim fStream as FileStream = File.Create ("C:\Ftest.Txt")
```

Now to try it out in code. Start by looking at the very top of the right pane in WinCV to get the namespace and object:

```
public sealed class System.IO.File :
```

So, first type `Imports System.IO` at the top of your code window to bring in the correct namespace. The object you are working with is `File`. Now, in the `Form_Load` event, type your line of code that creates a `FileStream`:

```
Dim fStream as FileStream = File.Create ("C:\Ftest.Txt")
```

Now that you have your `fStream` object, you can do things with it. What things? Use its methods. What methods? Rely on old Intellisense in the IDE to list and even describe them for you. Type the following in `Form_Load` just below the previous line of code:

```
With fStream
```

Then press Enter and the following line is added automatically:

```
End With
```

Now, between the `With` and `End With`, type a single period (.), as shown in Figure 5-7 (after you scroll down a bit).

Figure 5-7:
Intellisense
pops out
with its
list of
FileStream
members.

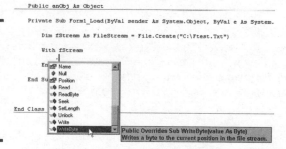

Click any of the members in the list shown in Figure 5-7 to see a description of that member's behavior.

Now complete this code by filling in some methods:

```
With fStream
        .WriteByte(65)
        .Close()
End With
```

Press F5, and then look on your hard drive for this file and double-click the filename. Notepad pops open, and you can see that byte 65 (the code for the letter A) has been stored here. And you did this entire job by decoding the class descriptions. Congratulations. The .NET Framework begins to open up for you. (If you want to save entire strings to a new file, look at the `File.CreateText` method. The `StreamWriter` object that you can use there has a `WriteLine` method to save entire strings, rather than single bytes, to a file.

The main point to remember here is that you now know how to translate the following line from WinCV:

```
public static System.IO.FileStream Create(string path);
```

You now know how to translate that line of code into the following usable line of VB.NET code:

```
Dim fStream As FileStream = File.Create("C:\Ftest.Txt")
```

Figure 5-8 graphically illustrates how to transform WinCV class listings into usable VB.NET source code.

Figure 5-8: These lines show you what goes where when you transform a class listing into working VB.NET source code.

```
public sealed class System.IO.File :
    object
{

    // Fields

    // Constructors

    // Methods


    public static System.IO.FileStream Create(string path);


Imports System.IO

Dim fStream As FileStream = File.Create("C:\Ftest.Txt")
```

Are you wondering why the code and pseudo-code listings in WinCV (and often in Help, for that matter) look so peculiar? What are those braces for? And why end every line with a semicolon? It's the influence of C. That language is the native language and generally the preferred language of people who write computer languages. So, when asked to document the language for VB.NET users (in Help or WinCV), these people often revert to their

C practices. In fact, WinCV is written in C#, an attempt to create a language with less confusing syntax than C itself. If you know VB, C# is actually pretty easy to pick up (as is Java). In fact, there's an online utility that translates C# source code into VB.NET code for you. Take a look at `www.kamalpatel.net/ConvertCSharp2VB.aspx`. With the Internet, the best advice is: Search and ye shall find.

Perhaps C# and Java are annoying to VB programmers in some ways (such as their reverse Polish syntax, all those unnecessary semicolons stuck around everywhere, and so on), but .NET represents a great coming-together of all computer languages, and what you are losing in simplicity, you are gaining in power. No longer does the VB.NET programmer have to consider his language in any way inferior to the capabilities offered by other languages. And, for people who write computer *programs* (as opposed to writing computer *languages*), VB.NET will doubtless prove by far the most popular language — as VB has for the last 12 years.

I have to confess that I envy people who are just starting on their voyage of discovery, either learning VB.NET as their first language or making the transition from other languages to VB.NET. (I consider earlier versions of VB to be in that category of "other languages.")

I envy you because I've made this transition myself, and it's rather like getting your first bicycle. Your early attempts are wobbly at best, and you're bound to fall now and then. But as time goes on, you realize that you have much more freedom than you had before, and that a big and very interesting world is out there for you to explore.

**Book VII
Chapter 5**

Exploiting the .NET Framework

Appendix: A Dictionary of VB.NET

Both experienced Visual Basic programmers and those new to the language can make good use of this appendix.

Showing Traditional VB Commands and Their .NET Equivalents

This appendix — which is the size of a small book — contains an alphabetized list of VB.NET features, including new techniques, differences between VB 6 (and earlier versions) and VB.NET, and the best ways to use VB.NET. I wrote this appendix during the past 18 months while I was learning VB.NET. I knew traditional VB quite well, but making the adjustment to VB.NET took time. VB.NET has many new features, and some of them take getting used to (such as streaming I/O, printing, file access, and so on). But VB.NET gives you much greater, finer control. After you get to know VB.NET capabilities (such as the `ArrayList`), you see how they are superior to traditional VB features.

Throughout this appendix, you can find code examples that you can try out to get a deeper understanding of the many facets of VB.NET.

VB.NET 2003

Tip: If you have upgraded to VB.NET 2003, you will find that there are only two significant changes to the language in this version: the bit shifting operators << and >> have been added, and you can initialize a loop counter. You can declare a loop counter variable within the line that starts the loop, like this:

```
For i As Integer = 0 To 10
```

instead of the traditional style:

```
Dim i as Integer
For i = 0 To 10
```

However, the VB.NET 2003 Help system is significantly improved, offering many more tested, working code samples, and additional narrative descriptions showing you how to accomplish various jobs. The IDE is also better, particularly because it now separates procedures and other zones visually with a thin, gray line. This makes it easier to scroll through your source code and locate what you're looking for.

Using Classic Functions

Many classic VB built-in functions are still available in VB.NET, held in *wrappers*. Generally, there is no difference between the classic function's behavior and the new .NET wrapper version. For example, if you want to convert a variable to a string-type variable, you can either use the classic `CStr` function or the new VB.NET `ToString` method.

The VB.NET equivalents of these legacy wrappers, though, are generally *methods*. For instance, the classic VB `LEN` function tells you how long a string variable is: `Len(string)`.

But in VB.NET, the optional replacement is the `Length` method of the string object: `string.Length`.

For the VB.NET equivalents of all the string functions (`Mid`, `Instr`, and so on), see "String Functions Are Now Methods" in this appendix.

Sometimes, if you want to use a classic function, you must add this line at the very top of your code window:

```
Imports Microsoft.VisualBasic
```

This is the *compatibility namespace,* and it includes many traditional VB commands. However, this namespace isn't required when you use wrapped functions such as `Len`. (See "Imports" in this appendix.) The main point is that if you try to use a classic function and you get an error message from VB.NET, you should add the `Imports` line to see whether that cures the problem.

To see the classic VB commands, press F2 in the VB.NET editor to open the Object Browser utility. You may have to press Ctrl+Alt+J instead.

Click the + next to Microsoft Visual Basic .NET Runtime to open its tree list, and then click the + next to Microsoft Visual Basic to open its list of general categories. Keep drilling down in these tree lists until you locate the classic VB command that you are interested in. Then click the Member in the right pane of the Object browser to see the proper syntax. For example, if you click the `FileSystem` object in the left pane and then click the `CurDir` member in the right pane, you see this syntax:

```
Public Shared Function CurDir() As String
     Member of Microsoft.VisualBasic.FileSystem
```

With this syntax, you can then extrapolate the actual code that you would need to write to find out the current directory (CurDir's job):

```
Private Sub Form1_Load(ByVal sender As System.Object, ByVal e
    As System.EventArgs) Handles MyBase.Load

        Dim s As String
        s = CurDir()
        MsgBox(s)

End Sub
```

Run this code, and VB.NET will display the current directory.

+= (See "Optional Operation Shorthand")

AND, OR, XOR, and NOT

Before VB.NET

AND, OR, NOT, and XOR work on the bit level.

VB.NET

Early in the development of VB.NET, there were plans to make the commands And, Or, Not, and XOr logical rather than bitwise operators. The plan was to include a new set of operators to deal with bitwise operations. This plan was abandoned and these four operators now work the same way that they always have within VB. Traditional operator precedence is also retained.

Two new operators, AndAlso and OrElse, can be used if you need to make a logical comparison. (These new operators work only on Boolean types.)

These four operators now are "overloaded," which means they can work both ways, depending on the parameters passed to them. They perform a logical exclusion operation if you pass two Boolean expressions, or a bitwise exclusion if you pass two numeric expressions.

Traditional operator precedence is also retained.

If you are using VB.NET 2003, bit shifting operators have been added to the language: << and >>.

App Object

In traditional VB, you could use the App object to find out information about the currently running app, such as App.EXEName. However, in VB.NET, you get the .exe name this way:

```
Dim s As String
s = Environment.CommandLine 'running program
MsgBox (s)
```

For additional data that you can get from the Environment object, see "Directory (Current)."

Array Declarations

Other .NET languages declare array sizes differently than VB. In other languages, the following declaration results in an array with 10 elements indexed from X(0) up to X(9):

```
Dim X(10)
```

In other words, the number in parentheses describes the total number of elements in the array.

However, that same line of code in VB has always resulted in an array with 11 elements indexed from X(0) up to X(10). In traditional VB, the number in parentheses represents the highest index number that can be used with this array, not the total number of elements.

Early in the development of the .NET languages, VB.NET was going to be made to conform to the rest of the .NET languages in this issue, but that attempt was abandoned. VB.NET will retain the traditional VB approach to array declaration. For more on this topic, see "Zero Index Controversy" and the various source code examples where the Dim command is used.

For information on how you can simultaneously declare and initialize an array, see "Dim and ReDim: New Rules."

Array Dimensioning Changes

See "Zero Index Controversy."

Array of Objects

In VB.NET, you can create an array of objects. The trick is to first declare an array object variable and then instantiate each object in the array. The following example illustrates how to create an array of seven objects:

```
Public Class Form1

    Inherits System.Windows.Forms.Form
```

```
(Windows Form Designer generated code)

Dim arrRecipe(6) As recipe 'create the array object variable

Private Sub Form1_Load(ByVal sender As System.Object, ByVal e
    As System.EventArgs) Handles MyBase.Load

    Dim i As Integer

    'instantiate each member of the array:
        For i = 0 To 6
            arrRecipe(i) = New recipe()
        Next

' set the two properties of one of the array members
        arrRecipe(0).Title = "MyZeroth"
        arrRecipe(0).Description = "MyZeroth recipe goes like
    this"


    End Sub
End Class

Public Class recipe
    Private _Title As String
    Private _Description As String

    Public Property Title() As String
        Get
            Return _Title
        End Get
        Set(ByVal Value As String)
            _Title = Value
        End Set
    End Property

    Public Property Description() As String
        Get
            Return _Description
        End Get
        Set(ByVal Value As String)
            _Description = Value
        End Set
    End Property

End Class
```

ArrayList (Replacing the Array Command)

The new VB.NET `ArrayList` is a powerful tool. Familiarize yourself with it if you expect to ever need to manipulate arrays in your programming, and you want to take advantage of the many features of this new object. For one thing, it can dynamically resize itself, so you don't have to resort to `ReDim` and other tortured techniques.

Before VB.NET

No real equivalent of the `ArrayList` existed before VB.NET, but there was the rather simple `Array`.

For most of the 10-year VB history, there was no function that created an array and then allowed you to add some data to it during runtime. Then, in VB 6, the `Array` function was added to do just that. (Those of you familiar with early, 1980s forms of Basic will recall the similar `DATA` statement that was used to insert items of data into an executing program.)

You could use the `Array` command in VB 6 to stuff some data into an array, like this:

```
Private Sub Form_Load()

Arx = Array("key", "Name", "Address")
MsgBox (Arx(2))

End Sub
```

VB.NET

The `Array` function has been deleted from the language, presumably because it returns a variant variable type, and variants are disallowed in the .NET framework.

The new `ArrayList` object, however, does what the `Array` function used to do, and much, much more.

Here's a VB.NET equivalent to the old `Array` command:

```
Dim MyArray as new ArrayList

myArray.Add ("key")
myArray.Add ("Name")
myArray.Add ("Address")
Msgbox (MyArray(2))
```

You can also stuff data into an array during its declaration using the following strange method in VB.NET:

```
Dim Month() As Integer = {1, 2, 3, 4, 5, 6, 7, 8, 9, 10, 11, 12}

msgbox(month(4))
```

Running this code results in a messagebox displaying 5 (the "fourth" index item in the array, because arrays start with a 0 index).

This is strange code because Visual Basic has never in its history used the brace characters { and }. The C languages, of course, use braces everywhere.

The ArrayList powerhouse

But back to our regular programming. The new `ArrayList` is excellent.

To see it in action, start a new VB.NET Windows-style project and put a ListBox on the form. Then add four buttons to the form, as well. Each button will do a different `ArrayList` trick.

First, create a variable (shown in bold) near the top of the form:

```
Public Class Form1
    Inherits System.Windows.Forms.Form

    Dim arrList As New ArrayList()
```

Then type in the following procedures:

```
    Public Function addOne() As String

        ListBox1.Items.Clear()
        ListBox1.Items.AddRange(arrList.ToArray)
        Me.Text = arrList.Count.ToString

    End Function


Private Sub Button1_Click(ByVal sender As System.Object,
    ByVal e As System.EventArgs) Handles Button1.Click
        Dim s As String = InputBox("Please type something")
        If s <> "" Then
            arrList.Add(s)
            addOne()
        End If
    End Sub
```

```
Private Sub Button2_Click(ByVal sender As System.Object,
ByVal e As System.EventArgs) Handles Button2.Click
    arrList = ArrayList.Repeat("Sandy", 12)
    addOne()
End Sub

Private Sub Button3_Click(ByVal sender As System.Object,
ByVal e As System.EventArgs) Handles Button3.Click

    arrList.Reverse()
    addOne()
End Sub

Private Sub Button4_Click(ByVal sender As System.Object,
ByVal e As System.EventArgs) Handles Button4.Click

    Dim s As String = InputBox("Search ArrayList for
...?")

    If arrList.Contains(s) Then
        MsgBox("Yes, " + s + " was in the array list.")
    End If
        End Sub
```

The first function clears out the ListBox, displays the array in the ListBox, and then displays the count (the total number of items in the ArrayList) in the title bar of the form.

When you run this program, Button1 illustrates how to add a single item to an ArrayList. Button2 shows how to fill an ArrayList with any number of duplicate objects. Button3 reverses the order of the objects in the ArrayList, and Button4 searches the ArrayList.

An ArrayList can do many more things. Search Help for ArrayList to see all of its methods and properties.

Array Search and Sort Methods

You can now have arrays search themselves or sort themselves. Here's an example showing how to use both the sort and search methods of the array object. The syntax for these two methods is as follows:

```
Array.Sort(myArray)
```

And:

```
anIndex = Array.BinarySearch(myArray, "trim")
```

To see this feature in action, put a Button and a TextBox control on a form, and change the TextBox's `MultiLine` property to `True`:

```
Private Sub Button1_Click(ByVal sender As System.Object,
    ByVal e As System.EventArgs) Handles Button2.Click

        Dim myarray(3) As String

        myArray.SetValue("zoo", 0)
        myArray.SetValue("brief", 1)
        myArray.SetValue("area", 2)
        myArray.SetValue("trim", 3)

        Dim x As String
        Dim show As String

        x - chr(13) & chr(10)

        Dim i As Integer

        For i = 0 To 3
            show = show & myarray(i) & x

        Next

        textbox1.text = show & x & x & "SORTED:" & x

        Array.Sort(myArray)

        show = ""
        For i = 0 To 3

            show = show & myarray(i) & x

        Next

        textbox1.text = textbox1.text & show

        Dim anIndex As Integer

        anIndex = Array.BinarySearch(myArray, "trim")
        show = CStr(anIndex)
        msgbox("The word trim was found at the " & show & "
    index within the array")


    End Sub
```

Of course, like most objects in VB.NET, the array object has many members. In addition to the common properties and methods that most objects have (such as ToString), there are several members unique to the array class (reverse, GetUpperBound, and so on). To see all the capabilities of the array class, search for Array members in the VB Help feature. Here is a list of all the members of the array class: `IsFixedSize` , `IsReadOnly` , `IsSynchronized` , `Length` , `LongLength`, `Rank` (the number of dimensions), `SyncRoot` , `BinarySearch` , `Clear` , `Clone` , `Copy` , `CopyTo` , `CreateInstance` , `Equals` , `GetEnumerator` , `GetHashCode` , `GetLength` , `GetLongLength`, `GetLowerBound` , `GetType` , `GetUpperBound` , `GetValue` , `IndexOf` , `Initialize` , `LastIndexOf` , `Reverse` , `SetValue` , `Sort` , and `ToString`.

Auto List Members

The Auto List Members feature, which shows you a list of all the methods and properties of an object, has become essential in VB.NET.

If you do not see certain events or other members automatically listed — such as when you're creating a new UserControl — go to Tools⇨Options⇨ Text Editor⇨Basic⇨General, and deselect Hide Advanced Members.

AutoRedraw Is Gone

In previous versions of VB, you could force drawn (or printed) content on a form to persist (to remain visible even after the form was minimized and restored or temporarily covered by another window). You set the `AutoRedraw` property to `True`. This property is unavailable in VB.NET. Alternatively, you could put code in the `Paint` event that would redraw your content each time the background was repainted.

Here's one way to make drawn content persist in VB.NET. Create a sub like this that overrides (overrules) the existing `OnPaint` method:

```
Protected Overrides Sub OnPaint(ByVal e As
System.Windows.Forms.PaintEventArgs)

    With e.Graphics
        .DrawString("Name", Me.Font, Brushes.Black, 25,
25)
        .DrawString("Address", Me.Font, Brushes.Black,
25, 50)
        .DrawString("State", Me.Font, Brushes.Black, 25,
75)
    End With

End Sub
```

ByVal Becomes the Default

There are two ways to pass parameters to a function. Traditionally, VB defaulted to the ByRef style, unless you specifically used the ByVal command.

Here's an example of how both ByVal and ByRef work. By default, in traditional VB, any of the variables passed to a function (or sub) can be changed by the function.

However, you can prevent the function from making a change to a variable if you use the ByVal command to protect that variable. When you use ByVal, the passed variable can still be used for information (can be read by the function) and even changed temporarily while within the function. But when you return to the place in your program from which you called the function, the value of the variable passed ByVal will not have been changed.

In the following example, X will not be changed, no matter what changes might happen to it while it's inside the function; Y, however, can be permanently changed by the function:

```
Public X, Y

Private Sub Form_Load()
X = 12
Y = 12
Newcost X, Y
MsgBox "X = " & X & "  Y = " & Y
End Sub

Function Newcost(ByVal X, Y)
X = X + 1
Y = Y + 1
End Function
```

This results in X = 12 Y = 13.

We defined X and Y as Public — making them form-wide in scope. Both of these variables can therefore can be changed within any procedure unless passed by ByVal. You sent both X and Y to your function, but X is protected with the ByVal command. When the function adds 1 to each variable, there is a permanent change to Y, but X remains unaffected by activities within the function because you froze it with the ByVal command.

VB.NET

The default has been changed to ByVal. Therefore, by default, if a procedure modifies a passed parameter, the change will not be visible to the caller (the procedure that passed the parameter).

Appendix

A Dictionary of VB.NET

Some parameters still default to ByRef

Not all parameters default to `ByVal` (this kind of inconsistency makes life interesting for us programmers): References to classes, interfaces, arrays, and string variables all still default to `ByRef`.

The fact that `ByVal` is now the default might require considerable rewriting to older VB code — depending on how much the programmer relied on the use of public variables and the assumption that all variables were passed by default using the `ByRef` style.

ParamArrays

Any procedure containing a `ParamArray` argument used to be able to accept any number of arguments, and it could also modify the value of any of those arguments. The calling routine used to be able to see any modifications. Now, in VB.NET, you can still use `ParamArrays`, but any modifications to the values will not be seen by the caller. This new approach is in keeping with the default to the `ByVal` style for most parameters. You cannot change this behavior by employing the ByRef or ByVal keywords. For information on how to use several different argument lists with a single procedure, see "Overloaded Functions, Properties, and Methods (Overloading)" in this appendix.

Caption Changes to Text

Versions prior to VB.NET used a `Caption` property for forms and various controls:

```
Form1.Caption = "THIS"
Label1.Caption = "That"
```

But now there is a `Text` property for all forms and controls:

```
Me.Text = "THIS"
Label1.Text = "That"
```

Case-Sensitivity

Before VB.NET

VB 6 and earlier was not case-sensitive. Variable names and methods or properties could be capitalized any way you wanted:

```
Dim ThisVar as String
```

You could later reference it as `Thisvar`, `thisvar`, `THISVAR`, or any other combination, and it would still be recognized by VB as the same variable.

VB.NET

If you want your objects to be usable by other languages in the Visual Studio group (namely C and its offspring, such as C++, Java, and C#), you must take care that you capitalize your objects' member names (the objects' properties, methods, or events) using precisely the same capitalization. In other words, you must be case-sensitive. In the C world, `ThisVar` and `Thisvar` represent two entirely different entities.

CheckBox.Value Becomes CheckBox.Checked

The headline says it all: What used to be the *value* property, indicating whether or not a CheckBox was checked, in VB.NET has become the `checked` **property.** `Circle, Line, Shape, PSet,` **and** `Point All Changed.`

Before VB.NET

These various graphics controls and commands have all been removed from the language.

VB.NET

The `System.Drawing.Graphics` class includes various methods that replace the older controls and commands. In this case, what you give up in convenience, you gain in flexibility.

Here's an example that illustrates how to use the new VB.NET graphics features to draw a square outline (which uses a *pen*), and then to fill that square (which uses a *brush*):

```
Private Sub Button1_Click_1(ByVal sender As System.Object,
    ByVal e As System.EventArgs) Handles Button1.Click
        'create graphics object
        Dim grObj As System.Drawing.Graphics
        grObj = Me.CreateGraphics

        'create a red pen
        Dim penRed As New
    System.Drawing.Pen(System.Drawing.Color.PaleVioletRed)

'make it fairly wide
        penRed.Width = 9
```

```
'draw a square
grObj.DrawRectangle(penRed, 12, 12, 45, 45)

'create a brush (to fill the square)
Dim brushBlue As System.Drawing.Brush
brushBlue = New SolidBrush(Color.DarkBlue)

grObj.FillRectangle(brushBlue, 12, 12, 45, 45)


    End Sub
```

Note that there are many other methods you can use with a graphics object besides the `DrawRectangle` and `FillRectangle` methods illustrated in this example. Use `DrawEllipse` to draw circles and other round objects, and also try `DrawLine`, `DrawPolygon`, and others.

The four arguments at the end of this line of code describe the horizontal (12) and vertical (15) point on the form where the upper-left corner of your rectangle is located, and the width (36) and height (45) of the rectangle:

```
    grObj.FillRectangle(brushBlue, 12, 15, 36, 45)
```

The `PSet` and `Point` commands, which allowed you to manipulate individual pixels in earlier versions of VB, can be simulated by using the `SetPixel` or `GetPixel` methods of the `System.Drawing Bitmap` class.

You can create a solid graphic (a square, circle, and so on) by simply using a brush to fill the area, without first using a pen to draw an outline.

Circle, Line, Shape, PSet, and Point All Changed

The familiar VB.NET graphics commands `Circle`, `Line`, `Shape`, `PSet`, and `Point` are all now removed from the language. Instead, you draw graphics using a *graphics object* and its various methods. To outline a shape you use a *pen,* and to fill a shape with color or texture, you use a *brush.* This is all very new to VB programmers, but it is more flexible and powerful than the old techniques. See "Drawing Directly on a Control" in this appendix. For an in-depth discussion of drawing graphics, see Chapter 1, Book VI of this book.

Clipboard Becomes a Clipboard Object

Before VB.NET

To retrieve text contents from the Windows Clipboard, you used this code in VB Version 6 and earlier:

```
Text1.Text = Clipboard.GetText
```

VB.NET

You can bring text in from the clipboard using this code:

```
Dim txtdata As IDataObject =
Clipboard.GetDataObject()

' Check to see if the Clipboard holds text
If (txtdata.GetDataPresent(DataFormats.Text)) Then
    TextBox1.Text =
txtdata.GetData(DataFormats.Text).ToString()

End If
```

To export or save the contents of a TextBox to the clipboard, use this code:

```
Clipboard.SetDataObject(TextBox1.Text)
```

Closing Event

VB.NET includes a new Closing event for a form. In this event, you can trap — and abort — the user's attempt to close the form (by clicking the x in the top right or pressing Alt+F4).

Here's an example that traps and aborts closing:

```
Private Sub Form1_Closing(ByVal sender As Object, ByVal e As
    System.ComponentModel.CancelEventArgs) Handles
    MyBase.Closing

    Dim n As Integer
    n = MsgBox("Are you sure you want to close this
form?", MsgBoxStyle.YesNo)

    If n = MsgBoxResult.No Then
        e.Cancel = True
        MsgBox("This form will remain open.")
    End If

End Sub
```

Appendix

A Dictionary of VB.NET

To see all the events available to the Form object, drop down the list at the top left of the code window. Select (Base Class Events), or if you are using VB.NET 2003, select (Form1 Events) and then drop the list at the top right of the code window to see all the events.

Compile

See "Deployment."

Constants Drop VB Prefix

Built-in language constants such as VB 6 `vbGreen` (and a whole slew of other color constants), `vbKeyLeft` (representing the left-arrow key, plus a whole slew of other key constants), and all other built-in sets of constants no longer use that `vb` prefix in VB.NET.

For example, in VB.NET what was `vbGreen` is now simply `Green` and `vbKeyLeft` is `KeyLeft`.

If this sounds to you like a simplification, don't jump to conclusions. Here's how it looks in VB.NET:

```
Private Sub Button1_Click_1(ByVal sender As System.Object,
    ByVal e As System.EventArgs) Handles Button1.Click
        form1.BackColor = color.green

End Sub
```

As you can see, you must *qualify* the constant by using the term `color` (a *namespace*). You must know the class (the library) to which the constant belongs in order for the constant to actually work in your programming. Things can get a bit complex in VB.NET. For example, in VB 6, you tested which key was pressed when the user entered text into a TextBox, like this:

```
Private Sub Text1_KeyDown(KeyCode As Integer, Shift As
    Integer)

If KeyCode = vbKeyC Then
MsgBox ("They entered C")
End If

End Sub
```

However, VB.NET doesn't supply a `KeyCode` to the TextBox `KeyDown` event. Instead, it looks like this:

```
Private Sub TextBox1_KeyDown(ByVal sender As Object, ByVal e
    As System.Windows.Forms.KeyEventArgs) Handles
    TextBox1.KeyDown

        If e.KeyCode = keys.C Then
```

```
        msgbox("They entered C")

    End If
End Sub
```

So you must look at the KeyEventArgs variable, and you must look at its KeyCode property. However, at the current time, the key constants aren't working the same way as the color constants (simply dropping the vb prefix). Rather than KeyLeft, you must use keys.left.

Similarly, the VB.NET control characters (such as CRLF, which is used in a message box to force the message text to appear down one line), requires the ControlChars namespace:

```
Dim s As String = "This line."
s += ControlChars.CrLf + "Next line."
Debug.Write(s)
```

See "Imports" for more information on this topic.

Constructors Are Now "Parametized"

When you instantiate (create) a new structure or object in VB.NET, you, the programmer, sometimes have the option of assigning a value (or sometimes multiple values) to that new object.

Here's a similar technique that you might be familiar with. In VB.NET, you can simultaneously declare a variable or array and assign a value to it:

```
Dim s As String = "Alabama"
```

However, there is a related technique — new in VB.NET — called *parametized constructors*. This technique is very important to object-oriented programming. In previous versions of VB, the Initialize event could not take parameters. Therefore, you could not specify the state of an object during its initialization. (See "Initializers" in this appendix.)

Now switch viewpoints. Programmers sometimes write code that will be used by other programmers. That's the case when you write a class — it will later be used (by a programmer or by you) to generate objects that will be useful in the application you are designing. It's often very important to be able to force the person who uses your classes to provide initial information — to provide, in other words, parameters.

Think of it this way: When you write a function, you often *force* the user of that function to provide an initial parameter (or several):

```
Function AddNumbers(ByVal numone As Integer, ByVal numtwo As
    Integer) As Integer

        Return numone + numtwo

End Function
```

It would make no sense to permit a programmer to use this `AddNumbers` function in his or her code without providing the two parameters that it needs to do its job. Likewise, when you write a class, it is often necessary to require that a user of your class provide parameters when that class instantiates an object. By *require,* I mean that VB.NET will display an error message if the programmer attempts to generate an object without the required parameters.

To repeat: When you define a class in your source code, you might want to force any programmer who later uses your class to pass a value or values. A *constructor* is a method of a class that is automatically executed when that class is instantiated. The purpose of a constructor is to initialize the object during its *construction*. Here's a class that requires any programmer who uses it to pass it an ID number as a parameter. A method named `New` is always a constructor in a class:

```
Public Class Codecs

    Private mID As String 'property named mID

    Sub New(ByVal initValue As String) 'make them pass a
    string
        MyBase.New()
        mID = initValue ' store the string as the mID
    End Sub

    Public ReadOnly Property TheID()
        Get
            TheID = mID 'let them read the value
        End Get
    End Property

End Class
```

In this example, the `New` method (the constructor) requires that a string be passed to this object when the object is initialized. If the programmer tries to instantiate a `Codecs` object without passing that string, VB.NET will display an error message and refuse to instantiate. Here's how you would correctly instantiate this class:

```
Private Sub Form1_Load(ByVal sender As System.Object, ByVal e
    As System.EventArgs) Handles MyBase.Load
```

```
        Dim c As Codecs
        c = New Codecs("DaraLeen112")
        MsgBox("The programmer passed this value: " +
    c.TheID)
End Sub
```

When you press F5 and run this, the MsgBox shows you that the value
"DaraLeen112" was indeed passed to the constructor and stored in the
TheID property.

Permitting multiple parameters

You can also employ more than one constructor if you wish. That allows the
user to choose between more than one kind of parameter list. (VB.NET dif-
ferentiates between these parameter lists by noting their different variable
types or noting that they contain a different *number* of parameters.)

VB.NET executes the constructor (the method named New in your class) that
matches whatever parameters the programmer passes. (This is quite similar
to *overloading*, which you can read about elsewhere in this appendix.)

For example, your class could have these two different constructors:

```
    Sub New()
        MyBase.New()
        mID = Now.ToString ' generate an ID if they don't
    pass one
    End Sub

    Sub New(ByVal initValue As String) 'let them pass a
    string
        MyBase.New()
        mID = initValue ' use the string as the ID
    End Sub
```

Now the programmer has a choice. He or she can instantiate but pass no
argument:

```
        c = New Codecs()
```

In this case, the New ( ) procedure here with no parameters would then be
executed and the other New(ByVal initValue As String) would be
ignored. (In this example, the first New ( ) constructor generates an ID
automatically using the Now command.)

Or, if the programmer *does* pass a parameter, the second constructor,
New(ByVal initValue As String, will be executed instead.

In fact, your class can have as many constructors as you want, as long as each one has a unique argument list. Here are two additional constructors for this example (shown in boldface):

```
Public Class Codecs

    Private mID As String 'ID property value

    Sub New()
        MyBase.New()
        mID = Now.ToString ' generate an ID if they don't
pass one
    End Sub

    Sub New(ByVal initValue As String) 'let them pass a
string
        MyBase.New()
        mID = initValue ' use the string as the ID
    End Sub

    Sub New(ByVal initValue1 As String, ByVal initValue2 As
String) 'let them pass two strings
        MyBase.New()
        mID = initValue1 + initValue2 ' combine them to form
the ID
    End Sub

    Sub New(ByVal initValue As Integer) 'let them pass an
integer
        MyBase.New()
        mID = initValue.ToString ' convert their integer to a
string
    End Sub

    Public ReadOnly Property TheID()
        Get
            TheID = mID 'let them read the value
        End Get
    End Property

End Class
```

This concept is discussed further in the section titled "Overloaded Functions, Properties, and Methods (Overloading)" in this appendix.

ContainsFocus Property

A new property tells you whether or not this control (or a child control on it) has the focus, meaning that the next key pressed on the keyboard will be sent to this control. If you want to know whether the control has focus regardless of whether or not any of its child controls have the focus, use the Focused property instead.

ContextMenu Property

You can add context menu controls to your form from the Toolbox. A particular context menu control can be assigned to a control by specifying the context menu's name property in the ContextMenu property.

Control Arrays Are Gone

Before VB.NET

When you have several controls of the same type performing similar functions, grouping them into a control array was a valuable feature, allowing you to manipulate them efficiently. Also, a control array was the only way to create a new control (such as a brand-new TextBox or a new group of buttons) while a program is running.

Grouping controls into an array lets you manipulate their collective properties quickly. Because they're now labeled with numbers, not text names, you can use them in loops and other structures (such as Select Case) as a unit, easily changing the same property in each control by using a single loop.

There were several ways to create a control array, but probably the most popular was to set the index property of a control during design time. During runtime, you can use the Load and Unload commands to instantiate new members of this array.

Each control in a control array gets its own unique index number, but they share every event in common. In other words, one Click event, for example, would be shared by the entire array of controls. An Index parameter specified which particular control was clicked. So you would write a Select Case structure like the following within the shared event to determine which of the controls was clicked and to respond appropriately:

```
Sub Buttons_Click (Index as Integer)

Select Case Index
Case 1
    MsgBox ("HI, you clicked the OK Button!")
Case 2
    MsgBox ("Click the Other Button. The one that says OK!")
End Select
End Sub
```

Appendix

A Dictionary of VB.NET

There is a way to simulate this all-in-one event that handles all members of a control array in VB.NET. I describe this simulation in the upcoming section titled "Multiple handles."

VB.NET

Control arrays have been removed from the language. However, in VB.NET you can still do what control arrays did. You can instantiate controls during runtime and also manipulate them as a group.

To accomplish what control arrays used to do, you must now instantiate controls (as objects) during runtime and then let them share events (even various different *types* of controls can share an event). Which control (or controls) is being handled by an event is specified in the line that declares the event (following the `Handles` command, as you can see in the next example). Instead of using index numbers to determine what you want a control to do (when it triggers an event), as was the case with control arrays, you must now check an object reference. (Each instantiated control should be given its own, unique name; programmer-instantiated controls do not automatically get a `Name` property specified for them by default.) You are also responsible for creating events for runtime-generated controls. The `Name` property can now be changed during runtime.

Here's an example showing how you can add new controls to a form while a program is running.

Adding a button to a form

Let's assume that the user clicked a button asking to search for some information. You then create and display a TextBox for the user to enter the search criteria, and you also put a label above it describing the TextBox's purpose:

```
Public Class Form1

    Inherits System.Windows.Forms.Form

    Dim WithEvents btnSearch As New Button()


Private Sub Button1_Click(ByVal sender As Object, ByVal e As
    System.EventArgs) Handles Button1.Click

        Dim textBox1 As New TextBox()
        Dim label1 As New Label()


        ' specify some properties:
        label1.Text = "Enter your search term here..."
```

```
        label1.Location = New Point(50, 55) 'left/top
        label1.Size = New Size(125, 20) ' width/height
        label1.AutoSize = True
        label1.Name = "lable1"

        textBox1.Text = ""
        textBox1.Location = New Point(50, 70)
        textBox1.Size = New Size(125, 20)
        textBox1.Name = "TextBox1"

        btnSearch.Text = "Start Searching"
        btnSearch.Location = New Point(50, 95)
        btnSearch.Size = New Size(125, 20)
        btnSearch.Name = "btnSearch"


        ' Add them to the form's controls collection.
        Controls.Add(textBox1)
        Controls.Add(label1)
        Controls.Add(btnSearch)


    'display all the current controls

        Dim i As Integer, n As Integer
        Dim s As String
        n = Controls.Count


        For i = 0 To n - 1

            s = Controls(i).Name

            Debug.Write(s)

            Debug.WriteLine("")

        Next


    End Sub



Private Sub btnSearch_Click(ByVal sender As System.Object,
    ByVal e As System.EventArgs) Handles btnSearch.Click

        MsgBox("clicked")

    End Sub


End Class
```

When adding new controls at design time, you want to at least specify their name, size, and position on the form — especially their `Name` property. Then, use the `Add` method to include these new controls in the form's controls collection.

VB.NET programmers will expect VB.NET to assign names to dynamically added controls. However, be warned that VB.NET does *not* automatically assign names to new controls added at design time. Therefore, the `Name` property remains blank unless you specifically define it, as you did in the preceding example (`textBox1.Name = "TextBox1"`).

Here's how to go through the current set of controls on a form and change them all at once. The following example turns them all red:

```
n = Controls.Count

For i = 0 To n - 1
    Controls(i).BackColor = Color.Red
Next
```

Of course, a control without any events is often useless. To add events to runtime-created controls, you must add two separate pieces of code. First, up at the top (outside any procedure, because this declaration cannot be local), you must define the control as having events by using the `WithEvents` command, like this:

```
Dim WithEvents btnSearch As New Button()
```

Then, in the location where you want to provide the code that responds to an event, type the following:

```
Private Sub btnSearch_Click(ByVal sender As System.Object,
    ByVal e As System.EventArgs) Handles btnSearch.Click

        MsgBox("clicked")

End Sub
```

This event code is indistinguishable from any other "normal" event in the code. Notice that unlike the all-in-one event shared by all the controls in the entire control array in VB 6, VB.NET expects you to give each newly created control its own name and then use that name to define an event that uses `"Handles" Name.Event`, as illustrated by the `Click` event for `btnSearch` in the previous example.

Multiple handles

If you're wildly in favor of the all-in-one event, you can do some curious things in VB.NET that permit it. Here's an example that handles the `Click` events for three different controls by declaring their names following the Handles command:

```
Private Sub cmd_Click(ByVal sender As System.Object, ByVal e
    As
System.EventArgs) Handles cmdOK.Click, cmdApply.Click,
    cmdCancel.Click
        Select Case sender.Name
            Case "cmdOK"
                'Insert Code Here to deal with their
clicking the OK button
            Case "cmdApply"
                'Insert Code Here for Apply button clicking
            Case "cmdCancel"
                'Insert Code Here for Cancel button clicks
        End Select
    End Sub
```

In addition to the multiple objects listed after Handles, notice another interesting thing in this code. There's finally a use for the sender parameter that appears in every event within VB.NET. It is used in combination with the .NAME property to identify which button was, in fact, clicked. This event handles three Click events. Sender tells you which control raised (triggered) this event at any given time. In most VB.NET code, the Sender object is the same as both the name of the event and the name following the Handles:

```
Private Sub Button1_Click(ByVal sender As System.Object,
    ByVal e As System.EventArgs) Handles Button1.Click
        MsgBox(sender.Name)
End Sub
```

VB.NET creates the event in the code window for you, if you wish. Your btnSearch doesn't show up in the Design window, so you cannot double-click it there to force VB.NET to create a Click event for it. However, you can use the drop-down lists. After you have declared a control WithEvents (Dim WithEvents btnSearch As New Button()), drop the list in the top left of the code window, and locate btnSearch. Click it to select it. Then drop the list in the top right, and double-click the event that you want VB.NET to create for you in the code window.

Appendix

Each Form has a collection that includes all the controls on that form. You access the collection, as illustrated previously, using Me.Controls or simply Controls. The collection can be added to, as shown in the previous example, or can be subtracted from:

```
Me.Controls.Remove(Button1)
```

Note, too, that the Me.Controls collection also has several other methods: Clear, Equals, GetChildIndex, GetEnumerator, GetHashCode, GetType,

A Dictionary of VB.NET

SetChildIndex, ShouldPersistAll, and ToString. There are also three properties available to Me.Controls: Count, Item, and IsReadOnly.

Controls Property

This new property represents a collection of any child controls within the current control.

Converting Data Types

VB.NET offers four ways to change one data type into another. The .ToString method is designed to convert any numeric data type into a text string.

The second way to convert data is to use the traditional VB functions: CStr(), CBool(), CByte(), CChar(), CShort(), CInt(), CLng(), CDate(), CDbl(), CSng(), CDec(), and CObj(). Here is an example:

```
Dim s As String
Dim i As Integer = 1551
s = CStr(i)
MessageBox.Show(s)
```

The third way is to use the Convert method, like this:

```
Dim s As String
Dim i As Integer = 1551
s = Convert.ToString(i)
MessageBox.Show(s)
```

The fourth way uses the CType function, with this syntax:

```
Dim s As String
Dim i As Integer = 1551
s = CType(i, String)
MessageBox.Show(s)
```

See "Option Strict and Option Explicit" for more information.

CStr Changes to .ToString

Many classic VB built-in functions are still available in VB.NET. Often there is no difference between the classic function's behavior and the new .NET version. For example, if you want to convert a variable to a string-type variable, you can either use the classic CStr or the new VB.NET ToString method:

```
Dim n As Integer
    n = 12

    MsgBox(CStr(n))
    MsgBox(n.ToString)
```

Note that, by default, VB.NET doesn't insist that you make these conversions; it will display 12 if you merely use this code:

```
MsgBox(n)
```

However, if you want to enforce strict conversion rules, making explicit conversion from one data type to another a requirement, add this line at the very top of your code window:

```
Option Strict On
```

For more information about `Option Strict`, see "Option Strict and Option Explicit."

Yet another way to convert variables from one type to another is to use the `Convert` method:

```
Dim s As String
Dim i As Integer = 1551
s = Convert.ToString(i)
MessageBox.Show(s)
```

Also see "Converting Data Types."

Currency Data Type Is No More

Before VB.NET

The currency data type (a scaled integer) used the symbol @ and could hold the following range of numbers:

```
-922,337,203,685,477.5808 to 922,337,203,685,477.5807
```

It specialized in large numbers that needed only four decimal places of precision.

VB.NET

The `Currency` data type has been removed from the language. You are advised to rely on the `Decimal` data type in its stead. See "Data Types" in this appendix for more information.

Cursor Property

The new Cursor property is what used to be called the MouseIcon property, and it determines what the mouse pointer looks like when it's on top of the TextBox (if you want to change it from the default pointer). I advise against changing this property — unless you're sure you will not confuse the user.

Data Types

There is no variant data type in VB.NET. There are some other changes to the traditional VB data types. A new Char type, which is an unsigned 16-bit type, is used to store Unicode characters. The Decimal type is a 96-bit signed integer scaled by a variable power of 10. No currency type is included any more (use the Decimal type instead).

The VB.NET Long data type is now a 64-bit integer. The VB.NET Short type is a 16-bit integer. And in between them is the new VB.NET Integer type, which is a 32-bit value. If you are working with programming where these distinctions will matter, memorize these differences from the way that integers were handled in traditional VB programming.

Use the Integer type when possible, because it executes the fastest of the comparable numeric types in VB.NET.

Here are all the VB.NET data types:

Traditional VB Type	New .NET Type	Memory Size	Range
Boolean	System.Boolean	4 bytes	True or False
Char	System.Char	2 bytes	0-65535 (unsigned)
Byte	System.Byte	1 byte	0-255 (unsigned)
Object	System.Object	4 bytes	Any Type
Date	System.DateTime	8 bytes	01-Jan-0001 to 31-Dec-9999
Double	System.Double	8 bytes	+/-1.797E308
Decimal	System.Decimal	12 bytes	28 digits
Integer	System.Int16	2 bytes	-32,768 to 32,767
	System.Int32	4 bytes	+/-2.147E9
Long	System.Int64	8 bytes	+/-9.223E18
Single	System.Single	4 bytes	+/-3.402E38
String	System.String	CharacterCount * 2 (plus 10 bytes)	2 billion characters

Also see "Converting Data Types."

Date and Time: New Techniques

Before VB.NET

The `Date` function used to give you the current date (for example: 11/29/00). The `Time` function used to give you the current time.

VB.NET

Now you must use the `Today` and `TimeOfDay` functions instead. Also note that the old `DATE$` and `TIME$` functions have been eliminated.

In Visual Basic 6.0 and previous versions, a date/time was stored in a double (double-precision floating point) format (four bytes). In VB.NET, the date/time information uses the .NET framework `DateTime` data type (stored in eight bytes). There is no implicit conversion between the `Date` and `Double` data types in VB.NET. To convert between the VB 6 `Date` data type and the VB.NET `Double` data type, you must use the `ToDouble` and `FromOADate` methods of the `DateTime` class in the `System` namespace.

Here's an example that uses the `TimeSpan` object to calculate how much time elapsed between two `DateTime` objects:

```
Dim StartTime, EndTime As DateTime
Dim Span As TimeSpan

        StartTime = "9:24 AM"
        EndTime = "10:14 AM"

        Span = New TimeSpan(EndTime.Ticks - StartTime.Ticks)
        MsgBox(Span.ToString)
```

Notice the `Ticks` unit of time. It represents a 100-nanosecond interval.

Here's another example illustrating the `addhours` and `addminutes` methods, how to get the current time (`Now`), and a couple other methods:

```
Dim hr As Integer = 2
Dim mn As Integer = 13


Dim StartTime As New DateTime(DateTime.Now.Ticks)
Dim EndTime As New DateTime(StartTime.AddHours(hr).Ticks)

EndTime = EndTime.AddMinutes(mn)

        Dim Difference = New TimeSpan(EndTime.Ticks -
    StartTime.Ticks)
```

```
      Debug.WriteLine("Start Time is: " +
StartTime.ToString("hh:mm"))
      Debug.WriteLine("Ending Time is: " +
EndTime.ToString("hh:mm"))
      Debug.WriteLine("Number of hours elapsed is: " +
Difference.Hours.ToString)
      Debug.WriteLine("Number of minutes elapsed is: " +
Difference.Minutes.ToString)
```

The following sections provide some additional examples that illustrate how to manipulate date and time.

Adding time

Here's an example of using the `AddDays` method:

```
Dim ti As Date = TimeOfDay 'the current time
      Dim da As Date = Today 'the current date
      Dim dati As Date = Now 'the current date and time


      da = da.AddDays(12) ' add 12 days
      Debug.WriteLine("12 days from now is:" & da)
```

Similarly, you can use `AddMinutes`, `AddHours`, `AddSeconds`, `AddMilliseconds`, `AddMonths`, `AddYears`, and so on.

Using the old-style double DateTime data type

There is an OA conversion method for currency data types and for date data types. (*OA* stands for *Ole Automation,* a legacy technology that still keeps popping up.) Here's an example showing how to translate to and from the old double-precision date format:

```
      Dim dati As Date = Now 'the current date and time
      Dim da as Date
      n = dati.ToOADate ' translate into double-precision
format
      n = n + 21 ' add three weeks (the integer part is the
days)
      da = Date.FromOADate(n) ' translate the OA style into
.NET style
      Debug.WriteLine(da)
```

Use `Now`, not `Today`, for these OA-style data types.

Finding days in month

2004 is a leap year. Here's one way to prove it:

```
Debug.WriteLine("In the year 2004, February has " &
Date.DaysInMonth(2004, 2).ToString & " days.")
Debug.WriteLine("In the year 2005, February has " &
Date.DaysInMonth(2005, 2).ToString & " days.")
```

Debug.Print Changes

If you're one of those programmers who likes to use Debug.Print while testing your project, note that that feature has been changed in VB.NET to Debug.Write. If you want to force a linefeed, use Debug.WriteLine.

Also, instead of displaying its results in the Immediate window (as in previous versions of VB), Debug.Write now writes to the Output window.

Default Control Names Are Now Longer

Before VB.NET

When you added a TextBox to a form, it was given a default name Text1. Similarly, when you added a ListBox, it was named List1. It doesn't work this way anymore.

VB.NET

For reasons I don't understand, VB.NET now provides longer default names: TextBox1, ListBox1, and so on.

Default Properties Are No More

You can no longer use code like this, because default properties (such as Text1.Text) are no longer permitted with controls:

```
Text1 = "This phrase"
```

Instead, in VB.NET, you must specify the property:

```
Text1.Text = "This phrase"
```

See the sections "Property Definitions Collapse (Property Let, Get, and Set Are Gone)" or "Object Instantiation" in this appendix for more information.

Deployment

You have ways to give others your WinForm-based and WebForm-based applications. See VB.NET Help for ways to deploy your solutions. However, if you are wondering how to write a little utility program in VB.NET and run it in your local computer, you'll doubtless notice that the usual File⇨Make .EXE or File⇨Compile .EXE option is missing in VB.NET.

Don't despair, though. Whenever you press F5 to test your VB.NET WinForm-style project, it is compiled into an .exe program with the same name as your project. You can find this .exe file in: `C:\Documents and Settings\` `YourIdentityName\MyDocuments\Visual Studio Projects\` `YourProjectsName\Bin`.

Dim and ReDim: New Rules

Before VB.NET

The `Dim` command could either dimension an array or declare a variable (or a group of variables).

The default variable type was the variant, so if you wanted to use a different type, you had to explicitly declare it using `Dim` or one of the other declaring commands such as `Public`. (Variants are not permitted in VB.NET.)

You could dim a list of different variables:

```
Dim X As String, Y As Integer, Z
```

In this example, `Z` would default to variant because you didn't specify a data type.

Or you could use the `DefType` commands to change the default from `Variant` to, say, `Integer`:

```
DefInt A-Z '(all variables become integer types unless
    otherwise declared).
```

The `ReDim` command could be used two ways: to resize arrays, or to declare variables.

VB.NET

The `DefType` commands have been removed from the language, as has the `Variant` data type. The now-removed `DefType` commands are: `DefBool`, `DefByte`, `DefCur`, `DefDate`, `DefDbl`, `DefDec`, `DefInt`, `DefLng`, `DefObj`, `DefSng`, `DefStr`, and `DefVar`.

You can mix types within a Dim list, but *all* variables are required to have an As clause defining their type (if you set Option Strict On). This next line of code is not permitted because of the Z:

```
Dim X As String, Y As Integer, Z
```

This is allowed:

```
Dim X As String, Y As String, z As Integer
```

Or:

```
Dim X, Y As String
```

Note that in VB 6, the X (because no As phrase defines it) would have been a variant type. In VB.NET, X is a string type.

If you leave Option Strict Off, and you don't attach an As clause, the variable will default to the object type:

```
Dim X
```

See "Option Strict and Option Explicit" for more details.

You *must* declare every variable and every array. You must use Dim (or use another declaring command such as Private or Public). Option Explicit is built into the language as the default. (Option Explicit requires that every variable be declared, though you can turn it off.) The default type is now object instead of variant, but you must declare even this "default" type.

You can no longer implicitly declare a variable merely by assigning a value to it, like this:

```
X = 12
```

However, VB.NET does allow you to assign a value in the same statement that declares the variable:

```
Dim X As Integer = 12
```

Also, if you are using the latest version, VB.NET 2003, you can even declare a loop counter variable within the line that starts the loop, like this:

```
For i As Integer = 0 To 10
```

instead of the traditional style:

```
Dim i as Integer
For i = 0 To 10
```

You can no longer use `ReDim` in place of the `Dim` command. Arrays must be first declared using `Dim` (or similar); `ReDim` cannot create an array. You can use `ReDim` only to redimension (resize) an existing array originally declared with the `Dim` (or similar) command. (See "ArrayList (Replacing the Array Command)" for a superior way to let VB.NET handle arrays that must dynamically change size. `ArrayList` also does other neat tricks.)

You can declare arrays in a similar way. Here's a two-dimensional array declaration:

```
Dim TwoArray(3, 4) As Integer
```

Use empty parentheses to declare a dynamic array:

```
Dim DynArray() As Integer
```

You are allowed to declare the same variable name in more than one location. This can cause problems that are not flagged by any error messages. Here's an example: Assume that you originally declared n within the `Form_Load` event (so that it's local to that event only). However, you decide you need to make it `Public` so that other procedures can use its contents as well. Therefore, you type in a `Public` declaration at the top, outside of any event or procedure. But you forget to erase the local declaration. Unfortunately, you get hard-to-track-down bugs because the local declaration will remain in effect and n will lose its contents outside the `Form_Load` event. Here's an example:

```
Public Class Form1
    Inherits System.Windows.Forms.Form
    Public n As Integer '(holds the number of files being
    renamed)

    Private Sub Form1_Load(ByVal sender As System.Object,
    ByVal e As System.EventArgs) Handles MyBase.Load

        Dim myfile As String
        Dim mydir As String
        Dim n, i As Integer
...
End Sub
```

Strongly typed

VB.NET is *strongly typed*. Several changes to the language support this new approach. For one thing, the `As Any` command has been deleted from the language. You can no longer declare a function `As Any` (meaning that it can return any kind of data type). For additional details, and an alternative approach, see "Overloaded Functions, Properties, and Methods (Overloading)" elsewhere in this appendix.

Declaring arrays

You declare an array in a way similar to the way you declare a variable. To create an array that holds 11 values, ranging from `MyArray(0)` through `MyArray(10)`, type the following:

```
Dim MyArray(10)
```

You can simultaneously declare and initialize (provide values to) an array (see "Initializers" in this appendix). You use the braces punctuation mark, which has never before been used in Visual Basic. Here's how to initialize a string array with two elements, `MyArray(0)` and `MyArray(1)`, which contain `"Billy"` and `"Bob"`:

```
Dim MyArray() As String = {"Billy", "Bob"}
MsgBox(MyArray(0) + MyArray(1))
```

Notice that you are not permitted to specify the size of an array when you initialize it with values, as illustrated in the previous example: `MyArray()`. This array has two elements: `(0)` and `(1)`.

Multidimensional arrays are declared as you would expect. The following array has two dimensions, each with elements ranging from 0 to 3:

```
Dim MyArray(3,3)
```

Declaring with symbols

You can still use symbols when declaring some data types in VB.NET. For example, the following declares `N` as an `Integer` variable:

```
Dim N%
```

The following code is equivalent:

```
Dim N as Integer
```

Here are the symbols you can use in VB.NET:

Symbol	VB 6	VB.NET
%	16-bit Integer	32-bit Integer
&	32-bit Long Integer	64-bit Long Integer
!	Single Floating Point	Single Floating Point
#	Double Floating Point	Double Floating Point
@		Decimal
$	String	String

DIM As New

Before VB.NET

Here's an example of how `Dim` was used before VB.NET:

```
Dim MyObj as New MyClass
```

You could always access the members of this object because VB handled the references automatically.

VB.NET

An instance of an object is created only when the procedure in which it is declared AS NEW is called. Other references to this object's properties or methods will not instantiate it automatically, as before. So you must now explicitly test whether or not the object exists:

```
If MyObj Is Nothing Then
```

Use the old VB 6 syntax and VB.NET gives you the following error message:

```
This keyword does not name a class.
```

DIM Gets Scoped

Before VB.NET

The `Dim` command worked the same no matter where you put it inside a given procedure. These two uses of `Dim` behaved the same:

```
Private Sub Form_Load()

For I = 2 To 40
    Dim n As Integer
    n = n + 1
Next I
End Sub



Private Sub Form_Load()
Dim n As Integer

Do While n < 40
    n = n + 1
Loop

End Sub
```

In traditional VB, the compiler first searches through procedures like those in the example to find any Dim commands. Then it carries out the Dim commands first, before other code in the procedure. It doesn't matter *where* in the procedure these Dim commands are located. There was no scope narrower than a single procedure.

VB.NET

Now Dim can have a narrower scope than you ever imagined. Dim, when located within a code block (such as If...Then) has scope only within that code block. That's right: Dim inside a code block doesn't have procedure-wide scope; it works only within the block. So, if you've been in the habit of sticking your Dim statements here and there in your code, you'll have to clean up your act and place them at the top of procedures or outside of procedures in what used to be the General Declarations section of a form. In other words, you'll have to check each Dim in your existing code to ensure that it has the scope you want it to have.

Directory (Current)

Before VB.NET

To find out information about the currently executing application in VB 6, you could use the App object for some info and make API calls for other info.

VB.NET

In VB.NET, you can find the current directory (the one that your application is running in, for example) with this code:

```
Debug.WriteLine(System.Environment.CurrentDirectory)
```

The System.Environment object allows you to find out many other aspects of the environment (the currently executing process) as well:

```
Private Sub Button1_Click(ByVal sender As System.Object,
    ByVal e As System.EventArgs) Handles Button1.Click

        Debug.WriteLine(Environment.CurrentDirectory)
        Debug.WriteLine(Environment.CommandLine) 'running
program
        Debug.WriteLine(Environment.MachineName)
        Debug.WriteLine(Environment.OSVersion)
        Debug.WriteLine(Environment.SystemDirectory)
        Debug.WriteLine(Environment.UserDomainName)
        Debug.WriteLine(Environment.UserName)
        Debug.WriteLine(Environment.Version)

    End Sub
```

This results in:

```
E:\Documents and Settings\Richard Mansfield.DELL\My
    Documents\Visual Studio Projects\WindowsApplication11\bin
"E:\Documents and Settings\Richard Mansfield.DELL\My
    Documents\Visual Studio
    Projects\WindowsApplication11\bin\WindowsApplication11.
    exe"
DELL
Microsoft Windows NT 5.0.2195.0
E:\WINNT\System32
DELL
Richard Mansfield
1.0.2914.16
```

Directory and File: Creating and Destroying

The following code illustrates how to create or delete directories and subdirectories:

```
Imports System.io

Public Function DestroyDirectory()

        Dim objDir As New DirectoryInfo("C:\TestDir")
        Try
            objDir.Delete(True)
        Catch
            Throw New Exception("Failed to delete")
        End Try


End Function


Public Function CreateDirectory() As String

        Dim objDir As New DirectoryInfo("c:\TestDir")

        Try
            objDir.Create()

        Catch
            Throw New Exception("Failed to create new
    directory")
        End Try
End Function

Public Function CreateSubDirectory() As String
```

```
        Dim objDir As New DirectoryInfo("c:\TestDir") 'parent
directory
        Try
            objDir.CreateSubdirectory("TestSubDir") 'name for
new subdiretory

        Catch
            Throw New Exception("Failed to create new
subdirectory")
        Fnd Try
End Function
```

A similar set of file copy, move, create, and destroy methods are available using code like this:

```
Dim fa As New FileInfo("c:\textq.txt")
fa.CopyTo("c:\testq.bak")
```

Directory-, Drive-, and FileListBoxes Are Gone

The venerable Directory-, Drive-, and FileListBox controls are now missing from the Toolbox. No great loss, because the SaveFileDialog and OpenFileDialog controls do a much better job of providing a dialog box that gives users access to hard drives.

Divide by Zero Equals Infinity

Dividing by zero is not an error in VB.NET (except for integers). Try the following:

```
Dim x As Single
Dim y As Single
y = 1 / x 'divide by zero
MsgBox(y)

If [Single].IsInfinity(y) Then
    MsgBox("yes, it's infinity")
End If
```

The first MessageBox will display Infinity. Then the second MessageBox pops up and says yes, it's infinity.

Note how you can test for "positive" or "negative" or either kind of infinity using the IsPositiveInfinity, IsNegativeInfinity, or IsInfinity methods of the Single or Double type. Also note the odd punctuation. This is the first time in Visual Basic that brackets have been used in the language. (New, as well, are braces — used when declaring and initializing an array. See "Dim and ReDim: New Rules.")

Dock Property

This new property specifies which side of the parent container (normally the form) this control attaches itself to.

Drawing Directly on a Control

In VB.NET, you can get pretty down and dirty and take charge of precisely how a control will look to the user. Here's how to frame a Button control with blue. First, up near the top, next to the Form's declaration, add this line (shown in boldface):

```
'Put this WithEvents line up with the Inherits line:

Public Class Form1

    Inherits System.Windows.Forms.Form

    Friend WithEvents Button1 As System.Windows.Forms.Button
```

Then put a Button control on your form and type this into its Paint **event:**

```
Private Sub Button1_Paint(ByVal sender As Object, ByVal e As
    System.Windows.Forms.PaintEventArgs) Handles
    Button1.Paint

    Dim g As Graphics = e.Graphics
    ControlPaint.DrawBorder(g, e.ClipRectangle, Color.Blue,
ButtonBorderStyle.Solid)

End Sub
```

Empty, Null, Missing, IsNull, IsObject, and IsMissing Are Gone

Before VB.NET

The traditional VB Variant data type could hold some special kinds of values: Null (not known), Empty (no value was ever assigned to this variable), and

`Missing` (this variable was not sent, for example, as part of a procedure's parameters).

`Null` was sometimes used to identify fields in databases that are not available (or unknown), while the `Empty` command was used to represent something that didn't exist (as opposed to simply not being currently available).

Some programmers used the `IsMissing` command to see if an optional parameter had been passed to a procedure:

```
Sub SomeSub(Optional SomeParam As Variant)
    If IsMissing(SomeParam) Then
```

VB.NET

The VB.NET object data type does not use `Missing`, `Empty`, or `Null`. There *is* an `IsDBNull` function that you can use with databases instead of the now-missing `IsNull` command. Similarly, an `IsReference` command replaces the `IsObject` command.

Optional parameters can still be used with procedures, but you must declare that `As Type` and you must also supply a default value for them. You cannot write code within a procedure that will tell you whether a particular parameter has been passed. For further details, see the section titled "Optional Parameter-Passing Tightened" in this appendix.

If you need to test whether an optional parameter has been passed, you can overload a procedure. *Overloading* is a new technique where a function (or indeed a method or property) can be made to behave differently based on what is passed to it. For more on overloading, see the section titled "Overloaded Functions, Properties, and Methods (Overloading)" in this appendix.

Also see "IsEmpty."

Appendix

Environment Information

See "Directory (Current)."

A Dictionary of VB.NET

Error Messages (Obscure)

Some .NET error messages can be confusing. They merely offer some general abstract comment, without telling you precisely the punctuation or syntax you must use to fix the problem.

For example, you might get an error message like this: `Value of type system.drawing.color cannot be converted to 1-dimensional array of system.drawing.color.`

This code results in that error message:

```
Dim ArrColor() As Color = Color.Gold
```

To fix the problem, enclose the color in braces:

```
Dim ArrColor() As Color = {Color.Gold}
```

Error Handling Revised

Before VB.NET

Don't panic. You can still use the familiar VB error-handling techniques (`On Error...`).

Thus, you don't have to revise this aspect of your older programs. But for new programs that you write in VB.NET, you might want to consider the possibility that a superior error-trapping and handling approach exists. They call it *structured* error handling, which implies that your familiar, classic VB error handling is ... well ... *unstructured*. For details and examples, see the section titled "Structured Error Handling" in Chapter 5.

If you try to write something traditional like `If Err Then`, however, you'll be informed that VB.NET doesn't permit the `ErrObject` to be treated as boolean (true/false). However, where there's a will, there's a way. You can test the `Err` object's `number` property. So, if you want to test the `Err` object within an `If...Then` structure, use this VB.NET code:

```
x = CInt(textbox1.Text)

If err.Number <> 0 Then

    textbox1.Text = "You must enter a number..."

End If
```

VB.NET

Consider using the new `Try...Catch...Finally` structure:

```
Sub TryError()
```

```
Try

        Microsoft.VisualBasic.FileOpen(5, "A:\Test.Txt",
OpenMode.Input)

    Catch er As Exception
        MessageBox.Show(er.ToString)
    Finally

    End Try


    End Sub
```

Code between the `Try` and `End Try` commands is watched for errors. You can use the generic `Exception` (which will catch *any* error) or merely trap a specific exception such as the following:

```
Catch er As DivideByZeroException
```

The term *exception* is used in C-like languages (and now in VB.NET) to mean error.

I used `er` but you can use any valid variable name for the error. Or you can leave that variable out entirely, and just use `Catch`, like this:

```
Try
        Microsoft.VisualBasic.FileOpen(5, "A:\Test.Txt",
  OpenMode.Input)

    Catch
        MessageBox.Show("problem")
    Finally

    End Try
```

If an error occurs during execution of the source code in the `Try` section, the following `Catch` section is then executed. You must include at least one `Catch` section, but there can be many such sections if you need them to test and figure out which particular error occurred. A series of `Catch` sections is similar to the `Case` sections in `Select...Case` structures. The `Catch` sections are tested in order, and only one `Catch` block (or none) is executed for any particular error.

You can use a `When` clause to further specify which kind of error you want to trap, like this:

```
Dim Y as Integer
Try
```

Appendix

A Dictionary of VB.NET

```
Y = Y / 0
Catch When y = 0
    MessageBox.Show("Y = 0")
End Try
```

Or you can specify a particular kind of exception, thereby narrowing the number of errors that will trigger this `Catch` section's execution:

```
Catch er As ArithmeticException
    MessageBox.Show("Math error.")
Catch When y = 0
    MessageBox.Show("Y = 0")
End Try
```

To see a list of the specific exceptions, use the VB.NET menu Debug⇨ Windows⇨Exceptions and then expand the Common Language Runtime exceptions. You may have to do a bit of hunting. For instance the `FileNotFound` error is located two expansions down in the hierarchy: Common Language Runtime⇨SystemException⇨IOException. So you have to expand all three (click the + next to each) in order to finally find `FileNotFoundException`.

Also notice in the Exceptions window that you can cause the program to ignore any of the exceptions (click the Continue radio button in the Exceptions window). This is the equivalent of `On Error Resume Next` in VB 6.

Here is a list of common errors you can trap in VB.NET. The following errors are in the `System` namespace:

```
AppDomainUnloadedException
ApplicationException
ArgumentException
ArgumentNullException
ArgumentOutOfRangeException
ArithmeticException
ArrayTypeMismatchException
BadImageFormatException
CannotUnloadAppDomainException
ContextMarshalException
DivideByZeroException
DllNotFoundException
DuplicateWaitObjectException
EntryPointNotFoundException
Exception
ExecutionEngineException
FieldAccessException
FormatException
IndexOutOfRangeException
```

```
InvalidCastException
InvalidOperationException
InvalidProgramException
MemberAccessException
MethodAccessException
MissingFieldException
MissingMemberException
MissingMethodException
MulticastNotSupportedException
NotFiniteNumberException
NotImplementedException
NotSupportedException
NullReferenceException
ObjectDisposedException
OutOfMemoryException
OverflowException
PlatformNotSupportedException
RankException
ServicedComponentException
StackOverflowException
SystemException
TypeInitializationException
TypeLoadException
TypeUnloadedException
UnauthorizedAccessException
UnhandledExceptionEventArgs
UnhandledExceptionEventHandler
UriFormatException
WeakReferenceException
```

The following errors are in the `SystemIO` category:

```
DirectoryNotFoundException
EndOfStreamException
FileNotFoundException
InternalBufferOverflowException
IOException
PathTooLongException
```

You can list as many `Catch` phrases as you want and respond individually to them. You can respond by notifying the user as you did in the previous example, or merely by quietly fixing the error in your source code following the `Catch`. You can also provide a brief error message with the following:

```
e.Message
```

Or, as you did in the previous example, use the following fully qualified error message:

```
e.ToString
```

Appendix

A Dictionary of VB.NET

Here's the full `Try...Catch...Finally` structure's syntax:

```
Try trystatements

[Catch₁ [exception [As type]] [When expression]
    catchStatements₁
[Exit Try]
Catch₂ [exception [As type]] [When expression]
    catchStatements₂
[Exit Try]
...
Catchₙ [exception [As type]] [When expression]
    catchStatementsₙ]
[Exit Try]
[Finally
    finallyStatements]
End Try
```

Recall that following the `Try` block, you list one or more `Catch` statements. A `Catch` statement can include a variable name and an `As` clause defining the type of exception or the general "all errors," *As Exception* (`er As Exception`). For example, here's how to trap *all* exceptions:

```
Try
Microsoft.VisualBasic.FileOpen(5, "A:\Test.Txt",
    OpenMode.Input)


Catch e As Exception

    'Respond to any kind of error.

Finally


End Try
```

And here is how to respond to the specific `File Not Found` error:

```
Try

Microsoft.VisualBasic.FileOpen(5, "A:\Test.Txt",
    OpenMode.Input)

Catch FileNotFoundE As FileNotFoundException

    'Respond to this particular error here, perhaps a
    messagebox to alert the user.
```

```
Finally

End Try
```

An optional `Exit Try` statement causes program flow to leap out of the `Try` structure and to continue execution with whatever follows the `End Try` statement.

The `Finally` statement should contain any code that you want executed after error processing has been completed. Any code in the `Finally` is *always* executed, no matter what happens (unlike source code following the `End Try` line, which may or may not execute, depending on how things go within the `Try` structure). Therefore, the most common use for the `Finally` section is to free up resources that were aquired within the `Try` block. For example, if you were to acquire a Mutex lock within your `Try` block, you would want to release that lock when you were done with it, regardless of whether or not the `Try` block exited with a successful completion or an exception (error). It's typical to find this kind of code within the `Finally` block:

```
objMainKey.Close()
objFileRead.Close()
objFilename.Close()
```

Use this approach when you want to close, for instance, an object reference to a key in the Registry, or to close file references that were opened during the `Try` section ("block") of code.

Here's how source code you put within the `Finally` section differs from source code you put following the `End Try` line.

If there *is* an error, here is the order in which code execution takes place:

1. `Try` section
2. `Catch` section (the `Catch` section that traps this error)
3. `Finally` section

If *no* error occurs, here is the execution order:

1. `Try` section
2. `Finally` section
3. Source code following the `End Try` line

Even if a Catch section has an Exit Sub command, the Finally section nevertheless will still be executed. Finally is *always* executed. However, the Exit Sub *does* get executed just *after* the Finally block.

Event Handlers

See "Handles" or "Multiple handles."

Executable

See "Deployment."

File I/O Commands Are Different

Before VB.NET

The familiar syntax is as follows:

```
Open filepath {For Mode}{options}As {#} filenumber {Len =
    recordlength}
```

For example:

```
Open "C:\Test.Txt" As 5
```

Some people refer to the filenumber as the channel.

VB.NET

To use the traditional VB file I/O commands, you must import the VB "Compatibility" namespace. So include this line at the top of your code window:

```
Imports Microsoft.VisualBasic
```

If you want to let your user decide which file to display or access, you want to use the handy and effective OpenFileDialog control found on the Toolbox.

VB.NET has a C-like "stream" (incoming or outgoing data) technique for reading or writing to a file. If you want to use this approach, the following sections cover some examples, beginning with how to read from a file.

Reading a file

Start a new VB.NET WinForm-style project, and then double-click TextBox in the WinForms tab of the Toolbox to add it to your Form1.VB. Double-click a Button to add it also.

Click the TextBox in the IDE (Design tab selected) so that you can see its properties in the Properties window. Change its `Multiline` property to `True`.

Now, double-click the Button to get to its `Click` event in the code window.

Type this in at the top of the code window:

```
Imports System.IO
```

The simplest example looks like this:

```
Private Sub Button1_Click_1(ByVal sender As System.Object,
    ByVal e As System.EventArgs) Handles Button1.Click

        Dim a As String

        Dim sr As New StreamReader("e:\test.txt")
        a = sr.ReadLine
        a += sr.ReadLine
        sr.Close()

End Sub
```

However, to see a more flexible approach, type this into the Button's click event:

```
Private Sub Button1_Click_1(ByVal sender As System.Object,
    ByVal e As System.EventArgs) Handles Button1.Click

        Dim strFileName As String = TextBox1.Text

        If (strFileName.Length < 1) Then
            msgbox("Please enter a filename in the TextBox")
            Exit Sub
        End If

        Dim objFilename As FileStream = New
    FileStream(strFileName, FileMode.Open, FileAccess.Read,
    FileShare.Read)

        Dim objFileRead As StreamReader = New
    StreamReader(objFilename)
```

```
While (objFileRead.Peek() > -1)
    textbox1.Text += objFileRead.ReadLine()
End While

objFileRead.Close()
objFilename.Close()
```

```
End Sub
```

Note the `End While` command, which replaces the VB 6 `Wend` command.

Finally, recall that you must add `Imports System.IO` up there at the top of the code window. If System IO is missing, the `FileStream` and `StreamReader` classes will be missing. Or you could create them by adding the name of the assembly (library) with this cumbersome usage:

`System.IO.StreamReader`

and:

`System.IO.FileStream`

Beyond that, you would find the compiler choking when it came to such "undeclared" items as `FileShare`, `FileMode`, and `FileAccess`, which, themselves, would each need the modifier `System.IO`. So, you should play by the rules and simply add `Imports` up top in the code window and avoid all the hassle. Right?

Consider the following line:

```
Dim objFilename As FileStream = New FileStream(strFileName,
    FileMode.Open, FileAccess.Read, FileShare.Read)
```

That line would look like the following without the `System.IO` import:

```
Dim objFilename As System.IO.FileStream = New
    System.IO.FileStream(strFileName,
    System.IO.Filemode.Open, System.IO.Fileaccess.Read,
    System.IO.Fileshare.Read)
```

Press F5, type a valid filepath to a .TXT file (such as `C:\myfile.txt`), and click the button to see the file's contents in the TextBox.

How do you know you're at the end?
When reading from a file, you have to know when you've reached the end. In the previous example, you used the following code:

```
While (objFileRead.Peek() > -1)
```

Alternatively, you can use this:

```
While (objFileRead.PeekChar()<> -1)
```

You can use yet another technique for reading (or writing, using the `FilePut` command). In this case, you test for the end of file with the venerable `EOF` property, `End Of File`. Also, you use the `FileGet` command to read from a file; in this case, you are reading individual characters. Start a new project, and put a TextBox on the form. Now type the following:

```
Private Sub Form1_Load(ByVal sender As System.Object, ByVal e
    As System.EventArgs) Handles MyBase.Load

    Dim objN As New ReadBytes()

    TextBox1.Text = objN.ReadAFile


End Sub

Public Class ReadBytes

    Private strRead As String

    Public Function ReadAFile()
        strRead = ""

        Dim chrHolder As Char
        Dim filenumber As Int16

        filenumber = FreeFile() ' whatever filenumber
isn't already used

        FileOpen(filenumber, "C:\test.txt",
OpenMode.Binary)

        Do While Not EOF(filenumber)
            FileGet(filenumber, chrHolder)
            strRead = strRead & chrHolder
        Loop
        FileClose(1)

        Return strRead

    End Function


End Class
```

Appendix

A Dictionary
of VB.NET

For your final trick, here's one more way to read from a file. This one does not require a loop:

```
Private Sub Form1_Load(ByVal sender As System.Object, ByVal e
    As System.EventArgs) Handles MyBase.Load

        Dim objFilename As FileStream = New
FileStream("C:\test.txt", FileMode.Open, FileAccess.Read,
FileShare.Read)
        Dim strRdr As New StreamReader(objFilename)

        TextBox1.Text = strRdr.ReadToEnd()
        TextBox1.SelectionLength = 0 'turn off the selection

    End Sub
```

This one relies on the `ReadToEnd` method of the `StreamReader` object. The one kink is that the text that is placed into the TextBox is selected (white text on black background). So, to deselect it, you set the `SelectionLength` property to zero.

The RichTextBox control has `LoadFile` and `SaveFile` methods, which are well explained in the VB.NET Help feature.

Writing to a file

The code that writes to a file is similar to the previous file-reading example (the one that used the *streaming* technique). First, be sure to add `Imports System.IO` as described previously.

The simplest approach is as follows:

```
Dim sw As New StreamWriter("test.txt")
sw.Writeline("My example line.")
sw.WriteLine("A second line.")
sw.Close
```

For a more flexible, advanced example, type the following:

```
Private Sub Button1_Click_1(ByVal sender As System.Object,
    ByVal e As System.EventArgs) Handles Button1.Click

        Dim strText As String = TextBox1.Text

        If (strText.Length < 1) Then
            MsgBox("Please type something into the TextBox so
we can save it.")
            Exit Sub
```

```
        Else
            Dim strFileName As String = "C:\MyFile.txt"
            Dim objOpenFile As FileStream = New
FileStream(strFileName, FileMode.Append,
FileAccess.Write, FileShare.Read)
            Dim objStreamWriter As StreamWriter = New
StreamWriter(objOpenFile)

            objStreamWriter.WriteLine(strText)

            objStreamWriter.Close()
            objOpenFile.Close()
        End If


    End Sub
```

Because you used the `FileMode.Append` property, each time you run this program new text will be added to any existing text in the file. If you want to overwrite the file, use `FileMode.Create` instead.

Alternatively, you can save to a file by borrowing functionality from the `SaveFileDialog` class (or the `SaveFileDialog` control), like this:

```
Dim sfd As New SaveFileDialog()
        Dim dlgResponse As Integer
        Dim strFname As String


        sfd.DefaultExt = "txt" '  specifies a default
    extension
        sfd.InitialDirectory = "C:"

        dlgResponse = sfd.ShowDialog

        If dlgResponse = 1 Then
            strFname = sfd.FileName
            msgbox(strFname)
        End If
```

(Then add code here to actually save this file.)

Yet another alternative reads and writes individual pieces of data. The size of these pieces is up to you when you define the variable used to write and when you define the read mode (as in `r.ReadByte()` versus `r.ReadBoolean` or `r.ReadInt32`, and so on).

This techique also requires `Imports System.IO`. Here's an example of how to create a file and store bytes into it:

```
Private Sub Form1_Load(ByVal sender As System.Object, ByVal e
    As System.EventArgs) Handles MyBase.Load


    Dim fs As FileStream = New FileStream("c:\test1.txt",
FileMode.Create)

    Dim w As BinaryWriter = New BinaryWriter(fs)

    Dim i As Byte

    ' store 14 integers in a file (as bytes)
    For i = 1 To 14
        w.Write(i)
    Next


    w.Close()

    fs.Close()
```

And here's how you read individual bytes from a file:

```
    ' Create the reader for this particular file:
    fs = New FileStream("c:\test1.txt", FileMode.Open,
FileAccess.Read)
    Dim r As New BinaryReader(fs)

    ' Read the data, in bytes, from the Test1.txt file:
    For i = 1 To 14
        Debug.WriteLine(r.ReadByte())
    Next i
    r.Close()
    fs.Close()
```

`BinaryReader` and `BinaryWriter` can read and write information in quite a few different data types. Type this line, and when you type the . (period), you see the list of data types:

```
Debug.WriteLine(r.
```

Also note that there are several `FileModes` you can define. The one used in the preceding example breaks with an error if the file already exists.

(To *replace* an existing file, use `FileMode.Create` instead of `FileMode.CreateNew`.)

Fixed-Length Strings Are Not Permitted

Before VB.NET

When using `Get` or `Put` for random-mode disk file access, you needed to employ strings of a fixed, known length. You could create one by using the following code:

```
A = String(20," ")
```

This code caused the string variable A to have 20 space characters. A more common way to create a fixed-length string, however, was by using `Dim A As String * 20`. When a string was defined to have a fixed length, any attempt to assign a shorter value resulted in the string being padded with spaces and any longer values were truncated to fit.

VB.NET

Fixed-length strings in VB.NET require a different declaration than they required in previous versions of VB. Consider this example:

```
Dim A As String * 20 'This is the pre-VB.NET way
```

That code now changes to the following new declaration syntax:

```
Dim A As VB6.FixedLengthString(20)
```

Additionally, to use this code, you must also use the "compatibility" `Imports` statement:

```
Imports Microsoft.VisualBasic
```

Or you can use the `PadRight` or `PadLeft` methods of the string object, like this:

```
Dim n As String = "Title 1"
        n = n.PadRight(75)
        MsgBox(n.Length)
```

Focus

Before VB.NET

If you wanted to force the focus to a particular control, you would use the `SetFocus` method:

```
TextBox1.SetFocus
```

VB.NET

SetFocus has been replaced by the Focus method:

```
TextBox1.Focus
```

Or you can use this alternative:

```
ActiveControl = TextBox1
```

Focused Property

This new property tells you whether the control has the focus.

Font Property Cannot Directly Be Changed at Runtime

Before VB.NET

Here's an example of how the Font property could be used at runtime prior to VB.NET:

```
Sub CommandButton1_Click()

Lable1.Font.Italic = True

End Sub
```

VB.NET

You can no longer simply change a property of a control's font (its name, size, boldness, and so on). To change these qualities at runtime, you have to take an indirect approach by creating a new Font object and then assigning it to a control's Font property, like this:

```
Private Sub Button1_Click(ByVal sender As System.Object,
    ByVal e As System.EventArgs) Handles Button1.Click

    ' Assign a Font object -- Name and Size are required.
    Label1.Font = New System.Drawing.Font("Courier New",
20)

    ' Assign additional attributes.

    Label1.Font = New System.Drawing.Font(Label1().Font,
FontStyle.Bold)
 End Sub
```

First, you must assign both name and size (both are *required*). Then in the next line, you can specify additional properties such as italic or bold, as illustrated in this example.

Inheriting container font properties

In VB.NET, if you change the font properties of the form, all the controls' font properties will also change to match their "parent" container form. However, if you specifically change the font of a control, any additional changes to the form's font properties will not be inherited by the "child" controls. Here's how to adjust all the controls' fonts by simply changing the form:

```
Me.Font = New System.Drawing.Font("Courier New", 20)
Me.Font = New System.Drawing.Font(Me.Font,
FontStyle.Italic)
```

Enumerating fonts

In VB 6, you used the `Screen.FontCount` to find out how many fonts were available, and you used the `Screen.Fonts` collection to list (eunumerate) them. Now, in VB.NET, there is no screen object. Instead, use the `System.Drawing.FontFamily` object, like this:

```
Dim F As System.Drawing.FontFamily

For Each F In System.Drawing.FontFamily.Families
    Debug.Write(F.Name)
    Debug.WriteLine("")
Next
```

Form Events Are Now Called "Base Class Events"

Before VB.NET

If you wanted to have VB type in a form's event for you, you dropped the listbox in the upper-left corner of the code window and selected the Form's Name (such as `Form1`). Then you dropped the listbox in the upper-right corner of the code window and clicked the event that you wanted to be typed in. For instance, following these steps and clicking the form's `KeyPress` event in the list would result in VB typing the following:

```
Sub Form1_KeyPress()

End Sub
```

Appendix

A Dictionary of VB.NET

VB.NET

To have VB.NET type in a form's event for you, you drop the listbox in the upper-left corner of the code window and select (Base Class Events). However, the newer VB.NET version 2003 changes this: If you are using VB.NET 2003, select (Form1 Events).

Then you drop the listbox in the upper-right corner of the code window and click the event that you want to be typed in. Clicking the Base Class Event named KeyPress in the top right list results in VB.NET typing the following:

```
Private Sub Form1_KeyPress(ByVal sender As Object, ByVal e As
    System.Windows.Forms.KeyPressEventArgs) Handles
    MyBase.KeyPress

End Sub
```

If you do not see events or other members automatically listed — such as when you're creating a new UserControl — go to Tools⇨Options⇨ Text Editor⇨Basic⇨General and deselect Hide Advanced Members.

Form References (Communication between Forms)

Before VB.NET (from inside the form)

You could reference a form's properties in code inside that form by merely specifying a property (leaving off the name of the form):

```
BackColor = vbBlue
```

Before VB.NET (from outside the form)

If you want to show or adjust properties of controls in one form (by writing programming in a second form), you merely use the outside form's name in your code. For instance, in a CommandButton_Click event in Form1, you can Show Form2, and change the ForeColor of a TextBox on Form2, like this:

```
Sub Command1_Click ()
Form2.Show
Form2.Text1.ForeColor = vbBlue
End Sub
```

VB.NET (from inside the form)

To reference a form's properties from code inside the form, you must use me:

```
Me.BackColor = Color.Blue
```

VB.NET (from outside the form)

Say that you want to be able to contact `Form2` from within `Form1`. You want to avoid creating clone after clone of `Form2`. If you use the `New` statement willy-nilly all over the place (`Dim F5 As New Form2`), you propagate multiple copies of `Form2`, which is not what you want. You don't want lots of windows floating around in the user's Taskbar, all of them clones of the original `Form2`.

Instead, you want to be able to communicate with the single, original `Form2` object from `Form1`. One way to achieve this is to create a public variable in `Form1`, like this:

```
Public f2 As New Form2

Private Sub Form1_Load(ByVal sender As System.Object, ByVal e
    As System.EventArgs) Handles MyBase.Load

        f2.Show()
        f2.BackColor = Color.Blue

End Sub
```

`Form1` is instantiated first when a VB.NET project executes (by default, it is the "startup object") in any Windows-style VB.NET project. So, by creating a `Public` variable that instantiates `Form1` (the `New` keyword does that), you can then reference this variable (`F2` here) any time you need to manipulate `Form2`'s properties or methods from within `Form1`. It's now possible for `Form1` to be a client of `Form2`, in other words.

The problem of communicating from `Form2` to `Form1`, however, is somewhat more complex. You cannot use the `New` keyword in `Form2` or any other form because that would create a *second* `Form1`. `Form1` already exists because it is the default startup object.

To create a way of accessing `Form1`, create an object variable in a `Module`; then assign `Form1` to this variable when `Form1` is created. The best place to do this assigning is just following the `InitializeComponent()` line in the `Sub New()` constructor for `Form1`.

Create a module (choose Project⇨Add Module). Modules are visible to all the forms in a project. In this module, you define a public variable that points to `Form1`. In the `Module`, type this:

```
Module Module1

    Public f1 As Form1()

End Module
```

Notice that the NEW keyword was not employed here. You are merely creating an object variable that will be assigned to point to Form1. Click the + next to "Windows Form Designer generated code" in Form1's code window. Locate Form1's constructor (Public Sub New) and just below the InitializeComponent() line, type this:

```
InitializeComponent()

F1 = Me
```

This assigns Me (Form1, in this case) to the public variable F1. Now, whenever you need to communicate with Form1 from any other form, you can use F1. For example, in Form2's Load event, you can have this code:

```
Private Sub Form2_Load(ByVal sender As System.Object, ByVal e
    As System.EventArgs) Handles MyBase.Load

        F1.BackColor = Color.Brown

End Sub
```

Formatting Strings

In VB.NET, you can format strings using a set of character symbols that represent typical formatting styles.

C for Currency

The following code gives a result of $44,556,677.00:

```
        Dim i As Integer = 44556677
        Dim s As String = i.ToString("c") ' use the "c" for
currency format
        Debug.Write(s)
```

There is also d for decimal, e for exponential, f for fixed point, n for number, p for percent, x for hex, and a whole variety of other symbols you can look up in VB.NET Help. To look them up, choose Help⇨Search, and then type the following line into the address field:

```
ms-help://MS.VSCC/MS.MSDNVS/cpguide/html/
    cpconformattingoverview.htm
```

Here's an example showing how various formatting symbols can be combined:

```
        Dim d As Double = 44.556677
        Dim s As String = d.ToString("%#.##")
        Debug.Write(s)
```

This results in:

```
%4455.67
```

If you're using a StringBuilder object, you can employ its `AppendFormat` method using one of the formatting symbols.

Frame Becomes Group Box

Before VB.NET

The *frame* was the control used to create subdivisions on forms, to option-ally label those subdivisions, and to enclose a set of option buttons (so that when the user clicked one button, the previously selected button was unselected).

In VB.NET

The frame is now named the *group box,* but it behaves the same way as the frame did.

Function Return Alternative

Before VB.NET

In traditional VB, a function returned a value to the caller by simply assign-ing that value to the function's name. For example, this function multiplied a number by 2 and then returned the result to the caller:

```
Public Function DoubleIt(passednumber As Integer)

passednumber = passednumber * 2

DoubleIt = passednumber 'assign the result to the function's
    name
'                          so it gets passed back to the caller

End Function
```

VB.NET

It's not mandatory, but if you want to use C-like syntax, you can now use the following way of returning a value to the caller:

```
Public Function DoubleIt(ByVal passednumber As Integer)
As Integer

    passednumber = passednumber * 2

    '   use the Return statement to pass the result
    '   back to the caller
    Return (passednumber)

End Function
```

I don't know about you, but I view this syntax as a real improvement over the way that VB has always returned function values. It's clearer and easier to read. I confess that *some* C-language diction and syntax are, to me, not as readable as traditional VB. But this one is an exception.

In the following function, the if ... then test will never execute:

```
Public Function DoubleIt(ByVal passednumber As Integer)
As Integer

    passednumber = passednumber * 2
    Return (passednumber)

If passednumber > 50 then msgbox ("Greater than 50")


End Function
```

The If...Then line comes after the Return, and anything following Return in a function is not executed. Return causes an immediate Exit Function.

Garbage Collection Debate

Before VB.NET

One of the most controversial changes in VB.NET is the way that objects are terminated. As defined by the Microsoft COM framework, when an object is instantiated (brought into being), it is automatically kept track of, and when it is no longer needed by the program, its Terminate event is triggered. (You can kill an object in this way: Set MyObject = Nothing.)

An object's Terminate event allows you to do any needed shutdown house-keeping chores (by putting such code into the Terminate event) and then the object is destroyed. This keeps things clean and, above all, frees up memory. (The use of a Terminate event in this fashion is called *deterministic finalization*.)

VB.NET

VB.NET does not keep track of objects in the COM fashion. Instead, .NET uses a *garbage collection* (GC) technique that checks things from time to time during a VB.NET program's execution. It checks its list of object references, and if an object is no longer in use, GC deletes them and thereby frees memory. This means that you, the programmer, cannot know when an object is destroyed, nor the order in which objects in an object hierarchy are destroyed. You cannot rely on a `Terminate` event.

If your VB 6 and older source code relies on an object's `Terminate` event or a predictable order of termination, you'll have to rewrite that object to give it a procedure that shuts it down. And if you need to keep a count of references, you also need to give it a procedure that opens the object and deals with this reference counting.

Technically, the garbage collection approach can prevent some problems such as memory leaks. And it also permits faster performance. However, many programmers (mostly C programmers, actually) are upset because the garbage collection approach not only requires quite a bit of rewriting to port older programs to VB.NET, but it also means that the programmer, not the computer, has the burden of adding open and close procedures for his or her objects. This is potentially a serious source of errors because the object no longer automatically handles its own termination. (Clients, users of the object, must specifically invoke the close event and ensure that the event doesn't itself spawn any unintended side effects — in other words, clients must error trap.) However, for VB programmers, it's best to just relax and let VB.NET handle this issue.

Global Is Gone

Before VB.NET

VB has had a `Global` command for years. It declares a variable with the widest possible scope — application-wide. Any form or module in the application can see and manipulate a `Global` variable. `Global` is no longer in the language.

VB.NET

The `Public` command is the equivalent of `Global`. Use `Public` instead.

GoSub, On . . . GoSub, and On . . . GoTo Are No More

Before VB.NET

The various GoSub and GoTo structures have been used in traditional VB for error trapping or for quick, convenient execution of a task that requires many parameters. GoSub or GoTo commands must be used *within* a given procedure. Therefore, if you have some code that you GoSub to, it would not be necessary to "pass" parameters to this task (the variables would all have local scope, and therefore would be usable by your task).

The On... commands were also sometimes used instead of Select...Case or If branching situations.

VB.NET

These three commands are removed from the language.

Handle Property

This new property gives you the window handle for this control.

Handles

In VB 6 and earlier, each event of each object (or control) was unique. When the user clicked a particular button, that button's unique event procedure was triggered. In VB.NET, each event procedure declaration ends with a Handles command that specifies which event *or events* that procedure responds to. In other words, you can create a single procedure that responds to multiple different object events.

To put it another way, in VB.NET an event can "handle" (have code that responds to) whatever event (or multiple events) that you want it to handle. The actual sub name (such as Button1_Click) that you give to an event procedure is functionally irrelevent. You could call it Bxteen44z_Click if you want. It would still be the click event for Button1 no matter what you named this procedure, as long as you provide the name Button1 following the Handles command.

In other words, the following is a legitimate event where you write code to deal with Button1's Click:

```
Private Sub Francoise_Click(ByVal sender As System.Object,
    ByVal e As System.EventArgs) Handles Button1.Click
```

The `Handles Button1.Click` code does the trick.

You can even gang up several events into one, like this:

```
Private Sub cmd_Click(ByVal sender As System.Object, ByVal e
    As
System.EventArgs) Handles cmdOK.Click, cmdApply.Click,
    cmdCancel.Click
```

For a working example of this ganging up, see the section in this appendix titled "Control Arrays Are Gone."

Runtime handles

If you want to get really fancy, you can attach or detach an object's events to a procedure during runtime. The following example illustrates this. Put three buttons on a form.

Now create this procedure to handle all three of these buttons' `Click` events:

```
Private Sub AllTheButtonClicks(ByVal sender As Object, ByVal
    e As System.EventArgs) Handles Button1.Click,
    Button2.Click, Button3.Click

    RemoveHandler Button1.Click, AddressOf AllTheButtonClicks

    MsgBox(sender.ToString)

End Sub
```

Press F5 to run this little program and click `Button1`. The MessageBox appears. Click `Button1` again and *nothing happens* because `Button1`'s `Click` event has been detached — so this procedure no longer responds to any clicking of `Button1`. `Button2` and `Button3` still trigger this procedure. To restore (or create for the first time) a procedure's ability to handle an object's events, use the `AddHandler` command, like this:

```
    AddHandler Button1.Click, AddressOf AllTheButtonClicks
```

HasChildren Property

This new property tells you if the control contains any child controls.

Height

See " Left, Top, Height, Width, and Move All Change."

Help System Fails

From time to time, you may notice that when you look up an entry (using Index, Search, it doesn't matter) in the VB.NET Help utility, you get an error message in the right view pane:

```
The page cannot be displayed
The page you are looking for is currently unavailable. The
    Web site might be experiencing technical difficulties, or
    you may need to adjust your browser settings.
Etc. etc.
```

It's the usual browser error message when you travel to an Internet address that no longer exists.

Or, you may simply see a blank right pane, no error message, and no help information.

The most likely cause for this problem is a filled browser cache. To cure the problem, open Internet Explorer, and choose Tools⇨Internet Options. On the General tab (the default) in this dialog box, click the Delete Files button under Temporary Internet Files. These files will be deleted (which can take several minutes). Then retry Help, and it should work fine once again.

Help (Using)

The .NET Help system can be used in a variety of ways to assist you when creating VB.NET projects. It's a significant resource, and it's becoming more useful as time goes on (more helpful descriptions, more bug-free source code examples). For an in-depth discussion on how to best exploit Help and other VB.NET resources, see Chapter 5, Book VII of this book.

IDE: The VB.NET Editor

The VB.NET IDE (Integrated Development Environment) is packed with features and options. You usually work with a *solution,* which can contain one or more individual *projects.* You can switch between projects, or right-click project names to adjust their properties, within the Solution Explorer (Ctrl+R).

You get used to the IDE and find your own preferred layout. My main piece of advice is to right-click the title bar of all the various windows and choose Auto Hide. That way, the Properties window, toolbox, Solution Explorer, output window, and so on are all quickly available (because they're tabs along the edges of your IDE). But they don't cover up the primary work surface: the Design and code window. You may need to set the Tabbed Documents option in the Tools⇨Options⇨Environment⇨General menu.

And while you're looking at the Environment section of the Options menu, you may want to click the Help section and switch from the default to *External Help.* That way, you get a full, separate window for your help searches rather than letting VB.NET try to fit help windows into your IDE.

Under Tools⇨Options⇨Text Editor⇨All Languages⇨General, you want to select Auto List Members and Parameter Information, unless you have a photographic memory and have read through the entire .NET class documentation. These two options are, for most of us, essential: They display the properties and methods (with their arguments and parameters) of each object as you type in your source code. Also, while you're on this page in the dialog box, uncheck the Hide Advanced Members. That way you get to see everything.

Implements Changes

Before VB.NET

VB 6 and earlier versions could inherit classes using the `Implements` command, but they could not create interfaces directly.

VB.NET

In VB.NET, you can give an inherited object's members (its methods and properties) any names you wish. The `Implements` command can be followed by a comma-separated list of names. (Typically, you would use only a single name, but you *can* use multiple names.)

The names you use in this fashion must be *fully qualified,* which means you need to supply the interface name, a period, and then the name of the member (method or property) that you want to be implemented. (VB prior to VB.NET used an underscore for the punctuation: `InterfaceName_MethodName`.)

Imports

The new VB.NET `Imports` command does not import anything. Based on its name, you're likely to assume that it adds a library of functions to your project. You'll probably think it's adding a "Reference" to a dynamic link library (DLL). (By the way, the term *DLL* isn't used any more; it's now called an *assembly*. A given assembly can contain multiple namespaces. In `System.Drawing.Color`, `System.Drawing` is an assembly and `Color` is a namespace within that assembly.)

Anyway, when you use `Imports`, all that happens is that it permits you to write shorter, more convenient source code. After importing, you can then leave out the namespace when referring to a function or object that sits inside the namespace referenced by that `Imports` statement. For example, include the following line at the top of your code window:

```
Imports System.Drawing.Color
```

With that line, you can then use the following shortcut when naming one of the VB.NET color constants:

```
Me.BackColor = Black
```

Or, if you don't use any `Imports` statement, you must specify the `Color` namespace within your source code whenever you use the `Black` constant:

```
Me.BackColor = Color.Black
```

Similarly, the VB.NET control characters (such as `CRLF`, which is used in a message box to force the message text to appear down one line) require the `ControlChars` namespace:

```
Dim s As String = "This line."
s += ControlChars.CrLf + "Next line."
Debug.Write(s)
```

A *namespace* is the new .NET term for a group of functions that are stored together (as a logical unit) within an assembly. Recall that there can be more than one namespace in a given assembly (a given code library).

You put `Imports` statements at the very top of your code window. When you do, you can thereafter simply refer in your source code to objects and functions (methods) residing in whatever your `Imports` statement specifies. VB.NET will be able to tell in which code library namespace the function is located — because you specified the namespace's name in the `Imports` statement.

Here's an example. Let's say that you want to write the following code that deletes a directory on the hard drive:

```
Public Function DestroyDirectory()

    Dim objDir As New DirectoryInfo("C:\TestDir")
```

```
        Try
            objDir.Delete(True)
        Catch
            Throw New Exception("Failed to delete")
        End Try

    End Function
```

If you simply type this into the VB.NET code window, it rejects the `DirectoryInfo` object because it doesn't recognize it. You can fix this problem by specifying the correct namespace adjectives in your source code line, as follows:

```
Dim objDir As New System.IO.DirectoryInfo("C:\TestDir")
```

That `System.IO` specifies the namespace adjectives so that VB.NET knows in which library to find the `DirectoryInfo` object and its methods. However, if you are going to be using `DirectoryInfo` or other IO functions several times, you may not want to keep having to type in that `System.IO` reference over and over. You can shorten your source code by putting this `Imports` statement at the top:

```
Imports System.IO
```

Now you can shorten the example line, merely using the `DirectoryInfo` command, without "qualifying" it by specifying the namespace where this command can be found. Here's how you can shorten this line of code:

```
Dim objDir As New DirectoryInfo("C:\TestDir")
```

With no `Imports` statement, you must "fully qualify" (use adjectives).

In earlier versions of VB, *all* the commands in the language were always available. You never needed to specify a namespace (there was no such concept as *namespace*).

In VB.NET, some namespaces are loaded in by default, so you need not use `Imports` for them. However, if you are trying to use a valid VB.NET command (such as `DirectoryInfo`) and you get the error message `"Type is not defined"` or something like it, consider that you might have to `Imports` a namespace for that command. (For example, when you work with certain database commands, you have to use `Imports`.)

To see the available namespaces, go to the top of your code window and type the following:

```
Imports System.
```

As soon as you type the . (period), you see a list. If you're working with databases, try the following:

```
Imports System.Data.
```

Now, when you type the second period (after `Data.`), you see another list of namespaces. If you are going to use SQL Server databases, you may then want to `Imports` all namespaces beginning with `SQL` (each namespace `Imports` statement must be on a separate line in your code window):

```
Imports System.Data.SqlClient
Imports System.Data.SqlDbType
Imports System.Data.SqlTypes
```

In this situation, however, your best bet is to get a good book and just follow its advice about which namespaces you need to `Imports`. See this book for information on namespaces to use for database, graphics, security, and other project categories. Otherwise, you just have to learn by trial and error for yourself.

If you look up a class in Help, such as `DirectoryInfo`, you frequently find a reference to its namespace *down at the bottom of the right pane* (be sure to scroll down as necessary to see if the namespace is mentioned in a section titled "Requirements").

Why namespaces?

Why are they using namespaces? It's a clerical thing. It prevents "name collisions" if there are two identically named functions that do two different things (and each function is in a different code library). Which one does the programmer mean to use? By adding `Imports` statements at the top of the code window (or by qualifying the function name each time it appears within the source code), you are saying: "Use the function in *this* namespace — not the other one that is in some other namespace." (You can even have multiple namespaces within a single assembly — a single library, a single DLL.)

Sometimes, you may find that you need to actually add a library of code to a VB.NET project. In other words, a function or functions that you want to use aren't part of the default set of libraries added to a VB.NET project. (To see which libraries are added by default, right-click the name of your project in Solution Explorer, choose Properties, and then select Imports in the Properties dialog box. To add a namespace to your VB.NET project, choose the menu item Project⇨Add Reference.)

What happens, you may say, if you use `Imports` to name two namespaces that have a pair of identically named objects? Now you *will* have a name collision — no doubt about it. `Imports` doesn't help you distinguish between these objects because you've used `Imports` for both namespaces.

For example, assume that you write code for a custom cursor class and put it into a namespace called `NewCursors` within your library `MyObjects`. Then you `Imports` it:

```
Imports MyObjects.NewCursors
```

And you also `Imports` the standard Windows objects namespace (which includes controls such as the TextBox, as well as other items such as cursors):

```
Imports System.Windows.Forms
```

You need not actually use `Imports System.Windows.Forms`; it's already imported by default by VB.NET, but I'm just showing you an example here.

Now, you have two namespaces in your project, each containing a (different) `cursor` class. The only way you can distinguish them is to forget about the `Imports` trick and just use the long form (fully qualify) whenever you use the cursor object:

```
Dim n As New System.Windows.Forms.Cursor("nac.ico")
```

or:

```
Dim n As New MyObjects.NewCursors.Cursor("nac.ico")
```

Practical advice about namespaces

Don't worry about using `Imports` to add whatever namespaces you may need: Namespaces neither increase the size of your executable (.EXE) program, nor do they slow execution.

VB.NET is a *huge* language. It includes more than 60 .NET assemblies, containing the hundreds of .NET namespaces. Each namespace contains many classes. In turn, these classes have multiple members (methods you can employ, properties you can read or change). Also, many of the methods are overloaded: They often permit you to provide a variety of arguments to make them behave in different ways. As you can see, there are hundreds of thousands of commands and variations of those commands in this language.

What to do? You can learn the important tools quickly — file I/O, printing, useful constants, interacting with the user, debugging, and so on. Most of these major programming techniques can be found in this appendix, as a matter of fact. Also, you can use VB.NET Help's Search and Index features as necessary. To see the format, syntax, punctuation, and, sometimes, code examples of the many classes, try this approach. Run the Help Index, and

Appendix

A Dictionary of VB.NET

then type the following into the Look For field (cutting and pasting doesn't work; you must type this in):

```
system.drawing.
```

You then see the massive number of classes listed in the left pane. Click on any of these classes to see its members and other information about how to use it. Each page contains hyperlinks that take you to more specific information about particular members.

The more you work with VB.NET, the more you learn about which namespaces you need to `Imports`. Often, you don't need to `Imports` any because the most common namespaces are automatically imported by VB.NET when you create a new project. These seven are imported by default: `Microsoft. VisualBasic` (a "compatibility" namespace, permitting you to use most VB 6 constants and functions, such as `InStr` rather than the new .NET equivalent, `IndexOf`); `System`; `System.Collections`; `System.Data`; `System.Diagnostics`; `System.Drawing`; and `System.Windows.Forms`.

You may remember some traditional VB constants, such as `vbBlue`. Well, they are not included in the `Microsoft.VisualBasic` compatibility namespace that's automatically imported by default. Use the new VB.NET constants instead:

```
Me.BackColor = Color.Black
```

The VB.NET color constants are in the `System.Drawing.Color` namespace, but you only have to use `Color` because `System.Drawing` is one of the seven automatically imported default assemblies. And, if you wish, you can avoid having to specify `Color` in your code by adding the following line at the top of your code window:

```
Imports System.Drawing.Color
```

The Object Browser

Press F2 or Ctrl+Alt+J. The Object Browser opens. Browse through the various assemblies and their namespaces to see what's available — which constants, properties, and methods are contained within which namespaces.

Inheritance

Some VB programmers have long wanted the language to have true inheritance, one of the big three features of object-oriented programming (the other two being encapsulation and polymorphism). Well, they got their wish.

Here's an example showing you how to inherit from the built-in TextBox class. In this example, you have a problem. Your daughter cannot speak or write without using the term "really" every few words. You want your TextBox to have a method that deletes all instances of the word "really" at the click of a button. Here's how:

```
Public Class Form1
    Inherits System.Windows.Forms.Form


    Dim t As New NewTextBox()
    Private Sub Form1_Load(ByVal sender As System.Object,
ByVal e As System.EventArgs) Handles MyBase.Load

        t.Multiline = True
        t.Size = New System.Drawing.Size(130, 130)
        t.Location = New System.Drawing.Point(10, 50)
        t.Name = "SpecialTextBox"
        Me.Controls.Add(t)
    End Sub

    Private Sub Button1_Click(ByVal sender As System.Object,
    ByVal e As System.EventArgs) Handles Button1.Click
        t.RemoveReally()
    End Sub
End Class

Public Class NewTextBox
    Inherits System.Windows.Forms.TextBox

    Public Sub RemoveReally()

        Dim s As System.Text.StringBuilder
        s = New System.Text.StringBuilder(Me.Text)

        s.Replace("really", "") ' get rid of any really's.
        Me.Text = s.ToString

    End Sub

End Class
```

The new TextBox class that you created inherits all the members (properties, events, and methods) in the ordinary VB.NET TextBox. But you define a new method, called RemoveReally, which replaces all instances of "really" in its Text property.

In the Page_Load event, you specify various properties of the new TextBox. Run this program by pressing F5, and then type in some text with the word "really" in various places. Then click the Button that invokes the RemoveReally method.

Initializers

VB.NET permits you to simultaneously declare a variable or array and assign a value to it:

```
Dim n As Integer = 12
```

or:

```
Dim strVisitors() As String = {"Morris", "Susan"}
```

Also, if you are using the latest version, VB.NET 2003, you can even declare a loop counter variable within the line that starts the loop, like this:

```
For i As Integer = 0 To 10
```

instead of the traditional style:

```
Dim i as Integer
For i = 0 To 10
```

Also see "Dim and ReDim: New Rules."

Instantiation

See "Object Instantiation."

InStr

See "String Functions Are Now Methods."

Integers and Long Double in Size

Before VB.NET

The Integer data type was 16 bits large, and the Long data type was 32 bits large.

VB.NET

Now Integer and Data are twice as big: Integer is 32 bits large and Long is 64 bits (it's an Integer, too, with no fractional control and no decimal point). If your program needs to use a 16-bit integer, use the new Short type.

So if you're translating pre-.NET VB code, you need to change any `As Integer` or `Cint` commands to `As Short` and `Cshort`, respectively. Similarly, `As Long` and `CLng` now must be changed to `As Integer` and `Cint`. See also "Data Types."

IsEmpty

In VB 6, if a variant variable had previously been declared in the source code, but not yet given any value (not initialized), you could check to see if the variant contained `empty` as its "value" (`IsEmpty`). The `IsEmpty` command is not available in VB.NET, nor is the variant type itself.

In VB.NET the default variable type is the `object`. An `object` variable has a default value of `nothing`.

IsNull

In VB 6, you could query to see if a variable held a `Null`, using the `IsNull` command. This command has been changed to `IsDBNull`, and the `Null` value is now `DBNull` and can only be used with database fields, not in other situations (such as string concatenation).

KeyPress

The following example shows how to use the `e.KeyChar` object in VB.NET to figure out which key the user pressed. You compare it to the `Keys` enumeration (a list of built-in constants that can be used to identify keypresses). The following code checks to see if the user presses the Enter key:

```
Private Sub TextBox1_KeyPress(ByVal sender As Object, ByVal e
    As System.Windows.Forms.KeyPressEventArgs) Handles
    TextBox1.KeyPress

        If Asc(e.KeyChar) = Keys.Enter Then
            MsgBox("ENTER")
        End If

    End Sub
```

The following example shows how to detect if the user presses Ctrl+N on the form (to set the Form's `KeyPreview` property to `True`):

```
Private Sub Form1_KeyDown(ByVal sender As Object, ByVal e As
    System.Windows.Forms.KeyEventArgs) Handles MyBase.KeyDown
```

```
                  If e.KeyCode = Keys.N And e.Control = True Then
                      'they pressed CTRL+N

                  searchnext() 'respond to this key combination

                  Exit Sub

            End If

      End Sub
```

LCase and UCase Change

Many traditional VB string functions — LCase, UCase, LTrim, RTrim, and Trim — have been changed to VB.NET methods. So, the following classic function syntax has changed:

```
Dim s As String = "Bob"
MsgBox(LCase(s))
```

You now use the syntax appropriate to a method, as follows:

```
Dim s As String = "Bob"
MsgBox(s.ToLower)
```

LCase, UCase, LTrim, RTrim, and Trim have been changed to, respectively, ToLower, ToUpper, TrimStart, TrimEnd, and Trim.

See "String Functions Are Now Methods" for additional information.

Left (LeftStr or Left$) Must Be "Qualified"

See "Right." Also see "String Functions Are Now Methods."

Left, Top, Height, Width, and Move All Change

Before VB.NET

You could specify a new position or size for a control like this:

```
CommandButton1.Left = 122
CommandButton1.Height = 163
```

VB.NET

In VB.NET, you have several ways to position or size items using code.

In the following code, the `With...End With` structure is used to provide references to other controls, in order to specify size and position:

```
With Button1
        .Left = btnSearch.Left
        .Top = txtTitle.Top
        .Width = btnSearch.Width
        .Height = txtTitle.Height + txtDesc.Height + 17
End With
```

Or you can use the traditional VB property names:

```
btnSearch.Left = 222
btnsearch.top = 155
```

However, you can no longer use `Left` or `Top` to position a form. Instead, use this:

```
    Me.Location = New Point(10, 12)
```

You can use the new (preferred) CLR-compatible (Common Language Runtime) property names in the Properties window:

```
Location.X, Location.Y, Size.Width and Size.Height
```

Or you can "qualify" your code, which means that you add various library references and object references to adjust position or size. (See "Imports" for more on namespaces.) Here are some examples for you to follow, if you want to change these qualities while your application is running:

```
Button1.Location = New System.Drawing.Point(256, 160)
Button1.Size = New System.Drawing.Size(120, 32)
```

Alternatively, you can use code like this if the `System.Drawing` namespace is already available to your code (because at the top of your code window, you include the line `Imports System.Drawing`):

```
Button1.Location = New Point(100, 125)
```

Line Control (And Command) Are Gone

See "Circle, Line, Shape, PSet, and Point All Changed."

LinkLabel Control

This new control displays an Internet URL, and then you can use its clicked property to run Internet Explorer and automatically go to the Web site described in the LinkLabel's Text property:

```
Private Sub LinkLabel1_LinkClicked(ByVal sender As
    System.Object, ByVal e As
    System.Windows.Forms.LinkLabelLinkClickedEventArgs)
    Handles LinkLabel1.LinkClicked

    System.Diagnostics.Process.Start("http://www.cnn.com")

End Sub
```

ListBox (And Others) Become Objectified

Before VB.NET

You could write code like this:

```
ListBox1.AddItem(n)
```

VB.NET

If you try using the AddItem method of a ListBox in VB.NET, you get an error message informing you that AddItem "is not a member of the System.WinForms.ListBox" object. Well, excuuuuuse me! AddItem used to be a member.

Little kinks like this pop up here and there as you're adjusting yourself to VB.NET programming. You then should look up the control in VB.NET Help to see what the proper diction is to accomplish your goal. In this example, you must use the Add method of the ListBox control's Items collection. Here's the solution:

```
ListBox1.Items.Add(n)
```

Also, if you want to clear the contents of a ListBox (or similar control), you must now use the Clear method of the Items collection, like this:

```
Listbox1.Items.Clear()
```

The ListBox control in previous versions of VB had its own Clear method (List1.Clear).

Another change in terminology involves the way that you access which item the user clicked within a ListBox. In traditional VB, you get the clicked item's index number like this:

```
Dim SelectedItem as Integer
SelectedItem = ListBox1.List(ListBox1.ListIndex)
```

But in VB.NET, you use the following code:

```
Dim SelectedItem as Integer
SelectedItem = ListBox1.Items(ListBox1.SelectedIndex)
```

Or, to get the actual string that was clicked (not the index), use the following code:

```
Dim SelectedItem as String
SelectedItem = ListBox1.Items(ListBox1.SelectedItem)
```

You probably assume that if you use an Add method to add items, there is a corresponding Remove method to remove items. Well, Dude, there used to be. The powers that control the language decided in their mysterious way to change this method's name to RemoveAt:

```
ListBox1.Items.RemoveAt (ListBox1.SelectedIndex)
```

Other changes to the ListBox include: It can now have multiple columns; its items are objects, not strings; and you can display any property of the objects in the ListBox. The following example shows how to list the Name properties of all the controls currently on the form in a two-column ListBox:

```
Private Sub Form1_Load(ByVal sender As System.Object, ByVal e
    As System.EventArgs) Handles MyBase.Load

        Dim n As Integer = Me.Controls.Count
        Dim i As Integer

        With listbox1

            .MultiColumn = True
            'make width of each column less than half of
listbox width
            .ColumnWidth = (.Width \ 2) - 10

        End With


        For i = 0 To n - 1
            ListBox1.Items.Add(Me.Controls(i).Name)
        Next

    End Sub
```

LoadPicture Replaced

Before VB.NET

To put a graphic into a VB PictureBox in VB 6, you used this code:

```
Set Picture1.Picture = LoadPicture("C:\Graphics\MyDog.jpg")
```

VB.NET

LoadPicture has been replaced with the following code:

```
PictureBox1.Image = Image.FromFile("C:\Graphics\MyDog.jpg")
```

Notice the various changes:

✦ The default name for a PictureBox is no longer Picture1 but rather PictureBox1.

✦ The Picture property has been changed to an Image property.

✦ Rather than LoadPicture, you now use Image.FromFile.

Location Property

This new property specifies the coordinates of the upper-left corner of the control, relative to the upper-left corner of its container (usually the form).

LSet and RSet Are Gone

If you need to pad strings, use the new PadRight and PadLeft commands.

You cannot use LSet or RSet to assign one data type to another.

For additional information see "User-Defined Type Changes to Structure" in this appendix.

LTrim

See "LCase and UCase Change" and "String Functions Are Now Methods."

Math Functions Change (ATN, SGN, ABS, and so On)

The various VB 6 math functions (such as `Atn`, `Sgn`, and `Sqr`) have been replaced by (often) differently named functions in VB.NET: `Atan`, `Sign`, and `Sqrt`, for example. What's more, they are now methods of the `System.Math` class. So, you must use them like this:

```
Private Sub Button1_Click_1(ByVal sender As System.Object,
    ByVal e As System.EventArgs) Handles Button1.Click

    Dim x As Double

    x = System.Math.Sqrt(16)
    msgbox(x)

End Sub
```

The obsolete VB 6 version looked like this:

```
MsgBox (Sqr(16))
```

Mathematical functionality is supplied by classes in the `System` namespace. The `Atn`, `Sgn`, and `Sqr` functions are replaced by the `Atan`, `Sign`, and `Sqrt` methods of the `Math` class. `System.Math` offers comprehensive mathematical support with its methods and fields.

Mid

See "String Functions Are Now Methods."

Move

See "Left, Top, Height, Width, and Move All Change."

Name Property Becomes Dynamic

In VB.NET, the `Name` property can be changed during runtime. This is useful when you create the VB.NET version of control arrays. See "Control Arrays Are Gone."

Namespace

See "Imports."

Null

See "IsNull."

Object Instantiation

Before VB.NET

A common format for instantiating (creating) an object in VB 6 and earlier is as follows:

```
Dim DataCon as New ADODB.Connection
```

However, some people argued that this wasn't good programming because it added overhead (inefficiency) to the execution (never mind why). Instead, you were asked to use this version:

```
Dim DataCon as ADODB.Connection
Set DataCon = New ADODB.Connection
```

VB.NET

The Set command has been removed from the language in VB.NET.

All three of the following syntaxes do the same thing in VB.NET (instantiate an object — bring it into existence):

```
Dim DataCon as New ADODB.Connection
```

```
Dim DataCon as ADODB.Connection = New ADODB.Connection
```

```
Dim DataCon as ADODB.Connection
DataCon = New ADODB.Connection
```

However, the third version gives you a bit more flexibility because the object is not created in the declare (Dim) statement. It's created in the line where you use the New command. This way, you can declare the object variable with Dim, but delay the actual instantiation of the object (with New) until you actually need that object. If this distinction means something to your programming, go ahead and use the most verbose format (version three in this example).

ObjPtr, VarPtr, and StrPtr Are Removed

Before VB.NET

Although you would search for them in vain in the VB Help engine, there were three "secret" commands in VB: `ObjPtr`, `VarPtr`, and `StrPtr`. You could use them to get a variable's address in memory. This isn't officially permitted in VB, so it's undocumented. However, using such commands, some extreme programmer jockeys were able to speed up their applications or add functionality that VB itself didn't directly offer. (Interestingly, although these three functions are missing from Help, their syntax *is* displayed to you if you've got the Auto Quick Info option set in the Tools⇨Options menu.)

Here's an example:

```
Private Sub Form_Load()

Dim books As String
books = "Dickens"
n = StrPtr(books)
MsgBox n 'display the variable's address in memory

End Sub
```

VB.NET

These functions have been removed. Like several other elements in VB 6 and earlier versions, these commands have simply been eliminated from the language (with no substitutions to provide a replacement for their functionality).

Optional Parameter-Passing Tightened

Before VB.NET

In VB 6 and earlier, you could freely change a default value for parameters in a procedure. For instance, if no parameter is passed to this sub, it will default to the value 101 for the `Books` parameter:

```
Private Sub CountBooks(Optional Books As Integer = 101)
```

Because VB used to check parameters and employ any necessary default parameters at *runtime,* it was possible to change a control to use a different default value and VB would respect that new value.

What's more, you could simply declare a parameter as `Optional` and not provide any default whatsoever, if you wished:

```
Private Sub CountBooks(Optional Books As Integer)
```

And, if the optional parameter is a `Variant` type, you could have used the `IsMissing` command to determine whether or not the parameter was passed at all.

VB.NET

VB.NET compiles any needed default values — and the result becomes hard-wired into the compilation. If the control is changed and a procedure is given new default parameter values, the original defaults will still be used. Any new defaults cannot take effect unless you completely recompile the program. The virtue of this approach is that it speeds things up at runtime. Also, VB.NET offers an alternative to optional parameters known as *overloading* (see the section titled "Overloaded Functions, Properties, and Methods (Overloading)" in this appendix).

In VB.NET, every optional parameter must declare a default value (it will be passed to the procedure if the calling code does not supply that parameter). The `IsMissing` command is no longer part of the VB language. Note, too, that you must include the `ByVal` command:

```
Private Sub CountBooks(Optional ByVal Books As Integer = 101)
```

OptionButton Is Renamed RadioButton

Option Strict and Option Explicit

Before VB.NET

In VB 6, you were not required to explicitly declare variables. You could simply assign a value to a variable, and that caused the variable to come into existence:

```
MyVariable = 12
```

Also, you were permitted to forget about variable types and let VB decide for you which type was required at any given place in the code, based on the context. For example, if `MyVariable` contained numeric 12, yet you wanted to display it in a TextBox, VB 6 would automatically transform this numeric integer data type into a text string type:

```
Text1 = MyVariable
```

This line would cause `Text1` to display the digit characters 12.

VB.NET

Many programmers believe that all variables should be explicitly declared. It's not enough to simply assign some value to a variable; you should declare it and declare its *type* as well:

```
Dim MyVariable As Integer
MyVariable = 12
```

Not only that, if you want to transform (*cast,* or *coerce*) a variable of one type into another type — such as changing an integer type into a string type — you should specifically do that transforming in your source code:

```
TextBox1.Text = CStr(MyVariable)
```

The `CStr` command is one of several commands that begin with `C` (`CInt`, `CByte`, and so on) that cast one variable type into another.

In VB.NET, if you attempt to use a variable before explicitly declaring it, VB.NET will inform you that you've made an error, that the variable name has not been declared. If you want to turn off this error message and use undeclared variables, type this line at the very top, on the first line, in your code window:

```
Option Explicit Off
```

However, you can avoid some kinds of bugs by explicitly declaring all your variables, and it doesn't take too much extra time to declare them.

Although VB.NET enforces `Option Explicit` by default, it does not enforce `Option Strict` by default. `Option Strict` governs whether an error message will be generated if you don't cast variables. You can use this line of code, even though the TextBox displays a string and `MyVariable` was declared as an Integer variable type:

```
TextBox1.Text = MyVariable
```

This is perfectly legal in VB.NET. No error message will be displayed when you execute this code. However, some programmers insist that casting is important. If you are one of those, you can enforce casting by typing this line at the top of your code window:

```
Option Strict On
```

Now, try to execute the following line:

```
TextBox1.Text = MyVariable
```

The VB.NET compiler does not like that line and displays the following error message:

```
Option strict disallows implicit conversions from
    System.Integer to System.String.
```

`Option Strict` does permit VB.NET to handle a few "safe" data type conversions itself. For instance, changing a 16-bit integer to a 32-bit integer cannot result in any loss of data, so it is permitted to take place automatically within VB.NET — no need for the programmer to explicitly do this conversion with special source code. The reverse, though (changing a 32-bit integer into a 16-bit version), is not permitted to take place automatically. You, the programmer, must use one of the data-conversion commands (see "Converting Data Types" in this appendix). Likewise, a floating-point data type (which may hold a value such as 12.335) is not permitted to automatically convert to an integer (which would strip off the $.335$ fractional portion of the number because integers have no decimal point). Is converting from an integer to a floating-point type permitted? Yes, because that is "safe."

Optional Operation Shorthand

Some programmers (users of the C language and its offspring) prefer a slightly abbreviated form of arithmetic, incrementation, and text concatenation. To some VB programmers, it can seem harder to read at first. This new syntax is optional, so you can stick with the traditional VB syntax if you prefer. But it can save some time and effort, particularly if you want to avoid repeating one of those long, heavily qualified, object names. For example, if you have this heavily qualified string object and you want to add the characters ED to it, in traditional VB you must type the object's name twice, like this:

```
MyAssem.MyNameSpace.MyObject = MyAssem.MyNameSpace.MyObject +
    "ED"
```

But in VB.NET, you can omit the second object name, thereby bringing the = and the + together into +=, like this:

```
MyAssem.MyNameSpace.MyObject += "ED"
```

It takes a little getting used to, but it's an improvement. The fundamental difference is that the C-style moves the operator (+, -, *, or whatever) way over next to the assignment (=) symbol.

So you get:

```
X += 1 '(The new C-style syntax)
```

instead of:

```
X = X + 1
```

With the VB-style, you must repeat the object (you must use that second X).

If you want to try out the C syntax, here are the variations:

```
X = X + Y     X +=Y
X = X - 5     X -= 5
X = X * 4     X *= 4
X = X / 7     X /= 7
X = X ^ 2     X ^= 2
String1 = String1 + "ing" String1 += "ing" (you can also use &)
```

Overloaded Functions, Properties, and Methods (Overloading)

Before VB.NET

Sometimes you may want to use the same function name but accomplish different tasks with it. Typically, you would do this by using optional parameters:

```
MyFunction (Optional SomeParam As Variant)

If IsMissing(SomeParam) Then

    'Do one task because they didn't send SomeParam

Else

'Do a different task because they did send SomeParam

End If
```

This way, the same `MyFunction` behaves differently based on what you pass to it.

You can still use optional parameters, but their utility has been reduced in VB.NET. Among other things, the `IsMissing` command is no longer part of the VB language. This puts a slight crimp in things if you attempt to write code like the previous example. For details about what has been removed or restricted concerning optional parameters, see "Optional Parameter-Passing Tightened" in this appendix.

VB.NET

You can use the same function name to do different tasks in VB.NET, but you employ a different technique than using the `optional` command. (Properties and methods can also be overloaded.)

In VB.NET, you can overload a function by writing several versions of that function. Each different version of the function uses the same function name but has a different argument list. The differences in the argument list can be different data types, or a different order, or a different number — or two or three of these variations at once.

The VB.NET compiler can tell which version of this function should be used by examining the arguments passed to the function (the order of the arguments, the number of arguments, and/or the different variable types of the arguments).

You can have multiple procedures with the same name. They are distinguished by the arguments (parameters) passed to them.

VB.NET employs overloading quite extensively in the language itself. You can see it whenever VB.NET lists various different argument lists you can choose from. The `MessageBox.Show` method, for example, is really overloaded: It will recognize 12 different kinds of argument lists. Try this. Type the following line into the code window within the `Form_Load` event:

```
messagebox.Show(
```

As soon as you type that left parenthesis, VB.NET pops up a gray box showing the first of the 12 different ways you can use the MessageBox object's show method. The box says: `1 of 12`. Use your keyboard's up- and down-arrow keys to see all the different ways that this overloaded method can be used.

Doing it yourself

Why should the people who wrote the VB.NET source code have all the fun? Here's an example of how you, too, can use overloading in your own VB.NET source code when writing your own applications.

Let's say that you want a function named `SearchBooks` that will give you a list of a particular author's book titles if you only provide the author's name. However, at other times you want `SearchBooks` to behave differently: You want a list limited to the author's books in a particular year if you also provide the year by passing that parameter to the function.

Create two overloaded functions with the same name, which accept different arguments:

```
Public Overloads Function BookList(ByVal AuthorName As
    String) As Object

        ' write code to find all books by this author

End Function

Public Overloads Function BookList(ByVal AuthorName As
    String, ByVal YearNumber As Integer) As Object

' write code to find all books written in the particular year

End Function
```

Some programmers like to use the overload feature to group a set of identically named functions that, as this example illustrates, handle different jobs. To me, this has the potential of making the source code harder to read and harder to maintain. If you want to accomplish two jobs, you can write *two* different functions — and give them descriptive names so that you can tell what they do when you read the source code:

```
Public Function GetBooksByYear (ByVal AuthorName As String,
    ByVal YearNumber As Integer) As String

Public Function GetAllBooksOfAuthor (ByVal AuthorName As
    String) As String
```

However, overloading can be of value to many programmers. VB.NET itself uses overloading extensively, as you can easily see by typing in a line like this in the code window:

```
console.WriteLine(
```

As soon as you type the parenthesis symbol, a small window opens with scrollable arrow symbols and displays 2 of 18, meaning that you are currently looking at the second of 18 different overloaded versions of the WriteLine function (method). Press your up- or down-arrow keys to scroll through all 18 different arugment lists for this WriteLine procedure.

.NET creates unique signatures for overloaded functions. These signatures are based on the name of the function and the number and types of the parameters.

As a side note, the signature is not affected by type modifiers (Shared or Private), parameter modifiers (ByVal or ByRef), the actual names of the parameters, the return type of the function, or the element type of a property. A function with three parameters, two of which are optional, will generate three signatures: one signature with all three parameters, one signature with the required parameter and one optional parameter, and one signature with just the required parameter.

Overloading is also used as a replacement for the As Any command. As Any has been deleted from the language, but you can use overloading to permit functions to return several different data types. However, you can no longer declare a function As Any (meaning it can return any kind of data type):

```
Public MyFunction (parameters) As Any
```

When you declare a function, every parameter and the function itself (the return type) must be specified.

As Any is gone

In Visual Basic 6.0, you could specify As Any for the data type of any of the parameters of a function, and for its return type. The As Any keywords disable the compiler's type checking and allow variables of any data type to be passed in or returned. The As Any command has been removed in VB.NET because As Any degrades type safety. If you want to permit more than one return type for a procedure, use overloading.

Parameters (If not Needed)

Before VB.NET

When passing traditional parameters to a function, you can omit parameters that you don't want to specify by simply leaving out their names. For example, if you wanted to specify the first and third parameters for a MessageBox, you could just leave out the second parameter, like this:

```
MsgBox("Your Name", , "Title")
```

VB understood that the empty area between commas in a parameter list meant that you wanted to use the default, or *no* parameter at all.

VB.NET

That tactic still works with many functions and methods in VB.NET, but not always!

Sometimes, you must use the word Nothing instead.

For example, when you want to sort a DataRow, the first parameter specifies a filter (such as "all dates after 12/12/01"). (The second parameter specifies the column to sort on, so you *do* want to specify that parameter.)

However, if you want to avoid using a filter — if you want *all* the rows sorted, for example — you must use Nothing in the parameter list. Leaving the first parameter out raises an error message:

```
        Dim fx As String - "title"
'dt is a DataTable in a DataSet
        myRows = dt.Select(, fx)
```

Instead, you must use Nothing:

```
        Dim fx As String = "title"
        myRows = dt.Select(Nothing, fx)
```

Parent Property

This new property specifies the parent container of this control.

Parentheses Now Required

Before VB.NET

The Call command is ancient. It has been used since the first versions of Basic more than 20 years ago. It indicates that you're calling a procedure.

Call is optional, but traditional VB has required that if you use it, you must enclose passed parameters within parentheses:

```
Call MySub (N)
```

But if you omitted the Call command, you did not use parentheses:

```
MySub N
```

You could also add extra parentheses, which had the same effect as using the ByVal command (the called procedure cannot then change any passed parameters):

```
Call MySub ((N))
```

```
MySub (N)
```

VB.NET

VB.NET requires parentheses in all cases (the `Call` command remains optional):

```
Call MySub (N)

MySub (N)
```

To translate VB 6 and earlier code to VB.NET, you must go through and add parentheses to any procedure call that doesn't employ them (that does not use the `Call` command).

Point Changed

See "Circle, Line, Shape, PSet, and Point All Changed."

Print Is No Longer Available

The `Print` command can no longer be used with a form. In other words, the following code doesn't work:

```
Print 12 * 3
```

In earlier versions of VB, if you put that code in your program, the number 36 would appear on the current form. No more.

VB 6 (and earlier) programmers often used this `Print` command to quickly test or debug their programs. It was a superior alternative to the `Debug.Print` command (which requires that you look for the results in a special Immediate window). The `Print` command put the results right there on your form as soon as you pressed F5.

This feature has been removed in VB.NET.

Printing to a Printer Has Changed

Before VB.NET

To print the contents of a TextBox to the printer, you typed the following:

```
Printer.Print Text1
```

To print a string, you typed the following:

```
Printer.Print "This."
```

To print a whole form (its graphic apprearance), you typed the following:

```
PrintForm
```

VB.NET

In VB.NET, you have greater control over what gets printed, but there is a cost. Some would say a *terrible cost.* You use a group of MFC (an API used by C programmers) members. You have to muster a fair amount of information (such as "brush" color, the height of each line of text, and so on), and you have to manage several other aspects of the printing process as well. For an in-depth examination of all issues related to printer management — word wrap, text measurement, preventing cut-off lines, calculating printable space, and so on — see Chapter 3, Book VI of this book.

Project Properties

If you want to change the name of the assembly, change which object (such as Form2) is supposed to be the startup object (the one that executes first when the project is run), or change other fundamental aspects of your project, you cannot do it from the menu system any more. In VB.NET, you must right-click the name of your project, and then choose Properties.

Property Definitions Collapse (Property Let, Get, and Set Are Gone)

Before VB.NET

To expose a property of an object, you used Property Get, Property Set, and Property Let procedures. Each of these was a separate, discrete procedure. Therefore, you could freely specify varying scopes for the different procedures. For example, you could define the Get (read) procedure as Public, but refuse to permit outsiders to change the property simply by making the Let (write) procedure Private. (The Friend scoping definition was particularly useful in this regard. You could use it to allow *your* procedures in your control have access to each other's properties, but block any code outside your control from having access to certain elements that you want to protect.)

Appendix

A Dictionary of VB.NET

VB.NET

Now in VB.NET, you must combine Get and Set within a single logical block of code. This has the effect of allowing you to define scope for the property as a whole (you cannot specify different scopes for Get and Set).

Whither Let?

Everything in VB.NET is an object, so the Let command disappears. You can only use Get and Set. Here's how you must now code a property:

```
Private m_MyProperty As String

Public Property MyProperty As String
Get
          MyProperty = m_MyProperty
End Get

Set
          M_MyProperty = MyProperty
End Set

End Property
```

And don't you dare suggest that this source code seems a little bit redundant, or that VB.NET could automatically fill in all this repetition for you, so that you would have to write only `Public Property MyProperty As String` and all the other stuff would be automatically inserted into the code window for you. It's true, but don't suggest it. Fortunately for us, somebody finally *did* suggest it, and VB.NET 2003, the latest version of the language, does fill in this entire property declaration template.

Specifying different scope levels

If you want different scope levels, you have to define two different properties, but have them manipulate the same internal variables. This is what we used to call a *workaround*. Here's an example that makes the read (Get) public, but restricts the write (Set) to Friend (control-internal only):

```
Private m_MyProperty As String

ReadOnly Public Property MyProperty As String
Get
          MyProperty = m_MyProperty
End Get
End Property
```

```
WriteOnly Friend Property SetMyProperty As String

Set
            M_MyProperty = MyProperty
End Set
End Property
```

PSet Changed

See "Circle, Line, Shape, PSet, and Point All Changed."

Public versus Property Procedures

Before VB.NET

Any changes made to a Public variable in a class are not seen by the calling procedure. For example, changes made by AFunction to TheObj.ItsVariable in the following code will not be seen by the calling procedure:

```
AFunction(TheObj.ItsVariable)
```

VB parses this function call and merely passes a temporary variable to AFunction. That temporary variable is *not* passed back to the calling procedure, so any modifications made to the variable are then lost.

If you want changes to a Public variable to persist in the calling procedure, you must first explicitly assign that variable's value to a different variable. This is how you could permit a called function to *modify* an object's property value (without using a Property procedure):

```
NewVariable = TheObj.ItsVariable
AFunction(NewVariable)
TheObj.ItsVariable = NewVariable
```

VB.NET

The workaround described in the previous code is unnecessary in VB.NET. Public variables within a class can be directly modified by a called function (In effect, a Public variable can be considered global to the project). Using the previous example, AFunction can change ItsVariable if you send simply and directly like this:

```
AFunction(TheObj.ItsVariable)
```

Permitting outside procedures to have direct access to Public variables in a class is something that you should probably avoid. I suggest you stick to using traditional property procedures to manage an object's properties and avoid this new VB.NET feature that exposes Public variables.

Reading the Registry

Before VB.NET

In VB 6 and before, you could use API commands such as `RegQueryValueEx` to query the Registry. Or you could employ the native VB Registry-related commands such as `GetSetting`, like this:

```
Print GetSetting(appname := "MyProgram", section := "Init",
    key := "Locale", default := "1")
```

VB.NET

In VB.NET, you can query the Registry using the `RegistryKey` object. However, you're not really supposed to use the Registry much in VB.NET. The idea of avoiding the Registry is that in VB.NET, you are supposed to steer clear of the traditional DLL problems (which version should be loaded if two applications use two different versions of a particular "dynamic link library?"). These problems have plagued us for many years.

In VB.NET, you put all support files (including code libraries, now called *assemblies*) in the same directory path as the VB.NET application. In other words, you put all the files needed by your application into its directory (or a subdirectory under that directory). That way, you can "photocopy" (make an X-copy, or directly just copy the VB.NET application's directory and all its subdirectories), and by simply doing this copy you deploy (transfer to another computer) your VB.NET application. No more need for Setup programs to install your application; no more need to modify the Windows Registry. (Of course all this assumes that the huge VB.NET runtime library — the CLR as it's called — is already installed on the other computer to which you are deploying your VB.NET application. At some point, Microsoft says, nearly everyone will have the CLR because it will be built into the operating system (Windows) or the browser (Internet Explorer) or otherwise made universally available.

Where, though, should a VB.NET programmer store passwords or other customization information (such as the user's choice of default font size) instead of the Registry that you've used for the past several years? What goes around comes around. Go back to using a good old .INI file or a similar simple text file. It's quick and easy, and it avoids messing with the Registry.

Using the Registry

If you must use the Registry, though, here's how to access it from VB.NET. Start a new VB.NET WinForm-style project, and then double-click TextBox in the WinForms tab of the Toolbox to add it to your Form1.VB. Double-click a Button to add it as well.

Click the TextBox in the IDE (Design tab selected) so that you can see its properties in the Properties window. Change its Multiline property to True.

Now, double-click the Button to get to its Click event in the code window. Type this into the Button's Click event:

```
Private Sub Button1_Click_1(ByVal sender As System.Object, _
    ByVal e As System.EventArgs) Handles Button1.Click

        Dim objGotValue As Object
        Dim objMainKey As RegistryKey = Registry.CurrentUser
        Dim objOpenedKey As RegistryKey
        Dim strValue As String


        objOpenedKey = _
objMainKey.OpenSubKey("Software\\Microsoft\\Windows\\
CurrentVersion\\Internet Settings")

        objGotValue = objOpenedKey.GetValue("User Agent")

        If (Not objGotValue Is Nothing) Then
            strValue = objGotValue.ToString()
        Else
            strValue = ""
        End If

        objMainKey.Close()

        TextBox1.Text = strValue

    End Sub
```

You must also add Imports Microsoft.Win32 up there at the top of the code window where all those other Imports are. The Microsoft.Win32 namespace contains the Registry-access functions such as the OpenSubKey method that you need in this example.

Press F5 to run this example, and click the button. If your Registry contains the same value for this key as my Registry contains, you should see a result similar to this:

Appendix

A Dictionary of VB.NET

```
Mozilla/4.2 (compatible; MSIE 5.0; Win32)
```

Note that the complete name (path) of the entire Registry entry is divided into three different locations in the example code (they are in boldface): first the primary key, CurrentUser, then the path of sub-keys, and finally the actual specific "name": objOpenedKey.GetValue("User Agent").

Writing to the Registry

The RegistryKey class includes a group of methods you can use to manage and write to the Registry. These methods include Close, CreateSubKey, DeleteSubKey, DeleteSubKeyTree, DeleteValue, GetSubKeyNames, GetType, GetValue, GetValueNames, OpenSubKey, and SetValue.

ReDim

Before VB.NET

You can use the ReDim command to initially declare a dynamic array. Simply using ReDim rather than Dim makes the array dynamic (changeable elsewhere in the code), and also declares (and dimensions) the array, just as Dim does.

VB.NET

All VB.NET arrays can be redimensioned, so there is no need for a special subset of "dynamic" arrays. ReDim can no longer be used as an alternative to the Dim command. Arrays must be first declared using Dim (or similar) — because ReDim cannot create an array. ReDim can be used only to redimension (resize) an existing array originally declared with Dim (or similar) command.

Also see " Dim and ReDim: New Rules."

References to Code Libraries

See "Imports."

Region Property

This new property specifies the region (an area within a window) that is used with this control.

ResizeRedraw Property

This new property specifies whether the control should be redrawn when it is resized. In some cases, a graphic or text on a resized control will need to be redrawn to appear correctly.

Return

Before VB.NET

To return a value from a function, you assigned that value to the function's name:

```
Function AddFive(ByVal N As Integer) As Integer
AddFive = N + 5
End Function
```

VB.NET

You now have the option of using the more readable Return command:

```
Function AddFive(ByVal N As Integer) As Integer
Return N + 5
End Function
```

Right Property

This new property tells you the distance between the right edge of the control and the left edge of its container.

Right (RightStr or Right$) Must Be "Qualified"

Before VB.NET

To access characters on the right side of a string, you used the right function, like this:

```
If Right(filepathname, 1) <> "\" Then filepathname =
    filepathname & "\"
```

VB.NET

The Form "object" now has a `right` property, which means that if you want to use the `right` function, you must add some qualifiers (adjectives describing the class to which this version of "right" belongs):

```
If Microsoft.VisualBasic.Right(filepathname, 1) <> "\" Then
    filepathname = filepathname & "\"
```

The same requirement applies if you want to use the `Left` function. VB 6 could tell the difference between these uses of the words `right` and `left` by looking at the context in the source code and distinguishing between a property and a function. In VB.NET, the burden of making this distinction shifts to the programmer.

When you use the qualifier `Microsoft.VisualBasic`, you are invoking the "compatibility" namespace, which provides for some backward compatibility with VB 6 programming code.

You can also use this compatibility namespace if you want to continue using the various traditional string-manipulation functions such as `Mid`, `Instr`, and so on. However, it is better to become familiar with all the new and more efficient .NET string functions and methods. See "String Functions Are Now Methods" in this appendix for details and the VB.NET equivalents of traditional techniques.

RND Has New Syntax (It's an Object Now)

Before VB.NET

In VB 6 and previous versions, you would generate a random number between 1 and 12 like this:

```
X = Int(Rnd * 12 + 1)
```

Or to get a random number between 0 and 12, you would use this code:

```
X = Int(Rnd * 13)
```

You used the `Rnd` and `Randomize` functions.

VB.NET

It's different now. You must use a `System.Random` object. The good news is that the `Random` object has useful capabilities that were not available via the old `Rnd` and `Randomize` functions.

Type this code into a form's `Load` event:

```
Private Sub Form1_Load(ByVal sender As System.Object, ByVal e
    As System.EventArgs) Handles MyBase.Load
        Dim i As Integer
        For i = 1 To 100
            Debug.Write(rand(i) & " ")
        Next
    End Sub
```

And elsewhere in that form's code window, type this function, which returns random numbers between 1 and 12:

```
    Function rand(ByVal MySeed As Integer) As Integer
        Dim obj As New system.Random(MySeed)
        Return obj.next(1, 12)
    End Function
```

When you press F5 to run this example, you see the `Debug.Write` results in the output window in the IDE.

Although the arguments say `1, 12` in the line `Return obj.next(1, 12)`, you will not get any 12s in your results. The numbers provided by the `System.Random` function in this case will range only from 1 to 11. I'm hoping that this error will be fixed at some point. However, even the latest version of VB.NET (2003) gives you results ranging only 1 to 11. I'm hoping even more strongly that this truly odd behavior is not the result of an intentional "feature" of the `Random.Next` method. It's just too tedious to hear justifications for confusing programmers with upper boundaries like this 12 that turn out — surprise! — not to be upper boundaries after all.

On a happier note, here's an example that illustrates how you can use the `NOW` command to seed your random generator. Put a Button control on your form, and then type in the following:

```
Private Sub Button1_Click_1(ByVal sender As System.Object,
    ByVal e As System.EventArgs) Handles Button1.Click


        Dim sro As New coin()
        Dim x As Integer
        Dim i As Integer

        For i = 1 To 100
            sro.toss()

            Dim n As String

            x = sro.coinvalue
            If x = 1 Then
```

```
                n = "tails"
        Else
                n = "heads"
        End If

        n = n & " "

        debug.Write(n)


    Next i



    End Sub

End Class


Class coin

    Private m_coinValue As Integer = 0

    Private Shared s_rndGenerator As New
    System.Random(Now.Millisecond)

    Public ReadOnly Property coinValue() As Integer
        Get
            Return m_coinValue
        End Get
    End Property

    Public Sub toss()
        m_coinValue = s_rndGenerator.next(1, 3)
    End Sub

End Class
```

As always in VB.NET, there is more than one way to do things. The next example ple uses the system.random object's next and nextdouble methods. The seed is automatically taken from the computer's date/time (no need to supply a seed as was done in the previous example, or to use the old VB 6 Randomize function). The next method returns a 32-bit integer; the nextdouble method returns a double-precision floating point number ranging from 0 up to (but not including) 1.

```
Private Sub Form1_Load(ByVal sender As System.Object, ByVal e
        As System.EventArgs) Handles MyBase.Load
        Dim r As New System.Random()
        Dim x As Integer
```

```
    Dim i As Integer

    For i = 1 To 10
        Debug.Write(r.Next & ", ")
    Next

    For i = 1 To 10
        Debug.Write(r.NextDouble & ", ")
    Next

End Sub
```

The following is a sample of what you see in the output window when you run this example:

```
519421314, 2100190320, 2103377645, 526310073, 1382420323,
    408464378, 985605837, 265367659, 665654900, 1873826712
0.263233027543515, 0.344213118471304, 0.0800133510865333,
    0.902158257040269, 0.735719954937566, 0.283918539194352,
    0.946819610403301, 0.27740475408612, 0.970956700374818,
    0.803866669909966
```

Any program that uses this technique can be guaranteed to get unique results each time it's executed. It's impossible to execute that program twice at the *same* time and date, just as you cannot kiss yourself on the face. (Even Mick Jagger can't.)

Of course, if you choose, you can still employ the older VB 6 version of the randomizing function:

```
Dim r As Double
    r = Rnd
    MsgBox(r)
```

It's not necessary in this case to invoke the `Microsoft.VisualBasic` namespace. The `Rnd` function is a *wrapper* like many other attempts at backward compatibility between VB.NET and earlier VB code (such as `MsgBox` rather than the new `MessageBox.Show`).

If you've used the `Rnd` function before, you may recall that it will provide identical lists of random numbers by default (which can be quite useful when attempting to, for example, debug a game). In fact, I use this feature in my unbreakable code system described in the Warning in the next section. If you want to get identical lists in VB.NET, you can seed the `Random` object, like this:

```
Dim r As New System.Random(14)
```

Filling an array

The `Random.NextBytes` method automatically fills an array of bytes with random numbers between 0 and 255. Here's how:

```
Dim r As New System.Random()
Dim i
Dim a(52) As Byte 'create the byte array

r.NextBytes(a) ' fill the array

For i = 0 To a.Length - 1
        Debug.WriteLine(i.ToString + ". " +
a(i).ToString)
        Next
```

Neither the old `Rnd` function nor the new `Random` object uses algorithms that are sufficiently sophisticated to be of direct use in most kinds of cryptology. Nonetheless, an unbreakable encryption system can be built upon them. (I describe and include an application that does this in my book *Hacker Attack* published by Sybex.) However, if you want to explore encryption in VB.NET, you would be well advised to check out the `System.Security.Cryptography` namespace and the objects it offers.

RTrim

See "LCase and VCase Change."

ScaleHeight and ScaleWidth Are Gone

Before VB.NET

You could get a measurement of the inside dimensions of a form (ignoring its frame) by using this code:

```
X = ScaleWidth
Y = ScaleHeight
```

VB.NET

Now you must use the following:

```
Dim X as Integer, Y as Integer

X = ClientSize.Width
Y = ClientSize.Height
```

The results, however, are only provided in pixels.

Scope for Modules

If you want to make some variables (or enums) visible throughout an assembly or throughout a "solution," put them in a module, but use `Public Module` rather than simply `Module`. Modules without the `Public` declaration are visible only within the project in which the module resides.

SelStart and SelLength Are Renamed (Selected Text)

Before VB.NET

You identified text that the user selected in a TextBox, like this:

```
        Text1.SelStart = WhereLoc - 1   ' set selection start
and
        Text1.SelLength = Len(SearchString)   ' set selection
length.
```

VB.NET

If you want to get a copy of selected text in a TextBox in VB.NET, use this code:

```
        Dim s As String
        s = TextBox1.SelectedText
```

You must go through a rather dramatic OOP acrobatic performance when you use the `ActiveControl` method. Also, `SelLength` becomes `SelectedLength`, `SelStart` becomes `SelectedStart`, and so on.

SendKeys Changes

You can use the `Shell` command to run an application, such as Notepad. `Shell` works much as it did in VB 6. An associated command, `SendKeys`, imitates the user typing on the keyboard. `SendKeys` works differently in VB.NET. This code will run an instance of Windows Notepad, and then "type" `This message` into Notepad:

```
Dim X As Object
X = Shell("notepad.exe", AppWinStyle.NormalFocus)
System.Windows.Forms.SendKeys.Send("This Message")
```

If you put this code in a Form_Load event, it will only send the T into Notepad (there are timing problems involved). So, put it into a different event, such as Button1_Click, and VB.NET will have enough time to get itself together and send the full message.

SET Is No More

Remove all uses of the Set command. Just write the same line of code as before, but without Set.

Before VB.NET

Here's an example of how the Set command was used:

```
Set MyDataConn = Server.CreateObject("ADODB.Connection")
```

To accomplish the preceding job in VB.NET, leave out the Set command.

Also note that if you tried to change an object variable so that it referenced a *different* object before VB.NET, you used this syntax:

```
Set CurrentObjVar = DifferentObjVar
```

Before VB.NET, you could not leave out the Set command, like this:

```
CurrentObjVar = DifferentObjVar
```

If you did, something entirely different occured. If the DifferentObjVar had no default property, an error was triggered. If it did have a default property, that default property was assigned to CurrentObjVar as *its* default property.

VB.NET

VB.NET doesn't have the Set command, and in general it doesn't allow default properties anyway. For example, you can no longer use X = Text1 as a way of assigning the text in a TextBox to the variable X. Instead, you must explicitly name any property, including what were previously "default" properties. In VB.NET, this works like so: X = Text1.Text.

However, just to make life interesting, *some* objects do have default properties that you can use in VB.NET. Specifically, objects that take arguments (the dictionary object, the Item property in a collection, parameterized properties, and so on) can be assumed to be defaults and explicit reference to the property can, in these few cases, be omitted from your source code.

Parameterized properties (properties that take parameters) are still permitted to be defaults in VB.NET. For example, in VB.NET most *collections* fall into this category. Here are some examples from the ADO data language:

```
Recordset object   (its default property is Fields)
Fields collection  (its default property is Item)
Field object       (its default property is Value)
```

For instance, this code illustrates two ways to reference the Item property of a recordset's field object:

```
Dim rs As Recordset
```

You can use the fully qualified code:

```
rs.Fields.Item(1).Value = "Hello"
```

Alternatively, you can omit the term Item because it is the default property of the Fields collection:

```
rs.Fields(1).Value = "Hello"
```

For more information on instantiating objects in VB.NET, see "Object Instantiation" in this appendix.

SetFocus

See "Focus."

Shape Control Is Gone

See "Circle, Line, Shape, PSet, and Point All Changed."

ShowFocusCues Property

This new property tells you if the form will currently display one of those visual cues (like the dotted gray rectangle inside a Button control) that indicates which control has the focus.

ShowKeyboardCues Property

This new property tells you if the form will currently display those keyboard shortcuts (underlined letters in the Text property of controls).

Size Property

This new property specifies the height and width of the control (in the format width, height).

Sorting a DataTable

See "Parameters (If not Needed)"

Static Procedures Are No Longer Available

Before VB.NET

Normally, if you use a variable only within a procedure, it lives and dies within that procedure. It's *scope* is said to be local — so no other procedures can read or change that variable. However, the value held in a local variable also evaporates when the procedure that contains it is no longer executing. Sometimes you want a variable to be local in scope, but you want its value to persist. (Another way to put this is that you sometimes want a variable to be visible only within its procedure, but you want it to have a lifetime greater than merely procedure-level.)

In traditional VB, you can cause a local variable's value to persist by using the Static command to declare it:

```
MySub DoSomething
Static X
X = X + 1
End Sub
```

Each time this procedure executes, the value in variable X will be increased by 1. However, if you omit the Static keyword, X will always reset to 0 when the procedure is finished executing; therefore X will simply change from 0 to 1 each time the procedure executes.

You could also declare all the variables in a procedure to be static at once by merely defining the entire procedure as static:

```
Static MyFunction()
```

This procedure use of Static is not supported in VB.NET.

VB.NET

The Static command can be used when declaring individual variables.

However, you cannot declare an entire procedure as Static in VB.NET.

String Functions Are Now Methods

A string used to be a variable type; now it's an object and it has many methods.

Where previous versions of VB used functions, VB.NET often uses *methods* — behaviors that are built into objects. In VB.NET, everything is an object, even a string variable. So, you shouldn't be surprised that to find the length of a string in VB 6, you used the function Len(*String*), but now in VB.NET, you use the method String.Length. Fortunately, the old functions such as Len still work in VB.NET, so usually the approach you choose — function or method — is up to you.

In addition to those described in the proceeding sections, you might want to check out VB.NET Help for information on how to use these new string methods, just so you know that they exist if you ever need them: Compare, Concat, Format, Chars, EndsWith, Insert, LastIndexOf, PadLeft, PadRight, Remove, Replace, Split, and StartsWith. There are others, such as Trim, that are discussed in the upcoming sections.

The various string methods or functions can manipulate text in many ways. Some of them take more than one argument. Arguments can include string variables, string literals, or expressions.

IndexOf or InStr

The traditional VB InStr format is as follows:

```
InStr([start, ]string1, string2[, compare])
```

InStr tells you where (in which character position) string2 is located within string1. Optionally, you can specify a starting character position and a comparison specification that you can ignore — the default is what you want for the comparison style.

This is a remarkably handy function when you need to *parse* some text (meaning that you need to locate or extract a piece of text within a larger body of text). InStr can enable you to see if a particular word, for example,

Appendix

A Dictionary of VB.NET

exists within a file or within some text that the user has typed into a TextBox. Perhaps you need to search a TextBox to see if the user typed in the words **New Jersey**, and if so, to tell them that your product is not available in that state.

InStr is case-sensitive by default; it makes a distinction between Upper and upper, for example.

What if you want to know whether more than one instance of the search string is within the larger text? You can easily find additional instances by using the result of a previous InStr search. InStr, when it finds a match, reports the location and the character position within the larger text where the search string was found, as in the following example:

```
Private Sub Form1_Load(ByVal sender As System.Object, ByVal e
    As System.EventArgs) Handles MyBase.Load

        Dim quot, MainText, SearchWord As String
        Dim X, Y, Z As Integer


        quot = Chr(34)

        MainText = "Masterpieces are built of pieces."
        SearchWord = "pieces"

        Do
            X = Y + 1
            Z = Z + 1
            Y = InStr(X, MainText, SearchWord)

        Loop Until Y = 0

        MsgBox("We found " & SearchWord & " " & Z - 1 & _
            " times inside " & quot & MainText & quot)


    End Sub
```

In this example, the loop continues to look through the MainText until the InStr function returns a zero (which indicates that the SearchWord isn't found any more). The variable Z is used to count the number of successful hits. The variable X moves the pointer one character further into the MainText (X = Y + 1). You can use this example as a template any time you need to count the number of occurrences of a string within another, larger string.

To merely see if, in the previous code, a string appears within another one, use this:

```
If InStr("Masterpiece", "piece") Then MsgBox "Yep!"
```

The preceding code line translates to: If "piece" is found within "Masterpiece," then display "Yep!"

There's also an `InStrRev` function that works in a similar way, but it starts looking at the last character and searches backward to the first character.

The equivalent VB.NET method is `IndexOf`. Here's an example that finds the first occurance of the letter n in a string:

```
Dim s As String = "Hello Sonny"
Dim x As Integer
x = s.IndexOf("n")
MsgBox(x)
```

`IndexOf` is case-sensitive. To specify the starting character position, add an integer to the argument list, like this:

```
x = s.IndexOf("n", x)
```

To translate the Masterpiece example, change these two lines:

```
Y = MainText.IndexOf(SearchWord, X)
Loop Until Y = -1
```

ToLower or LCase (String)

This traditional function removes any uppercase letters from a string, reducing it to all lowercase characters. `AfterWord` becomes `afterword`. Likewise, there's also a `UCase` function that raises all the characters in a string to uppercase.

The VB.NET `ToLower` method can be used instead of `LCase`, and VB.NET `ToUpper` replaces `UCase`.

Appendix

These functions or methods are used when you want to ignore the case — when you want to be case-insensitive. Usually, `LCase` or `UCase` is valuable when the user is providing input, and you cannot know (and don't care) how he or she might capitalize the input. Comparisons are case-sensitive:

```
If "larry" = "larry" Then MsgBox "They are the same."
```

A Dictionary of VB.NET

This message box will never be displayed. The L is not the same. You can see the problem. You often just don't care how the user typed in the capitalization. If you don't care, use `LCase` or `UCase` to force all the characters to be lowercase or uppercase, like this:

```
Private Sub Form1_Load(ByVal sender As System.Object, ByVal e
    As System.EventArgs) Handles MyBase.Load

    Dim reply As String
    Dim n As Integer

    reply = InputBox("Shall we proceed?")

    reply = UCase(reply)

    Dim x As Integer


    If reply = "YES" Then
        MsgBox("Ok. We'll proceed.")
    End If


    End Sub
```

Notice that it now does not matter how the user capitalized yes. Any capitalization will be forced into uppercase letters, and you compare it to a literal that is also all uppercase.

To translate this to VB.NET, change the following line:

```
reply = UCase(reply)
```

Replace it with the following line:

```
reply = reply.ToUpper
```

Substring or Left (String, Number)

The Left function returns a portion of the string, the number of characters defined by the Number argument. Here's an example:

```
Dim n As String

    n = Microsoft.VisualBasic.Left ("More to the point.",
    4)
    MsgBox(N)
```

This code results in More.

There's also a Right function. Both Left and Right require the Microsoft.VisualBasic qualifier, which was not necessary in previous versions of VB.

The VB.NET equivalent of `Left` or `Right` is the `SubString` method:

```
Dim n As String = "More to the point."

        n = n.Substring(0, 4)
        MsgBox(n)
```

Or to get a string from the right side, the following code retrieves all characters from the 12th character to the end of the string:

```
n = n.Substring(12)
```

Length or Len (String)

This function tells you how many characters are in a string. You may want to let users know that their response is too wordy for your database's allotted space for a particular entry. Or perhaps you want to see if they entered the full telephone number, including their area code. If they did, the number will have to be at least 10 characters long. You can use the less-than symbol (<) to test their entry, like this:

```
        If Len(TextBox1.Text) < 10 Then
            MsgBox("Shorter")
        End If
```

The VB.NET equivalent is the `Length` method:

```
        If TextBox1.Text.Length < 10 Then
```

The Trim Method or LTrim (String)

`LTrim` (and its brother `RTrim`) removes any leading (or trailing) space characters from a string. The uses for this function are similar to those for `UCase` or `LCase`: Sometimes people accidentally add extra spaces at the beginning or end of their typing. Those space characters will cause a comparison to fail because computers can be quite literal. `" This"` is not the same thing as `"This"`. And if you write the code `If " This" = "This"`, and the user types in `" This "`, the computer's answer will be no.

The VB.NET equivalent is the `Trim` method. Here's an example that removes four leading spaces:

```
        Dim s As String = "    Here"
        s = s.Trim
        MsgBox(s & s.Length)
```

Substring or Mid

The `Mid` format is:

```
Mid(String, StartCharacter [, NumberOfCharacters])
```

You find yourself using this function or method surprisingly often. It's a little like the `Left` and `Right` functions, except `Mid` can extract a substring (a string within a string) from anywhere within a string. `Left` and `Right` are limited to getting characters on one end of a string or the other. The VB.NET `Substring` method does all of these things.

The `Mid` function works like this:

```
MsgBox(Mid("1234567", 3, 4))
```

This results in 3456. You asked `Mid` to begin at the third character and extract four characters, and that's exactly what you got.

The VB.NET `Substring` equivalent is:

```
Dim s As String = "1234567"
MsgBox(s.Substring(2, 4))
```

Notice that to start with the third character in this string (the digit 3), you must specify 2 in your `Substring` argument. Absurd isn't it? This nonsense is because the `Substring` method begins counting characters with 0. Somebody who worked on designing VB.NET thinks we should start counting with 0 instead of 1.

The VB 6 `Mid` function begins counting characters with 1, as we humans do. In this case, VB.NET takes a step backward by counting from 0 in the `Substring` method.

The StartsWith Method

This method gives you a quick way of telling whether or not a string begins with a particular character or substring:

```
Dim s As String = "narop"
If s.StartsWith("na") Then MessageBox.Show("Yes")
```

String Manipulation Using the StringBuilder

Before VB.NET

The string was simply a variable type.

To display a large amount of text in Visual Basic, it's sometimes necessary to resort to a process that builds strings. Rather than assigning a paragraph-long piece of text to a string variable, you instead use the & operator to *build* a large string out of smaller strings, like this:

```
StrLabelText = "Thank you for submitting your information."
StrLabelText = StrLabelText & "We appreciate your input. "
StrLabelText = StrLabelText & "If all our customers were as
    responsive and submissive "
```

Then you assign the string to a label or display it in some other way to the user:

```
LblResponse.Text = strLabelText
```

VB.NET

The string, like most everything else, is an *object* and it has many methods. VB.NET also offers you a more efficient (faster executing) way of manipulating strings, called the *StringBuilder*. Use it when you are going to do some heavy-duty manipulations of a string.

Instead of creating a new string each time you modify a string, the StringBuilder does not spawn multiple string objects (as do ordinary VB.NET string methods, such as ToUpper). Why? In VB.NET, when you create a string, it is *immutable* — meaning it cannot be changed. If you ask for a change (like "make this string all uppercase" with the ToUpper method), a brand new string is created with all uppercase letters, but the old string hangs around until garbage collection cleans things up. Asking VB.NET to create new strings each time you manipulate a string wastes time and space. (The StringBuilder is not efficient when you are only reading or querying the contents of a string — such as IndexOf. The StringBuilder is useful when you are *changing* a string, not merely reading it.)

If you are writing some source code involving repeatedly changing a string, you can speed up your program's execution by creating a StringBuilder object rather than using normal strings. After you are through with the manipulations, you can turn the StringBuilder's products back into normal strings. The StringBuilder sets aside some memory for itself when you instantiate it — then it does its work directly on the string data within that memory block. No nasty little abandoned strings hanging around waiting for the garbage truck to make its rounds.

Also the StringBuilder is *extremely rich* with features. You'll want to use it.

To create a StringBuilder, you first Imports the System.Text namespace up at the top of your code window. In a WebForm, for example, you use this code:

```
<%@ Import Namespace="System.Text" %>
```

or in a WinForm, type this:

```
Imports System.Text
```

Then you declare a new StringBuilder. The StringBuilder offers six different *constructors* (read about this in "Constructors Are Now Parametized" in this appendix). In other words, when you declare a new StringBuilder object, you can choose from *six* different kinds of parameter lists to use:

✦ Pass no parameters:

```
Dim sb As New System.text.StringBuilder()
```

✦ Pass a single string:

```
Dim s As String = "This"
Dim sb As New System.text.StringBuilder(s)
```

✦ Pass no string, but set aside memory for the specified number of characters (12 in the following example), and permit the string to be enlarged only up to the maximum specified number of characters (44). If you do manipulate this StringBuilder in a way that exceeds your specified maximum, an exception (error) is triggered:

```
Dim sb As New System.text.StringBuilder(12,44)
```

✦ Pass no string, but set aside memory for the specified number of characters (258 in the following example):

```
Dim sb As New System.text.StringBuilder(258)
```

✦ Pass a string, and also specify the initial size:

```
Dim sb As New System.text.StringBuilder("Norma Jean",
    258)
```

✦ Pass a substring ("cd" in this example), and also specify the initial size:

```
Dim s As String = "abcde"
Dim startindex As Integer = 2 'start with b in
abcde.
Dim length As Integer = 2 'get just bc out of
abcde
Dim capacity As Integer = 14 ' set initial size
of sb as 14 characters
Dim sb As New System.text.StringBuilder(s,
startindex, length, capacity)
```

```
Dim ns As String = sb.ToString

MsgBox(ns)
```

Not only are there those six constructors, but you also find that many of the StringBuilder's methods are heavily overloaded, which means you can pass a variety of different parameter lists to the methods.

The following sections describe a few of the more interesting StringBuilder methods.

The Append method

Here's how to use the StringBuilder's Append method to concatenate (this is a WebForm example that builds a string for use with HTML code):

```
Sub btnSubmit_OnClick(Sender As Object, E As EventArgs)

Dim strLabelText As StringBuilder = new StringBuilder()


strLabelText.Append("Thank you for submitting your
    information.")
strLabelText.Append("<br /><br />")
strLabelText.Append("We appreciate your input. ")
strLabelText.Append("If all our customers were as responsive
    and submissive! ")
strLabelText.Append("<br /><br />")
strLabelText.Append("(We don't call it a SUBMIT button for
    nothing!")
```

Finally, you use the ToString method to transform the StringBuilder object into actual text and assign it to your label's Text property, like this:

```
lblResponse.Text = strLabelText.ToString()

End Sub
```

Replace and Insert methods

The StringBuilder is marvelously flexible. It easily replaces the classic VB InStr, Mid, and other functions. Here's an example that puts the StringBuilder through some of its paces, using a traditional Windows form (WinForm):

```
Private Sub Form1_Load(ByVal sender As System.Object, ByVal e
    As System.EventArgs) Handles MyBase.Load

    Dim s As System.Text.StringBuilder
```

```
        s = New System.Text.StringBuilder("My original
string.")

        s.Replace("My", "This") ' Edit the string by
replacing a word.
        s.Replace(".", "") ' Edit the string by removing
punctuation
        s.Append(" has now been extended and modified.") '
append some words
        s.Insert(0, "Attention! ", 2) ' insert two copies at
the start (character position zero)
        MessageBox.Show(s.ToString)

    End Sub
```

String$ Dropped

Instead of the traditional VB `String$` function, you now use the more flexible VB.NET `String` object. It has various methods. For example, use this to create a string with 12 spaces:

```
Dim S As String
S = New String(Chr(32), 12)
MsgBox(S & "!")
```

Tag Property Is Gone

Before VB.NET

Some programmers liked to use the `Tag` property to store information about a control, as a way of identifying controls used in MDI Forms and other highly specialized situations. I never used `Tag`, so I won't miss it.

VB.NET

Tag is removed from the language.

TextBox and Clipboard Changes

See "SelStart and SelLength Are Renamed (Selected Text)."

TextBox Change Event Changes

The TextBox `Change` event has now become the `TextChanged` event.

TextBox Text is Selected

Sometimes when you assign text to a TextBox, that text is selected (black on white). To deselect it so that it looks normal, set the SelectionLength property to zero.

```
TextBox1.SelectionLength = 0 'turn off the selection
```

Timer Interval Extended

Before VB.NET

The Timer's Interval property was limited by the range of numbers that could be held in an unsigned Integer data type: 65,535. Because the Interval property measures time in milliseconds, this worked out to be a maximum duration of a little over a minute. To use longer intervals, you had to employ a static variable in the Timer's Timer event and count up the minutes until that variable reached the number of minutes you wanted.

VB.NET

A VB.NET Timer's Interval property can range from 0 to 2,147,483,647 milliseconds. (The Interval in VB.NET is a signed 32-bit Integer data type, Int32, which can hold a number plus or minus 2,147,483,647.)

In practical terms, this means that you can set the Interval to anything between 1 millisecond and 35,791 minutes (which is 596 hours, or almost 10 days). This amount of time should do for most applications.

Timer Tick Event

Before VB.NET

The Timer's Timer event was one of the most badly named traditional VB objects. Both the control (the Timer control) and its event (the Timer control's Timer event) had the same name. Bad idea. It was always confusing.

VB.NET

Some feel that many of the changes made to traditional VB diction in VB.NET are arbitrary and not helpful (SetFocus becomes Focus, for example). However, renaming the Timer's Timer event to Tick is an improvement and was worth changing.

Triggering an Event

Before VB.NET

If you wanted to trigger the code in an event procedure, all you had to do was name that event and its code would execute:

```
CommandButton1_Click()
```

VB.NET

Now, events require two arguments, so you must include these paramters within the parentheses:

```
Button1_Click(sender, e)
```

Literally using `sender` and `e` works just fine. No need to declare these parameters, give them values, or otherwise pay any attention to them.

True Is Still -1

Before VB.NET

The number -1 was always a fairly weird number to represent `True`, but that's been the VB way since its inception in 1991. False has always been 0, which is intuitive enough, but `True` = -1 is strange.

An attempt was made early in the VB.NET design to make VB.NET conform to the other .NET languages by making 1 stand for `True`. Thus, when the Boolean data type (true/false) was converted to other numeric data types, `True` would equal 1 and `False` would equal 0. However, when any numeric data type was converted to `Boolean`, 0 was to become false, but *any* other number besides 0 was to become 1 (`True`).

This change was abandoned, and the traditional VB `True` = -1 was preserved in VB.NET. Presumably this was done for backward compatibility.

VB.NET

`True` remains -1.

This does not cause any compatibility problems between VB.NET and other .NET languages. When a `True` value is passed from VB.NET to other .NET languages, such as C#, `True` will be passed as 1.

Try . . . Catch . . . End Try

See "Error Handling Revised."

ToolTipText Property Becomes a Control

Many controls in VB 6 had a ToolTipText property that you could set to pop
up a brief description if the user paused the mouse pointer over the control.
In VB.NET, this property is no longer avaiable. However, a ToolTip control is
on the Toolbox, but at the time of this writing, the ToolTip control is not
operative.

Top

See " Left, Top, Height, Width, and Move All Change."

TopLevelControl Property

This new property specifies the top-level control that contains the current
control. Usually the form is as follows:

```
MsgBox(Button3.TopLevelControl.ToString)
```

Trim

See "String Functions Are Now Methods" or "LCase and VCase Change."

Type . . . End Type Gone

See "User-Defined Type Changes to Structure."

UCase

See "LCase and VCase Change."

User-Defined Type Changes to Structure

Before VB.NET

You could use the `Type` command to create a user-defined type:

```
Private Type MyDataType
```

A user-defined type can include a combination of variables of different types (integer, long, and so on). This is known as a *struct* in the C language, so can you guess why `Type` is now called `Structure` in VB.NET?

VB.NET

You now declare this entity with the `Structure` command. No fixed-length arrays are allowed. Also, you can no longer use the `Lset` command to copy a variable of one user-defined `Type` to another variable of a different user-defined `Type`. `LSet` is eliminated from the language.

```
Public Structure VariableName
    Dim nas As Integer
End Structure
```

Also note that it was common to use fixed-length strings in user-defined types. Now you cannot do that anymore. You can only use what they call "primitive" data types in a Structure — and a fixed-length string isn't primitive. One workaround is to use the new `PadRight` command (formerly `LSET`) to ensure that a particular string is precisely a particular length:

This is VB 6 code:

```
Type MyType
RefNo As Integer
Comment As String*30
End Type
```

To translate that code to VB.NET, use the following code:

```
Structure MyType
Public RefNo As Integer
Public Comment As String
End Structure
```

And, because the `Comment` variable is now a variable-length string, if you need it to be a predictable length of characters, you must do that with your programming:

```
Dim strRec As MyType
StrRec.Comment = Space$(30)' set the length
StrRec.Comment = "Here is a description."
StrRec.Comment.PadRight(30)
```

The `Structure` object is more powerful than the `Type`. A `Structure` can have private members, including both properties and methods. It can have a constructor. A *constructor* is what allows a programmer to specify initial values when instantiating the `Structure` or object. Here's an example of how a programmer can pass values while instantiating:

```
        Dim strNumbers As New Numbers(22, 33) 'create
structure & set default values.
```

A `Structure` is almost a *class* in flexibility and features (however, limited inheritance and no initializers). Here's an example showing you how to create a simple structure that holds three-column rows (three field records). It also illustrates how to create an array of structures:

```
 Private Sub Button1_Click(ByVal sender As System.Object,
ByVal e As System.EventArgs) Handles Button1.Click
      Dim strRecipe(200) As Recipe
      strRecipe(0).Cuisine = "Mexican"
      strRecipe(0).Title = "Corn Slump"
      strRecipe(0).Recipe = "Mix Mexicorn into boiled
tamales."

      With strRecipe(1)
          .Cuisine = "Chinese"
          .Title = "Egg Drop Soup"
          .Recipe = "Dribble a beaten egg into 1 qt.
chicken stock. Add 1 t. soy sauce. Add 2 T. cornstarch
mixed into 3 T. cold water. Add 1 t. yellow food
coloring."
      End With

      MsgBox(strRecipe(1).Recipe)
End Sub

 Private Structure Recipe ' similar to a VB 6 Type
      Public Cuisine As String ' Mexican, Chinese etc.
      Public Title As String
      Public Recipe As String
End Structure
```

This next example shows you how to use private variables and properties:

```
      Private Structure Car
          Public Year As String
```

```
            Private theMake As String
            Public Property Make() As String
                Get
                     Make = theMake
                End Get
                Set(ByVal Value As String)
                     theMake = Value
                End Set
            End Property
        End Structure
```

Finally, the following example shows you how to overload a structure's method and how to use a constructor to permit the specification of initial values when instantiating this structure (see "Overloaded Functions, Properties, and Methods (Overloading)" in this appendix):

```
    Private Sub Button1_Click(ByVal sender As System.Object,
    ByVal e As System.EventArgs) Handles Button1.Click

        Dim strNumbers As New Numbers(22, 33) 'create
    structure & set default values
        Dim s As String
        s = strNumbers.Larger
        MsgBox(s & " is the largest number now in this
    structure.")
        s = strNumbers.Larger(2)
        MsgBox(s)
    End Sub


     Private Structure Numbers ' Structure with constructor
    and method
        Public s As Integer
        Public t As Integer
        ' this constructor will initialize the values when
    the Structure is declared:
        Sub New(ByVal InitialS As Integer, ByVal InitialT As
    Integer)
            s = InitialS
            t = InitialT
        End Sub

        ' here's the method. It returns the larger
        Function Larger() As String
            If s > t Then
                Return s.ToString
            Else
                Return t.ToString
            End If
        End Function
```

```
      ' here's how to overload Larger. This one compares
the submitted string to both S & T
      Function Larger(ByVal NewNumber As Integer) As String
          If NewNumber > s And NewNumber > t Then
                Return NewNumber.ToString & " is larger than
s or t."
          Else
                Return NewNumber.ToString & " is smaller than
s or t."
          End If
      End Function
End Structure
```

Validate Event Changes

The VB 6 `Validate` event has now been replaced by `Validating` and `Validated` events.

From the `Validating` event, you can call a routine that validates user input. For example, on a textbox you can validate the user input to make sure that it represents the format of an e-mail address. If the text does not validate, you can set `e.cancel` to true (within the validating event) and cancel the event so that the user can fix the entry. The `Validated` event fires after the control has been validated.

Variable Declaration Changes

Before VB.NET

You declared multiple variables on the same line like this:

```
Dim X As Integer, Y As Integer
```

VB.NET

You can omit repetitive `As` clauses because VB.NET assumes that a list of declared variables all on the same line are the same variable type. The VB.NET equivalent to the previous example is as follows:

```
Dim X, Y As Integer  '(Both X and Y are Integers)
```

Note that if you used `Dim X, Y As Integer` in VB 6, X would be a Variant type, not an Integer. Undefined variables in VB 6 default to the Variant type. (There is no Variant type in VB.NET.)

Variant Variable Type Is Gone

Before VB.NET

All variables defaulted to the Variant variable type. You could, of course, use coercion ("casting") commands such as `CBool`, or declare variables `As Integer`, `As String`, or whatever. But if you didn't, a variable defaulted to the variant type.

VB.NET

VB.NET does not use the Variant data type. Each variable inherits from a base object. An object variable type (one declared `As Object`) can hold any data type (just as a Variant could).

If the `Option Explicit` is turned off in VB.NET, *all* variables not declared as a particular type default to the object type.

The Variant type, efficient though it often was, had two fatal flaws from the VB.NET designers' perspective. First, in some cases, VB had a hard time figuring out which type the Variant should change to — resulting in an error. Second, the other languages in the .NET universe do not use variants — and the .NET philosophy requires conformity between its various languages (at least on the fundamental issues, such as variable typing). Therefore, the Variant variable is no longer part of the VB language. It has been banished in VB.NET.

VarType Replaced

The VB 6 `VarType` function, which used to tell you the variable type of a variable (or object), has been replaced by this:

```
obj.GetType.FullName
```

While . . . Wend Changes to While . . . End While

Before VB.NET

VB has always had a looping structure that worked somewhat the same way as the `Do While...Loop` structure:

```
While X = 5

'source code that does something

Wend
```

VB.NET

The new `While...End While` structure works exactly the same as the older `While...Wend`; it simply changes the word `Wend` into `End While`:

```
While X < 222

'source code that does something

End While
```

Width

See " Left, Top, Height, Width, and Move All Change."

"Windowless" Controls Removed

Before VB.NET

To save processor time and memory, VB programmers sometimes employed label or image controls. These so-called *windowless* controls were drawn on the form instead of being a formal window with a "handle." Windowless controls take up fewer resources. (Only the label and image were windowless; all other controls are windows.)

VB.NET

The image control has been dropped entirely and the windowless label control is now a fully windowed control. In place of the image control, use the picturebox control.

Unfortunately, the picturebox control doesn't offer some of the features available via an image control (stretching or shrinking the contained image — which is useful for creating thumbnail views, zooming, and other graphic manipulations). If you've written programs relying on these special features of the image control, you have to resort to API calls to get the same effect using pictureboxes.

There are also some other additions to the VB 6 repertoire of controls. Check out the new VB.NET HelpProvider, PrintPreview, ErrorProvider, PageSetupDialog, CrystalReportViewer, LinkLabel, Button (formerly known as CommandButton), MainMenu, RadioButton (formerly OptionButton), DomainUpDown, NumericUpDown, and ContextMenu.

Appendix

A Dictionary of VB.NET

Zero Index Controversy

We humans almost always count from 1. It's natural to our way of describing, and therefore *thinking*, about numbers and groups. When the first person arrives at your party, you don't say "Welcome, you're the zeroth one here!" And when your child is one year old, you don't send out invitations titled "Jimmy's Zeroth Birthday Party!!"

It makes little logical or linguistic sense to humans to begin counting from zero when working with lists, collections, or indeed arrays. We quite properly think of zero as meaning *nothing* — absence, nonexistence.

However, it was decided early in the development of computer languages that it would be more "computer-like" if we started indexing arrays (and some other collections) using zero as the starting number: Array(0), Array(1), and so on. In fact, a zero-based counting system *is* more computer-like, but that's no compelling argument for using it in a computer language, which is a tool created for use by people. There are technical reasons why a zero-based counting system was used to save computer memory — but this reason has long since lost any validity.

Many programmers — having learned to adjust to zero-based lists — want to perpetuate this unfortunate practice. Zero-based lists have resulted in countless man-years of debugging problems (mismatching loops to upper array boundaries — should it be `For I = 1 to 10` or `For I = 1 to 9`? — and such). And it continues to this day. Some sets in computer languages start their index with 1 (*some* but not *all* collections of objects, for instance) while other sets start with 0 (traditional arrays).

Visual Basic improved on this counterintuitive mixup by permitting programmers to use the `Option Base 1` command, which forced all arrays to begin sensibly, using an index of 1 as their first element. (You could also force an initial index of 1 by this kind of array declaration: `Dim MyArray(1 To 100)`.

VB.NET

The `Option Base` command has been deleted from the language and can no longer be used. All arrays must now begin with 0. Also, you can no longer use the `(1 To 100)` format when dimensioning an array to make the array be one-based. What's more, VB has traditionally counted characters using one-based lists. No longer.

This VB 6 function returns `ABC` because when you specify that you want the string starting at the first character (`,1`), you *mean* the first character — A in this case:

```
Dim x As String
x = Mid("ABC", 1)
 MsgBox(x)
```

When you run this example, you get `ABC` as you would expect.

Now, what do you suppose happens when you use the equivalent VB.NET function `Substring` and specify 1 as the first character?

```
Dim x As String = "ABC"
MsgBox(x.Substring(1))
```

Perhaps you're not stunned, but I was. When I first tried this example, I thought I was saying to VB.NET that I wanted a string starting at the first character (1), which would give me back `ABC`. Nope. You get `BC`! In VB.NET, this (1) means (2). The string that is returned to you starts with the second character, even though you used (1) in the source code. This phenomenon, they tell me, is deliberate, by design, and, in some way, good. How it's good escapes me.

It should be noted that in VB.NET, `Mid("ABC", 1)` still returns `ABC`.

I expect that when psychoergonimics are, at long last, introduced into computer-language design, we'll get rid of inane, human-unfriendly usages like the zero-based set. There is simply no reason at all to transfer to us humans the burden of describing *some* sets in computer programming as beginning with 1 and *other* sets as beginning with 0. All groups should begin with 1, obviously. Why should we memorize exceptions to a rule that is a very bad rule in the first place?

Appendix

A Dictionary of VB.NET

Index

U

W

Web, 283
Web farm, 267
Web Matrix Project, 269
Web pages
  allowing access, 316
  binding to databases,
    310–312
  controls, 110
  dynamic content, 262
  HTML, 263
  interactive, 263
  as objects, 279–280
  passing data between,
    283–286
  permissions, 316
  plain HTML version, 92
  positioning controls, 272
  posted back, 282
  preserving values, 282–283
  programming for, 262–263
  requested, 282
  zones, 291–292
Web programming, 289
Web programs, 90–94
Web projects, 91, 95
Web Service template, 322
Web Services, 261, 317
  allowing applications to use
    functions, 320
  backward compatibility, 321
  calling, 317
  client access, 323
  communicating with text, 318
  connecting to database,
    325–326
  connecting Windows project
    to, 331–333
  controls, 321
  creation of, 321–324
  cross-platform
    communication, 321
  current time and date,
    322–323
  data connection controls, 321
  decreasing inefficiencies, 320
  firewalls, 320

free of constraints, 319
versus functions, 317
how to call, 329–333
imitating access to, 323
importance of, 318–319
listing available, 332
messaging security, 321
name of, 323
overview, 319
passing parameters, 317,
  327–329
platform independence, 318
rebuilding before retesting,
  333
as set of functions, 320
SOAP , 319–320, 329
stateless, 318
testing multiple methods,
  327–329
viruses, 320
Visual Studio .NET, 319
XML, 317, 319, 320, 326
Web sites, 283–286
WebApplication1 project, 91
Web.Config file, 96
WebControls, 110
WebForm applications, 92
WebForm container, 16
WebForm design window, 271,
  343
WebForm projects, 109–111,
  310
WebForm1 WebForm, 286,
  335–336
WebForm1.aspx, 284–285, 344
WebForm2 WebForm, 284–286,
  286
WebForm2.ASPX Web page,
  284
WebForm3 Web page, 342
WebForm-based applications,
  654
WebForms, 110, 261, 268, 357
  absolute positioning, 272
  Button control, 93, 193, 272,
    344

code window, 310
code-behind file, 272
controls, 110–111, 277
deleting button, 193
design mode, 284
displaying ads, 298–300
event procedures, 192–194
FlowLayout property, 272
Label control, 272, 344
ListBox control, 310
PageLayout property, 272
Page_Load event, 282
RangeValidator control, 344
TextBox control, 272, 344
<WebMethod( )> element, 323
WebRequest class, 182
WebService element, 323
Wend command, 672
WhatsThisHelpID property,
  108
WhatTimeIsIt Web Service,
  325
When clause, 665
WHERE clause, 471, 479
whichway argument, 237
While loop, 530, 533
While...End While loop,
  174–175, 748–749
While...Wend structure,
  748–749
Width property, 106, 297, 520,
  698–699
wildcards, 480–481
WinCV, 615–617, 620–621
windowless controls, 749
windows, 75, 125–126
Windows 2000, 269
Windows applications
  attaching database, 464–465
  predictable relationship, 289
Windows Components Wizard,
  270–271
Windows current directory, 51
Windows Forms tab, 474
Windows Integrated Security,
  358

Notes

Notes

FOR DUMMIES®

The easy way to get more done and have more fun

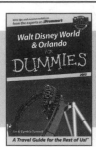

FOR DUMMIES®

Plain-English solutions for everyday challenges

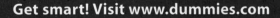